Economic Report of the President

Transmitted to the Congress
February 1998

TOGETHER WITH
THE ANNUAL REPORT
OF THE
COUNCIL OF ECONOMIC ADVISERS

UNITED STATES GOVERNMENT PRINTING OFFICE

WASHINGTON : 1998

For sale by the U.S. Government Printing Office
Superintendent of Documents, Mail Stop: SSOP, Washington, DC 20402-9328
ISBN 0-16-049419-2

CONTENTS

For a detailed table of contents of the Council's Report, see page 11

ECONOMIC REPORT
OF THE PRESIDENT

ECONOMIC REPORT OF THE PRESIDENT

To the Congress of the United States:

For the last 5 years this Administration has worked to strengthen our Nation for the 21st century, expanding opportunity for all Americans, demanding responsibility from all Americans, and bringing us together as a community of all Americans. Building a strong economy is the cornerstone of our efforts to meet these challenges.

When I first took office in 1993, the Federal budget deficit was out of control, unemployment was unacceptably high, and wages were stagnant. To reverse this course, we took a new approach, putting in place a bold economic strategy designed to bring down the deficit and give America's workers the tools and training they need to help them thrive in our changing economy.

Our strategy has succeeded: the economy has created more than 14 million new jobs, unemployment is at its lowest level in 24 years, and core inflation is at its lowest level in 30 years. Economic growth in 1997 was the strongest in almost a decade, and the benefits of that growth are being shared by all Americans: poverty is dropping and median family income has gone up nearly $2,200 since 1993. We also saw the biggest drop in welfare rolls in history. Many challenges remain, but Americans are enjoying the fruits of an economy that is steady and strong.

THE ADMINISTRATION'S ECONOMIC STRATEGY

From the beginning, this Administration's economic strategy has had three crucial elements: reducing the deficit, investing in people, and opening markets abroad.

Deficit reduction. In 1993 this Administration's deficit reduction plan set the Nation on a course of fiscal responsibility, while making critical investments in the skills and well-being of our people. When I took office, the deficit was $290 billion and projected to go much higher. This year the deficit will fall to just $10 billion and possibly lower still. That is a reduction of more than 95 percent, leaving the deficit today smaller in relation to the size of the economy than it has been since 1969. And this year I have proposed a budget that will eliminate the deficit entirely, achieving the first balanced budget in 30 years.

Beyond that, it is projected that the budget will show a sizable surplus in the years to come. I propose that we reserve 100 percent of the surplus until we have taken the necessary measures to strengthen the Social Security system for the 21st century. I am committed to address-

3

ing Social Security first, to ensure that all Americans are confident that it will be there when they need it.

Investing in our people. In the new economy, the most precious resource this Nation has is the skills and ingenuity of working Americans. Investing in the education and health of our people will help all Americans reap the rewards of a growing, changing economy. Those who are better educated, with the flexibility and the skills they need to move from one job to another and seize new opportunities, will succeed in the new economy; those who do not will fall behind.

That is why the historic balanced budget agreement I signed into law in 1997 included the largest increase in aid to education in 30 years, and the biggest increase to help people go to college since the G.I. Bill was passed 50 years ago. The agreement provided funds to ensure that we stay on track to help 1 million disadvantaged children prepare for success in school. It provided funding for the America Reads Challenge, with the goal of mobilizing a million volunteers to promote literacy, and it made new investments in our schools themselves, to help connect every classroom and library in this country to the Internet by the year 2000.

The balanced budget agreement created the HOPE scholarship program, to make completion of the 13th and 14th years of formal education as widespread as a high school diploma is today. It offered other tuition tax credits for college and skills training. It created a new Individual Retirement Account that allows tax-free withdrawals to pay for education. It provided the biggest increase in Pell grants in two decades. Finally, it provided more funds so that aid to dislocated workers is more than double what it was in 1993, to help these workers get the skills they need to remain productive in a changing economy.

But we must do more to guarantee all Americans the quality education they need to succeed. That is why I have proposed a new initiative to improve the quality of education in our public schools—through high national standards and national tests, more charter schools to stimulate competition, greater accountability, higher quality teaching, smaller class sizes, and more classrooms.

To strengthen our Nation we must also strengthen our families. The Family and Medical Leave Act, which I signed into law in 1993, ensures that millions of people no longer have to choose between being good parents and being good workers. The Health Care Portability and Accountability Act, enacted in 1996, ensures that workers can keep their health insurance if they change jobs or suffer a family emergency. We have also increased the minimum wage, expanded the earned income tax credit, and provided for a new $500-per-child tax credit for working families. To continue making progress toward strengthening families, the balanced budget agreement allocated $24 billion to provide health insurance to up to 5 million uninsured chil-

4

dren—the largest Federal investment in children's health care since Medicaid was created in 1965.

Opening markets and expanding exports. To create more good jobs and increase wages, we must open markets abroad and expand U.S. exports. Trade has been key to the strength of this economic expansion—about a third of our economic growth in recent years has come from selling American goods and services overseas. The Information Technology Agreement signed in 1997 lowers tariff and other barriers to 90 percent of world trade in information technology services.

To continue opening new markets, creating new jobs, and increasing our prosperity, it is critically important to renew fast-track negotiating authority. This authority, which every President of either party has had for the last 20 years, enables the President to negotiate trade agreements and submit them to the Congress for an up-or-down vote, without modification. Renewing this traditional trade authority is essential to America's ability to shape the global economy of the 21st century.

SEIZING THE BENEFITS OF A GROWING, CHANGING ECONOMY

As we approach the 21st century the American economy is sound and strong, but challenges remain. We know that information and technology and global commerce are rapidly transforming the economy, offering new opportunities but also posing new challenges. Our goal must be to ensure that all Americans are equipped with the skills to succeed in this growing, changing economy.

Our economic strategy—balancing the budget, investing in our people, opening markets—has set this Nation on the right course to meet this goal. This strategy will support and contribute to America's strength in the new economic era, removing barriers to our economy's potential and providing our people with the skills, the flexibility, and the security to succeed. We must continue to maintain the fiscal discipline that is balancing the budget, to invest in our people and their skills, and to lead the world to greater prosperity in the 21st century.

THE WHITE HOUSE
FEBRUARY 10, 1998

THE ANNUAL REPORT
OF THE
COUNCIL OF ECONOMIC ADVISERS

LETTER OF TRANSMITTAL

COUNCIL OF ECONOMIC ADVISERS

Washington, D.C., February 10, 1998

MR. PRESIDENT:

The Council of Economic Advisers herewith submits its 1998 Annual Report in accordance with the provisions of the Employment Act of 1946 as amended by the Full Employment and Balanced Growth Act of 1978.

Sincerely,

Janet L. Yellen,
Chair

Jeffrey A. Frankel,
Member

Rebecca M. Blank,
Member-Nominee

C O N T E N T S

LIST OF CHARTS

LIST OF BOXES

CHAPTER 1

Promoting Prosperity in a High-Employment Economy

THE PAST YEAR SAW THE NATION'S ECONOMY turn in its best performance in a generation. Over the course of 1997, output growth and job creation remained vigorous while inflation declined. Real (inflation-adjusted) gross domestic product (GDP) grew 3.9 percent, and employment rose by 3.2 million, for an average rate of 267,000 jobs per month. The unemployment rate dropped below 5 percent for the first time in 24 years, yet core inflation (as measured by the consumer price index, excluding its volatile food and energy components) averaged only 2.2 percent, its lowest rate in over 30 years. This exceptional economic performance occurred during a period of historic deficit reduction: the Federal budget deficit, which reached $290 billion in the 1992 fiscal year, declined to only $22 billion in fiscal 1997. And the Administration has submitted a budget for fiscal 1999 that projects a balanced budget for the first time since 1969.

As 1998 begins, the prospects for continued growth with high employment and low inflation remain excellent. The economy is remarkably free of the symptoms that often presage an economic downturn—such as an increase in inflation, an accumulation of inventories, or evidence of financial imbalance. Inflation fell in 1997, and developments in East Asia, by reducing U.S. import prices, are likely to exert additional downward pressure on U.S. inflation in 1998. Economic turmoil in East Asia could affect the global economy, but if international efforts to restore stability there succeed, the main effect on the U.S. economy could simply be to allow continued growth and job creation with a more moderate outlook for interest rates. Another sign that an expansion is nearing its end would be a sudden accumulation of inventories, as businesses find their sales falling short of production. Yet sales were strong in 1997, and inventory-sales ratios are near historical lows. Financial imbalances can also threaten to disrupt an expansion. But today banks and other financial institutions do not appear overextended, as they did in the late 1980s and early 1990s, and the stock market shrugged off a one-day plunge in October (although its continuing high valuation relative to earnings is a source of concern to some). Although the business cycle may not have been vanquished, the economy is in fundamentally sound shape and well-equipped to handle any unexpected bouts of rougher weather.

A principal force behind the current expansion has been private fixed investment. Almost none of the growth in GDP over this expansion has come from increased government spending, whereas close to one-third has come from greater private fixed investment (Chart 1-1). Because of the Administration's deficit reduction efforts, the contribution of government spending to overall growth has been much lower than in most previous postwar expansions (real Federal Government spending has actually declined), while that of private fixed investment has been substantially higher. One benefit of this burst of investment has been a rapid expansion of industrial capacity: over the past 3 years average annual capacity growth has exceeded every previous growth rate since 1968.

Policies such as deficit reduction have contributed to an investment-led recovery and a climate conducive to sustained economic

Chart 1-1 **Investment and Government Spending in Overall GDP Growth**
Real GDP growth during this expansion has been driven by private spending, particularly on fixed investment.

Share of real GDP change (percent)

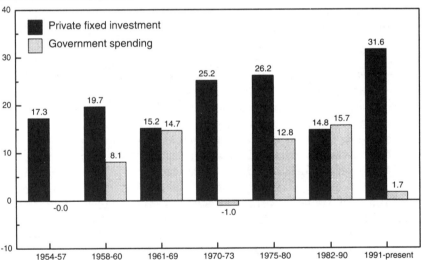

Note: Change in component expressed as fraction of overall change in real GDP.
Sources: Department of Commerce (Bureau of Economic Analysis) and National Bureau of Economic Research.

growth. But the lion's share of the credit for the economy's performance goes to American workers and firms, who have risen to the challenges of a competitive global economy and rapidly changing technology. The role of government in such an economy is not to prop up economic growth with government spending but, more subtly, to provide individuals and businesses with the tools they need to flourish through their own efforts. The range of appropriate government policies in such an economy includes promoting private investment through sound macroeconomic policies, encouraging the formation of skills through training and education, securing opportunity for the marginalized members of our society, and—where necessary—providing assistance to the most vulnerable. Using government to complement, not replace, the market and the private sector has been a fundamental, guiding principle of this Administration's economic strategy from the very beginning. And it is this strategy that has borne fruit over the last 5 years.

Despite the economy's recent exemplary performance, a number of challenges remain. The first is to preserve and nurture the successes achieved so far. And although progress has been made in addressing the longer term problems that have affected the economy since the productivity slowdown of the early 1970s—problems like slow growth in wages and incomes and widening income inequality—more needs to be done. This chapter describes the principles and policies of this Administration for achieving its two basic, overarching goals: securing high and rising living standards now and in the future, and ensuring that the benefits of a higher standard of living are extended to all Americans.

THE ADMINISTRATION'S ECONOMIC STRATEGY

The Employment Act of 1946 (which created the Council of Economic Advisers), together with its later amendments, gave the Federal Government responsibility for stabilizing short-run economic fluctuations, promoting balanced and noninflationary economic growth, and fostering low unemployment. This Administration's strategy in pursuing this mandate has focused on getting the fundamentals right: reducing the budget deficit, investing in technology and the American people, and opening markets at home and abroad. These were the right policies for encouraging the job creation needed to move the economy to full employment, and they are the right policies for attacking the longer term problems of sluggish productivity growth and widening income inequality that began to afflict the economy in the early 1970s.

But there is more to the Administration's policy agenda than can be measured by aggregate economic statistics alone. Getting the fundamentals right means removing the barriers that block people from realizing their potential; it means promoting their sense of individual responsibility and giving them the tools to succeed. Getting the fundamentals right also means fostering a personal commitment by all Americans to help others, a sense of shared responsibility for our Nation's children, and a sense of community in an increasingly multiethnic society.

A CREDIBLE PLAN FOR DEFICIT REDUCTION

The policy course set in 1993 has contributed to the Nation's recent economic health and strength. In 1993 the economy was still recovering from the 1990-91 recession, and it labored under the burden of a Federal budget deficit that had ballooned to $290 billion, an all-time record. The linchpin of the Administration's economic strategy was a credible budget plan that could achieve substantial deficit reduction over the longer term, yet be balanced and gradual enough to allow the economy to gather strength and move toward full employment in the short term. The success of this program rested on achieving an interest rate environment conducive to investment, which would allow the economy to grow in the face of a contractionary fiscal policy. This in turn required that financial markets correctly anticipate an appropriately accommodative monetary policy. In large measure, that is exactly what happened. Long-term interest rates fell to 25-year lows in 1993, spurring a pickup in economic growth.

A key feature of the Administration's deficit reduction plan was its credibility. A credible and realistic program for deficit reduction—one that observers and financial markets judged likely to be fully implemented—was a precondition for the reduction in interest rates that spurred investment-led growth. Fundamental to the plan's credibility was the adoption of a set of economic projections that represented conservative, mainstream forecasts of future growth and inflation. These projections eschewed the "rosy scenarios" of previous budgets, which invariably fell short of reality; they were not meant to indicate the best that the economy could do, but rather how the economy was most likely to perform given past experience. In fact, the economy's performance has been stronger than the Administration projected.

In the 1980s expansive fiscal policy required relatively tight monetary policy in the form of high interest rates to prevent the economy from overheating. This policy mix is particularly unfavorable from the standpoint of fostering longer term growth: high interest rates impede capital formation, while burgeoning government deficits depress national saving and contribute to more borrowing from abroad. The net result of deficit reduction in the 1990s has been to promote a more balanced mix of fiscal and monetary policy. Deficit reduction has also had an important collateral benefit, namely, a restoration of Americans' confidence in the ability of their government to manage its own affairs.

INVESTING IN PEOPLE AND TECHNOLOGY

The primary purpose of deficit reduction, however, is to encourage investment. Hence, this Administration recognized from the outset that a plan that balanced the budget at the expense of the government's own productive investments would ultimately be self-defeating. Far from curtailing public investment, the

Administration has given investment in people and technology a major place in its economic agenda.

Government invests in people by promoting public health and safety, encouraging opportunity and individual responsibility, and assisting in the formation of human capital through education and training. This last function is especially vital in today's high-technology economy, where a skilled work force is an essential condition for future growth. Education is critical if Americans are to capitalize on the opportunities created by new technologies and more open global markets. And education and training programs are of particular importance in the present economic environment as a means of preventing poverty and ensuring opportunity for all. The return to education has risen dramatically since the late 1970s; today, highly skilled workers command a large premium in the labor market over their less skilled counterparts. This rising skill premium is an important reason why earnings inequality is greater today than it was in the late 1970s. Governments have an important role to play in ensuring that all Americans have the opportunity to accumulate the skills necessary for economic success. This requires initiatives to improve public education at the primary and secondary levels, as well as programs to make higher education more accessible. It also requires recognizing that learning must be a lifelong activity in an economy where technological change is ongoing.

Investing in basic research and the development of new technologies is another important function of government. The private sector spends billions of dollars every year on research and development. But economists have long recognized that private sector spending alone in these areas will be less than the optimum. Since the fruits of a new scientific discovery, for example, are enjoyed not merely by the discoverer but by society as a whole, the private incentive for pursuing scientific research falls short of the total social benefit. Moreover, new theories of economic growth place a special emphasis on advances in knowledge through research and development as the motive force behind long-run increases in living standards. This analysis implies that the return to government investment in basic research and technology is likely to be especially high.

OPENING MARKETS AT HOME AND ABROAD

A third major component of the Administration's economic agenda is the promotion of freer and more competitive markets at home and abroad. Domestically, this has involved the pursuit of initiatives directed at enhancing competition—particularly in such industries as telecommunications, electric power, financial services, and health care—and a vigorous approach to antitrust enforcement. It has also meant addressing market failures in such areas as health care and environmental protection. In some cases the effect of these initiatives is a one-time boost to the *level* of output, through greater efficiency

23

and lower costs. But these policies can also sometimes lead to a faster *rate* of economic growth. For example, past experience provides evidence that sensible deregulation can not only help raise efficiency, but also spur continued innovation through greater competition. Moreover, some benefits of these policies are not captured in the GDP statistics at all, but rather take the form of improvements in our quality of life.

The Administration is also committed to reducing the burden of government regulation and ensuring that the benefits of new regulations justify their costs. Many government regulations apply to industries in which technological change is rapidly altering the nature of market competition. A key precept of this Administration's approach to regulation, therefore, is that the regulatory process must be dynamic, with regulatory policies under constant review so as to minimize their burden on consumers and businesses. Another important precept is to refrain from policies that regulate through government fiat in favor of policies that use market-based incentives to attain the desired outcome. Experience with such policies as permit trading for sulfur dioxide emissions suggests that this approach can help ensure that compliance with socially beneficial goals is achieved efficiently and cost-effectively.

This Administration has also worked hard to open markets abroad by encouraging fairer and freer international trade. From his earliest days in office, the President has advocated an outward-looking, internationalist trade policy. During the Administration's first 4 years the United States concluded over 200 trade agreements with other countries. Some of these agreements, such as the North American Free Trade Agreement (NAFTA) and the Uruguay Round agreement of the General Agreement on Tariffs and Trade, were comprehensive in scope, whereas others had much more limited aims—but all are vital to our Nation's competitive future.

Economists generally recognize that an open economy offers both static and dynamic advantages. First, trade benefits an economy by allowing it to specialize in what it does best—a point that economists have made since the early 1800s. Even if a country is more efficient than its neighbors at producing every good it consumes, it can still benefit from trade by specializing in the production of goods in which it is *relatively* more efficient, and then trading its surplus production for whatever else it wants to consume. In addition, a new view of international trade argues that increased trade actually raises an economy's rate of growth, because increased competition and larger markets spur the acquisition of new skills and the development of new technologies. If so, the case for trade liberalization becomes even more compelling, since raising the economy's growth rate—even by a few tenths of a percentage point per year—has vastly more significance for long-run living standards than even a relatively large one-time increase in the level of output.

A RECORD OF ACCOMPLISHMENT

Focusing on the fundamentals in shaping economic policy has paid off by helping to produce an economy that is stronger than it has been in decades. This past year alone saw a drop in the unemployment rate to its lowest level in a generation and the forging of a budget agreement that promises to bring the Federal deficit under control for the first time in decades. Last year also saw significant advances in this Administration's economic agenda along other fronts.

BENEFITS OF A HIGH-EMPLOYMENT ECONOMY

Driven largely by strong growth in business fixed investment, growth in real GDP and employment picked up in the second half of 1993 and persisted in 1994. This robust growth led to a series of monetary policy tightenings over the course of 1994, which resulted in more moderate growth in 1995. In retrospect, 1995 may have been the pause that refreshes. Economic growth exceeded expectations in 1996, and strong growth continued through 1997. The result has been a high-employment economy with the potential to overcome some of the longer term problems of productivity growth and income distribution that built up in the 1970s and 1980s.

A high-employment economy brings enormous economic and social benefits. Essential to personal economic security is the knowledge that work is available to those who seek it, at wages sufficient to keep them and their families out of poverty. A tight labor market increases the confidence of job losers that they will be able to return to work, lures discouraged workers back into the labor force, enhances the prospects of those already at work to get ahead, enables those who want or need to switch jobs to do so without a long period of joblessness, and lowers the duration of a typical unemployment spell. Returning the economy to full employment yields a direct benefit by ensuring that the economy's resources—human and material—are not squandered by needless cyclical unemployment. On average, reducing the unemployment rate by a percentage point raises output by approximately 2 percent; in 1997, 2 percent of GDP was $160 billion, or roughly $600 for every American man, woman, and child. Wasted resources from not producing at potential, together with the human cost of unemployment, are intolerable; the elimination of this waste is the principal benefit of a sustained return to full employment.

But a high-employment economy in which jobs are plentiful and labor markets tight yields other benefits as well. Short-term economic conditions can affect long-term structural unemployment. A tight labor market encourages participation by those who might otherwise be forced to sit on the sidelines, and makes it easier to absorb less skilled or younger and more inexperienced workers into the labor force. These new labor market entrants gain much-needed job experience, building the skills they will need to hold down a job in the future. The importance of this can be seen from the experience of some European countries: prolonged stagnation or recession may have led to a permanent increase in unemployment there, as the unemployed and the never-employed have seen their skills atrophy or become obsolete. Running a high-employment economy, then, may be one of the surest ways to ensure that an unacceptably large fraction of our citizens are not consigned to long-term joblessness and economic marginalization.

From the 1980s until the early 1990s, the economy's ability to reduce poverty through growth alone was hampered by a strong headwind: sustained declines in wages at the low end of the earnings distribution that offset the benefits of an expanding economy for the poorest Americans. As a result, holding a job no longer ensured that a less skilled worker would be able to lift his or her family out of poverty. This adverse secular trend raises even further the stakes of maintaining a high-employment economy.

Keeping the unemployment rate low and job growth high is also necessary if we are to move current welfare recipients into the work force. Early, indirect evidence here is encouraging: employment and labor force participation rates among single women who maintain families—about two-thirds of whom have children under 18—have increased in the past few years. This is probably in part the result of recent welfare reform: the greatest acceleration in employment rates has occurred among those single women most likely to be affected by welfare reform, namely, those with young children. Nevertheless, it is obvious that fostering an economy in which job opportunities are plentiful plays a crucial part in aiding the transition from welfare to work.

We have begun to see heartening signs that the current expansion is yielding gains in living standards for all Americans, especially those at the bottom of the income distribution. The poverty rate fell to 13.7 percent in 1996, from 15.1 percent in 1993; the poverty rate for black Americans is at a historical low, and in 1997 unemployment among blacks fell to its lowest rate since 1973. Since 1993, household income has grown in each quintile of the income distribution, with the largest percentage increase going to the poorest members of our society (Chart 1-2). Maintaining a full-employment economy is essential if this progress is to continue.

DEFICIT REDUCTION: COMPLETING THE TASK

The most significant economic policy event of 1997 was the passage of a deficit reduction package that will finish the task of balancing the Federal budget by 1999. This will be the first balanced budget since 1969, and only the ninth since World War II (Chart 1-3).

Some have claimed that the expanding economy, not government policy, deserves all the credit for vanquishing the deficit. It is cer-

26

tainly true that ups and downs in the business cycle have an important effect on both revenues and outlays, leading to fluctuations in the deficit. But even when cyclical factors are thus accounted for, it

Chart 1-2 **Real Household Income Growth by Quintile, 1993-96**
From 1993 to 1996, households in the lowest quintile of the income distribution enjoyed the fastest growth in real incomes.

Average annual percent change

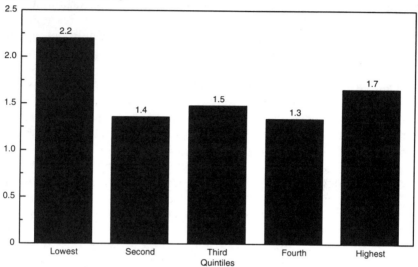

Source: Department of Commerce (Bureau of the Census).

Chart 1-3 **Federal Budget Deficit as a Percent of GDP**
The budget is projected to be in balance in fiscal 1999 for the first time since 1969.

Percent of GDP

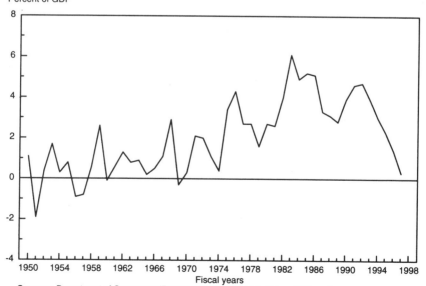

Fiscal years

Sources: Department of Commerce (Bureau of Economic Analysis) and Office of Management and Budget.

27

is evident that policy has played a major role in bringing the deficit under control. It is also worth noting that in January 1993, before the 1993 deficit reduction package was adopted, the Federal deficit was projected to reach $350 billion in fiscal 1998 and to rise to $650 billion in fiscal 2003, even when the economy was projected to be at full employment. Finally, it is difficult to imagine that the economy's performance would have been anywhere near as strong as it has been without a credible and successful attempt to put the government's fiscal house in order. Improvements in economic conditions have played a part in reducing the deficit, but a balanced budget would not now be in sight had the Nation remained on the fiscal course in place in 1992.

Although a balanced budget is often taken as the goal of fiscal policy, from an economic standpoint the motivation for deficit reduction is to raise national saving, thereby augmenting society's future consumption possibilities. When the government's budget is in surplus, in the sense that revenues exceed outlays, the government makes a positive contribution to national saving. As discussed in Chapter 2 of this *Report,* a case for higher national saving can be based on the high return on saving in the United States and the fact that private saving remains low. A higher rate of national saving now would lead to a larger economy when the baby-boom generation retires, thus making it easier to provide for their retirement without imposing undue burdens on younger generations. Although a balanced budget does not add to the government's outstanding debt to the public, which past deficits have ballooned, it does not subtract from it either. Leaving a large public debt in place implies that a sizable portion of existing government resources will continue to be absorbed by interest payments, leaving less for all other spending. Indeed, one legacy of the runup in the national debt that accompanied the deficits of the 1980s and early 1990s has been a sharp increase in the share of total outlays that must be used to make interest payments on the debt (Chart 1-4).

POLICIES TO RAISE GROWTH, REDUCE INEQUALITY, AND INCREASE OPPORTUNITY

A significant part of the Administration's economic agenda also involves investment in people: in a broad sense, this encompasses education and training, measures to promote health, and policies that extend opportunity to all Americans. A number of policies have been put in place to ensure that these investments are made.

Education

The 1997 balanced budget agreement included the largest Federal investment in education in a generation, in the form of initiatives to improve the quality and accessibility of primary, secondary, *and* higher education.

Chart 1-4 **Net Interest as a Share of Federal Outlays**
Net interest payments now represent twice as large a share of total outlays as they did in the 1970s.

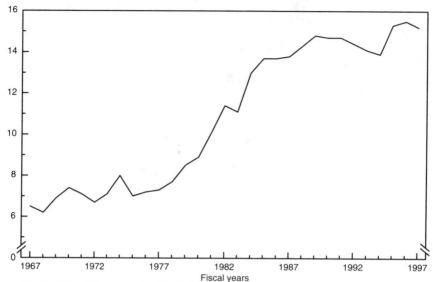

Percent

Fiscal years

Source: Office of Management and Budget.

Higher education is a particular priority. The earnings of college graduates have risen sharply relative to those of workers with only a high school education; in today's economy, a college degree has become as vital for success as a high school diploma was a generation ago. Even post-high school education that does not lead to a bachelor's degree (such as an associate's degree program or vocational or technical training) boosts earnings substantially over just completing high school (Chart 1-5).

Moreover, learning must be a lifelong process. A fundamental characteristic of our economy is constant technological change. Such progress holds the promise of higher living standards for all, but it also requires workers to adapt to employers' demands for a well-trained, highly skilled work force. It is therefore critical to provide all individuals—including those not traditionally thought of as "school age"—with access to additional education or training.

The President's higher education initiatives reflect these principles. Specific measures include:

- *The largest Pell grant increase in 20 years.* The balanced budget agreement raises the maximum Pell grant by over 10 percent, to $3,000. Approximately 3.7 million students receive Pell grants, and close to a quarter of a million families will become eligible for the grant for the first time.

29

Chart 1-5 **Returns to Education**
Earning an associate's degree raises earnings significantly.

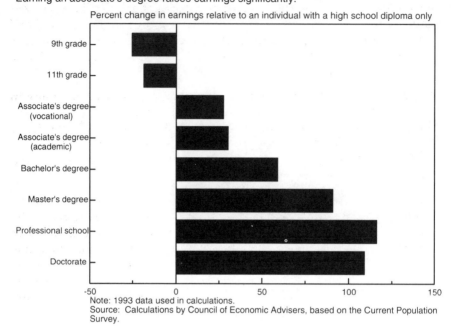

Percent change in earnings relative to an individual with a high school diploma only

Note: 1993 data used in calculations.
Source: Calculations by Council of Economic Advisers, based on the Current Population Survey.

- *HOPE scholarships for post-high school education.* In his 1997 State of the Union address, the President called for making the 13th and 14th years of education as universal as a high school education is today. The HOPE scholarship program accomplishes this by providing a tax credit for higher education expenses of as much as $1,500, enough to cover tuition at a typical community college.

- *A tuition tax credit for Americans of all ages.* A 20-percent tax credit for post-high school tuition expenses will be available for the first $5,000 (and after 2002, $10,000) of qualified education expenses. This tax credit is offered not just to school-age Americans but to those already working as well, to permit workers to upgrade their skills at any time during their life.

- *Tax exemptions for employer-provided education benefits.* The budget agreement extends Section 127 of the tax code for 3 years, allowing workers to exclude up to $5,250 of employer-provided education benefits from their taxable income.

- *A tax deduction for interest on student loans.* Up to $1,000 of interest payments on loans for higher education expenses will be tax-deductible in any given tax year, starting in 1998. This deduction will rise by $500 each year until 2001.

Because public education in the United States is largely administered by local authorities, the Federal Government's ability to

30

influence primary and secondary education is somewhat less direct. Nevertheless, this Administration recognizes that there is much that the Federal Government *can* do to improve our public schools, and has worked to enact programs that will ensure that our children have access to the best possible primary and secondary education. These initiatives include:

- *Establishing national standards.* Research shows that students in countries that have standardized, mandatory examinations do better than students in countries that do not. The Administration's voluntary national testing program has received full funding; this will allow for the development of national fourth-grade reading and eighth-grade mathematics examinations.

- *Expanding Head Start.* The balanced budget agreement raised funding for Head Start by $374 million, to $4.4 billion, to reach the Administration's goal of having 1 million children in the Head Start program by 2002. Since 1993, funding for this program, which has shown great success in preparing low-income preschoolers to enter school, has increased by 57 percent. The program will serve over 830,000 children and their families in 1998, including 40,000 infants and toddlers in the Early Head Start program.

- *Establishing a comprehensive literacy strategy.* Every child should be able to read by the third grade. To meet this basic goal, the President's comprehensive literacy strategy will receive nearly $46 million in new funding in 1998 for State teacher training, family literacy, and tutoring efforts; $210 million was provided in an advance appropriation to be available in 1999, contingent on authorization of a literacy initiative such as the America Reads Challenge.

- *Increasing funding for charter schools.* The President set a goal of having 3,000 locally designed public charter schools in operation by early in the next century. Funding for charter schools is increased by over 50 percent in the balanced budget agreement, to allow the Department of Education to support nearly 1,000 charter schools by the end of 1998.

Health

This Administration has made promoting health, increasing access to health insurance, and improving the functioning of health insurance markets a major priority. The Balanced Budget Act of 1997 allocates $24 billion over 5 years to assist States in providing health insurance for up to 5 million children through Medicaid or State programs. This represents the single largest investment in children's health since Medicaid was begun in 1965. The Administration's 1999 budget proposes to expand access to health insurance further by allowing uninsured Americans between 62 and 65 years old, as well as 55- to 61-year-olds who have been laid off or displaced from their jobs, to buy into the Medicare program. These measures are fully off-set so as not to increase the cost of Medicare to the government.

The Balanced Budget Act also takes important steps toward ensuring that Medicare itself remains viable. Structural reforms—such as expanded choice among health care plans and the restructuring of payment systems—will help save $115 billion over 5 years. Recently passed legislation also provides additional funding for preventive care, such as mammograms, which can help keep health care expenses down by catching and treating health problems before they become serious. These and other measures will keep the Medicare trust fund solvent for at least the next decade. The Balanced Budget Act also created a commission to examine long-term solutions to the problems that will face Medicare as a result of the demographic changes coming in the 21st century.

The Administration has also promoted policies to improve the functioning of health insurance markets, increase consumer protection, and improve access to new pharmaceuticals. The Health Insurance Portability and Accountability Act of 1996 helps workers who change jobs by making it easier to carry their health insurance with them to the new job. In 1997 the President's Commission on Consumer Protection and Quality in the Health Care Industry, established to advise the President on changes in the health care system, responded to the President's request to develop and recommend a "Consumer Bill of Rights and Responsibilities." The President urged the Congress to pass appropriate and necessary legislation to ensure that a range of protections are extended to all Americans. And the Food and Drug Administration Modernization Act of 1997, which codifies a number of initiatives taken by this Administration as part of the reinventing government initiative, will help ensure the timely availability of safe and effective new drugs. These policies and others are considered in greater detail in Chapter 5 of this *Report*.

Finally, teenage tobacco use is one of the most important public health concerns that the Nation faces, and it has been rising in recent years. The increase in the tobacco tax passed last year not only will help fund the expansions in children's health insurance coverage described above, but also will help reduce teen smoking. The rise in the tax complements recent Food and Drug Administration rules to limit advertising targeted at youth. Finally, the Administration has indicated its support for national legislation designed to achieve large reductions in teen smoking, with strict financial penalties on the tobacco industry if specific targets in this effort are not met.

Welfare Reform and Poverty Alleviation

Welfare reform presents an ongoing challenge: to ensure that our neediest citizens can maintain a decent standard of living without creating incentives that encourage a life of dependency. This Administration has committed itself to a policy that combines work incentives and community efforts to move people off of welfare and into employment. This has contributed to the largest reduction in welfare rolls in history.

The same long-term changes in the wage structure that give greater rewards to education and skill also imply that some workers will find it difficult to raise themselves and their families out of poverty, even with a full-time job. To make work pay, all those who work must be guaranteed a minimum level of earnings. The Administration has made an expansion of the earned income tax credit (EITC), which raises the take-home pay of eligible low-income workers, a cornerstone of its strategy to promote work and reduce poverty (Box 1-1). This expansion has occurred alongside two increases in the minimum wage (the second

---

Box 1-1.—Poverty Alleviation, the Earned Income Tax Credit, and the Minimum Wage

A typical cash assistance program guarantees its maximum benefit to those who receive no income, then phases out this benefit as the recipient's income from other sources (usually labor) rises. The disincentive to work that such programs create has been a major concern—perhaps *the* major concern—of policymakers with regard to welfare policy. These disincentives will persist so long as we confine ourselves to considering policies with this structure.

One way to avoid these work disincentive effects is to design programs that add to the wages of low-income workers. One such program, the earned income tax credit, was expanded substantially in 1993. Under the EITC, eligible low-wage workers receive a credit against their income and payroll tax liability; this credit is rebated in cash if the worker's income tax liability is zero. The EITC differs from the typical cash assistance program in that no benefits are paid to those who do not work, and benefits rise as earnings increase (up to some threshold earnings level). It therefore largely eliminates the typical program's work disincentive effects.

The minimum wage complements and enhances the EITC. When used by itself to guarantee a subsistence level of income, the minimum wage must be set very high. But an excessively high minimum wage (that is, substantially above the current one) could discourage hiring. On the other hand, using the EITC alone to guarantee an income floor would require payment of a large subsidy, which would then have to be phased out slowly to minimize the disincentive to earn additional income. This makes the program much more costly. Hence, the minimum wage and the EITC are best employed jointly in designing an optimal assistance package.

of which, in September 1997, raised the minimum wage from $4.75 to $5.15 an hour).

In August 1996 the President signed into law a comprehensive, bipartisan welfare reform bill, which established the Temporary Assistance for Needy Families program. This created a new system of block grants to States and dramatically altered the nature and provision of Federal welfare benefits in America. This legislation has changed the Nation's welfare system into one that requires work in exchange for time-limited assistance and provides support for families moving from welfare to work.

Although these policies have helped shrink the welfare rolls significantly since 1993, much remains to be done. To that end, two additional initiatives have been put in place to advance this Administration's strategy for moving welfare recipients into employment. The first is a tax credit for employers who hire long-term welfare recipients; the credit rebates to employers up to $3,500 in wages paid in the first year and up to $5,000 in the second. The second initiative is the Welfare to Work Job Challenge Fund, which will assist States and communities in moving long-term welfare recipients into lasting, unsubsidized employment. A hallmark of this fund, for which $3 billion has been earmarked, is that it is targeted to those areas of the country most in need of poverty alleviation.

The Child Tax Credit

The Administration proposed a tax cut to help working families with the expense of raising their children. The Taxpayer Relief Act of 1997 will reduce taxes for 26 million families by providing a tax credit of $500 per child. This credit will benefit over 40 million children under age 17, including over 10 million children from working families with incomes below $30,000. Because the credit is partly refundable, large families who have paid significant out-of-pocket payroll taxes can benefit even if they have little or no income tax liability.

STRENGTHENING CITIES AND COMMUNITIES

This Administration has worked to make Federal resources available for investment in our Nation's cities and communities. First, the Administration has sought to expand the number of Empowerment Zones and Enterprise Communities. The initial round of competition, in 1994, led to the establishment of 95 Enterprise Communities and 9 Empowerment Zones; both urban and rural areas were represented. The Taxpayer Relief Act of 1997 established 22 additional Empowerment Zones. To compete for these designations, communities submitted strategic plans for revitalization; this requirement is intended to mobilize local communities and encourage them to harness their talents and resources in framing a plan for local economic development. Designated zones and communities receive tax benefits and flexible grants and are entitled to apply for waivers of certain Federal regulations; the underlying principle of the program is that communities know best how to solve their own problems but may lack the necessary resources.

The Administration has also worked to promote fair access to loans and investment capital for residents of low- and moderate-income areas. Reform of the Community Reinvestment Act regulations required banks to focus on performance—actual lending, investments, and services—rather than paperwork. Since 1993, conventional home mortgage lending to black Americans has increased by 67 percent, lending to Hispanic borrowers is up nearly 50 percent, and lending activity in low- and moderate-income communities has risen by 37 percent. The Administration also obtained $80 million in funding for Community Development Financial Institutions, which make investment capital and other financial products available to low- and moderate-income communities. The President's 1999 budget requests an additional $45 million for this program.

In addition, the President signed into law the "brownfields" program, which will provide tax incentives for the restoration of urban land contaminated by pollution. These incentives will leverage more than $6 billion for nationwide private sector cleanups and the redevelopment of 14,000 contaminated and abandoned sites in economically distressed urban areas.

Several basic principles inform these policies. First, they seek to equip communities with the tools they need in order to flourish—they are helping hands, not handouts. Second, they place the principal responsibility for community development with the communities themselves, because they are closest to their problems. Third, they emphasize private sector engagement rather than government mandates. And finally, they stress results over process: the Enterprise Communities/Empowerment Zones program, for example, gives communities broad scope to determine for themselves the best path for development; similarly, the reformed regulations implementing the Community Reinvestment Act use criteria based on actual outcomes to judge compliance with its provisions.

STRENGTHENING THE PERFORMANCE OF DOMESTIC MARKETS

As part of this Administration's commitment to free and open markets, the Antitrust Division of the Department of Justice has worked together with the Federal Trade Commission to vigorously enforce the Nation's antitrust laws. Recent cases and investigations reveal that the Department of Justice and the Federal Trade Commission have both pursued an aggressive but balanced approach in enforcing antitrust law; in particular, both agencies have sought to ensure the continued growth and competitiveness of high-technology industries.

Chapter 6 of this *Report* describes how the antitrust agencies have worked to attain these goals in several recent cases.

OPENING FOREIGN MARKETS

Progress was also made in 1997 toward opening foreign markets to U.S. goods, as a number of important international trade initiatives were made final. Trade agreements affecting three important sectors were reached, concluding some unfinished business from the Uruguay Round of multilateral negotiations. The first of these agreements, the Information Technology Agreement (ITA), will eliminate tariffs on a large array of information technology products, in which U.S. firms tend to be highly competitive. Also successfully concluded were an agreement covering financial services, which will foster broad liberalization of banking, securities, and insurance markets, and a key agreement to liberalize basic telecommunications services (including telephone services). Chapter 7 of this *Report* considers the Administration's trade policies in more detail.

These negotiations illustrate an important point about trade liberalization. Even though all three agreements involved sectors in which the United States is generally thought to have a competitive advantage, other countries were willing nevertheless to agree to their liberalization. They did so because they recognized that the entry of efficiently produced foreign products in these markets would improve the competitiveness of their own economies: securing goods of the highest quality at the lowest possible price is good for any economy.

PROMOTING AN ECONOMICALLY SOUND ENVIRONMENTAL AGENDA

The Administration took several important steps in 1997 to protect the environment. These included efforts to address global climate change and to improve air quality. In December representatives of the United States and some 160 other countries, meeting in Kyoto, Japan, agreed to establish binding limits on industrial countries' greenhouse gas emissions. These limits are intended to stem the disruptive effects of climate change by stabilizing atmospheric concentrations of greenhouse gases. (Because developing countries will emit an increasing share of global greenhouse gases, the President has indicated that the Kyoto agreement will not be submitted for ratification without meaningful developing-country participation.)

The Administration has proposed several market-based approaches to meeting the Kyoto limits. Domestically, tax incentives for energy-efficient technologies and research and development will spur early efforts to reduce emissions. A national system of tradable permits for greenhouse gas emissions, patterned after the successful permit trading program for sulfur dioxide emissions, will be implemented later under the President's proposal. In addition, the Kyoto agreement allows for trading in greenhouse gas emissions permits on an international scale, as well as opportunities for firms in the industrial countries to receive emissions credits for investing in climate-friendly technologies in developing countries. All of these efforts will help the United States attain its greenhouse gas emissions target in a cost-effective way.

In July 1997 the Environmental Protection Agency (EPA) issued a significantly more stringent standard for ground-level ozone and a new standard for fine particulate matter in the atmosphere. Although the Clean Air Act does not allow for the consideration of costs in setting these standards, under the President's policy the EPA must implement these health-based standards in a cost-effective manner. The Administration's plan for achieving the new air quality standards departs from traditional command-and-control approaches by designing regional strategies that will complement local efforts, and encouraging the development of trading programs for emissions of nitrogen oxides, which are ozone precursors. The nitrogen oxide trading program, like the acid rain program and the trading program envisioned for greenhouse gas emissions, enlists market incentives in controlling pollution and should reduce pollution more cheaply than do traditional regulatory approaches. Chapter 5 of this *Report* provides a detailed assessment of the Administration's environmental policies.

FACING THE CHALLENGES AHEAD

In many ways the U.S. economy today is very different from that in which our parents and grandparents lived and worked. Today, 24 percent of families are headed by a single parent, compared with 14 percent 25 years ago. And three in five married mothers with children under 6 are in the work force—twice as large a share as in 1970. This makes affordable, quality child care a pressing concern for most families. Meanwhile the nature of the labor market has changed significantly: few American workers expect to be working for the same employer—or even to be in the same career—when they retire. Industry has also changed radically: in the 1950s the information technology industry barely existed; today it employs a larger share of the labor force than the automobile industry did in the 1950s and 1960s. And the U.S. population is aging, implying that in the next century there will be fewer workers for every retiree.

This Administration's economic agenda is designed to deal with these changes and the challenges they pose. If the American economy is to maintain its preeminence as the strongest and most dynamic in the world, both policymakers and citizens will have to meet and overcome a number of challenges in the 21st century.

Several such challenges already loom large for this Administration and Congress. Perhaps the most important is preparing for the aging of the population, which requires reforming Medicare and Social Security and promoting retirement security more generally. As reported above, some progress was made in addressing Medicare's immediate problems, but comprehensive reforms are still needed to ensure the program's long-term viability. Likewise, steps will have to be taken to strengthen the finances of the Social Security system.

For almost 60 years Social Security has provided Americans with income security in retirement and protection against loss of family income due to disability or death. A large share of elderly Americans, particularly those with low incomes, rely on Social Security as their primary source of pension income in retirement. The system has enjoyed dramatic success in reducing poverty rates among older Americans. However, many Americans now fear that Social Security will not be there for them when they are ready to retire. This concern reflects the widespread recognition that, under current "intermediate" projections of the Social Security trustees, the system faces a long-term funding gap: beginning in 2012, unless the system is reformed by then, the government will be unable to pay current Social Security benefits in full out of current payroll taxes; it will then have to draw down the system's trust fund, and by 2029 those funds will be exhausted. If still nothing has been done, the government would then face several options which it could adopt singly or in combination: it could reduce benefits until they are in line with collections, raise payroll taxes to cover an unchanged level of benefits, or finance the shortfall from other parts of the budget, by raising other taxes, cutting expenditures on other programs, or borrowing and allowing the budget deficit to increase. One or more of these measures will have to be taken so long as no changes are made to the present system.

Although the seriousness of the financial imbalance facing Social Security should not be downplayed, its magnitude is not so large as to be insurmountable, particularly if early action is taken. For example, even if nothing is done and the trust fund is exhausted, payroll taxes will still be sufficient to permanently finance roughly 75 percent of benefits. Put another way, the difference between the anticipated income and the anticipated expenditures of the Old Age, Survivors', and Disability Insurance program over the next 75 years amounts to around 2¼ percentage points of taxable payroll, or approximately 1 percent of GDP. (The imbalance is somewhat larger when viewed over a longer horizon.) These facts suggest that the problem of placing Social Security on a sound financial footing can admit of eventual resolution, and the President has proposed a process to devise an appropriate solution over the next 2 years. The President has also proposed that any budget surpluses should be reserved until Social Security reform is achieved.

Medicare reform presents a somewhat thornier problem, in terms of both its complexity and its scale. Unlike Social Security, Medicare promises not just the payment of a sum of money but the delivery of

38

a service: health insurance. The government has little influence over the rate of increase in the cost of providing this service, which has been rising faster than general inflation for decades, largely driven by technological advances in medical care. Higher costs for medical care are projected to account for the bulk of the increase in Medicare expenditures for the next 25 years or so, after which the aging of the baby-boom generation will act to raise expenditures still further through increases in program enrollment. Hence, any long-term reform will have to involve slowing both the rise in health care prices and the growth in volume and intensity of use of covered services. Neither will be accomplished easily.

Before last year's budget legislation was enacted, the trust fund for the component of Medicare that covers hospital costs was projected to fall to zero in 2001. The 1997 reforms will delay the trust fund's depletion until 2010. The legislation also calls for the establishment of a bipartisan commission to assess and recommend the structural changes that will be needed to ensure Medicare's long-term viability.

A second major policy challenge involves continuing the drive for more open international markets. Preferential trade agreements are being negotiated among countries around the world at a rapid pace, and the United States could easily be left behind through inaction. Since 1992, countries in Latin America and Asia have negotiated 20 preferential trade arrangements that exclude the United States. One of these is MERCOSUR, a customs union among four South American countries. The European Union has begun a process intended to culminate in a free trade agreement with Brazil, Argentina, and the other MERCOSUR nations; the President of one European nation has even gone so far as to declare that the economic interests of Latin America lie with Europe, not the United States. Meanwhile the MERCOSUR nations are attempting to extend their preferential trade arrangement to the entire continent. It is clear that now, more than ever, continued engagement with the world trading system will require an active effort on the part of the United States.

In 1997 the Senate voted to move forward on extending the President's so-called fast-track negotiating authority. This authority allows the President to negotiate trade agreements and submit them to the Congress for a yes-or-no vote, without amendments. However, in the House of Representatives the vote to renew fast-track was postponed. Some have voiced concern that free trade hurts American workers and contributes to the U.S. trade deficit. As discussed in Chapter 7, however, market-opening initiatives do not cause net job losses to the U.S. economy as a whole, although they do result in a reallocation of jobs into expanding, export-oriented industries. As the chapter documents, the jobs created by increased trade are good jobs, offering high pay. But some workers are indeed hurt by more open markets, just as some workers are harmed by technological innova-

39

tion, even though market-opening initiatives unambiguously benefit the economy as a whole.

This Administration has realized from the beginning that the government can minimize the impact of dislocations affecting workers who lose their jobs, by speeding the adjustment process. For example, one of the key provisions of NAFTA involved monitoring those industries that were in danger of being adversely affected by the agreement, and the Administration committed itself early on to providing for dislocated workers through retraining programs. The President's 1999 budget includes proposals to expand the scope of trade adjustment assistance and to increase funding for these programs. More generally, the Administration's commitment to investing in people through education and training serves as a strong complement to its policy of trade liberalization.

A widespread misconception is that one of the benefits of increased trade comes in the form of an improved balance of trade. Economic policies do indeed affect the current account (the broad measure of U.S. international transactions that includes investment income and transfers as well as trade in goods and services), but it is budget, saving, and investment policies, not trade liberalization policies, that do so. The Nation's current account deficit equals its borrowing abroad to finance any excess of investment over domestic saving. The current account is therefore a macroeconomic phenomenon that mirrors the gap between what we as a Nation invest and what we save. The large Federal budget deficits of the 1980s and early 1990s were a form of negative saving, or dissaving, which reduced the total amount of national saving available to cover the Nation's investment in plant and equipment. In an important sense, the Nation was overconsuming in the 1980s, financing its consumption binge by borrowing from foreigners. The result was a large and persistent current account deficit.

We still have a current account deficit today, but for a very different reason. The near elimination of the budget deficit has left more saving available for investment in plant and equipment by the private sector. National saving has risen. But because of the investment boom during this expansion, the gap between investment and saving has persisted. Once again, this shortfall is made up by borrowing from abroad, and the result is a current account deficit. But there is a big difference between borrowing to invest—as the Nation is doing now—and borrowing to consume, as it did in the 1980s. In fact, running a trade deficit in order to expand the Nation's productive capacity is not new to American history—we did much the same thing in the last century, to build up the Nation's infrastructure, most notably during the railroad construction boom. Ironically, therefore, today's trade deficit reflects the economy's current success in growing more rapidly than our trading partners and investing so much—and *not* our free trade policies.

It is always difficult to explain this macroeconomic perspective on the trade deficit to those who are primarily concerned with the microeconomics of their daily lives. But making the case in favor of trade is particularly important now, because real danger threatens should countries turn their backs on a progressive and integrated world economic order. Besides postponing the renewal of the President's traditional trade-negotiating authority, the Congress chose not to support the sort of financial participation in international institutions that is vital for the sound functioning of the international system. Meanwhile financial crises in East Asia have made U.S. international engagement more important, rather than less. Other emerging-market countries are themselves in danger of reacting to the East Asian crises by turning inward. It is important for their economic well-being, as well as our own, that they continue along the path toward an outward-oriented market system, on which they had until recently been making such astonishing progress. This will require difficult macroeconomic and structural adjustments on their part, including reducing their dependence on foreign borrowing. As a result, these countries will have to reduce their trade deficits, and in some cases even turn them into trade surpluses. This will inevitably lead to an increase in U.S. bilateral trade deficits with some East Asian countries. Again, however, such deficits are not the proper gauge of the success or failure of U.S. trade policy.

The Nation faces other, broader challenges in shaping economic policies for the 21st century. First, we must act to help families address the problems they face in today's economy. More American workers today are faced with the need to juggle the demands of the workplace with the demands of family and home. Government must act to ease this burden by ensuring that families have access to quality child care and health care. For this reason the President's 1999 budget includes a $21 billion increase in funding for child care, to make it accessible to more families and raise its quality. An important part of this proposal is increased tax credits for 3 million working families to help them pay for child care, as well as an increase in block grants to States that will directly subsidize child care for low-income families. In addition, the proposal calls for a new Early Learning Fund, along with support for the enforcement of State child care health and safety standards, scholarships for up to 50,000 child care providers per year, and funding for research and consumer education.

We must also continue to invest in our Nation's children. Chapter 3 of this *Report* shows that the last 3 years have witnessed notable improvements in children's well-being along several fronts, including decreases in child poverty, increases in consumption of basic health care services, and improvements in health status and in some measures of educational achievement. However, many children remain economically vulnerable. One in five children in the United States lives in a family whose income is below the poverty line, one in seven

41

does not have access to health insurance, and a large proportion of children fail to achieve basic levels of proficiency in science, mathematics, and reading. Chapter 3 considers ongoing and proposed Administration initiatives that address these problems.

Finally, this country's longstanding goal of achieving equality of opportunity among racial and ethnic groups has not yet been attained. Chapter 4 of this *Report* reviews differences in economic status among blacks, Hispanics, non-Hispanic whites, Asians, and American Indians. Although there has been progress in narrowing these gaps in the postwar period, it has been very uneven, with rapid progress in the 1960s and early 1970s followed by 20 years of stagnation from the early to mid-1970s to the early 1990s. For example, since the mid-1970s the wages of young black college graduates have fallen relative to those of their white counterparts. Although the current expansion has brought signs of renewed progress, substantial disparities in economic status persist. For example, the median wealth of white families is by some estimates 10 times that of black and Hispanic families. More needs to be done to promote equality of opportunity for all Americans. Many of the Administration's current and proposed policies, such as those that encourage community empowerment and education, are intended to address these disparities. And this Administration has pledged itself to furthering a dialogue on race in America.

CONCLUSION

The United States today enjoys some of the most favorable economic conditions in a generation: high growth and low unemployment combined with low and stable inflation. And the success of Americans in adapting to the new economy in which they find themselves has been truly remarkable. But that success—and the economy's present strength—cannot be taken for granted. Recent developments do not herald the end of inflation, the conquest of the business cycle, or the permanent reversal of such secular trends as weak productivity growth and rising income inequality. Rather, there are still long-term changes at work that demand action by individuals, businesses, and governments alike. This Administration has put in place a set of policies that has allowed the economy to grow and to flourish—in particular by putting the Nation's fiscal house in order. But we must continue to pursue sound policies aimed at opening markets at home and abroad, promoting private and public investment, and ensuring that all Americans, regardless of age or origin, have the skills they need to prosper in a world of change and opportunity.

CHAPTER 2

Macroeconomic Policy and Performance

MACROECONOMIC PERFORMANCE over the past 5 years has been excellent, and the record in 1997 was truly remarkable. In general, the behavior of the economy last year bore out the analysis of macroeconomic conditions presented in last year's *Economic Report of the President*, which was confident that the economy would continue to grow without rising inflation. What was not anticipated fully at that time, however, was how rapidly the economy would grow or how strong the pace of job creation would be—or that inflation would actually *decline*.

Last year the Administration forecast 2-percent growth during 1997 with an average unemployment rate of 5.3 percent. This forecast was not meant as an assessment of the best the economy could do. Rather, it represented a conservative and credible set of economic assumptions to be used for forecasting Federal revenues, outlays, and deficits in the preparation of the budget. Last year's *Report* recognized that the actual outcome could be even better. And it was, with growth at nearly 4 percent and the unemployment rate averaging only 4.9 percent. More jobs were created in 1997 than in either of the 2 previous years. Yet inflation remained subdued, with the consumer price index (CPI) rising just 1.7 percent during the year.

This chapter's analysis of macroeconomic policy and performance concludes that the economy should continue to grow with low inflation in 1998. The chapter begins with a review of macroeconomic performance and policy in 1997, to show in some detail where the year's growth came from and how inflation remained so tame. The second section examines the important question of whether our understanding of inflation and our ability to predict it have changed in significant ways. This question is part of a broader inquiry into whether the economy has changed in such fundamental ways that standard analyses of how fast it can grow without inflation need to be replaced with a new view. The conclusion reached here is that no sea change has occurred that would justify ignoring the threat of inflation when the labor market is as tight as it is now; however, the unemployment rate at which rising inflation becomes a serious threat appears to be lower than it was in the 1980s, and the rate of growth of potential output may be higher.

Prudence dictates keeping a wary eye on inflationary pressures, but, as discussed in Chapter 1, the economy remains remarkably free of the kinds of imbalances that often appear at the end of expansions. For example, the analysis in the third section of this chapter indicates that the financial condition of households remains fundamentally sound, even though they took on considerable debt in 1997. Two cautionary notes are introduced. First, the rise in the stock market over the first 7 months of 1997 put price-earnings ratios and other measures of stock market valuation near historical highs. Second, households are continuing to consume a very high proportion of their disposable income and are saving little. The implications of this low saving rate for long-term growth are explored in the fourth section of the chapter, which also assesses the positive contribution of deficit reduction. The chapter concludes with the Administration's forecast and outlook.

OVERVIEW OF 1997: A BURST OF GROWTH

Economic growth exceeded expectations in 1997, and the unemployment rate declined to a 24-year low. Households and firms both increased their spending at robust rates as continued low inflation, low unemployment, declining costs of business equipment, and lower long-term interest rates contributed to a favorable economic environment for both consumers and producers. Federal Government purchases of goods and services declined in real terms, and purchases by State and local governments increased only modestly. Net exports continued to be a restraining influence on growth.

Strong investment in new productive capacity in the past few years has helped the economy accommodate higher spending without rising inflation. But inflation has also been held in check by several other favorable developments that have kept prices from accelerating even as wage growth has picked up. Chief among these have been the rise in the value of the dollar on foreign exchange markets (which makes imports cheaper), unusually steep declines in prices for computers, and continued moderation in employer costs of health insurance.

Late in 1996 the economy was already operating near the consensus estimate of its noninflationary potential. Continued robust economic growth in the latter part of 1996 and early 1997 promised to increase resource utilization rates even further, raising concerns that inflationary pressures would build, and the Federal Reserve raised short-term interest rates in March. With inflation low and stable—and in light of the turmoil in Asian financial markets that began to emerge in mid-1997—the Federal Reserve made no further interest rate moves.

AGGREGATE SPENDING IN 1997

An accounting of the sectoral contributions to growth in 1997 shows that increases in private domestic spending for consumption and investment combined exceeded growth in gross domestic product (GDP; Table 2-1). Modest increases in State and local government expenditures accounted for the increase in total government spending. Net exports became more negative.

TABLE 2-1.—*Components of GDP and Growth in GDP, 1997*

Item	Billions of dollars	Percent of GDP	Contribution to growth	
			Percentage points	Percent of total change
Personal consumption expenditures...............	5,488.6	67.9	2.5	65.2
Gross private domestic investment...............	1,237.6	15.3	1.5	38.4
Fixed investment....................................	1,173.0	14.5	1.1	27.3
Nonresidential...................................	845.4	10.5	.8	21.3
Structures.....................................	230.2	2.8	-.0	-.6
Producers' durable equipment...............	615.2	7.6	.9	21.9
Residential.......................................	327.5	4.1	.2	6.0
Change in business inventories..................	64.6	.8	.4	10.9
Net exports of goods and services...............	-96.7	-1.2	-.4	-10.0
Exports...	958.8	11.9	1.2	31.7
Imports...	1,055.5	13.1	-1.6	-41.9
Government consumption expenditures and gross investment..............................	1,453.9	18.0	.2	6.1
Federal...	524.8	6.5	-.0	-.0
State and local.....................................	929.1	11.5	.2	6.1
GROSS DOMESTIC PRODUCT...............	8,083.4	100.0	3.9	100.0
MEMORANDUM: FINAL SALES...............	8,018.8	99.2	3.5	89.1

Note.—Data are preliminary estimates. Contribution to growth is measured fourth quarter to fourth quarter.
Sources: Department of Commerce (Bureau of Economic Analysis) and Council of Economic Advisers.

Private Domestic Spending

The factors traditionally thought to determine household spending are household income, consumer sentiment, and household net worth in the current and recent years. Signals were favorable for all of these fundamentals through most of 1997: real disposable personal income grew 3.7 percent over the four quarters of the year, consumer sentiment remained at or near record highs for most of the year, and year-end stock market values were up about 30 percent from a year earlier. Outlays grew even faster than income, and as a result, the personal saving rate edged down.

Although consumption was robust over the past year, it was not smooth. Real consumption grew in excess of a 5-percent annual rate in the first and third quarters, but at only a 0.9-percent annual rate in the second. No reason for this volatility is apparent; neither fluctuating income, changes in consumer confidence, nor ups and downs in the stock market explain it. Although the stock market dipped in

April after the Federal Reserve's interest rate hike, it had fully recovered by mid-May. At the same time, consumer sentiment continued to rise. Most of the volatility was in goods consumption; services consumption grew at around a 4- to 5-percent annual rate in each quarter. Durable goods, which rose at double-digit annual rates in the first and third quarters but fell at a 5-percent annual rate in the second, accounted for much of the quarter-to-quarter fluctuations in growth. Light motor vehicle sales of roughly 15 million units in 1997 were about the same as in each of the past 3 years; over this 4-year period, sales of light motor vehicles were just shy of the record 4-year pace set in the mid-1980s.

Like those for consumption, the signals for the traditional determinants of business investment—lagged GDP growth, cash flow growth, and the cost of capital—were strongly favorable throughout 1997. Several special factors added further impetus to investment spending. Business equipment grew 12 percent over the four quarters of the year, with strong demand for most types of equipment. Industrial equipment grew a healthy 7 percent over the year, and transportation equipment advanced 10 percent, with particularly rapid growth in aircraft purchases.

The standout categories of business equipment investment in 1997 were office and computing equipment and telecommunications equipment. Growth in real computer spending was fueled in part by price declines that were even sharper than normal (32 percent over the past year). Real spending on telecommunications equipment increased 10 percent. One factor possibly boosting sales in this industry is the rapidly expanding capacity and availability of cellular telephone and other wireless services. Although nominal spending on computers and telecommunications equipment represents about 25 percent of investment in equipment, measured relative declines in computer prices have been rapid, so that these categories now account for a rising fraction of real equipment purchases.

In contrast to the strength in equipment spending, investment in nonresidential structures was about flat last year, following solid gains in 1996. Construction of new office buildings made solid gains, as the strength in the economy allowed the sector to grow out from under an overhang of empty office buildings at the beginning of the decade. These gains were offset by small declines in the construction of industrial, utility, and mining structures.

A pickup in inventory investment added 0.4 percentage point to real GDP growth over the four quarters of 1997, with an especially large buildup in the first quarter. The demand for inventories was probably a result of strong final sales, which increased faster than inventories over the first three quarters of the year. As a result, stocks remained lean in relation to sales.

Residential construction increased 6 percent over the four quarters of 1997, with much of that growth occurring in the fourth quarter. The

pickup toward the end of year reflected in part the pattern of mortgage rates, which after rising through April, fell more than 1
percentage point later in the year. Falling mortgage rates, together
with strong real income growth, resulted in an increase in housing
affordability in the second half of the year. In addition to new home
construction, real estate commissions moved up over the year, as
sales of existing homes grew by 3 percent over 1997 as a whole to
their highest level ever.

When consumption and investment are combined, real private
domestic demand grew 4.8 percent over the four quarters of 1997; this
was somewhat faster than plausible estimates of the sustainable long-
run growth rate of the economy. The impact of this surge of private
spending was muted, however, by an erosion in net exports, a continuing decline in real Federal Government spending, and slow growth in
spending by State and local governments.

Government Spending and Fiscal Policy

Government expenditures made only a modest contribution to
growth in real GDP in 1997—and all of that came from expenditures
by State and local governments. Real Federal Government expenditures were lower last year than in 1996. Fiscal policy was tight in
1997, with the adjusted structural budget deficit (the deficit measured at a standardized level of economic activity) declining by $54
billion in fiscal 1997 from $112 billion in fiscal 1996.

These developments reflected ongoing efforts to restore Federal fiscal responsibility, which culminated in the Balanced Budget Act of
1997. The Federal Government's unified budget deficit for fiscal 1997
was $22 billion, a reduction of $86 billion from 1996. The Federal budget position has now improved in each of the last 5 years, the longest
unbroken period of improvement since 1948. Last year's unified
deficit was just 0.3 percent of GDP, the smallest by this measure since
1970. Relative to the size of the economy, last year's general-government deficit (the combined deficit of all levels of government) is
estimated to have been smaller than that of any other large industrial country except Canada. Moreover, last year's primary Federal
surplus (defined as revenues less outlays other than net interest) was
$221 billion; as a share of GDP this was the largest since the 1950s.
It reveals that the overall budget would have shown a substantial
surplus last year were it not for the interest obligations on debt run
up during the period of large deficits.

Much of the long-term progress on the deficit can be traced to the
effects of the Omnibus Budget Reconciliation Act of 1993. However,
last year's improvement in the deficit was considerably greater than
had been anticipated; as recently as February 1997 the projected
deficit for fiscal 1997 was $126 billion.

The continuing vigor of the economy is clearly responsible for part
of this progress toward a balanced budget. Of course, sound policies—

47

including a credible commitment to deficit reduction—have nurtured the expansion. About $30 billion of the improvement in the deficit resulted from lower-than-expected expenditures. Robust economic growth also was responsible for some of the $76 billion in unanticipated revenues collected by the Treasury. However, revenues increased even more than would have been predicted on the basis of observed economic growth (Box 2-1).

Box 2-1.—Accounting for the Deficit Surprise During Fiscal 1997

In last year's budget the current-services deficit for fiscal 1997 was projected at $127.7 billion. (The current-services deficit assumes no change in law. The President's budget, which includes policy proposals, was projected at $125.6 billion.) The actual budget deficit was $21.9 billion—or $105.8 billion lower than the current-services projection. Although a full accounting for this deficit surprise will not be possible for several years, the table below summarizes what is now known.

Of the $105.8 billion difference between the actual and the current-services deficit, $30.3 billion was accounted for by lower-than-expected outlays. About one-quarter of these savings were in income security programs such as food stamps, unemployment insurance, and family support programs; spending on all of these programs is typically linked to economic performance.

The remaining $75.5 billion of the difference was attributable to unexpectedly high revenues. Only $12.3 billion of this revenue surprise was accounted for by higher-than-expected collections of corporate, social insurance, excise, and other taxes. Most ($63.2 billion) of the unanticipated revenues came from individual income taxes. A large portion of the unanticipated individual income tax revenue, $28.2 billion, came in as payments on 1997 obligations. A full accounting of this surprise will have to wait until 1997 tax returns are processed, but a large share of the unanticipated collections on 1997 liabilities is likely related to better-than-expected economic growth in 1997. Approximately $6.0 billion in additional individual tax receipts came from payment of back taxes or from taxes on trusts.

Another $29.0 billion of the revenue surprise arrived in the form of higher-than-anticipated final payments and lower-than-anticipated refunds on 1996 individual income tax liabilities. The largest identifiable contributing factor was higher-than-anticipated tax liability on capital gain realizations, which accounted for $20.1 billion of the $29.0 billion in unanticipated

---

Box 2-1.—continued

payments on 1996 obligations. The remaining $8.9 billion came from higher-than-expected tax liabilities on pensions, dividends, distributions from Individual Retirement Accounts, interest payments, and wages and salaries, which were partially offset by higher-than-anticipated deductions.

Accounting for the Fiscal 1997 Deficit Surprise
[Billions of dollars]

Item	Actual minus projected[1]
Outlays	-30.3
Income security programs	-7.3
Other	-23.0
Receipts	75.5
Individual income taxes	63.2
On 1996 liability	29.0
Wages and salaries	.8
Capital gains	20.1
Pension and IRA distributions	4.1
Interest income	5.3
Dividend income	1.9
Itemized deductions	-3.2
On 1997 liability	28.2
Back taxes and fiduciaries	6.0
Corporate income taxes	6.1
Social insurance taxes	3.6
Excise taxes	2.9
Other	-.3
Increase in surplus or reduction in deficit	105.8

[1] Current-services projection.
Sources: Department of the Treasury and Office of Management and Budget.

In national income accounting terms, the slowdown in the growth of government expenditures and the improving general-government budget balance have exerted a moderating influence on overall aggregate demand that has partly offset the robust stimulus coming from private consumption and investment. Nevertheless, the combined impetus from private and government spending exceeded the increase in domestic aggregate production, so that net exports declined further.

Net Exports and the Current Account

U.S. exporters had a good year in 1997, as real exports rose 10.9 percent. However, robust growth in domestic demand pushed real

49

imports up by 13.3 percent. Real net exports fell by $35.8 billion over the course of the year, and their contribution to growth in real GDP was –0.4 percentage point.

One useful perspective on the performance of real net exports comes from looking at the pattern of growth in the global economy. At least four major locomotives matter for global economic growth: North America, Europe, Japan, and—in the past decade—the East Asian industrializing economies. Expectations at the end of 1996 were that

---

Box 2-2.—Turmoil in Asian Economies

The outbreak of financial crisis in Asia was one of the most notable—and troubling—developments in the global economy during 1997. Events began in midyear as a currency crisis and intensified over the rest of the year, spilling over to the real sectors of the affected economies as well as to the rest of the world.

By May 1997 Thailand was in the throes of the fourth speculative attack on its currency, the baht, since August 1996. By then the buildup of financial difficulties and balance of payments pressures had reached such a point that efforts to defend the baht could not be sustained. Pressures soon spilled over to other emerging Asian economies (especially Indonesia, Malaysia, and South Korea), most of which also had some balance of payments weaknesses, as well as to Eastern Europe. These countries' difficulties shook financial market confidence elsewhere in Asia and in emerging markets around the world, even those with sounder policies and economic fundamentals, in a contagion effect.

Since June, four of the countries in the region (Indonesia, the Philippines, South Korea, and Thailand) have requested and received assistance from the International Monetary Fund (IMF). In each instance the adjustment programs developed by the domestic authorities and the IMF have included a heavy emphasis on financial and structural adjustment measures (for example, to reform bank lending practices and further liberalize the economy), as well as the more traditional macroeconomic adjustments necessary to restore financial market stability. For each of the affected economies, the question of when their financial and balance of payments situations will stabilize depends, first and foremost, on whether and how aggressively they implement their policy commitments, and second, on the easing of the contagion effect from those economies that continue to experience difficulties. In the medium term the return of these economies' strong growth performance will depend significantly upon the degree to which structural and financial sector reforms are implemented.

growth would slow in the United States and that the other regions (except Japan) would easily outpace it. Instead, the United States (and Canada) saw higher growth rates in 1997 (about 4 percent each), while growth among our trading partners in the other regions slowed. In Japan the recovery from the recession of the early 1990s came to a standstill. In Europe growth continued in 1997, especially in a northern tier composed of the British Isles and the Nordic countries. In the developing economies of East Asia, slowing growth turned to financial crisis in the second half of the year (Box 2-2).

Growth rates in the United States and its trading partners, along with exchange rates, are major determinants of short-run fluctuations in real net exports. The fact that income increased more rapidly here in 1997 than it did in most other advanced industrial economies worked to increase U.S. imports from those economies more rapidly than their imports from the United States. The negative effects of the East Asian crunch on U.S. net exports to developing countries had barely begun to materialize at the end of the year.

In analyzing the components of real growth, it is appropriate to look at real net exports. But the focus generally shifts to nominal imports and exports when examining current income flows between the United States and the rest of the world. The comprehensive measure of such flows is the current account balance, which comprises not only the trade balance in goods and services but also net investment income and transfers.

In a fundamental sense, trends in the current account balance reflect movements in saving and investment. When the demand for investment in the United States exceeds the pool of national saving, the difference is made up by borrowing from foreigners. Conversely, when saving exceeds investment, the surplus is invested abroad. The United States first experienced large current account deficits during the mid-1980s, when net investment fell as a share of national income and net national saving fell even faster. The deficit shrank briefly as investment collapsed in the 1990-91 recession, but it has reemerged in the current expansion. The good news in this expansion is that investment has been booming. But saving does not appear to have kept pace. (The interpretation of current trends in saving, investment, and the current account is complicated by the statistical discrepancy between GDP measured as the sum of all spending on output and GDP measured as the sum of all income generated in producing that output.)

The current account deficit for the first 9 months of 1997 was about $8.7 billion greater than in the comparable period in 1996, and the deficit for the year is likely to be moderately higher than the $148 billion (1.9 percent of GDP) recorded in 1996. Much of the increase reflects the emergence of a deficit in the balance on investment income. As a result of past deficits, foreign holdings of U.S. assets are now sufficiently large that the investment income paid to foreigners now exceeds investment income earned on U.S. holdings of foreign assets. The balance on all goods and services may show little change at all from last year's $111 billion. The modest size of the increase in the trade deficit last year is probably related to changes in the exchange rate of the dollar.

The effect of exchange rates on the nominal trade balance last year is complicated. The trade-weighted exchange rate of the dollar rose about 3 percent during the first quarter of the year (that is, the dollar strengthened against a weighted average of the currencies of our trading partners). In the long run the effect of a stronger dollar is to slow exports and probably raise spending on imports, thereby depressing the trade balance. But in the short run the effects on the nominal trade balance may go the other way. This is because, with a stronger dollar, importers do not have to pay out as many dollars to obtain the foreign currency they need to pay for previous quantities of imports (in what is called a valuation effect), and because it takes time for the quantity demanded to adjust. There can be a lag of 2 years or more before price changes have their full effect on trade volumes, but when they do they dominate the valuation effect. (This pattern of response is often called the J-curve, because the dollar value of imports at first declines with a stronger dollar but later rises.) The difficulty in interpreting what happened in 1997 is due to the fact that in 1996, before the most recent appreciation, the dollar had also increased in value. Thus the lagged effects from that earlier appreciation may have partly canceled out the immediate effects from the 1997 appreciation. The delayed effects of the dollar's appreciation, together with the other effects of the East Asian financial crisis, are likely to show up in a more marked increase in the trade deficit, by all measures, in 1998.

MONETARY POLICY AND FINANCIAL MARKETS

The Federal Reserve raised its target Federal funds rate by 25 basis points in March, to 5.5 percent. The proximate cause of the rate increase was the perception that strong demand would boost utilization rates, which were already approaching levels that in the past had been associated with rising inflation. The mild deceleration in GDP prices in the second half of the year translated into a slight upward drift in the real Federal funds rate as 1997 came to a close, putting the real rate slightly above its mid-1995 peak. Moreover, the rise in the real short-term rate did not appear to feed through to intermediate- and long-term real rates, which remained essentially unchanged—or, by some measures, even declined—in the second half of the year.

Short-term interest rates fluctuated within a narrow range over the course of the year, whereas long-term rates rose slightly early in the year but then declined, finishing the year roughly 50 basis points (half a percentage point) lower. Long-term interest rates remain very low. The yield on 10-year Treasury notes remained within 50 basis points of its 30-year low, while the 30-year Treasury yield stood near its lowest level since that bond's introduction in 1977. This largely reflects two related factors: continued progress in deficit reduction, which lowers nominal interest rates by reducing expected future real rates, and market participants' expectations of low future inflation, which act to reduce nominal rates. In addition, turmoil in foreign asset markets in the second half of the year helped make U.S. securities more attractive to investors; this "flight to quality" probably boosted demand for U.S. assets, putting additional downward pressure on nominal interest rates. The net result was a flattening of the yield curve, with the spread (the difference in interest rates) between 3-month Treasury bills and 10-year Treasury notes falling to roughly 60 basis points by the end of 1997. This spread is now well below its historical average of 135 basis points and is roughly equal to the level that prevailed during the 1960s.

The risk premium on corporate debt—measured as the spread between the yield on Baa-rated corporate bonds and the 30-year Treasury bond yield—averaged roughly 125 basis points in 1997 (a Baa rating denotes bonds of intermediate credit quality); this spread remains quite narrow by historical standards. The spread between riskier, high-yield corporate debt ("junk" bonds) and 10-year Treasury securities also remained narrow in 1997 but began to rise toward the end of the year. Taken as a whole, these low risk premiums suggest that market participants perceive the financial and business sectors to be quite healthy; most relevant statistics provide support for this view. In the banking sector, business loan charge-offs and delinquency rates remained low, while bank capital ratios remained high. Although business failures increased in 1997, a large portion of this increase appears to reflect special, one-time factors, not a permanent change in trend.

For equity markets 1997 was a noteworthy year. The rise in stock prices was checked only slightly following the Federal Reserve's March tightening, and even sharp declines in some foreign stock markets were unable to do more than temporarily slow the market's advance. All three major stock price indexes—the Dow Jones Industrial Average, the Standard & Poor's (S&P) 500, and the NASDAQ composite—shattered previous records; the S&P 500, for example, peaked in October at 983.12, a record high and 40 percent above its October 1996 average. The runup in stock prices appeared to be fueled by continued high profitability in the corporate sector and forecasts of strong future earnings growth, and it pushed aggregate price-earnings ratios up sharply. By some measures price-earnings ratios are at levels not seen in decades.

Declines in foreign stock markets spread to domestic markets later in the year, causing them to retreat from these record highs. On October 27th the Dow posted a 554-point decline—the 12th-largest in percentage terms in its history. The drop was steep enough to cause the New York

Stock Exchange's system of "circuit breakers" to suspend trading temporarily for the first time ever (Box 2-3). The day after the plunge saw the volume of shares traded on the New York Stock Exchange reach a record high of 1.2 billion (the market made up much of its previous day's decline that day). The stock market rebounded quickly following its October losses, with the S&P 500 index and the Dow finishing 1997 near their highs for the year. Turmoil in East Asia apparently continued to be a source of downward pressure on stock prices for the remainder of the year.

The rise in stock prices in 1997 represents the continuation of a trend that has seen major indexes more than double over the past 3 years. One explanatory factor is market expectations of strong future corporate earnings. Another possible factor is a reduction of the premium that investors require to hold stocks in lieu of less risky assets. Such a reduction could occur if the perception has become more widespread that stocks represent an attractive, high-return asset, or if investors' interest in longer term investments for retirement has grown. Still other possible explanations are a reduction in investors' expectations of future inflation or of future real interest rates, or the effect of financial innovations in channeling a larger share of savings into the stock market by way of mutual funds and pension funds.

There is some scattered evidence that investors have come to view stocks as a less risky investment: for example, a survey of individuals' attitudes toward the stock market shows a marked decline in the perceived riskiness of stocks since 1994. Similarly, participants in the largest private retirement savings plan in the United States have directed an increasing fraction of their retirement saving contributions to equities since 1986; however, it is unclear how much this reflects a reduction in participants' tolerance for risk, a change in their perception of the riskiness of the stock market, or other factors. If the risk premium on stocks has declined, this could explain why price-earnings ratios are at historically high levels; a simple calculation indicates that even a relatively small change in the risk premium is sufficient to raise price-earnings ratios sharply. Nevertheless, the possibility exists that price-earnings ratios will eventually return to more normal levels, given that periods in which price-earnings ratios are high tend to be followed by slower future growth in stock prices.

INFLATION AND THE LABOR MARKET

Inflation remained remarkably subdued in 1997. Both GDP and core CPI inflation (a measure of inflation that excludes the volatile food and energy components) fell over the course of the year, continuing a decline that began in 1995. Surprisingly, this deceleration of prices occurred in an economic environment that was characterized by extremely low unemployment: as 1997 came to a close, the unemployment rate had been at or below 5.5 percent for almost 2 years, and at or below 5 per-

Box 2-3.—Circuit Breakers

"Circuit breakers" are rules that automatically halt trading on a securities exchange when prices move by a given amount. The boards of a number of major exchanges, including the New York Stock Exchange (NYSE) and the Chicago Mercantile Exchange, set up circuit breakers in the wake of the 1987 stock market crash. The NYSE circuit breakers provide a good example of how such rules operate. Before the October 27th stock market decline, the circuit breakers were set to halt trading for 30 minutes if the Dow Jones Industrial Average declined more than 350 points from its morning opening price, and for another hour if the Dow were to fall an additional 200 points. Both of these limits were hit on October 27th, and the circuit breakers operated as designed and closed the market twice (the second event occurred less than an hour before the closing bell and thus ended trading for the day).

When they were introduced, it was argued that circuit breakers would reduce the chance of a major market disruption in three ways: by preventing an overload of the exchanges' trading systems during periods of extraordinary price movements; by reducing the possibility that sharp (and possibly unchecked) declines in stock prices would leave market participants unable to make good on their trading commitments; and by providing a forced pause in trading—a chance for market participants to "take a deep breath."

Many observers and market participants criticized the role that the circuit breakers actually played on October 27th. The trigger limits had only been adjusted once since 1988, and the percentage declines in the Dow that they reflected were only about a third as large as they were when the triggers were set up in 1988. Furthermore, the securities exchanges now have enormously greater capacity to process trades than they did in 1987; by all accounts the record trading volumes on October 27th and 28th did not remotely threaten to overload the system. And concerns about fulfillment of trading commitments appear to have been at least partially allayed, because traders now have greater access to emergency credit. The "deep breath" argument is more difficultto assess, because nobody knows what would have happened had the markets not closed early on October 27th. But some critics argue that circuit breakers can add to market volatility by causing a race to the exit—a sharp selloff in shares—as stock prices approach the threshold for a trading halt. Indeed, many traders argue that that is just what happened when the NYSE reopened after the first of its two shutdowns on October 27th. The NYSE has announced that it will propose modifications to the rule in 1998.

cent for 9 months. The unemployment rate fell from 5.3 percent in the fourth quarter of 1996 to 4.7 percent in the fourth quarter of 1997; all major demographic groups participated, with declines of 1.0 percentage point among blacks, 0.6 percentage point among whites, and 0.6 percentage point among Hispanics.

The pace of job creation was quite rapid. More than 3.2 million jobs were created in 1997, for an average of 267,000 new jobs per month—a substantially faster rate than in either of the 2 preceding years. Factory employment rose significantly, by 230,000 new jobs, while employment at construction sites rose by 210,000 jobs following a slightly larger gain in 1996. Among the service-producing industries growth was particularly rapid in computers and data processing (which increased 13 percent) and engineering and management services (which increased 7 percent).

These hiring gains were matched by large increases in industrial capacity. Nevertheless, tightness in labor markets was reflected in a continued acceleration of wages during the year. Hourly wages as measured by the employment cost index (ECI) rose by 3.9 percent in 1997, 0.5 percentage point faster than in 1996. The ECI for total hourly compensation accelerated by a slightly smaller amount, and continued slow growth in the cost of benefits—particularly health insurance—kept the growth rate of total hourly compensation 0.5 percentage point lower than that for hourly wages. Trend unit labor costs (defined as compensation growth relative to trend productivity growth) continued to rise moderately through the year, while overall price inflation fell slightly (Chart 2-1).

Chart 2-1 **Inflation and Trend Unit Labor Costs**
Inflation has dropped below growth in trend unit labor costs.

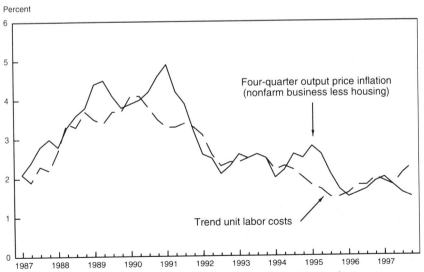

Note: Trend unit labor costs defined as the four-quarter percent change in compensation as measured by the employment cost index minus 1.1 percentage points.
Sources: Department of Commerce (Bureau of Economic Analysis), Department of Labor (Bureau of Labor Statistics), and Council of Economic Advisers.

PRODUCTIVITY

Growth in output per hour worked picked up sharply in 1997: over the first three quarters of the year the official measure of productivity in the nonfarm business sector rose at an average annual rate of 2.6 percent. This measure has exceeded its trend rate of growth in all but one of the past eight quarters. These recent gains were sufficient to offset the earlier weak performance of this product-side measure of productivity, bringing it back to its post-1973 trend. (Trend growth in productivity is discussed in the "Forecast and Outlook" section of this chapter.) Part of the surge in productivity probably reflected special factors: productivity growth in the third quarter of 1997 was boosted in part by a decline in hours worked by self-employed workers; these data tend to be more volatile and somewhat less reliable than measures of hours worked by employees. However, even when self-employed workers are excluded, measured productivity growth in the third quarter remains over twice as fast as its trend rate. The pickup in productivity growth is significant because it occurred at the same time that hourly compensation showed some signs of accelerating. This has kept growth in unit labor costs from rising by as much as compensation, thus eliminating a potential source of inflationary pressure.

EXPLAINING RECENT INFLATION PERFORMANCE

Inflation continued to moderate in 1997 even as the unemployment rate reached a 24-year low. To what extent can recent inflation performance be explained with the traditional tools of macroeconomic forecasting and analysis?

RECENT INFLATION PERFORMANCE AND THE NAIRU

The present combination of low and declining inflation and sustained low unemployment would appear to pose a challenge to models of price inflation based on the concept of a NAIRU, or nonaccelerating-inflation rate of unemployment. As discussed in the 1997 *Economic Report of the President*, historical experience indicates that the chances are high that inflation will rise in periods when the unemployment rate is very low, and fall when unemployment is unusually high. The NAIRU can therefore be defined as the unemployment rate at which—absent special factors—the odds of falling and rising inflation are roughly balanced. Although a specific value of the NAIRU represents a forecaster's best estimate of the rate of unemployment that can be sustained on average without causing an increase in inflation, any estimate of the NAIRU is subject to some degree of imprecision, inasmuch as there will be periods when inflation is falling even though unemployment is below the NAIRU, and vice versa. In addition, the NAIRU itself is not invariant over time, but is instead affected by such factors as the demographic composition of the labor force and changes in the structure of labor and product markets.

The 1997 *Report* indicated that reasonable estimates for the NAIRU lie between 5 and 6 percent, with a midpoint of 5.5 percent. In 1997 the unemployment rate averaged 4.9 percent, about one-half percentage point below the midrange estimate of the NAIRU. A forecasting model built around a NAIRU of 5.5 percent would therefore have predicted some acceleration in prices over the course of 1997; one reasonable estimate would have been a 0.3-percentage-point increase in core CPI inflation. Instead, core CPI inflation finished the year roughly 0.4 percentage point below its year-earlier rate, although 0.1 percentage point of this deceleration can be accounted for by methodological changes introduced into the calculation of the CPI.

The observed decline in inflation is consistent with the view that changes in inflation are influenced by other factors besides labor market slack (measured here by the gap between the actual unemployment rate and the NAIRU). A number of factors did in fact help mitigate inflationary pressure in 1997. First, the costs of providing workers with nonwage compensation (such as health insurance) continued to rise at a very low rate; as mentioned above, this helped keep growth in labor costs from adding to inflation. Second, also as noted above, computer prices have recently declined at a faster-than-average rate; without this decline, overall inflation would have risen steadily since early 1994 (Chart 2-2). Although it is always possible to find components of GDP whose prices are growing faster or slower than the average, relative price changes for computers are particularly noteworthy in that they are largely driven by technological change, as opposed to cyclical forces such as shortages in raw materials, bottlenecks in production, or rising labor costs.

Chart 2-2 **Computer Prices and Total Inflation**
Declines in computer prices have helped to keep overall inflation from increasing in recent years.

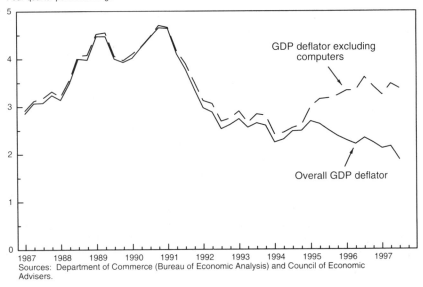

Four-quarter percent change

Sources: Department of Commerce (Bureau of Economic Analysis) and Council of Economic Advisers.

Overall price inflation has been further reduced by sharp declines in the relative price of imported goods, particularly non-oil merchandise imports. Since the second quarter of 1995 the relative price of all imported goods has fallen by 14 percent, and the relative price of non-oil merchandise imports has declined by 15 percent. In part this decline in import prices reflects two interrelated factors: significant excess capacity—and hence low rates of inflation—abroad, and the dollar's appreciation against other major currencies. It is difficult to determine precisely what effect this has had on overall inflation, but some estimates indicate that this factor could have reversed much if not all of the increase in inflation that would have been predicted solely from the gap between the actual unemployment rate and the estimated NAIRU.

Judged from the perspective of a NAIRU model, therefore, it seems possible that the economy is currently operating at an unemployment rate that is inconsistent with stable inflation over the long run, but that the influence of special, possibly transitory factors has prevented prices and labor costs from accelerating. Although this is a plausible explanation for recent inflation performance, it is certainly not the only one; an alternative hypothesis is that structural changes in labor and product markets have led to further declines in the NAIRU. If true, this would imply that at least some portion of the recent decline in the unemployment rate can be sustained without an eventual increase in inflation.

The rate of unemployment consistent with stable inflation would be expected to vary over time in response to such factors as shifts in labor force demographics, changes in the relation between workers' real wage demands and their productivity, and structural shifts that alter the degree of mismatch between workers and jobs (both sectorally and regionally). For a number of reasons, however, it is difficult at present to justify a large additional reduction in the estimated NAIRU on the basis of recent experience. First, the presence of fortuitous supply shocks clouds the inflation picture significantly; although it is evident that these shocks have contributed to lower inflation, the exact extent of this contribution cannot be perfectly gauged. Second, although inflation in goods and services prices has not risen as unemployment has fallen below 5.5 percent, some acceleration in wages has occurred (Chart 2-3), which might reflect labor market tightness. Finally, the unemployment rate has been below 5.5 percent for too short a time to allow any certainty that the risk of a gradual buildup of inflationary pressure is entirely absent.

However, a small downward revision to the estimated range of the NAIRU is indeed justifiable. A portion of recent inflation performance cannot be explained by special factors; moreover, the fact that prices have not accelerated as the unemployment rate has fallen below 5.5 percent suggests that the estimated range should be shifted down. A model that accounts for supply shocks such as recent declines in relative import prices and that allows the NAIRU to vary over time indicates that a reasonable range for the NAIRU now has a midpoint of 5.4 percent, 0.1 percentage point lower than in previous estimates. The Administration's budget forecast has been revised to reflect this slightly lower estimated midpoint of the NAIRU's range.

Chart 2-3 **Wage Growth and the Unemployment Rate**
Wages have accelerated as the unemployment rate has fallen.

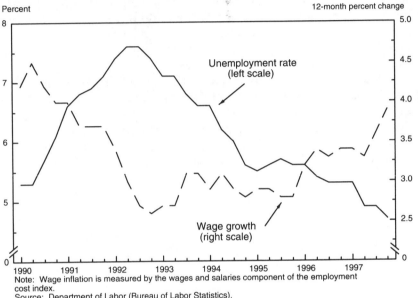

Note: Wage inflation is measured by the wages and salaries component of the employment cost index.
Source: Department of Labor (Bureau of Labor Statistics).

ALTERNATIVE MEASURES OF UTILIZATION AND CAPACITY

The unemployment rate is a useful predictor of future inflation in that it can directly indicate the potential for rising inflationary pressure on the cost side, as excess demand in the labor market tends to raise nominal wages and thus nominal labor costs. The unemployment rate can also proxy for the state of aggregate demand in the economy, and thus help assess the degree of excess demand in product markets. However, the unemployment rate is not the only indicator of resource utilization and demand (even for the labor market), nor does it necessarily provide the best forecast of future inflation. It is therefore of interest to consider what other measures of resource utilization and labor market tightness suggest about the current degree of inflationary pressure in the economy.

Several plausible indicators—such as the State insured unemployment rate, the demographically adjusted unemployment rate, and the unemployment rate for men of prime working age—imply a degree of

60

labor market tightness that exceeds that which has historically been associated with stable inflation. In addition, an index of help-wanted advertising (which can be considered a proxy for the job vacancy rate) fails to reveal a large degree of slack in the labor market at present; earlier in the expansion some observers argued that this measure indicated a weaker labor market than did the unemployment rate. The picture painted by these labor market variables is therefore one in which the potential for inflationary pressure is relatively high.

The effects of a tight labor market on wages may have been muted by the presence of widespread worker insecurity, which has been evident since the 1990-91 recession. Despite a strong job market and a high level of consumer confidence, surveys indicate that workers' fears of job loss remain high relative to the level that prevailed before the recession. Quit rates are low as well, which could reflect workers' unwillingness to leave their current jobs in the hope of "trading up" to better jobs. And strike activity is at a low ebb, although this is related at least in part to declines in unionization rates. These factors suggest that workers may be relatively unwilling to press for the wage gains that they could normally command in a labor market as tight as that of today.

One indicator that tempers somewhat the general conclusion that labor and product markets are tight is the rate of capacity utilization (both in the manufacturing sector alone and for all industry). Capacity utilization remains below its peak for this expansion and is roughly at the level historically associated with stable inflation. It is also noteworthy that core producer price inflation, which more closely reflects the output price measure that is relevant to manufacturing capacity utilization, has declined rapidly since the end of 1995. This suggests that industry has not yet reached the point where production bottlenecks or other capacity constraints are putting upward pressure on inflation. Gains in capacity, which have followed an increase in real private investment growth, have helped keep capacity utilization in the noninflationary zone; measured capacity growth increased sharply after 1993 and has stayed high as real business fixed investment growth has remained strong. In fact, recent revisions to the capacity utilization data indicate that the economy had more industrial capacity over the past 4 years than was previously thought (Box 2-4), making the recent declines in core producer price inflation somewhat less of a mystery. However, manufacturing represents only about 20 percent of total output, and although total goods output (which includes manufacturing as well as trade and mining) accounts for a larger fraction (40 percent), it is still less than half of the economy. The possibility of overheating in the economy as a whole, therefore, should not be dismissed.

> **Box 2-4.—Recent Revisions to Capacity and Utilization**
>
> In December the Federal Reserve revised its estimates of capacity and industrial production, on the basis of improved source data. For the preceding 2 years estimates of industrial capacity and utilization had largely been extrapolated from national accounts data on real investment. The recent revision incorporates direct estimates of utilization based on survey data and industry reports, as well as more comprehensive data on physical output and labor and other inputs.
>
> The new data indicate that industrial capacity has been growing about 1 percentage point faster than previously estimated. Over the past 3 years capacity has grown at an average annual rate of 4.7 percent. In each of the past 3 years average annual capacity growth has exceeded every previous growth rate since 1968. Similarly, recent estimates of the rate of capacity utilization were revised downward by more than a percentage point. Currently, production as a share of total capacity is about 83 percent; this is only slightly higher than the series' long-term average.

A NEW ERA FOR THE ECONOMY?

To summarize the chapter thus far, the past few years have seen rapid growth in output with stable inflation, gradual declines in the NAIRU, strong growth in profits and stock prices, and a pickup in productivity that, if sustained, would herald a significant departure from past productivity trends. Indeed, economic performance in recent years has been so extraordinary that some have wondered whether it reflects fundamental structural change in the economy— change so great that a "new paradigm" is needed to describe an economy that is in a "new era."

Many such assessments are extreme and unsupportable. In particular, any claim that the business cycle has been vanquished must be viewed with considerable skepticism. Nevertheless, it is possible to identify a number of areas in which fundamental changes are probably influencing the economy's current performance, in many cases favorably.

First, U.S. producers face increased foreign and domestic competition. Exports and imports today play a greater role in the U.S. economy than at any other time in history. And here at home, deregulation has taken place or is under way in a number of industries, including telecommunications, transportation, electricity, and banking. Increased competition and more open markets contribute to greater efficiency, thus helping raise the *level* of output. But it is possible that greater competition also fosters a faster pace of innovation, inducing long-run improvements in productivity and thus a higher *rate* of output growth.

Labor and product markets have also changed in significant ways. Since the early 1980s the unionization rate has dropped by nearly half, continuing a decline in union membership that began in the late 1960s. In addition, the use of temporary and contingent employees is much higher than it was 15 years ago. Although this has probably made labor markets more flexible, it might also have contributed to an increase in worker anxiety. Information technology might prove as revolutionary as the steam engine or the automobile. Adoption of just-in-time inventory management by manufacturers also represents a significant development, since changes in inventories have often been an important source of business-cycle fluctuations. Whether just-in-time inventories will be able to dampen future business cycles, however, remains to be seen.

Even the public sector has been transformed in recent years. Our system of social welfare has been changed to help welfare recipients make the transition to employment. The end of the Cold War saw a vast amount of defense-related resources freed up for civilian uses. The government itself is being reinvented to make it more efficient and responsive. Perhaps most important, deficit reduction has increased private sector investment; this recent expansion in capital investment raises productivity by providing workers with more modern and efficient workplaces.

Not all of these changes represent unalloyed boons. Nor is it possible to quantify the effects of these changes on the economy or on specific groups or sectors with any degree of precision (although these factors would have to be very large to reverse the post-1973 productivity slowdown to any significant degree). And even if these changes are having a significant influence on recent economic performance, it may imply not that a new model of the economy is needed, but rather that certain key parameters of the current model, such as the NAIRU or trend productivity growth, have changed. Hence one cannot declare with any certainty that the old rules no longer apply. But the factors just described suggest that the economy may be experiencing some important structural changes that will shape our economic analysis and forecasts in the years ahead.

THE ECONOMIC CONDITION OF HOUSEHOLDS

Both aggregate statistics and consumer surveys painted an exceptionally favorable picture of the economic circumstances of American households in 1997. The tight labor market that led to a 24-year-low in the unemployment rate also lured enough new workers into the labor market to set an all-time record for the labor force participation rate. The combination of healthy wage growth and increasing employment helped push real disposable personal income up a solid 3 percent over the year. Despite the stock market volatility witnessed in the second half of the year, at year's end all major market indexes remained sharply above their levels at the end of 1996, representing a substantial boost to household net worth. Largely reflecting this combination of favorable circumstances and the low inflation rate, consumer sentiment reached record highs in early summer and remained near those levels for the rest of the year. Growing income and wealth together with buoyant sentiment led to a 3.8-percent rate of spending growth over the four quarters of 1997—outpacing even the robust growth of disposable income.

Against this backdrop of general prosperity only a few potentially worrisome trends were discernible. The first was the drop in the personal saving rate implied by the excess of consumption growth over income growth. A temporary shortfall in personal saving would not necessarily be a problem, but the personal saving rate has remained low for about a decade now, raising questions about whether American households are preparing adequately for the future. A second persistent concern has been the ongoing buildup of household debt. Upon analysis, however, this growth in debt does not appear very menacing, both because household assets have risen even faster, and because households still appear to be able to service their rising debt loads comfortably. A final potential concern has been the continuing rise in personal bankruptcies despite the robust economy, which might seem to suggest an increase in the number of households experiencing sudden financial shocks. However, the bankruptcy rate has been trending upward for about 20 years now, and the available evidence suggests that the uptrend is attributable to a complex mix of economic, legal, and social developments rather than a dramatic worsening of the economic shocks hitting households.

THE CONFIDENT CONSUMER

Early in the summer of 1997 the Index of Consumer Sentiment constructed by the University of Michigan reached an all-time high; it remained near that record level for the remainder of the year (Chart 2-4). Some observers have suggested that consumers have become overly optimistic, and that a return to more normal levels of confidence could have adverse economic consequences. But a major part of the surge in consumer sentiment in 1997 can be explained by the simultaneously favorable values of all four of the indicators that have historically influenced consumer sentiment: the inflation rate, the unemployment rate, the performance of the stock market, and, to a lesser extent, the growth rate of household income. Moreover, although Chart 2-4 shows that the actual level of sentiment in 1997 has been even higher than would be predicted given the values of these indicators, the size of the underprediction is not large compared with typical past prediction errors.

The Michigan index comprises two subindexes: one for current conditions and one for expected future conditions. Recently, both have been hovering near record levels. Roughly two-thirds of the increase in the index of expected conditions over 1997 can be attributed to the favorable economic environment, and the remaining underprediction is not large by historical standards. This suggests that consumers are not unrealistically optimistic about future developments. However, very little of 1997's increase in the index of current conditions can be explained by changes in observed aggregate variables. Again, the magnitude of underprediction is not very large; moreover, there are good reasons not to attribute this prediction error to irrational confidence on the part of consumers. Because the current conditions index largely reflects consumers' answers to questions about their own individual financial circumstances, a plausible interpretation of the prediction error is simply that economy-wide variables such as the inflation rate and the unemployment rate do not fully capture the complex elements that influence consumers' assessments of their personal financial situation. It therefore seems more appropriate to accept consumers' rosy assessments of their personal financial circumstances at face value. And judging by past episodes when sentiment has exceeded the predicted value, the danger appears modest of a sudden sharp plunge in sentiment that would quickly return it to the level that aggregate indicators would predict.

Chart 2-4 **Consumer Sentiment**
Much of the increase in consumer sentiment recently can be explained by the exceptional performance of the economy.
Index, 1966:Q1 = 100

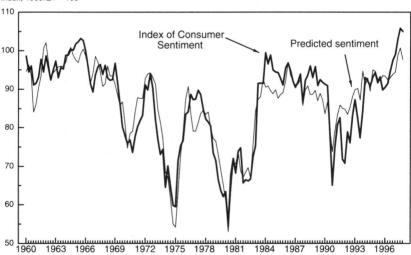

Note: Predicted sentiment is calculated from a model in which the inflation rate, the unemployment rate, stock market performance, and wages and salaries are independent variables.
Sources: University of Michigan and calculations by Council of Economic Advisers.

Other measures of consumer attitudes also reflect optimism. The Conference Board's Consumer Confidence Index, the main alternative to the Michigan index, rose to a 28-year record in December; as with the Michigan index, a large part of the improvement in the Conference Board index can be attributed to observable economic conditions. Both the Michigan and the Conference Board surveys contain many questions that are not incorporated in their overall indexes, and answers to these other survey questions have also generally been quite favorable. For example, throughout the year consumers interviewed for the Michigan survey said they expected low inflation rates to continue and believed it was a good time to buy automobiles and houses.

THE CONDITION OF HOUSEHOLD BALANCE SHEETS

The exceptional performance of the stock market appears to be one of the factors contributing to consumers' sanguine assessments of their financial circumstances. The rise in the stock market boosted total household net worth by around $2.6 trillion over the course of 1997, following similarly strong gains in 1995 and 1996. Higher stock prices lifted the ratio of household net worth to disposable income to record levels (Chart 2-5).

Chart 2-5 **Ratio of Household Net Worth to Disposable Personal Income**
The stock market boom helped boost the household net-worth-to-income ratio to a record level in 1997.

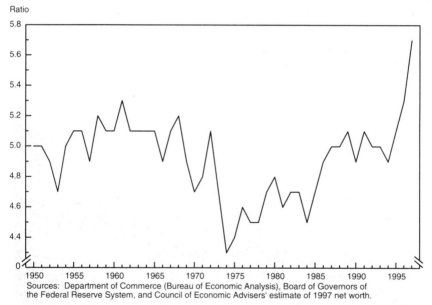

Sources: Department of Commerce (Bureau of Economic Analysis), Board of Governors of the Federal Reserve System, and Council of Economic Advisers' estimate of 1997 net worth.

Despite the recent boost to stock market wealth, the family home is still the most valuable single asset most American households own. On this front, too, 1997 brought encouraging news: the rate of home-ownership reached a new all-time record, boosted by robust income

66

growth and relatively low mortgage interest rates. Another factor that has likely contributed to the increase in the homeownership rates in the 1990s is the increasing availability of sub-prime mortgage loans, which do not meet traditional industry lending guidelines. Such loans carry a higher interest rate to compensate lenders for the extra risk. For example, home buyers who put up less than the traditional 20-percent down payment usually have to purchase private mortgage insurance to guarantee repayment of the loan; the premium for this insurance rises as the size of the down payment declines. Indeed, mortgages that require no down payment at all are now available for consumers willing to pay very high rates.

Home buyers who take advantage of these loans, of course, take on more debt than was typical of past buyers who put up a traditional down payment of 20 percent. The relaxation of down payment constraints is therefore probably part of the explanation for the runup in mortgage debt depicted in Chart 2-6. Some of this rise, however, is attributable to the increasing popularity of home equity borrowing. A substantial part of new home equity borrowing likely reflects the growing use of home equity loans to buy motor vehicles, to pay for home repairs and additions, and to finance other large expenses that might previously have been financed by separate consumer loans. Home equity loans are an attractive way of financing such expenditures because their interest is tax deductible, whereas the interest on traditional consumer loans lost its tax-deductible status with the tax reform of 1986.

Chart 2-6 **Household Debt by Type**
The ratio of household debt to disposable income has risen sharply since the mid-1970s, mostly in the form of higher mortgage debt.

Percent of disposable personal income

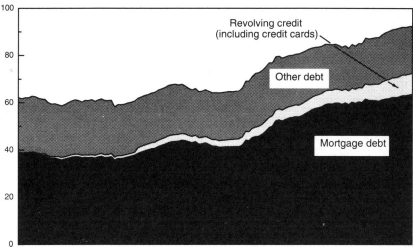

Sources: Department of Commerce (Bureau of Economic Analysis) and Board of Governors of the Federal Reserve System.

The increasing substitution of mortgage debt for other kinds of debt suggests that any assessment of the aggregate household balance sheet needs to look at the value of all debts combined, not just mortgage debt. As Chart 2-6 shows, the uptrend in overall household debt is somewhat less dramatic than that for mortgage debt alone; the ratio of total debt to disposable income increased from 77 percent in 1986 to 92 percent in 1997. Nevertheless, the ratio of overall debt to disposable personal income has been trending upward since the mid-1970s, except for pauses around the recessions of the early 1980s and early 1990s.

The chart does not support the common perception that aggregate credit card borrowing has soared out of control. Although revolving debt (which consists mainly of credit card debt) has grown more rapidly than other kinds of borrowing, it still represents only a modest fraction of consumers' debt load. Most of the runup in total debt instead reflects the sharp rise in mortgage debt.

Chart 2-7 **Household Debt Delinquency Rates**
After rising from 1994 to 1996, delinquency rates on credit cards and consumer loans have stabilized. Mortgage delinquencies edged down to the lowest rate since 1980.

Percent

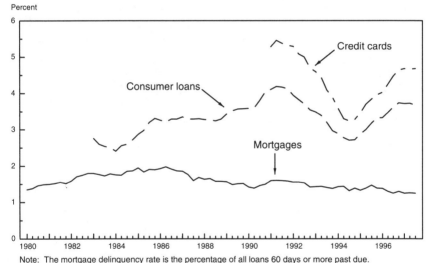

Note: The mortgage delinquency rate is the percentage of all loans 60 days or more past due.
The consumer loan and credit card delinquency rate is the percentage of loan balances that are 30 days or more past due or nonaccruing.
Sources: Board of Governors of the Federal Reserve System and Mortgage Bankers Association.

The dominance of mortgage debt in household balance sheets implies that the mortgage delinquency rate is a particularly important indicator of the magnitude of debt repayment problems. Chart 2-7 shows that the mortgage delinquency rate has actually edged down over the last year and remains well below rates posted in the mid-1980s, suggesting that comparatively few consumers have found their rising mortgage debt insupportable. The chart also shows that although delinquency rates on credit card borrowing and consumer loans have gone up, they remain below their peak levels of the early 1990s and appear to have flattened off in the past year or so.

One probable reason why the continuing runup in debt has not caused greater repayment problems is that interest rates have fallen, reducing the payments required to service the outstanding stock of debt (the debt service burden). The debt service burden has also been lightened by an increase in the average duration of loans. Chart 2-8 shows that although the aggregate debt service burden has risen substantially since its trough in 1993, it is still below the level attained in the late 1980s and certainly does not exhibit the relentless uptrend evident in the ratio of total debt to disposable income.

Chart 2-8 **Household Debt Service Payments**
The debt service burden fell after the 1990-91 recession but has risen since 1994. Although high by historical standards, it remains below late-1980s levels.

Percent of disposable personal income

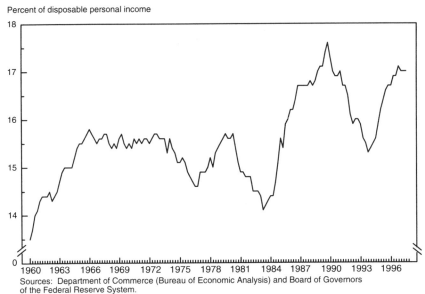

Sources: Department of Commerce (Bureau of Economic Analysis) and Board of Governors of the Federal Reserve System.

On the whole, then, aggregate statistics paint a favorable picture of the financial condition of households. Although household debt has risen, the aggregate value of household assets has risen even more, leading to a net gain in aggregate household net worth. Judging from mortgage delinquency rates, the recent rise in the debt service burden does not seem to be causing unusual strain. And although credit card debt has been growing, this category still represents a relatively minor fraction of the aggregate debt households owe.

Aggregate statistics, however, can sometimes mask divergent trends among different subgroups of the population. If, for example, the rise in household assets were occurring entirely among the affluent, and if the rise in household debt were concentrated among lower income households, then the increase in aggregate household net worth would not provide much reassurance about the ability of the indebted households to repay their debt. In practice, however, household-level data do not seem to be telling a story very different from that told by the aggregate data. Although affluent households still hold disproportionate amounts of stock, the surging popularity of mutual funds and the rise of 401(k) and other tax-sheltered retirement plans have considerably increased the fraction of households who benefit directly from stock market gains. Indeed, a recent poll found that roughly half of American families own stock in some form. And as Table 2-2 shows, although the debt service burden for the median household increased somewhat between 1983 and 1989, by 1995 the combination of falling interest rates and lengthening debt maturities had reduced the median household's burden to near its 1983 level; the fraction of households with high or very high debt service burdens (defined as debt service payments greater than 30 and 50 percent of income, respectively) was actually lower in 1995 than in 1983.

TABLE 2-2.—*Household Debt Service Burden*

Item	1983	1989	1995
Debt service burden of the median household (percent of income) [1]	12.8	15.2	13.1
Percent of households with debt service burden:			
Over 30 percent	18.8	23.1	16.3
Over 50 percent	6.4	7.9	5.6

[1] Debt service burden is required debt service payments as a percent of income.

Note. — Data are for households whose heads are employed.

Sources: Board of Governors of the Federal Reserve System and calculations of the Council of Economic Advisers.

THE PERSONAL SAVING RATE

The personal saving rate has been trending downward since the mid-1980s. According to the preliminary figures currently available, the personal saving rate in 1997 was only 3.8 percent, down from 4.3 percent in 1996. Given the exuberant level of consumer sentiment and the large gains in household wealth last year, the fact that there was a modest decline in the saving rate from 1996 to 1997 is neither surprising nor disturbing; such modest annual fluctuations are of little consequence. The longer term decline in personal saving, however, has aroused considerable concern among academic economists and policymakers, for at least three reasons. First, because national saving is the sum of personal, business, and government saving, low personal saving contributes to a low national saving rate, and low national saving has a variety of negative consequences, which are discussed in more detail later in this chapter. Second, the falling saving rate raises questions about whether many American consumers are preparing adequately for their retirement. Finally, families with too little savings may be unprepared to deal successfully with financial emergencies such as a spell of unemployment or large medical expenses.

Personal Saving and Retirement

One of the most obvious reasons for households to save is to provide for a comfortable standard of living in retirement. One way to judge whether personal saving is too low, then, is to ask whether consumers appear to be saving enough for retirement. Several recent studies have examined whether the baby-boom generation, in particular, is doing enough retirement saving. One set of studies has concluded that typical baby-boomers need to roughly triple their saving rates if they hope to maintain their living standards in retirement. Another study, however, asserts that even if they do not change their saving behavior at all, the majority of boomers probably will not experience a sharp drop in living standards upon retirement.

These different conclusions largely reflect a difference in approach. The first set of studies begins by calculating the gap between the income that baby-boomers can expect to receive from the combination of Social Security and traditional pensions, and the income that would be required to maintain their preretirement standard of living. These studies then calculate the "target" saving rates that baby-boomers would need to achieve to plug that income gap, and show that the saving rates of typical baby-boom households are only about a third of the target rates, leading to a "baby boom retirement adequacy index" of 33 percent.

Critics point out that this approach can be misleading, in part because it is not a measure of the consequences if consumers decide *not* to increase their saving. In particular, an index value of 33 percent does not imply that retirement spending will have to be one-third the level of preretirement spending. For example, consider a household for whom Social Security and pensions will provide sufficient retirement income to finance spending at 80 percent of preretirement income, and suppose that the household only needs 85 percent of preretirement income to maintain its accustomed standard of living. (Spending needs could decline in retirement for several reasons, notably the decline in commuting and other work-related expenses.) Such a household could save nothing, and therefore would have an index value of zero, yet would only experience about a 5-percent decline in its standard of living at retirement.

An alternative way to evaluate the adequacy of retirement saving is to calculate the ratio of the level of sustainable retirement spending to the level of spending necessary to maintain standards of living. Using this measure of retirement adequacy, a recent study calculated that, under plausible assumptions about the rate of return on savings, and assuming no changes in saving behavior or in the Social

Security system, almost half of married-couple baby-boomer households in which the husband works full-time are saving enough to maintain their standard of living in retirement. (Single baby-boomers are probably not faring as well, however.) And only about a third of these married-couple baby-boomer households are projected to suffer large cuts in their standard of living. These figures improve if home equity is included in the measure of retirement savings, although there is some debate whether including home equity is appropriate. The recent runup in the stock market would improve the picture further, although most of the improvement would likely be concentrated among the third of households who are already best prepared for retirement to the extent that they hold a disproportionate share of equity investments.

Even the optimists, however, acknowledge that current saving rates of most baby-boom households are not high enough to provide much of a cushion against the many uncertainties that they face. In particular, if their retirement savings earn low rates of return, or if rising medical costs or other unexpected expenses increase their spending needs in retirement, or if retirement income from sources other than personal savings falls substantially short of the projections made on the basis of current pension and social insurance programs, then many baby-boomers may end up wishing they had saved much more. And even under optimistic assumptions, it appears likely that unless they boost their saving, most unmarried boomers will reach normal retirement age with insufficient assets to fully maintain their preretirement standard of living.

On the whole, therefore, it does appear that unless their saving rates rise, a very substantial proportion of the baby-boom generation is at risk of reaching retirement age with insufficient assets to maintain their standard of living. One response may be for them to delay retirement. Since Social Security and many other pension benefits are adjusted upward for those who delay retirement, some of the boomers who are not saving enough to retire at the normal retirement age may nevertheless be able to retire in relative comfort several years later. Of course, those who have saved little but whose state of health or line of work prevents them from remaining in the work force may have no choice but to accept significantly lower living standards in their retirement years.

Personal Saving and Financial Emergencies

When consumers are asked about their primary reasons for saving, the most common answer is that saving is important in order to build up resources that can be drawn upon in case of emergency. Although precautionary saving of this kind cannot plausibly explain either the practice of regular payroll deductions for pension plans or the accumulation of wealth held by the richest few percent of households, it can account for the consistent finding by consumer surveys that most households usually have on hand an amount of liquid assets that corresponds to between a few weeks' and a few months' worth of spending.

It is difficult to judge whether these liquid assets are enough to cushion consumers against financial emergencies. Certainly, they alone would not be enough to fully maintain spending through the worst possible emergencies such as a long spell of unemployment. But most households could probably substantially cut their spending during an extended unemployment spell. Also, in today's economy most consumers have the option of credit card, home equity, or other kinds of borrowing to finance emergency spending. Indeed, a potential partial explanation of the drop in the personal saving rate over the past decade is that some consumers have decided that credit cards or other consumer credit sources can help fill the buffer role traditionally served by liquid assets.

Unquestionably, credit card availability has risen in recent years. Particularly notable has been the increase in availability of credit cards to consumers in lower income and wealth brackets: in 1983 only 28 percent of consumers with annual incomes of less than $15,000 (in 1992 dollars) held credit cards, but by 1995 the ownership rate for that group had increased to 44 percent. In addition, those groups of consumers who already had credit cards in 1983 have seen a large increase in their credit limits in recent years: the median total credit limit among all consumers with cards increased from about $6,000 in 1989 to over $9,000 in 1995 (both in 1992 dollars).

As might be expected, credit card borrowing has increased as credit has become more available. But the increases in borrowing have been fairly modest compared with the increases in credit limits. Table 2-3 shows the distribution of credit balances (the part of the credit card bill that consumers choose not to pay off at the end of the month) as a percentage of income for employed working-age consumers in 1983, 1989, and 1995. Whereas the median ratio of credit card balance to income was close to zero in all 3 years, consumers at the 75th and 95th percentiles of the distribution had increasingly large balances relative to their incomes. Still, even in 1995 consumers at the 95th percentile of the distribution had credit card debt equal to only 22 percent of annual income—a substantial but by no means unbearable burden.

TABLE 2-3.—*Household Credit Card Balances as a Percent of Income*

Point in distribution [1]	1983	1989	1995
Median household	0	0	1
Household at 75th percentile	2	3	6
Household at 95th percentile	7	14	22

[1] Distribution is that of households according to credit card balances as a fraction of income.
Note. — Data are for households whose heads are employed.
Sources: Board of Governors of the Federal Reserve System and calculations of the Council of Economic Advisers.

The available data are consistent with the idea that the expanding availability of credit card debt may have somewhat reduced the need for consumers to hold buffer stocks of liquid assets, and thus may have contributed at least modestly to the drop in the personal saving rate. But for most households credit availability appears to have increased considerably more than credit use, so that there appears to be little reason to worry that typical households have less capacity to withstand financial shocks. Even the small subset of consumers who have run up quite substantial credit card debts could plausibly expect to be able to repay those debts, if they do not experience a major disruption to their income or a large unavoidable expenditure. On the other hand, consumers with large credit card debts who do experience a major financial blow may be forced into bankruptcy.

THE LONG-TERM UPTREND IN THE BANKRUPTCY RATE

After remaining roughly stable over much of the 1960s and 1970s, the personal bankruptcy rate began rising sharply sometime around the late 1970s or early 1980s. Some have argued that this uptrend resulted from passage of the Bankruptcy Act of 1978, which eased some of the burdens of bankruptcy. Other analysts argue that the approximate correspondence between passage of that act and the beginning of the uptrend in bankruptcies is just a coincidence, and that rising bankruptcy rates reflect other social and economic developments that would have led to a rising bankruptcy rate even if the law had remained unchanged.

One intuitively plausible explanation is that the rise in bankruptcies reflects the increasingly aggressive marketing of credit cards to high-risk consumers who previously would not have been granted credit at all. As noted above, it is true that some households have borrowed increasingly large amounts on credit cards. Some of those highly indebted individuals presumably end up in bankruptcy if they lose their jobs or experience other large financial shocks. But there are reasons to doubt that increased availability of credit cards provides a full explanation of the rise in bankruptcies. First, some suggestive evidence indicates that credit card debt is not a large fraction of the total debt of consumers who declare bankruptcy; consumers who end up in bankruptcy court must therefore have borrowed heavily from non-credit card sources. Second, much of the increase in bankruptcy appears to have come not from low-income consumers who until recently could not get cards, but from the kinds of middle-income consumers who have presumably had access to credit cards all along.

If excessive credit card borrowing is not a complete explanation for the rising bankruptcy rate, what does explain the rise? One possibility is that an increasing number of consumers are simply taking on more debt than they can manage, in non-credit card form as well as with credit cards. On its face, this explanation seems plausible in light of the large increases in aggregate household debt over the past 15 years, depicted in Chart 2-6. But as noted above, although the aggregate debt service burden has climbed recently, it remains below its late-1980s levels, yet the bankruptcy rate has continued to rise. And as shown in Table 2-2, the proportion of households who had either high or very high debt service burdens was actually lower in 1995 than in 1983. Hence, the available data do not seem to support the theory that bankruptcy has risen simply because increasingly large numbers of ordinary consumers have unwisely taken out so much debt that any financial shock will send them into bankruptcy.

Unfortunately, the evidence on alternative explanations is scant, and no consensus has emerged among experts. One researcher points out that, under the post-1978 bankruptcy law, up to 15 percent of households could increase their net worth by declaring bankruptcy; this researcher and others argue that the rise in the bankruptcy rate over time largely reflects consumers learning about the costs and benefits of declaring bankruptcy, perhaps partly through advertising by bankruptcy lawyers. A related hypothesis is that there has been a decline in the stigma associated with bankruptcy. This theory is consistent with evidence showing that, controlling for other factors, people who live in areas where the bankruptcy rate has been high in the past are more likely to declare bankruptcy.

Other authors have suggested that increasing divorce rates, skyrocketing medical costs, or large legal judgments or settlements may have contributed to the rise in the bankruptcy rate. However, although each of these factors is clearly important in many individual bankruptcy cases, none appears to be sufficient to explain more than a small fraction of the increase in bankruptcies. For example, the divorce rate stabilized in the mid- to late-1980s, yet bankruptcies have continued to rise. And some evidence indicates that only a modest fraction of bankrupt consumers have significant amounts of medical debt or large legal judgments against them.

Whatever is driving the increase in bankruptcies, the rising bankruptcy rate has focused attention on the bankruptcy system. In response, in 1994 the Congress established a commission to recommend reforms in the bankruptcy system. The National Bankruptcy Review Commission released its final report in October 1997 (Box 2-5).

LONG-TERM GROWTH: BUDGET DEFICITS AND NATIONAL SAVING

Since its first budget proposal in 1993, this Administration has demonstrated a strong commitment to reducing the Federal budget deficit. As a result, the deficit has declined from $290 billion in 1992 to only $22 billion in 1997, or from 4.7 percent to 0.3 percent of GDP.

In August 1997 the President and the Congress sealed a historic agreement that was projected to lead to a balanced budget by 2002; the continuing robust performance of the economy since August has improved the outlook further, leading the President to propose a balanced budget for fiscal 1999.

Balancing the budget has been achieved in large part through a combination of expenditure restraint and increases in income taxes for the 1 percent of households with the highest incomes. Both budget cuts and tax increases are difficult and painful measures. Why did the Administration judge that taking such measures was so important? Principally because persistent budget deficits as large as those of the 1980s and early 1990s constitute an unacceptable drain on national saving.

To see why budget deficits reduce national saving, it is useful to imagine the private saving of all Americans as flowing into a common national pool. This pool of saving is then made available to borrowers. The budget deficit measures how much of this pool of saving is drawn down by the government; national saving is the amount left in the pool after the government has borrowed what it needs to pay for that portion of current expenses that exceed its current revenues.

Because of the reduction in Federal borrowing, net national saving (gross national saving less depreciation of the private and public capital stock) has increased from 3.1 percent of GDP in 1992 to 6.4 percent in 1997 (on the basis of incomplete data for the year). But even this net national saving rate is far below the 10-percent average over the period 1960-80.

Given the Nation's favorable recent economic performance even without a high national saving rate, it might be tempting to conclude that the low national saving rate does not matter. But such a conclusion would be a mistake. There are still good reasons to believe that the benefits of boosting national saving would outweigh the short-term pain of cutting back on spending.

SAVING IN A CLOSED ECONOMY

One way of thinking about whether more saving would make the Nation better off is to ask whether the aggregate capital stock is at the "golden rule" level—the level that maximizes sustainable per capita consumption. (Economists call this the golden rule level because every generation must resist the temptation to consume more than its share and thereby leave less for future generations.)

Whether an economy is at the golden rule level can be determined by comparing the net extra output that would be produced by more capital against the cost of equipping the growing work force with that extra capital. If the extra output is greater than this cost, then total national output could be increased by adding to the capital stock. In the United States, economists estimate that the before-tax rate of return on additional capital is much higher than the cost of equipping the work force with extra capital, implying that the Nation's capital stock is well below the golden rule level.

The golden rule, however, is an imperfect way to judge whether saving should be higher. The principal problem is that the rule provides no way to weigh the short-term pain from lower current consumption against the long-term gain from eventually higher future consumption. A more flexible framework is provided by the "modified golden rule," which makes explicit assumptions about how current consumption should be traded off against future consumption. The modified golden rule assumes that society as a whole is slightly impatient, in the sense of preferring current consumption to future consumption, and that consumers prefer gradual changes in the level of consumption and dislike abrupt changes. But under plausible assumptions about the before-tax rate of return, the rate of impatience, and the degree to which one year's consumption is substitutable for another year's, even the modified golden rule implies that the saving rate is too low.

SAVING IN AN OPEN ECONOMY

In an economy closed to foreign trade and capital, all domestic investment must be financed by domestic saving. One of the principal benefits of increasing globalization of trade and capital markets is that the ability to borrow and lend in foreign markets relaxes the need to balance national saving with national investment in every year. If attractive investment opportunities are available at home but domestic saving is insufficient to pursue them, foreign investors can step in; the resulting excess of investment over national saving is manifested in a current account deficit. This aspect of globalization has been a favorable development for the United States, because it has allowed the economy recently to invest in capital equipment at high rates despite the persistently low national saving rate. The high rates of investment in capital equipment over the past few years have been critical in preventing the kinds of production bottlenecks that have ᴖfᴖᴖ led to rising inflation rates at comparable points in past busi- cycles.

But maintaining national investment above national saving over long periods does come at a price: growing indebtedness to foreign investors. In the long run, increased foreign indebtedness means that a portion of the extra future output generated by the extra invest- ment will be needed to pay a return to foreign lenders. In light of the demands that will be placed on the economy over the next 30 or 40 years by the retirement of the baby-boom generation, and considering that countries that are currently lending to us face similar demo- graphic challenges, there remains a strong argument that it would be better to finance our high investment rates more through higher national saving and less by borrowing abroad.

IMPLICATIONS

This Administration has believed from the beginning that the case for a higher national saving rate is compelling. That conviction led to the Administration's steadfast commitment to reducing the budget deficit. But as important as the progress on the budget deficit has been, the net national saving rate is still too low. One important pri- ority for the Administration and the Nation is to address the actuarial imbalance in the Nation's entitlement programs in a way that increases the national saving rate and thereby increases the resources available to meet the impending demographic crunch.

FORECAST AND OUTLOOK

THE ADMINISTRATION FORECAST

The Administration projects GDP growth over the long term at about 2.4 percent per year—a figure consistent with the experience so far during this business cycle as well as with reasonable growth rates of its supply-side components. From the business-cycle peak in the third quarter of 1990 until the third quarter of 1997, real output growth has averaged 2.4 percent per year. This figure is the average of real growth rates of the product side (gross domestic product, 2.3 percent) and the income side (gross domestic income, 2.6 percent). Because the unemployment rate fell by 0.1 percentage point per year over this period, the empirical regularity known as Okun's law suggests that these growth rates overstate the growth of trend output by 0.2 percentage point—a calculation that results in a backward-looking estimate of 2.2-percent growth of potential output.

This estimate is likely understated by about 0.2 percentage point because of methodological problems with the CPI that have been or will soon be corrected (Box 2-6). By lowering measured inflation while leaving nominal GDP unaffected, these methodological changes will boost measured real output (and better capture its true value).

Box 2-6.—Methodological Changes in the Consumer Price Index

The Bureau of Labor Statistics has recently made several methodological changes that have improved the accuracy of the consumer price index; a few more changes are planned over the next several years (Table 2-4). Most of these improvements have reduced the measured increase in the CPI, and many of these also will affect the deflation of nominal output, and therefore will raise the growth rate of measured real GDP. Changes made through 1997 include the substitution of generic drugs when patents expire on proprietary brands; the correction of a problem in rotating new stores into the survey through a procedure called "seasoning" (a problem that was corrected first in the food category and later in other categories of goods); the modification of the formula for measuring increases in rent; and a change to measuring transaction rather than list prices for hospital services. Changes scheduled to be made in the next 2 years include a switch to measuring computer prices by their intrinsic characteristics ("hedonics"); an update of the market basket from 1982-84 to 1993-95; the use of geometric rather than arithmetic means to address substitution bias within categories; and more frequent rotation of the items sampled in categories with many new product introductions.

The changes made through 1997 have a combined effect of lowering the CPI inflation rate by 0.28 percentage point per year, and raising real GDP growth by 0.06 percentage point per year. The post-1997 changes lower CPI inflation by 0.41 percentage point per year and raise real GDP growth by 0.14 percentage point per year.

In addition, continued capital deepening may add a bit to productivity growth as the net capital stock grows faster than GDP. This would not happen in a steady state where capital and output are growing at the same pace. But the economy is projected not to reach a steady state during the forecast period, as the relative price of capital is expected to continue to fall.

TABLE 2-4.—*Expected Effects on Changes in the CPI and Real GDP of CPI Methodological Changes*

Change in method	Year introduced	Percentage-point effect on:	
		CPI percent change	Real GDP percent change
Pre-1998		-0.28	0.06
Generic prescription drugs	1995	-.01	.00
Food at home seasoning	1995	-.04	.0
Owners' equivalent rent formula	1995	-.10	.00
Rent composite estimator	1995	.03	.00
General seasoning	1996	-.10	.06
Hospital services index.	1997	-.06	.00
1998 and after		-.41	.14
Personal computer hedonics	1998	-.06	.00
Updated market basket	1998	-.15	.02
Geometric means	1999	-.15	.09
Rotation by item	1999	-.05	.03
Total		-.69	.20

Sources: Department of Labor (Bureau of Labor Statistics) and Council of Economic Advisers.

COMPONENTS OF LONG-TERM GROWTH

After rising rapidly in the 1970s and 1980s, the labor force participation rate was relatively flat between 1990 and 1996. But the participation rate rose 0.3 percentage point to 67.1 percent in 1997—the first year in which it surpassed the 1990 level (after correcting for the redesign of the Current Population Survey). One might interpret the pickup in participation in 1997 as a return toward the rapid growth of earlier decades, but other explanations, which suggest that the increase in the rate of participation growth will not endure, are also likely. Given the strong growth of labor demand, it seems that some of last year's labor force pickup ought to be interpreted as a cyclical response to a tight labor market.

The welfare reform law passed in the summer of 1996 may also have boosted labor force participation growth last year and can be expected to do so for several years to come. The legislation requires that, by 2002, States either reduce their welfare caseloads by 50 percent or have 50 percent of the caseload either working or engaged in work-related activities (such as vocational or job skills training), or some combination or the two (with some exemptions). This legislation also set a 2-year time limit on any spell of welfare recipiency and a 5-year lifetime limit, except that 20 percent of a State's caseload may be exempted from this requirement. Rough calculations suggest that the requirement for work-related activities and the 2-year limit on welfare spells together could cause the labor force participation rate to grow by almost 0.1 percentage point per year over the next several years.

At the same time, the long-term demographic forces that have restrained growth in labor force participation in the 1990s are expected to remain in place. The stalling of the overall participation rate in the 1990s is accounted for largely by a deceleration in the participation rate of women; the participation rate for men has fallen no faster than in earlier years. The child dependency ratio (the number of children per woman aged 20-54) fell between the late 1960s and the early 1980s, echoing the earlier pattern in the birth rate. The decline in this ratio allowed an increasing fraction of women to enter the labor force between the mid-1970s and the 1980s, but its subsequent flattening in the late 1980s has limited further increases in participation.

Balancing these influences, the Administration's long-term outlook includes a 0.1-percent per year increase in the participation rate through 2007. Together with population growth of 1.0 percent per year for the working-age population, this implies labor force growth of 1.1 percent per year (Table 2-5).

PRODUCTIVITY

A good way to begin the analysis of productivity growth is by examining the recent past. Labor productivity (that is, worker output per hour) can be measured using either the product-side or the income-side measure of output (Chart 2-9). By the product-side measure, labor productivity has grown at a 1.1-percent annual rate since the business-cycle peak in the third quarter of 1990, whereas the income-side measure shows productivity growth at a more robust 1.5-percent annual rate. Because neither of these two measures is perfect, an argument can be made for averaging them, to yield an estimated annual rate of 1.3 percent over this business cycle.

By either measure, productivity growth was particularly rapid over the first three quarters of 1997, as noted earlier. An acceleration in productivity is not usually observed in the latter part of an expansion (Chart 2-10); historically, productivity growth has tended to slow as the economy returns to full employment. This tendency could reflect several factors, such as overly optimistic hiring decisions by firms, or firms' having to hire less productive workers as the labor market tightens. Whatever the explanation, the fact that no such slowdown is now apparent is evidence that none of these imbalances are currently present, and that the economy is behaving as if it remains in a mid-expansion phase, rather than an end-of-expansion phase.

81

TABLE 2-5.—*Accounting for Growth in Real GDP, 1960-2005*

[Average annual percent change]

Item	1960 II to 1973 IV	1973 IV to 1990 III	1990 III to 1997 III	1997 III to 2005
1) Civilian noninstitutional population aged 16 and over	1.8	1.5	1.0	1.0
2) PLUS: Civilian labor force participation rate [1]........................	.2	.5	.0	.1
3) EQUALS: Civilian labor force [1]..	2.0	2.0	1.1	1.1
4) PLUS: Civilian employment rate [1]...	.0	-.1	.1	-.1
5) EQUALS: Civilian employment [1]...	2.0	1.9	1.2	1.0
6) PLUS: Nonfarm business employment as a share of civilian employment [1,2]..	.1	.1	.2	.1
7) EQUALS: Nonfarm business employment	2.1	2.0	1.4	1.1
8) PLUS: Average weekly hours (nonfarm business)	-.5	-.4	.1	.0
9) EQUALS: Hours of all persons (nonfarm business)...	1.6	1.7	1.5	1.1
10) PLUS: Output per hour (productivity, nonfarm business)..	2.9	1.1	1.1 [3](1.5)	1.3
11) EQUALS: Nonfarm business output...	4.5	2.8	2.7 [3](3.0)	2.4
12) LESS: Nonfarm business output as a share of real GDP [4]...	.3	.1	.4 [3](.4)	.1
13) EQUALS: Real GDP...	4.2	2.7	2.3 [3](2.6)	[5]2.3

[1] Adjusted for 1994 revision of the Current Population Survey.
[2] Line 6 translates the civilian employment growth rate into the nonfarm business employment growth rate.
[3] Income-side definition.
[4] Line 12 translates nonfarm business output back into output for all sectors (GDP), which includes the output of farms and general government.
[5] GDP growth is projected to fall below its long-term trend (2.4 percent) as the employment rate is projected to fall 0.1 percent per year over this period.

Note.—Detail may not add to totals because of rounding.
Except for 1997, time periods are from business-cycle peak to business-cycle peak to avoid cyclical variation.

Sources: Council of Economic Advisers, Department of Commerce (Bureau of Economic Analysis), and Department of Labor (Bureau of Labor Statistics).

Because hours worked usually reacts to changes in output with a lag, hours probably have not caught up with the acceleration in GDP in 1997. As a result, the growth of productivity over the four quarters ending in the third quarter of 1997 likely exceeded its trend rate, as it often does midway through an expansion. A better estimate of trend productivity growth comes from a model that takes this lagged adjustment into account. This procedure estimates that the trend rate of productivity thus far in this business cycle has been similar to the 1.1-percent annual rate that has prevailed since 1973. Looking ahead, measured productivity can be expected to grow at a 1.3-percent annual rate because of the 0.2-percentage-point effect that the CPI methodological adjustments will have on real GDP.

Chart 2-9 **Alternative Measures of Productivity**

Since the last business-cycle peak, the income-side measure of productivity has grown significantly faster than the product-side measure.

Index, 1990:Q3 = 100 (ratio scale)

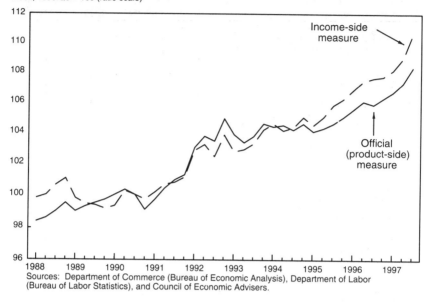

Sources: Department of Commerce (Bureau of Economic Analysis), Department of Labor (Bureau of Labor Statistics), and Council of Economic Advisers.

Chart 2-10 **Productivity Growth and the End-of-Expansion Effect**

Nonfarm business productivity growth has slowed in the late stages of almost all previous postwar expansions. Over the past year, productivity accelerated.

Average annual percent change

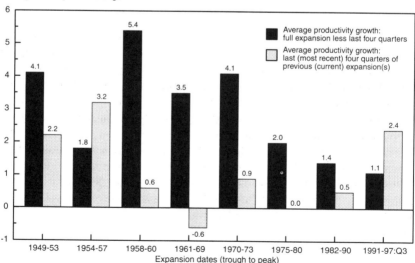

Sources: Department of Labor (Bureau of Labor Statistics) and National Bureau of Economic Research.

INFLATION CONSIDERATIONS

Continued labor market tightness can be expected to put some upward pressure on inflation. With the relative price of investment goods continuing to fall, strong growth of investment is expected to keep industrial capacity relatively more ample than labor supply. And the future development of inflation will also be affected by the factors that have thus far suppressed it. The restructuring of the Asian economies virtually guarantees that the price of imports from these economies will remain low and may fall further. The relative price of computers will continue to fall, although the rate of decline is expected to return to the roughly 15-percent annual rate that has prevailed over much of the 1990s. Finally, the methodological changes to the CPI planned to be implemented before 2000 are eventually expected to lower annual CPI inflation by another 0.4 percentage point, and the price index for GDP by 0.1 percentage point. With these considerations in mind, the Administration projects CPI inflation to creep up by about 0.3 percentage point over the next few years, to 2.3 percent by 2000.

THE DEMAND FOR HOUSING

A surge in the fourth quarter raised residential investment growth above that of GDP during the past year. New home construction (housing starts and shipments of mobile homes) was roughly unchanged in 1997 from its year-earlier pace, despite a jump in the fourth quarter. Demographic trends indicate stable demand for housing during the next decade.

The current shape of the age distribution reflects the legacy of the baby boom and the baby bust. Because most new households are formed by young adults, the passage of the first wave of baby-boomers into the prime years of household formation in the late 1970s was associated with a rapid pace of home construction and rising house prices. But household formation fell to an annual rate of about 1.1 million per year during the first half of the 1990s as the smaller baby-bust cohort moved into adulthood. Demographic forecasts project a similar rate of household formation over the second half of the 1990s.

In addition to growth in the number of households, demand for new homes is created by the replacement of homes that are scrapped or destroyed and by the increase in the number of second homes and vacant homes (Table 2-6). Replacement demand (which can be estimated over long periods only) has averaged about 300,000 units per year. The increase in "vacant" homes (which includes second homes) is highly cyclical and has reflected the general economic strength of recent years, but tends to average about 200,000 units per year. Altogether, housing demand has averaged 1.53 million units per year thus far in the 1990s and, in light of the demographic forecast, is expected to continue at a similar pace for the next decade.

This projection of the long-run demand for housing is slightly stronger than what has prevailed thus far in the 1990s, but not quite as strong as demand in the past 2 years. As Table 2-6 shows, long-run demand is consistent with a rate of housing starts of roughly 1.40 million units per year, slightly below the 1.48-million-unit pace of homebuilding in 1997. Of course, economic conditions can push housing starts away from their demographic fundamentals. Recessions generally slow the pace of both home construction and household formation as young people remain longer in their parents' homes—this is what happened in 1990. In good times, people spend more on larger homes and second homes. If the current good times continue, homebuilding could exceed these projections of its demographic determinants.

TABLE 2-6.—*Contribution of Selected Determinants of Demand and Supply for New Homes*
[Millions, annual average]

Determinant	1970s	1980s	1990-96	1996-2006
Demand:				
Household growth	1.73	1.26	1.05	1.10
Change in vacancies	.20	.40	.18	.24
Net removals	.30	.30	.30	.30
Total demand	2.23	1.96	1.53	1.64
Supply:				
Single-family homes	1.14	.99	1.05	1.08
Multifamily homes	.62	.51	.24	.30
Mobile homes	.37	.25	.26	.26
Total supply	2.12	1.75	1.54	1.64
Measurement error	.11	.21	-.01	.00

Note. — Detail may not add to totals because of rounding.
Sources: Department of Commerce (Bureau of the Census) and Council of Economic Advisers.

THE NEAR-TERM OUTLOOK

Both supply- and demand-side considerations argue for some moderation in real GDP growth from its rapid 3.6-percent annual pace of the past 2 years (Table 2-7). On the supply side, the unemployment rate has fallen about a percentage point over the past 2 years, and it is therefore doubtful whether a further decline of this magnitude could be accommodated without inflationary consequences. Labor force growth has not kept up with demand in the past 2 years, nor can it be expected to keep up with a repetition of that kind of demand growth.

On the demand side, some restraint is likely to come from the international economy, where the recent rise in the dollar and the restructuring of several Asian economies may slow the demand for American-built products. Because the direction of trade responds with a lag to changes in the exchange rate, the large rise in the dollar over the past 2 years is likely to boost demand for imports and limit growth of our exports. The recent movements of the Asian currencies are particularly dramatic and will make imports from these economies less expensive. Even so, the cloud formed by the Asian restructuring has a silver lining: aggressive competition from foreign producers is likely to restrain domestic inflation—as it has during the past 2 years.

TABLE 2-7.—*Administration Forecast*

Item	Actual		1998	1999	2000	2001	2002	2003	2004
	1996	1997							
	Percent change, fourth quarter to fourth quarter								
Nominal GDP	5.6	¹5.8	4.0	4.1	4.3	4.6	4.6	4.6	4.7
Real GDP (chain-type)	3.2	¹3.9	2.0	2.0	2.0	2.3	2.4	2.4	2.4
GDP price index (chain-type)	2.3	¹1.8	2.0	2.1	2.2	2.2	2.2	2.2	2.2
Consumer price index (CPI-U)	3.2	1.9	2.2	2.2	2.3	2.3	2.3	2.3	2.3
	Calendar year average								
Unemployment rate (percent)	5.4	4.9	4.9	5.1	5.3	5.4	5.4	5.4	5.4
Interest rate, 91-day Treasury bills (percent)	5.0	5.1	5.0	4.9	4.8	4.7	4.7	4.7	4.7
Interest rate, 10-year Treasury notes (percent)	6.4	6.4	5.9	5.8	5.8	5.7	5.7	5.7	5.7
Nonfarm payroll employment (millions)	119.5	¹122.3	124.0	125.4	126.8	128.4	130.4	132.5	134.5

¹ Preliminary.
Sources: Council of Economic Advisers, Department of Commerce, Department of Labor, Department of the Treasury, and Office of Management and Budget.

Other factors also are expected to slow the growth of demand. Business purchases of capital goods have been growing faster than the overall economy, and because the relative price of equipment investment is falling, this trend is expected to continue. However, some moderation of the recent torrid pace is expected as business demand for capital goods becomes more sated. A similar effect may limit expenditures on consumer durables, where—given the length and strength of this expansion—pent-up demand has been exhausted.

The rate of inventory investment was particularly strong during the first half of 1997 and remained high despite tapering off somewhat in the second half of the year. Because output grew so rapidly, inventories remain lean with respect to sales, and certainly no overhang of excess inventories exists at this point. Still, the rate of inventory growth during 1997, at about 5 percent, is in excess of what will be needed once demand moderates to its trend. As a result, inventory investment is also expected to restrain near-term growth in demand.

86

As in recent Administration projections, a moderation in output growth to 2.0 percent is projected in the near term—slightly below the economy's long-run growth rate, but in line with the consensus of professional economic forecasters. The balance of the Administration's forecast is built around a growth rate for potential output of 2.4 percent per year. The Administration does not think that 2.4-percent annual real growth is the best that the economy can do; rather, this projected growth reflects a conservative estimate of the effects of Administration policies to promote education and investment and to balance the budget. The outcome could be even better—as it has been in the past 2 years. But the Administration's forecast is used for a very important purpose: to project Federal revenues and outlays and the Federal budget deficit. For this purpose excessive optimism is dangerous and can stand in the way of making difficult but necessary budget decisions. In the final analysis, the most important goal is the creation of a sound forecast that accurately captures likely economic trends.

As of December 1997 the current expansion had lasted 81 months, making it the third longest in the postwar record. There is no foreseeable reason why this expansion cannot continue. As the 1996 *Report* argued, expansions do not die of old age. Instead, recent postwar expansions have ended because of rising inflation, financial imbalances, or inventory overhangs. None of these conditions exists at present. The most likely prognosis is therefore for sustained job creation and continued noninflationary growth.

CHAPTER 3

The Economic Well-Being
of Children

AFTER DROPPING SHARPLY IN THE 1960s, the official poverty rate among children trended upward from 1969 to 1993, reflecting
increases in the share of children in single-parent families and
declines in real wages at the bottom of the income distribution.
Recently, however, the picture has improved, as the child poverty
rate declined by 2.2 percentage points from 1993 to 1996.

Other measures of children's material well-being have improved
recently as well. Since the early 1990s the share of children in households reporting that they did not have enough food to eat has
decreased, the share of households with children living in inadequate housing has fallen, and children's use of basic health services
has increased. Continued declines have also been recorded in infant
and child mortality rates, and some measures of children's educational achievement have improved.

Nevertheless, many children remain economically vulnerable. In
1996 one in five children was officially poor; in 1995 one in nine lived
in households paying more than half of their income for housing, and
one in seven did not have health insurance; and in 1994 one in 56
lived in households where children experienced hunger due to inadequate resources for food. These factors place children at risk of both
current and future hardship, as many of these factors may be critical to children's long-term development.

This Administration has adopted a range of strategies to improve
the economic and social well-being of children. The first of these is to
put in place a system that guarantees that children's basic needs are
met. For this reason the Administration has supported major initiatives to expand health insurance, child care, and subsidized housing
and has substantially strengthened the child support enforcement
system. The second strategy is to provide financial support to needy
families in a way that promotes work and personal responsibility. To
achieve these goals the Administration proposed and the Congress
enacted increases in the minimum wage, an expansion in the earned
income tax credit (EITC), and a major restructuring of the welfare
system. The third strategy is to invest in programs that enrich children's educational opportunities, by expanding the Head Start
program and encouraging higher standards for elementary and secondary schools.

This chapter begins by describing recent economic and demographic trends that have influenced the economic well-being of children,
and recent programs designed to improve the economic status of families with children. The second section reports on changes in two key
components of children's material well-being: food sufficiency and
housing conditions. The third section describes recent changes in children's health outcomes, access to health care, and health insurance
coverage rates. The concluding section discusses child care and educational programs for children.

TRENDS IN THE ECONOMIC WELL-BEING
OF CHILDREN

THE LINK BETWEEN INCOME AND
CHILDREN'S WELL-BEING

The adequacy of family income is a critical predictor of both the present and the future well-being of children. Children who grow up in
low-income families score lower on standardized academic achievement tests, are less likely to complete high school, complete fewer
years of school, and are likely to have lower earnings when they enter
the labor market than children who grow up in higher income families. Most studies find that family income is more strongly correlated
with children's achievement than parental schooling or family structure.

Low family income might affect children's well-being for any of several reasons. One is that low-income parents may not be able to afford
to invest as much in the things that improve their children's well-
being, such as food, shelter, medical care, and education. A second is
that the poor are more likely to live in neighborhoods with a high concentration of poverty and thus may face higher crime rates, poorer
quality schools, and more limited connections to mainstream economic activity. A third is that low-income families may experience higher
levels of emotional distress, due to the economic pressures of living on
a limited income.

Finally, income may be highly correlated with children's achievement not because income directly affects child well-being, but because
income is associated with some other, hard-to-measure factor that
does affect child well-being, such as the value that parents place on
education. For example, children from high-income families may perform better on standardized academic tests than children from
low-income families not because they have higher incomes but
because their parents encouraged them to work harder in school. If
this is so, increasing family income will not necessarily increase children's academic achievement unless it also increases parents'
commitment to their children's education. A recent study found that
more sophisticated techniques that control for potential differences

across families produced lower estimated impacts of family income on child well-being than suggested by simple correlations of family income and child well-being.

MEASURING TRENDS IN CHILD POVERTY RATES

One of the most commonly used measures of the adequacy of family income is the poverty rate. The poverty rate is the percentage of the population who live in families with before-tax cash incomes below a defined level of need, called the poverty line. The official poverty line in use today was devised in the early 1960s and based on the minimum cost of a nutritionally adequate diet. This amount was multiplied by three, because data from the late 1950s suggested that the typical family spent one-third of its income on food. Since then the poverty line has been updated annually for inflation using the consumer price index for all urban consumers. In 1996 the poverty line for a family of two adults and two children was $15,911. Many people have argued that the official poverty measure should be modified to account for family income and family income requirements differently. Box 3-1 describes a recent proposal by the National Research Council to change the way we measure poverty.

Box 3-1.—How Does Our Poverty Measure Affect Our Conception of Poverty?

A 1995 report by the National Research Council (NRC) recommended a number of changes in the way we measure poverty. Its recommendations include the following:

- *Defining income.* On the one hand, the definition of family income should be expanded to include other important sources of purchasing power, such as the EITC, food stamps, and housing subsidies. On the other hand, some necessary expenditures that reduce a family's resources available for basic consumption needs should be subtracted from income, such as taxes, necessary child care and other work-related expenditures, child support payments, and out-of-pocket medical expenditures.
- *Setting a threshold.* Poverty thresholds should be adjusted to provide a more accurate measure of family income requirements. First, the consumption bundle used to derive thresholds should be based on food, clothing, and shelter, not food consumption alone. Second, thresholds should reflect regional variations in housing costs. Third, thresholds should be adjusted for family size in a more consistent way than currently. Finally, thresholds should be updated to reflect changes in expenditure patterns over time.

Chart 3-1 shows that the poverty rate for children declined sharply from 1960 to 1969 and has since trended upward, with peaks in 1983 and 1993. (Throughout this chapter "children" refers to persons under age 18 except where stated to the contrary.) Chart 3-1 also illustrates an experimental poverty measure developed by the Bureau of the

Chart 3-1 **Poverty Rates of Children**
The child poverty rate rose between 1978 and 1993 after falling steeply in the 1960s. It has declined again since 1993, especially after including taxes and in-kind benefits.

Percent

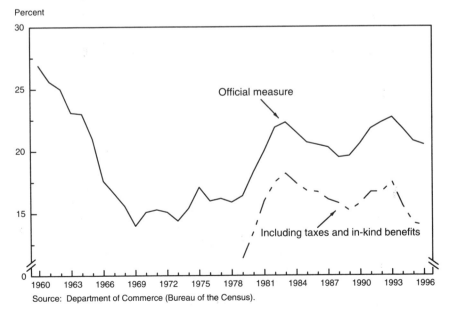

Source: Department of Commerce (Bureau of the Census).

92

Census, which includes taxes and in-kind transfers in family income. Including taxes and transfers reduces the estimated poverty rate in each year but does not substantially affect the trend in poverty from 1979 to 1993. Since 1993, poverty rates have declined more rapidly under the experimental than under the official measure. This is largely attributable to recent expansions in the EITC, which affect the experimental but not the official measure of poverty.

Estimates of changes in the poverty rate are sensitive to the method used to adjust the poverty line for inflation. Some have argued that the price index used in the official poverty measure has overestimated the actual level of inflation. (See the *1997 Economic Report of the President* for a discussion of this issue.) Under some alternative estimates of poverty that incorporate different inflation estimates, poverty trends for children are flat or down over the last several decades.

Table 3-1 shows poverty rates for children of different ages, races, family status, and incomes in 1996. In that year 20.5 percent of all children were poor, 9.0 percent were in extreme poverty (defined here

TABLE 3-1.—*Children with Family Incomes Below Different Income Cutoffs, 1996*
[Percent of children in each category]

Demographic category	Family income		
	Less than half of poverty line	Less than poverty line	Less than twice poverty line
Age of child:[1]			
Under 6	10.5	22.7	46.2
6-17	7.4	18.3	40.7
Race/ethnicity of child:			
White	6.6	16.3	38.2
Black	20.6	39.9	68.0
Hispanic	14.7	40.3	72.0
Family status:			
Female-headed	25.8	49.3	76.3
Married couple	2.8	10.1	31.0
All children	9.0	20.5	43.2

[1] Children in families.
Note.—Income is before-tax cash income.
Source: Department of Commerce (Bureau of the Census).

as family income less than half the poverty line), and 43.2 percent were poor or near poor (defined here as family income less than twice the poverty line). The poverty rate for children under age 6 was 1.25 times that for children aged 6-17, the rate for black and Hispanic children was 2.5 times that for white children, and the rate for children in female-headed households with no husband present was nearly five times that for children in married-couple families. Over one-quar-

93

ter of children in female-headed families lived in families with incomes below half the poverty line, and over three-quarters of this group lived in families with incomes below twice the poverty line.

EXPLAINING RECENT CHANGES IN CHILD POVERTY

Changes in family structure, labor market opportunities, and transfers are all likely to have an important influence on child poverty. This section briefly describes each of these three factors. It then estimates the relative influence of these factors on changes in child poverty since 1979.

Family Structure

Changes in family structure are likely to have had a substantial influence on child poverty rates over the past few decades. The percentage of children living with their mother only has nearly tripled since 1960. This reflects increases both in the percentage of children living with a mother who is divorced or who is married but not currently living with her husband and in the percentage living with a never-married mother (Chart 3-2). Because children in female-headed households have poverty rates nearly five times those of children in married-couple households, an increase in the percentage of children in female-headed households is likely to increase child poverty.

Chart 3-2 **Children Living with Their Mother Only, by Marital Status of Mother**
The percent of children living with their mother only has nearly tripled since 1960.

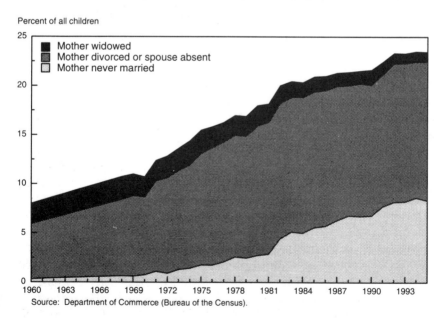

Percent of all children

Source: Department of Commerce (Bureau of the Census).

Children in female-headed households have a higher risk of living in poverty for two reasons. First, most single mothers do not receive

94

child support and must therefore rely on a single income. Nearly two-thirds of all divorced, separated, or never-married women with children did not receive child support payments in 1991. Second, that single income is likely to be lower in a female-headed than in a male-headed household, because women typically earn less in the labor market than men. In 1996 the median earnings of full-time, year-round workers were about 25 percent lower for women than for men.

Macroeconomic and Labor Market Conditions

Both macroeconomic and labor market conditions can affect child poverty because they influence the quality and quantity of jobs available to parents. Table 3-2 shows how changes in child poverty rates are related to two key indicators of macroeconomic performance: the unemployment rate and the economic growth rate, as measured by annual growth in real gross domestic product per capita. The marked decline in child poverty from 1959 to 1969 coincided with both high economic growth rates and decreases in unemployment. Some studies have attributed the decline in poverty over this period to these strong macroeconomic conditions.

TABLE 3-2.—*Changes in Child Poverty Rate and
Selected Macroeconomic Indicators*

Period	Change in official poverty rate of children (percentage points)	Average annual growth rate in real GDP per capita (percent)	Change in unemployment rate (percentage points)
1959-69	-13.3	3.0	-2.0
1969-79	2.4	2.1	2.3
1979-89	3.2	1.8	-.5
1989-93	3.1	.3	1.6
1993-96	-2.2	1.8	-1.5

Sources: Department of Commerce (Bureau of the Census and Bureau of Economic Analysis) and Department of Labor (Bureau of Labor Statistics).

Despite continued strong rates of economic growth, the child poverty rate increased during the 1970s and 1980s. This was partly a result of the increase in the unemployment rate from 1969 to 1979, and partly attributable to an increase in wage inequality since the 1970s. (See Chapter 4 of the 1997 *Economic Report of the President* for a discussion of these trends.) Two recent studies have concluded that the increases in overall poverty in the 1980s were largely attributable to increases in wage inequality and to decreases in the real wages of low-wage workers.

During the 1990s changes in child poverty have been more closely aligned with changes in unemployment and economic growth rates. The increase in child poverty from 1989 to 1993 coincided with increases in unemployment and low economic growth rates, whereas the decrease from 1993 to 1996 coincided with lower unemployment and higher rates of economic growth.

Changes in Transfer Policy

One other factor that has had an important influence on child poverty is changes in the generosity of the tax-and-transfer system. The real value of cash transfers available to low-income families with children has deteriorated significantly since the 1970s. This reflects a decline in the real value of benefits under the Aid to Families with Dependent Children (AFDC) program, the main cash assistance program for low-income families with children until 1996. Although this decline was offset somewhat by expansions in food stamps, combined benefits from both AFDC and food stamps have also decreased (Chart 3-3).

Since 1993, expansions of the EITC have increased the transfers available to low-income working families. In addition, the welfare system has been restructured to promote work and family responsibility. These changes are described further below.

Chart 3-3 **Monthly AFDC and Food Stamp Benefits for a Family of Four**
The purchasing power of AFDC and food stamp benefits has eroded since 1970. AFDC payments alone have lost nearly half their real value.

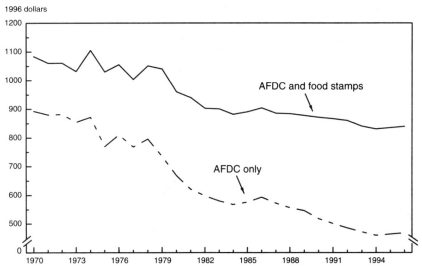

Note: Each data point represents the maximum benefit paid by the median State.
Sources: U.S. House of Representatives (Committee on Ways and Means), Department of Health and Human Services, and Department of Agriculture.

Assessing Relative Magnitudes—A Decomposition

Table 3-3 presents estimates of the impact of changes in family composition, earnings and other before-tax-and-transfer income, and taxes and transfers on the change in child poverty since 1979. It presents two measures of poverty: the official measure, which is based on before-tax cash income, and an alternative measure, which includes both taxes and means-tested food and housing transfers. These estimates may not accurately reflect the full impact of each of these factors on poverty over this period, because they assume that the observed changes in family composition have not been influenced by changes in underlying poverty rates for married couples and single-parent families. These estimates may also be sensitive to the order in which each income source is accounted for in the analysis.

The first line of the table shows the impact of changes in family structure on changes in the child poverty rate for various periods since 1979. It shows how changes in the percentage of children living in each of three family types—married couples, female householders with no husband present, and male householders with no wife present—would have affected child poverty in each period, if the poverty rates of each group had not changed. The second line shows the impact of market earnings. It shows the effect of changes in before-tax-and-transfer poverty rates of children in each family category. The third line shows the impact of cash transfers (social insurance and welfare payments). It shows the effect of changes in the percentage of children within each family category whose incomes are brought above the poverty line when cash transfers are included in income. The fifth and sixth lines show similar calculations for means-tested food and housing transfers and for taxes.

TABLE 3-3.—*Accounting for Changes in Child Poverty*
[Percentage points]

Factor	1979-89	1989-93	1993-96	1979-96
Change in official poverty measure attributable to changes in:				
Family structure	1.2	0.8	0.3	2.3
Earnings and other before-tax-and-transfer income	1.1	3.5	-3.0	1.6
Social insurance and welfare payments	1.0	-1.1	.5	.4
Total change in official poverty measure	3.2	3.1	-2.2	4.1
Change in extended poverty measure attributable to changes in:				
Means-tested food and housing transfers	.4	-.3	.0	.1
Taxes	.3	.0	-2.5	-2.2
Total change in extended poverty measure	4.0	2.9	-4.7	2.2

Note.—A positive number indicates an increase, and a negative number a decrease, in the child poverty rate resulting from that factor.
Detail may not add to totals because of rounding.
Sources: Department of Commerce (Bureau of the Census) and Office of Management and Budget.

These calculations imply that the increase of 3.2 percentage points in the official poverty rate from 1979 to 1989 is attributable to changes in family structure (1.2 percentage points), increases in before-tax-and-transfer poverty (1.1 percentage points), and decreases in social insurance and welfare payments (1.0 percentage point).

97

Changes in food and housing transfer payments further increased the extended poverty measure by 0.7 percentage point.

By contrast, the 2.9-percentage-point increase in the extended child poverty measure from 1989 to 1993 is mainly attributable to an increase in before-tax-and-transfer poverty (3.5 percentage points) and to changes in family composition (0.8 percentage point). These factors were offset by transfers, which tended to decrease poverty over this period.

Finally, the table suggests that the 4.7-percentage-point decline in the after-tax-and-transfer extended child poverty measure from 1993 to 1996 is attributable to both a 3.0-percentage-point decrease in before-tax-and-transfer poverty and a 2.0-percentage-point increase in the proportion of children moved out of poverty by taxes and transfers (primarily the EITC). Changes in family structure had a small impact on child poverty during this period, increasing the poverty rate by 0.3 percentage point from 1993 to 1996.

Overall, this table suggests that changes in family structure have put upward pressure on child poverty rates since 1979. The long-term increase in wage inequality has been reflected in an increase in before-tax-and-transfer poverty since 1979, although there have also been cyclical fluctuations in before-tax-and-transfer poverty in the 1980s and 1990s. Finally, the tax-and-transfer system did more to reduce child poverty in 1996 than in 1979. This largely reflects the recent expansion of the EITC.

POLICY INITIATIVES TO SUPPORT FAMILY INCOMES

This Administration has established a number of initiatives to expand the resources available to families with children in a way that creates positive incentives for work and personal responsibility. Recent policy initiatives include:

- *A higher minimum wage.* The Congress and the Administration increased the minimum wage from $4.25 to $4.75 per hour in October 1996, and to $5.15 per hour in September 1997, bringing the minimum wage to its highest level in real terms since 1984.
- *An expanded EITC.* In 1993 the Congress approved the Administration's proposal to expand the EITC. The EITC is a refundable tax credit designed primarily for low-income working families with children. In 1997 the maximum credit for a family with one child was $2,210 (a 54-percent increase since 1993), and that for a family with two or more children was $3,656 (a 140-percent increase since 1993).
- *Welfare reform.* The Personal Responsibility and Work Opportunity Reconciliation Act of 1996 dramatically restructured the welfare system to promote work and personal responsibility, and to allow States greater flexibility in designing welfare assistance programs. The law converted the Aid to Families with Dependent Children program into a new block grant, called Temporary Assistance for

Needy Families. To promote work and personal responsibility, the law includes new work requirements, a 5-year limit on the length of time that families can receive assistance, and new measures to strengthen child support enforcement. The law also expands funding for child care to make it easier for families to move from welfare to work. Even before the new welfare law was enacted, the Administration had granted waivers to 43 States to allow them to reform their welfare systems to require work, make work pay, and encourage parental responsibility.

Increased child support enforcement. Federal legislation in 1993, 1994, and 1996 included measures designed to make the child support enforcement system more effective. Key reforms include streamlined procedures to establish paternity, a new-hire reporting system to track delinquent parents across State lines, uniform interstate child support laws, computerized registries of statewide child support collections, and tough new penalties, such as revocation of the driver's licenses of delinquents.

These initiatives have already had noticeable effects. The combination of a higher minimum wage with an expanded EITC guarantees a more adequate income to working families with children. A single mother with two children can now earn enough, if she works full-time, to bring her income with the EITC above the poverty line. In addition, because the EITC benefit increases the financial reward to working, it encourages parents to enter the labor market. Research has shown that expansions in the EITC have been associated with increases in the employment rate of single mothers with children.

The changes to the welfare system have already been associated with a large decline in welfare caseloads. The number of children on welfare declined by 23 percent from January 1993 to June 1997. Research suggests that the decline in welfare caseloads from January 1993 to January 1997 was due to a strong economy and to recent State welfare reforms that the Federal waiver process facilitated.

Finally, the child support enforcement system has become more effective in guaranteeing that absent parents fulfill their obligations to pay child support. From 1992 to 1996, child support collections increased by 50 percent, to a record $12 billion. In addition, the number of paternities established for children born to unmarried women rose to 1 million in 1996, almost double the number in 1992. These changes are reflected in a substantial increase from 1992 to 1996 in the percentage of never-married mothers who received child support payments.

OTHER MEASURES OF
CHILDREN'S MATERIAL WELL-BEING

Two alternative measures of the adequacy of housing conditions and the sufficiency of household food supply suggest that the material well-being of children has improved since 1989. These trends are consistent with the reduction in child poverty over this period, under the extended measure of child poverty that includes taxes and means-tested food and housing benefits.

AVAILABILITY OF FOOD

One alternative measure of children's material well-being is the adequacy of household food supply. It has been shown that households that report having an insufficient food supply consume smaller quantities of essential nutrients than other households.

Estimates from the Department of Agriculture's Continuing Survey of Food Intakes by Individuals (CSFII) provide information on the percentage of children living in households where there sometimes or often was not enough to eat in the last 3 months. These estimates may overstate the prevalence of hunger among children, if many adults typically go without food before they let their children go hungry. Estimates from the CSFII suggest that the percentage of children living in households without enough to eat has fallen from 4.1 percent in 1989-91 to 3.0 percent in 1994-96 for all children, and from 13.5 percent to 9.4 percent for children in households with incomes below 130 percent of the poverty line (Table 3-4).

TABLE 3-4.—*Children in Households Reporting That There Was Sometimes or Often Not Enough to Eat During the Last 3 Months*
[Percent]

Category	1989-91	1994-96
Children in households at or below 130 percent of poverty line	13.5	9.4
Children in households above 130 percent of poverty line	.8	.6
All children	4.1	3.0

Source: Department of Agriculture.

The Department of Agriculture's Food and Nutrition Service has recently developed a detailed questionnaire that makes it possible to separately identify whether children or adults in the household experienced hunger. This questionnaire was incorporated into the April 1995 Current Population Survey. The survey found evidence that hunger is more likely among adults than among children: among households with children, 4.3 percent had adult members who had been hungry in the last year due to insufficient resources, but only 1.8

percent had children who had been hungry in the last 12 months because the parents could not afford to buy more food. This survey also suggests that it is unusual for children to go without food for an extended period: 0.9 percent of households with children reported that at least one of their children had skipped a meal in the past year, and 0.2 percent reported that their children had not eaten for a whole day at least once in the past year because of insufficient resources.

ADEQUACY OF HOUSING

Estimates from the Annual Housing Survey and the American Housing Survey present a mixed picture of the changes in housing conditions of households with children. On the one hand, the percentage of these households that have high rent burdens has increased substantially. The percentage of households with children that spend more than half their income on housing has increased from 6.5 percent in 1978 to 11.5 percent in 1995 (Table 3-5). For renters with very low incomes (defined as households with incomes below 50 percent of the median income for their area), this figure has increased from 31.0 percent to 37.6 percent.

TABLE 3-5.—*Housing Problems Among Households with Children*
[Percent of all households with children]

Housing cost or condition	1978	1989	1993	1995
All households with children:				
Housing costs more than 50 percent of income	6.5	8.7	10.9	11.5
Housing costs 31-50 percent of income	8.3	15.1	15.6	16.7
Severe physical problems with housing	3.1	3.2	2.0	2.2
Moderate physical problems with housing	5.6	5.5	5.1	5.0
Crowding (more than 1 person per room)	9.4	7.0	6.3	6.6
Very low income households with children:				
Housing costs more than 50 percent of income	31.0	36.1	38.2	37.6
Housing costs 31-50 percent of income	28.0	30.6	29.1	30.6
Severe physical problems with housing	7.5	5.8	3.6	3.4
Moderate physical problems with housing	10.5	12.0	10.1	9.5
Crowding (more than 1 person per room)	21.9	16.7	14.2	17.0

Note.—Income is before-tax cash income. Very low income is defined as family income below half the median for the area.
Source: Department of Housing and Urban Development (Office of Policy Development and Research).

On the other hand, measures of housing quality for households with children have shown improvement. The percentage of all households with children living in housing with either moderate or severe physical problems fell from 8.7 percent in 1978 to 7.2 percent in 1995, and from 18.0 percent to 12.9 percent for very low income renters. In addition, households with children were less likely to live in crowded living situations in 1995 than in 1978: the percentage living in housing with more than one person per room dropped from 9.4 percent to 6.6 percent for all households and from 21.9 percent to 17.0 percent for very low income renters.

These findings are consistent with the results of a recent study which found that many measures of the housing quality of children in households in the bottom income quintile had improved since the early 1970s. These children were more likely to live in modern (that is, post-1940 vintage) housing and more likely to have air conditioning in the 1990s than in the early 1970s. On the other hand, this study also found that children in the bottom household income quintile were more likely to live in neighborhoods where their parents reported that crime was a serious problem in 1991-93 than in 1973-75.

NEW HOUSING POLICY INITIATIVES

This Administration will continue to make housing quality and affordability high priorities in fiscal 1999. Key initiatives include:

- *Expanding the low-income housing tax credit.* The low-income housing tax credit gives States the authority to allocate a fixed pool of tax credits to developers of affordable housing. For fiscal 1999 the President has proposed increasing the total amount of tax credits available to each State from $1.25 to $1.75 per State resident.
- *The HOME Investments Partnerships Program.* The Administration has expanded funding for the HOME program by 50 percent since 1993, to $1.5 billion in fiscal 1999. This program offers funding to States, cities, and counties to develop affordable housing options for low-income families. These funds can be used for rehabilitation of existing housing, new housing development, and tenant-based rental subsidies. To date, almost 310,000 families have been awarded assistance through this program.

HEALTH STATUS AND HEALTH INSURANCE

HEALTH OUTCOMES

Over the past 10 years infant and child mortality rates have continued to decline. Other measures, however, such as the incidence of chronic health conditions and of low birthweight, are stable or increasing.

One of the most frequently cited measures of children's health status is the infant mortality rate. Infant mortality has continued its decades-long decline in the 1990s, falling from 9.8 deaths per thousand live births in 1989 to 7.2 per thousand in 1996 (Chart 3-4). During the same period the incidence of low birthweight (weight at birth below 2,500 grams, or about 5.5 pounds) has increased slightly, from 7.0 percent of live births in 1989 to 7.3 percent in 1995. This shows that the improvement in infant mortality in the 1990s has been entirely due to factors other than reductions in low-birthweight births. This improvement has been attributed in part to two key interventions. First, new medical treatments have been developed for infant respiratory disorders, an important cause of mortality among preterm infants. Second, there has been a marked decline in sudden infant death syndrome since researchers discovered that these deaths could be prevented by placing babies on their backs to sleep.

The slightly increased incidence of low birthweight since the mid-1980s is due in part to an increase in multiple births and births to older women. Failure to prevent low-birthweight births is costly to society because many of these infants require more-expensive medical interventions than do infants born at normal weight. In addition, low-birthweight infants have a much higher risk of infant mortality. In 1995 nearly two-thirds of all infant deaths occurred among the 7.3 percent of all infants born at low birthweight.

Chart 3-4 **Infant Mortality Rates and Incidence of Low Birthweight**
Infant mortality has continued to decrease since 1989 despite an increase in low-birthweight births.

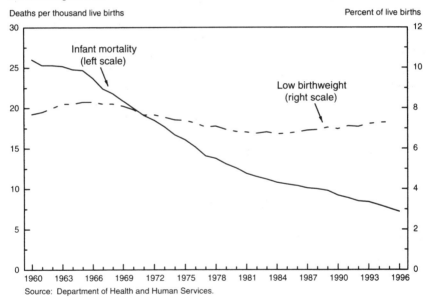

Source: Department of Health and Human Services.

Mortality rates of older children have also fallen throughout the 1990s, continuing a steady decline since 1960 (Chart 3-5). Much of the decline in the 1960s has been attributed to medical interventions, which have minimized the risk of death from such conditions as congenital anomalies of the heart, infectious diseases, and certain childhood cancers. By contrast, the reduction in mortality during the

1980s has been primarily attributed to a decline in injury-related mortality.

The one exception to this pattern is among those aged 15-19, whose mortality rates have increased since 1985. This largely reflects the more than doubling in homicides among adolescents since 1985. The homicide rate for black male adolescents has nearly tripled since 1985, and in 1994 it was nearly seven times higher than the homicide rate for all adolescents.

Other indicators of child health have shown less progress in the 1980s and 1990s. The prevalence of asthma among children has increased substantially since the mid-1980s. The prevalence of most other chronic health conditions has fluctuated, without a consistent upward or downward trend.

Chart 3-5 **Child and Youth Mortality Rates**
Mortality rates have continued to decline since the mid-1980s for all children and youths except those aged 15-19.

Deaths per hundred thousand

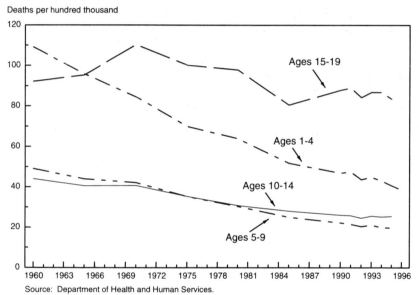

Source: Department of Health and Human Services.

HEALTH INSURANCE

One of the critical determinants of children's access to health care is whether or not they have health insurance. Research has shown that children with health insurance coverage are more likely to receive preventive and primary care, and more likely to have a regular relationship with a primary care provider, than uninsured children. Insured children are also more likely to receive treatment for such conditions (when they are present) as injury, asthma, and acute earache. They are less likely to be hospitalized for conditions that appropriate outpatient care could have prevented, and they receive less intensive hospital services when admitted to the hospital.

Since 1987 the Congress and the Administration have substantially expanded children's access to health insurance through Medicaid, the primary government program offering health insurance to low-income children. Before 1987 Medicaid was mainly restricted to children in very low income, single-parent families. Since then a series of legislative initiatives have extended Medicaid to much broader groups of children. By 1996 all pregnant women and all children under age 6 who had family incomes below 133 percent of the poverty line, and all children age 13 and younger with family incomes below 100 percent of the poverty line, were eligible for Medicaid. Coverage will continue to be phased in for all children born after September 1983 until poor children of all ages are covered. In addition, many States have expanded children's eligibility for Medicaid beyond these federally required levels.

The net result of these expansions is that a much larger share of the child population are now enrolled in Medicaid. Estimates from the Current Population Survey suggest that the proportion of children who are enrolled in Medicaid increased from 16 percent in 1989 to 23 percent in 1995 (Table 3-6). For children under age 6 the increase in Medicaid coverage was even larger, and by 1995, 30 percent of all children under age 6 were covered by Medicaid.

TABLE 3-6.—*Children with Health Insurance, by Age of Child and Type of Coverage*
[Percent]

Age of child	Any insurance		Medicaid		Private insurance	
	1989	1995	1989	1995	1989	1995
Current Population Survey:						
Under 6	87.2	86.7	20.3	29.6	70.6	60.4
6-17	86.4	86.0	13.2	19.9	75.3	69.1
All children	86.7	86.2	15.7	23.2	73.6	66.1
Health Interview Survey:						
Under 6	84.9	88.4	18.7	28.2	67.9	60.1
6-17	85.5	85.7	10.9	16.6	74.0	68.7
All children	85.3	86.7	12.8	20.6	71.8	65.7

Sources: Department of Commerce (Bureau of the Census) and Department of Health and Human Services (National Center for Health Statistics).

At the same time that Medicaid eligibility has increased, there has been a reduction in children's private insurance coverage. This decline is likely to have been driven in part by a general reduction in employer-provided health insurance, which has affected both low- and high-income families. It may also have resulted in part from newly eligible families dropping their private insurance coverage in order to enroll in Medicaid.

Studies have tried to estimate the extent to which the expansion in Medicaid eligibility has crowded out private insurance coverage. These studies have produced a wide range of estimates. One study found that at least one person dropped private insurance coverage for every two persons made eligible for Medicaid. Two other studies estimated that anywhere between 0 and 25 percent of new Medicaid coverage displaced existing private coverage.

Table 3-6 presents estimates of the change in insurance coverage for children from 1989 to 1995 from two large household-based surveys, the March Current Population Survey and the Health Interview Survey. Both surveys suggest that the percentage of children under age 18 with health insurance from any source remained constant from 1989 to 1995. These surveys provide a somewhat different picture, however, of the change in total insurance coverage for young children. Whereas the Health Interview Survey finds a moderate increase in insurance coverage for children under age 6, the Current Population Survey finds no increase for this group. This may result from changes in question content in the Health Interview Survey in 1990. It may also reflect differences in the way the two surveys ask about health insurance coverage.

Even though there have not been substantial increases in the percentage of children with health insurance, the recent increase in the percentage of children covered by Medicaid may have important implications for the quality of children's medical care. On the one hand, since Medicaid requires no copayments from the insured, covers prescription drugs, and in many States covers services such as dental care, it may promote greater utilization of medical care than private insurance. On the other hand, since provider reimbursement levels tend to be much lower under Medicaid than under other insurance plans, fewer providers may be willing to provide care to children with Medicaid coverage than to children with private insurance.

Although research to date on the impact of the recent Medicaid expansion on children's utilization of medical care is inconclusive, Table 3-7 suggests that basic medical care services received by low-income children have increased. The average number of physician visits per year rose by more than 30 percent for poor children in fair or poor health, and by more than 10 percent for poor children in excellent or good health, from 1987-89 to 1993-95. By contrast, during the same period the average annual number of physician visits decreased for children with family incomes above twice the poverty level.

TABLE 3-7.—*Average Number of Physician Contacts in Last Year for Children Under 15, by Family Income*

[Number of contacts]

Family income	Good or excellent health		Fair or poor health	
	1987-89	1993-95	1987-89	1993-95
Below poverty line	3.6	4.0	10.8	14.2
Poverty line to twice poverty line	3.8	3.9	15.2	16.2
Above twice poverty line	5.0	4.9	22.6	20.7

Note.—Income is before-tax cash income.
Source: Department of Health and Human Services (National Center for Health Statistics).

This evidence is also consistent with data pointing to an increase in the share of pregnant women and children receiving at least a minimal level of primary care. The percentage of children under age 5 who did not see a doctor during the previous year fell from 8 percent in 1983 to 5 percent in 1994, while the comparable percentage of children aged 5-17 decreased from 27 percent to 21 percent (Chart 3-6). In addition, the percentage of pregnant women who initiated care in the first trimester of pregnancy increased to a record high of 82 percent in 1996, from 76 percent in 1989.

Chart 3-6 **Children Without Physician Visit Within Past Year**
Fewer children went without regular doctor visits in the mid-1990s than a decade before.

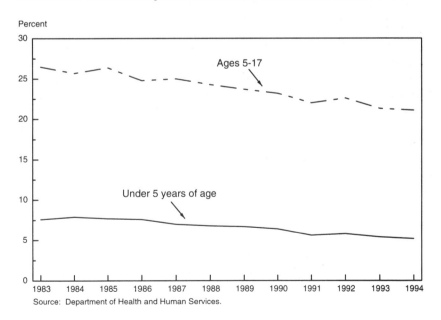

Source: Department of Health and Human Services.

107

RECENT INITIATIVES TO EXPAND CHILDREN'S ACCESS TO HEALTH INSURANCE

Despite recent efforts to expand children's access to health insurance, a large share of children remain uninsured. Estimates from the Current Population Survey suggest that 15 percent of all children did not have health insurance in 1996. Table 3-8 presents estimates from the Current Population Survey on the characteristics of these children. Roughly 21 percent are potentially eligible for Medicaid, because they

TABLE 3-8.—*Uninsured Children by Family Income, 1996*

Family income and age of child	Percent of all uninsured children
Below poverty line	32.6
Under 6	9.8
6-11	10.9
12-17	12.0
Between 100 and 150 percent of poverty line	20.0
Between 150 and 200 percent of poverty line	16.4
Above twice poverty line	30.9

Note.—Income is before-tax cash income.
Source: Department of Commerce (Bureau of the Census).

are under age 12 and have family incomes below the poverty level. An additional 48 percent either are poor children aged 12 and over or have family incomes between 100 percent and 200 percent of the poverty level. Their family incomes are low enough so that the cost of health insurance may pose a significant barrier, but probably not low enough to guarantee them eligibility for Medicaid.

This Administration has developed a two-pronged effort to continue progress in increasing insurance coverage for low-income children. The first component is to extend insurance coverage to more low-income children through the new Children's Health Insurance Program (CHIP). This program offers $24 billion in new Federal funding to States over the next 5 years to expand health insurance programs for uninsured low-income children. States have the option of using the funding to expand children's health insurance coverage through Medicaid, separate State programs, or a combination of the two. In general, States must use their allocation to cover children in families below twice the poverty level, or within 50 percent of the State's current Medicaid income limits for children if the State already covers children at or near twice the poverty level. States must contribute some of their own funds to the program in order to receive these Federal funds, and they must maintain Medicaid eligibility standards at least equal to those in effect in June 1997.

In addition, the President will make enrolling eligible uninsured children in both Medicaid and CHIP a priority. In partnership with the States, health care providers, and business and community groups, the Administration will identify and encourage successful outreach campaigns to enroll up to 5 million uninsured children. To facilitate this effort, the proposed budget for fiscal 1999 includes an option for States to determine presumptive eligibility for Medicaid among children at sites such as schools and day care centers. It will also allow States to receive Federal funding for outreach activities at a 90-percent matching rate from a fixed pool of funds. These legislative proposals will be complemented by administrative actions to simplify enrollment of uninsured children.

CHILD CARE AND EDUCATION

CHILD CARE

Over the past two decades the adequacy and affordability of day care have become increasingly salient issues, as a growing proportion of mothers with young children have entered the work force. Whereas 30 percent of married mothers with one or more children under age 6 were working in 1977, by 1997 that figure had risen to 61 percent. This increase in employment of women with young children has translated into a substantial increase in nonparental child care. Between 1977 and 1993 the number of children under 5 in nonparental child care whose mother was working more than doubled. By 1993, 47 percent of young children with employed mothers had their primary day care arrangement in a day care center or a family day care home, and only 5 percent were cared for by a nonrelative in the child's home.

The affordability of child care is an especially critical issue for low-income working families. Although Federal programs subsidize day care costs for low-income families, a large share of these families do not have access to subsidized care. Approximately 1 million low-income children under 13 received federally subsidized care in fiscal 1995. This compares with the approximately 10 million children under 13 with employed mothers and family incomes below 200 percent of the poverty level.

For families without access to subsidies, the cost of child care can represent a substantial financial burden. In 1993 child care expenditures represented 25 percent of annual income for those families with annual incomes below $14,400 with employed mothers and preschool children in paid child care. Comparable families with annual incomes above $54,000 spent only 6 percent of their income on child care.

The quality of child care is also a critical issue. Two recent studies of regulated child care providers offer reason for concern. One study found that 86 percent of child care centers surveyed provided mediocre or poor care when judged from the perspective of child development, and 12 percent were of such poor quality that the children's health and safety needs were only partly met. The second

109

study, of family day care homes, found that 91 percent were of only adequate quality or less.

The President's fiscal 1999 budget includes a dramatic increase in Federal investments in child care to increase its affordability and quality. Key initiatives would:

- *Expand child care subsidies.* The proposed budget builds on the increases in child care subsidies legislated in 1996, by expanding funding for the Child Care and Development Block Grant Program by $7.5 billion over 5 years. These new funds, combined with funds provided in welfare reform, would allow States to provide child care subsidies to more than 2 million low-income children by 2003— more than double the number of children served in fiscal 1995.
- *Increase tax credits for child care expenses.* The proposed budget would increase tax subsidies for working parents who pay for child care expenditures, by expanding the child and dependent care tax credit. The President's proposal would offer more help to 3 million families with annual incomes below $59,000, providing nearly $5 billion in aid over the next 5 years. The President's proposal also includes a new tax credit for private employers that offer child care services for their employees.
- *Expand after-school care for school-age children.* The President's proposed budget includes $800 million in new funding over 5 years to dramatically expand the 21st Century Community Learning Program. This program provides funding to school-community partnerships to establish or expand before- and after-school programs for school-age children. The program will serve up to half a million children each year.
- *Improve early learning and child care quality.* The President's proposed Early Learning Fund would provide $3 billion over 5 years in challenge grants to communities for programs that improve early learning and the quality and safety of child care for young children. The President's proposed budget also includes funding for scholarships for up to 50,000 child care providers per year, and for improved enforcement of State health and safety standards.

EARLY CHILDHOOD EDUCATION

Early childhood education programs can play a critical role in preparing children aged 3-5 for entry into school and can have an important effect on children's short-run and long-run development. Research has found that children who participate in early childhood education programs show large short-run gains in IQ, which persist until entry into kindergarten. Research has also linked early childhood education to a number of longer term outcomes, such as grade retention and placement in special education programs. Studies of a smaller number of programs have also shown early childhood education to be associated with increases in high school graduation rates and post-high school monthly earnings, and with a lower probability of teen pregnancy.

One of the principal Federal programs supporting early childhood education for disadvantaged children is the Head Start program. The major focus of Head Start is support for enriched preschool programs and development services for children aged 3-5. Federal guidelines require that 90 percent of all children served be from families with incomes below the poverty line. Head Start offers disadvantaged children and their parents a range of services that focus on education, social and emotional development, and health and nutrition. With the establishment of the Early Head Start program in 1994, for which disadvantaged children under age 3 are eligible, the range of Head Start services was extended to younger children as well.

A recent nationwide study found that participation in Head Start was associated with increased performance on the Peabody Picture Vocabulary Test and a reduction in grade repetition for white and Hispanic children, although it did not find similar gains for black children. The study also found that both white and black children who participated in Head Start were more likely to be immunized against measles than nonparticipating children from the same family.

The President's proposed budget includes $3.8 billion in additional funding over 5 years to help reach the goal of expanding participation in Head Start to 1 million children in 2002, from 714,000 in fiscal 1993. This funding would also allow a doubling of participation in Early Head Start, to 80,000 children by 2002.

ELEMENTARY AND SECONDARY EDUCATION

One of our society's most important investments in children is elementary and secondary education. Elementary and secondary schools play a critical role in preparing children for college and for entry into the labor market. Research has shown that increases in educational attainment are associated with increases in labor market earnings: each year invested in elementary or secondary education is estimated to increase annual earnings by 5 to 12 percent. Investments in elementary and secondary education can also achieve other important social goals, such as the development of an informed electorate.

Measures of Student Performance

One of the key tools used in assessing the performance of our elementary and secondary school students is the National Assessment of Educational Progress (NAEP). The NAEP has two parts: the long-term trends assessment, which has repeated the same set of questions since the early 1970s to provide a consistent record of progress over time, and the main assessment, a more recent set of tests designed to reflect current testing methodology and educational content. The main assessment also groups students into three levels of achievement based upon collective judgments about what students should know and be able to do in each subject area.

Evidence from the NAEP long-term assessment suggests that achievement in science, mathematics, and reading has improved since the late 1970s. Charts 3-7 and 3-8 show average NAEP long-term

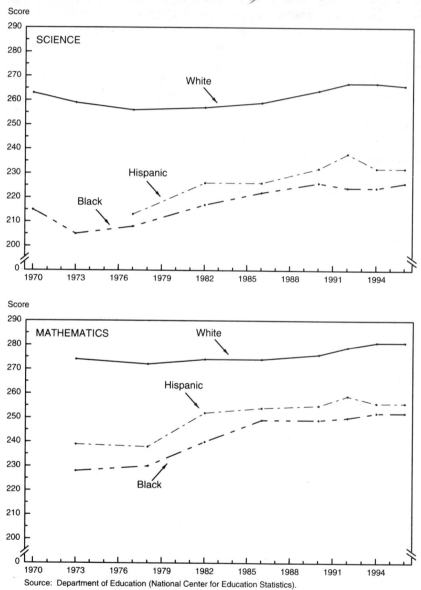

Chart 3-7 **NAEP Long-Term Trend Assessment: Science and Mathematics Scores**
Science and mathematics achievement scores have improved modestly since the mid-1970s for white, black, and Hispanic 13-year-olds.

Source: Department of Education (National Center for Education Statistics).

assessment scores for 13-year-old white, black, and Hispanic students in these subjects. Chart 3-7 reveals increases in mathematics and science scores since the late 1970s, which have been larger for black and Hispanic than for white children. Improvement in reading scores has been somewhat less dramatic overall (Chart 3-8), but both white and black children have recorded measurable improvement since 1971.

Despite these recent gains, significant challenges remain for the Nation's educational system. Evidence from the main NAEP assessments suggests that many students do not achieve basic competency in mathematics, science, or reading. The most recent main assessments found that 38 percent of eighth-grade children performed below the basic level in mathematics, as did 40 percent in science and 30 percent in reading. In addition, U.S. students do not perform well in comparison with students in other countries. According to the Third International Mathematics and Science Study, a study of half a million children in 41 countries, U.S. eighth-graders had average mathematics scores that were below those of 20 other countries. Although U.S. eighth-graders performed better in science, they were still outperformed by students in nine other countries.

A second challenge facing the Nation's educational system is the substantial variation in the performance of schools across the country. A recent study of first-grade students found that those attending the top quarter of schools with respect to student performance had average scores in both reading and mathematics nearly 75 points

Chart 3-8 NAEP Long-Term Trend Assessment: Reading Scores
Reading achievement scores have changed little for white and Hispanic 13-year-olds and improved modestly for black 13-year-olds since 1971.

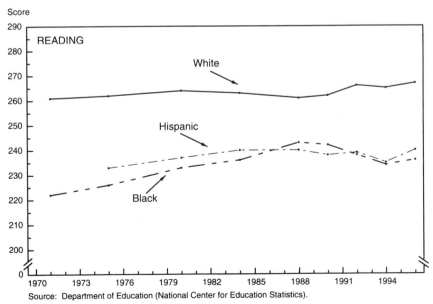

Source: Department of Education (National Center for Education Statistics).

113

higher than those of students in the bottom quarter. This difference is approximately equal to the average achievement gain of students from the spring of first grade to the spring of second grade. In other words, by the end of second grade the average student's achievement in the bottom-ranked schools will just about equal that of students finishing first grade in the top schools.

Differences in student performance are evident across States as well. For example, in 1994 the share of fourth-graders in public schools who scored at or above the basic level in reading ranged across 39 States from a low of 40 percent to a high of 75 percent, and in 1996 the share of eighth-graders in public schools who attained at least the basic level of proficiency in mathematics ranged across 40 States from a low of 36 percent to a high of 77 percent.

Impact of School Inputs on School Performance

A substantial body of research has investigated the extent to which school quality is related to measurable inputs, such as expenditures per pupil, pupil-teacher ratios, or the level of teacher training. This research has had mixed results. On the one hand, most studies that attempt to relate school resources to students' achievement on standardized tests tend to find only weak evidence that these resources do influence school quality. This may be because most research in this area is based on samples that are not large enough to find a statistically measurable effect. A recent study which combined the results from a large number of other studies found stronger evidence that school expenditures per pupil are positively associated with student achievement.

On the other hand, studies that estimate the relationship between school resources and students' earnings later in life tend to find much larger effects. A recent study used data from the 1980 Census to estimate the relationship between the average level of school resources in the State in which workers were born and their subsequent earnings. This study found that workers who had been born (and probably attended school) in States with more abundant school resources earned higher rates of return to each additional year of schooling than other workers. A decrease in the pupil-teacher ratio by five students was associated with an increase in the rate of return to each additional year of school of 0.4 percentage point, and a 10-percent increase in teachers' pay was associated with a 0.1-percentage-point increase. (The average rate of return for all workers in the sample was 5 to 7 percent.)

This literature also found that there are important dimensions of school and teacher quality that are unrelated to school expenditure patterns. After controlling for student and parent characteristics likely to affect student performance, and even after controlling for measurable characteristics of schools and classrooms, it is clear that students in particular schools, or enrolled in particular teachers' classes, consistently perform better than average. This suggests that certain aspects of teacher or school quality that are not easily measured, such as the teacher's level of enthusiasm or the school's management style, may be critically related to student performance.

Recent Federal Initiatives in Primary and Secondary Education

Recognizing that the quality of primary and secondary education can have an important influence on children's later economic opportunities, the Administration has developed and supported a number of initiatives to improve the quality of America's schools. In his 1998 State of the Union address the President proposed two major new initiatives that would increase the financial resources available to public schools:

- *Smaller classes with qualified teachers in grades 1-3.* The President is proposing that $12.4 billion be devoted over 7 years ($7.3 billion over 5 years) to reducing class sizes in public schools in grades 1 to 3 from a nationwide average of 22 pupils to an average of 18, and to helping local school districts hire an additional 100,000 well-prepared teachers. The initiative will also provide funds to States and local school districts to test new teachers, develop more rigorous teacher testing and certification requirements, and train teachers in effective reading instruction. This initiative will help ensure that every child receives personal attention, learns to read independently, and gets a solid foundation for further learning.
- *New construction and renovation of school buildings.* The President is proposing Federal tax credits to pay interest on nearly $22 billion in bonds to build and renovate public schools. This initiative provides more than double the assistance of the Administration's earlier school construction proposal, which covered half the interest on an estimated $20 billion in bonds. Half of this new bond authority would be allocated to the 100 school districts with the largest number of low-income children, and the other half would be allocated to the States.

These proposals build on a number of ongoing Administration efforts to improve the quality of primary and secondary education. To increase the educational opportunities of disadvantaged children, the Administration has expanded the Title I program, which targets resources to children in high-poverty schools. In addition, since it is clear that some important differences in the quality of individual teachers and schools are not directly related to the level of a school's financial resources, the Administration has supported initiatives to change the way schools operate, to better reward performance, and to grant schools more flexibility in meeting measurable performance standards. These are the key emphases of the Goals 2000 and the

Charter Schools programs. Finally, the Administration has developed two new initiatives to improve literacy and to increase students' access to the Internet:

- *Title I—Education for the Disadvantaged.* Title I provides funds to raise the achievement of disadvantaged children. In 1994 the President proposed, and the Congress adopted, changes to Title I to focus resources on schools with a high percentage of children from poor families, to raise standards of achievement for disadvantaged students, and to give schools greater flexibility in helping students meet these standards. The appropriation for Title I grants to local education agencies was increased by about 20 percent from fiscal 1993 to fiscal 1998.

- *Goals 2000.* Enacted in 1994, the Goals 2000 program encourages States to set rigorous academic standards for student performance and to determine whether students are making progress in meeting these goals. It also provides funding to support reform of individual schools and for parental information and resource centers in each State, to help parents become more involved in their children's education.

- *Charter Schools.* The Federal Charter Schools program supports the efforts of parents, teachers, and communities to develop innovative public schools that are free from most of the rules and regulations that apply to most public schools and are held accountable for raising student achievement. Since the program's inception in 1995 over 700 charter schools have been established, and Federal funding has increased from $6 million in fiscal 1995 to $80 million in fiscal 1998.

- *The America Reads Challenge.* The proposed America Reads program is a multipronged effort to help States and communities ensure that all children are reading well and independently by the end of the third grade. Key initiatives include recruiting and training volunteer reading tutors and helping families help their children build literacy skills. In addition, the Administration has recruited work-study students in 800 universities to help with tutoring initiatives.

- *Technology.* The Technology Literacy Challenge Fund and the Technology Innovation Grants program are aimed at meeting four goals: to connect all schools to the Internet, to provide teachers with professional development in the use of technology, to put modern computers in all schools, and to provide challenging software that encourages children to learn more. These initiatives should help prepare our children for the 21st century and keep the Nation competitive in a global economy.

CONCLUSION

It is clear that children have shared in the benefits of the economic recovery of the past 3 years. The child poverty rate fell from 1993 to 1996, and under an extended poverty measure that includes taxes and means-tested food and housing benefits, the rate was lower in 1996 than in 1989. Other measures of well-being, such as health status, educational achievement, food sufficiency, and housing quality have also shown improvements during the 1990s. Yet many children remain vulnerable, either because they have low family incomes, or because they lack access to health insurance, or because they are not learning basic mathematics, science, and reading skills in school. For this reason the Administration will continue to invest in initiatives to improve the well-being of children. Key initiatives for fiscal 1999 will focus on increasing access to child care and early childhood education, improving the quality of primary and secondary education, and increasing access to affordable housing for families with children.

CHAPTER 4

Economic Inequality
Among Racial and Ethnic Groups

THIRTY-FOUR YEARS AGO the signing of the Civil Rights Act of 1964 set the Nation on a course toward racial equality. As the economy surged, income differences narrowed for a full decade. The sharp recessions of the mid-1970s and early 1980s hit black and Hispanic Americans particularly hard, however. And in the expansion of the 1980s, economic growth was accompanied by sharp increases in overall income inequality. As a result, despite the economic growth of this period, income differences between black and Hispanic families on the one hand, and non-Hispanic white families on the other, did not diminish. The recession of the early 1990s brought further economic hardship, as the poverty rate climbed to near a 30-year high.

Since 1993, incomes have once again been rising. But the present recovery differs from those of the 1970s and 1980s in one important respect: economic growth has not been accompanied by sharp increases in income inequality. Moreover, this recovery has been accompanied by a narrowing of some measures of racial inequality. The median black family income reached a new high, and the poverty rate for blacks fell to a new low. After nearly 20 years of stagnation, these developments have again raised hope for sustained progress toward economic equality among racial and ethnic groups.

This chapter reviews statistics on the differences in economic status among racial and ethnic groups—whites, blacks, Hispanics, Asians, and American Indians—and evaluates various explanations for those differences (Box 4-1). Three themes are developed in this review. First, although some narrowing of gaps in economic status among racial and ethnic groups has occurred, it has been uneven—faster in some periods and for some groups than others—and substantial differences persist. The median incomes of non-Hispanic white families and of Asian families are nearly double those of black and Hispanic families. The median wealth of non-Hispanic white households is 10 times that of blacks and Hispanics. Poverty rates among Hispanics and blacks are more than triple those of non-Hispanic whites. Unemployment rates for blacks are twice those for whites.

Second, the sources or causes of current differences in economic status across racial and ethnic groups are numerous and complex. The economic status of a person, a household, or a family reflects a

119

mixture of current conditions, such as the state of the economy, and more permanent characteristics, such as educational background, occupational experience, and family background, which have antecedents in constraints faced in childhood and by previous generations. This commingling of short-term and long-term influences poses a challenge for the interpretation of trends in racial inequality. For example, current progress toward racial equality is due both to the recent effects of the strong economy and to longer term developments such as improvements in educational attainment and reduced discrimination over the past half-century. The complexity of these social and economic processes cautions against a simple explanation of trends in racial and ethnic economic equality.

A third theme of the chapter is that racial inequality and related policy issues are intertwined with the long-term general increase in economic inequality that extends beyond racial differences. Lack of progress toward racial economic equality between the early to mid-1970s and the early 1990s coincided with marked increases in inequality both overall and within racial and ethnic groups.

Box 4-1.—Racial and Ethnic Identity and Classification

The identification and classification of persons by race and ethnicity are complex and controversial issues. The concepts of race and ethnicity lack precise and universally accepted definitions. Their economic significance depends on a variety of factors, including how individuals identify themselves racially or ethnically, and how others identify and treat them. Most of the data presented in this chapter classify persons by race or ethnicity on the basis of responses to questions about race and Hispanic origin in the decennial Census and other household surveys.

Whenever possible, data for five mutually exclusive racial and ethnic groups are presented in this chapter:

- Hispanics, who may be of any race
- Non-Hispanic whites
- Blacks not of Hispanic origin
- Asians, including Pacific Islanders, not of Hispanic origin
- American Indians, including Alaska Natives
  (Alaskan Eskimos and Aleuts), not of Hispanic origin.

The term "black" rather than "African American" has been used in government statistics for more than two decades. The tables, charts, and references to statistics in this chapter that rely on these classifications use the term "black."

Hispanic identification is determined by responses to a question about Hispanic origin. Therefore, in tables, figures and discussion of related statistics the term "Hispanic" is used.

The increase in income inequality has two major implications. First, since blacks, Hispanics, and American Indians are disproportionately represented at the bottom of the income distribution, they are affected disproportionately by developments that make all those at the bottom worse off relative to the middle or the top. A second and more subtle implication is that inequality within racial and ethnic groups has grown relative to inequality between such groups. Growing income inequality within the previously largely impoverished black population is partly a product of black economic progress: by some measures more than half of black families have attained middle-class incomes or higher. Despite persistent gaps in income between blacks and whites, the growth of the black middle class, combined with widening inequality within the white population and the general slowdown of economic growth in the 1970s and 1980s, may have fueled opposition to measures or programs perceived to benefit members of minority groups without regard to individual economic circumstances.

Box 4-1.—continued

The terms "American Indian" and "Native American" are often used synonymously in speech and writing. In this chapter "American Indian" rather than "Native American" is used to avoid confusion caused by the use in some Federal programs of the term "Native American" to include Native Hawaiians and Pacific Islanders.

On October 30, 1997, the Office of Management and Budget announced its decision to revise the standards for classifying Federal data on race and ethnicity. The new standards recognize the growing diversity of the American population by permitting respondents to mark more than one race on survey questionnaires. In addition, the "Asian or Pacific Islander" category has been divided into two categories, "Asian" and "Native Hawaiian or Other Pacific Islander," making a total of five racial categories ("Hispanic" is an ethnic category). The "black" category has been changed to "black or African American." The ethnicity question will include two categories: "Hispanic or Latino" and "Not Hispanic or Latino." Federal agencies will produce data on the number of individuals who mark only one racial category, as well as those who mark more than one.

Published statistics are not always available for all the groups listed above. At times statistics are lacking because survey sample sizes are too small to yield reliable estimates for small populations such as American Indians or Asians. Specialized surveys or samples are required to remedy this problem.

The chapter begins with a brief description of recent and projected changes in the racial and ethnic composition of the population. The most prominent of these changes are the increase in the proportion of the population that is Asian or Hispanic and the decrease in the proportion that is non-Hispanic white. The chapter then provides a detailed description of differences among racial and ethnic groups in traditional indicators of economic status: family income, poverty, and wealth. The next two sections of the chapter review the evidence and the economic literature in two arenas critical to the determination of economic status: education and the labor market. The chapter ends with a review of evidence of contemporary racial discrimination.

Although it is difficult to quantify the precise contribution of contemporary acts of discrimination to the wide economic disparities across racial and ethnic groups, there is substantial evidence that such discrimination persists in many areas of the economy. Such evidence highlights the need for racial reconciliation, as promoted in the President's Initiative on Race as well as the President's proposals to strengthen enforcement of the civil rights laws (Box 4-2).

POPULATION COMPOSITION

Since 1970 the percentage of the population that is non-Hispanic and white has fallen substantially; the percentages that are Hispanic, American Indian, and Asian (including Pacific Islanders) have risen rapidly, and the percentage that is black has risen slowly (Table 4-1). The large increases in the Hispanic and Asian populations are largely due to immigration and reflect changes in immigration laws, especially the 1965 Immigration Act, which raised the ceiling on admissions and ended the system of national origin quotas that had restricted immigration from the developing world. The Immigration Reform and Control Act of 1986, which legalized a large number of immigrants, also contributed to these changes. Under the assumption that these trends will continue, the non-Hispanic white population, currently the majority, is projected to fall to about half of the total population in the middle of the next century. (These projections assume there will be no change in rates of intermarriage, although these rates have been increasing.)

These national population changes mask differences across and within regions. The geographic distribution of racial and ethnic groups is important both because it influences the potential for social and economic interaction among them, and because it affects their economic fortunes. For example, over this century employment has shifted from rural to urban areas and, within urban areas, from the central cities to the suburbs.

Hispanics and American Indians are heavily concentrated in the West and, to some extent, the South. Asians are concentrated in the West. Within the South, Hispanics are concentrated in Florida, Texas,

Box 4-2.—The President's Initiative on Race

On June 14, 1997, the President announced a new Initiative on Race. The President envisions an America based on opportunity for all, responsibility from all, and one community of all Americans. Race relations remains an issue that too often divides our Nation. The President's vision is to have a diverse, democratic community in which all Americans respect and even celebrate their differences while embracing the shared values that unite them. To reach this goal the President has launched a national effort to deal openly and honestly with our racial differences. The effort includes study, dialogue, and action to address the continuing challenge of how to live and work more productively together.

To further the goals of expanded opportunity and fairness for all Americans, and in conjunction with the President's Initiative on Race, the Vice President announced on January 19, 1998, in a Martin Luther King, Jr. Day address at the Ebenezer Baptist Church in Atlanta, a package of new civil rights enforcement initiatives. These proposed initiatives place an emphasis on prevention and nonlitigation remedies for discrimination, and on strengthening the ability of the Federal civil rights agencies to enforce antidiscrimination law. The Administration's plan increases resources for compliance reviews and technical assistance, and offers alternatives to litigation by funding expansion of alternative dispute resolution mechanisms. The plan would set performance goals for the Equal Employment Opportunity Commission to speed the processing of complaints and reduce case backlogs, and would provide for better coordination across Federal agencies and offices. The Administration's 1999 budget proposal contains $602 million for civil rights enforcement agencies and offices—an increase of $86 million, or more than 16 percent, over 1998 funding.

TABLE 4-1.—*Racial and Ethnic Composition of the U.S. Population*

[Percent of population]

Year	American Indian	Asian[1]	Black	Hispanic	Non-Hispanic white
1970	0.4	0.7	10.9	4.5	83.5
1997 (estimated)	.9	3.8	12.1	10.3	72.9
2050 (projected)	1.1	8.7	13.6	23.8	52.8
1990 by region[2]:					
Northeast	.2	2.5	10.3	7.4	79.4
Midwest	.5	1.3	9.5	2.9	85.8
South	.6	1.3	18.3	7.9	71.8
West	1.6	7.3	5.1	19.1	66.7

[1] Includes Pacific Islanders.

[2] Detail may not add to 100 percent because data for the category "other" are not shown.

Source: Department of Commerce (Bureau of the Census).

and Washington, D.C. And despite massive outmigration over much of the 20th century, the majority of blacks continue to live in the South. In fact, net black migration from the South to the North ended some time in the 1960s.

There are also differences within regions in the racial and ethnic distribution of populations. In 1990 Hispanics, Asians, and blacks were much more likely than whites or American Indians to live in the central cities of metropolitan areas. Hispanics, Asians, and whites were much more likely than blacks or American Indians to live in the parts of metropolitan areas outside the central city. Nearly half of American Indians lived in rural areas; 37 percent lived on reservations or other American Indian and Alaska Native areas.

ECONOMIC STATUS

FAMILY INCOME

Annual income is the most widely accepted indicator of current economic status. This section reports incomes for families, where a family is defined as two or more persons related by birth, marriage, or adoption who reside together. In 1996 the median income of Asian families was about $49,100, the highest among the groups considered in this chapter. Asians are followed closely by non-Hispanic whites ($47,100) and, with a $20,000 gap, by blacks ($26,500) and Hispanics ($26,200; Chart 4-1). Because of the smaller size of the American Indian population, reliable national data on their incomes are not available for every year. However, according to the most recent data (from the 1990 Census), American Indians had the lowest median family income (and the highest poverty rate) of the five racial and ethnic groups. With few exceptions these rankings have been stable over the past 25 years.

Black and non-Hispanic white real median family incomes are somewhat higher than they were 25 years ago, and Hispanic incomes are somewhat lower. Since 1972, when data for Hispanics first became available on an annual basis, real median family income has increased 14 percent among non-Hispanic whites and 9 percent among blacks, but has fallen 9 percent among Hispanics.

As a result of faster income growth for non-Hispanic whites, the Hispanic median family income has dropped sharply relative to non-Hispanic white income over the past 25 years, and the relative incomes of blacks has also dropped somewhat over the same period. However, the Hispanic population has grown tremendously over this period, primarily because of immigration. The relative decline in the Hispanic median income reflects, at least in part, compositional changes in the Hispanic population resulting from the immigration of persons with relatively little education. The median incomes of both

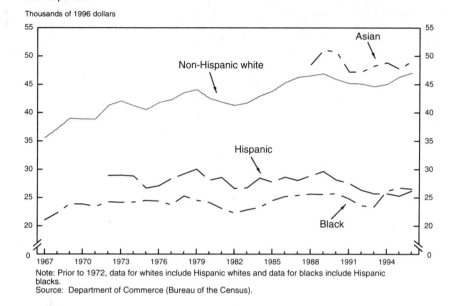

Thousands of 1996 dollars

Note: Prior to 1972, data for whites include Hispanic whites and data for blacks include Hispanic blacks.
Source: Department of Commerce (Bureau of the Census).

black and Hispanic families are about 56 percent of the non-Hispanic white median, lower than in 1972. Because these ratios vary by a fair amount from year to year, it is difficult to identify turning points precisely. But it is clear that, between the early to mid-1970s and the early 1990s, black and Hispanic family incomes declined relative to non-Hispanic white family incomes. Since 1993, however, black family incomes have increased faster than those of non-Hispanic white families.

Inequality Within Groups and the Growth of the Middle Class

Although a useful summary measure, median family income is an incomplete indicator of the economic status of entire groups. For example, trends in median income do not reveal the dramatic increases in overall income inequality between the early 1970s and the early 1990s, nor do they speak to inequality within groups. Consideration of other indicators of economic status may alter conclusions about the nature of economic inequality among racial and ethnic groups. For example, despite their higher median family income, the poverty rate for Asians exceeds the rate for non-Hispanic whites by nearly 6 percentage points, indicating that this population is economically heterogeneous.

Definitions of "middle class" are necessarily arbitrary. By one indicator—household income between two and five times the poverty line—a large middle class emerged among both blacks and whites between 1940 and 1970 (Charts 4-2 and 4-3). The poverty line used

125

here to adjust income corresponds to a 1960s' standard, since the poverty line was developed in the early 1960s and reflects societal standards of economic need at that time.

Chart 4-2 **Distribution of White Persons by Household Income**
Between 1940 and 1970 the white middle class grew. Since 1960 the percent of high-income whites has also grown substantially.

Percent

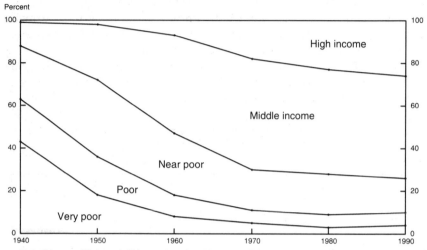

Note: "Very poor" is household income less than 50 percent of the poverty line, "poor" is 50 to 99 percent, "near poor" is 100 to 199 percent, "middle income" is 200 to 499 percent, and "high income" is 500 percent or higher.
Sources: University of Michigan Population Studies Center and Reynolds Farley, Russell Sage Foundation.

Chart 4-3 **Distribution of Black Persons by Household Income**
Between 1940 and 1970 the proportion of blacks who were poor or very poor fell, and the black middle class grew.

Percent

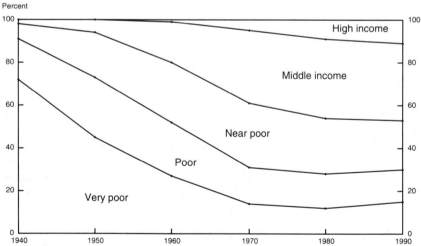

Note: "Very poor" is household income less than 50 percent of the poverty line, "poor" is 50 to 99 percent, "near poor" is 100 to 199 percent, "middle income" is 200 to 499 percent, and "high income" is 500 percent or higher.
Sources: University of Michigan Population Studies Center and Reynolds Farley, Russell Sage Foundation.

According to this measure, the white middle class expanded considerably in each decade from 1940 to 1970, whereas the expansion of the black middle class was greatest in the 1960s. Some scholars have pointed to figures such as these as evidence of tremendous black economic progress since 1940. However, that progress has not been steady. Progress clearly slowed in the 1970s and 1980s. Furthermore, although Chart 4-3 suggests that moderate growth of the black middle class continued over the 1970s, annual data show little growth between the early to mid-1970s and the early 1990s. In sum, a substantial economic expansion of the black middle class between the 1940s and the early 1970s was followed by 15 to 20 years of stagnation between the mid-1970s and the early 1990s, with perhaps a resumption of growth in the mid-1990s.

Chart 4-4 **Gini Index for Family Income**
Overall and within-group inequality grew steadily from the early 1970s to the early 1990s. Inequality has been consistently higher for blacks than for whites or Hispanics.

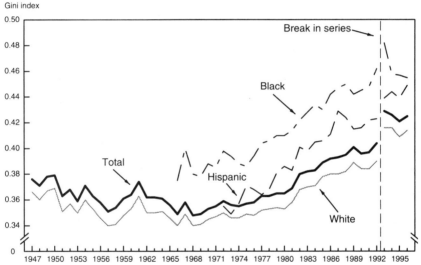

Note: The Gini index is a measure of inequality ranging from zero to one, where zero indicates perfect equality.
Source: Department of Commerce (Bureau of the Census).

Since the early 1970s, income inequality has increased not only overall but also within racial groups (Chart 4-4). However, only among Hispanics has increased inequality taken the form of growth in the proportions of both upper income and poor families at the expense of the middle. Although both whites and Hispanics experienced declines in the proportion of middle-income families, among whites there was rapid growth in the proportion at the top, and a small decline in the proportion at the bottom. The proportion of black families in the middle- and upper income groups combined has changed little since the mid-1970s, but by some measures there has been movement of families from the middle of the income distribution to the top.

127

Poverty

Gaps in poverty rates between non-Hispanic whites and Asians on the one hand, and blacks and Hispanics on the other, remain substantial (Chart 4-5). However, the gaps in poverty rates between blacks and whites have decreased since 1993, after remaining largely stagnant from the mid-1970s to the early 1990s. In 1996 the black poverty rate reached its lowest level ever, as did the difference in poverty rates between blacks and whites. The decline in the black poverty rate in the current recovery exceeds slightly the declines recorded in the recoveries of the 1970s and 1980s. The poverty rate for Hispanics fell slightly from 1993 to 1996, although it is still high, exceeding the rate for blacks. The poverty rate for Asians has been flat since 1994.

Chart 4-5 **Poverty Rates for Persons**
Poverty rates fell over the 1960s and early 1970s, and since then differences across groups have been relatively stable.

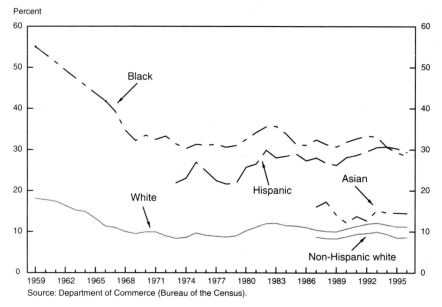

Source: Department of Commerce (Bureau of the Census).

Child Poverty

Differences across racial and ethnic groups in the prevalence of child poverty not only indicate inequality in the current well-being of children, but also represent differences in economic opportunity that contribute to future inequality among adults and in subsequent generations. Although child poverty is associated with health, developmental, and educational disadvantages, the importance of low family income per se as compared with parental education, family structure, or other characteristics associated with poverty remains in dispute (see Chapter 3).

Since 1993, child poverty rates have generally fallen, but they remain too high, and differences in child poverty rates across racial and ethnic groups are stark. Between 1993 and 1996 the poverty rate for white children fell 1.5 percentage points to 16.3 percent. The rate for black children fell even more, from 46.1 percent to 39.9 percent, the lowest rate in more than 20 years but still very high. The rate for Hispanic children fell marginally after 1993 and stood at 40.3 percent in 1996, higher than the rate for black children. The poverty rate for Asian children rose 1.3 percentage points, to 19.5 percent, between 1993 and 1996.

HOUSEHOLD WEALTH

Household wealth—the total value of a household's material and financial assets, minus its liabilities—contributes to economic well-being independently of income. Greater wealth allows a household to maintain its standard of living when income falls because of job loss, family changes such as divorce or widowhood, or retirement. Financial wealth may also be particularly important in the presence of borrowing constraints. For example, evidence that the receipt of an inheritance increases entry into self-employment suggests that a lack of personal financial capital limits small business ownership.

Wealth has been measured less frequently than income in government statistics. There are two major Federal sources of data on household wealth for the population: the Survey of Income and Program Participation (SIPP) and the Survey of Consumer Finances (SCF). Figures are not comparable across the two surveys for many reasons: for example, the SCF and the SIPP employ different definitions of "family" and "household."

Measures of wealth show even greater disparities across racial and ethnic groups than do measures of income. For example, according to data from the 1993 SIPP, the median net worth of white households ($47,740) was over 10 times that of black or Hispanic households ($4,418 and $4,656, in 1993 dollars, respectively). Figures from the 1995 SCF are $73,900 for non-Hispanic whites and $16,500 for all other groups combined (in 1995 dollars). Very substantial wealth gaps between whites on the one hand and blacks and Hispanics on the other are found even among families with similar incomes.

Differences in wealth result primarily from differences in lifetime labor market compensation, differences in saving rates and the return on those savings (including appreciation of the value of assets), and differences in inheritances or other transfers from relatives. Holdings among non-Hispanic whites in all major categories of wealth exceed those of blacks and Hispanics. Three important components of wealth for families are housing equity, holdings of stocks and mutual funds, and private pension wealth.

129

Home Equity

The most important asset for most households is the equity in their home. Differences in home equity arise from differences in homeownership rates, in home values, and, among homes of a given value, in the level of equity accumulated. Since 1993 there have been increases in homeownership among all groups, but the homeownership rate among non-Hispanic whites is more than 50 percent higher than that of blacks or Hispanics.

Some evidence suggests that gaps among racial groups in home values, although large, are narrowing. For example, between 1992 and 1995 the median value of the primary residence was unchanged at about $92,000 for non-Hispanic whites but increased from $54,200 to $70,000 for all other groups combined. In 1993 the median equity among homeowners was about $50,000 for whites (in 1993 dollars), $29,000 for blacks, and $36,000 for Hispanics. These values were $3,000 to $5,000 higher in 1993 than in 1991 (in 1993 dollars).

This Administration's efforts may have contributed to recent increases in homeownership and home values among blacks and Hispanics. The Administration has strengthened regulations under the Community Reinvestment Act and has stepped up enforcement of fair lending laws. Data collected under the Home Mortgage Disclosure Act show that, between 1993 and 1996, conventional home mortgage lending to blacks has increased 67 percent; such lending to Hispanics has increased 49 percent. These increases are much larger than the percentage increase in conventional home mortgage lending overall in this period.

Discrimination in Mortgage Lending

There are a variety of possible explanations for differences in homeownership rates among racial and ethnic groups. Research has documented substantially higher denial rates in applications for home mortgages among blacks and Hispanics than among whites. An analysis of lending practices in Boston found that applications from blacks and Hispanics were rejected about 28 percent of the time, compared with 10 percent for whites. However, applications from whites, blacks, and Hispanics differed along many economic dimensions—including income, loan-to-value ratios, and the presence of private mortgage insurance, as well as other characteristics of properties and applicants—which together explained about two-thirds of the difference in rejection rates. Still, about one-third of the gap remained unexplained by these factors.

The remaining gap has three possible explanations. The first is that some relevant economic characteristics correlated with race are observed by the lender but not by the analyst, and average differences in those characteristics across racial and ethnic groups account for the higher denial rate among minorities. However, the Boston study was careful to incorporate extensive controls, including all factors that lenders, underwriters, and others reported to be important in making lending decisions. The second explanation is that the higher denial rate reflects lenders' expectations of higher default rates among minorities with similar qualifications and other characteristics. This practice—rejecting applications on the basis of group characteristics—is known as statistical discrimination and is illegal. The third possible explanation, "noneconomic" or prejudice-based discrimination, in which lenders discriminate against minorities and lower their profits as a result, is also illegal.

The authors of the Boston study argue that no clear-cut evidence exists of differences by race in default rates, after adjusting for other characteristics of applicants and properties such as those measured in the study. However, this argument and the study itself have been challenged in subsequent studies, which claim to find evidence of higher default rates among minorities. Other researchers have argued in response that differences in default rates between minorities and whites may not be a good indication of their creditworthiness because, for example, whites might be treated more favorably in foreclosure proceedings. As discussed in the concluding section of this chapter, audit studies provide additional evidence of discrimination in home mortgage lending, although continued research is needed on the extent and nature of discrimination in this area.

Holdings of Major Financial Assets

Whites have higher rates of ownership of every kind of major financial asset than do blacks or Hispanics, and among those holding each kind of asset, holdings by whites are much more valuable. This is not surprising given whites' greater median wealth. But some gaps are particularly striking. For example, as of 1993 nearly 95 percent of black households owned no stocks or mutual funds, and 95 percent reported owning no private pension wealth (the corresponding figure for whites is about 75 percent in each category). Differences in stock ownership in 1993 are particularly important because between 1993 and 1997 the value of common stock appreciated enormously: for example, the Standard and Poor's 500 index roughly doubled in value. Another striking difference is in transaction accounts (such as checking accounts), which are held by the vast majority (92 percent) of non-Hispanic white families but by only 69 percent of all other racial and ethnic groups combined.

THE ROLE OF FAMILY STRUCTURE IN INCOME AND POVERTY

Increases in family income and decreases in poverty rates for both blacks and whites were rapid in the postwar period, especially in the 1960s. Blacks also made progress relative to whites in the 1960s. But black family income was flat from the early to mid-1970s to the early 1990s, and the ratio of black to white family income generally fell over this period. For example, since 1967 the ratio of black to white average income for all families has fallen slightly, from 0.65 to 0.62. However, black-white ratios of income *within* family types have increased, from 0.71 to 0.80 among married-couple families, and from 0.63 to 0.73 among female-headed families. (The overall ratio of income is lower than the ratios among these subgroups because a larger proportion of black families are female headed, a group with much lower average income than other family types.) During this period the shift toward female-headed families was faster for blacks than for whites (Chart 4-6). Some observers have suggested that these trends—particularly the rise of female-headed families—may largely explain the persistence of differences in family income and poverty rates among racial and ethnic groups. However, an adjustment for changes in family structure since 1967 suggests that such changes explain only about one-fifth of the income and poverty gaps between blacks and whites observed today. Moreover, this adjustment may overstate, perhaps greatly, the adverse effects of family structure on income if those with lower income or lower expected income are less likely to marry or to stay married.

Chart 4-6 **Family Structure**
Since 1970 all groups have experienced increases in the proportion of families headed by single women. The rise has been most pronounced for black families.

Percent

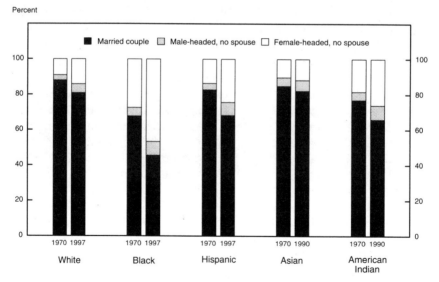

Source: Department of Commerce (Bureau of the Census).

The adjustment amounts to taking a weighted average in which the average income or poverty rate specific to a racial group and family type in 1996 is weighted by the corresponding percentage of families of that racial group and family type in 1967. The adjustment shows that if family structure for blacks and whites had not changed since 1967, in 1996 the black-white ratio of family income would have been 0.70 rather than 0.62, and the ratio of poverty rates would have been 2.6 rather than 3.0. Thus, these ratios indicate that roughly one-fifth of both the income gap and the poverty gap in 1996 is explained by changes in family structure after 1967. These are surprisingly modest effects when one considers that since 1967 the proportion of female-headed families increased from 28 percent to 47 percent among black families and from 9 percent to 14 percent among white families. (Results are similar if the difference in family incomes rather than their ratio is used to measure the income gap between blacks and whites; differences in poverty rates rather than ratios suggest a somewhat larger effect of family structure changes since 1967 on the poverty gap. Also, similar adjustments demonstrate that family structure can account for only a small portion of the difference in income and poverty between Hispanics and non-Hispanic whites.)

If the dramatic changes in family structure since the 1960s account for only a modest portion of current income gaps among whites, blacks, and Hispanics, what accounts for the remainder? Since the labor market is the most important source of family income, a later section of this chapter investigates gaps among racial and ethnic groups in labor market outcomes such as earnings and employment. However, such outcomes are linked to the skills that workers bring to the labor market, many of which are developed prior to labor market entry. The next section therefore discusses differences in education across racial and ethnic groups.

EDUCATION

Education is one of the most powerful predictors of economic status. Many dimensions of education are important, including the quality of schooling, the quantity of schooling (often called "attainment," for example the number of years completed), and student achievement or learning. The link between educational attainment and earnings has been well established, in part because data on attainment have been collected in the Census and in labor market surveys over a number of years. There is less agreement on the measurement and economic importance of other dimensions of education. Furthermore, the economic importance of a college education has increased dramatically over the past 20 years, as the relative demand for highly educated workers has risen sharply. The focus of this section is on secondary and postsecondary educational attainment. Of course, differences in later educational attainment among racial and ethnic groups can result from effects of discrimination and social and economic disadvantages experienced in early childhood or in elementary education. (Chapter 3 discusses early childhood and elementary education.)

DIFFERENCES AND TRENDS IN EDUCATIONAL ATTAINMENT

Differences

Substantial gaps in educational attainment persist among racial and ethnic groups. The most recent year for which comparable national data are available for all groups discussed in this chapter is 1990. Asians had the highest average attainment: in 1990, 40 percent of Asians 25 years and older had completed 4 or more years of college, compared with 22 percent of whites, 11 percent of blacks, and about 9 percent of Hispanics and American Indians. About 80 percent of whites and Asians had at least completed high school, versus two-thirds of American Indians and blacks and about half of Hispanics. For Hispanics, attainment also varies considerably between immigrants and the native-born. For example, Hispanic immigrants have much lower rates of high school completion than native-born Hispanics. Asian immigrants, on the other hand, have educational attainment similar to that of their native-born counterparts.

Trends

To provide an indication of recent changes in educational attainment across racial and ethnic groups, this section examines attainment for younger persons (those aged 25-29 years).

High school. High school completion rates have increased steadily over the 20th century. As educational attainment has increased, gaps in high school completion among racial and ethnic groups have generally narrowed, at least among the native-born. In 1967 the gap between blacks and whites in high school completion rates was 20 percentage points. This gap has narrowed considerably, but a 7-percentage-point difference remains between blacks and non-Hispanic whites (Chart 4-7). And although their high school completion rate has risen since the early 1970s, Hispanics lag far behind and have not gained ground relative to non-Hispanic whites. In interpreting these trends, however, it is important to recall that the composition of the Hispanic population has changed rapidly. The Hispanic population has roughly doubled in size between 1980 and 1996, and the fraction that is foreign-born has been growing. In fact, the slow progress in high school attainment among Hispanics is in large part explained by the increasing representation of immigrants with less education. For example, between 1980 and 1990 the proportion of 18- to 21-year-old dropouts (those who were neither enrolled in nor had completed high school) fell from 30 percent to 23 percent among native-born Hispanics, but remained at 47 percent for foreign-born Hispanics.

134

Still, as of 1990 a substantial gap in high school completion rates remained between native-born Hispanics and non-Hispanic whites.

Postsecondary education. Educational attainment beyond high school has increased dramatically for blacks, Hispanics, and whites over the past 30 years, although Hispanics have shown little increase in the 1980s and 1990s. The percentage of non-Hispanic whites with a bachelor's degree or higher is more than twice that of their black and Hispanic counterparts. High school completion rates, college enrollment rates among high school graduates, and college completion rates among college enrollees combine to determine rates of college completion. Some of the gaps in college completion rates reflect differences in high school completion rates. For example, the gap between blacks and Hispanics in completing 1 or more years of college is explained almost entirely by lower high school completion rates among Hispanics. But even among those who have completed high school, non-Hispanic whites are more likely to enter and to complete college than blacks or Hispanics. Again, Hispanics' low college attainment rates appear to be due partly to low rates among immigrants: between 1980 and 1990 the proportion of 18- to 24-year-olds enrolled in college increased from 18 percent to 28 percent among native-born Hispanics, but remained at about 16 percent for foreign-born Hispanics.

Among women aged 25-29, college completion gaps widened between whites on the one hand, and blacks and Hispanics on the other, over the 1980s. In fact, except among white women, there was

Chart 4-7 **High School Completion Rates for 25- to 29-Year-Olds**
High school completion rates have risen since the late 1960s, and blacks are closing the gap with whites. The completion rate for Hispanics remains low.

Percent

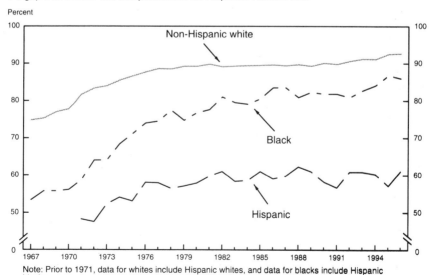

Note: Prior to 1971, data for whites include Hispanic whites, and data for blacks include Hispanic blacks.
Sources: Department of Commerce (Bureau of the Census) and Department of Education (National Center for Education Statistics).

relatively little increase in college completion rates over the 1980s for men or women of these ages (Charts 4-8 and 4-9). However, in the 1990s rates of college completion among black men and women began to pick up, reflecting an increase in college enrollment rates of black high school graduates in the mid-1980s. College completion also increased among white men in the early 1990s.

EXPLAINING EDUCATIONAL ATTAINMENT GAPS

High school completion rates increased sharply in the postwar period. Compared with the rather steady increase in high school completion, college attendance and completion have fluctuated, especially for males, although they have increased steadily since the mid-1980s. Increases in college attainment have been attributed to two developments. First, since the late 1970s growth in demand for highly educated workers has raised the relative wages of college graduates. Second, because educational attainment has generally increased over time, the parents of recent high school graduates tend to be better educated than the parents of high school graduates some years ago. This is important because parents' and children's education levels are highly correlated. Federal financial aid has also expanded dramatically in the 1990s, doubling in real terms since 1993. This expansion is expected to increase college enrollment and attainment among low-income students, but it is too early to assess the magnitude of this effect.

Levels

Most studies in the economics literature of gaps in college-level educational attainment among racial and ethnic groups have focused on college entry. Parental education and family income are important determinants of gaps in college entry among racial and ethnic groups. Both factors affect high school completion as well. For example, one detailed recent study concluded that differences among blacks, whites, and Hispanics in family background (primarily parental education and income) can account for all the gaps in rates of high school completion and college entry among racial and ethnic groups. The study found that among young people with similar family income and parental education, rates of college entry appear to be higher among blacks and Hispanics than among whites. The importance of family background and income differences is reduced when achievement test scores are controlled for, but the interpretation of this finding is the subject of great controversy. For example, low test scores result at least partly from disadvantages relating to family background and may therefore be a mechanism whereby such disadvantages are translated into low educational attainment.

136

Chart 4-8 Women Aged 25-29 with 4-Year College Degree or Higher
The fraction of women with at least a 4-year college degree has increased for
non-Hispanic whites, blacks, and Hispanics, but considerable gaps persist.

Percent

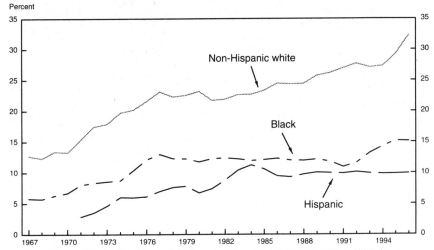

Notes: Prior to 1971, data for whites include Hispanic whites, and data for blacks include Hispanic
blacks. Data for blacks and Hispanics are 3-year centered averages. Prior to 1992, series shows
fraction of women completing 4 or more years of college.
Sources: Department of Commerce (Bureau of the Census) and Department of Education (National
Center for Education Statistics).

Chart 4-9 Men Aged 25-29 with 4-Year College Degree or Higher
The fraction of men with a 4-year college degree or higher has tripled for blacks and
nearly doubled for whites and Hispanics, but considerable gaps persist.

Percent

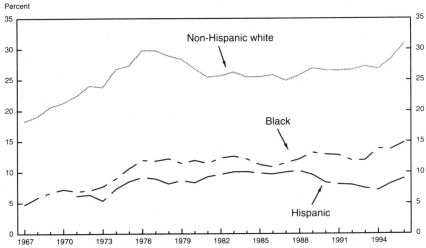

Notes: Prior to 1971, data for whites include Hispanic whites, and data for blacks include Hispanic
blacks. Data for blacks and Hispanics are 3-year centered averages. Prior to 1992, series shows
fraction of men completing 4 or more years of college.
Source: Department of Commerce (Bureau of the Census) and Department of Education (National
Center for Education Statistics).

137

Trends

More attention has been paid to explaining differences in educational attainment among racial and ethnic groups than to explaining their trends. Large inflows of less educated immigrants have kept the average educational attainment of Hispanics relatively flat. As noted above, high school graduation rates have increased for native-born Hispanics but continue to be much lower among immigrants. The narrowing of differences in high school attainment between blacks and whites over the past 30 years can be largely explained by increases relative to whites in black parental educational attainment.

As high school completion gaps between blacks and whites were decreasing steadily, differences in earnings between college and high school graduates of all races were increasing markedly. Naturally, attention has turned to explaining differences among racial and ethnic groups in college enrollment and completion. College attendance among high school graduates has increased for all groups. However, the enrollment rate among recent graduates began to increase for whites around 1980, about 5 years before the rate for blacks began to increase. Therefore, the disparity in college enrollment rates widened in the early 1980s and translated into wider differences in college completion among racial and ethnic groups in the late 1980s or early 1990s (Charts 4-8 and 4-9).

One possible explanation of these differences is the increasing direct costs of college. A recent study found that the schooling decisions of blacks are more sensitive than those of whites with similar incomes to tuition and other direct costs, perhaps because of lower wealth among blacks than among whites with similar incomes. It also found that the rise in the direct cost of higher education explains some, but no more than one-third, of the lower propensity of blacks to enter college in the 1980s. However, college tuition and other costs continued to increase in the late 1980s, a time when black college enrollment began to increase. The study concluded that the positive effects of rising parental education appear to have more than offset the negative effects of rising costs.

AFFIRMATIVE ACTION IN HIGHER EDUCATION ADMISSIONS

The term "affirmative action" encompasses a variety of activities and programs, ranging from outreach and recruitment efforts to programs that consider race as a factor in an evaluation process, which are intended to increase minority representation in employment, education, or contracting. Under the law, and as reflected in Department of Education guidelines, colleges and universities may not establish quotas for admission or set aside a certain number or percentage of admissions slots based on race. However, they may consider race or national origin as one factor in making admissions decisions, for the purpose of remedying the effects of past discrimination or achieving a diverse student body.

138

Affirmative action in admissions has been the subject of recent contention. The Board of Regents of the University of California voted in 1995 to prohibit universities within its system from considering race in admissions. The California Civil Rights Initiative, known as Proposition 209, prohibits the State from utilizing race- or gender-based affirmative action programs in State employment, public contracting, and education. In *Texas et al. v. Hopwood* the Court of Appeals for the Fifth Circuit held that the admissions procedure used by the University of Texas Law School in 1992 was unconstitutional. However, this Administration strongly supports affirmative action in higher education, and the practice remains widespread.

Such programs are intended to serve a variety of societal purposes, including to remedy past or present discrimination, to secure the educational benefits of a diverse campus community, to compensate for educational or other disadvantages faced by promising applicants, to prepare students for an increasingly diverse society, and to train students to serve the needs of diverse communities. But what are the more narrow economic effects of affirmative action in higher education admissions?

A recent study found that black and Hispanic students are more likely to be admitted to "elite" institutions of higher education (that is, those with average Scholastic Aptitude Test, or SAT, scores in the top 20 percent of 4-year institutions) than non-Hispanic white or Asian students with similar grade point averages (GPAs) and test scores. Of course, in assessing student merit and making admissions decisions, universities consider many criteria, such as letters of recommendation, extracurricular activities, region of residence, and adverse personal circumstances. The study also found no evidence of differences by race, after controlling for test scores and grades, in admissions to the less elite institutions where 80 percent of college students are educated. Nonetheless, admission to elite institutions is of interest because of the strong link between college selectivity and later earnings.

Critics of affirmative action programs in higher education admissions argue that some of the intended beneficiaries may actually be harmed by such policies. (The same criticism could also be made of programs for children of alumni or faculty.) They contend that affirmative action programs impede the academic performance of minority students and increase their college dropout rates by encouraging them to enter colleges for which they may not be well prepared. However, the study discussed above found little evidence of economic harm to these students, as measured by graduation rates and earnings. The key question this criticism raises is whether students admitted to elite institutions because of affirmative action would have fared better had they instead attended less selective institutions. In fact, attending an elite institution is associated with a lower college GPA, but a higher graduation rate and higher earnings, for all students, after controlling for SAT scores and high school GPA. The relationship between college selectivity and both college completion and earnings is similar for blacks and Hispanics and others.

The higher graduation rate among similar students attending more elite institutions raises questions about which practices at elite institutions increase graduation rates. Possibilities range from more engaging professors or classes to better support services. It is also possible that students expect a higher economic return to additional investment in education at an elite college and are therefore more highly motivated to obtain a degree.

The authors of the study argue that the number of applicants denied admission because of affirmative action programs is small. But many other students who are rejected may erroneously conclude that they would have been admitted in the absence of such programs. As a result, affirmative action in admissions may generate resentment far in excess of its actual aggregate effects. Nonetheless, individuals denied admission as a result of these policies may bear some costs—even if those individuals are difficult to identify and are few in number.

As an alternative to race-conscious admissions policies, some have called for "color-blind" policies that might target low parental income or education. Blacks and Hispanics are, of course, a minority of the population and account for a small minority of the population of youths with high SAT scores. As a result, although blacks and Hispanics are much more likely than whites to be poor, they make up a relatively small share of the low-income population with the SAT scores or GPA needed to gain admission to elite colleges. Therefore, targeting low-income applicants alone would very likely result in a dramatic reduction in minority representation at elite colleges. Class-based, color-blind admissions standards would not yield substantial numbers of blacks and Hispanics at most top-ranked institutions at present. Some commentators have therefore concluded that race-conscious admissions policies are needed to retain a semblance of racial diversity on elite college campuses.

LABOR MARKETS

The largest share of most families' income is derived from earnings from labor. Changes in labor markets can therefore have considerable effects on economic inequality across racial groups. Differences in labor market outcomes among racial and ethnic groups are intertwined with general developments in labor markets. Among the most important recent developments are technological changes that have increased the demand for highly educated labor, growing immigration and international trade, declining trade union membership, increased participation of women in the labor market, and, most recently, increases in the minimum wage and expansions of the earned income tax credit. (See Chapter 7 for a discussion of the effects of international trade on labor markets.) Developments that appear race-neutral may nonetheless affect racial and ethnic groups differently. For example, since Hispanics, on average, have much lower educational attainment than whites and blacks, they are more likely to be harmed by falling demand for less educated workers. However, lower demand for less skilled workers would not necessarily be expected to increase wage gaps among racial and ethnic groups for workers with similar levels of education.

In analyzing changes in racial inequality in labor markets it is important to bear in mind the growing economic diversity within racial groups that began to be observed in the mid-1960s. For example, the growing income inequality among blacks described above is mirrored in the labor market, with college-educated professionals at one extreme and labor force dropouts at the other. Although both groups face substantial barriers in the labor market related to race, the nature of these barriers could be quite different. The growing labor market diversity within racial groups cautions against the search for a single explanation for changes over time in differences among racial groups.

Three periods mark changes in black-white inequality in the labor market since 1960: a period of rapid progress from 1965 to the mid-1970s; a period of stagnation or erosion of gains between the mid-1970s and the early 1990s; and a period of mixed results since the early 1990s. The beginnings and ends of these periods are difficult to determine precisely because focusing on different data series and different subgroups can yield somewhat different results.

TRENDS IN LABOR MARKET OUTCOMES

Unemployment and Employment Gaps

The current economic recovery has reduced unemployment substantially for all groups. The overall unemployment rate has been below 6 percent for over 3 years and has been at 5 percent or below since April 1997. Improvement in the employment situation overall has been accompanied by a reduction in the difference in the unemployment rate between blacks and Hispanics on the one hand, and whites on the other. The proportion of black women employed has risen above that for white women in recent months. However, unemployment rates for blacks are more than double those for whites and fluctuate more sharply over the business cycle (Chart 4-10).

Men. In 1997 the unemployment rate for black men 20 years and older was 8.4 percent, its lowest annual average since 1974. At 3.6 percent, the white male unemployment rate for 1997 was also near a 20-year low. Although the ratio of black unemployment to white unemployment is thus more than 2 to 1, as it has been for many

141

years, for the past 3 years the difference in rates has been roughly 4 to 5 percentage points, smaller than the gaps that prevailed from 1975 to 1994. Among men aged 25-54, the labor force participation rate for blacks is about 84 percent, about 9 percentage points lower than the rate for whites. These rates have fallen in the past 25 years for both blacks and whites, although the decline has been somewhat larger among blacks.

Chart 4-10 **Unemployment Rates**
Unemployment rates for blacks and Hispanics are higher and increase more in recessions than unemployment rates for whites.

Percent

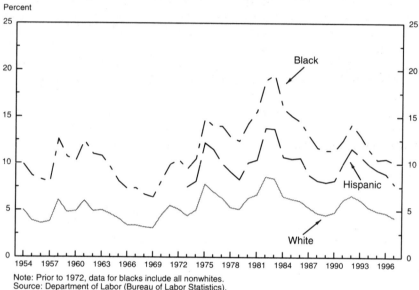

Note: Prior to 1972, data for blacks include all nonwhites.
Source: Department of Labor (Bureau of Labor Statistics).

Women. Labor market outcomes for women are important for understanding differences in economic well-being among racial groups, for two reasons. First, women's earnings have historically made up a larger proportion of two-parent family income among blacks than among whites. Second, because of their much higher rate of single parenthood, black families rely more heavily on female earnings than do white families. For women aged 20 and above the most striking employment trend is a long-term increase in labor force participation. Participation rates for black women have long exceeded rates for white women, but the difference has narrowed considerably and nearly disappeared by the early 1990s. However, beginning in 1995, participation rates of black women accelerated, reaching 64 percent in 1997. The rate for white women appears to have reached a plateau at about 60 percent. But because black women also have higher unemployment rates than white women, their employment-to-population ratios are much more similar than are their participation rates. Still, the black female employment-to-population ratio surpassed the white ratio in 1996. Labor force participation rates for Hispanic women are lower than those for either blacks or whites. Gaps (both ratios and differences) among racial groups in unemployment rates for women are similar to those for men. The black-white unemployment ratio for women has remained above 2, but the difference has been somewhat smaller in the 1990s than in the 1980s.

Occupations

Like educational attainment, occupation is regarded as an indicator of more permanent economic and social status than are wages or income in a single year or month. Workers in different occupations are affected differently by changes in the economy. For example, workers in blue-collar occupations are more likely than white-collar workers to be laid off in recessions.

Over the postwar period black men and women have both experienced tremendous change in the occupations in which they work. Some of these changes were experienced by all workers, black and white, but some are specific to blacks, due, for example, to reduction in the most overt forms of discrimination and to large migration flows out of the rural South.

Women. In 1940, 60 percent of employed black women worked in domestic service occupations, more than triple the percentage among all employed women. The proportion of black women employed in domestic service fell to 35 percent by 1960 and to 2 percent by 1996. Over the same period, black (and white) women moved in large numbers into other service occupations, as well as into clerical and sales jobs. The proportion of black women in managerial and professional occupations increased slowly between 1940 and 1960, then jumped in the 1960s and 1970s, reaching about 19 percent in 1980.

A major revision of the occupational classification system, implemented after 1982, makes tracking changes over the entire 1980s difficult. Since 1983 the fraction of black women employed in managerial and professional occupations grew steadily, but increased less than that of white women. As a result, the gap between white and black women in the percentage working in managerial and professional occupations widened by more than 2 percentage points over the past 15 years. Hispanic women are less likely than black or white women to be employed in managerial and professional occupations, and more likely to be employed in private household service and in the relatively low skill blue-collar occupations of operators and fabricators.

Men. In 1940, 41 percent of black men worked as farmers or farm laborers; that share had fallen to only 14 percent in 1960. (The corresponding percentages for all men were 22 percent and 8 percent, respectively.) By 1970 employed black men were more likely than other employed men to work in blue-collar occupations (60 percent compared with 48 percent). Black men were therefore concentrated in those occupations that were the most affected by the severe cyclical downturns of the 1970s and early 1980s, and at least until recently by the long-term decline in manufacturing employment. By 1996 only about 45 percent of employed black men and 38 percent of all employed men worked in blue-collar jobs.

In the period between 1960 and 1980 the percentages of black men and black women who worked in professional and managerial occupations were roughly equal, and both increased by about 10 percentage points. But since 1980 black men have not moved into professional and managerial occupations as rapidly as black or white women. In 1996 the share of black men working in managerial and professional occupations stood 6 percentage points behind that of black women, 11 percentage points behind that of white men, and 15 percentage points behind that of white women.

Hispanic men are the least likely of all the groups considered here to work in managerial and professional occupations. They are far more likely than black or white men to work in farming and related occupations, more likely than black men to work in precision production ("craft") occupations, and slightly less likely than black men to work in the lower skill blue-collar occupations.

Earnings Gaps

Black-white earnings gaps. By all available measures, the wages of blacks increased rapidly relative to those of whites in the 1960s and early 1970s, but progress slowed or reversed between the mid-1970s and the early 1990s (Charts 4-11 and 4-12). Trends in earnings inequality among racial groups in the 1990s are less clear. Most wage series show little progress in the pay of blacks relative to that of whites. However, one wage series—median annual earnings for full-time, year-round male workers—does show substantial recent progress among black men relative to white men, with the black-white ratio reaching a new high of about 0.8 in 1996. Firm conclusions about black-white pay gaps for men in the 1990s are therefore difficult to reach. Explanations for the narrowing of the pay gap in the 1960s, as well as the widening between the mid-1970s and the early 1990s, are discussed below. Researchers have just begun to examine the record of the 1990s.

Wage growth in the 1960s and early 1970s was faster for black women than for black men, both relative to white women (Chart 4-12) and relative to white men. Between 1967 and 1975 the gap in median wages between white and black women fell from about 20 to about 5 percentage points. Among younger women the differential disappeared, and there is even evidence that young, college-educated black women were paid more than comparable white women in the 1970s. But the earnings gap increased starting in the mid-1970s and stood at about 17 percentage points in 1997. Black and white women have both gained relative to white men.

144

Chart 4-11 **Ratios of Median Weekly Earnings of Male Full-Time Workers**
Since the 1970s, black men's earnings have held roughly constant relative to those of
white men, while Hispanic men have lost ground.

Percent of white male earnings

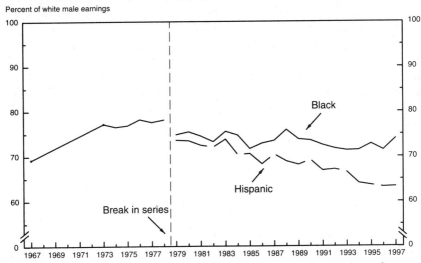

Notes: Prior to 1979, the series for blacks includes other nonwhites. Beginning in 1979 data are for
workers aged 25 and over.
Source: Department of Labor (Bureau of Labor Statistics).

Chart 4-12 **Ratios of Median Weekly Earnings of Female Full-Time Workers**
Black women nearly closed the pay gap with white women by the early 1970s, but
relative wages of black and Hispanic women have been falling since then.

Percent of white female earnings

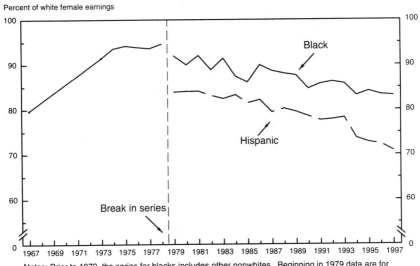

Notes: Prior to 1979, the series for blacks includes other nonwhites. Beginning in 1979 data are for
workers aged 25 and over.
Source: Department of Labor (Bureau of Labor Statistics).

As noted above, whites on average have higher educational attainment than blacks. But sizable pay gaps among racial and ethnic

145

groups remain for workers with similar educational attainment (Table 4-2). At least until the 1990s, these trends in black-white pay gaps were more pronounced for younger workers, who tend to bear the brunt of labor market adjustment. For example, the pay gap between blacks and whites narrowed most among young college graduates in the 1960s and early 1970s, and then widened most among this group after 1975.

TABLE 4-2.—*Ratios of Black and Hispanic to White Median Weekly Earnings, 1997*

Sex	Black-white ratio			Hispanic-white ratio		
	All workers	Workers with high school diploma only	Workers with bachelor's degree only	All workers	Workers with high school diploma only	Workers with bachelor's degree only
Men	0.74	0.75	0.74	0.63	0.78	0.86
Women	.83	.85	.90	.71	.86	.94

Note—Data are for full-time workers aged 25 and over.
Source: Department of Labor (Bureau of Labor Statistics).

Earnings gaps for other groups. Less information is available about differences in pay between whites and other minority groups. The pay of Hispanic men and women fell relative to that of whites over the 1970s and 1980s. Much of the deterioration in the pay of Hispanics is linked to educational differences and immigration. For example, differences in pay between Hispanics and whites with similar educational attainment are much smaller than the overall differences (Table 4-2). In fact, a recent study reported that, between 1980 and 1990, differences in pay between whites and minorities living in the same metropolitan areas, with comparable levels of schooling and working in similar occupations, widened by 2.5 percentage points for blacks and 4.1 percentage points for American Indians, but by less than 1 percentage point for Hispanics and Asians.

EXPLAINING EARNINGS GAPS

Differences in pay among racial and ethnic groups can result from differences in the average quantities of factors related to labor market success, such as educational attainment, and from differences in the "prices" of such factors, that is, their value in the labor market. Differences among racial and ethnic groups in the prices these factors command have been attributed to labor market discrimination. But differences in the quantities of these factors may also reflect discrimination outside the labor market or even within it. For example, if blacks with higher educational attainment are discriminated against in the labor market, their returns to investing in education may be artificially reduced. Facing a lower return, blacks may invest less in higher education.

146

Historically, blacks have received less schooling and attended schools with larger class sizes and smaller budgets than those attended by whites. Largely as a result of the 1954 Supreme Court decision in *Brown v. Board of Education*, the Civil Rights Act of 1964, and the 1968 decision in *Green v. County School Board*, which required active integration of schools, schools became increasingly integrated in the late 1960s and early 1970s. Schooling gains can account for perhaps 20 percent of the gains in black workers' relative earnings in the 1960s and early 1970s.

Other factors that explain trends in wage gaps among various racial groups include migration (especially before the 1960s), regional and industry demand conditions, macroeconomic shocks, and government intervention. Government intervention to increase economic opportunities for disadvantaged minorities has taken many forms, including education and training programs, the enactment and enforcement of civil rights and equal opportunity laws, requirements (under Executive Order 11246) that Federal contractors engage in affirmative action programs, and court-monitored affirmative action programs intended to remedy past practices of discrimination.

Changes to the Mid-1970s

Between 1920 and 1990 blacks experienced two periods of rapid progress relative to whites in the labor market: the first was during the wartime economy of the 1940s, and the second was the period from 1965 to 1975. Migration from the South was substantial in the 1940s, 1950s, and into the 1960s: 10 to 15 percent of all blacks and roughly 20 to 25 percent of young black men migrated in each of these decades. Wage gaps between blacks and whites were much larger in the South than in other regions. For example, in 1960 the black-white gap in wages was about twice as large in the South (50 to 60 percent compared with 20 to 30 percent outside the South).

Following passage of the Civil Rights Act of 1964, the relative wages of black workers increased sharply—more than can be explained by macroeconomic factors such as growth in gross domestic product. The improvement in relative wages was by far the greatest in the South, where State fair-employment laws were weakest, where institutional discrimination was greatest, and where Federal antidiscrimination efforts were focused. Although there was some progress in the relative earnings of blacks before 1964, the evidence is overwhelming that progress accelerated substantially in the period from 1964 to 1975, and that Federal attacks on racial exclusion in the South were critical to this acceleration.

As noted above, gains in years of schooling and school quality explain perhaps 20 percent of the gain in relative wages for blacks in this period. There were large increases in the economic returns to schooling for blacks. In principle, these could result from either increased quality of schooling or decreased discrimination in the labor

147

market. However, decreased discrimination is the more compelling explanation, since returns to education increased even among older cohorts whose education had been completed prior to 1965.

But part of the improvement in schooling and school quality is also attributable to Federal actions. The Supreme Court ruled in the *Brown* decision that segregated schools are unconstitutional. Yet despite the *Brown* decision and provisions of the Civil Rights Act that threatened to cut off Federal aid to segregated schools, in the mid-1960s black children in the South still overwhelmingly went to segregated schools. The dramatic changes came after the 1968 and 1969 Supreme Court decisions that required immediate integration. Therefore, improvements in school quality that resulted from school desegregation do not explain improvements in black wages in the South between 1965 and 1975.

Demand forces seem responsible for much of the improvement in relative wages between 1964 and 1975. Partly because Federal actions coincided with a strong economy, the precise role of Federal action, including the associated voluntary compliance, has been difficult to establish statistically. However, the observation that the most rapid progress came in the South, where Federal efforts were concentrated, supports the importance of the Federal role. Detailed studies show that blacks moved into industries in the South from which they had previously been excluded. For example, after 55 years of near-total exclusion, black employment advanced rapidly in South Carolina's textile industry from 1965 to 1975.

A recent evaluation of the impact of the Equal Employment Opportunity Act of 1972 confirms earlier findings of the importance of Federal equal opportunity law to the labor market progress of blacks. The act expanded civil rights coverage of Title VII of the Civil Rights Act to employers with 15 to 24 employees (previously only larger establishments were covered), as well as to State and local governments. Blacks employed in the newly covered small establishments in States where small employers were not already covered by State fair-employment practice laws, largely in the South, were most affected by this legal change. Blacks gained in relative employment, earnings, and occupational status in small establishments in Southern States after 1972.

Changes Since the Mid-1970s

Men. In the mid-1970s and 1980s, wages for less educated workers and for black and Hispanic workers deteriorated. Wage differences between blacks and whites grew fastest in the North Central region, where employment and earnings declined more generally. On the demand side, the heavy concentration of blacks in central-city manufacturing jobs in the Midwest in the 1970s made them particularly vulnerable to recessions and the decline of manufacturing employment. Ironically, then, the movement out of the South and into

148

manufacturing employment that had contributed so much to black economic progress in the 1960s and early 1970s also contributed to the deterioration of the late 1970s and 1980s.

Labor supply responses such as migration and training can help offset the effects of reductions in labor demand. Lower mobility will produce larger wage and employment declines in response to demand shocks. There appears to have been slower adjustment out of declining areas and industries among blacks and less educated workers, on average, although it is unclear whether this supply adjustment was slower for minorities than for whites with similar educational attainment.

Perhaps the most important change in the labor market over the past 25 years has been the increase in the demand for more educated workers. But wage inequality has generally increased even for workers with the same educational attainment. Although growing wage differences between blacks and whites could be a symptom of increased discrimination, the increase in general wage inequality makes this inference more difficult. The increase in general wage inequality for workers of the same age and educational attainment could lead to widening differences in wages between blacks and whites, as the following example illustrates. Suppose that in 1975 the median wage for black men aged 30 with a high school degree stood at the 35th percentile of the distribution of wages for the corresponding group of white men. Suppose further that wage inequality increased generally after 1975, so that by 1990, wages at the 35th percentile of the white wage distribution had fallen 10 percent relative to the white median (for this group). Then, even if the black median wage remained at the 35th percentile of the white wage distribution, the general growth of wage inequality would have resulted in a 10-percent decline in the black-white ratio of median wages.

Scholars have recently attempted to quantify these effects. Estimates vary, however, regarding the extent to which the widening of pay gaps between blacks and whites is accounted for by increasing general wage inequality. One early study concluded that such effects could account for the entire increase in black-white wage differences among young workers in the 1980s. But this conclusion has been challenged. For example, the increase in wage gaps between blacks and whites has been greatest among young, college-educated workers. But the median wages of black and white workers for this group were similar in the mid-1970s. Therefore, a general decline at the bottom of the wage distribution relative to the median cannot account for the fall of the black median relative to the white median for this group. For other groups of workers, however, increases in general wage inequality appear to be more important.

Researchers have also hypothesized that the increase in general wage inequality among workers of similar ages and education levels is due to the growing value in the labor market of "unmeasured skills" (skills not measured by years of schooling or age). Some have hypothesized further that the growth in wage differences between blacks and whites is related to differences in unmeasured skills between blacks and whites. For example, skills differences between blacks and whites with the same years of schooling might result from differences in the quality of the schools that blacks and whites attend. Some studies have attempted to explore this issue by directly examining school quality or measures of "skill" such as performance on tests of cognitive achievement or ability. However, important aspects of school quality may be difficult to measure. Studies find that differences in test scores can explain a substantial portion of black-white differences in wages in a given year, but have not been able empirically to account for the reversal in black-white wage convergence since the mid-1970s.

In addition, a recent study concludes that growing returns to unmeasured skills are simply not large enough to account for the stagnation of black economic progress after the mid-1970s. First, changes in school quality cannot explain the widening of pay gaps over time *within* cohorts whose schooling is of fixed quality over their lifetimes. In principle, an increase in the labor market return to school quality could lead to a widening of pay gaps between blacks and whites even within cohorts, if blacks attended lower quality schools. But second, the study found that even after differences in schooling, age, location, and unmeasured skills are taken into account, young, college-educated black men experienced at least a 13-percent drop in wages relative to their white counterparts in the 1980s.

In sum, black men's earnings fell relative to those of white men of similar age and educational attainment in the late 1970s and 1980s. The evidence available indicates that increasing overall wage inequality may have contributed to this deterioration and may be linked to unmeasured skill differences, but these explanations are incomplete. For example, this explanation does a poor job with young, college-educated black men, for whom the erosion of relative pay was substantial. These investigations therefore provide indirect evidence that discrimination also contributed to widening pay gaps across racial groups.

Women. Less attention has been paid to recent increases in the wage gap between black and white women. Since the early 1970s, working women have made substantial gains in earnings relative to men. The narrowing of the gender pay gap has been attributed to greater lifetime labor force participation among women and the dramatic increase in the value of education and work force experience.

As noted above, black women reached virtual pay parity with white women in the early 1970s, after a long period of steady improvement (Chart 4-12). Since the mid-1970s, however, the wages of young black women have fallen about 10 percentage points relative to those of young white women. The relative decline was more rapid among young college graduates. Chart 4-12 shows only ratios of weekly earnings of full-time workers, but the trends in pay gaps among racial and ethnic groups for women are similar in other data series (such as annual earnings of full-time, year-round workers) and for workers of similar ages and educational attainment.

Both labor force participation rates and attainment of a college degree rose more for white women than for black women in the 1980s. Over the 1980s the returns to education also increased. Changes in demand for specific occupations and the decline in unionization rates appear to have hurt black women relative to white women. Black women were also more likely to be employed in declining industries than white women.

Studies document a widening of pay gaps among racial groups for women of similar ages and educational attainment. But since white women's labor force participation rates have increased relative to those of black women (at least until the mid-1990s), their labor market experience at any age may also have increased relative to that of black women. And pay tends to rise with greater labor market experience. Thus, a possible yet unexplored explanation for the decrease in the pay of black women relative to white women since the mid-1970s is the increasing relative attachment of white women to the labor force. Discrimination could also have contributed to the decline in the black-white earnings ratio among women.

Affirmative Action in Employment

Aside from labor market changes that increased the demand for more skilled labor, weaker enforcement of antidiscrimination laws during the 1980s may have contributed to the decline in black workers' relative earnings between the mid-1970s and the late 1980s. There is evidence that enforcement of equal opportunity and affirmative action laws has an effect on hiring decisions.

Affirmative action programs have proved controversial, but their aggregate effects remain unclear. Because a variety of civil rights and antidiscrimination measures were undertaken in a relatively short time, it has been difficult to distinguish the effects of affirmative action from those of broader civil rights enforcement. The Office of Federal Contract Compliance Programs (OFCCP) is responsible for monitoring the hiring and promotion practices of Federal contractors. Large government contractors (those with 50 or more employees and $50,000 or more in Federal contracts) must develop an affirmative action program to remedy any underutilization of minorities and women and must make good faith efforts to implement the program. One approach to assessing the effects of affirmative action on employment, therefore, is to compare government contractors (who are covered by OFCCP enforcement) with firms that are not government contractors (noncontractors). This approach, however, is subject to biases that can lead it to overstate or understate the effects of affirmative action plans. On the one hand, noncontractors often take steps to ensure diversity and compliance with equal opportunity laws, even though they are not covered by OFCCP rules. This would lead the method to understate the effects of affirmative action. On the other hand, increased employment at contractor firms could also result from a shift of employment from noncontractors to contractors. In this case the difference between contractor and noncontractor hiring could overstate the employment effects of affirmative action.

According to these studies, active enforcement by OFCCP during the 1970s appears to be related to government contractors' increasing their hiring of minority workers, although the effect is relatively modest. For example, one study found that the employment share of black males in contractor firms increased from 5.8 percent to 6.7 percent between 1974 and 1980. In noncontractor firms the share increased from 5.3 percent to 5.9 percent. The literature also finds that OFCCP had a significantly positive effect on the employment of black females and a smaller but still positive effect on white females.

A 1996 study concluded that, in contrast to findings for the 1970s, there was no consistent evidence of the success of government antidiscrimination efforts in the 1980s. As noted, in the 1980s OFCCP enforcement was greatly weakened. Debarments of contractors found to be noncompliant, awards of back pay to affected employees, and conciliation agreements following violations all decreased during the decade. Enforcement has apparently increased in the 1990s as new initiatives have been adopted that focus enforcement on the worst offenders, target areas of obvious noncompliance, and strengthen sanctions.

DISCRIMINATION

No discussion of differences in economic status among racial and ethnic groups would be complete without a consideration of the ongoing importance of discrimination. Two statements appear to be true. First, discrimination is far less pervasive and overt today than it was before the Civil Rights Act of 1964. Second, audit studies and significant judgments in favor of victims of discrimination make it clear that discrimination against members of racial and ethnic minority groups persists in many areas of the economy. However, there is far less agreement about the degree to which current acts of discrimination are responsible for differences in economic status among racial and ethnic groups.

Many States' laws dictated a system of race-based classifications that placed blacks at a disadvantage in the economy, in education, and before the law. As late as the early 1960s overt racial discrimination was common. For example, newspaper advertisements clearly stated employer preferences for whites or blacks for specific jobs. The practice was common even in States like New York, where antidiscrimination legislation predated national civil rights legislation.

Evidence of continued racial discrimination takes a variety of forms. Perhaps the most convincing evidence comes from audit studies, in which similar white and minority candidates are sent to the same sources to seek jobs, rent apartments, or apply for loans for home mortgages. For example, a white and a black job seeker may be given similar résumés and sent to the same set of firms to apply for a job. These studies typically find that employers are less likely to interview or offer a job to minority applicants, and that minority applicants are treated less favorably by real estate agents and lenders and in some types of consumer purchases (such as automobiles and meals in restaurants). For example, one national study found that the incidence of unfavorable treatment in the housing market was 23 to 30 percentage points higher for a black or Hispanic auditor than for his or her "matched" white counterpart. In the area of housing discrimination the Department of Justice recently launched a national program to test housing developments, seeking evidence of discriminatory practices. Pairs of black and white persons are trained to pose as prospective tenants and sent to ask about the availability of units. In a case brought using evidence developed with this technique, the Department of Justice obtained a consent decree against housing providers in suburban Detroit that resulted in a $125,000 civil penalty paid to the Treasury and required the defendants to make $225,000 available to the victims of their discrimination.

Various Federal agencies also receive and resolve thousands of discrimination complaints each year. On the one hand, although a settlement of charges does not always involve admission of discriminatory practice, at a minimum the bringing of a charge indicates the perception that discrimination has occurred. On the other hand, only a portion of employees who experience discrimination actually bring charges. In fiscal 1996 alone, the Equal Employment Opportunity Commission, which is responsible for enforcing the principal Federal statutes prohibiting employment discrimination including Title VII of the Civil Rights Act of 1964, obtained $145 million in monetary benefits (excluding litigation awards) for parties bringing discrimination charges, through settlement and conciliation. From 1993 to 1997 the OFCCP conducted 19,852 compliance reviews and 3,192 complaint investigations and obtained over $158 million in financial settlements, including over $60 million in back pay for 30,171 victims of employment discrimination by Federal contractors. During the first term of this Administration, the Department of Housing and Urban Development (HUD) reached out-of-court settlements on 6,517 housing discrimination cases. HUD took enforcement action on 1,085 cases, either issuing housing discrimination charges or referring cases to the Department of Justice. During this period HUD obtained $17.8 million in compensation for victims of housing discrimination.

The Department of Justice settled major mortgage lending discrimination suits in the 1990s, including suits against large lenders in the Atlanta and Boston areas. In fiscal 1997 the Department of Education's Office of Civil Rights received 1,422 complaints alleging discrimination based on race, color, or national origin in access to equal educational opportunities. The office facilitated a change in 249 of these cases.

Less direct evidence of discrimination comes from earnings comparisons such as those described earlier in this chapter. As noted there, even after adjusting for many characteristics that affect earnings, these studies typically find that blacks are paid less than their white counterparts. The traditional interpretation is that the unexplained differential reflects discrimination in pay. However, these studies are not uniformly accepted as providing evidence of discrimination in the labor market: some researchers have argued that the studies fail to control adequately for differences in average characteristics between groups. Others argue that controlling for such characteristics may not be appropriate if differences in characteristics such as education and labor market experience are themselves partly the result of discrimination both outside and within the labor market.

More direct evidence of labor market discrimination, in addition to that from audit studies, comes from lawsuits that prove in a court of law a pattern and practice of discriminatory behavior. But these narrow, albeit powerful, pieces of evidence do not translate easily into estimates of the aggregate economic impacts on employment or economic well-being of discriminatory behavior. Significant analytical challenges, requiring a combination of approaches, remain in assessing the contribution of current acts of discrimination to current differences in economic status among racial and ethnic groups. For example, minorities who face discrimination by one employer may be able to find employment with another, nondiscriminatory employer. (But even in this case, discrimination imposes psychological costs and additional job search costs on minorities.) This example also suggests sthat, especially where discrimination is prevalent, reducing discrimination can yield substantial economic benefits, by increasing the number of nondiscriminatory employers.

It is an important goal of social and economic policy to ensure that discrimination does not limit the economic opportunities available to members of racial and ethnic minority groups. This Administration remains committed to ensuring equal opportunity for all Americans.

CHAPTER 5

Improving Economic Efficiency: Environmental and Health Issues

THE U.S. ECONOMY RELIES PRIMARILY on market forces and price signals to allocate economic resources efficiently. Economists have long recognized that a system of decentralized, competitive markets in which businesses and households act in their own best interest promotes economic growth and well-being. Market prices signal how resources should be used to produce goods and services of the highest value, and facilitate the distribution of these goods and services to those willing and able to pay the most for them. In a well-functioning market the price of a good or service reflects both its marginal value to the consumer and its marginal cost to the producer. So long as there is no divergence between the private and the social values and costs of these goods and services, the market system is likely to bring about the most efficient allocation of economic resources. Although economic efficiency is not the only concern of policymakers, it is important because it largely determines the total quantity of goods and services available. However, economists also recognize that sometimes prices might be distorted and that a market economy may fail to allocate resources efficiently. When market failures occur, appropriate government action may be able to improve upon market performance and enhance overall economic well-being. Examples of such action include protecting the environment, promoting health and safety, providing intellectual and physical infrastructure, and promoting competition.

Potential sources of market failure are:

- *Externalities.* An externality arises when production or consumption by one person or group provides a benefit to others (for example, by revealing a useful scientific discovery) without receiving compensation equal to the benefit, or imposes a cost on others (for example, by polluting the environment) without paying compensation for the full cost.

- *Incomplete or asymmetric information.* When two parties to an economic transaction do not have complete information, or do not have the same information, about the goods or services being exchanged, they may face distorted incentives that prevent markets from supplying the amount or the type of products most

155

desired. These information problems are especially prevalent in the market for health care, where incomplete or asymmetric information about a patient's health status or the value of a provider's services can adversely affect the decisions of both provider and consumer.

- *Public goods.* A public good is one that many people can use simultaneously without reducing its availability to others, and whose benefits are such that one person cannot exclude others from enjoying them. An example of a public good is national security, which, once provided, cannot be denied to anyone residing in the protected nation.

- *Imperfect competition.* Imperfect competition may result when a few suppliers or buyers can exercise market power to limit supply, keep prices high, and prevent new competitors from entering the market.

Economics provides important insights into the circumstances in which governments can act to improve upon market performance, how they can do so in a cost-effective manner, and how the costs and benefits of such actions are likely to be distributed. Economics has shown that market mechanisms can be a powerful instrument for achieving desired policy outcomes without incurring unnecessary costs. A prime example is the use of tradable pollution permits in environmental policy, described in detail later in this chapter.

This chapter presents several examples of market failures in the areas of environmental protection and health care and discusses new approaches to addressing them. Recent environmental initiatives include policies to improve air quality, address global climate change, and reduce non-point source water pollution from agriculture. These policies are designed to build upon the considerable success of past efforts in improving the quality of our environmental resources. In the domain of health care and consumer safety, rules governing health insurance and drug approval have been reformed, and new policies are being proposed to improve the performance of health maintenance organizations and reduce teenage smoking. These policies are intended to further enhance the health and well-being of our Nation's people. Recent antitrust reforms designed to increase market competition are discussed in Chapter 6.

COST-EFFECTIVE ENVIRONMENTAL PROTECTION

Achieving environmental targets at the lowest possible cost is an important policy objective. The President's Executive Order 12866, issued in 1993, directs Federal agencies to design regulations in the most cost-effective manner to achieve the regulatory objective and to propose or adopt a regulation only upon a reasoned determination that its benefits justify its costs. Further, the 1995 Unfunded Mandates Reform Act requires agencies either to certify that the regulatory approaches they adopt to achieve policy goals are the least burdensome, the most cost-effective, or the least costly among available alternatives, or to state the reasons for choosing an alternative approach.

TRADABLE EMISSIONS PERMITS

In implementing environmental policy, economists often advocate the use of market-based mechanisms such as tradable emissions permits for environmental pollutants, to encourage emissions reduction from those sources where the cost of emissions reduction is lowest and to foster innovation in emissions control technology. Tradable permits can be especially useful in achieving quantitative targets for emissions control or abatement.

Under the traditional regulatory approach to environmental protection, a regulatory agency may specify an allowable emissions level for each firm or facility or require firms to use specific technologies to reduce emissions. This is often inefficient because the cost of reducing emissions by a given amount differs from firm to firm. A tradable permit system instead caps total emissions from all firms but neither places limits on emissions by any one firm nor dictates how the reduction in emissions must be achieved. Instead the regulatory agency issues permits for emissions in a total amount equal to the cap and prohibits emissions without a permit. After their initial allocation (methods for which are discussed below), firms may freely buy and sell permits among themselves. Any firm that can reduce its emissions for less than the going price of a permit has an incentive to do so and then sell its unused permits to other firms for which emissions reduction is more costly. With tradable emissions permits, firms thus have more choices and can meet environmental standards at lower cost than under traditional regulation.

An emission permit trading system also gives firms an incentive to innovate. Firms that develop more effective and cheaper pollution control measures can sell not only their unused permits but the technology itself. Furthermore, trading systems that allow unused permits to be saved, or "banked," for future use encourage the early adoption of unanticipated technological improvements that lower the cost of emissions controls. These features lower the cost of emissions reductions still further.

Economists have identified some other key features of successful emissions permit trading programs. First, firms should perceive that owning a permit is like owning any other asset. A firm will purchase a permit only if it expects that the permit conveys a legitimate right to emit. Similarly, a firm will reduce emissions in order to sell unused permits only if it believes that the permit will be valuable to other firms. Thus, if there is a risk that the right to emit or the right to trade will be revoked, both the trading price and the volume of permits traded will be depressed, and some of the efficiency gains from permit trading will be lost. Of course, the government retains its authority to restrict or revoke trades for legitimate compliance and enforcement purposes under terms and conditions specified by law.

A second key feature is broad scope: because trading lowers costs, it should be permitted among all sources of emissions that cause the same type of environmental harm. Excluding some sources may raise costs if emissions from these sources can be reduced at relatively low cost. However, including all sources of a pollutant in the emissions cap may not always be practical. For example, emissions from natural sources and from other countries may affect our Nation's environment but be beyond the control of U.S. regulatory authorities. Even within our borders, measuring pollutant discharges from all sources may be prohibitively costly, especially when discharges are dispersed or affected by weather, as is the case with fertilizer and pesticide runoff from cropland. One way to broaden the scope of a program is to offer firms subject to the emissions cap a credit for emissions if they contract with uncapped sources to reduce their emissions. So long as a satisfactory means of measuring and verifying these reductions can be established, this approach can provide further opportunities to lower the cost of meeting environmental objectives.

To ensure the broadest possible scope for permit trading, permits should reflect units of environmental damage from emissions, not necessarily units of emissions. Permit trading then lowers costs by allowing trades in emissions that differ with respect to location, time period, chemical, or pathway (by air or by water, for example). If suitable conversion factors can be devised, trades in different emissions representing equivalent amounts of environmental damage can be made. This approach could also help prevent local environmental "hot spots" from developing. Suppose, for example, emissions from an area far upwind of a heavily polluted area have half the environmental effect there of local emissions of the same quantity of the contaminant. Then 2 tons of upwind emissions could trade for 1 ton of local emissions without changing total effects on the environment. Likewise, to the extent that different chemicals affect the environment similarly (as, for example, both carbon dioxide and methane contribute to the global greenhouse effect), the permit trading system could allow reductions in one pollutant to substitute for reductions in another by an amount that causes equivalent environmental effects. Finally, suppose a certain pollutant causes similar environmental damage whether it is introduced into lakes through the air or by surface water. Then permits for air emissions could be tradable for permits for water discharges, again encouraging reductions from those sources with the least costly control opportunities.

A final key feature of a successful emissions permit trading system is an effective compliance mechanism that ensures the integrity and fairness of the system and at the same time ensures that transaction costs are relatively low. The compliance mechanism will normally include monitoring and reporting requirements as well as enforcement provisions. Transaction costs include the costs of paperwork, recordkeeping, notification, and prior-approval requirements for permit trading. Although some requirements are inevitable in operating a credible trading system, they should be balanced against the need to keep transaction costs low. High transaction costs could discourage trading, thus eroding the potential gains from trade, and may make participation in the program prohibitively expensive for some firms.

Initial Allocation of Permits

A tradable permit system achieves its environmental benefit by capping pollutant emissions below the level that would otherwise occur. The costs of reducing emissions are then borne by the firms responsible for the emissions and (through higher prices) those who buy their products, as well as by suppliers of inputs such as labor and capital equipment to these firms. Firms and consumers in related markets, such as those for substitutes and complements of the goods produced by the regulated firms, will also be affected.

The government could arrange the initial allocation of permits in any of a number of ways, for example by auction, by free allocation in proportion to firms' historical emissions ("grandfathering"), or even by lottery. Anyone receiving permits may then sell all or some of them, or use them as needed to keep actual emissions within regulatory requirements. So long as a permit trading system imposes low transaction costs, the choice of allocation system does not generally affect the efficiency with which emissions reductions are achieved; after the permits are first allocated, the trading of permits itself minimizes the cost of pollution reduction. However, the choice of allocation method does have other consequences. If the method chosen yields revenue to the government, the program presents an opportunity to lower taxes, such as those on earnings from labor and investments, without affecting budget balance. Shifting the tax burden in this way, called "revenue recycling," could enhance economic efficiency and growth as lower taxes increase incentives to work and save. These economic benefits can significantly lower the net economic cost of reducing emissions.

The allocation system has further implications for who bears the cost of monitoring and reducing emissions. The extent to which firms can pass on some of the costs to consumers in the form of higher product prices depends on the degree of competition and the price elasticities of supply and demand for goods in the markets affected by the emissions constraint. In some cases, granting free permits to participants in the permit market could go beyond compensating them for their cost share of emissions reductions, leaving them better off than before the permit system was introduced.

Lessons from the Sulfur Dioxide Program

Practical experience in designing and implementing trading programs for pollution emissions permits is still limited. The highly acclaimed sulfur dioxide (SO_2) program—also called the acid rain program—administered by the Environmental Protection Agency (EPA) relies on, among other things, a system of tradable permits to reduce emissions of SO_2 from electric utilities. Trading of emissions permits began in 1992, and to date the program is the only emissions permit trading program that is national in scope. The SO_2 program is being implemented in two phases. The first phase covers the 110 most heavily polluting electric generating plants. Phase II, beginning in 2000, will impose a more stringent emissions cap and include a total of more than 2,000 units. The program has been successful in several ways: a large number of utilities engage in trading, SO_2 emissions and ambient concentrations have fallen, and the costs of reducing emissions have been considerably lower than originally forecast.

Why the early cost estimates were higher than the costs actually realized is a matter of considerable discussion. One contributing factor was a greater-than-expected decline in rail freight rates, which made low-sulfur coal from the Powder River Basin of Wyoming more competitive with locally mined, high-sulfur coal in Midwestern markets. Use of low-sulfur coal proved a less costly means of reducing SO_2 emissions than the smokestack scrubbers that utilities had anticipated using. A second factor was lower-than-predicted costs of using scrubbers, in part because of unexpectedly high utilization rates. The average cost of reducing SO_2 emissions using retrofitted smokestack scrubbers was about $270 per ton in 1995, far below early estimates of around $450 to $500 per ton.

One measure of the decline in cost relative to expectations is the trend in emission permit prices (Chart 5-1). Currently, at approximately $100 per ton of SO_2, permit prices are well below earlier estimates of around $250 to $400 per ton. These prices reflect the short-run marginal cost of reducing SO_2. Prices are low partly because firms, believing that permit prices would be much higher, overinvested in scrubbers. Average total control costs are likely to be higher than these short-run marginal costs.

The permit trading program also allows firms to bank unused emissions permits for future use, for example when emissions limits become more stringent in phase II. By banking, utilities can lower costs by timing their reductions according to their projections of emissions control costs and permit prices. If firms expect permit prices or control costs to go up, or if they want to take advantage of newly available control technology, they can adopt measures to reduce emissions sooner than they otherwise might.

160

Dollars per ton

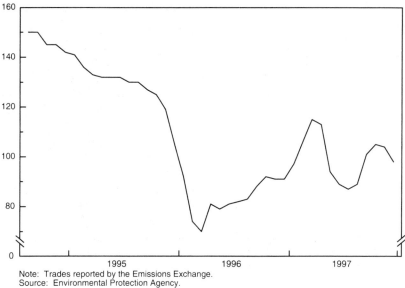

Note: Trades reported by the Emissions Exchange.
Source: Environmental Protection Agency.

Trading programs may not always bring cost savings as large as those achieved by the SO_2 program, nor will they always lead to the discovery of much cheaper control strategies. Programs that involve multiple pollutants or international cooperation will necessarily be more complex. However, the SO_2 experience does demonstrate how such programs offer market incentives to find cheaper ways of reducing emissions, and the flexibility to take advantage of them. Had regulators simply required all utilities to install scrubbers, utilities would not have been able to take advantage of the new availability of cheap, low-sulfur coal, and the costs of pollution abatement would have been much higher.

Another important lesson from the SO_2 program is that efforts to minimize transaction costs help ensure the successful operation of markets for pollution permits. But even so, it takes time to develop the institutions needed to facilitate trading and instill confidence in the value of credits so that markets run smoothly. The volume of trade in the market for SO_2 permits, a measure of the potential gains from such trade, started out quite small but has grown rapidly as utilities gained experience with the program. In addition, increased trading volume and the annual public permit auctions tightened the range of market prices for permits. In the program's fifth year about 7.9 million allowances were traded, up from 900,000 allowances in the second year (Chart 5-2).

We now turn to three other areas where the Administration is seeking to improve the environment in a cost-effective manner:

161

Million tons traded

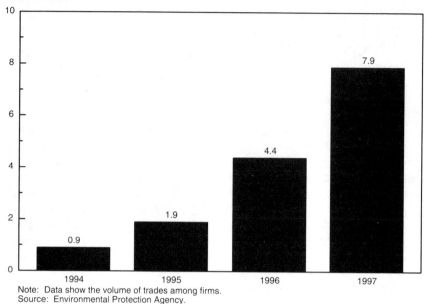

Note: Data show the volume of trades among firms.
Source: Environmental Protection Agency.

attainment of the new air quality standards, policies to address global climate change, and programs to reduce water pollution from agriculture.

AIR QUALITY STANDARDS

Air pollution has been linked to a variety of health problems ranging from decreased lung function to increased mortality risk. These adverse health effects are a classic externality: the emitter does not bear the full cost of its actions. Under the Clean Air Act, the EPA must periodically review, and may revise as appropriate, national air quality standards for pollutants. State agencies are largely responsible for developing programs (subject to EPA approval) to meet these standards. In July 1997 the EPA issued a more stringent standard for ground-level ozone and a new standard for fine airborne particulate matter. Under the act, these standards must be set so as to protect public health, with an adequate margin of safety. Courts have confirmed the EPA's interpretation of this to mean that consideration of costs or feasibility is excluded in setting the standard. However, under the President's policy the EPA is to implement these health-based standards cost-effectively.

Efforts to meet air quality standards have traditionally focused on controlling emissions within "nonattainment areas"—mostly urban areas where concentrations of pollutants exceed the standard. Although some States—California, for example—have set up trading

162

programs or used other market mechanisms to reduce the costs of compliance with air quality standards, most rely on traditional prescriptive approaches to controlling pollution. The Administration's plan for achieving the new air quality standards departs from these traditional approaches by designing regional strategies to complement local efforts, and by encouraging the development of nitrogen oxides (NO_x) trading programs among sources in different States.

Regional Strategies and Market-Based Approaches

Studies of air quality have found that high ground-level ozone concentrations are not just a local problem: under certain weather conditions, ozone and NO_x can travel hundreds of miles and contribute to nonattainment of standards in downwind areas. Under traditional regulatory approaches, nonattainment areas would have to make costly emissions reductions within their borders even if upwind reductions that would have similar environmental impact were available at lower cost. To address this problem, the plan for implementing the new standards will expand the geographic scope of the program. Under the Clean Air Act the EPA has the authority to require emissions reductions in any State that significantly contributes to nonattainment outside its borders. In November 1997 the EPA proposed a regional strategy that would require 22 Eastern States and the District of Columbia to reduce NO_x emissions by an average of 35 percent during May through September (when ozone levels are highest) by 2007. Reductions in NO_x emissions, apart from reducing ground-level ozone, may also reduce excess nutrients in waterways and the formation of airborne particles linked to adverse health effects. The design of a cost-effective regional strategy that contributes to attaining and maintaining the new standards will require careful attention to the effects of emissions on air quality. Later this year the EPA will also propose a rule to facilitate trading of NO_x emissions reductions among the States covered by the regional program.

Designing a Trading Program for Nitrogen Oxides

In designing a trading program for NO_x, the EPA faces a number of challenges. These include ensuring adequate scope for the trading program, ensuring that trading does not adversely affect the environment, and providing for necessary accountability and compliance.

As discussed above, the scope of trading programs like the NO_x program is an important determinant of their cost-effectiveness. As more emissions sources are included in the program, the increased opportunity to trade emissions permits tends to lower the cost of achieving a given level of emissions reduction. Utilities currently account for only about 30 percent of NO_x emissions, compared with about 65 percent of SO_2 emissions (Chart 5-3). Transportation accounts for 49 percent and nonutility combustion for 18 percent of NO_x emissions.

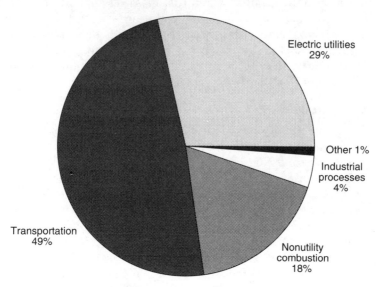

Electric utilities
29%

Other 1%

Industrial
processes
4%

Transportation
49%

Nonutility
combustion
18%

Note: Nonutility combustion includes residential and commercial heating.
Source: Environmental Protection Agency.

Thus, extending NO_x trading to nonutility sources could reduce costs. However, the scope of the program may be limited by the need to ensure accountability. For example, some smaller sources have considerably lower control costs than electric utilities, but their claimed emissions reductions may be more costly to monitor.

Including more sources from different sectors in the trading program may also have desirable distributional effects. Utilities are likely to pass the cost of compliance on to consumers in the form of higher electricity prices, and low-income households spend a higher share of their income on electricity bills than do households near the median income. Moreover, broader scope can decrease the average cost of pollution abatement, reducing the burden on all parties, including the poor.

Another challenge in designing a trading program for NO_x within the context of the regional ozone reduction strategy is to maintain broad geographic scope while ensuring that trading does not result in significant adverse environmental effects. The goal of this strategy is to improve air quality in nonattainment areas cost-effectively. In its simplest form, the problem of pollution transport can be thought of in terms of a single downwind nonattainment area that is affected by a number of upwind pollution sources located at varying distances from it along a line indicating wind direction. In this case, sources that are farther upwind will have less impact on the air quality of the area than sources that are closer, all other things being equal, and such differences may be as large as 10 to 1. It might then appear that emissions trading could undercut the effectiveness of pollution controls if it resulted in shifting emission reductions farther upwind. Trading ratios that weight the reductions made at different sources according to their distance from the downwind nonattainment area might be considered to address this problem. In reality, however, there are a large number of nonattainment areas spread out over the region, and several different weather patterns and wind conditions characterize the ozone pollution episodes that the program is trying to remedy. Sources affect multiple nonattainment areas in a variety of directions from them, and it affects any single nonattainment area differently under different weather conditions. The polycentric nature of this problem complicates the identification of a unique and stable set of trading ratios that would work for all relevant cases. Thus, striking the proper balance between achieving the cost savings from larger geographic scope and limiting the potentially significant adverse environmental effects of trading is an ongoing challenge.

Like most air pollution control programs, NO_x trading programs would require an estimate of emissions from each regulated source in order to ensure compliance. The estimation method can have significant implications for cost-effectiveness, both directly, through the cost of performing the estimate, and indirectly. One indirect implication is that more costly requirements may limit the number of sources that could meet the estimation requirements and participate in trading, and thereby raise costs. On the other hand, a more reliable estimation method may offer regulators and sources greater confidence in the permits, and thereby increase the willingness of sources to buy them or offer them for sale. For example, the SO_2 program requires continuous emissions monitoring to provide precise information on emissions. Such monitoring is expensive and impractical for many smaller sources and thus may effectively exclude such sources from participating. But such precise monitoring may not always be necessary. Methods for estimating emissions that provide unbiased, although less precise, estimates of emissions may be accurate enough to ensure accountability.

CLIMATE CHANGE

Climate change is a global environmental externality: warming of the earth's surface results from the accumulation of greenhouse gases from myriad sources worldwide, none of which presently pay the cost to others of warming's ill effects. The Intergovernmental Panel on Climate Change, jointly established by the World Meteorological Organization and the United Nations Environment Programme, concluded in 1995 that "the balance of evidence suggests that there is a discernible human influence on global climate." Current concentrations of carbon dioxide (SO_2), methane, nitrous oxide (N_2O), and other so-called greenhouse gases have reached levels well above those of

165

preindustrial times. Of these, CO_2 is the most important: net cumulative CO_2 emissions resulting from the burning of fossil fuels and deforestation account for about two-thirds of potential warming from changes in greenhouse gas concentrations related to human activity. If growth in global emissions continues unabated, the atmospheric concentration of CO_2 will likely double, relative to its preindustrial level, midway through the next century.

The accumulation of greenhouse gases poses significant risks to the world's climate and to human well-being. Potential impacts include a rise in sea levels, greater frequency of severe weather events, shifts in agricultural growing conditions from changing weather patterns, threats to human health from increased range and incidence of diseases, changes in availability of freshwater supplies, and damage to ecosystems and biodiversity.

Climate change is a complex, long-term problem requiring global cooperation and a long-term solution. No single country has an incentive to reduce emissions sufficiently to protect the global environment against climate change. Even if the United States sharply reduced its emissions unilaterally, greenhouse gas emissions from all other countries would continue to grow, and the risks posed by climate change would not be significantly abated. Since many of these gases remain in the atmosphere for a century or more, the climatic effects of actions taken today will primarily benefit future generations. But delaying action to reduce greenhouse gas emissions until the disruptive effects of climate change become widespread will considerably reduce the options for remedial or preventive measures.

The Framework Convention on Climate Change

The threat of disruptive climate change has led to coordinated international efforts to reduce the risks of global warming by reducing emissions of greenhouse gases. The first international agreement to address global warming was the Framework Convention on Climate Change signed during the Earth Summit in Rio de Janeiro in 1992. This convention established a long-term objective of limiting greenhouse gas concentrations and encouraged the established industrial countries to return their emissions to 1990 levels by 2000. Since then it has become clear that the United States and many other participating countries will not meet this goal.

To address the lack of progress among many industrial countries toward meeting this first target, the United States and approximately 159 other nations, in negotiations held in Kyoto, Japan, last December, agreed to take substantial steps to stabilize atmospheric concentrations of greenhouse gases. The Kyoto agreement, which requires the advice and consent of the Senate, would place binding limits on industrial countries' emissions of the six principal categories of greenhouse gases: CO_2, methane, N_2O, sulfur hexafluoride, perfluorocarbons, and hydrofluorocarbons. Each industrial country's "1990 baseline" is actually based on its 1990 emissions of CO_2, methane, and N_2O and its choice of 1990 or 1995 levels of the other three categories of gases. The United States agreed to a target of 7 percent below 1990 levels over 2008-2012. To meet that target, net U.S. emissions of greenhouse gases—all emissions minus removals of CO_2 by certain forest activities such as planting trees—must average no more than 1,484 million metric tons of carbon equivalent per year during that period (Chart 5-4). The targets for the European Union and Japan are 8 percent and 6 percent below 1990 levels, respectively. Australia, New Zealand, Norway, Russia, and Ukraine all have less stringent limits. In sum, over the period from 2008 to 2012, the industrial countries are

Chart 5-4 **U.S. Greenhouse Gas Emissions, Actual and Projected**
The U.S. emissions target under the Kyoto agreement is about 25 percent below current projections in 2008-2012.

Billion tons of carbon equivalent

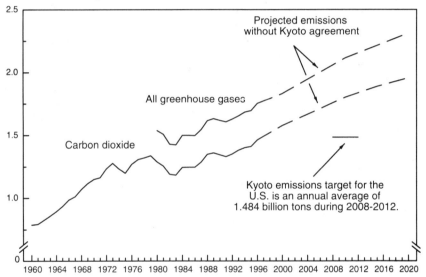

Notes: All greenhouse gases include carbon dioxide, methane, nitrous oxide, hydrofluorocarbons, perfluorocarbons, and sulfur hexafluoride. Carbon equivalence is calculated assuming a global warming potential over a 100-year time horizon. Targets can be met through forest activities that remove carbon from the atmosphere and international permit purchases and credits in addition to domestic emissions reductions.
Sources: Department of Energy, United Nations Framework Convention on Climate Change, and U.S. Climate Action Report 1997.

expected to reduce their average emissions of greenhouse gases to about 5 percent below their 1990 levels.

The Kyoto agreement provides opportunities for the industrial countries to trade rights to emit greenhouse gases with each other. They may also invest in "clean development" projects in the developing world and use these projects' certified emissions reductions toward meeting their targets. Both of these mechanisms allow for emissions reductions to occur where they are least expensive. Many of the details of these provisions will be worked out in subsequent negotiations.

167

Emissions Permit Trading for Greenhouse Gases

One component of the Administration's climate change proposal, announced last October by the President, is a domestic emissions permit trading program for greenhouse gases starting in 2008. As in the similar program for SO_2, permit trading would allow emissions targets to be met at a lower cost than under a traditional regulatory approach that sets fixed limits on individual firms' emissions.

As previously discussed, one consideration in designing an emissions permit trading program for greenhouse gases is how initially to distribute permits. The method of initial allocation would not generally affect the efficiency with which emissions reductions are achieved, but would have significant distributional implications. Another issue is where, in the marketing chain of products responsible for greenhouse gas emissions, permits would be required. One approach, called the permit-to-market approach, would impose the emissions limits at the point of first sale of the commodities responsible for greenhouse gases. In the case of SO_2 emissions, permits would be required for the sale of fossil fuels and specified in terms of the amount of SO_2 released in their combustion. The requirement would be imposed at the wellhead or the refinery (in the case of oil or natural gas), at the mine (in the case of coal), or at the port of entry (in the case of imported fossil fuels). Alternatively, a permit-to-emit approach would issue permits to consume these fuels or to sell products, such as automobiles, that do so. A hybrid of the two approaches may also be possible.

The design of an effective greenhouse gas permit system needs to take several other issues into account. First, a sufficient number of participants must be included in the domestic permit market to ensure that the market is competitive and efficient.

Second, the system should include a monitoring mechanism that assesses compliance in the most cost-effective manner possible. In the case of a permit-to-market system, since the amount of SO_2 emitted per barrel of oil or ton of coal consumed is relatively fixed, the task of measuring SO_2 emissions is straightforward. Moreover, for accounting purposes firms already collect information and keep records about their fuel transactions. Under the permit-to-emit approach, monitoring would likely involve a more complex combination of emissions calculation and measurement for all regulated greenhouse gas emitters.

Third, a permit system that would allow trades across all sectors of the economy would minimize total cost. If, for example, the incremental cost of reducing emissions is much lower in electric power generation than in transportation, one could reduce the cost of meeting the reduction target by allowing permit trading between the two sectors. The permit-to-market approach would generally allow trades across sectors. The permit-to-emit approach could also yield the same result, depending on how it is implemented.

Timing Flexibility in Meeting Emissions Reductions

Flexibility about *when* emissions reductions take place can further lower the cost of reducing greenhouse gas emissions. A system that allows participants to borrow emissions permits from the future or to save unused permits for future use would take advantage of differences in cost abatement opportunities across time.

Three features of the Kyoto agreement contribute to timing flexibility. First, the target for emissions reductions is based on a 5-year commitment period. For example, the target set for the United States of a 7-percent reduction in emissions below 1990 levels is specified as an annual average over 2008-2012. By averaging over 5 years instead of requiring the United States to meet the 7-percent target each year, the agreement provides flexibility in the timing of reductions that can lower costs, especially given an uncertain future. Averaging can smooth out the effects of short-term events such as fluctuations in the business cycle and energy demand. It can also lessen the impact of a year with a hard winter, when energy demand, and thus emissions, would increase. Further, if firms anticipate that a new technology will soon be available that lowers the cost of reducing emissions, they could emit more greenhouse gases in the early years of the period and less after the technology becomes available. Another advantage of this approach is that it may avoid forcing a costly rapid turnover of capital stock for electricity generation.

The Kyoto agreement allows countries to bank unused emissions rights from one commitment period for use in the next. Should investments in research and development yield some pleasant surprises in the form of cleaner and more efficient technologies, banking will encourage the early adoption of these technologies in order to save unused emissions permits for future periods when the costs of emissions abatement may be higher.

In addition to banking across commitment periods, countries may bank certified emissions reductions obtained through the "clean development mechanism" discussed below. Countries may use emissions reductions achieved through this mechanism over the 2000-2007 period to assist in complying with their targets in the first commitment period. This provides an incentive for firms in industrial countries to begin investing in energy-efficient technologies in developing countries before 2008.

International Trading in Greenhouse Gas Emissions

Building on the benefits of the domestic trading program just described, the Administration proposed in Kyoto an international trading program for greenhouse gas emissions permits. The Kyoto agreement established the right of countries assigned emissions targets to meet their commitments by trading among themselves. This establishment of the right to trade provides the foundation for a trading regime among industrial countries, but leaves the details to be agreed upon later. Since it is easier to reduce emissions in some countries than others, and given that greenhouse gas emissions have equivalent climate effects regardless of their location, allowing global trading would achieve climate change objectives at lower cost. Such a global approach would ideally allow trading among all sources of greenhouse gases in participating countries and could incorporate opportunities to *remove* greenhouse gases from the atmosphere, for example by issuing emissions credits (which could then be sold to other firms) for reforestation projects.

International trading could take place among firms that have been allocated permits through domestic trading programs. For countries that have no domestically tradable permits because they have opted for a command-and-control or a tax approach to controlling emissions, it may still be possible instead to arrange exchanges on a government-to-firm or government-to-government basis.

The setting of binding targets among all countries, together with international trade in permits, could in principle result in a global market price for permits for greenhouse gas emissions. For example, the permit price could be expressed in terms of dollars per ton of carbon equivalent emitted. Firms in all countries would reduce their emissions until the cost of further reductions exceeded this price, at which point they would buy additional permits. Large differences in both the patterns of energy use and the efficiency of energy technologies among countries imply that the cost savings from international permit trading would be large compared with a system without international trading. Put differently, even in comparison with a system with full domestic trading of emissions permits, international trading could substantially lower costs. Some models predict that the incremental cost of reducing CO_2 emissions may be as little as one-seventh of the cost of reductions from domestic trading alone. The gains from international trade in permits would be particularly large if developing countries were to participate.

The Importance of Developing-Country Participation

Negotiations leading up to the Kyoto agreement sought binding limits on greenhouse gas emissions among industrial nations. Developing countries have resisted committing themselves to binding limits on their emissions because of concern that to do so would severely constrain their economic growth, and because by far the greater part of accumulated greenhouse gases in the atmosphere is the result of past economic activity in the industrial countries (Chart 5-5). However, current forecasts project that greenhouse gas emissions from developing countries will surpass those from industrial countries around 2030, and even sooner if industrial countries are successful in limiting their emissions (Chart 5-6). Thus, eventual curbs on emissions from developing countries are essential in order to

Chart 5-5 Cumulative World Emissions of Carbon Dioxide, 1950-95
Industrial countries are responsible for the vast majority of accumulated carbon dioxide in the atmosphere.

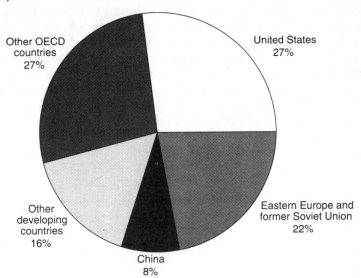

Note: Other OECD countries include the countries of the European Union, Australia, Canada, Iceland, Japan, New Zealand, Norway, Switzerland.
Source: Department of Energy.

Chart 5-6 Projected World Carbon Dioxide Emissions Without Kyoto Agreement
Around 2030, annual carbon dioxide emissions from developing countries are expected to surpass industrial countries' emissions.

Billion tons of carbon equivalent per year

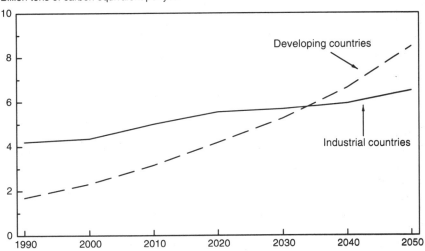

Note: These projections are consistent with the Intergovernmental Panel on Climate Change IS92A global projection through 2100.
Source: Unpublished calculations by A. Manne, Stanford University and R. Richels, Electric Power Research Institute.

stabilize the amount of greenhouse gases in the atmosphere. Moreover, some of the least cost opportunities for reducing greenhouse gas emissions are in developing countries, because those countries now use energy relatively inefficiently. Moreover, those that are industrializing rapidly have greater scope to build their industry around cleaner and more efficient energy technologies and fuels than do mature economies whose capital stock is already in place.

Failure to involve developing countries in an international agreement limiting greenhouse gas emissions could lead to a more rapid rate of increase in emissions in those countries than would occur without any agreement at all. This "leakage" effect of emissions reductions could come about in any of several ways. As industrial countries reduce their use of fossil fuels in response to emissions controls, future world oil and coal prices are likely to be lower than they would be otherwise. This is likely to increase energy consumption in countries not bound to limit their emissions. U.S. industries are also concerned about their international competitiveness if some countries remain outside an international agreement, since factories in those countries will face lower costs for producing goods that take relatively large amounts of energy to manufacture. Some may be concerned that energy-intensive industries might choose to relocate to countries not subject to emissions constraints, although there is little evidence to suggest that this would pose a significant problem in most industries. For example, energy costs for manufacturing industries average just 2.2 percent of total costs.

Given the projected growth of developing countries' emissions, the Administration's position is to seek meaningful participation by key developing countries in the reduction of greenhouse gas emissions as a condition for the United States taking on binding emissions reductions. The President has indicated he will not submit the Kyoto agreement for Senate ratification until there is meaningful participation by key developing countries.

Joint Implementation and the Clean Development Mechanism

To encourage participation by developing countries in the climate change initiative even before they formally sign on for binding emissions limits, the President has proposed a program known as joint implementation. This program would provide incentives to developing countries to reduce their emissions of CO_2 and other greenhouse gases. The Kyoto agreement embraces the President's proposal in its designation of a "clean development mechanism" (CDM): U.S. companies that undertake projects that reduce greenhouse gas emissions in developing countries could count those reductions to meet their commitments. Institutionalizing key elements of joint implementation through this mechanism would encourage firms in the United States to transfer a larger volume of cleaner and more energy-efficient technology to developing countries, especially in the electric power

172

generating industry, while providing substantial cost savings to U.S. firms. It would also provide incentives to expand forests, which absorb CO_2. In addition to the CDM, the agreement allows industrial countries to undertake joint implementation projects with each other.

A key issue is how to ensure that credits are awarded for actual, additional emissions reductions, and not simply for projects that would have been carried out anyway. The Kyoto agreement requires that emissions reductions occurring through the CDM be certified to provide real, measurable, and long-term benefits related to the mitigation of climate change, and that the emissions reductions achieved are additional to any that would occur in the absence of these projects. Future negotiations will focus on developing the rules for certifying and enforcing projects undertaken through the CDM.

Promoting Clean and Efficient Energy Technology

The President's plan to reduce greenhouse gases commits new resources to energy research and programs to promote the wider use of cleaner and more energy-efficient technologies in the U.S economy. The emissions permit trading system for greenhouse gases is also likely to encourage more private research and innovation, as companies seek to lower the cost of meeting environmental targets.

Government support for science and technology in general addresses an important market failure. Promising new technologies often fail to attract sufficient private sector interest if their technical risk is high and if they create economic and social benefits beyond what the investing firms can capture for themselves. Economic studies have shown that private firms, despite intellectual property protection, are able to appropriate only about half of the total economic benefits from their own research. This gap between social and private returns may be particularly large for research on cleaner and more efficient energy technology, when the environmental externalities associated with energy use have not been fully addressed by environmental and other regulatory policies.

The appropriability problem is not limited to basic research but frequently extends to precommercial research as well. Precommercial research is research that is close to yielding new products or processes, but still far enough away from commercialization that further development poses a substantial financial risk. New renewable energy industries (wind power, solar energy, and biomass energy, for example) may face particularly formidable constraints to commercialization. First-of-a-kind products often have high unit costs. High-volume production provides economies of scale, generates experience in manufacturing and operation, and opens new opportunities for incremental technological improvements—all of which may lead to lower costs.

The President's commitment to increase Federal support for new energy technology seeks to reverse a trend of declining national investment in energy research (Chart 5-7). One reason investment in energy research has declined since the late 1970s is falling or stagnant energy prices, which reduced the economic incentive to develop new sources of energy and improve efficiency. In the 1990s it is primarily private sector energy research that has declined. Increasing government investment in energy research is likely to be complemented by more private research: public research on longer term, basic scientific studies can open up new, profitable opportunities for applied research and commercial development by the private sector. An increase in support for research that raises the rate of progress in developing cleaner and more efficient technologies would lower the costs of reducing greenhouse gas emissions.

Chart 5-7 **Energy Prices and Private Energy Research**
Energy prices and private investment in energy research have followed similar trends since the 1970s.

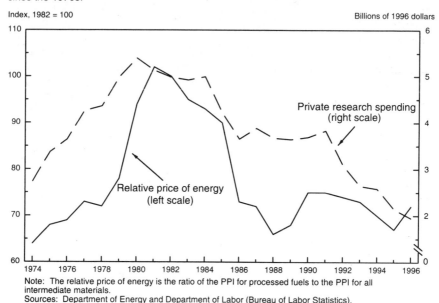

Note: The relative price of energy is the ratio of the PPI for processed fuels to the PPI for all intermediate materials.
Sources: Department of Energy and Department of Labor (Bureau of Labor Statistics).

The President's proposal also includes programs and tax incentives to encourage the wider adoption of existing technologies that can decrease greenhouse gas emissions. Of particular importance are technologies that reduce consumption of fossil fuels. In addition to encouraging clean and renewable energy sources, these programs will provide economic incentives and other forms of assistance (such as better information) for improving energy efficiency in industry, transportation, and homes. The President's plan to use Federal procurement policy to reduce greenhouse gas emissions is another way to increase market penetration of these technologies.

Until an emissions cap and trading system are in place, however, the economic incentive to use these technologies may be low, because at present the price of energy does not reflect the environmental cost of

CO_2 emissions. This environmental externality results in a market failure to make the most efficient use of new technologies that lower emissions. Many of these technologies are expected to be more profitable once a CO_2 emissions cap is in place and the environmental costs associated with energy use are more fully reflected in energy prices.

There is also evidence that many households and businesses fail to invest in some home and building improvements that appear profitable even at today's energy prices. More efficient home refrigerators and air conditioners, fluorescent lighting, and "low-E" glass for windows, for example, are available on the market and, by some accounts, offer potentially large energy and cost savings. By spending money now on these more efficient technologies, proponents argue, many consumers could quickly recoup their investments in the form of lower energy bills. But if such investments are in consumers' own economic interest, why don't they invest in them on their own? Insufficient knowledge and information may be a key factor: consumers may not be aware of new technologies that could reduce CO_2 emissions and save them money on energy bills, or may not be convinced of the economic benefits that could be realized from adopting them. Lack of up-to-date information on recent technological developments may also lead people to overestimate technical risks—they may doubt whether a new technology is as reliable as current methods, particularly if the new technology is not yet widely used.

On the other hand, even if a new technology is beneficial for many users, it may not be so for everyone. People differ in their willingness and ability to make investments today in order to realize savings in the future, especially if the initial expense is relatively large. In addition, some consumers may value a product for attributes other than its energy efficiency—for example, its convenience, size, or design. And not all consumers may achieve all of the promised energy savings, depending on the climate of the region where they live. These considerations reflect the great diversity of needs and preferences among businesses and households and help explain why new technologies may diffuse slowly over time.

Better information about the potential cost savings from improving energy efficiency may increase the use of technologies that already meet the market test—that is, that meet consumer standards for quality and dependability and offer real economic benefits. The Federal Government is working with the private sector to promote wider use of such technologies. For example, through the Green Lights program, the EPA provides technical information to private companies on the economic and environmental benefits of switching to new, fluorescent lighting systems. Energy Star is another EPA program, in which innovative products that use significantly less energy than older generation products are allowed to bear a special, readily identifiable label. More rapid diffusion of new emissions-saving technologies would make an important contribution toward meeting the goals of the Kyoto agreement.

175

NON-POINT SOURCE WATER POLLUTION

Protecting the quality of the Nation's water resources has been a major component of U.S. environmental policy since passage of the Clean Water Act in 1972. The act regulates water pollution from point sources—discrete, concentrated sources such as the discharge from factories and municipal sewage treatment plants—but not from non-point sources. Non-point source water pollution is the entry of pollutants into a body of water from a broad area, such as a cultivated field or the streets and lawns of a city. In recent years attention has increasingly turned to pollution from these non-point sources, especially runoff from agricultural operations. Since environmental regulation has already led to extensive control of point sources of water pollution, further improvements in water quality are likely to be less expensive if they address non-point sources. Recently, the Administration has given renewed emphasis to non-point source water pollution (Box 5-1).

Agriculture is one of the principal sources of non-point source pollution. The environmental problems caused by agriculture stem

---

Box 5-1.—The Clean Water Initiative

On the 25th anniversary of the passage of the Clean Water Act, in October 1997, the Vice President called for a new set of initiatives to further improve the quality of the Nation's water resources. These initiatives will address the principal remaining challenges, especially public health protection, polluted runoff, and community-based watershed management. Agencies will emphasize innovative approaches to control pollution, including the use of incentives and market-based mechanisms. The EPA and NOAA are directed to expedite the full implementation of the Coastal Zone Reauthorization Act Amendments. The Administration also challenged the Congress to help strengthen the Clean Water Act, especially for the control of non-point sources of water pollution.

---

mainly from the runoff of soil, agricultural chemicals, and livestock waste into lakes, rivers, and estuaries. These pollutants may cause undesirable algal blooms, impair recreation and fishing, and adversely affect wildlife. Pesticides and nutrients can also leach into groundwater, threatening drinking water supplies. Soil erosion from U.S. farmland raises the cost of municipal and industrial water use, shortens the life span of dams and hydroelectric projects, damages aquatic habitat, and can contribute to flooding. These off-farm damages from soil erosion have been estimated at $7 billion to $25 billion per year. In 1994 the EPA estimated that at least 6 percent of all U.S. river miles and 21 percent of lake surface areas were water-quality impaired (that is, unsuitable for their designated uses). The same study identified agriculture as a major contributor to impairment in about 60 percent of those river miles and 50 percent of those lakes and reservoirs.

Since these environmental effects are largely imposed on other users of the water resources, and not on the farms that caused them, agricultural non-point source water pollution is another example of an environmental externality that market forces alone are unlikely to solve. In a world of perfect and costless information, the efficient policy response would be to monitor the erosion and runoff from each farm and reduce it to the point at which the incremental cost of further reduction equals the incremental benefit to the environment. This textbook approach, however, is often unworkable because the cost of assessing the pollution caused by each farm can be prohibitive. Instead, public policies to address non-point source pollution from agriculture tend to focus on farmers' choice of farming practices, which is much more easily observed.

Non-point source pollution from agriculture, like many other environmental problems, raises the policy question of whether and how to encourage the adoption of environmentally friendly technologies. Examples of such practices include conservation tillage, integrated pest and nutrient management, precision farming, and buffer zones along waterways. These practices may actually be profitable for some farmers to adopt. As discussed above in the context of energy technology, direct subsidies for the adoption of existing technology improve ecomonic efficiency when the benefits to society at least equal the costs, including the social cost of subsidies. This section examines three policy approaches that have been used to encourage the adoption of farming practices that reduce non-point source pollution: incentive programs, regulations, and emissions trading programs.

Incentive Programs

The U.S. Government has implemented several programs that provide incentives to farmers and ranchers to limit their impacts on the environment. These include support for State programs through Section 319 of the Clean Water Act and several important components of the 1996 Federal Agriculture Improvement and Reform (FAIR) Act. Three programs account for the bulk of Federal spending on environmental incentive programs for agriculture: the Conservation Reserve Program (CRP), begun in 1985; the Wetland Reserve Program (WRP), initiated in 1990; and the Environmental Quality Incentives Program (EQIP), established by the FAIR act. The CRP and the WRP (both of which were reauthorized by the FAIR act) establish voluntary contracts with producers in which they agree to adopt certain practices on their land, including establishing long-term conservation easements and taking it out of production for a period of years. In return, the government provides incentive payments, subsidies for the cost of the practices, and technical assistance as needed. EQIP provides assistance for environmental and conservation improvements on the farm. The FAIR act requires new acres enrolled in the CRP to meet higher environmental and conservation criteria than land enrolled under earlier versions of the program, and funds for EQIP are intended to maximize the environmental benefits per dollar expended and help farmers and ranchers meet national, State, and local environmental standards. Other program provisions, such as Conservation Compliance, require farmers who cultivate highly erodible land to adopt conservation practices or else forgo benefits from other agricultural programs. All these programs differ significantly from traditional regulation in that they are voluntary: no requirements apply to producers who do not wish to participate.

Efforts to remove environmentally sensitive land from agricultural production and encourage the adoption of resource-conserving farming practices have met with much success in reducing soil erosion from cropland. Between 1982 and 1992, erosion from cropland is estimated to have declined by about one-third.

Regulatory Control of Agricultural Pollution

The Coastal Zone Act Reauthorization Amendments (CZARA) authorized the first federally mandated program requiring specific measures to address agricultural runoff as well as four other major non-point sources of water pollution. The EPA and the Department of Commerce's National Oceanic and Atmospheric Administration (NOAA) issued Federal guidelines for implementing CZARA in 1993. The guidelines set out certain requirements that State coastal non-point source pollution control programs must meet, but they allow States to tailor their programs to their own environmental concerns, geographic conditions, site characteristics, and farmer preferences. These programs, currently in the approval process, identify the set of management measures that may be required of individual farms in the State. This process is designed to provide enough flexibility to allow farmers and technical assistance providers to select the practices appropriate for a given farming operation, and to help keep farm compliance costs low. Existing sources of pollution, such as most agricultural sources, will have 3 to 8 years to comply from the time their State program is approved, adding further flexibility and cost-saving opportunities in the timing of implementation.

Trading Water Pollution Credits

To achieve water quality standards cost-effectively, several State and local governments have experimented with programs that are similar in principle to the air pollution trading programs discussed earlier, but do not involve marketed permits as such. Much like the joint implementation projects discussed in the context of climate change above, these programs allow point sources of pollution to meet environmental standards by paying non-point sources (such as farms) to adopt practices to reduce pollution. As already noted, it may be considerably less expensive to attain the same environmental outcome by reducing pollution from non-point sources than from point sources. But because verifying pollution reduction from farms is prohibitively expensive, the agencies administering these programs rely on verifying that farmers have adopted land management practices that are linked with pollution reduction, assessing credits based on the estimated amount of pollution reduced, and certifying the "trades." Most of these programs focus on fertilizer and animal waste pollution, including nitrogen and phosphorus compounds.

Cost savings from such exchanges, if fully implemented, could reach several billion dollars annually. But few trades have occurred to date. For example, the Dillon Reservoir program in Colorado provides opportunities for trading between point and non-point sources. Early estimates expected significant cost savings from trading for the four municipal sewage treatment facilities, but few trades between a point source and a non-point source have occurred since 1984.

The Tar-Pamlico Basin program, implemented in North Carolina in 1989, is not strictly a trading program. Rather, it allows an association of 14 point sources to average all of the members' nutrient discharges under one cap. Then, if total discharges exceed the cap, the association must contribute to a State program that subsidizes management practices on farmland to reduce non-point source pollution. To date, the association has not exceeded its cap, so no contributions to the non-point program have been required.

Trading has been limited both because the scope of trading opportunities has been constrained and because transaction costs have been high. To ensure that all sections of water bodies meet environmental standards, trading is often restricted to a local watershed or certain stretches of a river. Other policy constraints on trades may further limit the potential gains from discharge credit trading. For example, point sources are often required to adopt specific pollution control technologies before they may consider trading. This may limit the discharge reductions that they buy from other sources and reduce the potential gains from trading. In the Tar-Pamlico program, point sources receive only one unit of pollution credit for every two units of pollution reduction they buy from non-point sources. By explicitly requiring nonequivalent emissions to be traded, the program increases the cost of participation. Moreover, these point sources must pay a 10-percent administrative surcharge for every pollution credit they purchase. Finally, programs have often failed to provide assurances that the credits will continue to be honored in the future. This reduces the economic value of the credits and is another impediment to trading.

Although economic theory indicates that the costs of complying with environmental regulation can be significantly reduced through a trading system, the limited experience with water pollution credit trading has not yet provided substantial cost savings. So far the small size of the markets for trades, both geographically and in the number of potential traders, and the regulatory constraints on trades have generated extra costs that make trading less attractive.

IMPROVING HEALTH CARE AND HEALTH INSURANCE MARKETS

Without regulation, health insurance markets do not function well. A variety of policies have been implemented or proposed to address these shortcomings. This section discusses policy initiatives that this Administration has promoted to help improve the functioning of these markets. The Health Insurance Portability and Accountability Act (HIPAA) of 1996 helps workers maintain continuous insurance coverage by limiting exclusions of preexisting conditions, whereby insurers do not cover previously diagnosed conditions for some period, and by expanding guaranteed issue and renewability requirements, which prohibit insurers from denying coverage or renewal on the basis of health status or claims experience. The President's 1999 budget includes policies that improve access to affordable health insurance for people aged 55-65 and for small businesses. In addition, the Administration and the Congress are considering legislation to help ensure that consumers have enough information about health insurance plans and prescription drugs to make informed decisions. Finally, new initiatives to discourage teenage use of tobacco products are aimed at protecting those who may lack the maturity to make decisions about risky behaviors like smoking.

IMPROVING ACCESS AND PORTABILITY

Adverse Selection in Health Insurance Markets

A variety of concerns about health insurance markets relate to the problem of adverse selection, the danger that only those persons most likely to need insurance will purchase it. Adverse selection in insurance markets can arise because of asymmetric information: would-be customers typically know more about their likelihood of incurring high medical costs than do insurers. If insurance is priced to reflect the average risk of a particular population (a practice called community rating), some healthier people may choose to go without. The average risk (or expected medical costs) of the insured pool will then be higher than that for the whole population, and the insurer will lose money. Insurers will, therefore, seek ways to ensure that they do not attract a group that is particularly unhealthy. For example, they may avoid offering comprehensive coverage (by limiting access to specialists or not covering chronic conditions, for example). They may also engage in targeted marketing or change their health plans to appeal to healthier persons and discourage sicker ones from enrolling, by adding benefits, such as health club discounts or coverage for well-baby care, that are more attractive to persons in good health. In addition, in an unregulated market insurers may explicitly exclude higher risk individuals through exclusions of preexisting conditions or by simply denying coverage. Thus, adverse selection in health insurance markets can result in underinsurance among both younger, healthier individuals and the very sick.

Adverse selection is reduced when insurers can insure large groups of people whose purpose in associating is unrelated to their preferences for health insurance. Insurers can be reasonably sure that the members of such groups are not exceptionally unhealthy on average, and healthy people are not likely to leave the insured pool. Employee groups, particularly those of larger organizations, are a natural pool for spreading risk, and this, in part, explains why employer-based insurance is widespread. The lower premiums offered to such groups, the tax-preferred treatment of employer-provided insurance, employer subsidies, and the difficulty of obtaining coverage on the individual market all encourage healthy workers to purchase insurance through their employers, making adverse selection a much less serious problem.

Small firms might like to pool together to offer insurers larger risk pools and reduce administrative costs, but these pools may fall apart, as firms with healthier employees are likely to want to leave the pool to seek lower premiums on their own. The prevalence of employer-based insurance may also discourage self-employment or employment in smaller firms, where obtaining affordable insurance is more difficult.

Even if one could correct the problem of asymmetric information directly, by giving insurers the same information that their customers have, this may not lead to a better outcome, for two reasons. First, there may be a "missing market" for longer term contracts for health insurance. Most health insurance contracts are for 1 year, but purchasers might prefer to buy long-term insurance to avoid the possibility of high premiums or cancellation should they become sick. In addition, the government cares not only about efficiency and market failures in health insurance markets, but also about improving access to care. If insurers had more information, they could choose not to cover some individuals or could charge higher premiums, which is likely to reduce insurance coverage and access to care.

Employer-Based Insurance and "Job Lock"

Health insurance coverage in the United States is closely tied to employment: about 90 percent of the privately insured have employment-related coverage. Thus, changing jobs often means changing health plans. Before HIPAA, workers starting a new job often had to wait to qualify for coverage of preexisting conditions. In some cases, new hires faced waiting periods for any health insurance. However, one important drawback of employer-based insurance is reduced mobility between jobs, or "job lock." Waiting periods or preexisting condition exclusions make it difficult to ensure continuity of insurance coverage when changing jobs. This can be a barrier to job mobility, particularly for those with chronic conditions. Evidence on the extent of job lock is mixed: some studies find little or no effect, but one study estimates that employer-based health insurance can decrease job turnover rates by up to 25 percent. When a person obtains coverage through a new employer, he or she may be subject to preexisting conditions exclusions or waiting periods under the new plan. In addition to creating costs for individuals, who may stay with a particular employer in order to keep health insurance, job lock may also impose costs on the economy by preventing workers from moving to those jobs where they are most productive. Policies like HIPAA and the proposed Medicare buy-in may help improve mobility between jobs.

The Health Insurance Portability and Accountability Act

HIPAA contains a number of reforms designed to improve the operation of individual and group health insurance markets. It helps ease the transition between jobs and into self-employment and improves access to insurance for those who lack access to employment-based insurance and for small firms.

Guaranteed issue and renewability. HIPAA prohibits insurers from declining to cover individuals who were previously covered by a group plan and who have elected and exhausted their eligibility for extended coverage under COBRA (the Consolidated Omnibus Budget Reconciliation Act of 1985), which allows workers to buy into their former employer's plan for up to 18 months. HIPAA also prohibits insurers from refusing to renew coverage on the basis of health status, claims experience, genetic information, or other related factors. These provisions can help improve access to health insurance for small firms and individuals. However, HIPAA imposes no restrictions on the premiums that insurers may charge, so some individuals or firms may still be effectively excluded by prohibitively high premiums. In addition, insurers may try to find other ways to avoid selling insurance policies to high-cost individuals, through more targeted marketing or plan design as described above, for example. Newspaper accounts report that some insurers may even be instructing their agents in how to avoid enrolling higher risk applicants.

Limiting preexisting condition exclusions. HIPAA generally limits exclusion periods for preexisting conditions to 12 months. Some exclusions for preexisting conditions are appropriate, because otherwise people would have little incentive to purchase insurance when they are healthy, knowing that they could simply sign up after they get sick. Thus, it is important to design policies that increase accessibility without exacerbating this free-rider problem. HIPAA addresses this problem by requiring that individuals have continuous coverage in order to take full advantage of the limits on preexisting conditions exclusions. If a person was covered for a particular condition at one job and then changes jobs or elects to purchase individual insurance, he or she can "credit" the time covered under the previous plan against the preexisting condition period in the new plan. For example, someone who had 8 months of coverage could be required to wait no more than 4 months for coverage at a new job (assuming the employer offers insurance). In addition, those seeking insurance on the individual market must have 18 months of creditable coverage and must have exhausted coverage under COBRA (if eligible). Insurers offering coverage to these persons may not impose preexisting condition exclusions.

Proposals to Improve Access to Health Insurance for 55- to 64-Year-Olds

Americans aged 55-64 are one of the more difficult-to-insure populations: they have less access to and great risk of losing employer-based health insurance, and they are twice as likely as younger people to have health problems. Many lose their coverage when they lose their jobs as a result of company downsizing or plant closings. Still others lose insurance when their retiree health coverage is dropped unexpectedly.

To address these problems, the Administration has proposed three policies as part of its proposed 1999 budget. First, persons aged 62-64 who lack access to employer-provided insurance would be allowed to buy into Medicare. The premiums, which would be paid in two parts—one contemporaneously, the second after turning 65—would cover the full cost of participation, making the policy self-financing in the long run. Second, displaced workers aged 55 and older who have lost their employer-based insurance as a result of job loss could also buy into Medicare. Third, retirees aged 55 and older whose employer drops their retiree health coverage would be eligible to buy into their former employer's health insurance through COBRA. Retirees would pay a higher premium than do other COBRA participants, to reflect their higher costs. Each of these options provides a competitive alternative to individual insurance for people in this age group.

Voluntary Purchasing Cooperatives for Small Businesses

As described earlier, small businesses are at a disadvantage in purchasing health insurance. To address this problem the Administration has proposed giving States grants to establish voluntary purchasing cooperatives for small businesses. Small firms could then pool together to negotiate insurance rates that are more affordable than those offered to them individually. This policy could help the large numbers of individuals working for small firms who are presently uninsured.

CONSUMER PROTECTION AND QUALITY IN THE HEALTH CARE INDUSTRY

Health insurance plans are of two general types: fee-for-service plans pay providers for each service they perform, whereas managed care plans (such as health maintenance organizations) usually shift some financial risk to providers. Between 1980 and 1996, the share of workers enrolled in fee-for-service plans fell from 92 percent to 25 percent, primarily in response to rising health insurance costs. The expansion of managed care has helped slow the rate of growth in health insurance premiums by giving providers a greater incentive to control costs. But perceptions that the quality of care has suffered in managed care plans have made managed care the subject of criticism from consumer groups, the press, and the public. The last few years have seen a flurry of activity by the Congress and State legislatures, regulatory agencies, health plans, consumer advocates, and others to define a new set of consumer rights, protections, and responsibilities in response to consumers' concerns about the changing health care system. Although managed care has focused new attention on these issues, many of the concerns raised by these groups—and the actions they propose to address them—are equally important for traditional insurance plans.

The President's Commission on Consumer Protection and Quality in the Health Care Industry was established to advise the President on changes occurring in the health care system and, where appropriate, to make recommendations on how best to promote and ensure consumer protection and the quality of health care. The commission submitted a report, including a Consumer Bill of Rights and Responsibilities, to the President in November 1997. In addition, the Health Care Financing Administration (HCFA) has promulgated rules designed to protect Medicare and Medicaid managed care participants.

How Managed Care Works

Managed care organizations typically contract with a group of hospitals and doctors to care for their enrollees. Enrollees generally must seek care from providers in the plan's network, although point-of-service plans, which allow enrollees to see providers outside the network, with higher cost sharing, are growing in popularity. ("Cost sharing" refers to out-of-pocket payments, such as deductibles and copayments, required of insured individuals who receive care.) Whereas traditional fee-for-service plans control utilization mainly through cost sharing, managed care organizations rely on a number of "supply-side" utilization controls. For example, they may require enrollees to see a primary care physician, or "gatekeeper," before they can go to a specialist, or may limit the types of treatments that providers can offer. Another important feature of managed care plans is that providers often bear some of the financial risk. For example, managed care plans may pay providers a fixed ("capitated") payment for each member or use other mechanisms that give providers financial incentives to limit care.

Promises and Pitfalls in Consumer Protection Legislation

Managed care highlights a new challenge to policymakers, namely, how to protect consumers and promote their informed choice among health plans without undermining managed care's ability to control costs. More employers now offer their employees a choice of health plans—including managed care plans—and many of these ask employees to pay more for more expensive coverage. This can encourage plans to operate more efficiently, control costs, and provide higher quality care, but consumers need sufficient information to make good decisions about what features they want in a health plan—and how much they are willing to pay for them. Many of the activities of the President's commission have focused on addressing the need for more user-friendly information about health plan features and quality, and for strengthening consumer confidence in the health care system. In addition, government attempts to micromanage the practice of medicine—whether in the name of cost containment or in the name of consumer protection—are an unwise use of regulatory authority and would either waste valuable resources or run counter to the goal of a quality-focused system.

The commission includes consumers, health care providers, health insurers, health care purchasers, representatives of State and local governments, and experts in health care quality, financing, and administration. In drafting its Consumer Bill of Rights and Responsibilities, the commission was guided by four principles:

• *All consumers are created equal.* The rights and responsibilities outlined by the commission should apply to all participants in the health care system, including beneficiaries of public programs, government employees, persons with individual policies, and those with employer-based coverage, including self-funded coverage. In addition, to the extent possible, these rights should be accorded to those who have no health insurance but make use of the health care system.

185

Box 5-2.—Quality Data Collection for Medicare Managed Care

The Health Care Financing Administration has promulgated rules that will enable the agency to collect data on quality of care in and beneficiary satisfaction with Medicare managed care plans. The National Committee for Quality Assurance, in conjunction with HCFA, industry representatives, other purchasers, and beneficiary advocates, has developed 40 quality measures related to the Medicare population. These measures build on the Health Plan Employer Data and Information Set (HEDIS) developed by the National Committee for Quality Assurance for the under-65 population. HCFA will publish summary data to help beneficiaries choose among plans. Quality indicators will also allow HCFA to ensure that Medicare beneficiaries receive appropriate care from managed care providers, and will help identify areas for quality improvement.

Currently, managed care plans contracting with Medicare may have no more than 50 percent of their enrollment from Medicare. This provision was designed to help ensure that plans contracting with Medicare offer service of similar quality to that provided in the private sector. The Balanced Budget Act of 1997 eliminated this requirement, and new rules will allow HCFA to use actual quality data, rather than the 50-percent rule, in deciding which managed care organizations are eligible to contract with Medicare. This effort will improve HCFA's ability to ensure high-quality care and help beneficiaries make informed health plan decisions. In addition, more information about these plans could improve confidence in Medicare managed care, encouraging more beneficiaries to enroll in these plans.

- *Quality first.* In considering each proposal, the commission asked whether it would improve the quality of care and of the system that delivers that care.

- *Preserve what works.* Some elements of managed care and of fee-for-service plans must be changed to protect the rights of consumers. But each delivery system can also point to elements that have improved quality and expanded access.

- *Costs matter.* The need for stronger consumer rights must be balanced against the need to keep coverage affordable. Ultimately costs are borne by consumers and their families through higher health insurance premiums, higher prices, lower wages, fewer benefits, or less coverage.

186

Some reforms proposed by States and consumer groups would make managed care plans look more like traditional plans—for example, by requiring health maintenance organizations to accept all providers or limiting the use of financial incentives that may encourage physicians to limit treatment. To the extent that these regulations would prohibit practices that have helped managed care plans control utilization and spending, they could undermine the ability of health plans to control costs, and could ultimately reduce accessibility and affordability. However, to the extent that such policies improve the delivery of high-quality, efficacious care, they could improve health outcomes and may help offset cost increases.

Among the rights laid out by the commission is the right of consumers to "fully participate in decisions related to their medical care." In order for consumers to participate in decisions affecting their health care, both when choosing a health plan and when considering treatment, they need information. The commission recommended that plans should disclose all factors—for example, the method of provider compensation and the plan's ownership of or financial interest in health care facilities—that could influence providers' advice or treatment decisions. In addition, "gag clauses" and penalties on health care professionals who advocate on behalf of their patients should be eliminated, so that providers can freely discuss all treatment options with their patients, and so that patients can make decisions based on informed consent.

New Rules for Plans Serving Medicare and Medicaid

In 1996, HCFA adopted regulations limiting the use of some financial arrangements for health plans serving the Medicare and Medicaid populations. These rules prohibited plans from making payments to providers to limit necessary care, required plans to institute "stop-loss" provisions—which protect providers from very large financial losses—if the compensation method used places physicians or groups of physicians at substantial financial risk, and required disclosure of information about arrangements that transfer substantial financial risk to the health care provider. HCFA also banned the use of "gag clauses" for Medicare plans beginning in 1996 and Medicaid plans beginning in 1997. In addition, HCFA has sought new ways to ensure that Medicare managed care plans provide high-quality care by collecting data on quality and satisfaction in those plans (Box 5-2).

FOOD AND DRUG ADMINISTRATION REFORM

The Food and Drug Administration Modernization Act of 1997 is designed to ensure the timely availability of safe and effective new products that will benefit the public health. The act, which codifies a number of initiatives taken by the Administration as part of its reinventing government effort, includes important provisions that will

187

establish a clearly defined, balanced mission statement for the Food and Drug Administration (FDA), improve access to certain experimental drugs prior to their final approval, establish a fast-track approval process for drugs to treat life-threatening or serious diseases, and reauthorize the Prescription Drug Users Fee Act (PDUFA) of 1992, increasing the resources available for the drug approval process.

Why Drug Regulation Is Needed

Even without regulation, drug manufacturers would have some incentive to distribute honest and accurate information about their products. If a manufacturer repeatedly releases drugs that turn out to be ineffective or unsafe, its reputation will suffer, and it may have more difficulty selling new products in the future. The threat of litigation or a public relations crisis can further discourage drug companies from marketing unsafe products. However, drug companies are not likely to produce enough information about their products' safety and efficacy without regulation. The legal system may not provide adequate consumer protection, and regulation through litigation may come with high transaction costs. For example, companies could set up corporate subsidiaries to issue new drugs and shield the parent company from loss of reputation. Government regulation is then needed to remedy this underprovision of information by evaluating and approving drugs before they may be marketed.

Setting the Standard of Proof

Setting the standard of proof for new drug approvals entails balancing two risks. On the one hand, approval of unsafe drugs may cause injury or death, and approval of ineffective drugs may crowd out alternative treatments or increase wasteful medical spending. On the other hand, denials or delays in approval may prevent sick people from getting more effective treatment.

The FDA has historically focused primarily on minimizing the first type of risk (Box 5-3). In the late 1980s, however, the focus began to shift with respect to drugs for life-threatening illnesses, particularly AIDS. The FDA instituted a fast-track approval process for these drugs, and more patients were offered early access to these drugs before final approval. These policies recognize that the risk that a drug will prove unsafe or ineffective must be weighed against the risks of the disease itself. The FDA Modernization Act codifies and expands upon these reforms and establishes a mission for the FDA that explicitly emphasizes not only protecting the public health, by ensuring that products approved by the FDA meet high standards for safety and efficacy, but also designing a review process that does not unduly limit innovation or product availability.

Box 5-3.—History of Food and Drug Administration Regulation of Drugs

In 1937 an elixir of sulfanilamide, an antibiotic, killed 107 people, most of them children. This tragedy hastened the enactment, the following year, of food and drug legislation already pending: the Federal Food, Drug, and Cosmetic Act gave the FDA authority to regulate cosmetics, prescription drugs, and therapeutic devices. The act required that products be shown to be safe before they are marketed. During the 1940s and 1950s the Congress subjected a number of other products, including food additives and pesticides, to FDA approval and enacted other requirements.

In 1962 the sleeping pill thalidomide was linked to serious birth defects in Europe. Although concerns with thalidomide related to safety, not efficacy, and the drug had not been approved in the United States, the scare generated support for extending the FDA's mandate to determining the efficacy of new drugs. These events culminated in the passage of the 1962 Drug Amendments, which required drug manufacturers to show that drugs were not only safe but also effective. The effectiveness requirement was associated with a rapid increase in total drug development time (Chart 5-8).

Chart 5-8 **Clinical Trial and Drug Application Approval Times for New Drugs**
New drug development time has trended upward since the 1960s, although drug application approval time is at an all-time low.

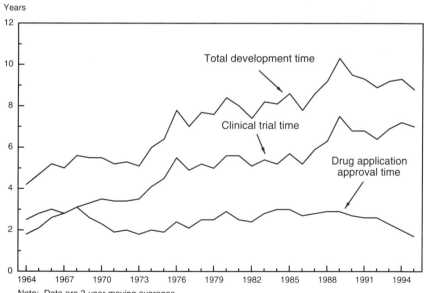

Years

Note: Data are 3-year moving averages.
Source: Tufts Center for the Study of Drug Development, Tufts University.

189

Box 5-4.—The Prescription Drug Users Fee Act of 1992

Between 1980 and 1991 the Congress enacted 34 laws that placed additional demands on the FDA. Yet the agency's budget resources have not always kept pace with growth in the number of products it reviews. The Prescription Drug Users Fee Act (PDUFA) of 1992 helped address this problem by allowing the FDA to assess fees on manufacturers seeking approval for drugs. PDUFA also set ambitious performance goals for reducing approval time for new drug applications and required that the fees not offset current funding.

Although faster NDA approval is important, it represents only a fraction of the total time necessary to develop and approve new drugs. Nor do shorter NDA approval times necessarily translate month for month into shorter total drug development times. The standard of proof for approval determines how many trials and how much analysis must be completed and is an important determinant of the time it takes a drug to travel from the laboratory to the medicine cabinet. In addition, total drug development time may rise or fall in response to a variety of other factors, from the efficiency of laboratory analysis to the chemical complexity of the drug.

Growth in total development time appears to have slowed nevertheless, and PDUFA is widely viewed as a success. The FDA has hired more than 600 new reviewers, and NDA approval times have fallen to record lows. As a result, PDUFA and its recent reauthorization have garnered broad industry support. In fiscal 1995 the FDA reported that 100 percent of the application backlog had been eliminated. In addition, the agency has met and exceeded PDUFA's performance goals for action on NDAs.

Improving Efficiency in the Drug Approval Process

Whatever the standard of proof for approval, rapid processing of new drug applications (NDAs) reduces the health costs associated with delay. Over the last several years the FDA has endeavored to streamline the NDA approval process and reduce unnecessary delays, and NDA approval times have declined significantly, especially for "priority" medications expected to have important therapeutic value. For example, seven drugs for AIDS and other life-threatening illnesses were approved in under 6 months in 1995. After rising since the early 1960s, the growth in total drug development time seems to have stabilized in the 1990s (Chart 5-8).

The FDA Modernization Act builds on the success of these initiatives to further streamline the approval process and reduce costly delays in drug application reviews. The act reauthorizes the Prescription Drug Users Fee Act of 1992, ensuring that the FDA has the resources to review drug applications quickly and efficiently (Box 5-4).

REDUCING TEENAGE SMOKING

The mere fact that people engage in hazardous behavior is not by itself evidence of market failure. But an externality exists if their behavior imposes costs on others, and an information market failure exists if they are not aware of the full costs to themselves of the activity. Smoking, especially by teenagers, arguably illustrates both types of market failure. In addition, because the cigarette manufacturing industry is highly concentrated, with just four firms accounting for the bulk of sales, market power is also a concern—although the higher prices that might result discourage smoking and ameliorate the other possible market failures. This section reviews important tobacco policy developments in 1997 and assesses them with respect to the rationale for government action based on market failure.

Last year marked a historic turning point in the long-running battle between tobacco companies and public health advocates over the harmful effects of cigarettes. First, a landmark rule by the FDA to protect children from the damage of tobacco products was upheld by a Federal judge in North Carolina. Next, the 1997 Balanced Budget Act took a first step toward reducing teen smoking by increasing the Federal excise tax on cigarettes. Revenue from this tax increase will help fund the State Children's Health Insurance Program. In addition, a proposed national tobacco settlement was reached last June between the major tobacco companies and a group of state attorneys general. Following an Administration review of the proposed settlement, the President challenged the Congress to pass sweeping tobacco legislation to reduce teen smoking. Full congressional consideration of such legislation was postponed until this year.

A major objective of both the FDA rule and the proposed settlement is to reduce access to and use of tobacco products by minors. The FDA rule prohibits the sale of nicotine-containing cigarettes and smokeless tobacco to persons under age 18 and imposes a number of restrictions on manufacturers, distributors, and retailers to limit easy access to cigarettes and other tobacco products and to decrease the amount of positive advertising imagery that makes these products appealing to children and teenagers. The proposed settlement goes beyond these prohibitions: it would increase the price of cigarettes and impose penalties on the industry if specific targets for reducing youth smoking are not met. Teens are more sensitive to the price of cigarettes than adult smokers. Estimates suggest that for every 10-percent increase in the price of cigarettes, the number of teenage smokers falls by 7 percent, versus about 4 percent for adults. The President's call for legislative action sought a comprehensive plan to reduce teen smoking, including even tougher penalties than under the proposed settlement if targets are not met.

The Rationale for Regulating Smoking

Tobacco use is one of the most important preventable causes of illness and premature death in the United States. Tobacco use is responsible for over 400,000 deaths each year—about 20 percent of all deaths. The average smoking-related death costs its victim up to 15 years of life. These facts alone might justify an active antismoking effort on public health grounds. But to make an economic case for discouraging smoking based on market failure requires evidence that people are unaware of the risks of smoking or that their smoking imposes costs on others. This case is less obvious than the public health case. It is hard to argue, for example, that people do not know that smoking is hazardous to their health. Indeed, at least one study suggests that people generally perceive the risks from smoking to be even greater than is consistent with scientific evidence. Another study finds that light and moderate smokers' assessments of the impact of their smoking on life expectancy are realistic, whereas heavy smokers significantly underestimate the risks. Similarly, it is widely recognized that smoking is habit-forming and most likely addictive. Yet mature adults are generally given the freedom to make choices that involve trading off the best possible health for other pleasures (like playing dangerous sports, overeating, overdrinking, or sitting on a couch watching too much TV).

The economic case for discouraging smoking based on incomplete information focuses therefore on the decision by teenagers to start smoking. To the extent that young people have short time horizons and are influenced by industry advertising, they may discount too heavily the risks of smoking and the difficulty of quitting. The studies cited above of people's perceptions of the risks associated with smoking did not include teenagers. The finding that heavy smokers underestimate the risks included only 50- to 62-year-olds; it is likely that teenagers' assessments are even more unrealistic. Society may legitimately wish to limit to adults the right to make such a risky decision as whether or not to smoke.

Tobacco use also imposes externalities. To the extent that the costs of treating smoking-related illnesses are not reflected in the insurance premiums paid by smokers, or in their tax and premium contributions to programs such as Medicare and Medicaid, smokers impose uncompensated costs on the rest of society. One influential study suggests that these costs are offset to some extent by the social savings in reduced pension and Social Security payments due to the premature death of smokers; it also suggests that existing excise taxes cover the net external costs of smoking. However, this study does not include the costs of all diseases in which smoking has been implicated, nor does it consider such additional, potentially large external effects as illness and death from second-hand smoke.

Thus, reasonable economic grounds exist for policies aimed at regulating and discouraging smoking. Until last year, the tobacco industry was able to mount a largely successful effort to limit such efforts. It did, however, face the prospect of numerous lawsuits, including several State-initiated class action suits, aimed at recovering damages for smoking-related State Medicaid expenditures. Although the industry had a good record of winning such lawsuits, the ongoing litigation costs and the huge potential costs of an adverse verdict apparently made it worthwhile to the tobacco companies to seek a settlement.

Economics of the Proposed Settlement

The proposed tobacco settlement reached last June illustrates some of the issues that will have to be addressed in any tobacco legislation. The settlement would impose a one-time $10 billion charge on tobacco firms plus an annual payment, which would be adjusted for inflation and for the quantity of tobacco sold in the United States. In effect, the annual payment would function like an excise tax. Although the figure of $368.5 billion is often cited as the industry's total payment, this number is misleading in several respects. First, $368.5 billion is the simple sum of the $10 billion initial payment and the base value of the first 25 years of annual payments (in constant 1997 dollars). A more economically meaningful approach would calculate the discounted present value of the stream of payments expected from the settlement, recognizing that a dollar paid 25 years from now is worth far less than a dollar paid today. For example, using a conservative discount rate of 3 percent, the present value of the first 25 years of payments described in the proposed settlement would be about $260 billion at current sales volumes. Second, the base payment does not represent the amount that would actually be paid. Because the annual payment functions like an excise tax, the quantity of cigarettes sold will decline to the extent that the payment is passed on to consumers through higher cigarette prices. The payment collected will fall accordingly. (On the other hand, other features of the proposed settlement, such as the surcharge for not meeting youth smoking targets and an "excess profits" provision, could increase the payment.) Third, because it is anticipated that the settlement payment will be fully reflected in the price of cigarettes, the incidence of the annual payment will fall primarily on continuing smokers, not on the tobacco companies.

A Federal Trade Commission analysis of the proposed settlement raises additional concerns about its antitrust implications. The tobacco industry is highly concentrated, as noted above. Gross profit margins are also high. But even in highly concentrated industries, where prices may be higher than would prevail under perfect competition, rivalry among firms and the illegality of explicit collusion tend to keep prices below the level that would maximize industry profits. Numerous economic studies have found an elasticity of demand for cigarettes in the range of about 0.4 to 0.5 in the short run—meaning that each 10-percent increase in the price of cigarettes leads to a 4- to 5-percent decline in the number of packs sold. This implies that a price increase would raise industry profits: not only would the increase in price be more than enough to offset the decline in the quantity sold, but total costs would also fall with the reduction in quantity. Since demand is inelastic, if firms were free to collude they would have an incentive to raise prices substantially. The Federal Trade Commission's analysis points to certain aspects of the settlement, most notably its broad antitrust exemption, that could reduce rivalry and increase collusion. In general, the antitrust laws forbid collusion to fix prices because higher prices increase industry profits at the expense of consumer welfare and economic efficiency. In the case of cigarettes, however, higher prices could further the social policy goal of reducing smoking. Nevertheless, granting a broad antitrust exemption is neither the most direct nor the most socially desirable way of achieving higher cigarette prices.

This Administration believes that tobacco legislation must include stiff penalties that give the tobacco industry the strongest possible incentive to stop targeting young smokers. The proposed settlement includes targets to cut teen smoking by 30 percent in 5 years, 50 percent in 7 years, and 60 percent in 10 years. Legislation should further impose financial penalties that hold tobacco companies accountable to meet those targets. The Administration supports penalties that are non-tax-deductible, uncapped, and escalating—so that the penalties get stiffer and the price increases greater the more the companies miss their targets. Recognizing that one of the surest ways to reduce youth smoking is to increase the price of cigarettes, the President has called for a combination of industry payments and penalties that could add up to $1.50 per pack to the price of cigarettes over the next decade. The Administration also supports a number of nonprice strategies for reducing youth smoking through tobacco settlement legislation, including public education, counteradvertising, stronger and more visible warning labels, and expanded efforts to prevent youth access to tobacco products.

CHAPTER 6

Recent Initiatives in Antitrust Enforcement

DURING THIS ADMINISTRATION the Federal antitrust enforcement agencies have been aggressive in enforcing the Nation's antitrust laws. The Antitrust Division of the Department of Justice has imposed record fines—over $200 million in fiscal 1997—and the Justice Department and the Federal Trade Commission (FTC) have both pursued many important cases and investigations, involving such firms as Microsoft, Archer Daniels Midland, Toys "R" Us, and Staples and Office Depot, as well as traders on the NASDAQ over-the-counter stock market. This more aggressive stance does not, however, return Federal antitrust philosophy to an earlier era in which big was viewed as inherently bad. Recent cases and investigations suggest that the Justice Department and the FTC have taken a balanced approach to antitrust enforcement, bringing an action only when thorough investigation and analysis reveal a substantial threat to competition. In doing so, these agencies are guided by their mission to protect the competitive process, recognizing that free markets are likely to provide the best outcomes for society.

This chapter reviews how these agencies have analyzed market competition in a number of recent cases. In so doing it attempts to explain some apparent paradoxes in antitrust enforcement—why, for example, in 1997 the FTC stopped Staples and Office Depot from merging, even though the vast majority of office products are sold by neither company, but allowed a merger between the two leading U.S. manufacturers of large commercial aircraft in an already highly concentrated industry. The chapter begins with a broad overview of the origins and principles of antitrust efforts in the United States and then proceeds to survey several recent developments. The most striking of these has been the growth in corporate merger filings to record levels. The chapter explores the efforts of the antitrust enforcement agencies to allow those mergers that reduce costs, without allowing firms to gain the power to raise prices. Next the chapter discusses the potential impact of electronic commerce on competition. Although electronic commerce will in many cases make competition work more smoothly, it may also make it easier to establish price-fixing agreements. The chapter also surveys the efforts of antitrust enforcers to ensure the continued growth and competitiveness of high-technology industries. Finally, the chapter discusses international antitrust enforcement, an aspect of antitrust policy that has become increasingly important as global trade has expanded.

ORIGINS AND PRINCIPLES OF ANTITRUST

As the American economy shifted from agriculture toward industry during the 19th century, large corporations and trusts began to emerge, eventually dominating or threatening to dominate a number of industries. Public opposition to these monopolies mounted, and in 1889 alone, 12 States passed antitrust or antimonopoly statutes. The Congress followed swiftly. In 1890 it passed the Sherman Act by an overwhelming margin: 52 to 1 in the Senate and 242 to 0 in the House of Representatives. The broad contours of American antitrust law were completed in 1914 with the passage of the Federal Trade Commission Act and the Clayton Act.

The Sherman Act contains broad bans—with both criminal and civil penalties—on monopolization, price-fixing agreements, and other unreasonable restraints on trade. The Clayton Act contains more specific prohibitions of mergers and of certain forms of price discrimination, exclusive dealing agreements, and tie-in sales (sales conditioned on the purchase of another product) when the effect may be to substantially lessen competition or to tend to create a monopoly. The Justice Department and the FTC have overlapping but distinct authorities: the Justice Department may bring actions under the Sherman Act and the FTC under the Federal Trade Commission Act, but either may bring actions under the Clayton Act. In addition, the major regulatory agencies, such as the Federal Communications Commission, the Federal Energy Regulatory Commission, and the Surface Transportation Board, all review mergers under their own statutory authority.

The antitrust laws' primary objection to monopolies, cartels, and other restrictive practices and restraints of trade is that they injure consumers by increasing prices. Another concern, which has been a particular focus of economists, is that these high prices inappropriately curtail consumption of the monopolized good. Inefficiencies arise when sellers charge monopoly prices, because consumers lose more from the price increase than sellers gain.

Another objection to monopoly was expressed by Judge Learned Hand, who argued that "Unchallenged economic power deadens initiative, discourages thrift and depresses energy," and that "immunity from competition is a narcotic, and rivalry is a stimulant, to industrial progress." In a similar vein, the British economist John Hicks wrote that "the best of all monopoly profits is a quiet life." This complacency on the part of monopolists can impede economic progress.

The concern that firms with market power—the power to raise prices above their production costs—can limit innovation has become an important part of antitrust enforcement during this Administration.

The choice between competition and monopoly is easy. Unfortunately, however, that is not usually the choice that antitrust enforcers face. The industries in which antitrust issues tend to arise can seldom be appropriately classified as either perfectly competitive or monopolized. Usually they lie somewhere in between. Firms typically have some market power, but they also have competitors. Mergers and restrictive practices may create or enhance market power, but they may also promote efficiencies and hence can benefit consumers. Identifying corporate conduct whose primary effect is to lessen competition is the task of antitrust enforcers—a task that often presents a formidable analytical challenge.

MERGERS

Another challenge for the antitrust enforcement agencies during this Administration has been the dramatic increase in merger activity. As Chart 6-1 shows, after a lull in the early 1990s the merger market has come roaring back to life. Both the 1996 and 1997 fiscal years set new records for the number of merger filings.

Chart 6-1 **Mergers Filed with the Antitrust Agencies**
Large mergers must be filed with the U.S. antitrust enforcement agencies. Fiscal 1997 was the second consecutive year of record filings.

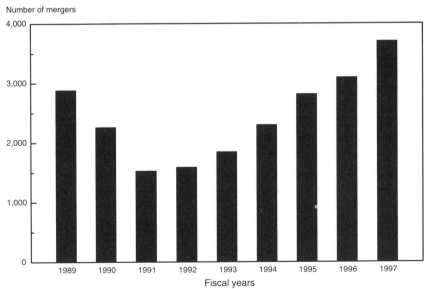

Number of mergers

Fiscal years

Sources: Department of Justice (Antitrust Division) and Federal Trade Comission.

In evaluating these mergers and deciding which ones to challenge, the enforcement agencies must strike a fine balance. A merger may yield significant cost savings, but it may also threaten to increase industry concentration (that is, reduce the number of firms in the industry) and stifle competition, allowing the remaining firms to increase prices and reduce output. The impact on concentration and competition is particularly difficult to evaluate in the many indus-tries now experiencing rapid structural and technological change, such as the defense industry, considered in Box 6-1. The enforcement agencies must consider who will be the merged firm's competitors in the future, not just today.

A merger does not have to create a monopoly in order to result in higher prices and lower output. By increasing concentration, a merg-er may increase the likelihood of successful collusion, either overt or tacit, among the remaining firms. Greater concentration may make it easier for each firm to communicate its intentions to the others, and

Box 6-1.—continued

"firewalls" between merging companies. An example of the first remedy is provided by the 1995 merger of Lockheed Corp. with Martin Marietta Corp. This merger raised antitrust concerns because the companies had entered into exclusive teaming agreements with Hughes and Northrop Grumman Corp., respectively. In the wake of a merger, these agreements would raise the prospect that there might be only one bidder on space-based infrared early warning satellite systems, since Hughes and Northrop Grumman were the leading providers of electro-optical sensors for these satellites. To promote competition in this market, the FTC's consent order forbade Lockheed Martin from enforcing the exclusivity provisions.

Likewise, Raytheon Co.'s $5.1 billion acquisition of Hughes Aircraft Co. might have substantially lessened competition in both infrared sensors and electro-optical systems had the Justice Department not forced Raytheon to make a large divestiture. Raytheon agreed to sell off the infrared sensor business it had acquired from Texas Instruments Inc., as well as electro-optical systems businesses that it would otherwise have acquired with the purchase of Hughes. Raytheon also agreed to a firm price on an Air Force missile to compensate for the lost competition from Hughes. Finally, Raytheon agreed to maintain an information firewall to preserve the independence of Raytheon and Hughes as competitors for a new Army antitank missile.

the interests of the firms may be less likely to diverge. The smaller number of firms may also reduce the benefits and increase the cost of cheating on the collusive agreement. For example, mergers make price cutting less profitable because the merger eliminates one firm from which customers might be attracted away by the price cut. It may also become easier for colluding firms to detect and punish those firms that deviate from the agreement.

Mergers may result in price increases even when firms do not collude in any sense. For example, a firm with market power by virtue of control over a large portion of industry capacity will enhance that power, and may therefore raise prices, if it acquires still more capacity by merging with a competitor. Another important example of such a "unilateral competitive effect" arises when formerly standardized products become differentiated, giving rise to market power as consumers develop brand preferences. Such power is limited by the availability of competing brands; hence a merger between firms selling competing brands relaxes the constraint that competition places on prices. The merged firm recognizes that some of the sales lost through a price increase on one brand will be recaptured by the other brand, and therefore be retained by the firm. This encourages the merged firm to raise the price of both brands. When the brands are particularly close substitutes, the firm may want to raise both prices substantially.

Enforcement agencies must balance these concerns about market power against the efficiencies in production that mergers can make possible. There are several ways in which mergers can reduce the average cost of production in an industry. A merger may allow one firm to take advantage of another's superior technology. Where production processes are composed of multiple distinct activities, a merger can allow each of the merging firms to specialize in those activities that it does best. Mergers may also increase efficiency in industries subject to economies of scale, that is, those in which average production cost declines as output increases. In these industries a merger may reduce costs by eliminating duplicative fixed costs or allowing longer production runs.

Consumers benefit from the merger as well if merging firms pass these savings along in the form of lower prices. The challenge for antitrust enforcement, then, is to prevent those mergers that would harm consumers by enhancing market power, but to allow those that create substantial benefits. To evaluate the market power and the efficiency effects of mergers, the FTC and the Justice Department use the framework that they jointly established in the 1992 Horizontal Merger Guidelines, which were partially revised in 1997. According to the guidelines, the steps to be taken in a merger review for a merger among competitors are as follows:

- define the relevant market and calculate its concentration before and after the merger

- assess whether the merger raises concerns about adverse competitive effects

- determine whether entry by other firms into the market would counteract those effects, and

- consider any expected efficiency gains.

This chapter discusses each step in turn below.

MARKET DEFINITION

The first step is to determine the relevant market and whether the merger will increase concentration significantly in that market. The Merger Guidelines state that the relevant market is generally the smallest group of products and geographical area such that a hypothetical monopolist in that market would raise the price significantly, taking into account the reduction in demand caused by consumers curtailing their purchases. Having defined the relevant market, the agencies determine the market shares of all firms identified as market participants, and use these market shares to calculate an index of market concentration. Mergers that would increase concentration significantly tend to attract more scrutiny from the enforcement agencies, because these mergers are more apt to lead to large price hikes. Typically, therefore, the narrower the relevant market, the more likely it is that a merger will be investigated.

In 1997 the FTC challenged the merger of Staples Inc. and Office Depot Inc. because it believed that the relevant product market was "the sale of consumable office supplies through office superstores," and these firms were the two largest in that market. Staples countered that the relevant market was all sales of office products, including sales by discount stores, drugstores, and wholesale clubs. The combined firm would have accounted for less than 6 percent of this broader market, which suggested that the firm could not have raised prices significantly after the merger if this market definition were indeed correct. The FTC maintained, however, that even though most individual items could themselves be bought from many retailers, the size, selection, and inventory offered by office superstores distinguish them from other office supply retailers. The FTC's statistical analysis showed that, when the presence of other potential competitors was controlled for, Staples' prices were over 5 percent higher in cities where it did not face competition from other office supply superstores. The FTC took this as evidence that nonsuperstore sellers of office supplies do not constrain superstores' prices effectively. This pricing evidence led the court to accept the FTC's market definition and conclude that the merger would significantly increase concentration in the office superstore market and so be anticompetitive.

The key issue in defining the relevant market in a recent merger between two gypsum drywall producers was not the type of seller, but rather the sellers' geographic location. In 1995 Georgia-Pacific Corp., which had 10 drywall plants nationwide, including one each in New York and Delaware, proposed to acquire nine drywall plants from a Canadian-based competitor, Domtar Inc. Two of the nine plants were located in New Hampshire and New Jersey. The Justice Department determined that if the relevant geographic market was national, the acquisition would likely not have raised competitive concerns. However, the merger would have increased concentration significantly in the Northeastern States, so that if the relevant market were localized to that region, the merger likely would have led to price increases there.

To determine the relevant geographic market, the Justice Department examined whether a small but significant local price increase by Northeastern producers would be profitable, taking into account the extent to which customers could switch to producers outside the region. The agency considered such factors as current shipping patterns, constraints on production capacity outside the region, and transportation costs. Gypsum drywall is heavy, bulky, expensive to ship, and likely to break during transport if handled excessively. The Justice Department found that drywall plants in the Northeastern States accounted for the majority of sales to consumers in those states; sales from plants outside the region were comparatively small. Furthermore, drywall plants outside the Northeast had relatively little excess capacity. From this evidence, the Justice Department determined that customers in the Northeast could not have switched to out-of-region producers in sufficient quantities to make a local price increase unprofitable. The agency therefore decided that the relevant geographic market was regional, and Georgia-Pacific, to satisfy the Justice Department's concerns, agreed that it would divest its New York and Delaware plants.

COMPETITIVE EFFECTS

Defining the market and assessing its concentration are only the beginning of the merger review process. The next step is to determine whether the merger would have adverse competitive effects. The 1992 Merger Guidelines recognize that mergers may lessen competition through either collusion or unilateral effects. Indeed, unilateral effects received new prominence in the 1992 Merger Guidelines and have been the dominant concern in several recent mergers.

One recent example where the analysis of unilateral effects suggested significant harm to competition is the acquisition of Continental Baking Co. by Interstate Bakeries Corp. Continental's Wonder Bread brand competed against various Interstate brands in several regions. Although these two firms were by no means the only producers of white bread in these regions, the Justice Department concluded that white bread is a highly differentiated product, with various brands commanding significant customer loyalty, and that after the merger Interstate would likely have raised prices on its brands even if other bakers kept their prices constant. Interstate would no longer be discouraged from raising prices on its own brands by the risk of customers switching to Wonder Bread, since after the merger Interstate would own Wonder Bread. Likewise, whereas Continental was discouraged from raising the price of Wonder Bread by the prospect of customers switching to Interstate's brands, after Interstate bought Wonder Bread this would no longer be a worry. Simulations based on estimated demand elasticities helped convince the Justice Department that significant price increases would likely follow the merger, even in the absence of coordination among the remaining firms. To avoid these price increases, the Justice Department entered into a consent decree requiring the merged firm to divest a brand of bread in each of five geographic regions.

Sometimes the antitrust authorities can limit a merged firm's power to raise prices without requiring a divestiture, as illustrated in the merger of Time Warner Inc. with Turner Broadcasting System Inc. In 1995 Time Warner proposed to acquire Turner in a deal valued at over $7 billion. Both companies were important providers of programming to local cable system operators. Time Warner owned Home Box Office (HBO), the leading cable movie channel, and Turner owned Cable News Network (CNN). Both these channels are "marquee" channels that cable operators have a strong desire to carry in order to attract and retain subscribers. The FTC was concerned that if Time Warner controlled both these marquee channels it would increase the prices it charged to cable operators. To limit the anticompetitive effects of the merger, the FTC's consent order prohibited Time Warner from "bundling" HBO with Turner channels, and CNN with Time Warner channels. The bundling restriction required that the Time Warner and Turner channels be offered separately at prices that do not depend on whether the other is purchased.

It may not be immediately apparent why restrictions on bundling can sometimes be an appropriate remedy; after all, once the merged firm controls the price of both channels it could simply implement an across-the-board price increase. However, a hypothetical example demonstrates that when a merged firm sells goods that are substitutes for each other, prohibiting bundling can limit price increases. Consider a cable operator in a city with 50,000 potential subscribers, and assume that the cable operator earns a dollar in profits from each subscriber. Suppose that 20,000 of the potential subscribers like movies: they will subscribe only if the cable system offers a movie channel. Another 20,000 like news and will subscribe only if a news channel is offered. The remaining 10,000 like both movies and news and will subscribe if either is offered. In this city the cable operator would be willing to pay up to $30,000 for either movies or news, since in each case 30,000 people will subscribe. However, as soon as the cable operator buys a movie channel and gets all the subscribers who like movies, it will be willing to pay only $20,000 for a news channel, since the only additional subscribers it will attract are the 20,000 people who like news but not movies. Similarly, a cable operator that already offers news would be willing to pay only $20,000 for movies. Since some people subscribe if either a movie channel or a news channel is offered, the two channels are substitutes from the point of view of the cable operator. If movies and news can be sold as a bundle, they can be sold for $50,000, because a total of 50,000 people will subscribe. On the other hand, if bundling is forbidden and each channel must be for sale individually, the merged firm will not be able to charge that much.

Suppose, for instance, that the merged firm tried to sell each channel for $25,000. The cable station would respond by buying only one of the channels; since the channels are substitutes, once the cable station purchases one channel, its willingness to pay for the other channel diminishes to $20,000. If the channels are sold separately, the most the merged firm could sell them for is $40,000 ($20,000 each). For this reason, restrictions on bundling such as those in the FTC's consent order can sometimes limit the exploitation of market power, even when the firm can charge whatever it likes for its products individually.

ENTRY

The analysis of a merger does not end with defining the market and determining whether the increase in concentration would allow the merged firm to raise prices. Entry can in principle constrain the merged firm's ability to raise prices: a merger that leads to increased prices may also create opportunities for new firms to enter the market, charge a lower price to gain market share, and still earn profits. Loss of sales to new entrants could cause the anticompetitive price increase to be unprofitable. As a result, entry or the threat of entry can in some cases prevent any appreciable price increase after a merger.

One difficulty with entry analysis is that it can be highly speculative. It is easy to be overly optimistic and assume that entrants will materialize and eradicate the anticompetitive effects of a merger. Accordingly, the antitrust enforcement agencies have taken seriously the Merger Guidelines' caution that entry must be timely, likely, and sufficient to counter the merger's adverse competitive effects.

One merger where entry seemed unlikely to offset the effects of increased concentration was the proposed 1995 acquisition of Intuit Inc. by Microsoft Corp. Each of the two software firms produced a popular personal finance program: Microsoft's Money and Intuit's Quicken together accounted for more than 90 percent of the personal finance software market. Here the question faced by the Justice Department was whether other firms were likely to enter this market in sufficient force to constrain Microsoft's market power once it owned both programs. Two important features of software markets limited the likelihood of entry: the importance of reputation and the "lock-in effect." Purchasers of personal finance software generally prefer a product that is widely accepted as reliable and successful and that has a reputation for performance and customer support. It can take many years and a significant investment for an entrant to develop such a reputation. Even Microsoft had considerable difficulty overcoming the initial success of Intuit. After 4 years of effort, the market share of Microsoft's Money remained far less than that of Quicken, and Microsoft had yet to achieve a positive return on its investment. The fact that consumers have to put considerable time and effort into learning to use a given program gives rise to the lock-in effect. Users of existing software may be reluctant to incur the switching costs of learning another program. Future purchasers may likewise hesitate to invest time and effort in learning to use an entrant's new and untested product because of the risk that the product may not succeed in the marketplace, requiring the customer to eventually switch to the established product.

To make the deal acceptable to the antitrust authorities, Microsoft planned to transfer part of its assets in Money to another software developer. Even so, the Justice Department felt that the importance of reputation and the lock-in effect, among other factors, meant that entry could not be relied upon to offset the high concentration that a merger of Microsoft and Intuit would have caused. The merger was challenged, and Microsoft decided not to pursue it.

EFFICIENCIES

The final major step in the merger review process is to consider the efficiencies promised by the merger. Economists have long recognized the potential benefits of such efficiencies, and in recent years the antitrust agencies have been increasingly willing to consider these benefits when reviewing mergers. Most recently, in April 1997 the Justice Department and the FTC issued revisions to the section of the Merger Guidelines devoted to efficiencies. These revisions reflect the balanced approach of current antitrust enforcement. Under the revised guidelines, the agencies consider the creation of efficiencies, but only verifiable, merger-specific efficiencies. Many studies have suggested that mergers may not produce the synergies and cost savings claimed by managers. Since the agencies understand that it is easier for firms to claim efficiencies than to realize them, they subject efficiency claims to careful scrutiny. If the agencies determine that the claimed efficiencies are likely to be realized and are of sufficient magnitude that the merger is not likely to be anticompetitive, they will not challenge the merger.

The proposed merger between Staples and Office Depot illustrates the increased consideration and scrutiny of efficiencies in antitrust enforcement. The two firms claimed that by merging they would be able to take advantage of large cost reductions and efficiencies in purchasing, distribution, operations, and marketing, and that these savings would be passed on to customers in the form of lower prices. Consistent with the revised Merger Guidelines, the court deciding the case considered whether these efficiencies would offset the presumed anticompetitive effects of the merger. The court refused to accept cost savings that were not merger-specific and dismissed those that could not be verified. Also at issue was the degree to which Staples and Office Depot would pass any cost savings through to consumers. The companies projected that for every dollar of cost savings their prices would go down by about 67 cents. However, the FTC presented evidence that historically Staples had passed through only 15 to 17 percent of its achieved cost savings. Accordingly, the court found that the merger's efficiencies would not offset its anticompetitive effects. It granted the FTC's request for an injunction, leading Staples and Office Depot to terminate their merger agreement.

ELECTRONIC COMMERCE

The potential impact of electronic commerce on competition is dramatic, as described in a recent White House report titled *A Framework for Global Electronic Commerce*. Electronic commerce is already common in several industries. Travelers, for example, buy airline tickets from travel agents who use computer reservation systems. Over-the-counter stocks are traded on a computerized system. And consumers can buy everything from books to automobiles over the Internet.

The potential for electronic commerce to make the economy function better is clear. Computer networks can inform buyers about products available in other States or, just as easily, in foreign countries. Cheap information about wide-ranging markets means that buyers can buy products that they would not otherwise have known about, and can pay lower prices as well. A seller who is the only supplier in a given area may have little power to raise prices if buyers can easily compare prices around the country or around the world. Music stores in Philadelphia will find it pointless to conspire to sell compact discs at high prices if buyers can easily locate competing dealers around the country. Putting cheap information in the hands of consumers thus seems likely to make markets more competitive. One might well wonder if electronic commerce could lessen the need for antitrust enforcement in many markets.

However, two cases that the Justice Department recently filed and settled—one against a group of U.S. airlines, and the other against so-called market makers who execute over-the-counter stock trades—highlight a straightforward problem with electronic commerce. Computers do increase the information available in the marketplace, but not just to consumers; they also make more information available to producers and other sellers. Sellers may be able to use this wealth of information to form or maintain cartels.

For a cartel to raise prices successfully, the members must somehow come to an agreement about what prices to charge and must figure out a way to maintain that agreement. The airline and stock trading cases illustrate how computer networks can sometimes help a cartel solve both these problems. They suggest that, rather than lessening the need for antitrust authorities, the growth of electronic commerce may in some cases increase it.

In 1994 the Justice Department reached a final settlement in a price-fixing case involving eight major airlines and the Airline Tariff Publishing Company (ATP). According to the Justice Department, the airlines had used ATP's computerized fare dissemination services to negotiate increases in fares and to trade fare changes in certain markets for changes in other markets.

The alleged collusive arrangement worked as follows. Each airline submitted its fare changes or planned future changes to ATP. In turn, ATP reported the changes to all the other airlines. The resulting data base was enormous, as each airline offered numerous fares, under various terms and conditions, on each of thousands of city pairs. Moreover, these fares changed frequently. In such a complex system it would seem difficult for the airlines to negotiate or maintain any price-fixing agreement, much less a covert one. With so many interrelated fares and fare changes, one might ask how one airline would distinguish, for example, whether another's price change was an attempt to cheat on a collusive agreement, an attempt to punish a third airline for deviating from an agreement in another market, or simply a normal response to increased costs. The Justice Department alleged that such confusion was avoided by linking fare changes with alphanumeric footnote designators and by the judicious use of first ticket dates. Since the ATP data were computerized, this mass of information could be analyzed by sophisticated computer programs each day. Aided by these computer analyses, airlines could engage in intricate but camouflaged negotiations and could monitor cheating on agreements. The settlement that the Justice Department entered into with the airlines barred them from using footnote designators, first ticket dates, and other devices to communicate with each other.

According to one study, price leadership in the airline industry cost air travelers $365 million per year during the 1980s. Others have estimated that the cost of such behavior in the airline industry, had it been left unchecked, could have reached several billion dollars per year. These figures suggest that the Justice Department's attempts to eliminate anticompetitive practices in the airline industry could yield large dividends for consumers.

The stock trading case, which resulted in a 1996 consent decree, involved transactions in over-the-counter stocks over the automated quotation system operated by the National Association of Securities Dealers (the NASDAQ system). This case also revealed how computerized information networks can sometimes make it easier for firms to maintain agreements to sell at high prices. When an investor places a buy or sell order for shares of a company traded on NASDAQ, special traders called "market makers" typically execute the trade. These intermediaries make their profits from the bid-ask spread, the difference between the price at which they buy a stock and the price at which they sell it.

In the NASDAQ case the Justice Department alleged that NASDAQ market makers had agreed to a strategy, or convention, for quoting stocks that essentially limited their incentives to narrow spreads. Also working to support the agreement was the fact that the

NASDAQ computer network provided sellers with ready (essentially instantaneous) information about the strategies other sellers were using to quote prices. Market makers that were observed to deviate from the convention were harassed by other market makers and threatened with economic harm.

Traditional economic theory predicts that the price-fixing agreement alleged by the Justice Department and the Securities and Exchange Commission (SEC) could not have been maintained on NASDAQ, because entry barriers were low and any of over 100 firms could enter the market for any security. If a price-fixing agreement kept the bid-ask spread high, some market maker would have been tempted to offer the security at a price below the best asking price, or to buy it at a price above the best bid, in an effort to increase market share. But the rules and common practices that governed the way in which NASDAQ securities were traded could have combined to deter market makers from undermining the agreement in this way, with the computer network used for trades playing a key role.

NASDAQ market makers may decline to trade a security at the price quoted by other market makers. But if a market maker does execute a trade, the NASD's best-execution rule requires it to make the trade at the best price quoted on the NASDAQ network. A key feature of trading on NASDAQ is the widespread practice of preferencing. A preferencing arrangement between a broker and a market maker commits the market maker to execute trades submitted by the broker. In combination with the NASD's best-execution rule, this practice could have sharply limited the benefits that any market maker could have anticipated from cheating on any anticompetitive agreement, and so significantly enhanced the ability of a cartel to maintain collusion. A market maker that attempted to cheat on an agreement would not expect to significantly increase its market share, because other firms would, in effect, match its prices instantaneously and retain their preferenced order flow. Thus, a practice that initially seemed to offer a great deal to investors—a guarantee of the best price available, regardless of which market maker executes the order—in fact may have tended to support an anticompetitive agreement.

In 1996 the Justice Department entered into an agreement with NASDAQ market makers. The market makers agreed not to fix prices in the future and to commit resources to an ongoing monitoring effort to ensure that they adhere to the antitrust laws.

The lesson of the airline and NASDAQ cases is that computer networks can sometimes make it easier for sellers to form and maintain price-fixing agreements, by providing sellers with information about the prices that other sellers charge. Agreements negotiated by posting prices on computer networks may prove difficult for the antitrust authorities to ferret out. In the airline case there was sufficient ancillary information—in particular the use of annotations linking one fare proposal to another—to convince the Justice Department that a negotiation was taking place. In contrast, when one firm tries to take advantage of the fact that prices can be quickly and easily changed on computer systems and raises price for a few instants (at a small cost) in the hope that others will follow, most antitrust experts believe that there is no violation of antitrust laws, even if other firms do follow. Simple price leadership is not banned by the Sherman Act, in part because there is no adequate way to frame a remedy. Firms in collusion and firms in competition may both move prices in concert. Antitrust authorities can only try to prevent sellers from negotiating and offering each other mutual assurances in order to form price-fixing agreements.

It has always been difficult to tell whether firms are being forced by competition to charge the same prices, or whether they have agreed to fix prices. The task could become steadily more troublesome as the electronic age progresses. Antitrust authorities in the electronic age need to maintain vigilance in seeking out and enjoining illegal agreements. Electronic commerce may make antitrust enforcement more challenging—and more important.

HIGH-TECHNOLOGY INDUSTRIES, INNOVATION, AND INTELLECTUAL PROPERTY

Many of the fastest growing and fastest changing U.S. industries are to be found in such high-technology fields as aerospace, computer hardware and software, and telecommunications. These industries present several additional challenges for antitrust enforcers. One is that antitrust enforcers must promote both competition and innovation in these fields through a balanced treatment of intellectual property. Another is to account for the tendency for network externalities, common in many high-technology fields, to create a strong potential for market dominance. A third challenge is to anticipate future developments in these fast-paced industries and conduct antitrust policy accordingly.

INNOVATION AND INTELLECTUAL PROPERTY

The key assets in high-technology industries are often not factories or machines but intangibles such as scientific ideas or the algorithms contained in computer programs. These assets, unlike physical assets, can be used by any number of people at once. Without intellectual property protection, firms and individuals would have insufficient incentive to produce these assets, because they are costly to produce but cheap to copy or imitate. In recognition of this problem, the U.S. Constitution empowers the Congress to "promote the Progress of Science and useful Arts, by securing for limited Times to Authors and Inventors the exclusive Right to their respective Writings and Discoveries." Patent and copyright laws do just that.

209

An important initiative of this Administration has been its use of antitrust enforcement to further encourage innovation and to clarify the role of intellectual property in antitrust law. The Administration recognizes that the licensing of intellectual property for use by persons other than its creator can benefit society both directly, by allowing the more widespread use of intellectual properties, and indirectly, by increasing the return to such assets and thereby encouraging innovation. Such licenses, however, sometimes contain restrictions that limit competition and actually discourage innovation. These restrictions may violate the antitrust laws.

The recent case involving the British firm Pilkington plc, the world's largest float glass producer, provides one example of the Justice Department's attempts to use antitrust enforcement to encourage innovation. Beginning in 1962, after acquiring hundreds of patents worldwide on glass production processes, Pilkington entered into licensing agreements with all of its principal competitors. These agreements generally included territorial restrictions, so that each licensee could construct and operate float glass plants in only one country or group of countries. These restrictions allegedly limited the incentives of Pilkington's competitors to innovate in glass processing, by geographically restricting their opportunities to exploit such innovations. Their incentive to innovate was allegedly further limited by requirements to report any improvements in float glass technology and to cede the rights to such improvements back to Pilkington. In 1994 the Justice Department entered into a consent decree with Pilkington, which, among other prohibitions, enjoined Pilkington from enforcing its licensing restrictions against U.S. licensees. The Justice Department's case was strengthened by the fact that Pilkington's principal patents had expired long before the complaint was filed. The Department does not, however, in general limit its attention to restrictions that outlive the life of patents.

The 1995 Antitrust Guidelines for the Licensing of Intellectual Property explain the balanced approach taken by the antitrust agencies. The guidelines recognize that intellectual property licensing can create efficiencies by allowing firms to combine complementary factors of production. However, licensing arrangements such as those used by Pilkington may contain restrictive terms that reduce competition among alternative technologies, and the antitrust agencies have sought to eliminate such anticompetitive arrangements. In evaluating the licensing of intellectual property, the agencies balance the procompetitive and anticompetitive effects.

NETWORK EXTERNALITIES

Many high-technology industries such as computers and communications exhibit network externalities: that is, consumers derive more value from the products of these industries the more people use them. For example, a computer program often becomes more valuable as its network of users grows, because users like to trade data files and exchange ideas about how to use the program effectively. Network externalities can sometimes therefore make entry difficult, because small firms may be unable to compete effectively against large ones, whose products enjoy additional value from widespread usage.

The challenge for antitrust policy is to preserve the benefits of network externalities for consumers while preventing firms from exploiting the market power to which these externalities can give rise. When sellers agree to standards, consumers benefit because the products of different sellers are then compatible. Unfortunately, however, firms can sometimes manipulate the standards-setting process to their own advantage, as the FTC claimed happened in a 1995 action against Dell Computer Corp.

Dell was a member of the Video Electronics Standards Association (VESA), a standards-setting organization in the computer industry. In 1992 VESA set a new standard for the design of computer bus hardware (the hardware that transmits information between a computer's components). According to the FTC, before the standard was approved, Dell certified that it did not violate any of its intellectual property rights, but after the standard was implemented the company announced that the standard did violate one of its patents. Since by then over a million computers using the standard had already been sold, other computer manufacturers could not switch to an alternative design without creating a compatibility problem. This would have put Dell in a good position to collect substantial royalties on its patent, were it not for a settlement with the FTC, in which Dell agreed not to enforce its patent rights against computer manufacturers using the standard.

FAST-PACED TECHNOLOGICAL CHANGE

The fast pace of change in high-technology industries makes it hard for antitrust enforcers to anticipate the impact of future developments when deciding the proper course of action. For example, a merger that seems innocuous today may eliminate future competition. Alternatively, a merger may increase concentration significantly today but may not pose anticompetitive problems, either because of entry, as discussed earlier, or because of exit, as revealed by the 1997 merger between Boeing Co. and McDonnell Douglas Corp.

Although the Boeing-McDonnell Douglas merger reduced the number of sellers of large commercial aircraft worldwide from three to two, thereby sharply increasing concentration, the FTC decided that McDonnell Douglas's 5-percent market share overstated the company's likely future competitive significance, because this market share reflected only the filling of old orders. Extensive interviews by the FTC revealed that advances in aviation design had left McDonnell Douglas behind: since the firm had not invested as much as its competitors in improving the technology of its aircraft, the vast majority of airlines no

211

longer considered purchasing its aircraft. As a result, the merger did not eliminate viable future competition in the commercial aircraft market. Moreover, after consulting with the Department of Defense, the FTC concluded that there were no prospects for Boeing and McDonnell Douglas to bid on the same defense projects. Having concluded that the merger raised antitrust concerns in neither commercial nor defense markets, the FTC did not challenge the merger.

Future competition was a critical issue in the investigation of Bell Atlantic Corp.'s 1997 acquisition of NYNEX Corp. The merger did not increase current concentration in any local telephone market, because neither Bell Atlantic nor NYNEX competed in each other's markets at the time of the merger. However, the Justice Department and the Federal Communications Commission (FCC) needed to assess the likelihood that, in the absence of the merger, each company would someday enter the other's geographic market, and the likely extent of other firms' entry. One focus of the Justice Department's investigation was the effect of the merger on future competition in local service in New York City and nearby portions of NYNEX's service area. NYNEX was the dominant supplier in that area, whereas Bell Atlantic was one of many potential entrants.

After carefully studying the plans of other potential entrants, such as AT&T Corp. and MCI Communications Corp., the Justice Department concluded that the prospect for entry by a number of experienced, capable, and well-financed competitors was significant. Therefore it was by no means clear how much the loss of Bell Atlantic as an independent competitive force would adversely affect consumers, particularly given the evidence concerning efficiencies. The Justice Department concluded that it could not meet its burden of proving that the loss of Bell Atlantic as an independent entrant was likely to have so significant a market impact as "substantially to lessen competition," the test of a violation under Section 7 of the Clayton Act.

The FCC, on the other hand, which also had authority to review the Bell Atlantic-NYNEX merger, operates under a different statute with a different substantive standard. Under the FCC's interpretations of the Communications Act of 1934, the merging parties had the burden of proving that the merger would on balance enhance competition and be in the public interest. The FCC concluded that the merger would not enhance competition, and it exercised its power to place conditions on its approval of the merger. To remedy the merger's possibly anticompetitive effects, and to advance the goal, set forth in the Telecommunications Act of 1996, of opening local telephone markets to competition, Bell Atlantic offered to make several market-opening commitments, which the FCC accepted before approving the merger.

THE GLOBAL MARKETPLACE AND INTERNATIONAL ANTITRUST EFFORTS

The emergence of a global marketplace for many goods and services has important implications for U.S. antitrust policy. On the one hand, as transportation costs and trade barriers fall, many problems in antitrust become easier. Mergers that would have led to significant concentration in the absence of international trade may not do so once one accounts for foreign competitors. Also, domestic price-fixing agreements will be undermined if foreign competitors are willing to sell in the U.S. market at a lower price. On the other hand, international price-fixing agreements are more difficult than domestic ones for U.S. antitrust enforcement agencies to police; success often requires cooperation with foreign governments or international organizations.

Unlike in the 1980s, when most antitrust fines were imposed in domestic bid-rigging cases, the vast bulk of the over $200 million imposed by the Justice Department's Antitrust Division during fiscal 1997 was collected in judgments against large international price-fixing conspiracies. This suggests that even though international trade may make price fixing more difficult, it will probably remain a serious concern for some time to come.

Criminal prosecution in international price-fixing conspiracies is generally much more difficult and complex than prosecuting domestic conspiracies. First, the antitrust authorities must demonstrate that U.S. antitrust law applies. In 1997 the Justice Department made significant headway on this point, when the First Circuit Court of Appeals held that Section 1 of the Sherman Act applies to "wholly foreign conduct which has an intended and substantial effect in the United States," regardless of whether the case is civil or criminal. Even when U.S. antitrust laws do apply, crucial evidence or culpable individuals or firms may be located outside the United States and be beyond the jurisdiction of U.S. courts.

These jurisdictional problems make it imperative that U.S. antitrust enforcement authorities coordinate their activities and cooperate with authorities abroad. In several recent investigations, the United States made good use of its mutual legal assistance treaties with a number of foreign countries: the Justice Department sought and received assistance in cartel investigations from several countries, including Japan and Canada.

In 1994 the Congress passed the International Antitrust Enforcement Assistance Act (IAEAA), which empowered the U.S. antitrust enforcement agencies to negotiate reciprocal agreements with foreign antitrust enforcers. Under these agreements each government will assist the other in obtaining evidence located in the country of the former, while ensuring confidentiality. Unfortunately, foreign antitrust authorities have been slow in following the U.S. lead in negotiating these agreements, in many cases because they lack similar legislative authorization from their own governments. In April 1997 the United States nonetheless managed to negotiate its first proposed agreement under the IAEAA, with Australia. The United States has also been pursuing discussions with the Organization for Economic Cooperation and Development toward a formal recommendation by that body that would encourage its member countries to enter into mutual assistance agreements that would permit more sharing of evidence with foreign antitrust authorities.

At the same time the United States has also worked to improve international antitrust enforcement through the so-called positive comity approach. This approach is used in cases where markets outside U.S. jurisdiction are affected by anticompetitive behavior that harms U.S. interests. Under a positive comity agreement, if one country believes that its firms are being excluded from another's markets by the anticompetitive behavior of firms there, it will conduct a preliminary analysis and then refer the matter to the foreign antitrust authority for further investigation and, if appropriate, prosecution. In April 1997 the Justice Department announced its first formal request to the European Union under a 1991 positive comity agreement. The Justice Department asked the Directorate General IV (DG IV), the European Union's antitrust arm, to investigate possible anticompetitive conduct by European airlines that may be preventing U.S.-based computer reservation systems from competing effectively in Europe. DG IV has announced that it is actively pursuing the matter.

Another notable ongoing effort in this domain is the competition advocacy program undertaken jointly by the Justice Department and the FTC. The two agencies are working together, in programs funded by the U.S. Agency for International Development, to educate and otherwise assist governments of developing countries in setting up antitrust enforcement programs. This assistance has included helping countries to draft competition laws, setting up implementation procedures, training their staffs, and, in some countries, placing long-term U.S. advisers in the antitrust office. Several countries in Eastern Europe have benefited from this extensive interaction with the U.S. agencies, and the program has now expanded into countries of the former Soviet Union and Latin America.

Although significant progress has been made in international antitrust enforcement, the growing importance of international trade makes it imperative that the antitrust enforcement agencies continue their efforts in this area. To this end, the Justice Department has established the first-ever International Competition Policy Advisory Committee, comprised of distinguished business, labor, academic, economic, and legal experts, to advise it on these cutting-edge issues. Investing in expanded enforcement and globalization of antitrust principles will lead to better protection of competition worldwide, and will yield substantial benefits that can be shared by many.

CHAPTER 7

The Benefits of Market Opening

THE UNITED STATES HAS LONG RECOGNIZED that open domestic markets and an open global trading system are superior to trade protection and isolationism at promoting broad-based growth and prosperity. For decades our open economy and successful U.S. leadership in liberalizing global trade and investment have generated important benefits for the American people, in the form of stronger growth and improved employment opportunities. The opportunity to acquire goods and services from abroad both encourages us as producers to stay competitive and allows us as consumers to raise our standard of living. In the 1990s, openness to trade and investment, combined with U.S.-led liberalization of world markets, has been essential to our economy's sustained expansion.

This contemporary picture of a prosperous America in an increasingly open world economy contrasts powerfully with the economic climate and international trade policies that prevailed at home and abroad some six and a half decades ago. In the early 1930s widespread isolationism had reduced world trade to a level only one-third that of 1929. Fortunately the Nation's leaders of that era saw that the path of economic isolation and tit-for-tat protectionism had no exit. During the 1930s and after, the Administration and the Congress worked together, through such measures as the Reciprocal Trade Agreements Act of 1934, the precursor of later fast-track legislation, to revive international trade, just as the programs of the New Deal worked to restart the domestic economy. World War II disrupted these early efforts, but after the war the U.S.-led campaign to open markets worldwide enjoyed a series of outstanding successes. Those countries that joined us in welcoming market opening, in particular through participation in the General Agreement on Tariffs and Trade, have grown and developed at impressive rates. True, these countries might have experienced growth even without open markets, but the history of this century has made it increasingly clear that strong growth is more likely in open than in closed economies.

Bearing this history in mind, this Administration's strategy for economic growth includes a campaign to foster the continued liberalization of markets worldwide. Although much has been accomplished in the postwar period, much remains to be done. As the United States currently enjoys the benefits of relatively open markets at home, this campaign reflects an export-driven agenda aimed

215

at opening markets abroad, reducing current asymmetries in countries' openness. This chapter surveys the primary elements of this campaign. It also reviews the impact that international trade has had on national economies including our own and on the distribution of the benefits of trade within economies (especially among workers). This discussion underscores the need for a strong commitment to trade liberalization not only by the United States, but by all of our trading partners. The chapter concludes with a presentation of recent developments in a second important dimension of open international markets, namely, foreign direct investment, and discusses the implications of the growth of U.S. direct investment abroad and of foreign investment in the United States. The chapter begins, however, with a review of recent trends in U.S. trade.

TRENDS IN U.S. INTERNATIONAL TRADE

The role of international trade in the U.S. economy today is unprecedented. Until 1970, U.S. exports and imports combined rarely amounted to more than one-tenth of gross domestic product (GDP; Chart 7-1). Since 1970, the real volume of trade has grown at more than twice the rate of output, so that by 1997 exports alone were 12 percent of GDP, and imports were equivalent to 13 percent.

Yet trade remains a much smaller component of the U.S. economy than in most countries: in 1995 only four countries had smaller ratios of

Chart 7-1 **Exports and Imports as a Percent of GDP**
Trade is an increasingly important component of the U.S. economy, although close to nine-tenths of U.S. expenditure is still on domestic goods and services.

Percent of GDP

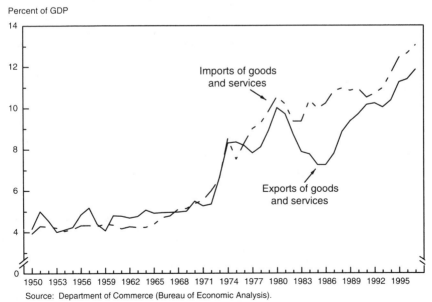

Source: Department of Commerce (Bureau of Economic Analysis).

trade to GDP than the United States. This does not reflect high U.S. trade barriers, but rather such factors as the size of our economy and the diversity of our endowments, which favor self-sufficiency, and our geographic location, relatively distant from most trading partners. Estimates that adjust for such factors have often found that the United States is more open to imports than are most other major countries. But the point remains that the United States feels the effects of trade and pressures for globalization much less than do most other countries.

The rising importance of trade in the U.S. economy is part of a worldwide phenomenon. Technological advances in transportation and communications have contributed to a rapid expansion of the global exchange of goods and services. There is also strong evidence that policy reforms in many countries, in particular the removal of trade barriers and other protectionist measures, have played a significant role in this explosion of trade. The history of the United States during the interwar period points to the importance of policy in stimulating or inhibiting trade. In the years between 1920 and 1930, technological progress continued, but policy moved in a different direction: average U.S. tariff rates more than doubled. The fact that the volume of trade in those years fell by half rather than rose reveals the important role that government policies can play.

THE SECTORAL COMPOSITION OF U.S. TRADE

The composition of U.S. trade, both exports and imports, has also changed markedly. Exports of services have enjoyed particularly strong growth in recent years, rising from $48 billion (18 percent of total exports) in 1980 to $237 billion (28 percent) in 1996. Over the same period exports of agricultural merchandise have risen only from $42 billion (15 percent of the total) to $61 billion (7 percent). In part these trends reflect Engel's law (as the incomes of households rise, the share devoted to food falls) and the evolution of U.S. comparative advantage in more skill-intensive goods and services. But the impact of market opening may be discerned in these trends as well. Innovations in global communications infrastructure and the liberalization of services trade in many countries have promoted greater trade in services. Large tariff reductions on manufactured products, negotiated in a series of rounds within the General Agreement on Tariffs and Trade (GATT), have lowered export costs in that sector. However, agriculture remains relatively protected in most countries.

Exports of both consumer and capital goods have enjoyed rapid sustained growth since the 1980s (Chart 7-2). These two sectors also represent the fastest-growing components of U.S. imports. But whereas growth in exports of these goods has tended to occur relatively evenly across industries, growth of imports has been more concentrated, with especially dramatic increases in such categories as computer goods.

217

Chart 7-2 U.S. Exports and Imports by Category in 1986 and 1996
Both exports and imports, most notably in services and in consumer and capital goods, have grown rapidly, due in part to market opening.

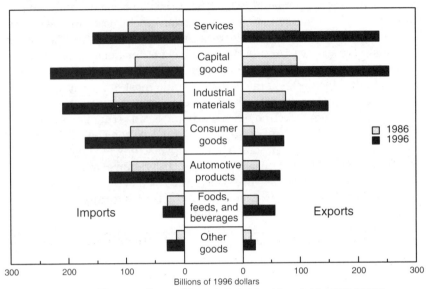

Billions of 1996 dollars

Sources: Department of Commerce (Bureau of Economic Analysis) and Council of Economic Advisers.

The fact that growth is occurring in both imports and exports of consumer and capital goods may seem contrary to the conventional logic of international trade theory, which is based on specialization according to countries' comparative advantage. In fact, this trend reflects the changing nature of trade. Imports and exports today often grow in tandem even within very narrowly defined product categories: that is, an increasing share of trade is intraindustry rather than interindustry. In 1996, for example, 57 percent of U.S. trade occurred within, rather than between, four-digit SITC commodity groupings (the SITC is a standard classification of goods in international trade; four-digit categories in this system represent highly disaggregated product groups), and this share has risen from 51 percent in 1989. Whereas interindustry trade (for example, the exchange of Chinese sweaters for U.S. computers) is associated with traditional notions of comparative advantage, intraindustry trade (for example, in automobiles and auto parts) is thought to arise principally from fixed costs in production and consumer tastes for variety.

THE GEOGRAPHIC COMPOSITION OF U.S. TRADE

Canada and Japan remain the United States' leading trade partners, together accounting for one-third of both our exports and our imports. In recent years Mexico and China have risen quickly to the third and fourth positions; together they represent about 13 percent of total U.S. merchandise trade. When trade is broken down by world region, Europe represents one-fifth of both U.S. exports and imports

(Chart 7-3). The Asia-Pacific region has experienced an explosion in growth of both trade and output over the past two decades and now accounts for more than one-third of total U.S. trade. This trade is principally with other industrial countries, although trade with developing economies in the region is also among the fastest growing anywhere. Trade with Latin America and the Caribbean is also growing but remains less than 10 percent of the total.

Chart 7-3 **U.S. Goods Exports and Imports by World Region in 1986 and 1996**
Imports from developing Asia have risen rapidly, but are less important than growing exports and imports with industrialized partners.

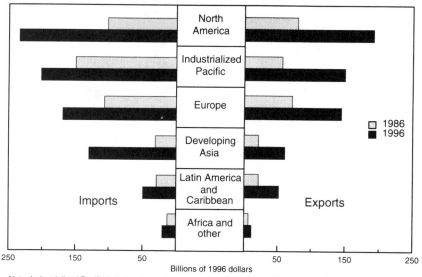

Note: Industrialized Pacific includes Australia, Japan, Hong Kong, Korea, Singapore, and Taiwan.
Sources: Department of Commerce (Bureau of Economc Analysis) and Council of Economic Advisers.

U.S. TRADE BY DOMESTIC REGION

In a country as large as the United States, the regional distribution of the gains from trade is a relevant concern. The North Central and Pacific States remain the largest sources of exports, and both regions continue to enjoy strong export growth (Chart 7-4). However, the highest rates of export growth have recently been recorded in regions and States in the center of the country. This is a positive sign, suggesting that the benefits of trade are being realized throughout the country, not just in the coastal and border States. The impact of the North American Free Trade Agreement (NAFTA) on regional trends in production and exporting has no doubt been significant and may be partly responsible for the rapid growth in exports from the Mountain, Southern, and North Central regions. These statistics suggest that the export opportunities presented by market-opening agreements can benefit the Nation as a whole.

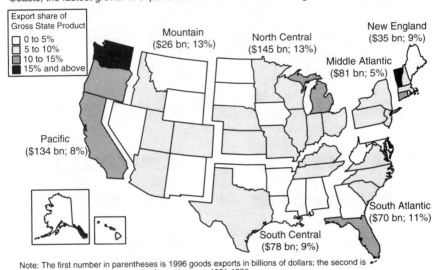

Chart 7-4 **Exports of Goods by U.S. Region**
Although exports are a larger share of Gross State Product on the East and West Coasts, the fastest growth in exports has come from the central regions of the country.

Export share of Gross State Product
☐ 0 to 5%
☐ 5 to 10%
▨ 10 to 15%
■ 15% and above

Mountain ($26 bn; 13%)

North Central ($145 bn; 13%)

New England ($35 bn; 9%)

Middle Atlantic ($81 bn; 5%)

Pacific ($134 bn; 8%)

South Atlantic ($70 bn; 11%)

South Central ($78 bn; 9%)

Note: The first number in parentheses is 1996 goods exports in billions of dollars; the second is average annual growth in exports in the region over 1991-1996.
Sources: Department of Commerce (Bureau of the Census and Bureau of Economic Analysis) and Council of Economic Advisers.

INITIATIVES IN MARKET OPENING

This Administration's primary focus in its conduct of international economic relations is on the continued opening of markets worldwide to trade. However, experience has shown that there is no universal solvent for trade barriers: no single strategy works in all situations to open foreign markets. Accordingly, the Administration has pursued an active trade liberalization agenda on several fronts. While recognizing the importance of an internationally coordinated effort to reduce trade barriers on a broad multilateral and reciprocal basis, the Administration is supplementing these negotiations with liberalization efforts at the regional level. In addition, since market access impediments may be peculiar to a single country, and may not be of the type traditionally dealt with in a multilateral forum, the United States sometimes needs to pursue bilateral negotiations to remove these obstacles to trade.

As this brief survey shows, the Administration is pursuing greater market access for both U.S. and other countries' exports in a number of arenas. The importance of this undertaking is highlighted by the extent to which large portions of the world economy have previously been exempt from formal negotiations. Although the trade-liberalizing initiatives described above are generally reciprocal in nature, they tend to lower foreign barriers more than they do our own. This is the result of the relatively open position taken by the United States throughout most of the postwar period, which has resulted in U.S. barriers that are already lower on average than those of our major trading partners. What is more, the United States has led the way toward the deregulation of domestic industries. In many cases this earlier deregulation in the United States has produced highly competitive U.S. industries, well poised to benefit from deregulation abroad.

TRADE-NEGOTIATING AUTHORITY

The U.S. Constitution places ultimate authority to regulate international trade with the legislative branch. However, for the better part of this century the Congress has provided the executive branch considerable authority to negotiate trade agreements with foreign nations. Most recently, between 1974 and 1993, the Congress repeatedly passed legislation giving the President so-called fast-track negotiating authority. This legislation allows the President to negotiate sensitive and complex trade agreements with other countries, and commits the Congress to either accept or reject the entire agreement, without amendment. In this way the Congress retains its constitutionally mandated final authority to regulate international trade, while turning over the task of negotiating agreements to the executive branch, which is organizationally better suited for that role.

Fast-track authority lends credibility to U.S. commitments in trade negotiations. Foreign parties to a trade agreement with the United States know that the agreed-upon package cannot later be reopened for renegotiation of individual provisions, which in effect would reopen the entire package, undermining commitments made by executive branch negotiators. In the absence of fast-track authority, this possibility is real and can have the effect of preventing other countries from engaging in negotiations with the United States.

The history of executive branch trade-negotiating authority has its roots in the 1930s, a time when international trade flows were heavily restricted by high tariffs throughout much of the world. The Congress granted President Franklin D. Roosevelt power to negotiate tariff reductions. This shift in authority came in the form of the Reciprocal Trade Agreements Act (RTAA) of 1934, which allowed the President to reduce U.S. tariffs on a bilateral basis by up to 50 percent in exchange for reductions in barriers faced by U.S. exports. The RTAA was used often in the 1930s and was repeatedly renewed. The resulting agreements generated large reductions in tariff barriers and embodied some of the same principles that formed the basis for GATT after World War II and, more recently, the World Trade Organization (WTO).

Under the RTAA and later under GATT, tariffs of participating countries were reduced from more than 40 percent in the 1930s to less than 6 percent by the late 1980s. By the 1960s negotiations had expanded to cover nontariff barriers (NTBs) to trade as well. These

221

include price controls, quantitative restrictions (such as import quotas), and quality control measures. But because the RTAA provided no authority to reduce these barriers, complications arose in congressional ratification of the Kennedy Round GATT agreement in the late 1960s. The Congress's refusal to implement the entire agreement as negotiated undermined the credibility of the President's negotiating efforts. The Nixon Administration confronted this problem by pursuing expanded negotiating authority prior to undertaking a round of negotiations in which nontariff barriers figured prominently.

For this reason, in 1974 the Congress passed the first fast-track legislation. The primary difference between this new authority and that granted under the RTAA was that fast-track extended presidential authority to agreements covering NTBs as well as tariff barriers. Fast-track bills have also generally called for extensive consultations between the executive branch and both houses of the Congress and with private sector advisory committees during the negotiations. The Congress must also be notified in advance of the intention to conclude an agreement. In return, the Congress promises to introduce the implementing bill in both houses, with language unchanged, and to vote on the unamended bill within 60 days. Through these provisions, the Congress has historically exerted influence over the negotiations—and hence over the resulting agreements—prior to submission of the implementing legislation. Fast-track has thus proved successful at facilitating negotiations while keeping the Congress involved in the process and preserving its ultimate authority to regulate trade.

Since the inception of fast-track, two extremely successful rounds of GATT negotiations have taken place: the Tokyo Round, signed by WTO members in December 1979, and the Uruguay Round, concluded in 1993 and signed in April 1994. Agreements resulting from other negotiations have also been approved by the Congress under fast-track procedures, including the free trade agreement with Israel in 1985, the U.S.-Canada Free Trade Agreement in 1988, and the North American Free Trade Agreement in 1993.

MULTILATERAL INITIATIVES

By the conclusion of the Uruguay Round negotiations, participants recognized that pursuing multilateral liberalization exclusively in the context of negotiating "rounds" was insufficient. Thus, the final Uruguay Round agreement included a "built-in agenda" for future, more focused talks within the WTO. This agenda provides a mandate and an opportunity to continue the liberalization process within the new organization's regular work program. In some cases the built-in agenda calls for the review and updating of the rules of the multilateral system, including its dispute settlement mechanism (Box 7-1); in other areas the goal is the further opening of markets and the reform or elimination of practices that distort or restrict trade. In the few years since the Uruguay Round agreement was concluded, negotiations toward further liberalization have occurred—or are occurring—in several sectors. Some of these negotiations were launched as a result of commitments contained within existing WTO agreements. Others are the result of forward-looking initiatives given impetus by the United States and its trading partners within the Asia-Pacific Economic Cooperation (APEC) forum and other international organizations.

Box 7-1.—The WTO Dispute Settlement Process and U.S. Trade Policy

The WTO Dispute Settlement Understanding (DSU), part of the Uruguay Round package of agreements, improves on GATT dispute settlement proceedings by expediting decisionmaking and instituting an appeals process. It also establishes procedures to ensure the implementation of dispute panel rulings, one of which is the acceptance of cross-sector retaliation for countries that choose not to abide by the ruling. In the 3 years since its institution, many countries have made efficient use of the reformed dispute settlement mechanism, largely to the satisfaction of all involved.

The introduction of a strengthened multilateral dispute settlement system in the WTO, together with new WTO agreements covering the protection of intellectual property rights and trade in services, has brought about a shift in U.S. tactics for resolving trade disputes. During the 1980s the United States frequently resorted to the bilateral negotiations and unilateral sanctions authorized in Section 301 of U.S. trade law to resolve differences with other countries. This approach was used in particular in the areas of agriculture, intellectual property protection, and services, which GATT covered barely or not at all. Beginning in 1995, however, the DSU and new WTO rules have permitted the United States to use multilateral dispute settlement procedures to address the overwhelming majority of issues that have been the subject of Section 301 investigations. The results of 35 complaints filed by the United States suggest that the DSU process has proved very effective, with the United States prevailing in 9 out of 10 rulings to date. The United States has also reached a bilateral settlement prior to a formal ruling in eight cases. Seventeen petitions are still pending. Section 301 investigations can now more often make use of multilateral dispute settlement, at least for disputes with WTO members in areas subject to WTO commitments. All nine of the Section 301 investigations initiated during 1996, and three of the six investigations initiated in 1997, have involved resort to the WTO dispute settlement procedures; a fourth was terminated before WTO consultations were initiated. As Chart 7-5 shows, the DSU process has been used against a variety of countries, the majority of which are our major trading partners.

The Success of Single-Sector Initiatives

The success of multilateral negotiations in the 4 years since the Uruguay Round ended has in some ways been remarkable. The traditional practice of conducting negotiations in comprehensive, multisector rounds had been based on the belief that only an agreement covering many sectors simultaneously could gain enough political support to be viable. Usually when two or more countries seek reciprocal trade liberalization, the easiest approach is to find one sector that is heavily protected in one country and another sector that is heavily protected in the other. By agreeing to liberalize both sectors simultaneously, each country can please at least one group of domestic producers.

Chart 7-5 **U.S.-Initiated WTO Dispute Settlement Cases by Target Country**
Since their inception in 1995, the WTO dispute settlement procedures have been broadly used by the United States.

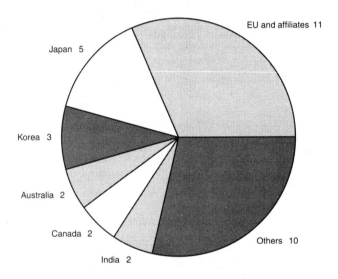

Source: Office of the U.S. Trade Representative.

However, recent WTO agreements in financial services, telecommunications, and information technology represent significant departures from this traditional negotiating format, in that each sector was negotiated separately from the others. Because the United States is believed to be highly competitive in all three of these sectors, one would have thought that U.S. concessions in some other sector would be necessary to reach an agreement. But a common element in all three sectors is that they are key inputs into production in other sectors, and are necessary for economic development and profitable participation in an advanced, information-driven global economy. Industrialists in emerging-market countries, for example, understand that a modern telecommunications infrastructure is

224

essential to economic development. Hence, liberalization of these sectors enjoys weighty domestic support in most countries, so that cross-sector tradeoffs proved unnecessary. As transportation services are also important inputs to trade and production in the modern global economy, it is hoped that the future resumption of single-sector negotiations in this area will bear fruit. Other sectors slated for individual negotiation under the built-in agenda are agriculture and government procurement.

Services

Two of the new WTO agreements—those in financial services and telecommunications—deal with trade in service industries. For most of its history GATT did not cover trade in most types of services. Thus the conclusion of a new General Agreement on Trade in Services (GATS) was an important contribution of the Uruguay Round. The new agreement made it possible for the first time to undertake the negotiations that led to the recent financial services and telecommunications agreements, and should eventually lead to the liberalization of other services.

GATS provides for the first time a solid framework of trading rules and obligations for services and the continued expansion and refinement of those rules in multilateral negotiations. However, the pledges from WTO member countries within GATS itself to liberalize their services sectors are fairly narrow in scope. Out of some 150 individual service activities identified, most countries have committed themselves to liberalize fewer than 100. Moreover, most of these commitments are in services where countries have either little domestic production or little domestic protection. Although it is typical in trade negotiations for countries to liberalize first where the domestic impact is smallest, in this case it means that GATS as written falls well short of comprehensive liberalization. This was acknowledged by the signatories at the time. They therefore included in the agreement specific deadlines for future negotiations in key areas. Some success has been achieved in financial services and telecommunications; the maritime negotiations, on the other hand, have been suspended until more comprehensive services negotiations take place in 2000.

Financial services. Multilateral negotiations on a broad range of financial services resumed in April 1997. (An earlier attempt had ended in 1995 with only an interim solution, as the United States had found some other countries' offers inadequate.) In continuing these negotiations, the United States emphasized the need for agreement on four principles. Foreign-based firms should be assured of retaining any rights they had acquired prior to the agreement, of the right to establish new operations, of the right of full majority ownership, and of substantially full national treatment (that is, legal and regulatory treatment equivalent to that received by domestic firms).

These talks were successfully concluded on December 13 and produced agreement among 102 WTO member countries on broad liberalization of their banking, securities, insurance, and financial data services sectors. The commitments apply to about $18 trillion in global securities assets, $38 trillion in global bank lending, and about $2.2 trillion in worldwide insurance premiums.

Telecommunications. On February 15, 1997, the United States and 69 other WTO members successfully concluded negotiations on basic telecommunications services, such as telephone service. The agreement commits countries to provide market access and national treatment to service suppliers from other WTO members. Sixty-five countries also agreed to a set of specific procompetitive regulatory principles. The agreement eliminates certain restrictive practices in countries that account for 95 percent of world telecommunications revenues, estimated at about $600 billion in 1996. Before the agreement, activities representing only 17 percent of telecommunications revenues in the top 20 markets were open to U.S. companies. The opening of these markets to foreign providers offers enormous opportunities for U.S. telecommunications firms. Whereas telecommunications markets in many countries continue to be served by inefficient government monopolies, markets in the United States have been largely deregulated. Deregulation, along with a large internal market, has resulted in a position of competitive advantage and technological leadership in this area for U.S. suppliers.

Information Technology

Information technology products are often "enablers" for the efficient production of goods in other sectors. Liberalization of this sector therefore takes on added importance as a source of growth worldwide. Concluded in Singapore in December 1996, the Information Technology Agreement (ITA) will liberalize trade in this half-trillion-dollar market. The agreement covers global information technology products such as semiconductors, telecommunications equipment, computers and computer equipment, and software. Signatories include countries accounting for over 90 percent of trade in this sector. The agreement also covers office machines and unrecorded electronic media (such as computer diskettes and CD-ROMs). Each of the 43 participating countries has agreed to eliminate tariffs on these products by 2000, although some countries were granted an extended phaseout of tariffs for a limited number of products. The agreement will benefit all the countries participating, but it is especially important for the United States as a major exporter of information technology products. The ITA also calls for further negotiations to extend country and product coverage and eliminate NTBs under an expanded agreement, dubbed ITA-II. These negotiations are scheduled to conclude by the summer of 1998.

Agriculture

Some agricultural tariffs were reduced in various GATT negotiations over the decades, but as in the case of services, comprehensive agricultural trade barriers only recently became a central focus of GATT talks. The result was the historic Uruguay Round Agreement on Agriculture, the first comprehensive agreement to reduce barriers to trade in agriculture. Among other commitments, the agreement specifies cuts in agricultural export subsidies, reduces aggregate support to farmers, converts NTBs to tariffs, binds all tariffs at levels that imply reductions in previously existing tariffs, and provides for minimum access quotas for products whose trade had been largely eliminated by past protection. Reflecting a general interest in further liberalization, agricultural negotiations are a part of the WTO's built-in agenda, with talks scheduled to resume by January 2000.

Government Procurement

Government procurement and contracting account for up to 15 percent of economic activity in some countries, yet are often subject to policies that discriminate against foreign suppliers. Many countries maintain explicit preferences for goods and services provided by domestic firms over those from foreign competitors. Bias toward domestic producers can manifest itself in many other subtle ways, for instance in limited advertising for bids and a reluctance to spell out selection criteria in advance. Governments may also specify contracts in terms of a certain process or method rather than in terms of the final product. Different firms often develop products that serve the same purpose, but by different processes. If only domestic firms use a particular process, and foreign firms another, governments can in effect exclude foreign suppliers by specifying that process.

Government procurement has historically been excluded from international trade rules; the nondiscrimination principles contained in the original GATT of 1947 do not apply. To address this situation, a group of countries consisting principally of members of the Organization for Economic Cooperation and Development (the OECD, which is composed mainly of high-income industrial countries) negotiated the 1979 GATT Agreement on Government Procurement during the Tokyo Round of multilateral trade negotiations. That agreement was renegotiated and expanded during the Uruguay Round, and the resulting WTO Agreement on Government Procurement (GPA) went into effect on January 1, 1996. The GPA requires signatories to accord nondiscriminatory treatment to the goods and services, including construction services, of other signatories and to follow transparent government procurement procedures. The agreement presently applies to government purchases estimated to be worth over $400 billion annually.

Although the GPA was a significant achievement, only 26 countries participate in it, most of them OECD countries; many of the world's emerging markets in Asia, Latin America, and elsewhere are not signatories. Given the size of the worldwide market (with an estimated value over $3.1 trillion) and its importance for U.S. exporters, the United States has long sought to extend rules on government procurement to all participants in the multilateral system. Largely at the United States' urging, WTO members agreed in 1996 to establish the WTO Working Group on Transparency in Government Procurement. Formal negotiations are scheduled to begin by January 1999.

REGIONAL INITIATIVES

During the 1980s the United States turned an eye toward bilateral and regional liberalization initiatives, not with the purpose of supplanting the multilateral talks, but rather to supplement and spur progress on that front. Regional agreements can be beneficial, but they raise some valid concerns: although such agreements can generate new trade by lowering barriers between participating countries, they may also inefficiently divert trade from nonparticipants that would otherwise supply goods and services more cheaply. From the participants' perspective, whether the benefits of trade creation outweigh the costs of trade diversion depends on how the agreement is structured. There are reasons to believe trade creation will predominate when the agreement encompasses countries that geography has made natural trading partners: when costs of transportation are included, countries in close proximity are more likely to be each other's low-cost suppliers, minimizing the scope for trade diversion. But for countries on the outside, regional agreements are more likely to impose costs than provide direct benefits.

Sometimes regional agreements can exert a positive influence on the multilateral process (Box 7-2) or support the participants' foreign policy positions. For example, the benefits for the United States of the free trade agreement with Israel, negotiated in 1985, were more symbolic than economic. The agreement reinforced political ties between the two countries, and Israel did reap important economic benefits from it as well. Similarly, although economic motivations were significant in the formation of what is now the European Union, a contributing factor was the desire to engender a sense of community that might prevent another intra-European war. The promotion of democracy and political stability as well as economic stability and development is also a factor in the Free Trade Area of the Americas initiative, discussed below.

In the last 10 years the United States has initiated and signed a number of important regional initiatives. The agenda for the remainder of this century and beyond includes laying the foundation for open trade in the Americas as well as moving toward expanded trade throughout the Pacific Rim.

Box 7-2.—Regional Trade Agreements: Building Blocks or Stumbling Blocks for the Multilateral Process?

Does regionalism accelerate or slow the momentum of multilateral liberalization? Some compelling arguments suggest that the formation of regional blocs can serve as a building block—or act as a stumbling block—to the multilateral process.

Perhaps the most compelling theoretical argument for protectionism—and the primary mechanism by which regionalism might act as a stumbling block—is the optimal tariff argument. Imposing tariffs may enable a country to exploit some monopsony power in its import markets, and so achieve more favorable terms of trade with the rest of the world. Moreover, a group of countries setting this optimal tariff in concert may have more success, because of their combined market power, than if each acted alone. Fortunately, Article XXIV of GATT, which governs regional trading arrangements among members, prohibits increases in tariffs against nonparticipants. (GATS now extends the same principle to services.) A regional trading arrangement may also undermine the multilateral process if special interests can manipulate the arrangement's more technical aspects (such as exemptions, phaseouts, and rules of origin) to their advantage, or if regional initiatives divert political capital and energy from multilateral initiatives.

On the other hand, regional arrangements can serve as building blocks for multilateralism in several ways. They can lock in countries' unilateral reforms, simplify negotiations by reducing the number of countries involved, and set in motion a process of competitive liberalization in which reluctant countries are prodded into liberalizing by the threat of exclusion from a regional agreement.

The history of NAFTA provides an example of how regionalism can lock in reforms. By entering into NAFTA, the then-President of Mexico hoped to prevent his successors from undoing the unilateral liberalizations his government had undertaken since the mid-1980s. Mexico's reaction to the peso crisis of 1994-95 showed that this lock-in strategy worked. Unlike in the 1982 debt crisis, when Mexico raised trade barriers against all its trading partners, in the 1994-95 crisis Mexico continued to reduce tariffs for its NAFTA partners (while raising tariffs against some other countries).

Negotiating with 150 other countries over dozens of sectors, as WTO negotiators must do, can be inefficient and difficult. The process can be made more efficient if countries can join into customs unions and thus negotiate as a larger unit. Also, within

Box 7-2.—*continued*

such a group it may be easier to test out innovative agreements in certain areas—such as services, investment, dispute settlement, and competition policy—before introducing their provisions into the multilateral negotiations.

The events of 1993 demonstrate the power of competitive liberalization. The Administration is said to have made a "triple play" that year, with the passage of NAFTA, the pathbreaking APEC summit, and the conclusion of the Uruguay Round. These not only were landmark achievements in themselves but interacted with each other in advantageous ways. By pushing NAFTA through the Congress despite strong opposition, the President revealed the political will to make free trade commitments stick. Combined with the upgrading of APEC negotiations to a high-profile leaders' meeting in Seattle, the passage of NAFTA sent a strong signal to the Europeans that the United States had serious regional alternatives should the Uruguay Round of GATT negotiations fall apart. German policymakers have reportedly stated that this was part of their motivation for prevailing on their EU partners to make certain concessions that allowed the GATT negotiations to be successfully concluded in December 1993.

These examples show that there are both positive and negative links between regionalism and the multilateral negotiations. Every regional bloc will have its share of each. In the end, however, the evidence suggests that the recent growth of regionalism has served more to foster than hinder progress toward liberalization. Those groups of countries that have participated in regional liberalization have often tended to reduce their barriers against nonmembers at the same time that they do so internally.

The Free Trade Area of the Americas

The idea of a free trade area encompassing all of the Americas took its first step toward realization in December 1994, when the President of the United States and leaders of 33 other Western Hemisphere countries met in Miami for the first hemispheric summit since 1967. There they committed their governments to concluding the negotiation of a comprehensive free trade agreement no later than 2005, with concrete progress due by the end of the century. The Miami Summit led to three meetings of the countries' trade ministers, at which 12 working groups were established to lay the foundation and begin preparations for actual negotiations toward a Free Trade Area of the Americas (FTAA).

The United States has championed this regional initiative and remains actively engaged in it, as a means of fostering closer political and economic ties with and further trade liberalization in our hemispheric neighbors. Building on unilateral liberalizations undertaken in the late 1980s, many Latin American countries have already negotiated preferential trading arrangements with each other. Examples include MERCOSUR (which includes Argentina, Brazil, Paraguay, and Uruguay), the revitalized Central American Common Market, and the Andean Community. Their dismantling of trade barriers, both unilaterally and in the context of regional agreements, reflects a significant shift away from traditionally inward-oriented trade policies toward more liberalized regimes. Although generally reflective of progressive policy programs, the preferential nature of these arrangements is of concern to the United States, because it means that other countries are gaining favored access to some of our most natural trading partners. As these arrangements proliferate, the potential benefits to the United States of participating in them—and the costs of remaining outside—are rising. Chile, for example, is now linked in preferential trading agreements with every major country in the hemisphere except the United States. For this reason, U.S. exports to Chile remain subject to tariffs averaging 11 percent, while exports from other Western Hemisphere countries increasingly enjoy duty-free access. Although Chile is only one country, it is a salient example of a growing trend.

An FTAA will bring substantial benefits to all countries in the region, which had a combined GDP of over $9 trillion and a market of 756 million people in 1995. These benefits include not only a significant reduction of import barriers but also deeper geopolitical ties. The general lowering of trade barriers will be particularly beneficial to the United States, since our market already is much more open than most. Although this benefit could in principle be achieved through the multilateral process, regional action probably offers more immediate and complete liberalization.

Asia-Pacific Economic Cooperation

Created in 1989, the APEC forum began to take on deeper significance in November 1993, when the President hosted the first-ever summit of the leaders of the member countries, in Seattle. This meeting elevated the importance of the organization and set the stage for a second summit, in Bogor, Indonesia, in 1994. There the leaders announced the goal of achieving "free and open trade and investment in the region" by 2010 for the developed-country members and by 2020 for the developing countries in the group (Box 7-3). In Osaka, Japan, the following year, an agenda was laid out for achieving that goal, and in 1996, in discussions at Subic Bay in the Philippines, implementation of the agenda got under way. The most immediate result of the Subic Bay meeting was a call by the APEC leaders for the elimination of all tariff barriers among member countries to trade in the information technology sector. This declaration laid the foundation for the Information Technology Agreement described above.

Box 7-3.—APEC Tariff Reductions and Other Initiatives

Although APEC members have not yet engaged in formal negotiations over tariff reductions, many have already implemented dramatic reductions in their tariff levels. Between 1988 and 1996 the average applied tariff among APEC members fell by more than a third, from 15.4 percent to 9.1 percent (Table 7-1).

The progressive lowering of tariff barriers is only one aspect of the APEC Action Agenda. This agenda details steps that APEC members have agreed to take to promote greater economic interaction throughout the region. Other agenda items include reducing barriers to competition in the fast-growing air transport market, and a variety of measures designed to reduce the cost of doing business in the region. These include the development of an infrastructure opportunity data base, the promotion of uniform customs classifications and procedures, and advances in the harmonization of standards.

TABLE 7-1.—*Tariff Rates of Asia-Pacific Economic Cooperation Members*
[Percent, simple average]

Economy	1988	1996
Australia	15.6	6.1
Brunei	3.9	2.0
Canada	9.1	6.7
Chile	19.9	10.9
China	40.3	23.0
Chinese Taipei (Taiwan)	12.6	8.6
Hong Kong	.0	.0
Indonesia	20.3	13.1
Japan	7.2	9.0
Malaysia	13.0	9.0
Mexico	10.6	12.5
New Zealand	15.0	7.0
Papua New Guinea	(^{1})	(^{1})
Philippines	27.9	15.6
Singapore	.4	.0
South Korea	19.2	7.9
Thailand	40.8	17.0
United States	6.6	6.4
Average	15.4	9.1

[1] Not available.
Sources: Institute for International Economics.

Fundamental to relations within APEC is the pledge of "open regionalism." APEC seeks to serve as a building block to the multilateral system of liberalization and not a stumbling block. As a start toward implementing this vision, in November 1996 APEC served as a catalyst for the ITA. APEC members are engaged in a process that builds upon the success achieved in the ITA. At the most recent summit, in November 1997 in Vancouver, Canada, the APEC leaders agreed to expand APEC's role as a catalyst for global market opening, by endorsing liberalization initiatives in 15 sectors. Among these are environmental services and technology, medical equipment and instruments, and chemicals—sectors in which the United States is a major exporter. APEC will thus capitalize upon the fact that its collective size and importance in world trade will help in leveraging multilateral agreements that will cut trade barriers globally. The leaders' decision recognizes the importance of taking APEC sectoral initiatives into the WTO where appropriate, and including binding global agreements, as was done with the ITA.

With its member countries now accounting for approximately half of world output and trade, the APEC region has grown in significance for the United States. Already the share of U.S. exports going to APEC members has increased from 52 percent in 1986 to 70 percent in 1996. APEC is also demonstrating its importance in other ways: in November 1997 APEC leaders embraced a strategy for dealing with the ongoing currency crisis in East Asia.

BILATERAL INITIATIVES

As successful as these multilateral and regional initiatives have been, significant barriers to U.S. exports remain, in some countries more than others. The reduction of formal barriers to trade worldwide often exposes cross-country differences in institutions and norms that also serve to limit trade. To the extent these practices are country-specific, it is sometimes easier to address them on a bilateral rather than a multilateral or regional basis. This Administration has a record of actively pursuing remedies to trade barriers abroad. These efforts are designed not only to liberalize markets for American products, but to provide broad market access for all would-be exporters.

China

China is the world's 10th-largest trading nation and the United States' fourth-largest trading partner. U.S. exports to China have nearly quadrupled in the last decade. However, China's wide array of barriers to trade, together with the relocation of the source of many of our imports to China, has resulted in a U.S. trade deficit with China of over $39.5 billion in 1996, an increase of more than $5.7 billion from 1995. Trade data from 1996 show that, when both goods and services are included, our recorded deficit with China exceeds our deficit with Japan. U.S. exports to China grew a slight 8 percent in 1997 (through November), compared with 21-percent growth in U.S. imports from China. Further opening the Chinese market to our exports is an important goal of U.S. bilateral and multilateral negotiations with China.

Negotiating the terms of China's accession to the WTO is a major part of the Administration's effort to address this trade imbalance. The focus of the WTO access negotiations rests on opening China's market to foreign goods and services and bringing China's trade regime into conformity with international trade rules. The United States is also pursuing an active bilateral agenda with China to resolve outstanding issues ranging from market access for U.S. agricultural exports (including citrus, wheat, and meat) to protection for intellectual property rights.

European Union

The trading relationship between the United States and the European Union is important and strong, but it has had its frictions. The U.S.-EU Agreement on Mutual Recognition of Product Testing or Approval Requirements, concluded in June 1997, is evidence of this strength. When fully implemented, the agreement will require each government to recognize the results of product testing and certification requirements set by the other, thus eliminating the need for duplicative testing, inspection, and certification requirements for products in trans-Atlantic trade. The agreement reduces trade barriers in six areas—telecommunications, medical devices, electromagnetic compatibility, electrical safety, recreational craft, and pharmaceuticals—covering approximately $50 billion in two-way trade. The agreement will allow products and processes to be assessed in the United States for conformity to European standards, and vice versa, saving U.S. exporters more than a billion dollars annually.

In recent years, however, longstanding divides between the United States and the European countries have reemerged, along with new areas of disagreement. In 1997 alone the United States has had to deal with disputes resulting from decisions made and deadlines set by the European Commission. The first involved a European ban on products made with so-called specified risk materials; these are foodstuffs that the European Union considers potentially contaminated with the agent that causes bovine spongiform encephalopathy, or mad cow disease. The other disputes involved restrictions on the imports of furs obtained through the use of leghold traps, the biogenetic alteration of corn, and the process by which wine for export to Europe is made. The fur dispute was resolved by an agreement to phase out the use of certain traps in the United States; the other issues remain outstanding.

Japan

Japan is our second-largest trading partner. Our two countries share a long history of negotiated access to the Japanese market for U.S. goods. A series of agreements have sought to address a range of structural features of the Japanese economy that act as market access barriers; these include closed distribution systems, overregulation, lack of transparency in procurement practices, and exclusionary business practices. In addition, the two countries have negotiated sectoral agreements on semiconductors, wood products, cellular phones, construction, and other goods and services.

Since the beginning of this Administration the United States and Japan have negotiated 33 trade agreements. Under the U.S.-Japan Framework for a New Economic Partnership Agreement, reached in 1993, the two countries have negotiated sectoral agreements covering such sectors as automobiles and auto parts, insurance, financial services, telecommunications, medical technology, and flat glass. These are generally sectors in which the United States is competitive but in which our share of the Japanese market often lags behind our shares in the same sectors in other industrial countries' markets. These agreements included objective criteria to guide the two countries in evaluating their success. Under the Framework Agreement, bilateral agreements on structural issues including deregulation, investment, and intellectual property rights also were reached.

Although noteworthy progress has been made under many of these agreements, progress has fallen short in some areas. The United States places priority on full implementation of its bilateral agreements with Japan and believes that more vigorous enforcement is necessary to ensure that their goals are achieved. In addition, the United States continues to seek new market access agreements with Japan to address barriers in specific sectors. Market opening is consistent with a larger deregulation program currently under way within Japan. Under the Enhanced Initiative on Deregulation and Competition Policy, to which the President and the Japanese Prime Minister agreed in June, four sectors—financial services, telecommunications, housing, and medical devices and pharmaceuticals—were identified as the focus of efforts in this area.

The United States also sees the WTO dispute settlement process as useful in addressing specific Japanese market access barriers. In December 1997 the United States reached a settlement with Japan regarding Japan's compliance with a WTO decision against its discriminatory taxation of distilled spirits. The United States is also pursuing a case against Japan's varietal testing requirements for fruit. On another front, the United States challenged an array of measures that Japan has put in place over the past 30 years to restrict imports of photographic film and paper, but the WTO panel did not rule favorably.

Negotiations in both regional and multilateral fora have also generated real market opening in Japan. The WTO agreements on information technology, basic telecommunications, and financial services will increase U.S. market access to many WTO members, including Japan.

THE EFFECTS OF MARKET OPENING

This Administration's efforts to open markets worldwide, reviewed in the previous section, are part of a long U.S. tradition of leadership in market liberalization. These efforts have been remarkably successful: barriers to international transactions, on average, are at a mere fraction of their 1930s levels. But it is not enough to measure the extent to which markets have been opened. The bottom line for the United States is the net benefits this opening brings, not just for the U.S. economy as a whole but for typical American workers and consumers. This section discusses the sources of benefit from international trade and some estimates of the impact of trade on U.S. GDP. This is followed by a discussion of international trade's impact on U.S. workers.

THE BENEFITS OF TRADE LIBERALIZATION

The benefits to an economy from international trade are of two types: static gains provide a one-time increase in income, whereas dynamic gains result in a more or less permanent increase in the economy's rate of growth. The former can be significant, but it is the accumulation over time of the latter that can generate much larger improvements in living standards.

The primary source of the static gains from trade is specialization, which allows resources to be used more efficiently. When one country produces and exports those goods that it can produce relatively cheaply (for instance, wheat in the United States) and imports those that are relatively cheap to produce abroad (for example, coffee from Brazil), this trade can boost living standards on both sides of the transaction. Such trade can be beneficial even in cases where one country could produce both goods more efficiently. This notion, commonly referred to as comparative advantage, is straightforward when applied to individuals—each of us sometimes purchases from others some goods or services that we could make or perform even better ourselves, because we realize that our time is most profitably spent doing those things we do best. But the principle applies equally well to countries. When each country specializes in what it produces relatively more efficiently, the resources of both are put to use where they generate the greatest economic value. Free trade thus is a positive-sum, not a negative- or a zero-sum, game.

The benefits of more efficient resource allocation are augmented when economies of scale are present. For some goods, such as automobiles, the average cost of production falls as more of the good is produced. Again, opening markets to trade allows production of such goods to be concentrated in those countries that produce them relatively well. They can then produce more of those goods, exploiting these economies of scale. This helps explain why the United States trades more with similar countries (Canada and Europe, for example) than dissimilar ones: such countries presumably have similar resource endowments, and this limits the potential gains from more efficient allocation, but they can still gain from exploiting scale economies. Such trade often offers yet another benefit: besides making goods cheaper, it increases the variety of goods available to both consumers and producers.

By encouraging continuous productivity improvements, international trade can increase an economy's growth rate; this is the source of the dynamic gains from trade. Trade stimulates productivity improvements most directly through its procompetitive effects. By subjecting domestic firms to foreign competition, trade gives them an incentive not only to lower prices, but also to strive to enhance productivity, which further reduces prices by lowering average cost. These gains from increased competition differ from the other gains from trade in that they are recurring: although competition is only introduced once, it leads to a cycle of productivity improvements and quality enhancements that continue to benefit the economy indefinitely. Trade (and international investment, discussed below) can also lead to increases in the growth rate by facilitating the transfer of technology between countries. Although the protection of intellectual property rights in the short term is important for maintaining the incentive to conduct research and development, over the longer term the free flow of technological advances across borders will encourage ever more efficient utilization of the world's scarce resources.

MEASURING THE GAINS FROM TRADE

How are the benefits from liberal trade policies to be gauged in practice? The difficulty in measuring the effects of international trade agreements is that they are but one event among many. In an economy the size of the United States, GDP both rises and falls in response to many factors, most of which have nothing to do with trade agreements.

NAFTA provides a prime example of the problems involved. NAFTA entered into force in January 1994. The following December, Mexico experienced a deep economic and financial crisis for reasons unrelated to the agreement. The result, in 1995, was a steep fall in output in Mexico, an increase in unemployment, and a drop in real wages there. A natural side effect of the crisis was a dramatic decline in Mexico's imports, brought on by greatly reduced domestic income and

237

demand, higher import prices due to devaluation of the peso, and, to a limited extent, higher tariff barriers against non-NAFTA trading partners. Despite this crisis-induced decline in trade with Mexico, it is possible to discuss gains for the U.S. economy derived from NAFTA. Because of the agreement, Mexico did not raise tariff barriers against the United States or Canada, but only against other countries. As a consequence, not only did U.S. exports to Mexico not decline by as much as they might have, but some believe the agreement sped the general recovery of the Mexican economy and of imports from the United States. Seeking to take the extraneous effects of the crisis into account, the Administration commissioned a report, which estimated that NAFTA increased U.S. income by $13 billion in 1996.

Despite the difficulty of disentangling the many causes of national income growth, a large number of studies have assessed the benefits of trade liberalizations, real and hypothetical. Some have examined the potential benefits from removing existing restrictive measures. A recent study of the costs of protection in the United States, for example, suggests potential consumer gains of approximately $70 billion in 1990 (1.3 percent of GDP) from removing existing barriers. A drawback of these studies is their inability to incorporate all the benefits of international trade enumerated above. Although they do capture the static costs of inefficient resource allocation, these studies are incapable of quantifying the value of forgone varieties, quality improvements, or productivity enhancements that would take place in the absence of trade barriers. Thus, studies of this type understate the benefits from trade.

Another approach to understanding the benefits of trade is to examine the statistical correspondence between openness and growth rates across a large sample of countries. Such cross-country studies hold constant other well-known determinants of growth, such as investment and education. The common empirical finding is that increased trade is associated with higher income. For example, one recent study, using data from 123 countries, estimated that every percentage-point increase in openness (measured as the sum of imports and exports, expressed as a percentage of GDP) was associated with a 0.34-percent increase in real income per capita between 1960 and 1985. Since 1960, U.S. openness by this measure has increased by 12.7 percent of GDP; this estimate would imply that the increase in trade was responsible for approximately a 4.3-percent increase in U.S. income per capita by 1997.

TRADE AND THE AMERICAN WORKER

The public debate over trade liberalization tends not to focus on whether trade brings benefits for the economy as a whole. It is widely conceded that it does. Instead, recent concerns have focused on the distributional impact of increased trade. This issue arises from the tendency of increased trade to favor some domestic industries while putting others at a disadvantage. As export-oriented industries expand, they draw resources away from the rest of the economy, resulting in a relative decline in other industries. This reallocation of resources will in all likelihood benefit some groups and injure others. Of particular concern are the impacts on workers, including average wages, the wages received by low-skilled relative to more highly skilled workers, the availability of jobs in the economy, and the extent to which workers suffer from job dislocation due to trade. This section discusses first the effects of trade on wages, and then the effects on employment. In each case we begin by discussing effects in the aggregate (on average wages and total employment) and then turn to distributional and individual effects that can be masked by the aggregates.

TRADE AND AVERAGE WAGES

Throughout the first half of the postwar era, real average hourly wages for U.S. production and nonsupervisory workers increased at an average rate of about 2 percent per year. Between 1974 and 1996, however, this measure of real wages fell by roughly 10 percent, retreating to 1965 levels. The early 1970s also saw a dramatic acceleration in the growth of world trade, to rates that (since 1972) have consistently outpaced that of world income growth. This trend was especially striking in the United States, where growth in trade exceeded growth in output by approximately 3.5 percentage points per year following 1972. The coincidence of increasing trade and falling real average hourly earnings suggested to many that international forces were the source of this decline.

This inference is probably wrong, however. To begin with, it is more appropriate to focus on the level of total compensation (wages of all workers plus nonwage compensation) than on wages of production and nonsupervisory workers alone. Wages of production workers have recently grown less rapidly than overall wages. Nonwage compensation, which includes health care benefits, pension costs, and other fringe benefits, has grown relative to wages in recent decades—so much so that total real compensation has increased by almost 8 percent since 1974, despite the decline in real wages. Although this represents slower growth of total compensation than in the 15 years before 1974, this slowdown is more appropriately explained by factors other than international trade, in particular by a slowdown in productivity growth.

The compensation of labor is generally believed to be determined by worker productivity. Between 1959 and 1973, nonfarm business productivity (output per worker hour in the nonfarm business sector) grew at a rate of 2.9 percent per year. Productivity growth slowed, however, between 1973 and 1990 to approximately 1.0 percent per year. Given the productivity slowdown, one would expect a slower rate of increase in real compensation during this period. Adjusting compensation by the consumer price index will not necessarily reveal this relationship: to producers—the ones making the hiring decisions—the real output of their workers must be judged only in terms of the prices received for their goods, not the prices of all goods and services that consumers buy. This implies that a more appropriate deflator is the nonfarm business implicit price deflator. And indeed when this measure of prices is used, a remarkable correlation is observed between productivity growth and growth in compensation over both periods (Chart 7-6). Policies aimed at increasing productivity growth, rather than at reducing international competition, are therefore more likely to increase the growth rate of real compensation.

Chart 7-6 **Real Wages and Labor Compensation, and Productivity**
Using the implicit price deflator, real compensation has kept pace with productivity growth. Using the consumer price index as a deflator, real compensation has lagged.

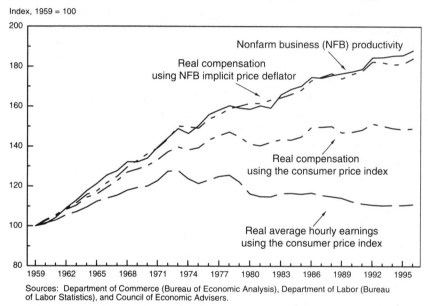

Sources: Department of Commerce (Bureau of Economic Analysis), Department of Labor (Bureau of Labor Statistics), and Council of Economic Advisers.

Although total compensation is thus driven by overall productivity growth, there is an additional effect related to the industry in which workers are employed. Standard theories of wage determination assume perfectly competitive labor markets, in which workers of similar skill should earn comparable compensation even when employed in different industries. These assumptions, however, are not borne out in reality. There has long been a relationship between industry and compensation, such that individuals with similar characteristics tend to earn more in some industries and less in others (Box 7-4). This

240

raises the possibility that some workers could increase their pay simply by moving to another industry.

A recent study indicates that jobs associated with goods exports tend to pay wages approximately 12.5 to 18 percent higher than other jobs. As exporters typically employ relatively skilled workers, a part of this figure is due to differences in observable skills. But even after this factor is accounted for, a significant wage differential remains: the adjusted wages of unskilled workers are approximately 7 percent higher, and those of skilled workers approximately 5 percent higher, in export-oriented industries than in the rest of the economy; accounting for differences in nonmonetary compensation results in differentials that are larger still. Working in export industries thus has the potential to benefit workers—and to benefit unskilled workers even more than skilled workers.

TRADE AND RELATIVE WAGES

Some commentators have pointed to growing differences in the relative wages of skilled and unskilled workers as an indictment of free trade. During the 1980s, a time when U.S. trade volumes were rising, the wages of skilled workers rose between 8 and 15 percent relative to those of unskilled workers (depending on how one defines "skilled"). Given the rough coincidence of these changes, it is tempting to single out international trade as responsible for this increasing wage disparity. Moreover, a significant source of the expansion in world trade has been the entry into the world marketplace of many Asian economies well endowed with unskilled workers. Thus, casual observation seems to support the claim that free trade is detrimental to unskilled U.S. workers: these workers now compete with a vast pool of unskilled workers abroad, and the expected result of this competition is a decline in their wages.

Most careful analysis of the direct evidence does not strongly support the notion that international trade is the major source of increasing wage inequality. Skill-biased technological change, for instance the use of computers and robotics, has been a more important source. The nature of this technological change has reduced demand for unskilled workers and increased demand for skilled workers. This phenomenon can be expected to reduce the wages of unskilled workers relative to those of skilled workers, and perhaps reduce them absolutely. Although the contribution of international trade to observed productivity changes has yet to be established, recent research indicates that international trade is responsible for only perhaps 10 to 15 percent of the observed increase in wage inequality during the 1980s.

Furthermore, U.S. trading patterns are inconsistent with the notion that trade liberalization is substantially depressing the wages of unskilled workers. Although the surge of imports from some low-wage

Box 7-4.—Industry-Related Differences in Wages

Basic economic theory tells us that equally productive workers ought to receive equivalent compensation. But there has long been a fairly stable pattern of differences in wages for similar workers across U.S. industries, as Table 7-2 illustrates. The table shows that a worker in the petroleum industry, for example, can expect to receive about 53 percent more in compensation than the average U.S. worker with similar characteristics (such as education, race, and geographic location). Similarly, workers employed in private household services can expect compensation that is 51 percent below the national average for similar workers.

There is no single reason for these differences in compensation levels. However, a number of possible explanations do present themselves:

- *Compensating wage differentials.* The work environment tends to differ from industry to industry. Work may be more pleasant or safe in some industries, less so in others. Workers in unhealthy or dangerous environments, for instance, may receive compensation that exceeds that in otherwise similar jobs.

- *Unobserved productivity differences.* Our ability to assess the productive characteristics of workers from survey data is limited. Workers may have skills not reflected in measures of education. In addition, firms may provide their workers with training that makes them more productive on the job, and their level of compensation may reflect this on-the-job training.

- *Efficiency wages.* Providing increased compensation may raise worker productivity, for example by increasing motivation and effort, and may reduce the probability that workers will quit. To the extent that the benefit to employers of paying higher wages differ across industries, compensation levels will differ.

- *Monopoly rents.* Competition is weaker, and therefore profitability higher, in some industries than in others. Workers may be able to extract some fraction of these higher profits in the form of higher compensation. Differences in the profitability of firms and the bargaining power of workers can thus give rise to differences in compensation across industries.

In the case of compensating wage differentials or exogenous skill differences, moving a worker from one job to another will not make that worker better off. In the first case the worker is merely being compensated for bearing an additional burden,

242

TABLE 7-2.—*Industry Compensation Premiums, 1984*
[Percent]

Top 10 industries		Bottom 10 industries	
Industry[1]	Premium	Industry[1]	Premium
Petroleum	53.3	Leather	-11.8
Tobacco	42.6	Repair services	-12.3
Communications	37.1	Entertainment	-14.9
Public utilities	34.2	Apparel	-15.0
Transportation equipment	28.2	Other retail trade	-17.3
Mining	27.7	Education services	-19.4
Primary metals	26.2	Personal services	-22.3
Chemical	23.1	Eating and drinking	-28.3
Paper	19.9	Welfare services	-32.8
Machinery, except electrical	18.2	Private household services	-50.8

[1] Two-digit Census Industrial Classification industries.

Note.—The premium is calculated as the percentage by which compensation in the industry (wages plus benefits) exceeds the national average for all industries, after accounting for worker characteristics.

Source: Katz, Lawrence F., and Lawrence H. Summers, "Industry Rents: Evidence and Implications," *Brookings Papers: Microeconomics 1989.*

countries has received tremendous attention, the United States still buys the bulk of its imports from other advanced industrial countries, whose workers have similar skills and wages. If we define low-wage countries as those whose average wage is half or less that in the United States, trade with such countries in 1990 was roughly the same as it was in 1960, when Japan and much of Europe qualified as low-wage countries. Imports from low-wage countries were 2.2 percent of GDP in 1960 and rose to only 2.8 percent of GDP by 1990. In addition, the trade-weighted average hourly manufacturing wage of U.S. trade partners was 88 percent of that in the United States in 1990; this seems much too small a difference to have produced the observed changes in relative wages.

This raises a more subtle but no less valid point: in order for international trade to result in a decrease in the wages of low-skilled workers, the price of low-skill-intensive imports must necessarily fall. But prices of such imports actually rose during the 1980s and 1990s.

In short, while trade may contribute a bit to the widening wage gap between skilled and unskilled workers, the evidence does not suggest that it is the prime source of the gap, nor that it hurts unskilled workers in an absolute sense.

TRADE AND AGGREGATE EMPLOYMENT

Much of the debate over trade has been over jobs. Critics of more open trade have claimed that trade destroys jobs; advocates often argue that trade creates them. According to basic economic theory, however, in general trade does neither. Today the United States is close to full employment. In such times, market opening means that opportunities will decrease in some industries and increase in others. The effect of export growth in this circumstance is not to increase the number of jobs but rather to increase the number of "good" jobs.

There are circumstances, however, in which trade can lead to job gains: when unemployment rates are high, the expansion in exporting industries can be accomplished by hiring unemployed workers. In January 1993 U.S. unemployment was still 7.1 percent (even though the recession had ended 2 years earlier). During the next 2 years the number of American jobs supported by exports rose by 446,000, helping reduce unemployment to its present level below 5 percent. As the economy comes closer to full employment, however, trade's positive effect on aggregate U.S. real incomes shows up less in the form of higher employment and more in the form of higher real compensation for workers.

TRADE AND JOB DISPLACEMENT

As reported in the 1997 *Economic Report of the President*, public opinion polls continue to reveal a low sense of job security among American workers. This is surprising in that, historically, periods of robust economic activity such as the present one have been characterized by much less anxiety over job loss. This anxiety is also evidenced by a relatively low propensity for workers to quit their jobs—a low quit rate suggests uncertainty about the prospects of finding a new job. Rightly or wrongly, workers may associate much of their concern about job security with the expansion of trade. These concerns must be addressed. This means going beyond aggregate measures of expanding employment that might mask individual hardship.

The evidence suggests that, for a variety of reasons, trade is not a primary contributor to total job displacements. Because the U.S. economy is highly dynamic, a great deal of job turnover occurs as new firms go into business or expand and others drop out or contract. Data from the 1980s reveal that trade contributed at most 10 percent of the observed displacements from manufacturing in the worst year of that decade; in most years it contributed significantly less. Most of the job loss resulted from other forces, principally technological change.

Trade can lead to increased displacements because an increase in imports is likely to displace workers in import-competing domestic industries. However, expanded export opportunities may reduce the incidence of displacements in other sectors. Some evidence suggests that expanded export opportunities have been sufficient to offset the effect of growing imports on total displacements. When the effects of increased imports and exports over the 1980s are combined, there is evidence that changing trade patterns over this period left the total volume of displacements relatively unchanged. This is possible because, over time, the displacements resulting from imports were generally offset by expansion in export-oriented industries, which served to reduce the number of displacements. The net effect was then only a reshuffling of displacements across industries and across time.

Although trade may not have increased the number of displaced workers in the 1980s, in some cases it may have increased the hardship associated with displacement. By shifting production from one industry to another, international trade brings about a shift in employment from one industry to another. This change in the distribution of employment, although it generally increases the quality of jobs available, can lead to greater transitional hardship than some other causes of displacement, for instance the closure of an inefficient plant in an otherwise thriving industry, because it is more likely to involve finding a job in a new industry.

In recognition of the relationship between imports and labor displacements, U.S. trade laws have included provisions for trade adjustment assistance since 1962. This assistance offers cash benefits, in the form of extended unemployment insurance benefits, and retraining to workers who lose their jobs as a result of trade. It also pays for job search assistance and relocation expenses. Since the inception of these programs, about 2 million workers have been certified as eligible. A smaller number have actually received benefits, as many found jobs in the meantime.

The Administration is conscious of the need to provide support for workers injured by international trade, but also aware that not all workers deserving of such support are now getting it. Accordingly, the President has made significant reform of the existing trade adjustment assistance programs a priority. One such reform is to extend adjustment assistance to all workers displaced from firms that have shifted production to another country. The NAFTA legislation already provides such assistance to workers displaced from companies that have shut down their plants and moved production to Mexico or Canada. Also in need of assistance are displaced secondary workers—those employed as subcontractors or in businesses that provided services to plants that have moved abroad. The

NAFTA legislation offered benefits for these workers as well, but most have been unaware they were entitled to the same types of benefits as other dislocated workers. These extensions of assistance, coupled with efforts to streamline the certification process, should significantly improve the quantity and quality of assistance provided to workers displaced by trade and investment liberalization.

THE U.S. TRADE BALANCE

A popular measure of the impact of trade policies is the trade balance, or the difference between exports and imports of goods and services. But use of the trade balance as a measure of the success of market-opening endeavors is problematic. Changes in the trade balance are seldom related to specific market-opening efforts; indeed, the trade balance is generally determined by macroeconomic factors, not microeconomic barriers to trade.

National income accounting identities demonstrate that the difference between exports and imports must equal the difference between national saving and domestic investment. In practice this relationship applies to the current account balance rather than to the trade balance. Trade in goods and services is by far the largest component of the current account, but it also includes overseas investment income and transfers. Measurement issues can also intrude to obscure the accounting identity. In particular, the existence in recent years of a large statistical discrepancy between the income- and the product-side measures of GDP has led to a situation in which the gap between official measures of saving and investment has narrowed as the current account has widened (Chart 7-7). The source of the statistical discrepancy is, by definition, unknown at present. But if, for example, the current account and investment are being measured relatively accurately, the current official measure of saving is too high.

Measurement issues aside, in periods when domestic investment exceeds national saving, the current account balance will necessarily be in deficit, whatever the state of trade policy. Whether the Nation is borrowing to finance a consumption binge or an investment boom, the current account deficit that results will represent the inevitable consequence of these aggregate borrowing decisions—not the failure of market-opening policies.

Until the 1980s the current account of the U.S. balance of payments was seldom far from balance. Since then, however, both the trade balance and the current account balance have been in substantial deficit, as growth in imports has largely exceeded growth in exports. These deficits have not arisen because we in the United States have expanded access to our markets while our trading partners have not done the same. In fact, over this period our major trading partners have

Chart 7-7 **Saving, Investment, and the Current Account Balance**
The current account deficit grew in the mid-1980s as saving fell faster than investment.
In the 1990s, however, both investment and saving are increasing.

Percent of GDP

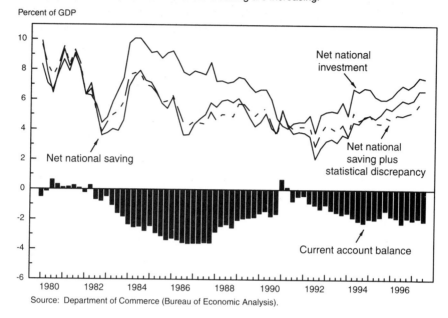

Source: Department of Commerce (Bureau of Economic Analysis).

reduced their trade barriers more than has the United States. Rather, the explanation is macroeconomic. As Chart 7-8 shows, changes in the trade deficit have often closely followed movements in the real exchange rate. The exchange rate, in turn, reflects global demand for U.S. dollars by those who want to buy U.S. goods and assets, and the supply of dollars from those who want to use them to buy foreign goods and assets.

The trade deficit grew in the early 1980s as the Federal Government maintained a mix of tight monetary policy and expansionary fiscal policy. Growing Federal budget deficits were a drain on the pool of domestic saving, requiring new investment to be financed increasingly through borrowing on international capital markets. In particular, the saving shortfall and tight monetary policy raised U.S. interest rates, which in turn caused the real exchange rate of the dollar to strengthen. As the dollar appreciated, imports became cheaper for Americans and U.S. exports more expensive for foreigners, so that the U.S. trade balance went deep into deficit. The deficit was thus financed by borrowing abroad. This problem was often referred to as the "twin deficits," emphasizing the role of the Federal budget deficit (that is, negative Federal Government saving) in the low overall national saving rate and the resulting trade deficit.

Since 1992 the Federal budget deficit has fallen steadily and national saving has increased, yet the trade deficit has once again grown. This is because of the strong boom in investment. Moreover,

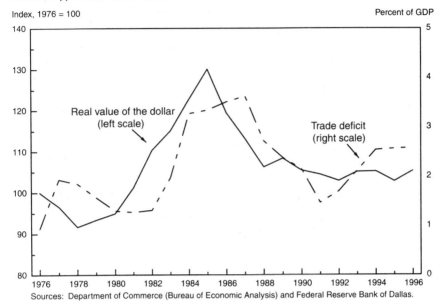

Chart 7-8 Real Value of the Dollar and the Trade Deficit
The trade deficit is a macroeconomic phenomenon: increases in the deficit typically follow an appreciation of the dollar.

Index, 1976 = 100   Percent of GDP

Sources: Department of Commerce (Bureau of Economic Analysis) and Federal Reserve Bank of Dallas.

the trade deficit tends to widen when the economy is growing rapidly. As Chart 7-9 shows for the United States, import growth is strongly correlated with growth in national income (as measured by GDP)—as our incomes rise, we demand more goods and services generally, including more foreign goods and services. The faster our incomes are rising relative to foreign incomes, the more our demand for imports can be expected to accelerate relative to that for our exports (which are foreigners' imports). The result is a growing trade deficit here at home. Arguably, a current account deficit is less worrisome when it is accompanied by rising saving and investment.

At the beginning of 1997 it seemed likely that the U.S. growth rate would fall behind that of our trading partners in Asia and elsewhere, which would help reduce the U.S. trade deficit. Instead, U.S. growth and import demand remained unusually strong, while much of the rest of the world grew less rapidly than expected. However, as discussed in Chapter 2, the dollar appreciated, keeping the nominal trade deficit from widening. The currency crisis and slower growth that hit East Asia in the second half of the year suggest that the U.S. deficit is likely to grow in 1998.

The current trade deficit reflects decisions by households and businesses, policy choices, and the strength of the U.S. economy, particularly in the context of financial instability and slowing growth abroad. In theory, a smaller deficit might be realized with a different mix of fiscal and monetary policy, but it would bring problems of its own. In particular, under current conditions of very low unemployment, an increase in the trade balance would simply crowd out growth in other sectors. The additional demand for U.S. goods and services would put upward pressure on inflation and interest rates, and other sectors would have to contract to make room for the rising net exports. In other words, the trade deficit has acted as a safety valve for the current economic expansion. Imports of goods have kept inflation low, while imports of capital have kept interest rates low, helping to sustain rapid income growth. In the strongly expanding full-employment economy that the United States now enjoys, it should be easier for Americans to see that trade deficits do not necessarily reduce output and employment.

Chart 7-9 **Growth in Real Imports and GDP**
Growth in demand for imports is strongly correlated with income growth.

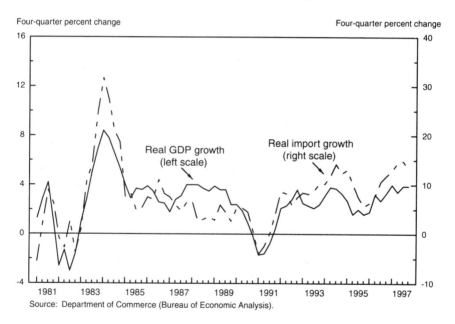

Four-quarter percent change

Four-quarter percent change

Source: Department of Commerce (Bureau of Economic Analysis).

FOREIGN DIRECT INVESTMENT

Although trade has been a primary focus of the *Economic Report of the President* since its inception, capital flows have become increasingly predominant in international transactions. A significant share of these flows has taken the form of foreign direct investment (FDI), wherein the investor acquires or increases foreign assets in which it then has some lasting interest or influence. In recent years growth in recorded FDI has outpaced even the rapid growth of trade. In the last decade nominal FDI outflows from the United States rose an average of 17 percent per year to reach $88 billion in 1996; growth in FDI inflows averaged 8 percent per year to $77 billion (Chart 7-10).

Chart 7-10 **Foreign Direct Investment Flows**
The 1980s saw a surge in foreign direct investment into the United States. In the 1990s, however, outflows of FDI have once again surpassed inflows.

Billions of dollars

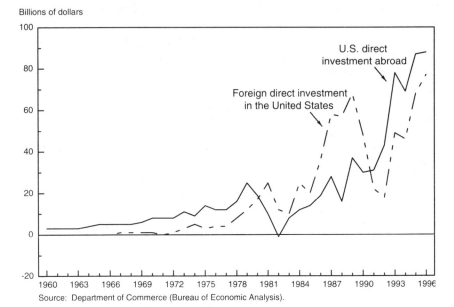

Source: Department of Commerce (Bureau of Economic Analysis).

Commentators tend to speak in universal terms about the motivations for FDI, but in reality no single factor determines why a firm chooses to become a multinational enterprise and operate affiliates in foreign countries. It may be to take advantage of unique opportunities only available overseas (for example, to develop new oil fields), to lower production costs by exploiting international comparative advantage, or to gain or improve access to foreign markets by avoiding trade barriers and transportation costs. Although a firm always has alternatives to FDI, such as exporting or licensing foreign firms to produce its goods, sometimes it is more cost-effective to internalize operations within the firm's command-and-control structure rather than conduct arm's-length transactions. This is especially true as telecommunications technology has improved, making the coordination of foreign operations easier.

FDI and trade are interlinked in a number of ways. Often, FDI is a substitute for exporting: firms invest in operations abroad in response to tariffs or other barriers that hinder the export of goods to those markets. But FDI and trade are also complementary. In 1994 reported intrafirm trade—the cross-border transactions between affiliated units of multinational companies—accounted for one-third of U.S. exports and two-fifths of U.S. imports of goods. An understanding of the large and growing role of FDI in modern trade

250

patterns may be useful in assessing the benefits of this important aspect of our integrating world economy.

As the importance of international direct investment has increased, countries have moved to negotiate a set of rules for FDI along the lines of those for trade. Unfortunately, many misunderstandings remain regarding FDI, which threaten to hinder these efforts (Box 7-5). Before reporting on the progress of these efforts, this section reviews recent trends in FDI flows and the ways in which both the home and the host country benefit from FDI.

Box 7-5.—Fears and Facts about Foreign Direct Investment

In the 1980s concerns arose in the United States that the rapid rise in inward FDI would have adverse effects on American workers. Some feared that foreign-controlled affiliates that displaced U.S. firms might change the composition of employment, moving "good" jobs to the home country and offering only "bad" jobs in the United States. In fact, foreign multinationals in the United States pay higher than average wages, suggesting that in fact they provide good jobs. When net FDI flows turned outward during the 1990s, the concern became that U.S. companies would begin outsourcing much of their production to other countries, again at the expense of jobs and wages at home. This seeming contradiction—that inward and outward FDI would have similar effects on U.S. workers—may reflect how little was actually known about the effects of FDI.

Unlike trade, which has been the subject of study for hundreds of years, FDI has been subjected to little rigorous study until recently. As more has been learned about FDI, many of these initial fears have subsided. The following are some fears that have been recently expressed about FDI, and the facts that we now know.

Fear: Won't U.S. industries leave for low-wage developing countries?

Fact: During the NAFTA debate, some voiced concern that lowering barriers to investment in Mexico would result in a large movement of U.S. industry there, as firms exploited low Mexican wages. But since the passage of NAFTA in 1993, Mexico's share of the U.S. outward FDI position has decreased. The reason there has been no mass exodus of U.S. industry to Mexico or to other low-wage countries is simple: there is no free lunch—for multinationals as for the rest of us. Real wages may vary significantly across countries, but studies show that these differences are linked to productivity differences, just as economic theory would predict. Low wages are not a sufficient reason to move production to a foreign country, if low pro

---

Box 7-5.—*continued*

ductivity there raises the labor cost per unit of output to a level close to that of the United States. The vast majority of U.S. FDI continues to be with other high-wage countries, so clearly other motivations than the potential for low-wage outsourcing are behind the greater part of FDI.

Fear: Are U.S. firms that invest abroad exporting jobs?

Fact: It may seem reasonable to suppose that a U.S. firm that hires workers in an overseas affiliate is contributing to U.S. unemployment, since the firm could be hiring U.S. workers to do the same job here. Evidence shows, however, that generally this is not the case: increases in employment in foreign affiliates of U.S. firms are often associated with increases in employment at the parent as well. What employment substitution there is seems to be occurring entirely offshore, between countries competing for U.S. FDI, not between U.S. parents and their foreign affiliates. Far from exporting jobs, it appears that creating jobs overseas creates jobs at home as well.

Fear: Doesn't U.S. FDI abroad represent domestic investment forgone?

Fact: With the surge in outward FDI in recent years, FDI outflows now amount to more than 10 percent of gross private nonresidential fixed investment. However, when a U.S. firm invests abroad, that does not necessarily mean it would have invested here instead if FDI had not been an option. It might then have chosen not to invest at all. Moreover, two-thirds of recorded outflows in 1996 were actually the reinvested earnings of foreign affiliates, not capital originating in the United States. Considering only actual capital outflows, a recent study estimated that outward FDI averaged only 0.9 percent of nonresidential fixed investment between 1970 and 1990—and the share has been trending downward. Capital outflows are also largely compensated by foreign investment inflows. Evidence suggests that a complementarity may exist between the investment decisions of domestic and foreign firms, which would imply that reciprocal direct investment between the United States and other industrial countries increases total investment in all countries that participate.

In short, opponents of FDI have incorrectly framed it as a zero-sum venture, where for one country to gain, another must lose. Both the theoretical arguments of the benefits of FDI and the evidence now available suggest that FDI can provide net gains for all parties.

CURRENT TRENDS IN FDI

The United States remains both the largest source of and the largest host to FDI in the world. Throughout most of the postwar period the United States has been a net direct investor overseas, with FDI outflows exceeding inflows (Chart 7-10). However, in 1981 the balance of U.S. FDI flows turned inward for the first time, led by a large expansion of investment in the United States by Japanese and U.K. firms. This direct investment by foreign firms in the United States grew rapidly throughout the 1980s, peaked in 1989, and then dropped sharply in the early 1990s. Investment abroad by U.S. firms has increased tremendously in the 1990s, so that since 1991 the balance of FDI flows has once again been outward. These trends continue: in the first three quarters of 1997, FDI outflows in the balance of payments accounts rose to $94 billion, $14 billion more than inflows and already surpassing the level for all of 1996 ($88 billion).

By 1996 the cumulative direct investment position of foreign firms in the United States (the inward FDI stock), measured on a historical cost basis, had reached $630 billion, an increase of 60 percent since 1990. There are some accepted problems in measuring FDI precisely. U.S. balance of payments accounting rules define FDI as financial flows from a parent company to an overseas affiliate in which it has at least 10 percent ownership. Thus, investment in foreign affiliates not financed directly by the parent company is excluded. In addition, historical cost positions are measured at the book value of purchases each year and therefore do not adjust for capital gains (including those due to inflation). Estimates that attempt to adjust for increases in the market value of assets are almost double the 1996 historical cost measure. However, historical cost measurements do indicate the distributional changes of FDI across countries and sectors.

More than half of the reported FDI stock in the United States has come from three countries: the United Kingdom holds the largest share, followed by Japan and the Netherlands. The United Kingdom is also the largest host to U.S. direct investment abroad, followed by Canada. European countries are host to half of the stock of U.S. investment abroad. In 1996 U.S. firms directly controlled overseas assets of $797 billion, again valued at historical cost; member countries of the OECD were home to over 73 percent of this investment. Much of the rest was in Bermuda, the Caribbean, and some Asian newly industrializing economies such as Hong Kong; this investment is concentrated in sectors such as wholesale trade, finance, real estate, and services. China, the second-largest host to worldwide FDI, still represents only a negligible share of U.S. direct investment abroad. However, between 1992 and 1996 the U.S. position in China increased at an average rate of 50 percent per year. FDI in other

Asian developing countries has been increasing as well; however, the majority of growth has come from investment in the higher income economies that are still host to 75 percent of U.S. FDI in the region.

Among developing countries, Brazil, Mexico, and Panama are the largest hosts to recorded U.S. FDI. Annual FDI flows to these countries represent about 10 percent of the total, but the stock of U.S. FDI in all of Latin America is still less than 12 percent of the total U.S. position abroad. Nevertheless, the brightening economic prospects in Latin America have been accompanied by a pronounced expansion of the U.S. direct investment position in the region. The emerging markets there are poised to become increasingly important to U.S. investors in the future, especially if investment barriers are liberalized under the proposed Free Trade Area of the Americas.

Although wages are lower in developing countries, these do not always entail the cost advantages many people assume (Box 7-5). Rather, the developing countries that receive the most FDI are usually those regarded as potentially large future markets. This suggests that companies investing in these countries hope to establish a market presence, in the expectation of profitable future sales, and are not simply outsourcing production for reexport to other markets.

Although the public image of FDI in the United States is often one of large manufacturing multinationals, manufacturing accounts for only one-third of both the inward and the outward FDI stock. Much FDI in manufacturing occurs in motor vehicles, electronic and electrical equipment, office machines and computers, and chemicals and allied products. In 1996 these sectors accounted for over half of both the U.S. FDI position abroad in manufacturing and almost half of the foreign position in the United States (Table 7-3).

The industrial composition of U.S. FDI has evolved in tandem with that of the U.S. economy. Much of U.S. outward FDI in past decades was motivated by the opportunity to use U.S. technology to extract foreign raw material resources such as oil, coal, and natural gas: in 1980 the petroleum industry accounted for roughly 22 percent of the outward U.S. FDI position. But this share has been falling steadily, and in 1996 the figure was less than 10 percent. Between 1980 and 1990 FDI became associated with the relocation of manufacturing activities abroad, in part because of the rapid expansion of foreign firms in the U.S. manufacturing sector. More recently, a growing share of FDI is in service industries—primarily finance, insurance, and real estate but also wholesale and retail trade and banking—mirroring the evolution of the U.S. economy from a manufacturing to a services economy. In 1996 service industries accounted for 52 percent of the U.S. position abroad, exceeding the share of the entire manufacturing sector. However, these figures may overstate the role of services, which include sectors such as finance where large holdings of "paper assets" are the norm.

TABLE 7-3.—*Inward and Outward Foreign Direct Investment, by Industry, Selected Years*

[Billions of dollars]

Industry	U.S. direct investment abroad			Foreign direct investment in the United States		
	1980	1990	1996	1980	1990	1996
Petroleum	47.6	52.8	75.5	12.2	42.9	42.3
Manufacturing	89.3	170.2	272.6	33.0	152.8	234.3
Food and kindred products	8.3	15.6	36.2	4.9	22.5	28.1
Chemicals and allied products	18.9	38.0	69.4	10.4	45.7	74.8
Primary and fabricated metals	6.3	10.5	13.6	3.6	13.7	18.7
Industrial machinery and equipment	16.1	30.9	35.0	2.9	11.5	16.3
Office and computing machines	9.3	22.2	21.7	.4	2.6	2.7
Electronic and other electric equipment	7.3	15.6	29.5	4.1	16.1	20.8
Motor vehicles and equipment	11.8	20.4	31.6	.7	3.1	12.3
Other manufacturing	20.6	39.3	57.2	6.4	40.1	63.3
Services	66.3	194.5	410.7	34.4	179.6	323.6
Wholesale and retail trade	25.9	50.7	84.3	15.2	60.2	92.9
Banking	7.3	20.7	32.5	4.6	18.4	31.9
Finance (excluding banking), insurance, and real estate ..	27.5	109.7	257.2	13.5	70.4	159.9
Other services	5.6	13.4	36.7	1.1	30.6	38.9
Other industries	12.2	13.1	37.7	3.4	19.6	29.7
Communications and public utilities	1.3	4.4	20.4	.1	3.3	11.4
All industries	215.4	430.5	796.5	83.0	394.9	630.0

Note.—Detail may not add to totals because of rounding.
Source: Department of Commerce (Bureau of Economic Analysis).

Employment in foreign-owned U.S. affiliates rose from 2 million in 1980 to almost 5 million in 1995. This represents an average annual increase of more than 6 percent, over three times the rate of growth in nonfarm U.S. employment over the same period, and led to an increase in the share of U.S. private industry employment in foreign-controlled firms from less than 3 percent to 5 percent of total employment. The share of private industry GDP accounted for by foreign-owned U.S. affiliates has increased from 3 percent in 1980 to 6 percent in 1995. However, these increases largely represent growth during the 1980s and early 1990s; in fact, by both measures the foreign presence in U.S. industry has been constant or decreasing in recent years.

THE BENEFITS OF FDI

The benefits of FDI to the economy as a whole seem less clear than the benefits of trade. Yet in a world where trade results from differences in relative factor abundance, capital mobility should act as a substitute for trade. This corresponds with the notion that FDI occurs in response to trade barriers and suggests that capital flows have welfare implications similar to those of trade. Capital mobility can also have macroeconomic benefits by relaxing the tradeoff between investment and consumption. However, the benefits of FDI go beyond increased capital mobility: FDI has direct impacts on both the host and the home countries that have little in common with other types of international investment, such as portfolio asset flows.

Benefits to the Host Country

The nature of the benefits of FDI to the host country is likely to depend on whether the country is developed or developing, and on the reasons why FDI is taking place. FDI in the higher income countries is often a response to market access concerns. By establishing operations closer to customers, a firm may be able to increase the quality of support services and the ability to match products to local tastes. The presence of multinationals also entails all the traditional benefits of local investment, creating jobs and fostering demand from local suppliers.

When FDI occurs in developing countries, the gains from fostering demand from local industry may be even greater. "Big push" theories of industrialization emphasize that the profitability to a single firm of adopting new technological advances often depends on other firms' decisions to do likewise. For example, an automobile assembly plant requires dependable suppliers of parts and machinery, but these are not likely to exist locally if no automobile plants exist. In this scenario the gap between developed and developing countries occurs because the former have managed to overcome this coordination problem. By internalizing such transactions, often by using already established global supply networks, multinationals can overcome the coordination problem and provide the first step toward industrialization in a developing country.

FDI may have additional advantages in developing countries, particularly over portfolio investment. The ability to own a foreign firm directly rather than through passive stock holdings may increase the incentive to invest in countries that offer attractive opportunities but little domestic entrepreneurial experience. Furthermore, since the commitments involved in direct ownership imply greater adjustment costs than under stock ownership when conditions turn unfavorable, FDI can create a more stable investment atmosphere by discouraging capital flight like that which plagued developing economies in Southeast Asia in 1997. When investors are forced to weather financial storms, a country's market volatility and macroeconomic instability are reduced, and this may help the storms pass more quickly.

Lastly, through direct control of their affiliates, multinationals provide crucial links in the international dissemination of technology and best practices. This promotes more efficient production and resource use in home countries and rising incomes throughout the world. The recent literature on economic growth emphasizes the

256

importance of an expanding common pool of ideas in increasing growth rates in all countries. As new trade and investment agreements are negotiated to strengthen global intellectual property rights, these transfers of knowledge can proceed without destroying the incentive to innovate or sacrificing the profitability of innovating firms. FDI is frequently shown to be an important vehicle for increasing productivity in host countries, in some cases contributing relatively more to growth than does domestic investment. Although developing countries that now employ outdated technologies may have the most to gain from new ideas brought in by foreign multinationals, they are not the only beneficiaries. The resurgent competitiveness of the U.S. automotive industry in the 1990s is often attributed in part to the adoption of just-in-time inventory practices used successfully by Japanese production facilities located in the United States.

Benefits to the Home Country

It might seem natural that foreign investment helps foreigners, but what is less apparent is that the activities of multinationals can promote growth in their home countries as well (see Box 7-5). By developing and expanding foreign markets, multinationals provide an important benefit to the home country, because growth in a country's trade partners means growth in its export opportunities. And in many cases, as firms expand their operations overseas, they expand their management and support operations at home also, increasing employment both at home and abroad.

Moreover, multinationals create trade by moving goods and services between parents and their foreign affiliates. As already noted, this intrafirm trade now plays a significant role in total U.S. trade. Although the move from arm's-length to intrafirm transactions need not represent "new" trade, evidence suggests that FDI is likely to increase trade. This can be considered a benefit in itself, by promoting the interchange of goods. FDI often plays an important role in promoting trade when barriers to traditional exports exist. A recent study shows that, in 1992, 70 percent of U.S. exports to Japan were intrafirm exports, as were 74 percent of exports to Switzerland and 64 percent to Russia. By contrast, only 12 percent of U.S. exports to Taiwan, our seventh-largest foreign market, were intrafirm exports.

Arguably, intrafirm trade might not be beneficial if it represents the foreign outsourcing of goods for production and reexport to the home country. If this were the case, we might expect to see an intrafirm trade deficit equal to the amount of value added overseas. But U.S. intrafirm trade is in surplus: U.S. multinationals export more to their overseas affiliates than they import from them. This suggests that, on balance, shipments to foreign affiliates represent goods to be sold in the overseas market (perhaps after final assembly there) rather than outsourcing for reexport. In a rapidly changing world environment, firms hoping to enter foreign markets are increasingly coming to realize that establishing a direct presence in those markets may be the best way to compete.

CURRENT U.S. INITIATIVES IN INVESTMENT POLICY

Evidence has shown that a stable policy environment is a good determinant of the amount of FDI a country attracts. Countries that are prone to nationalization, corruption, and political instability are less likely to receive foreign investment, whereas those that protect foreign investors and intellectual property rights do better. This suggests that there are benefits to achieving multilateral standards for investment rules.

Under the auspices of the OECD, the United States has joined other countries in negotiations toward a Multilateral Agreement on Investment (MAI) that will set "high standards for the liberalization of investment regimes and investment protection...with effective dispute settlement procedures." The goal is to eliminate discrimination in investment by achieving a uniform set of rules for all signatories, thereby removing market distortions and facilitating the investment process.

The MAI is being negotiated principally among the 29 OECD countries that account for the vast majority of worldwide FDI flows. But the MAI is being designed as a free-standing international treaty to which other nations may accede. Even though the negotiations are primarily among similar countries with similar objectives, the negotiations have been difficult at times.

Meanwhile over 1,000 bilateral investment treaties already exist, primarily between developed and developing countries. The United States has signed 40 such treaties to date (Box 7-6). With these treaties the United States has been able to establish deeper agreements more quickly with more countries than it could by negotiating a single agreement with a large number of countries.

Another recent initiative in which the United States has been active is the international effort to combat corruption. Corruption is a particularly thorny problem for multinationals in many developing countries, and its presence may offset much of the benefit to multinationals of locating in those countries. One recent study estimated that the effects of corruption were equivalent to an increase in the marginal tax rate for foreign investors of as much as 21 percentage points. Given the benefits of FDI to both home and host countries, this strong disincentive to investment is likely to reduce the welfare of both. It has also had important legal ramifications for U.S. investors abroad, who are prohibited under the Foreign Corrupt Practices Act from bribing foreign officials. This legislation has made it even more difficult for U.S. multinationals to establish and maintain businesses in countries with pervasive corruption.

Box 7-6.—Bilateral Investment Treaties

For much of the last decade the United States has been actively pursuing the negotiation of bilateral investment treaties with emerging-market countries around the world. The U.S. government places priority on negotiating such treaties with countries undergoing economic reform where it believes the United States can have a significant impact on the adoption of liberal policies on the treatment of FDI. The structure of these treaties has also laid the policy groundwork for broader multicountry initiatives in the OECD (the MAI) and eventually the WTO. The structure of our bilateral investment treaties provides U.S. investors with the following six basic guarantees:

- treatment that is as favorable as that received by their competitors—this implies the better of national or most-favored-nation treatment
- clear limits on the expropriation of investments, and fair compensation when expropriation does occur
- the right to transfer all funds related to an investment into and out of the country without delay, at the market rate of exchange
- limits on the ability of the host government to impose inefficient and trade-distorting performance requirements
- the right to submit an investment dispute with the host government to international arbitration
- the right of U.S. investors to engage the top managerial personnel of their choice, regardless of nationality.

In cases where national treatment is the binding standard, the treaty ensures that U.S. investors are treated in a manner equivalent to domestic investors; where it is most-favored-nation treatment, U.S. investors are assured treatment no worse than investors from any third country receive. To date, the United States has successfully negotiated bilateral investment treaties with some 40 countries (Table 7-4) and is actively engaged in pursuing a multilateral version of the treaty under the auspices of the OECD.

TABLE 7-4.—*Countries with Which the United States Has Bilateral Investment Treaties*

Country and date	Country and date	Country and date	Country and date
Albania .... pending	Croatia .... pending	Jordan .... pending	Romania 1994
Argentina 1994	Czech Republic 1992	Kazakhstan 1994	Russia .... pending
Armenia 1996	Ecuador 1997	Kyrgyzstan 1994	Senegal 1990
Azerbaijan .... pending	Egypt 1992	Latvia 1996	Slovakia 1992
Bangladesh 1989	Estonia 1997	Moldova 1994	Sri Lanka 1993
Belarus .... pending	Georgia 1997	Mongolia 1997	Trinidad and Tobago 1996
Bulgaria 1994	Grenada 1989	Morocco 1991	Tunisia 1993
Cameroon 1989	Haiti .... pending	Nicaragua .... pending	Turkey 1990
Congo (Brazzaville) 1994	Honduras .... pending	Panama 1991	Ukraine 1996
Congo (Kinshasa) 1989	Jamaica 1997	Poland 1994	Uzbekistan .... pending

Note.—Years are those when the treaty entered into force.
Source: Office of the U.S. Trade Representative.

In late 1997 the member countries of the OECD finalized a draft treaty to outlaw bribery of foreign public officials. Holding multinationals of all nationalities to similar standards will put pressure on foreign officials to abide by legal and transparent procedures in doing business with foreign companies, rather than allow them to promote a "race to the ethical bottom" among companies seeking government contracts or licensing. It is hoped that, together with the establishment of a common set of investment rules in the MAI, the reduction of corruption abroad will act as an incentive to FDI, bringing increased benefits to both home and host countries worldwide.

CONCLUSION

Economies that are open to international trade and investment are more likely to experience a rising standard of living than are economies with significant barriers to cross-border economic activities. Consumers in open economies benefit from a wider variety of goods at lower prices than do consumers in economies that resist competition from foreign suppliers. The economy as a whole benefits from an increased ability to devote its scarce resources to economic activities that it performs relatively efficiently. Over time, through both international trade and international investment, open economies benefit from higher rates of productivity growth and innovation that result from increased participation in international markets.

Many, however, fear that international transactions will disadvantage certain segments of the economy. As this chapter has shown, it is difficult to associate cross-border interactions with declining real wages of workers, or even of particular groups of workers. Indeed, there is evidence that adjustments resulting from growth in international trade have the potential to make workers better off. In the United States, jobs with exporting firms pay between 5 percent and 10 percent more than do jobs in other sectors of the economy. At the same time, the Administration recognizes that the transition from one job to another is not always easy and that assistance must be provided to those most affected by displacement.

As the United States is already among the most open economies in the world, the Administration's activities have been directed toward opening foreign markets to imports not only from the United States but from other exporters as well. This goal has been actively and successfully pursued in multilateral, regional, and bilateral forums. Partly reflecting these pursuits, U.S. imports and exports have increased significantly since 1993. Although much has been accomplished, the Administration maintains an active international policy agenda promoting free trade throughout the Americas, across the Pacific, and around the world.

Appendix A
REPORT TO THE PRESIDENT ON THE ACTIVITIES
OF THE
COUNCIL OF ECONOMIC ADVISERS DURING 1997

LETTER OF TRANSMITTAL

COUNCIL OF ECONOMIC ADVISERS
Washington, D.C., December 31, 1997

MR. PRESIDENT:

The Council of Economic Advisers submits this report on its activities during the calendar year 1997 in accordance with the requirements of the Congress, as set forth in section 10(d) of the Employment Act of 1946 as amended by the Full Employment and Balanced Growth Act of 1978.

Sincerely,

Janet L. Yellen, *Chair*

Jeffrey A. Frankel, *Member*

Rebecca M. Blank, *Member-Nominee*

Council Members and Their Dates of Service

Name	Position	Oath of office date	Separation date
Edwin G. Nourse	Chairman	August 9, 1946	November 1, 1949.
Leon H. Keyserling	Vice Chairman	August 9, 1946	
	Acting Chairman	November 2, 1949	
	Chairman	May 10, 1950	January 20, 1953.
John D. Clark	Member	August 9, 1946	
	Vice Chairman	May 10, 1950	February 11, 1953.
Roy Blough	Member	June 29, 1950	August 20, 1952.
Robert C. Turner	Member	September 8, 1952	January 20, 1953.
Arthur F. Burns	Chairman	March 19, 1953	December 1, 1956.
Neil H. Jacoby	Member	September 15, 1953	February 9, 1955.
Walter W. Stewart	Member	December 2, 1953	April 29, 1955.
Raymond J. Saulnier	Member	April 4, 1955	
	Chairman	December 3, 1956	January 20, 1961.
Joseph S. Davis	Member	May 2, 1955	October 31, 1958.
Paul W. McCracken	Member	December 3, 1956	January 31, 1959.
Karl Brandt	Member	November 1, 1958	January 20, 1961.
Henry C. Wallich	Member	May 7, 1959	January 20, 1961.
Walter W. Heller	Chairman	January 29, 1961	November 15, 1964.
James Tobin	Member	January 29, 1961	July 31, 1962.
Kermit Gordon	Member	January 29, 1961	December 27, 1962.
Gardner Ackley	Member	August 3, 1962	
	Chairman	November 16, 1964	February 15, 1968.
John P. Lewis	Member	May 17, 1963	August 31, 1964.
Otto Eckstein	Member	September 2, 1964	February 1, 1966.
Arthur M. Okun	Member	November 16, 1964	
	Chairman	February 15, 1968	January 20, 1969.
James S. Duesenberry	Member	February 2, 1966	June 30, 1968.
Merton J. Peck	Member	February 15, 1968	January 20, 1969.
Warren L. Smith	Member	July 1, 1968	January 20, 1969.
Paul W. McCracken	Chairman	February 4, 1969	December 31, 1971.
Hendrik S. Houthakker	Member	February 4, 1969	July 15, 1971.
Herbert Stein	Member	February 4, 1969	
	Chairman	January 1, 1972	August 31, 1974.
Ezra Solomon	Member	September 9, 1971	March 26, 1973.
Marina v.N. Whitman	Member	March 13, 1972	August 15, 1973.
Gary L. Seevers	Member	July 23, 1973	April 15, 1975.
William J. Fellner	Member	October 31, 1973	February 25, 1975.
Alan Greenspan	Chairman	September 4, 1974	January 20, 1977.
Paul W. MacAvoy	Member	June 13, 1975	November 15, 1976.
Burton G. Malkiel	Member	July 22, 1975	January 20, 1977.
Charles L. Schultze	Chairman	January 22, 1977	January 20, 1981.
William D. Nordhaus	Member	March 18, 1977	February 4, 1979.
Lyle E. Gramley	Member	March 18, 1977	May 27, 1980.
George C. Eads	Member	June 6, 1979	January 20, 1981.
Stephen M. Goldfeld	Member	August 20, 1980	January 20, 1981.
Murray L. Weidenbaum	Chairman	February 27, 1981	August 25, 1982.
William A. Niskanen	Member	June 12, 1981	March 30, 1985.
Jerry L. Jordan	Member	July 14, 1981	July 31, 1982.
Martin Feldstein	Chairman	October 14, 1982	July 10, 1984.
William Poole	Member	December 10, 1982	January 20, 1985.
Beryl W. Sprinkel	Chairman	April 18, 1985	January 20, 1989.
Thomas Gale Moore	Member	July 1, 1985	May 1, 1989.
Michael L. Mussa	Member	August 18, 1986	September 19, 1988.
Michael J. Boskin	Chairman	February 2, 1989	January 12, 1993.
John B. Taylor	Member	June 9, 1989	August 2, 1991.
Richard L. Schmalensee	Member	October 3, 1989	June 21, 1991.
David F. Bradford	Member	November 13, 1991	January 20, 1993.
Paul Wonnacott	Member	November 13, 1991	January 20, 1993.
Laura D'Andrea Tyson	Chair	February 5, 1993	April 22, 1995.
Alan S. Blinder	Member	July 27, 1993	June 26, 1994.
Joseph E. Stiglitz	Member	July 27, 1993	
	Chairman	June 28, 1995	February 10, 1997.
Martin N. Baily	Member	June 30, 1995	August 30, 1996.
Alicia H. Munnell	Member	January 29, 1996	August 1, 1997.
Janet L. Yellen	Chair	February 18, 1997	
Jeffrey A. Frankel	Member	April 23, 1997	

264

Report to the President on the Activities of the Council of Economic Advisers During 1997

The Council of Economic Advisers was established by the Employment Act of 1946 to provide the President with objective economic analysis and advice on the development and implementation of a wide range of domestic and international economic policy issues.

The Chair of the Council

Janet L. Yellen was appointed Chair on February 18, 1997. Dr. Yellen replaced Joseph E. Stiglitz, who left the Council to become Senior Vice President of Development Economics and Chief Economist of the World Bank. Before becoming Chair of the Council, Dr. Yellen served as a Member of the Board of Governors of the Federal Reserve System. Dr. Yellen is on leave from the Haas School of Business at the University of California, Berkeley, where she is the Bernard T. Rocca, Jr. Professor of International Business and Trade. Dr. Yellen is responsible for communicating the Council's views on economic matters directly to the President through personal discussions and written reports. Dr. Yellen also represents the Council at Cabinet meetings, meetings of the National Economic Council (NEC), daily White House senior staff meetings, budget team meetings with the President, and other formal and informal meetings with the President, senior White House staff, and other senior government officials. Dr. Yellen is the Council's chief public spokesperson. She directs the work of the Council and exercises ultimate responsibility for the work of the professional staff.

The Members of the Council

Jeffrey A. Frankel is a Member of the Council of Economic Advisers. Dr. Frankel is on leave from the University of California, Berkeley, where he is Professor of Economics. He previously directed the program on International Finance and Macroeconomics at the National Bureau of Economic Research and is a former Senior Fellow at the Institute for International Economics.

Alicia H. Munnell was a Member of the Council of Economic Advisers until August 1997. Dr. Munnell currently holds the Peter F. Drucker Chair in Management Sciences at Boston College's Carroll School of Management. The President has nominated Rebecca M. Blank to succeed Dr. Munnell as a Member of the Council. While awaiting confirmation, Dr. Blank has been serving as Chief Economist. She is on leave from Northwestern University, where she is Professor of Economics. Dr. Blank previously served as the first Director of the Northwestern University/University of Chicago Joint Center for Poverty Research and was a faculty affiliate at Northwestern University's Institute for Policy Research.

The Chair and Members work as a team on most economic policy issues. Dr. Frankel and Dr. Munnell shared responsibility for domestic macroeconomic analysis, the Administration's economic forecast, and budget and tax issues. Dr. Frankel is primarily responsible for international economic issues and certain microeconomic issues, including those relating to natural resources, the environment, and industrial organization. Dr. Munnell was primarily responsible for retirement, health care, welfare reform, and labor issues. Dr. Blank has taken over responsibility for these issues. She is also responsible for child and family policy issues and is working closely with the President's Initiative on Race. The Chair and Members participate in the deliberations of the NEC, and Dr. Yellen is a member of the NEC Principals Committee.

WEEKLY ECONOMIC BRIEFINGS

Dr. Yellen and the Members continued during 1997 to conduct a weekly economic briefing for the President, the Vice President, and the President's other senior economic and policy advisers. The Council, in cooperation with the Office of the Vice President, prepares a written *Weekly Economic Briefing of the President,* which provides analysis of current economic developments, more extended discussions of a wide range of economic issues and problems, and summaries of economic developments in different regions and sectors of the economy. This document serves as a basis for the oral economic briefing of the President.

MACROECONOMIC POLICIES

A primary function of the Council is to advise the President on all major macroeconomic issues and developments. The Council prepares for the President, the Vice President, and the White House senior staff almost daily memoranda that report key economic data and analyze current economic events.

The Council, the Department of the Treasury, and the Office of Management and Budget—the Administration's economic "troika"—are responsible for producing the economic forecast that underlies the Administration's budget proposals. The Council, under the leadership of the Members, initiates the forecasting process twice each year. In preparing these forecasts, the Council consults with a variety of outside sources, including leading private sector forecasters.

In 1997 the Council continued to take part in discussions about the President's balanced budget plan. The Council also participated in meetings on a range of budget issues including Medicare reform, discretionary spending priorities, and the Administration's tax proposals. The Council participated in discussions regarding proposals to strengthen the Social Security system, and in an interagency effort to develop a package of proposed reforms to the private pension system to promote higher rates of national saving and greater retirement security.

The Council participates in the Working Group on Financial Markets, an interagency group that monitors developments related to financial markets and the banking sector. The group includes representatives from the Treasury, the Federal Reserve, the NEC, and various regulatory agencies.

The Council continued its efforts to improve the public's understanding of economic issues and the Administration's economic agenda through regular briefings with the economic and financial press, frequent discussions with outside economists, and presentations to outside organizations. Drs. Yellen, Frankel, Munnell, and Blank also regularly exchanged views on the macroeconomy with the Chairman and Members of the Board of Governors of the Federal Reserve System.

INTERNATIONAL ECONOMIC POLICIES

The Council was an active participant in 1997 in the international economic policymaking process through the NEC and the National Security Council, providing both technical and analytical support and policy guidance. In particular, the Council has helped assess the economic impact of international sanctions against foreign nations, and the efficacy of relaxing restrictions in the U.S.-Japan civil aviation market. The Council has taken an active role on a range of other international economic issues, including evaluating and explaining the case for trade liberalization, the Administration's policy approach to Asia's financial turmoil, U.S. trade remedy laws (antidumping, countervailing duties, safeguards, and Section 301 actions), and the agendas of multilateral and regional forums such as the World Trade Organization, the Asia-Pacific Economic Cooperation forum, and the proposed Free Trade Area of the Americas.

The Council played a significant role in preparing both the Administration's *1997 Study on the Operation and Effects of the North American Free Trade Agreement* and the 1997 *APEC Economic Outlook*. The *Weekly Economic Briefing of the President* also regularly included articles on international events and issues.

Because of the growing importance of international economic issues to the U.S. economy, the Council often represents the United States at international meetings and forums. In November Dr. Yellen gave the keynote address at the U.S.-R.O.C. Economic Council Plenary Session. Also in November Dr. Frankel participated in the annual meeting of the APEC Senior Economic Advisers, a meeting initiated in 1996 by the Council during the APEC Leaders Summit. At this meeting Dr. Frankel presented a Council paper on the long-term determinants of growth. In December Dr. Frankel participated in the Joint Economic Development Group with Israel. The Council also continued annual meetings with the Economic Planning Agency of Japan and the State Planning Commission of China, the Council's counterparts in those countries.

The Council is a leading U.S. participant in the Organization for Economic Cooperation and Development (OECD), the principal forum for economic cooperation among the high-income industrial countries. The Council heads the U.S. delegation to the semiannual meetings of the OECD's Economic Policy Committee; Dr. Yellen serves as that committee's chair. In 1997 Dr. Frankel participated in Working Party 3 on macroeconomic policy coordination. Dr. Steven N. Braun, Director, Macroeconomic Forecasting at the Council, led the U.S. delegation to the OECD annual examination of the United States, and to the Short-term Economic Forecasters' Meeting. Dr. Christopher Carroll, Senior Economist at the Council, led the U.S. delegation to the Working Party 1 meeting on structural issues.

MICROECONOMIC POLICIES

During 1997 the Council was an active participant in a range of microeconomic policy discussions. The Council participated in various interagency policy discussions on labor market issues, health care, education, child care, and welfare reform; in the development of the Child Health Insurance Program; in interagency discussions of proposals to increase health insurance coverage for older workers; and in a working group investigating alternative measures of poverty. The Council also participated in working groups on the minimum wage, training initiatives for displaced workers, and unemployment insurance reform.

The Council has been actively involved in the President's Initiative on Race and is coordinating production of a document that will present important indicators of social and economic well-being by race and ethnicity for use by a national audience including educators and policymakers.

In May the Council issued a report titled *Explaining the Decline in Welfare Receipt, 1993 to 1996.* The report examined the causes of the 20-percent decline (2.75 million recipients) in the welfare caseload that took place between 1993 and 1996 and concluded that roughly 40 percent of the decline was due to the stronger economy, roughly 30 percent to welfare reform policies, and the remainder to other factors such as the earned income tax credit.

The Council was involved in White House conferences on early childhood development and child care. In conjunction with the early childhood development conference, the Council released a white paper titled *The First Three Years: Investments That Pay*. This report documented the importance of programs to encourage children's development in the first 3 years of life and the high long-term payoff of such investments.

As a follow-up to the White House child care conference, the Council issued a report titled *The Economics of Child Care*. This report reviewed the economics literature regarding the availability, cost, and quality of child care and the importance of policies to support access to affordable, quality care.

In the areas of regulation and competition policy, the Council helped develop important Administration initiatives to improve the performance of markets, both domestically and internationally. On the domestic front the Council took part in interagency efforts to increase competition in electric power markets in a manner consistent with important environmental and social objectives. The Council contributed to the Administration's analysis of whether and how much to reform product liability law, and to discussions of the Federal Communications Commission's methods for pricing telecommunications services. The Council also worked with the Federal Trade Commission, the Department of Justice, and the Department of the Treasury to consider questions raised by the proposed industry-wide tobacco settlement. In addition, the Council worked with the Treasury, the Department of Education, and the Office of Management and Budget to develop reforms of the college financial aid system to make it fairer and more efficient.

With respect to international regulation and competition policy, the Council cooperated with the Department of State and other agencies to bring more competition to the satellite communications industry, to support the OECD's adoption of principles for economically sound regulation, to promote efficient infrastructure development in the Asia-Pacific region, and to coordinate merger policy with the European Union.

The Council was also active in a range of policy discussions on natural resources and the environment. The Council took part in the interagency evaluation of National Ambient Air Quality Standards for ozone and particulate matter under the Clean Air Act and the implementation plans for the revised standards. The Council was actively involved in the development and analysis of the Administration's global climate change policy.

The Staff of the Council of Economic Advisers

The professional staff of the Council consists of the Chief of Staff, the Senior Statistician, 11 senior economists, 5 staff economists, and 3 research assistants. The professional staff and their areas of concentration at the end of 1997 were:

Chief of Staff and General Counsel

Michele M. Jolin

Senior Economists

Steven N. Braun	Director, Macroeconomic Forecasting
Christopher D. Carroll	Macroeconomics and Aging
Aaron S. Edlin	Regulation, Industrial Organization, and Antitrust
Keith O. Fuglie	Agriculture and Natural Resources
Maria J. Hanratty	Health Care and Labor
Jon D. Haveman	International Economics
Sanders D. Korenman	Labor, Welfare, and Education
Randall W. Lutter	Regulation and Environment
Adele C. Morris	Environment and Natural Resources
Jeremy B. Rudd	Macroeconomics
Charles F. Stone	Macroeconomics and Editor, *Weekly Economic Briefing of the President*

Senior Statistician

Catherine H. Furlong

Staff Economists

Joseph E. Aldy	Environment and Natural Resources
Amy N. Finkelstein	Labor and Public Finance
Mark R. Hopkins	International Economics
Mark C. Rainey	Industrial Organization and Regulation
Sarah J. Reber	Health Care and Environment

Senior Research Assistant

Ha Yan Lee............................	Macroeconomics

Research Assistants

Zachary M. Candelario..........	*Weekly Economic Briefing of the President,* Labor, and Environment
Daniel K. Chang	*Weekly Economic Briefing of the President* and International Economics

Statistical Office

Mrs. Furlong directs the Statistical Office. The Statistical Office maintains and updates the Council's statistical information, oversees the publication of the monthly *Economic Indicators* and the statistical appendix to the *Economic Report,* and verifies statistics in Presidential and Council memoranda, testimony, and speeches.

Susan P. Clements	Statistician
Linda A. Reilly	Statistician
Brian A. Amorosi	Research Assistant

Administrative Officer

Catherine Fibich

Office of the Chairman

Alice H. Williams	Executive Assistant to the Chairman
Sandra F. Daigle	Executive Assistant to the Chairman and Assistant to the Chief of Staff
Lisa D. Branch	Executive Assistant to Dr. Frankel
Francine P. Obermiller	Executive Assistant to Dr. Blank

Staff Secretaries

Mary E. Jones	International Economics, Labor, and Health Care
Rosalind V. Rasin	Environment, Industrial Organization, and Public Finance
Mary A. Thomas	Macroeconomics

Mrs. Thomas also served as executive assistant for the *Weekly Economic Briefing of the President*.

Michael Treadway provided editorial assistance in the preparation of the 1997 *Economic Report*. Michael A. Toman, Resources for the Future, served as a consultant during the year.

Student interns during the year were Aryeh J. Aslan, Elizabeth T. Burns, Carol L. Capece, Quindi C. Franco, Robert K. Kaproth, Mark N. Levine, Jennifer A. Meyers, Andrew J. Miller, Praveen Rangnath, Katharine S. Rogers, Ravi K. Sandill, Kristen M. Scarafia, Courtney A. Sweeney, Harsh N. Trivedi, and Jennifer H. Yoon. The following student interns joined the Council in January to assist with the preparation of the *Economic Report*: Keith H. Monk, Jenny E. Pippin, and Samuel G. Steckley.

DEPARTURES

The Council's senior economists, in most cases, are on leave of absence from faculty positions at academic institutions or from other government agencies or research institutions. Their tenure with the Council is usually limited to 1 or 2 years. Most of the senior economists who left the Council during 1997 returned to their previous affiliations. They are Timothy J. Brennan (University of Maryland, Baltimore County, and Resources for the Future), William B. English (Board of Governors of the Federal Reserve System), Phillip B. Levine (Wellesley College), John D. Montgomery (International Monetary

271

Fund), Raymond Prince (Department of Energy), Christopher J. Ruhm (University of North Carolina, Greensboro), Jason F. Shogren (University of Wyoming), and David L. Sunding (University of California, Berkeley). Mark J. Mazur became Senior Policy Adviser and Chief Economist at the Department of Energy.

Staff economists are generally graduate students who spend 1 year with the Council and then return to complete their dissertations. Those who returned to their graduate studies in 1997 are Carrie S. Cihak (University of Michigan), Cynthia K. Gustafson (University of California, Berkeley), Andrea Richter (London School of Economics), Cristian J. Santesteban (Stanford University), and Caroline M. Thompson (Princeton University). Jason L. Furman accepted a position with the World Bank. Thomas A. Rhoads accepted a position with Resources for the Future and has since returned to graduate studies at the University of Wyoming. After serving as research assistants at the Council, Jennifer C. Daskal accepted a position at the Center on Budget and Policy Priorities, and Diane M. Whitmore began graduate studies at Princeton University.

Elizabeth A. Kaminski and Margaret L. Snyder retired in 1997 after serving the Council for 32 and 36 years, respectively. Mrs. Kaminski served most recently as Administrative Officer, and Mrs. Snyder retired from the Statistical Office.

Public Information

The Council's *Annual Report* is an important vehicle for presenting the Administration's domestic and international economic policies. It is now available for distribution as a bound volume, on CD-ROM, and on the Internet, where it is accessible at http://www.access.gpo.gov/eop. The Council also has primary responsibility for compiling the monthly *Economic Indicators,* which is issued by the Joint Economic Committee of the Congress. The Internet address for the *Economic Indicators* is www.access.gpo.gov/congress/cong002.html.

Appendix B
STATISTICAL TABLES RELATING TO INCOME, EMPLOYMENT, AND PRODUCTION

CONTENTS

NATIONAL INCOME OR EXPENDITURE:

275

276

General Notes

Detail in these tables may not add to totals because of rounding.

Because of the formula used for calculating real gross domestic product (GDP), the chained (1992) dollar estimates for the detailed components do not add to the chained-dollar value of GDP or to any intermediate aggregates. In addition, the Department of Commerce (Bureau of Economic Analysis) no longer publishes chained-dollar estimates prior to 1982, except for selected series. This change is reflected in these tables.

Unless otherwise noted, all dollar figures are in current dollars.

Symbols used:
     ᵖ Preliminary.
    .... Not available (also, not applicable).

Data in these tables reflect revisions made by the source agencies from February 1997 through early February 1998.

NATIONAL INCOME OR EXPENDITURE

TABLE B–1.—*Gross domestic product, 1959–97*

[BILLIONS OF DOLLARS, EXCEPT AS NOTED; QUARTERLY DATA AT SEASONALLY ADJUSTED ANNUAL RATES]

Year or quarter	Gross domestic product	Personal consumption expenditures				Gross private domestic investment							Change in business inventories
							Fixed investment						
									Nonresidential				
		Total	Durable goods	Non-durable goods	Serv-ices	Total	Total	Total	Struc-tures	Pro-ducers' durable equip-ment	Resi-dential		
1959	507.2	318.1	42.7	148.5	127.0	78.8	74.6	46.5	18.1	28.3	28.1		4.2
1960	526.6	332.2	43.3	152.9	136.0	78.8	75.5	49.2	19.6	29.7	26.3		3.2
1961	544.8	342.6	41.8	156.6	144.3	77.9	75.0	48.6	19.7	28.9	26.4		2.9
1962	585.2	363.4	46.9	162.8	153.7	87.9	81.8	52.8	20.8	32.1	29.0		6.1
1963	617.4	383.0	51.6	168.2	163.2	93.4	87.7	55.6	21.2	34.4	32.1		5.7
1964	663.0	411.4	56.7	178.7	176.1	101.7	96.7	62.4	23.7	38.7	34.3		5.0
1965	719.1	444.3	63.3	191.6	189.4	118.0	108.3	74.1	28.3	45.8	34.2		9.7
1966	787.8	481.9	68.3	208.8	204.8	130.4	116.7	84.4	31.3	53.0	32.3		13.8
1967	833.6	509.5	70.4	217.1	222.0	128.0	117.6	85.2	31.5	53.7	32.4		10.5
1968	910.6	559.8	80.8	235.7	243.4	139.9	130.8	92.1	33.6	58.5	38.7		9.1
1969	982.2	604.7	85.9	253.2	265.5	155.0	145.5	102.9	37.7	65.2	42.6		9.5
1970	1,035.6	648.1	85.0	272.0	291.1	150.2	148.1	106.7	40.3	66.4	41.4		2.2
1971	1,125.4	702.5	96.9	285.5	320.1	176.0	167.5	111.7	42.7	69.1	55.8		8.5
1972	1,237.3	770.7	110.4	308.0	352.3	205.6	195.7	126.1	47.2	78.9	69.7		9.9
1973	1,382.6	851.6	123.5	343.1	384.9	242.9	225.4	150.0	55.0	95.1	75.3		17.5
1974	1,496.9	931.2	122.3	384.5	424.4	245.6	231.5	165.6	61.2	104.3	66.0		14.1
1975	1,630.6	1,029.1	133.5	420.6	475.0	225.4	231.7	169.0	61.4	107.6	62.7		–6.3
1976	1,819.0	1,148.8	158.9	458.2	531.8	286.6	269.6	187.2	65.9	121.2	82.5		16.9
1977	2,026.9	1,277.1	181.1	496.9	599.0	356.6	333.5	223.2	74.6	148.7	110.3		23.1
1978	2,291.4	1,428.8	201.4	549.9	677.4	430.8	403.6	272.0	91.4	180.6	131.6		27.2
1979	2,557.5	1,593.5	213.9	624.0	755.6	480.9	464.0	323.0	114.9	208.1	141.0		16.9
1980	2,784.2	1,760.4	213.5	695.5	851.4	465.9	473.5	350.3	133.9	216.4	123.2		–7.6
1981	3,115.9	1,941.3	230.5	758.2	952.6	556.2	528.1	405.4	164.6	240.9	122.6		28.2
1982	3,242.1	2,076.8	239.3	786.8	1,050.7	501.1	515.6	409.9	175.0	234.9	105.7		–14.5
1983	3,514.5	2,283.4	279.8	830.3	1,173.3	547.1	552.0	399.4	152.7	246.7	152.5		–4.9
1984	3,902.4	2,492.3	325.1	883.6	1,283.6	715.6	648.1	468.3	176.0	292.3	179.8		67.5
1985	4,180.7	2,704.8	361.1	927.6	1,416.1	715.1	688.9	502.0	193.3	308.7	186.9		26.2
1986	4,422.2	2,892.7	398.7	957.2	1,536.8	722.5	712.9	494.8	175.8	319.0	218.1		9.6
1987	4,692.3	3,094.5	416.7	1,014.0	1,663.8	747.2	722.9	495.4	172.1	323.3	227.6		24.2
1988	5,049.6	3,349.7	451.0	1,081.1	1,817.6	773.9	763.1	530.6	181.3	349.3	232.5		10.9
1989	5,438.7	3,594.8	472.8	1,163.8	1,958.1	829.2	797.5	566.2	192.3	373.9	231.3		31.7
1990	5,743.8	3,839.3	476.5	1,245.3	2,117.5	799.7	791.6	575.9	200.8	375.1	215.7		8.0
1991	5,916.7	3,975.1	455.2	1,277.6	2,242.3	736.2	738.5	547.3	181.7	365.6	191.2		–2.3
1992	6,244.4	4,219.8	488.5	1,321.8	2,409.4	790.4	783.4	557.9	169.2	388.7	225.6		7.0
1993	6,558.1	4,459.2	530.2	1,370.7	2,558.4	876.2	855.7	604.1	176.4	427.7	251.6		20.5
1994	6,947.0	4,717.0	579.5	1,428.4	2,709.1	1,007.9	946.6	660.6	184.5	476.1	286.0		61.2
1995	7,265.4	4,957.7	608.5	1,475.8	2,873.4	1,038.2	1,008.1	723.0	200.6	522.4	285.1		30.1
1996	7,636.0	5,207.6	634.5	1,534.7	3,038.4	1,116.5	1,090.7	781.4	215.2	566.2	309.2		25.9
1997 ᴾ	8,083.4	5,488.6	659.4	1,592.7	3,236.5	1,237.6	1,173.0	845.4	230.2	615.2	327.5		64.6
1992: I	6,121.8	4,127.6	474.1	1,303.1	2,350.4	755.2	755.4	544.1	171.6	372.5	211.3		–.2
II	6,201.2	4,183.0	481.3	1,308.4	2,393.3	790.7	780.5	556.8	170.4	386.3	223.7		10.2
III	6,271.7	4,238.9	492.5	1,326.3	2,420.1	799.7	788.1	561.0	167.6	393.4	227.1		11.6
IV	6,383.1	4,329.6	506.2	1,349.5	2,473.9	816.1	809.7	569.6	167.1	402.5	240.1		6.5
1993: I	6,444.5	4,365.4	506.4	1,354.4	2,504.6	854.3	823.5	580.5	171.7	408.9	243.0		30.7
II	6,509.1	4,428.1	524.2	1,366.3	2,537.6	857.4	842.9	598.8	175.2	423.6	244.1		14.5
III	6,574.6	4,488.6	537.2	1,373.9	2,577.4	872.8	858.8	606.4	177.8	428.6	252.4		14.0
IV	6,704.2	4,554.9	553.1	1,388.0	2,613.8	920.3	897.5	630.6	180.7	449.9	266.8		22.9
1994: I	6,794.3	4,616.6	563.2	1,404.4	2,649.0	963.4	911.0	634.6	175.4	459.3	276.4		52.4
II	6,911.4	4,680.5	572.4	1,416.0	2,692.2	1,017.9	941.7	652.9	185.2	467.7	288.7		76.3
III	6,986.5	4,750.6	583.3	1,439.5	2,727.8	1,007.1	956.9	667.4	186.8	480.6	289.5		50.2
IV	7,095.7	4,820.2	599.3	1,453.7	2,767.2	1,043.1	977.0	687.5	190.7	496.8	289.5		66.2
1995: I	7,168.9	4,871.7	596.9	1,462.7	2,812.2	1,050.8	998.7	710.9	197.7	513.2	287.8		52.1
II	7,209.5	4,934.8	602.8	1,472.4	2,859.6	1,024.0	999.6	722.5	201.1	521.4	277.1		24.5
III	7,301.3	4,990.6	616.0	1,480.4	2,894.2	1,028.8	1,009.4	725.4	202.8	522.6	284.0		19.4
IV	7,381.9	5,033.8	618.4	1,487.8	2,927.5	1,049.1	1,024.6	733.1	200.7	532.4	291.4		24.5
1996: I	7,467.5	5,105.8	626.7	1,508.1	2,970.9	1,060.5	1,049.4	750.7	205.7	545.0	298.8		11.1
II	7,607.7	5,189.1	638.6	1,532.3	3,018.2	1,105.4	1,082.0	769.3	210.6	558.7	312.7		23.4
III	7,676.0	5,227.4	634.5	1,538.3	3,054.6	1,149.2	1,112.0	798.6	217.7	580.9	313.5		37.1
IV	7,792.9	5,308.1	638.2	1,560.1	3,109.8	1,151.1	1,119.2	807.2	227.0	580.2	312.0		31.9
1997: I	7,933.6	5,405.7	658.4	1,587.4	3,159.9	1,193.6	1,127.5	811.3	227.4	583.9	316.2		66.1
II	8,034.3	5,432.1	644.5	1,578.9	3,208.7	1,242.0	1,160.8	836.3	226.8	609.6	324.6		81.1
III	8,124.3	5,527.4	667.3	1,600.8	3,259.3	1,250.2	1,201.3	872.0	232.9	639.1	329.3		48.9
IV ᴾ	8,241.5	5,589.3	667.6	1,603.9	3,317.9	1,264.5	1,202.4	862.3	233.7	628.5	340.1		62.1

See next page for continuation of table.

TABLE B–1.—*Gross domestic product, 1959–97*—Continued

[Billions of dollars, except as noted; quarterly data at seasonally adjusted annual rates]

Year or quarter	Net exports of goods and services			Government consumption expenditures and gross investment					Final sales of domestic product	Gross domestic purchases [1]	Addendum: Gross national product [2]	Percent change from preceding period	
					Federal								
	Net exports	Exports	Imports	Total	Total	National defense	Non-defense	State and local				Gross domestic product	Gross domestic purchases [1]
1959	−1.7	20.6	22.3	112.0	67.2	55.7	11.5	44.8	503.0	508.9	510.1	8.5	9.0
1960	2.4	25.3	22.8	113.2	65.6	54.9	10.8	47.6	523.3	524.1	529.8	3.8	3.0
1961	3.4	26.0	22.7	120.9	69.1	57.7	11.4	51.8	541.9	541.5	548.4	3.5	3.3
1962	2.4	27.4	25.0	131.4	76.5	62.3	14.2	55.0	579.1	582.8	589.4	7.4	7.6
1963	3.3	29.4	26.1	137.7	78.1	62.2	15.9	59.6	611.7	614.1	621.9	5.5	5.4
1964	5.5	33.6	28.1	144.4	79.4	61.3	18.1	65.0	658.0	657.6	668.0	7.4	7.1
1965	3.9	35.4	31.5	153.0	81.8	62.0	19.7	71.2	709.4	715.3	724.5	8.5	8.8
1966	1.9	38.9	37.1	173.6	94.1	73.4	20.7	79.5	774.0	785.9	793.0	9.5	9.9
1967	1.4	41.4	39.9	194.6	106.6	85.5	21.0	88.1	823.1	832.2	839.1	5.8	5.9
1968	−1.3	45.3	46.6	212.1	113.8	92.0	21.8	98.3	901.4	911.8	916.7	9.2	9.6
1969	−1.2	49.3	50.5	223.8	115.8	92.4	23.4	108.0	972.7	983.4	988.4	7.9	7.8
1970	1.2	57.0	55.8	236.1	115.9	90.6	25.3	120.2	1,033.4	1,034.4	1,042.0	5.4	5.2
1971	−3.0	59.3	62.3	249.9	117.1	88.7	28.3	132.8	1,116.9	1,128.4	1,133.1	8.7	9.1
1972	−8.0	66.2	74.2	268.9	125.1	93.2	31.9	143.8	1,227.4	1,245.3	1,246.0	9.9	10.4
1973	.6	91.8	91.2	287.6	128.2	94.7	33.5	159.4	1,365.2	1,382.0	1,395.4	11.7	11.0
1974	−3.1	124.3	127.5	323.2	139.9	101.9	38.0	183.3	1,482.8	1,500.0	1,512.6	8.3	8.5
1975	13.6	136.3	122.7	362.6	154.5	110.9	43.6	208.1	1,636.9	1,617.1	1,643.9	8.9	7.8
1976	−2.3	148.9	151.1	385.9	162.7	116.1	46.6	223.1	1,802.0	1,821.2	1,836.1	11.5	12.6
1977	−23.7	158.8	182.4	416.9	178.4	125.8	52.6	238.5	2,003.8	2,050.5	2,047.5	11.4	12.6
1978	−26.1	186.1	212.3	457.9	194.4	135.6	58.9	263.4	2,264.2	2,317.5	2,313.5	13.0	13.0
1979	−24.0	228.7	252.7	507.1	215.0	151.2	63.8	292.0	2,540.6	2,581.5	2,590.4	11.6	11.4
1980	−14.9	278.9	293.8	572.8	248.4	174.2	74.2	324.4	2,791.9	2,799.1	2,819.5	8.9	8.4
1981	−15.0	302.8	317.8	633.4	284.1	202.0	82.2	349.2	3,087.8	3,130.9	3,150.6	11.9	11.9
1982	−20.5	282.6	303.2	684.8	313.2	230.9	82.3	371.6	3,256.6	3,262.6	3,273.2	4.1	4.2
1983	−51.7	277.0	328.6	735.7	344.5	255.0	89.4	391.2	3,519.4	3,566.2	3,546.5	8.4	9.3
1984	−102.0	303.1	405.1	796.6	372.6	282.7	89.9	424.0	3,835.0	4,004.5	3,933.5	11.0	12.3
1985	−114.2	303.0	417.2	875.0	410.1	312.4	97.7	464.9	4,154.5	4,294.9	4,201.0	7.1	7.3
1986	−131.5	320.7	452.2	938.5	435.2	332.4	102.9	503.3	4,412.6	4,553.7	4,435.1	5.8	6.0
1987	−142.1	365.7	507.9	992.8	455.7	350.4	105.3	537.2	4,668.1	4,834.5	4,701.3	6.1	6.2
1988	−106.1	447.2	553.2	1,032.0	457.3	354.0	103.3	574.7	5,038.7	5,155.6	5,062.6	7.6	6.6
1989	−80.4	509.3	589.7	1,095.1	477.2	360.6	116.7	617.9	5,407.0	5,519.1	5,452.8	7.7	7.0
1990	−71.3	557.3	628.6	1,176.1	503.6	373.1	130.4	672.6	5,735.8	5,815.1	5,764.9	5.6	5.4
1991	−20.5	601.8	622.3	1,225.9	522.6	383.5	139.1	703.4	5,919.0	5,937.2	5,932.4	3.0	2.1
1992	−29.5	639.4	669.0	1,263.8	528.0	375.8	152.2	735.8	6,237.4	6,274.0	6,255.5	5.5	5.7
1993	−60.7	658.6	719.3	1,283.4	518.3	360.7	157.7	765.0	6,537.6	6,618.8	6,576.8	5.0	5.5
1994	−90.9	721.2	812.1	1,313.0	510.2	349.2	161.0	802.8	6,885.7	7,037.9	6,955.2	5.9	6.3
1995	−86.0	818.4	904.5	1,355.5	509.6	344.6	165.0	846.0	7,235.3	7,351.4	7,270.6	4.6	4.5
1996	−94.8	870.9	965.7	1,406.7	520.0	352.8	167.3	886.7	7,610.2	7,730.9	7,637.7	5.1	5.2
1997 p	−96.7	958.8	1,055.5	1,453.9	524.8	350.8	174.0	929.1	8,018.8	8,180.1		5.9	5.8
1992:I	−8.9	632.4	641.3	1,247.9	521.8	372.8	149.0	726.1	6,122.1	6,130.8	6,138.3	8.2	7.8
II	−29.0	635.9	664.9	1,256.4	523.2	374.1	149.1	733.2	6,191.0	6,230.2	6,212.2	5.3	6.6
III	−37.6	640.2	677.8	1,270.7	532.0	380.9	151.1	738.7	6,260.1	6,309.2	6,281.1	4.6	5.2
IV	−42.7	649.1	691.8	1,280.0	535.0	375.3	159.7	745.1	6,376.6	6,425.8	6,390.5	7.3	7.6
1993:I	−46.6	647.1	693.7	1,271.5	521.3	363.6	157.7	750.1	6,413.8	6,491.1	6,468.1	3.9	4.1
II	−57.5	661.2	718.7	1,281.2	517.8	361.7	156.1	763.4	6,494.7	6,566.7	6,525.3	4.1	4.7
III	−72.1	646.8	718.9	1,285.3	515.7	358.0	157.7	769.6	6,560.6	6,646.7	6,596.9	4.1	5.0
IV	−66.6	679.4	746.0	1,295.5	518.5	359.4	159.1	777.0	6,681.3	6,770.8	6,717.1	8.1	7.7
1994:I	−76.6	678.5	755.1	1,291.0	506.9	344.9	162.0	784.1	6,741.9	6,870.9	6,811.2	5.5	6.0
II	−87.9	710.1	797.9	1,300.8	505.3	348.5	156.8	795.5	6,835.1	6,999.2	6,920.3	7.1	7.7
III	−103.4	732.6	836.0	1,332.3	520.4	359.7	160.7	811.9	6,936.3	7,090.0	6,992.3	4.4	5.3
IV	−95.6	763.7	859.2	1,328.0	508.3	343.6	164.7	819.6	7,029.6	7,191.3	7,096.8	6.4	5.8
1995:I	−98.3	784.5	882.8	1,344.7	513.6	346.3	167.3	831.1	7,116.8	7,267.2	7,175.1	4.2	4.3
II	−105.4	807.7	913.1	1,356.0	511.2	348.1	163.0	844.8	7,185.0	7,314.8	7,220.6	2.3	2.6
III	−80.4	831.6	912.0	1,362.2	512.9	347.3	165.5	849.3	7,281.8	7,381.7	7,298.3	5.2	3.7
IV	−60.1	849.9	909.9	1,359.2	500.6	336.5	164.1	858.6	7,357.4	7,442.0	7,388.5	4.5	3.3
1996:I	−83.0	850.2	933.2	1,384.2	516.4	348.4	168.0	867.8	7,456.4	7,550.5	7,475.3	4.7	6.0
II	−93.8	865.0	958.7	1,407.0	524.6	357.3	167.3	882.4	7,584.3	7,701.5	7,610.5	7.7	8.2
III	−114.0	836.7	977.6	1,413.5	521.6	354.8	166.8	891.9	7,638.9	7,790.0	7,669.1	3.6	4.7
IV	−88.6	904.6	993.2	1,422.3	517.6	350.6	167.0	904.7	7,761.0	7,881.5	7,796.1	6.2	4.8
1997:I	−98.8	922.2	1,021.0	1,433.1	516.1	343.3	172.8	917.0	7,867.4	8,032.4	7,919.2	7.4	7.9
II	−88.7	960.3	1,049.0	1,449.0	526.1	350.6	175.5	923.0	7,953.2	8,123.1	8,013.6	5.2	4.6
III	−111.3	965.8	1,077.1	1,457.9	525.7	352.1	173.6	932.3	8,075.3	8,235.6	8,103.5	4.6	5.7
IV p	−87.9	986.9	1,074.8	1,475.6	531.1	357.1	174.0	944.4	8,179.3	8,329.4		5.9	4.6

[1] Gross domestic product (GDP) less exports of goods and services plus imports of goods and services.
[2] GDP plus net receipts of factor income from rest of the world.

Source: Department of Commerce, Bureau of Economic Analysis.

281

TABLE B–2.—*Real gross domestic product, 1959–97*

[Billions of chained (1992) dollars, except as noted; quarterly data at seasonally adjusted annual rates]

Year or quarter	Gross domestic product	Personal consumption expenditures				Gross private domestic investment							Change in business inventories
						Total	Fixed investment						
								Nonresidential					
		Total	Durable goods	Non-durable goods	Services		Total	Total	Struc-tures	Pro-ducers' durable equip-ment	Resi-dential		
1959	2,210.2	1,394.6				271.7							13.2
1960	2,262.9	1,432.6				270.5							10.5
1961	2,314.3	1,461.5				267.6							8.6
1962	2,454.8	1,533.8				302.1							19.5
1963	2,559.4	1,596.6				321.6							17.8
1964	2,708.4	1,692.3				348.3							15.6
1965	2,881.1	1,799.1				397.2							30.3
1966	3,069.2	1,902.0				430.6							42.4
1967	3,147.2	1,958.6				411.8							32.0
1968	3,293.9	2,070.2				433.3							26.9
1969	3,393.6	2,147.5				458.3							27.0
1970	3,397.6	2,197.8				426.1							5.4
1971	3,510.0	2,279.5				474.9							22.3
1972	3,702.3	2,415.9				531.8							24.7
1973	3,916.3	2,532.6				595.5							37.7
1974	3,891.2	2,514.7				546.5							23.4
1975	3,873.9	2,570.0				446.6							-10.2
1976	4,082.9	2,714.3				537.4							29.8
1977	4,273.6	2,829.8				622.1							38.8
1978	4,503.0	2,951.6				693.4							43.3
1979	4,630.6	3,020.2				709.7							23.4
1980	4,615.0	3,009.7				628.3							-10.2
1981	4,720.7	3,046.4				686.0							33.1
1982	4,620.3	3,081.5	285.5	1,080.6	1,728.2	587.2	610.4	464.3	207.2	260.3	140.1		-15.6
1983	4,803.7	3,240.6	327.4	1,112.4	1,809.0	642.1	654.2	456.4	185.7	272.4	197.6		-5.7
1984	5,140.1	3,407.6	374.9	1,151.8	1,883.0	833.4	762.4	535.4	212.2	324.6	226.4		75.3
1985	5,323.5	3,566.5	411.4	1,178.3	1,977.3	823.8	799.3	568.4	227.8	342.4	229.5		30.2
1986	5,487.7	3,708.7	448.4	1,215.9	2,041.4	811.8	805.0	548.5	203.3	345.9	257.0		11.1
1987	5,649.5	3,822.3	454.9	1,239.3	2,126.9	821.5	799.4	542.4	195.9	346.9	257.6		26.4
1988	5,865.2	3,972.7	483.5	1,274.4	2,212.4	828.2	818.3	566.0	196.8	369.2	252.5		11.7
1989	6,062.0	4,064.6	496.2	1,303.5	2,262.3	863.5	832.0	588.8	201.2	387.6	243.2		33.3
1990	6,136.3	4,132.2	493.3	1,316.1	2,321.3	815.0	805.8	585.2	203.3	381.9	220.6		10.4
1991	6,079.4	4,105.8	462.0	1,302.9	2,341.0	738.1	741.3	547.7	181.6	366.2	193.4		-3.0
1992	6,244.4	4,219.8	488.5	1,321.8	2,409.4	790.4	783.4	557.9	169.2	388.7	225.6		7.0
1993	6,389.6	4,343.6	523.8	1,351.0	2,468.9	863.6	842.8	600.2	170.8	429.6	242.6		22.1
1994	6,610.7	4,486.0	561.2	1,389.9	2,535.5	975.7	915.5	648.4	172.5	476.8	267.0		60.6
1995	6,742.1	4,595.3	583.6	1,412.6	2,599.6	991.5	962.1	706.5	179.9	528.3	257.0		27.3
1996	6,928.4	4,714.1	611.1	1,432.3	2,671.0	1,069.1	1,041.7	771.7	188.7	586.0	272.1		25.0
1997 ᵖ	7,191.4	4,869.7	645.8	1,459.3	2,765.2	1,192.2	1,122.3	846.7	195.4	657.4	279.7		62.2
1992: I	6,175.7	4,173.8	476.1	1,314.4	2,383.2	758.2	758.3	544.4	172.7	371.7	213.9		-.5
II	6,214.2	4,196.4	481.1	1,312.0	2,403.2	792.8	782.4	557.5	171.0	386.4	224.9		11.0
III	6,260.7	4,226.7	491.9	1,321.1	2,413.6	798.5	787.3	560.6	167.4	393.1	226.7		12.0
IV	6,327.1	4,282.3	505.0	1,339.8	2,437.6	812.2	805.8	569.1	165.6	403.5	236.7		5.6
1993: I	6,327.9	4,286.8	504.0	1,337.5	2,445.3	845.5	814.8	577.8	168.0	409.8	237.0		32.3
II	6,359.9	4,322.8	519.3	1,347.8	2,455.9	846.1	831.1	595.1	170.3	424.9	236.1		16.6
III	6,393.5	4,366.6	529.9	1,356.8	2,480.0	858.6	844.5	602.3	171.7	430.7	242.2		15.3
IV	6,476.9	4,398.0	542.1	1,361.8	2,494.4	904.0	880.8	625.6	173.1	452.9	255.1		24.2
1994: I	6,524.5	4,439.4	550.7	1,378.4	2,510.9	939.9	887.8	626.2	166.3	460.6	261.3		53.1
II	6,600.3	4,472.2	555.8	1,385.5	2,531.4	987.8	913.2	641.2	174.5	467.3	271.5		75.9
III	6,629.5	4,498.2	561.7	1,393.2	2,543.8	972.2	922.7	653.2	174.0	480.0	269.4		49.7
IV	6,688.6	4,534.1	576.6	1,402.5	2,555.9	1,003.0	938.5	672.9	175.0	499.1	265.9		63.6
1995: I	6,703.7	4,551.3	572.2	1,408.4	2,571.2	1,005.8	955.8	695.7	179.0	518.1	261.2		48.5
II	6,708.8	4,583.5	577.7	1,411.6	2,594.5	977.5	954.0	705.4	180.9	525.9	250.4		21.6
III	6,759.2	4,612.9	590.8	1,413.9	2,608.7	982.0	962.3	708.2	181.2	528.5	255.5		17.0
IV	6,796.5	4,633.5	593.7	1,416.3	2,623.8	1,000.8	976.3	716.8	178.6	540.5	260.8		22.2
1996: I	6,824.4	4,669.4	600.7	1,422.5	2,646.5	1,012.2	1,001.5	736.9	182.1	557.4	266.1		8.0
II	6,926.0	4,712.2	614.8	1,431.6	2,666.5	1,059.2	1,035.7	759.7	185.6	577.1	277.2		21.3
III	6,943.8	4,718.2	611.9	1,433.9	2,672.8	1,100.3	1,060.9	789.3	190.0	602.9	274.1		37.9
IV	7,017.4	4,756.4	617.1	1,441.2	2,698.2	1,104.8	1,068.7	800.8	196.9	606.7	271.1		32.9
1997: I	7,101.6	4,818.1	637.8	1,457.8	2,723.9	1,149.2	1,079.0	808.9	195.9	616.6	273.3		63.7
II	7,159.6	4,829.4	629.0	1,450.0	2,749.8	1,197.1	1,111.4	837.0	193.5	649.3	278.2		77.6
III	7,214.0	4,896.2	656.1	1,465.5	2,776.1	1,204.6	1,149.3	874.5	196.7	685.3	280.1		47.5
IV ᵖ	7,290.3	4,935.0	660.3	1,464.1	2,811.0	1,217.9	1,149.6	866.5	195.3	678.5	287.1		59.9

See next page for continuation of table.

[Billions of chained (1992) dollars, except as noted; quarterly data at seasonally adjusted annual rates]

Year or quarter	Net exports of goods and services			Government consumption expenditures and gross investment					Final sales of domestic product	Gross domestic purchases[1]	Addendum: Gross national product[2]	Percent change from preceding period	
					Federal								
	Net exports	Exports	Imports	Total	Total	National defense	Non-defense	State and local				Gross domestic product	Gross domestic purchases[1]
1959	....	71.9	106.6	618.5	....	....	....	....	2,206.9	2,268.0	2,222.0	7.4	7.8
1960	....	86.8	108.1	617.2	....	....	....	....	2,264.2	2,304.1	2,276.0	2.4	1.6
1961	....	88.3	107.3	647.2	....	....	....	....	2,318.0	2,354.3	2,329.1	2.3	2.2
1962	....	93.0	119.5	686.0	....	....	....	....	2,445.4	2,503.0	2,471.5	6.1	6.3
1963	....	100.0	122.7	701.9	....	....	....	....	2,552.4	2,604.2	2,577.3	4.3	4.0
1964	....	113.3	129.2	715.9	....	....	....	....	2,705.1	2,745.9	2,727.8	5.8	5.4
1965	....	115.6	143.0	737.6	....	....	....	....	2,860.4	2,932.1	2,901.4	6.4	6.8
1966	....	123.4	164.2	804.6	....	....	....	....	3,033.5	3,134.0	3,087.8	6.5	6.9
1967	....	126.1	176.2	865.6	....	....	....	....	3,125.1	3,221.1	3,166.4	2.5	2.8
1968	....	135.3	202.5	892.4	....	....	....	....	3,278.0	3,382.7	3,314.5	4.7	5.0
1969	....	142.7	214.0	887.5	....	....	....	....	3,377.2	3,485.6	3,413.3	3.0	3.0
1970	....	158.1	223.1	866.8	....	....	....	....	3,405.5	3,478.5	3,417.1	.1	-.2
1971	....	159.2	235.0	851.0	....	....	....	....	3,499.8	3,602.4	3,532.1	3.3	3.6
1972	....	172.0	261.0	854.1	....	....	....	....	3,689.5	3,806.2	3,726.3	5.5	5.7
1973	....	209.6	272.6	848.4	....	....	....	....	3,883.9	3,989.3	3,950.1	5.8	4.8
1974	....	229.8	265.3	862.9	....	....	....	....	3,873.4	3,928.6	3,930.2	-.6	-1.5
1975	....	228.2	235.4	876.3	....	....	....	....	3,906.4	3,875.9	3,903.3	-.4	-1.3
1976	....	241.6	281.5	876.8	....	....	....	....	4,061.7	4,124.6	4,118.8	5.4	6.4
1977	....	247.4	311.6	884.7	....	....	....	....	4,240.8	4,345.7	4,314.5	4.7	5.4
1978	....	273.1	338.6	910.6	....	....	....	....	4,464.4	4,574.9	4,543.7	5.4	5.3
1979	....	299.0	344.3	924.9	....	....	....	....	4,614.4	4,674.6	4,687.4	2.8	2.2
1980	....	331.4	321.3	941.4	....	....	....	....	4,641.9	4,581.5	4,670.8	-.3	-2.0
1981	....	335.3	329.7	947.7	....	....	....	....	4,691.6	4,693.1	4,769.9	2.3	2.4
1982	-14.1	311.4	325.5	960.1	429.4	316.5	113.3	531.4	4,651.2	4,619.3	4,662.0	-2.1	-1.6
1983	-63.3	303.3	366.6	987.3	452.7	334.6	118.5	534.9	4,821.2	4,864.3	4,844.8	4.0	5.3
1984	-127.3	328.4	455.7	1,018.4	463.7	348.1	115.9	555.0	5,061.6	5,276.2	5,178.0	7.0	8.5
1985	-147.9	337.3	485.2	1,080.1	495.6	374.1	121.8	584.7	5,296.9	5,482.8	5,346.7	3.6	3.9
1986	-163.9	362.2	526.1	1,135.0	534.4	393.4	125.2	616.9	5,480.9	5,663.9	5,501.2	3.1	3.3
1987	-156.2	402.0	558.2	1,165.9	534.4	409.2	125.3	631.8	5,626.0	5,816.7	5,658.2	2.9	2.7
1988	-114.4	465.8	580.2	1,180.9	524.6	405.5	119.1	656.6	5,855.1	5,986.1	5,878.5	3.8	2.9
1989	-82.7	520.2	603.0	1,213.9	531.5	401.6	130.1	682.6	6,028.7	6,147.8	6,075.7	3.4	2.7
1990	-61.9	564.4	626.3	1,250.4	541.9	401.5	140.5	708.6	6,126.7	6,199.8	6,157.0	1.2	.8
1991	-22.3	599.9	622.2	1,258.0	539.4	397.5	142.0	718.7	6,082.6	6,101.6	6,094.9	-.9	-1.6
1992	-29.5	639.4	669.0	1,263.8	528.0	375.8	152.2	735.8	6,237.4	6,274.0	6,255.5	2.7	2.8
1993	-70.2	658.2	728.4	1,252.1	505.7	354.4	151.2	746.4	6,368.9	6,459.0	6,408.0	2.3	2.9
1994	-104.6	712.4	817.0	1,252.3	486.6	336.9	149.5	765.7	6,551.2	6,712.7	6,619.1	3.5	3.9
1995	-98.8	791.2	890.1	1,251.9	470.3	322.6	147.5	781.6	6,712.7	6,837.5	6,748.7	2.0	1.9
1996	-114.4	857.0	971.5	1,257.9	464.2	317.8	146.1	793.7	6,901.0	7,037.7	6,932.0	2.8	2.9
1997 ᵖ	-142.1	964.4	1,106.5	1,270.6	457.8	309.0	148.3	812.9	7,124.2	7,323.4	....	3.8	4.1
1992: I	-14.8	633.0	647.8	1,258.5	525.1	374.2	150.8	733.5	6,175.8	6,190.3	6,192.0	4.7	4.5
II	-32.5	635.8	668.3	1,257.5	523.3	373.3	150.0	734.2	6,203.8	6,246.9	6,225.2	2.5	3.7
III	-30.8	639.7	670.5	1,266.5	529.6	378.7	150.9	736.9	6,249.5	6,291.7	6,270.3	3.0	2.9
IV	-40.0	649.1	689.1	1,272.5	534.0	376.8	157.1	738.5	6,320.7	6,367.0	6,334.6	4.3	4.9
1993: I	-54.7	647.2	701.9	1,250.1	525.1	359.2	152.9	738.0	6,297.3	6,382.3	6,351.3	.1	1.0
II	-62.6	660.1	722.7	1,253.1	507.8	356.7	151.1	745.3	6,344.9	6,422.0	6,375.9	2.0	2.5
III	-83.1	646.3	729.4	1,250.5	501.5	351.1	150.3	749.1	6,379.3	6,475.6	6,415.3	2.1	3.4
IV	-80.5	679.1	759.7	1,254.7	501.3	350.8	150.4	753.4	6,453.8	6,556.2	6,489.7	5.3	5.1
1994: I	-97.6	676.0	773.6	1,241.9	487.2	335.1	151.9	754.7	6,473.0	6,620.2	6,540.5	3.0	4.0
II	-103.9	704.1	808.0	1,243.3	481.2	335.9	145.1	762.2	6,526.7	6,701.8	6,609.3	4.7	5.0
III	-111.1	722.1	833.2	1,268.1	496.4	347.0	149.4	771.7	6,580.4	6,737.5	6,635.6	1.8	2.1
IV	-105.9	747.3	853.2	1,255.8	481.7	329.6	151.7	774.1	6,624.8	6,791.3	6,691.2	3.6	3.2
1995: I	-113.5	760.4	873.9	1,257.7	480.4	328.7	151.4	777.3	6,654.3	6,813.2	6,711.3	.9	1.3
II	-112.8	777.4	890.3	1,257.3	474.9	327.4	147.3	782.3	6,685.3	6,817.3	6,721.0	.3	.2
III	-92.9	802.4	895.4	1,255.0	473.4	324.0	149.1	781.5	6,739.3	6,848.9	6,758.3	3.0	1.9
IV	-76.1	824.6	900.7	1,237.7	452.6	310.3	142.1	785.1	6,771.9	6,870.4	6,804.2	2.2	1.3
1996: I	-100.8	828.2	929.0	1,243.2	460.9	314.9	145.7	782.4	6,815.0	6,923.2	6,834.7	1.8	3.1
II	-112.6	847.4	960.0	1,265.1	470.7	323.2	147.2	794.4	6,902.3	7,033.6	6,930.1	6.0	6.5
III	-138.9	851.4	990.2	1,261.5	465.7	319.4	146.0	795.9	6,905.0	7,075.3	6,940.2	1.0	2.4
IV	-105.6	901.1	1,006.6	1,261.8	459.6	313.6	145.7	802.3	6,981.7	7,118.4	7,023.1	4.3	2.5
1997: I	-126.3	922.7	1,048.9	1,260.5	452.8	303.9	148.5	807.7	7,034.1	7,220.9	7,091.8	4.9	5.9
II	-136.6	962.5	1,099.1	1,270.1	460.1	309.4	150.2	810.1	7,077.7	7,286.9	7,144.4	3.3	3.7
III	-164.1	973.0	1,137.1	1,273.4	458.8	310.3	148.0	814.7	7,160.3	7,364.6	7,198.8	3.1	4.3
IV ᵖ	-141.4	999.3	1,140.8	1,278.5	459.5	312.6	146.6	819.0	7,224.6	7,421.2	....	4.3	3.1

[1] Gross domestic product (GDP) less exports of goods and services plus imports of goods and services.
[2] GDP plus net receipts of factor income from rest of the world.

Source: Department of Commerce, Bureau of Economic Analysis.

TABLE B-3.—*Quantity and price indexes for gross domestic product, and percent changes, 1959–97*

[Quarterly data are seasonally adjusted]

Year or quarter	Gross domestic product (GDP)							
	Index numbers, 1992=100				Percent change from preceding period [1]			
	GDP (current dollars)	Real GDP (chain-type quantity index)	GDP chain-type price index	GDP implicit price deflator	GDP (current dollars)	Real GDP (chain-type quantity index)	GDP chain-type price index	GDP implicit price deflator
1959	8.12	35.39	22.95	22.95	8.5	7.4	1.0	1.0
1960	8.43	36.24	23.27	23.27	3.8	2.4	1.4	1.4
1961	8.72	37.06	23.54	23.54	3.5	2.3	1.2	1.2
1962	9.37	39.31	23.84	23.84	7.4	6.1	1.3	1.3
1963	9.89	40.99	24.12	24.12	5.5	4.3	1.2	1.2
1964	10.62	43.37	24.48	24.48	7.4	5.8	1.5	1.5
1965	11.52	46.14	24.95	24.96	8.5	6.4	1.9	2.0
1966	12.62	49.15	25.66	25.67	9.5	6.5	2.8	2.8
1967	13.35	50.40	26.48	26.49	5.8	2.5	3.2	3.2
1968	14.58	52.75	27.64	27.64	9.2	4.7	4.4	4.4
1969	15.73	54.35	28.94	28.94	7.9	3.0	4.7	4.7
1970	16.58	54.41	30.48	30.48	5.4	.1	5.3	5.3
1971	18.02	56.21	32.05	32.06	8.7	3.3	5.2	5.2
1972	19.81	59.29	33.42	33.42	9.9	5.5	4.2	4.2
1973	22.14	62.72	35.30	35.30	11.7	5.8	5.6	5.6
1974	23.97	62.32	38.46	38.47	8.3	-.6	8.9	9.0
1975	26.11	62.04	42.09	42.09	8.9	-.4	9.4	9.4
1976	29.13	65.38	44.55	44.55	11.5	5.4	5.8	5.8
1977	32.46	68.44	47.42	47.43	11.4	4.7	6.5	6.5
1978	36.69	72.11	50.88	50.89	13.0	5.4	7.3	7.3
1979	40.96	74.16	55.22	55.23	11.6	2.8	8.5	8.5
1980	44.59	73.91	60.34	60.33	8.9	-.3	9.3	9.2
1981	49.90	75.60	66.01	66.01	11.9	2.3	9.4	9.4
1982	51.92	73.99	70.18	70.17	4.1	-2.1	6.3	6.3
1983	56.28	76.93	73.16	73.16	8.4	4.0	4.3	4.3
1984	62.49	82.32	75.92	75.92	11.0	7.0	3.8	3.8
1985	66.95	85.25	78.53	78.53	7.1	3.6	3.4	3.4
1986	70.82	87.88	80.58	80.58	5.8	3.1	2.6	2.6
1987	75.14	90.47	83.06	83.06	6.1	2.9	3.1	3.1
1988	80.87	93.93	86.10	86.09	7.6	3.8	3.7	3.7
1989	87.10	97.08	89.72	89.72	7.7	3.4	4.2	4.2
1990	91.98	98.27	93.64	93.60	5.6	1.2	4.4	4.3
1991	94.75	97.36	97.32	97.32	3.0	-.9	3.9	4.0
1992	100.00	100.00	100.00	100.00	5.5	2.7	2.8	2.8
1993	105.02	102.32	102.64	102.64	5.0	2.3	2.6	2.6
1994	111.25	105.87	105.09	105.09	5.9	3.5	2.4	2.4
1995	116.35	107.97	107.76	107.76	4.6	2.0	2.5	2.5
1996	122.29	110.95	110.22	110.21	5.1	2.8	2.3	2.3
1997 P	129.45	115.17	112.46	112.40	5.9	3.8	2.0	2.0
1992: I	98.04	98.90	99.14	99.13	8.2	4.7	3.4	3.4
II	99.31	99.52	99.81	99.79	5.3	2.5	2.8	2.7
III	100.44	100.26	100.17	100.17	4.6	3.0	1.4	1.5
IV	102.22	101.32	100.88	100.88	7.3	4.3	2.8	2.9
1993: I	103.20	101.34	101.85	101.84	3.9	.1	3.9	3.9
II	104.24	101.85	102.38	102.35	4.1	2.0	2.1	2.0
III	105.29	102.39	102.83	102.83	4.1	2.1	1.8	1.9
IV	107.36	103.72	103.52	103.51	8.1	5.3	2.7	2.7
1994: I	108.81	104.49	104.16	104.13	5.5	3.0	2.5	2.4
II	110.68	105.70	104.74	104.71	7.1	4.7	2.2	2.2
III	111.88	106.17	105.39	105.39	4.4	1.8	2.5	2.6
IV	113.63	107.11	106.07	106.09	6.4	3.6	2.6	2.7
1995: I	114.80	107.36	106.93	106.94	4.2	.9	3.3	3.3
II	115.45	107.44	107.49	107.46	2.3	.3	2.1	2.0
III	116.92	108.24	108.03	108.02	5.2	3.0	2.0	2.1
IV	118.22	108.84	108.60	108.61	4.5	2.2	2.1	2.2
1996: I	119.59	109.32	109.35	109.39	4.7	1.8	2.8	2.9
II	121.83	110.92	109.86	109.84	7.7	6.0	1.9	1.7
III	122.93	111.20	110.59	110.54	3.6	1.0	2.7	2.6
IV	124.80	112.38	111.10	111.05	6.2	4.3	1.9	1.9
1997: I	127.05	113.73	111.78	111.71	7.4	4.9	2.4	2.4
II	128.66	114.66	112.27	112.22	5.2	3.3	1.8	1.8
III	130.10	115.53	112.67	112.62	4.6	3.1	1.4	1.4
IV P	131.98	116.75	113.10	113.05	5.9	4.3	1.5	1.5

[1] Percent changes based on unrounded data. Quarterly percent changes are at annual rates.

Source: Department of Commerce, Bureau of Economic Analysis.

TABLE B–4.—*Percent changes in real gross domestic product, 1959–97*

[Percent change from preceding period; quarterly data at seasonally adjusted annual rates]

Year or quarter	Gross domestic product	Personal consumption expenditures				Gross private domestic investment				Exports and imports of goods and services		Government consumption expenditures and gross investment		
						Nonresidential fixed								
		Total	Durable goods	Nondurable goods	Services	Total	Structures	Producers' durable equipment	Residential	Exports	Imports	Total	Federal	State and local
1959	7.4	5.7	13.4	4.1	5.2	8.3	2.4	12.4	25.5	0.9	10.5	5.7	7.2	3.5
1960	2.4	2.7	2.0	1.5	4.4	5.6	7.9	4.1	-7.1	20.8	1.3	-.2	-3.1	4.1
1961	2.3	2.0	-3.8	1.8	4.1	-.9	1.4	-2.4	.3	1.7	-.7	4.9	3.9	6.2
1962	6.1	4.9	11.7	3.1	4.9	8.7	4.5	11.6	9.6	5.4	11.3	6.0	8.3	2.9
1963	4.3	4.1	9.7	2.1	4.5	5.0	1.1	7.6	11.8	7.5	2.7	2.3	-.4	6.0
1964	5.8	6.0	9.2	4.9	6.1	11.8	10.4	12.6	5.8	13.3	5.3	2.0	-1.7	6.8
1965	6.4	6.3	12.7	5.3	5.3	17.3	15.9	18.2	-2.9	2.0	10.6	3.0	.0	6.7
1966	6.5	5.7	8.5	5.5	5.1	12.1	6.8	15.5	-8.9	6.7	14.9	9.1	11.4	6.4
1967	2.5	3.0	1.6	1.6	4.8	-1.6	-2.5	-1.0	-3.1	2.2	7.3	7.6	9.9	4.9
1968	4.7	5.7	11.0	4.5	5.2	4.3	1.4	6.1	13.6	7.3	14.9	3.1	1.0	5.7
1969	3.0	3.7	3.6	2.7	4.8	7.2	5.4	8.3	3.0	5.5	5.7	-.6	-3.4	2.8
1970	.1	2.3	-3.2	2.4	4.0	-1.0	.3	-1.8	-6.0	10.8	4.3	-2.3	-7.1	2.8
1971	3.3	3.7	10.0	1.8	3.7	-.1	-1.6	.8	27.4	.7	5.3	-1.8	-7.1	3.3
1972	5.5	6.0	12.7	4.4	5.4	9.0	3.1	12.7	17.8	8.1	11.0	.4	-1.7	2.2
1973	5.8	4.8	10.3	3.3	4.5	14.6	8.2	18.5	-.6	21.8	4.5	-.7	-4.9	3.0
1974	-.6	-.7	-6.9	-2.0	2.4	.5	-2.1	2.1	-20.6	9.6	-2.7	1.7	-.6	3.6
1975	-.4	2.2	.0	1.5	3.5	-10.5	-10.5	-10.5	-13.0	-.7	-11.3	1.5	-.2	2.9
1976	5.4	5.6	12.8	5.0	4.2	4.8	2.5	6.1	23.6	5.9	19.6	.1	-1.0	.8
1977	4.7	4.3	9.3	2.6	4.2	11.8	4.9	15.6	21.2	2.4	10.7	.9	1.6	.4
1978	5.4	4.3	5.3	3.5	4.7	13.7	10.9	15.1	6.6	10.4	8.7	2.9	2.1	3.6
1979	2.8	2.3	-.5	2.3	3.2	9.6	12.6	8.1	-3.7	9.5	1.7	1.6	1.5	1.6
1980	-.3	-.3	-8.0	-.4	1.9	-.5	6.7	-4.4	-21.1	10.8	-6.7	1.8	4.2	.0
1981	2.3	1.2	1.2	.9	1.5	5.3	7.9	3.7	-8.0	1.2	2.6	.7	4.2	-2.0
1982	-2.1	1.2	-.1	.6	1.9	-4.4	-1.5	-6.4	-18.2	-7.1	-1.3	1.3	3.2	-.3
1983	4.0	5.2	14.7	2.9	4.7	-1.7	-10.4	4.6	41.1	-2.6	12.6	2.8	5.4	.7
1984	7.0	5.2	14.5	3.5	4.1	17.3	14.3	19.2	14.6	8.3	24.3	3.1	2.4	3.8
1985	3.6	4.7	9.7	2.3	5.0	6.2	7.3	5.5	1.4	2.7	6.5	6.1	6.9	5.3
1986	3.1	4.0	9.0	3.2	3.2	-3.5	-10.8	1.0	12.0	7.4	8.4	5.1	4.6	5.5
1987	2.9	3.1	1.5	1.9	4.2	-1.1	-3.6	.3	.2	11.0	6.1	2.7	3.1	2.4
1988	3.8	3.9	6.3	2.8	4.0	4.4	.5	6.4	-2.0	15.9	3.9	1.3	-1.8	3.9
1989	3.4	2.3	2.6	2.3	2.3	4.0	2.2	5.0	-3.7	11.7	3.9	2.8	1.3	4.0
1990	1.2	1.7	-.6	1.0	2.6	-.6	1.1	-1.5	-9.3	8.5	3.9	3.0	2.0	3.8
1991	-.9	-.6	-6.4	-1.0	.8	-6.4	-10.7	-4.1	-12.3	6.3	-.7	.6	-.5	1.4
1992	2.7	2.8	5.8	1.5	2.9	1.9	-6.8	6.2	16.6	6.6	7.5	.5	-2.1	2.4
1993	2.3	2.9	7.2	2.2	2.5	7.6	1.0	10.5	7.6	2.9	8.9	-.9	-4.2	1.5
1994	3.5	3.3	7.1	2.9	2.7	8.0	1.0	11.0	10.1	8.2	12.2	.0	-3.8	2.6
1995	2.0	2.4	4.0	1.6	2.5	9.0	4.3	10.8	-3.8	11.1	8.9	.0	-3.3	2.1
1996	2.8	2.6	4.7	1.4	2.7	9.2	4.8	10.9	5.9	8.3	9.1	.5	-1.3	1.6
1997 P	3.8	3.3	5.7	1.9	3.5	9.7	3.6	12.2	2.8	12.5	13.9	1.0	-1.4	2.4
1992: I	4.7	6.4	13.3	5.9	5.4	3.6	2.9	3.9	24.7	6.3	4.1	2.5	-1.4	5.4
II	2.5	2.2	4.3	-.7	3.4	10.0	-3.9	16.9	22.2	1.8	13.3	-.3	-1.4	.4
III	3.0	2.9	9.3	2.8	1.7	2.2	-8.1	7.1	3.3	2.5	1.3	2.9	4.9	1.4
IV	4.3	5.4	11.0	5.8	4.0	6.2	-4.3	11.0	18.7	6.0	11.6	1.9	3.4	.9
1993: I	.1	.4	-.7	-.7	1.3	6.2	6.0	6.4	.6	-1.2	7.6	-6.9	-15.4	-.3
II	2.0	3.4	12.6	3.1	1.7	12.5	5.5	15.6	-1.6	8.2	12.4	1.0	-3.3	4.0
III	2.1	4.1	8.4	2.7	4.0	4.9	3.4	5.5	10.8	-8.1	3.8	-.8	-4.9	2.1
IV	5.3	2.9	9.6	1.5	2.3	16.4	3.3	22.3	23.1	21.9	17.7	1.3	-.1	2.3
1994: I	3.0	3.8	6.4	5.0	2.7	.4	-14.8	7.0	10.0	-1.8	7.6	-4.0	-10.7	.7
II	4.7	3.0	3.8	2.1	3.3	9.9	21.1	5.9	16.6	17.7	19.0	.4	-4.9	4.0
III	1.8	2.3	4.3	2.2	2.0	7.7	-1.1	11.4	-3.1	10.6	13.1	8.2	13.3	5.1
IV	3.6	3.2	11.0	2.7	1.9	12.6	2.3	16.9	-5.0	14.7	9.9	-3.8	-11.3	1.2
1995: I	.9	1.5	-3.0	1.7	2.4	14.2	9.5	16.1	-7.0	7.2	10.0	.6	-1.1	1.7
II	.3	2.9	3.9	.9	3.7	5.7	4.3	6.2	-15.5	9.3	7.7	-.1	-4.5	2.6
III	3.0	2.6	9.3	.7	2.2	1.6	.7	2.0	8.4	13.5	2.3	-.7	-1.3	-.4
IV	2.2	1.8	2.0	.7	2.3	4.9	-5.8	9.4	8.5	11.5	2.4	-5.4	-16.4	1.9
1996: I	1.8	3.1	4.8	1.7	3.5	11.7	8.2	13.1	8.3	1.7	13.1	1.8	7.5	-1.4
II	6.0	3.7	9.7	2.6	3.1	13.0	7.9	14.9	17.9	9.6	14.1	7.2	8.8	6.3
III	1.0	.5	-1.9	.6	1.0	16.5	10.0	19.1	-4.5	1.9	13.2	-1.1	-4.2	.7
IV	4.3	3.3	3.5	2.1	3.9	5.9	15.3	2.6	-4.3	25.5	6.8	.1	-5.2	3.3
1997: I	4.9	5.3	14.1	4.7	3.9	4.1	-2.1	6.7	3.3	9.9	17.9	-.4	-5.8	2.7
II	3.3	.9	-5.4	-2.1	3.9	14.6	-4.7	23.0	7.4	18.4	20.5	3.1	6.6	1.2
III	3.1	5.6	18.4	4.3	3.9	19.2	6.7	24.1	2.7	4.4	14.6	1.1	-1.1	2.3
IV P	4.3	3.2	2.6	-.4	5.1	-3.6	-2.7	-3.9	10.4	11.3	1.3	1.6	.7	2.1

Note.—Percent changes based on unrounded data.

Source: Department of Commerce, Bureau of Economic Analysis.

285

[Percentage points, except as noted; quarterly data at seasonally adjusted annual rates]

Year or quarter	Gross domestic product (percent change)	Personal consumption expenditures				Gross private domestic investment						
							Fixed investment					Change in business inventories
								Nonresidential				
		Total	Durable goods	Non-durable goods	Services	Total	Total	Total	Structures	Producers' durable equipment	Residential	
1959	7.4	3.7	1.1	1.3	1.3	2.9	2.0	0.8	0.1	0.7	1.2	0.9
1960	2.4	1.7	.2	.4	1.1	−.1	.1	.5	.3	.2	−.4	−.2
1961	2.3	1.3	−.3	.5	1.1	−.2	−.1	−.1	.1	−.1	0	−.1
1962	6.1	3.1	.9	.9	1.3	1.8	1.2	.8	.2	.6	.5	.6
1963	4.3	2.5	.8	.6	1.2	1.0	1.0	.5	0	.4	.6	−.1
1964	5.8	3.7	.8	1.3	1.6	1.3	1.4	1.1	.4	.7	.3	−.1
1965	6.4	3.9	1.1	1.4	1.4	2.2	1.5	1.6	.6	1.1	−.2	.7
1966	6.5	3.5	.7	1.5	1.3	1.4	.8	1.2	.3	1.0	−.4	.6
1967	2.5	1.8	.1	.4	1.3	−.7	−.3	−.2	−.1	−.1	−.1	−.4
1968	4.7	3.5	.9	1.2	1.4	.8	1.0	.4	.1	.4	.5	−.2
1969	3.0	2.3	.3	.7	1.3	.9	.9	.7	.2	.5	.1	0
1970	.1	1.4	−.3	.6	1.1	−1.1	−.4	−.1	0	−.1	−.3	−.7
1971	3.3	2.3	.8	.5	1.0	1.7	1.1	0	−.1	.1	1.1	.6
1972	5.5	3.7	1.1	1.1	1.5	1.9	1.8	.9	.1	.8	.9	.1
1973	5.8	3.0	.9	.8	1.3	2.0	1.4	1.5	.3	1.2	0	.6
1974	−.6	−.4	−.6	−.5	.7	−1.4	−1.1	.1	−.1	.1	−1.1	−.4
1975	−.4	1.4	0	.4	1.0	−3.0	−1.8	−1.2	−.4	−.7	−.6	−1.3
1976	5.4	3.5	1.0	1.3	1.2	2.8	1.4	.5	.1	.4	.9	1.4
1977	4.7	2.7	.8	.7	1.2	2.5	2.2	1.2	.2	1.0	1.0	.3
1978	5.4	2.7	.5	.9	1.4	2.0	1.9	1.5	.4	1.1	.4	.2
1979	2.8	1.5	0	.6	.9	.4	.9	1.1	.5	.6	−.2	−.5
1980	−.3	−.2	−.7	−.1	.6	−2.2	−1.2	−.1	.3	−.4	−1.2	−.9
1981	2.3	.8	.1	.2	.5	1.5	.3	.7	.4	.3	−.4	1.2
1982	−2.1	.7	0	.1	.6	−2.6	−1.3	−.6	−.1	−.5	−.7	−1.3
1983	4.0	3.3	1.1	.7	1.5	1.4	1.1	−.2	−.5	.3	1.3	.3
1984	7.0	3.3	1.1	.8	1.4	4.6	2.6	1.9	.6	1.3	.6	2.0
1985	3.6	3.0	.8	.5	1.7	−.2	.8	.7	.3	.4	.1	−1.0
1986	3.1	2.6	.8	.7	1.1	−.3	.1	−.4	−.5	.1	.5	−.4
1987	2.9	2.0	.1	.4	1.5	.2	−.1	−.1	−.1	0	0	.3
1988	3.8	2.6	.6	.6	1.4	.1	.4	.5	0	.4	−.1	−.2
1989	3.4	1.5	.2	.5	.8	.6	.3	.4	.1	.3	−.2	.4
1990	1.2	1.1	−.1	.2	.9	−.8	−.5	−.1	0	−.1	−.4	−.4
1991	−.9	−.4	−.5	−.2	.3	−1.3	−1.1	−.6	−.4	−.3	−.5	−.2
1992	2.7	1.9	.4	.3	1.1	.8	.7	.1	−.2	.3	.5	.2
1993	2.3	2.0	.6	.5	1.0	1.2	.9	.7	0	.6	.3	.2
1994	3.5	2.2	.6	.6	1.1	1.7	1.1	.7	0	.7	.4	.6
1995	2.0	1.7	.3	.3	1.0	.2	.7	.8	.1	.7	−.2	−.5
1996	2.8	1.8	.4	.3	1.1	1.1	1.1	.9	.1	.8	.2	0
1997 ᴾ	3.8	2.2	.4	.4	1.4	1.6	1.0	.9	.1	.8	.1	.5
1992: I	4.7	4.3	1.0	1.2	2.0	−.3	1.1	.3	.1	.2	.8	−1.4
II	2.5	1.5	.3	−.2	1.3	2.3	1.6	.9	−.1	1.0	.7	.7
III	3.0	2.0	.7	.6	.7	.4	.3	.2	−.2	.4	.1	0
IV	4.3	3.6	.8	1.2	1.6	.9	1.2	.5	−.1	.7	.6	−.3
1993: I	.1	.5	−.1	−.2	.8	3.4	.9	.9	.3	.6	0	2.5
II	2.0	2.3	1.0	.7	.7	0	1.0	1.1	.1	1.0	−.1	−1.0
III	2.1	2.8	.7	.6	1.6	.8	.8	.4	.1	.4	.4	−.1
IV	5.3	2.0	.8	.3	.9	2.8	2.3	1.4	.1	1.3	.8	.6
1994: I	3.0	2.6	.5	1.0	1.0	2.2	.4	0	−.4	.5	.4	1.8
II	4.7	2.0	.3	.4	1.3	2.9	1.5	.9	.5	.4	.6	1.4
III	1.8	1.6	.3	.5	.8	−.9	.6	.7	0	.7	−.1	−1.5
IV	3.6	2.2	.9	.5	.7	1.8	.9	1.1	.1	1.1	−.2	.9
1995: I	.9	1.0	−.3	.3	.9	.2	1.0	1.3	.2	1.0	−.3	−.8
II	.3	1.9	.3	.2	1.4	−1.7	−.1	.6	.1	.4	−.7	−1.6
III	3.0	1.8	.7	.1	.9	.3	.5	.2	0	.1	.3	−.2
IV	2.2	1.2	.2	.1	.9	1.1	.8	.5	−.2	.6	.3	.3
1996: I	1.8	2.1	.4	.4	1.4	.6	1.4	1.1	.2	.9	.3	−.8
II	6.0	2.5	.8	.5	1.2	2.6	1.9	1.3	.2	1.0	.7	.7
III	1.0	.4	−.2	.1	.4	2.3	1.4	1.6	.3	1.3	−.2	.8
IV	4.3	2.2	.3	.4	1.5	.2	.4	.6	.4	.2	−.2	−.2
1997: I	4.9	3.6	1.1	.9	1.5	2.4	.6	.4	−.1	.5	.1	1.8
II	3.3	.6	−.5	−.4	1.5	2.5	1.7	1.4	−.1	1.6	.3	.8
III	3.1	3.8	1.4	.8	1.5	.4	2.0	1.9	.2	1.7	.1	−1.6
IV ᴾ	4.3	2.2	.2	−.1	2.0	.7	0	−.4	−.1	−.3	.4	.7

See next page for continuation of table.

TABLE B–5.—*Contributions to percent change in real gross domestic product, 1959–97—Continued*

[Percentage points, except as noted; quarterly data at seasonally adjusted annual rates]

Year or quarter	Net exports of goods and services							Government consumption expenditures and gross investment				
	Net exports	Exports			Imports			Total	Federal			State and local
		Total	Goods	Services	Total	Goods	Services		Total	National defense	Non-defense	
1959	-0.4	0	0	0.1	-0.5	-0.5	0	1.3	1.0	0.3	0.7	0.3
1960	.8	.8	.8	.1	-.1	0	-.1	0	-.4	-.2	-.2	.4
1961	.1	.1	0	.1	0	0	0	1.0	.5	.4	.1	.6
1962	-.2	.3	.2	.1	-.5	-.4	-.1	1.3	1.1	.6	.4	.3
1963	.2	.4	.3	.1	-.1	-.1	0	.5	0	-.3	.2	.6
1964	.4	.6	.5	.1	-.2	-.2	0	.4	-.2	-.4	.2	.7
1965	-.3	.1	0	.1	-.5	-.4	0	.7	0	-.2	.2	.7
1966	-.3	.3	.3	.1	-.7	-.5	-.2	1.9	1.3	1.3	0	.6
1967	-.2	.1	0	.1	-.3	-.2	-.2	1.7	1.2	1.2	0	.5
1968	-.3	.4	.3	.1	-.7	-.7	0	.7	.1	.2	-.1	.6
1969	0	.3	.2	.1	-.3	-.2	-.1	-.1	-.4	-.5	.1	.3
1970	.3	.5	.4	.1	-.2	-.1	-.1	-.5	-.8	-.8	0	.3
1971	-.3	0	0	.1	-.3	-.3	0	-.4	-.8	-.9	.1	.4
1972	-.2	.4	.4	0	-.6	-.6	0	.1	-.2	-.3	.2	.3
1973	.9	1.2	1.0	.2	-.3	-.3	.1	-.1	-.5	-.5	0	.4
1974	.9	.7	.5	.2	.2	.2	0	.4	-.1	-.2	.1	.4
1975	.9	-.1	-.2	.1	1.0	.9	.1	.3	0	-.1	.1	.4
1976	-1.0	.5	.3	.2	-1.5	-1.4	-.1	0	-.1	-.1	0	.1
1977	-.7	.2	.1	.1	-.9	-.8	-.1	.2	.1	0	.1	0
1978	0	.8	.7	.1	-.8	-.7	-.1	.6	.2	0	.2	.4
1979	.6	.8	.8	0	-.2	-.1	0	.3	.1	.1	0	.2
1980	1.7	1.0	.9	.1	.7	.7	0	.4	.4	.2	.1	0
1981	-.2	.1	-.1	.2	-.3	-.2	-.1	.1	.4	.3	0	-.2
1982	-.6	-.7	-.7	0	.1	.2	-.1	.3	.3	.5	-.2	0
1983	-1.4	-.2	-.2	0	-1.1	-1.0	-.1	.6	.5	.4	.1	.1
1984	-1.6	.6	.5	.2	-2.2	-1.8	-.4	.7	.2	.3	-.1	.4
1985	-.4	.2	.2	0	-.7	-.5	-.1	1.2	.7	.5	.1	.6
1986	-.3	.5	.3	.3	-.8	-.8	0	1.1	.4	.4	.1	.6
1987	.2	.8	.6	.2	-.6	-.4	-.2	.6	.3	.3	0	.3
1988	.8	1.2	1.0	.2	-.4	-.4	-.1	.3	-.2	-.1	-.1	.4
1989	.6	1.0	.8	.2	-.4	-.4	-.1	.6	.1	-.1	.2	.4
1990	.4	.8	.6	.2	-.4	-.3	-.1	.6	.2	0	.2	.4
1991	.7	.6	.5	.1	.1	0	.1	.1	0	-.1	0	.2
1992	-.1	.6	.5	.2	-.7	-.8	0	.1	-.2	-.4	.2	.3
1993	-.6	.3	.2	.1	-.9	-.9	0	-.2	-.4	-.3	0	.2
1994	-.5	.8	.7	.1	-1.3	-1.2	-.1	0	-.3	-.3	0	.3
1995	.1	1.1	.9	.2	-1.0	-.9	-.1	0	-.2	-.2	0	.2
1996	-.2	.9	.7	.2	-1.1	-1.0	-.1	.1	-.1	-.1	0	.2
1997 P	-.3	1.3	1.2	.2	-1.6	-1.4	-.2	.2	-.1	-.1	0	.3
1992: I	.2	.6	.4	.2	-.4	-.4	-.1	.5	-.1	-.5	.4	.6
II	-1.2	.2	.3	-.1	-1.4	-1.5	.1	-.1	-.1	-.1	-.1	.1
III	.1	.2	.2	0	-.1	-.6	.4	.6	.4	.4	.1	.2
IV	-.6	.6	.8	-.2	-1.2	-.6	-.6	.4	.3	-.1	.4	.1
1993: I	-1.5	-.2	-.7	.5	-1.3	-1.7	.4	-2.3	-2.2	-1.8	-.4	-.1
II	-.5	.8	.7	.1	-1.3	-1.2	-.1	.2	-.3	-.2	-.1	.5
III	-1.3	-.9	-.8	0	-.4	-.3	-.1	-.2	-.4	-.4	-.1	.2
IV	.2	2.0	1.9	.1	-1.8	-1.5	-.3	.3	0	0	0	.3
1994: I	-1.0	-.2	-.3	.1	-.8	-.8	-.1	-.8	-.9	-1.0	.1	.1
II	-.3	1.7	1.3	.4	-2.0	-1.9	-.1	.1	-.4	0	-.4	.5
III	-.4	1.0	1.0	.1	-1.4	-1.4	0	1.5	.9	.7	.3	.6
IV	.3	1.4	1.2	.2	-1.1	-1.1	0	-.7	-.9	-1.0	.1	.1
1995: I	-.4	.7	.5	.2	-1.1	-.6	-.4	.1	-.1	-.1	0	.2
II	.1	1.0	.9	.1	-.9	-1.0	.1	0	-.3	-.1	-.3	.3
III	1.1	1.4	.8	.6	-.2	-.1	-.2	-.1	-.1	-.2	.1	0
IV	1.0	1.2	1.0	.2	-.3	-.2	0	-1.0	-1.2	-.8	-.4	.2
1996: I	-1.3	.2	.3	-.1	-1.5	-1.2	-.3	.3	.5	.3	.2	-.2
II	-.6	1.1	.8	.3	-1.7	-1.6	-.1	1.3	.6	.5	.1	.7
III	-1.4	.2	.2	0	-1.6	-1.6	0	-.2	-.3	-.2	-.1	.1
IV	1.8	2.7	2.2	.4	-.8	-.8	0	0	-.4	-.3	0	.4
1997: I	-1.0	1.1	1.0	.1	-2.1	-1.7	-.5	-.1	-.4	-.6	.2	.3
II	-.4	2.0	1.9	.1	-2.5	-2.3	-.2	.6	.4	.3	.1	.1
III	-1.3	.5	.3	.2	-1.7	-1.6	-.1	.2	-.1	.1	-.1	.3
IV P	1.1	1.3	1.3	0	-.2	-.1	-.1	.3	0	.1	-.1	.2

Source: Department of Commerce, Bureau of Economic Analysis.

TABLE B–6.—*Chain-type quantity indexes for gross domestic product, 1959–97*

[Index numbers, 1992=100; quarterly data seasonally adjusted]

Year or quarter	Gross domestic product	Personal consumption expenditures				Gross private domestic investment					
		Total	Durable goods	Non-durable goods	Services	Total	Fixed investment				
							Total	Nonresidential			Residential
								Total	Structures	Producers' durable equipment	
1959	35.39	33.05	21.10	45.87	28.53	34.37	34.09	26.47	50.71	18.37	58.14
1960	36.24	33.95	21.53	46.56	29.78	34.22	34.36	27.95	54.74	19.12	54.01
1961	37.06	34.64	20.72	47.42	30.98	33.86	34.19	27.70	55.48	18.67	54.16
1962	39.31	36.35	23.14	48.91	32.52	38.23	37.28	30.11	57.98	20.83	59.35
1963	40.99	37.84	25.39	49.93	33.98	40.69	40.04	31.62	58.62	22.41	66.34
1964	43.37	40.10	27.73	52.39	36.04	44.06	43.87	35.34	64.71	25.23	70.20
1965	46.14	42.64	31.24	55.18	37.96	50.25	48.31	41.46	75.03	29.81	68.15
1966	49.15	45.07	33.88	58.19	39.88	54.48	50.94	46.50	80.17	34.43	62.05
1967	50.40	46.41	34.42	59.12	41.82	52.10	49.91	45.77	78.13	34.08	60.10
1968	52.75	49.06	38.20	61.80	43.98	54.82	53.37	47.76	79.24	36.15	68.29
1969	54.35	50.89	39.56	63.44	46.10	57.98	56.54	51.20	83.51	39.15	70.31
1970	54.41	52.08	38.29	64.99	47.96	53.91	55.16	50.70	83.78	38.46	66.10
1971	56.21	54.02	42.11	66.16	49.72	60.08	59.34	50.63	82.41	38.76	84.23
1972	59.29	57.25	47.46	69.06	52.40	67.28	66.41	55.16	84.94	43.69	99.20
1973	62.72	60.02	52.37	71.33	54.76	75.33	72.43	63.19	91.86	51.77	98.56
1974	62.32	59.59	48.77	69.94	56.08	69.14	67.68	63.52	89.94	52.84	78.21
1975	62.04	60.90	48.74	70.99	58.03	56.50	60.12	56.88	80.53	47.32	68.06
1976	65.38	64.32	54.96	74.50	60.47	67.99	66.07	59.61	82.50	50.22	84.09
1977	68.44	67.06	60.06	76.44	63.01	78.71	75.78	66.65	86.52	58.05	101.89
1978	72.11	69.95	63.21	79.11	65.96	87.73	84.34	75.75	95.96	66.80	108.62
1979	74.16	71.57	62.90	80.92	68.06	89.79	88.78	83.05	108.01	72.21	104.65
1980	73.91	71.32	57.85	80.58	69.34	79.49	82.77	82.66	115.27	69.01	82.52
1981	75.60	72.19	58.51	81.27	70.39	86.78	84.32	87.07	124.37	71.56	75.92
1982	73.99	73.02	58.44	81.75	71.73	74.29	77.91	83.23	122.50	66.97	62.10
1983	76.93	76.79	67.01	84.16	75.08	81.23	83.51	81.82	109.79	70.08	87.62
1984	82.32	80.75	76.75	87.14	78.15	105.43	97.32	95.97	125.44	83.52	100.39
1985	85.25	84.52	84.21	89.15	82.06	104.23	102.02	101.90	134.63	88.10	101.75
1986	87.88	87.89	91.79	91.98	84.72	102.71	102.76	98.32	120.16	88.99	113.95
1987	90.47	90.58	93.13	93.75	88.27	103.93	102.05	97.22	115.77	89.24	114.22
1988	93.93	94.14	98.97	96.41	91.82	104.77	104.45	101.46	116.35	94.99	111.96
1989	97.08	96.32	101.57	98.61	93.90	109.24	106.20	106.55	118.91	99.73	107.84
1990	98.27	97.92	100.98	99.56	96.34	103.11	102.86	104.90	120.18	98.24	97.80
1991	97.36	97.30	94.56	98.57	97.16	93.39	94.62	98.18	107.32	94.20	85.76
1992	100.00	100.00	100.00	100.00	100.00	100.00	100.00	100.00	100.00	100.00	100.00
1993	102.32	102.93	107.23	102.20	102.47	109.25	107.58	108.00	100.95	110.52	107.56
1994	105.87	106.31	114.87	105.15	105.23	123.44	116.86	116.22	101.94	122.66	118.39
1995	107.97	108.90	119.46	106.86	107.89	125.44	122.81	126.65	106.35	135.91	113.94
1996	110.95	111.71	125.09	108.36	110.86	135.26	132.97	138.33	111.51	150.77	120.64
1997 P	115.17	115.40	132.19	110.40	114.77	150.83	143.26	151.78	115.47	169.14	124.00
1992:I	98.90	98.91	97.45	99.44	98.91	95.93	96.79	97.58	102.07	95.62	94.84
II	99.52	99.45	98.49	99.26	99.74	100.30	99.87	99.93	101.07	99.42	99.71
III	100.26	100.16	100.70	99.95	100.17	101.02	100.49	100.48	98.97	101.14	100.53
IV	101.32	101.48	103.36	101.36	101.17	102.75	102.85	102.01	97.89	103.82	104.93
1993:I	101.34	101.59	103.18	101.19	101.49	106.96	104.00	103.57	99.32	105.43	105.08
II	101.85	102.44	106.29	101.97	101.93	107.05	106.08	106.67	100.66	109.32	104.67
III	102.39	103.48	108.47	102.64	102.53	108.63	107.79	107.96	101.50	110.80	107.38
IV	103.72	104.22	110.97	103.02	103.53	114.37	112.43	112.13	102.33	116.51	113.10
1994:I	104.49	105.21	112.72	104.28	104.21	118.91	113.32	112.25	98.31	118.51	115.84
II	105.70	105.98	113.77	104.81	105.06	124.96	116.56	114.94	103.13	120.37	120.37
III	106.17	106.60	114.99	105.40	105.58	123.00	117.78	117.08	102.86	123.49	119.44
IV	107.11	107.45	118.02	106.10	106.08	126.89	119.79	120.62	103.45	128.42	117.90
1995:I	107.36	107.86	117.13	106.55	106.72	127.25	122.01	124.70	105.82	133.30	115.80
II	107.44	108.62	118.25	106.79	107.68	123.66	121.78	126.44	106.93	135.31	111.02
III	108.24	109.32	120.93	106.97	108.27	124.24	122.83	126.95	107.12	135.98	113.29
IV	108.84	109.80	121.53	107.15	108.90	126.62	124.62	128.49	105.54	139.06	115.63
1996:I	109.32	110.65	122.95	107.62	109.84	128.06	127.84	132.10	107.63	143.41	117.96
II	110.92	111.67	125.84	108.30	110.67	134.00	132.20	136.19	109.68	148.48	122.91
III	111.20	111.81	125.25	108.48	110.93	139.21	135.42	141.48	112.32	155.10	121.51
IV	112.38	112.72	126.32	109.03	111.99	139.77	136.41	143.54	116.40	156.09	120.18
1997:I	113.73	114.18	130.55	110.29	113.05	145.39	137.73	145.00	115.79	158.63	121.17
II	114.66	114.45	128.75	109.70	114.13	151.45	141.86	150.03	114.39	167.05	123.36
III	115.53	116.03	134.31	110.87	115.22	152.40	146.70	156.75	116.26	176.32	124.19
IV P	116.75	116.95	135.16	110.76	116.67	154.08	146.74	155.33	115.45	174.57	127.29

See next page for continuation of table.

[Index numbers, 1992=100; quarterly data seasonally adjusted]

Year or quarter	Exports of goods and services			Imports of goods and services			Government consumption expenditures and gross investment				
							Total	Federal			State and local
	Total	Goods	Services	Total	Goods	Services		Total	National defense	Non-defense	
1959	11.24	11.53	9.78	15.94	13.06	28.14	48.94	68.29	81.85	38.65	34.90
1960	13.58	14.23	10.82	16.15	12.84	30.35	48.84	66.18	80.17	35.54	36.32
1961	13.80	14.30	11.54	16.05	12.83	29.83	51.21	68.76	83.51	36.44	38.57
1962	14.54	14.94	12.59	17.87	14.72	31.23	54.28	74.48	88.45	43.88	39.70
1963	15.64	16.11	13.39	18.34	15.32	31.18	55.54	74.21	86.22	47.89	42.09
1964	17.73	18.32	14.99	19.32	16.33	31.98	56.65	72.95	82.48	52.02	44.98
1965	18.08	18.41	16.17	21.37	18.64	32.92	58.36	72.96	80.84	55.56	48.00
1966	19.30	19.69	17.10	24.55	21.58	37.10	63.66	81.28	92.66	56.27	51.09
1967	19.72	19.79	18.60	26.34	22.72	41.64	68.49	85.34	104.71	55.66	53.58
1968	21.16	21.35	19.55	30.26	27.41	42.39	70.62	90.22	106.69	54.18	56.61
1969	22.31	22.47	20.76	31.99	28.91	45.06	70.22	87.11	101.56	55.41	58.17
1970	24.73	25.03	22.59	33.35	30.05	47.41	68.59	80.90	92.88	54.56	59.80
1971	24.90	24.94	23.60	35.13	32.57	46.06	67.34	75.19	83.49	56.70	61.75
1972	26.90	27.62	23.45	39.01	37.00	47.63	67.58	73.90	79.91	60.39	63.12
1973	32.78	33.96	27.58	40.76	39.61	45.70	67.14	70.29	74.82	60.11	65.03
1974	35.93	36.66	32.27	39.66	38.51	44.65	68.28	69.85	72.80	63.34	67.35
1975	35.69	35.81	34.40	35.19	33.65	42.32	69.34	69.68	71.78	65.13	69.32
1976	37.79	37.51	37.98	42.08	41.26	45.28	69.38	68.99	70.43	65.97	69.90
1977	38.69	38.00	40.46	46.59	46.28	47.02	70.01	70.09	70.89	68.55	70.18
1978	42.71	42.24	43.52	50.62	50.43	50.36	72.05	71.54	70.99	73.17	72.68
1979	46.77	47.23	43.99	51.47	51.30	51.08	73.18	72.59	72.13	74.04	73.87
1980	51.83	52.86	46.78	48.03	47.49	49.82	74.49	75.63	74.71	78.21	73.88
1981	52.43	52.32	51.66	49.28	48.46	52.68	74.99	78.77	78.77	79.09	72.41
1982	48.71	47.58	51.65	48.66	47.24	55.49	75.97	81.33	84.23	74.46	72.22
1983	47.44	46.20	50.76	54.81	53.66	59.97	78.13	85.74	89.05	77.85	72.69
1984	51.36	49.85	55.50	68.12	66.64	74.85	80.58	87.83	92.63	76.17	75.44
1985	52.76	51.65	55.65	72.53	70.84	80.37	85.47	93.87	99.55	80.02	79.47
1986	56.65	54.30	63.06	78.65	78.10	80.72	89.81	98.18	104.68	82.25	83.85
1987	62.87	60.28	69.94	83.44	81.72	91.14	92.26	101.21	108.89	82.32	85.87
1988	72.85	71.63	76.04	86.73	85.01	94.38	93.44	99.36	107.92	78.25	89.24
1989	81.36	80.61	83.20	90.13	88.58	96.88	96.06	100.67	106.86	85.45	92.78
1990	88.27	87.29	90.74	93.62	91.27	104.26	98.94	102.64	106.86	92.31	96.31
1991	93.82	93.43	94.77	93.01	91.23	100.97	99.55	102.16	105.79	93.28	97.68
1992	100.00	100.00	100.00	100.00	100.00	100.00	100.00	100.00	100.00	100.00	100.00
1993	102.94	103.35	101.96	108.89	110.49	101.91	99.08	95.78	94.32	99.33	101.45
1994	111.41	113.62	106.38	122.13	125.56	107.31	99.09	92.17	89.66	98.24	104.06
1995	123.74	127.91	114.27	133.05	137.50	113.82	99.06	89.08	85.84	96.88	106.23
1996	134.03	140.05	120.51	145.22	151.06	120.06	99.54	87.92	84.56	96.01	107.88
1997 P	150.82	161.77	127.12	165.40	173.27	131.77	100.54	86.71	82.24	97.46	110.48
1992: I	99.00	98.13	101.08	96.84	95.67	102.06	99.59	99.45	99.59	99.10	99.69
II	99.44	99.20	99.98	99.91	99.78	100.45	99.51	99.11	99.34	98.54	99.79
III	100.05	99.93	100.29	100.23	101.46	94.87	100.22	100.31	100.79	99.13	100.15
IV	101.52	102.75	98.65	103.02	103.10	102.62	100.69	101.14	100.28	103.23	100.37
1993: I	101.22	101.22	101.21	104.93	106.20	99.34	98.92	97.00	95.58	100.46	100.30
II	103.24	103.70	102.15	108.03	109.72	100.63	99.16	96.19	94.92	99.29	101.29
III	101.07	100.74	101.81	109.04	110.70	101.79	98.95	94.98	93.42	98.76	101.81
IV	106.21	107.75	102.68	113.56	115.32	105.89	99.29	94.95	93.36	98.81	102.40
1994: I	105.73	106.79	103.28	115.65	117.72	106.61	98.27	92.28	89.19	99.77	102.52
II	110.12	111.72	106.46	120.79	123.81	107.69	98.38	91.13	89.40	95.36	103.59
III	112.93	115.54	106.99	124.56	128.48	107.58	100.35	94.02	92.33	98.13	104.89
IV	116.88	120.44	108.79	127.54	132.22	107.34	99.37	91.23	87.71	99.69	105.21
1995: I	118.92	122.68	110.39	130.63	134.62	113.37	99.52	90.99	87.46	99.46	105.64
II	121.59	126.09	111.42	133.09	137.92	112.23	99.49	89.95	87.12	96.80	106.33
III	125.50	129.35	116.70	133.85	138.31	114.52	99.30	89.66	86.22	97.94	106.22
IV	128.96	133.54	118.59	134.65	139.15	115.14	97.94	85.72	82.56	93.33	106.71
1996: I	129.52	134.88	117.43	138.87	143.42	119.13	98.37	87.29	83.79	95.70	106.33
II	132.53	138.00	120.19	143.51	148.97	119.94	100.10	89.15	86.01	96.72	107.97
III	133.15	138.85	120.28	148.03	154.49	120.29	99.83	88.21	85.00	95.93	108.17
IV	140.92	148.48	124.14	150.48	157.37	120.90	99.85	87.04	83.44	95.69	109.04
1997: I	144.30	152.94	125.27	156.80	163.58	127.64	99.74	85.76	80.86	97.54	109.78
II	150.53	161.76	126.25	164.30	172.24	130.41	100.50	87.14	82.33	98.71	110.10
III	152.17	163.11	128.46	169.98	178.53	133.58	100.77	86.89	82.58	97.27	110.73
IV P	156.29	169.26	128.51	170.53	178.74	135.44	101.17	87.04	83.18	96.33	111.31

Source: Department of Commerce, Bureau of Economic Analysis.

289

TABLE B–7.—*Chain-type price indexes for gross domestic product, 1959–97*

[Index numbers, 1992=100, except as noted; quarterly data seasonally adjusted]

Year or quarter	Gross domestic product	Personal consumption expenditures				Gross private domestic investment					
		Total	Durable goods	Non-durable goods	Services	Total	Fixed investment				
							Total	Nonresidential			Residential
								Total	Structures	Producers' durable equipment	
1959	22.95	22.81	41.38	24.49	18.47	29.01	27.95	31.51	21.16	39.74	21.43
1960	23.27	23.19	41.18	24.84	18.96	29.13	28.08	31.61	21.13	39.99	21.58
1961	23.54	23.44	41.27	24.99	19.33	29.13	28.03	31.50	21.01	39.90	21.61
1962	23.84	23.69	41.47	25.18	19.62	29.11	28.03	31.48	21.18	39.66	21.65
1963	24.12	23.99	41.61	25.48	19.94	29.04	27.98	31.53	21.38	39.52	21.48
1964	24.48	24.31	41.82	25.80	20.28	29.21	28.15	31.69	21.68	39.50	21.65
1965	24.95	24.69	41.44	26.27	20.72	29.69	28.64	32.06	22.31	39.55	22.26
1966	25.66	25.34	41.25	27.14	21.32	30.29	29.25	32.55	23.11	39.67	23.07
1967	26.48	26.01	41.89	27.78	22.03	31.10	30.08	33.40	23.84	40.59	23.87
1968	27.64	27.04	43.28	28.85	22.97	32.30	31.31	34.59	25.03	41.70	25.14
1969	28.94	28.16	44.47	30.19	23.91	33.85	32.87	36.04	26.68	42.88	26.88
1970	30.48	29.49	45.44	31.66	25.20	35.27	34.28	37.76	28.42	44.48	27.74
1971	32.05	30.82	47.10	32.65	26.73	37.05	36.05	39.59	30.61	45.88	29.35
1972	33.42	31.90	47.60	33.74	27.91	38.69	37.64	41.00	32.83	46.51	31.14
1973	35.30	33.62	48.29	36.39	29.17	40.80	39.74	42.59	35.38	47.30	33.89
1974	38.46	37.03	51.35	41.59	31.41	44.91	43.69	46.75	40.24	50.85	37.39
1975	42.09	40.04	56.04	44.83	33.97	50.48	49.22	53.30	45.03	58.59	40.86
1976	44.55	42.32	59.16	46.53	36.50	53.33	52.12	56.33	47.22	62.19	43.49
1977	47.42	45.13	61.73	49.18	39.46	57.29	56.19	60.05	50.95	65.90	47.99
1978	50.88	48.41	65.23	52.59	42.62	62.10	61.09	64.38	56.30	69.59	53.72
1979	55.22	52.76	69.62	58.33	46.08	67.72	66.71	69.71	62.88	74.13	59.75
1980	60.34	58.49	75.56	65.30	50.96	74.18	73.03	75.96	68.66	80.67	66.22
1981	66.01	63.73	80.64	70.57	56.17	81.09	79.94	83.48	78.22	86.60	71.62
1982	70.18	67.40	83.81	72.81	60.80	85.38	84.47	88.28	84.45	90.24	75.45
1983	73.16	70.46	85.48	74.64	64.86	85.20	84.38	87.52	82.23	90.58	77.19
1984	75.92	73.14	86.71	76.71	68.17	85.87	85.01	87.48	82.94	90.04	79.41
1985	78.53	75.84	87.76	78.72	71.62	86.81	86.20	88.31	84.86	90.15	81.45
1986	80.58	78.00	88.91	78.73	75.28	88.97	88.56	90.22	86.47	92.24	84.87
1987	83.06	80.96	91.59	81.82	78.23	90.93	90.44	91.34	87.85	93.22	88.34
1988	86.10	84.32	93.28	84.83	82.16	93.46	93.25	93.73	92.10	94.59	92.06
1989	89.72	88.44	95.29	89.28	86.55	96.06	95.85	96.16	95.61	96.45	95.08
1990	93.64	92.91	96.59	94.62	91.22	98.37	98.24	98.42	98.78	98.23	97.80
1991	97.32	96.82	98.54	98.06	95.78	99.70	99.63	99.93	100.09	99.84	98.85
1992	100.00	100.00	100.00	100.00	100.00	100.00	100.00	100.00	100.00	100.00	100.00
1993	102.64	102.66	101.22	101.46	103.62	101.50	101.53	100.65	103.26	99.57	103.71
1994	105.09	105.15	103.27	102.77	106.85	103.32	103.40	101.89	107.00	99.86	107.11
1995	107.76	107.89	104.27	104.48	110.53	104.71	104.78	102.33	111.49	98.89	110.93
1996	110.22	110.47	103.83	107.15	113.76	104.50	104.70	101.26	114.09	96.62	113.64
1997 ᴾ	112.46	112.72	102.16	109.15	117.04	104.14	104.54	99.88	117.87	93.63	117.09
1992: I	99.14	98.90	99.59	99.15	98.63	99.61	99.60	99.91	99.35	100.15	98.82
II	99.81	99.70	100.09	99.74	99.60	99.80	99.80	99.92	99.66	100.02	99.52
III	100.17	100.30	100.10	100.39	100.29	100.10	100.10	100.07	100.07	100.06	100.20
IV	100.88	101.10	100.23	100.72	101.48	100.49	100.50	100.11	100.91	99.77	101.46
1993: I	101.85	101.83	100.47	101.26	102.43	101.06	101.08	100.49	102.15	99.80	102.54
II	102.38	102.46	101.00	101.38	102.35	101.42	101.45	100.66	102.90	99.72	103.41
III	102.83	102.80	101.38	101.27	103.93	101.65	101.69	100.66	103.56	99.45	104.25
IV	103.52	103.57	102.03	101.92	104.79	101.85	101.91	100.80	104.42	99.32	104.64
1994: I	104.16	104.00	102.28	101.90	105.50	102.57	102.64	101.36	105.46	99.69	105.79
II	104.74	104.68	103.02	102.23	106.37	103.10	103.19	101.89	106.16	100.15	106.36
III	105.39	105.61	103.85	103.31	107.24	103.63	103.71	102.20	107.37	100.14	107.45
IV	106.07	106.31	103.94	103.64	108.27	103.96	104.04	102.12	109.00	99.46	108.83
1995: I	106.93	107.05	104.35	103.85	109.37	104.43	104.48	102.21	110.40	99.09	110.17
II	107.49	107.69	104.43	104.32	110.23	104.86	104.90	102.61	111.19	99.35	110.65
III	108.03	108.19	104.25	104.70	110.96	104.82	104.88	102.40	111.92	98.83	111.15
IV	108.60	108.63	104.07	105.05	111.58	104.74	104.83	102.11	112.43	98.29	111.75
1996: I	109.35	109.34	104.25	106.02	112.27	104.57	104.70	101.74	112.97	97.60	112.29
II	109.86	110.13	103.89	107.04	113.20	104.31	104.50	101.29	113.50	96.84	112.80
III	110.59	110.80	103.72	107.29	114.29	104.63	104.85	101.21	114.58	96.38	114.37
IV	111.10	111.61	103.45	108.26	115.26	104.50	104.75	100.82	115.30	95.65	115.10
1997: I	111.78	112.21	103.27	108.90	116.02	104.23	104.52	100.31	116.11	94.72	115.68
II	112.27	112.49	102.50	108.89	116.70	104.07	104.47	99.93	117.23	93.88	116.65
III	112.67	112.91	101.74	109.24	117.42	104.11	104.55	99.73	118.44	93.27	117.57
IVᴾ	113.10	113.27	101.14	109.56	118.04	104.16	104.62	99.53	119.71	92.64	118.47

See next page for continuation of table.

TABLE B-7.—Chain-type price indexes for gross domestic product, 1959-97—Continued

[Index numbers, 1992=100, except as noted; quarterly data seasonally adjusted]

| Year or quarter | Exports and imports of goods and services | | Government consumption expenditures and gross investment | | | | | Final sales of domestic product | Gross domestic purchases[1] | | Gross national product | Percent change[2] | | |
| | Exports | Imports | Total | Federal | | | State and local | | Total | Less food and energy | | Gross domestic product | Gross domestic purchases[1] | |
				Total	National defense	Non-defense							Total	Less food and energy
1959	28.74	20.94	18.10	18.61	18.10	19.51	17.45	22.79	22.44		22.95	1.0	1.0	
1960	29.10	21.14	18.34	18.75	18.20	19.82	17.82	23.11	22.75		23.27	1.4	1.4	
1961	29.51	21.14	18.66	19.01	18.38	20.48	18.24	23.38	23.00		23.54	1.2	1.1	
1962	29.48	20.89	19.15	19.42	18.74	21.12	18.83	23.68	23.28		23.85	1.3	1.2	
1963	29.44	21.30	19.61	19.90	19.19	21.67	19.25	23.97	23.58		24.13	1.2	1.3	
1964	29.64	21.75	20.15	20.58	19.77	22.75	19.63	24.32	23.94		24.49	1.5	1.6	
1965	30.61	22.05	20.73	21.19	20.41	23.22	20.17	24.80	24.39		24.96	1.9	1.9	
1966	31.55	22.56	21.56	21.89	21.07	24.04	21.14	25.51	25.07		25.68	2.8	2.8	
1967	32.80	22.65	22.47	22.55	21.72	24.72	22.35	26.34	25.83		26.49	3.2	3.0	
1968	33.48	23.00	23.74	23.84	22.92	26.34	23.60	27.50	26.95		27.65	4.4	4.3	
1969	34.54	23.60	25.19	25.13	24.18	27.65	25.23	28.80	28.21		28.95	4.7	4.7	
1970	36.04	24.99	27.21	27.08	25.94	30.30	27.31	30.33	29.73		30.49	5.3	5.4	
1971	37.27	26.53	29.33	29.42	28.24	32.71	29.23	31.91	31.32		32.07	5.2	5.3	
1972	38.50	28.44	31.46	32.00	31.01	34.53	30.97	33.26	32.71		33.43	4.2	4.5	
1973	43.78	33.44	33.88	34.51	33.66	36.54	33.32	35.15	34.64		35.32	5.6	5.9	
1974	54.11	48.04	37.45	37.89	37.24	39.31	37.00	38.28	38.17		38.48	8.9	10.2	
1975	59.72	52.13	41.36	41.95	41.10	43.84	40.80	41.90	41.72		42.11	9.4	9.3	
1976	61.62	53.69	43.99	44.63	43.85	46.33	43.38	44.37	44.15		44.58	5.8	5.8	
1977	64.17	58.54	47.11	48.18	47.21	50.34	46.19	47.25	47.18		47.45	6.5	6.9	
1978	68.16	62.68	50.28	51.47	50.82	52.84	49.26	50.71	50.65		50.91	7.3	7.4	
1979	76.48	73.39	54.82	56.10	55.81	56.58	53.73	55.06	55.22		55.26	8.5	9.0	
1980	84.17	91.45	60.86	62.20	62.05	62.34	59.70	60.15	61.10		60.37	9.3	10.7	
1981	90.31	96.39	66.84	68.31	68.23	68.26	65.57	65.82	66.72		66.05	9.4	9.2	
1982	90.76	93.13	71.32	72.94	72.96	72.59	69.93	70.02	70.64	69.04	70.22	6.3	5.9	
1983	91.32	89.64	74.51	76.08	76.20	75.44	73.16	73.00	73.31	71.99	73.20	4.3	3.8	4.3
1984	92.30	88.90	78.23	80.36	81.23	77.53	76.40	75.77	75.90	74.65	75.97	3.8	3.5	3.7
1985	89.82	85.99	81.01	82.74	83.51	80.20	79.51	78.43	78.34	77.30	78.57	3.4	3.2	3.5
1986	88.54	85.95	82.69	83.96	84.49	82.16	81.59	80.51	80.40	80.10	80.62	2.6	2.6	3.6
1987	90.99	90.99	85.15	85.26	85.62	84.04	85.02	82.98	83.11	82.88	83.08	3.1	3.4	3.5
1988	96.00	95.35	87.39	87.18	87.30	86.75	87.52	86.06	86.13	86.09	86.12	3.7	3.6	3.9
1989	97.91	97.81	90.21	89.79	89.79	89.70	90.51	89.69	89.78	89.56	89.75	4.2	4.2	4.0
1990	98.74	100.37	94.06	92.92	92.92	92.84	94.91	93.62	93.83	93.35	93.66	4.4	4.5	4.2
1991	100.31	100.02	97.45	96.88	96.47	97.95	97.86	97.31	97.30	97.00	97.33	3.9	3.7	3.9
1992	100.00	100.00	100.00	100.00	100.00	100.00	100.00	100.00	100.00	100.00	100.00	2.8	2.8	3.1
1993	100.07	98.75	102.50	102.51	101.77	104.29	102.49	102.65	102.48	102.65	102.64	2.6	2.5	2.7
1994	101.24	99.39	104.85	104.84	103.63	107.70	104.85	105.11	104.85	105.16	105.08	2.4	2.3	2.4
1995	103.44	101.62	108.28	108.34	106.83	111.88	108.24	107.79	107.52	107.93	107.74	2.5	2.5	2.6
1996	101.61	99.41	111.83	112.03	111.02	114.47	111.71	110.28	109.86	110.06	110.19	2.3	2.2	2.0
1997 P	99.39	95.52	114.47	114.74	113.66	117.35	114.32	112.56	111.77	111.94	....	2.0	1.7	1.7
1992: I	99.86	98.95	99.16	99.38	99.61	99.82	99.00	99.14	99.04	99.04	99.14	3.4	3.2	3.8
II	100.10	99.60	99.92	100.01	100.23	99.48	99.86	99.81	99.76	99.76	99.81	2.8	2.9	2.9
III	100.07	101.03	100.33	100.44	100.58	100.09	100.25	100.17	100.28	100.25	100.17	1.4	2.1	2.0
IV	99.98	100.42	100.59	100.17	99.57	101.61	100.89	100.88	100.92	100.94	100.87	2.8	2.6	2.8
1993: I	99.97	98.82	101.71	101.79	101.23	103.15	101.65	101.85	101.71	101.82	101.84	3.9	3.2	3.5
II	100.22	99.45	102.24	101.94	101.39	103.27	102.44	102.38	102.28	102.43	102.37	2.1	2.3	2.4
III	100.04	98.55	102.77	102.83	101.97	104.89	102.74	102.84	102.64	102.88	102.83	1.8	1.4	1.8
IV	100.03	98.19	103.26	103.48	102.48	105.84	103.13	103.53	103.28	103.49	103.51	2.7	2.5	2.4
1994: I	100.44	97.64	103.95	104.04	102.90	106.73	103.90	104.17	103.80	104.10	104.16	2.5	2.0	2.4
II	100.99	98.87	104.61	104.97	103.65	108.08	104.39	104.75	104.46	104.86	104.73	2.2	2.6	3.0
III	101.40	100.34	105.07	104.83	103.68	107.57	105.21	105.41	105.24	105.50	105.38	2.5	3.0	2.5
IV	102.11	100.72	105.75	105.53	104.31	108.42	105.89	106.09	105.88	106.18	106.05	2.6	2.5	2.6
1995: I	103.21	101.12	106.92	106.89	105.37	110.44	106.93	106.95	106.66	107.03	106.90	3.3	3.0	3.2
II	104.09	102.82	107.85	107.59	106.30	110.61	108.00	107.50	107.33	107.70	107.46	2.1	2.5	2.6
III	103.57	101.77	108.55	108.33	107.20	111.03	108.67	108.05	107.79	108.22	108.00	2.0	1.7	1.9
IV	102.88	100.75	109.80	110.56	108.44	115.44	109.35	108.63	108.29	108.77	108.58	2.1	1.9	2.1
1996: I	102.50	100.28	111.27	111.85	110.38	115.28	110.92	109.39	109.01	109.38	109.33	2.8	2.7	2.3
II	102.14	99.83	111.23	111.47	110.58	113.63	111.08	110.91	110.50	110.67	110.83	1.9	1.8	1.1
III	101.47	98.76	112.07	112.05	111.16	114.25	112.07	110.65	110.15	110.34	110.55	2.7	2.4	2.5
IV	100.35	98.75	112.76	112.74	111.94	114.72	112.77	111.17	110.79	110.86	111.06	1.9	2.4	1.9
1997: I	99.90	97.42	113.74	114.10	113.14	116.44	113.54	111.85	111.32	111.36	111.73	2.4	1.9	1.8
II	99.72	95.52	114.11	114.46	113.46	116.87	113.95	112.37	111.55	111.81	112.22	1.8	.8	1.6
III	99.21	94.81	114.54	114.71	113.62	117.30	114.44	112.78	111.90	112.10	112.62	1.4	1.3	1.1
IV P	98.71	94.30	115.47	115.71	114.41	118.76	115.33	113.22	112.31	112.51	....	1.5	1.5	1.5

[1] Gross domestic product (GDP) less exports of goods and services plus imports of goods and services.
[2] Percent changes based on unrounded data. Quarterly percent changes are at annual rates.

Source: Department of Commerce, Bureau of Economic Analysis.

TABLE B-8.—*Gross domestic product by major type of product, 1959–97*

[Billions of dollars; quarterly data at seasonally adjusted annual rates]

Year or quarter	Gross domestic product	Final sales of domestic product	Change in business inventories	Goods								Services	Structures
				Total		Durable goods		Nondurable goods					
				Total	Final sales	Change in business inventories	Final sales	Change in business inventories	Final sales	Change in business inventories			
1959	507.2	503.0	4.2	252.0	247.8	4.2	92.3	3.1	155.5	1.1		192.7	62.5
1960	526.6	523.3	3.2	257.8	254.6	3.2	95.1	1.7	159.5	1.6		206.8	61.9
1961	544.8	541.9	2.9	260.4	257.5	2.9	94.3	-.1	163.2	3.0		220.8	63.6
1962	585.2	579.1	6.1	281.2	275.1	6.1	104.5	3.4	170.7	2.7		236.1	67.8
1963	617.4	611.7	5.7	292.7	287.1	5.7	111.0	2.7	176.1	3.0		252.0	72.7
1964	663.0	658.0	5.0	313.2	308.1	5.0	120.5	4.0	187.6	1.0		271.4	78.4
1965	719.1	709.4	9.7	342.9	333.3	9.7	133.3	6.7	199.9	3.0		291.5	84.7
1966	787.8	774.0	13.8	380.6	366.8	13.8	149.0	10.2	217.8	3.6		319.2	88.0
1967	833.6	823.1	10.5	394.5	384.0	10.5	153.8	5.5	230.2	5.0		349.5	89.6
1968	910.6	901.4	9.1	426.7	417.6	9.1	167.8	4.6	249.8	4.5		383.9	100.0
1969	982.2	972.7	9.5	455.8	446.2	9.5	178.6	6.3	267.6	3.2		418.2	108.3
1970	1,035.6	1,033.4	2.2	467.5	465.3	2.2	180.2	.0	285.1	2.2		458.5	109.7
1971	1,125.4	1,116.9	8.5	493.2	484.7	8.5	187.0	3.2	297.7	5.3		503.8	128.4
1972	1,237.3	1,227.4	9.9	539.8	529.9	9.9	209.3	7.2	320.6	2.7		550.5	146.9
1973	1,382.6	1,365.2	17.5	619.2	601.8	17.5	241.4	14.6	360.3	2.9		600.5	162.9
1974	1,496.9	1,482.8	14.1	665.7	651.6	14.1	256.7	11.0	394.9	3.1		665.6	165.6
1975	1,630.6	1,636.9	-6.3	718.1	724.5	-6.3	288.1	-7.5	436.4	1.2		745.8	166.7
1976	1,819.0	1,802.0	16.9	804.0	787.1	16.9	322.5	10.6	464.6	6.3		823.8	191.2
1977	2,026.9	2,003.8	23.1	883.7	860.6	23.1	366.9	10.2	493.7	12.8		916.4	226.8
1978	2,291.4	2,264.2	27.2	996.5	969.3	27.2	416.9	20.3	552.5	6.9		1,023.1	271.8
1979	2,557.5	2,540.6	16.9	1,115.2	1,098.2	16.9	475.0	12.5	623.3	4.3		1,131.7	310.6
1980	2,784.2	2,791.9	-7.6	1,191.1	1,198.7	-7.6	502.9	-2.7	695.8	-4.9		1,274.1	319.1
1981	3,115.9	3,087.8	28.2	1,342.6	1,314.5	28.2	546.0	7.5	768.4	20.6		1,423.3	350.0
1982	3,242.1	3,256.6	-14.5	1,333.2	1,347.7	-14.5	544.4	-15.5	803.3	1.0		1,566.9	342.0
1983	3,514.5	3,519.4	-4.9	1,426.9	1,431.8	-4.9	586.1	4.0	845.7	-8.9		1,720.9	366.8
1984	3,902.4	3,835.0	67.5	1,607.0	1,539.6	67.5	655.1	43.6	884.5	23.9		1,871.8	423.6
1985	4,180.7	4,154.5	26.2	1,669.8	1,643.6	26.2	713.2	8.6	930.4	17.6		2,054.6	456.3
1986	4,422.2	4,412.6	9.6	1,720.6	1,711.0	9.6	741.3	.6	969.7	9.0		2,224.2	477.4
1987	4,692.3	4,668.1	24.2	1,804.8	1,780.6	24.2	764.7	21.5	1,015.9	2.8		2,398.2	489.3
1988	5,049.6	5,038.7	10.9	1,942.9	1,932.0	10.9	837.0	16.4	1,095.0	-5.5		2,600.0	506.7
1989	5,438.7	5,407.0	31.7	2,124.0	2,092.3	31.7	907.3	21.3	1,185.0	10.5		2,795.3	519.4
1990	5,743.8	5,735.8	8.0	2,203.8	2,195.8	8.0	935.7	2.5	1,260.1	5.6		3,016.9	523.1
1991	5,916.7	5,919.0	-2.3	2,234.0	2,236.3	-2.3	926.6	-16.6	1,309.7	14.3		3,201.3	481.4
1992	6,244.4	6,237.4	7.0	2,321.0	2,314.0	7.0	965.9	-10.9	1,348.1	17.9		3,411.1	512.3
1993	6,558.1	6,537.6	20.5	2,422.1	2,401.6	20.5	1,012.7	16.1	1,388.9	4.4		3,589.5	546.5
1994	6,947.0	6,885.7	61.2	2,581.4	2,520.2	61.2	1,072.5	33.6	1,447.6	27.7		3,772.3	593.2
1995	7,265.4	7,235.3	30.1	2,667.9	2,637.8	30.1	1,133.9	29.1	1,503.9	1.0		3,980.7	616.8
1996 ᵖ	7,636.0	7,610.2	25.9	2,785.2	2,759.3	25.9	1,212.0	16.9	1,547.3	9.0		4,187.3	663.6
1997 ᵖ	8,083.4	8,018.8	64.6	2,945.1	2,880.6	64.6	1,284.9	30.8	1,595.7	33.8		4,432.8	705.5
1992: I	6,121.8	6,122.1	-.2	2,281.1	2,281.4	-.2	944.6	-18.8	1,336.8	18.5		3,338.4	502.3
II	6,201.2	6,191.0	10.2	2,301.3	2,291.0	10.2	955.7	1.1	1,335.4	9.1		3,387.5	512.4
III	6,271.7	6,260.1	11.6	2,329.4	2,317.8	11.6	969.2	-11.1	1,348.6	22.7		3,432.1	510.1
IV	6,383.1	6,376.6	6.5	2,372.3	2,365.8	6.5	994.2	-14.9	1,371.6	21.4		3,486.4	524.4
1993: I	6,444.5	6,413.8	30.7	2,388.3	2,357.5	30.7	980.8	20.6	1,376.7	10.1		3,527.4	528.8
II	6,509.1	6,494.7	14.5	2,408.7	2,394.2	14.5	1,014.9	7.0	1,379.3	7.4		3,561.8	538.6
III	6,574.6	6,560.6	14.0	2,412.0	2,398.0	14.0	1,009.4	14.2	1,388.6	-.2		3,612.4	550.2
IV	6,704.2	6,681.3	22.9	2,479.6	2,456.7	22.9	1,045.9	22.5	1,410.8	.4		3,656.1	568.5
1994: I	6,794.3	6,741.9	52.4	2,531.2	2,478.8	52.4	1,052.3	29.0	1,426.5	23.4		3,695.1	568.0
II	6,911.4	6,835.1	76.3	2,568.6	2,492.4	76.3	1,062.1	40.5	1,430.2	35.8		3,749.6	593.1
III	6,986.5	6,936.3	50.2	2,582.8	2,532.6	50.2	1,082.3	29.3	1,450.3	20.9		3,800.8	602.9
IV	7,095.7	7,029.6	66.2	2,643.0	2,576.9	66.2	1,093.4	35.6	1,483.5	30.6		3,843.9	608.8
1995: I	7,168.9	7,116.8	52.1	2,650.5	2,598.4	52.1	1,108.9	41.6	1,489.4	10.5		3,903.0	615.5
II	7,209.5	7,185.0	24.5	2,637.8	2,613.4	24.5	1,120.8	26.9	1,492.6	-2.5		3,961.4	610.2
III	7,301.3	7,281.8	19.4	2,673.3	2,653.9	19.4	1,143.9	21.6	1,510.0	-2.1		4,011.0	617.0
IV	7,381.9	7,357.4	24.5	2,710.2	2,685.7	24.5	1,162.1	26.2	1,523.6	-1.7		4,047.3	624.4
1996: I	7,467.5	7,456.4	11.1	2,733.2	2,722.1	11.1	1,183.4	17.2	1,538.7	-6.2		4,096.2	638.1
II	7,607.7	7,584.3	23.4	2,782.7	2,759.3	23.4	1,214.8	18.1	1,544.5	5.3		4,162.2	662.8
III	7,676.0	7,638.9	37.1	2,797.8	2,760.7	37.1	1,216.3	33.3	1,544.4	3.9		4,208.1	670.1
IV	7,792.9	7,761.0	31.9	2,826.9	2,795.0	31.9	1,233.5	-1.1	1,561.5	33.0		4,282.7	683.3
1997: I	7,933.6	7,867.4	66.1	2,904.6	2,838.4	66.1	1,248.0	31.8	1,590.4	34.3		4,338.2	690.8
II	8,034.3	7,953.2	81.1	2,936.0	2,854.9	81.1	1,275.3	46.8	1,579.6	34.4		4,400.1	698.2
III	8,124.3	8,075.3	48.9	2,952.1	2,903.2	48.9	1,305.3	18.6	1,597.9	30.3		4,462.3	709.8
IV ᵖ	8,241.5	8,179.3	62.1	2,987.9	2,925.7	62.1	1,310.9	25.9	1,614.8	36.2		4,530.4	723.2

Source: Department of Commerce, Bureau of Economic Analysis.

TABLE B–9.—*Real gross domestic product by major type of product, 1959–97*

[Billions of chained (1992) dollars; quarterly data at seasonally adjusted annual rates]

Year or quarter	Gross domestic product	Final sales of domestic product	Change in business inventories	Goods							Services	Structures
				Total			Durable goods		Nondurable goods			
				Total	Final sales	Change in business inventories	Final sales	Change in business inventories	Final sales	Change in business inventories		
1959	2,210.2	2,206.9	13.2	785.2							1,115.3	299.4
1960	2,262.9	2,264.2	10.5	796.8							1,167.1	296.5
1961	2,314.3	2,318.0	8.6	799.4							1,219.9	304.7
1962	2,454.8	2,445.4	19.5	857.8							1,277.5	322.2
1963	2,559.4	2,552.4	17.8	886.4							1,336.9	343.9
1964	2,708.4	2,705.1	15.6	940.8							1,406.3	367.0
1965	2,881.1	2,860.4	30.3	1,017.8							1,472.5	385.4
1966	3,069.2	3,033.5	42.4	1,106.9							1,557.8	385.9
1967	3,147.2	3,125.1	32.0	1,120.2							1,639.4	380.2
1968	3,293.9	3,278.0	26.9	1,170.8							1,712.0	403.6
1969	3,393.6	3,377.2	27.0	1,204.7							1,774.1	408.8
1970	3,397.6	3,406.5	5.4	1,188.8							1,824.0	391.1
1971	3,510.0	3,499.8	22.3	1,216.8							1,875.8	427.4
1972	3,702.3	3,689.5	24.7	1,305.9							1,936.1	459.0
1973	3,916.3	3,883.9	37.7	1,424.5							2,004.4	469.0
1974	3,891.2	3,873.4	23.4	1,403.1							2,063.3	420.5
1975	3,873.9	3,906.4	–10.2	1,380.2							2,123.5	382.3
1976	4,082.9	4,061.7	29.8	1,479.5							2,182.9	418.3
1977	4,273.6	4,240.8	38.8	1,555.1							2,250.5	458.7
1978	4,503.0	4,464.4	43.3	1,652.0							2,334.3	498.1
1979	4,630.6	4,614.4	23.4	1,706.0							2,391.3	511.7
1980	4,615.0	4,641.9	–10.2	1,689.7							2,441.4	475.9
1981	4,720.7	4,691.6	33.1	1,761.8							2,475.8	468.8
1982	4,620.3	4,651.2	–15.6	1,681.0	1,706.7	–15.6	604.4	–17.8	1,122.6	2.0	2,518.7	428.5
1983	4,803.7	4,821.2	–5.7	1,748.9	1,762.6	–5.7	637.6	4.9	1,142.6	–10.3	2,598.4	460.7
1984	5,140.1	5,061.6	75.3	1,926.4	1,853.3	75.3	703.1	49.7	1,160.9	26.1	2,678.0	523.1
1985	5,323.5	5,296.9	30.2	1,966.1	1,940.6	30.2	758.2	10.0	1,189.0	20.1	2,797.8	550.3
1986	5,487.7	5,480.9	11.1	2,018.8	2,011.7	11.1	793.6	.9	1,223.5	10.3	2,903.2	558.4
1987	5,649.5	5,626.0	26.4	2,077.9	2,055.0	26.4	819.8	23.5	1,239.2	2.4	3,011.6	554.6
1988	5,865.2	5,855.1	11.7	2,181.0	2,171.0	11.7	897.0	17.6	1,274.8	–6.1	3,128.6	550.8
1989	6,062.0	6,028.7	33.3	2,301.8	2,269.2	33.3	951.9	22.4	1,317.2	11.0	3,208.5	546.0
1990	6,136.3	6,126.7	10.4	2,304.8	2,295.4	10.4	963.9	2.7	1,331.3	7.6	3,295.4	533.3
1991	6,079.4	6,082.6	–3.0	2,262.7	2,265.9	–3.0	934.2	–16.6	1,331.8	13.4	3,332.3	484.5
1992	6,244.4	6,237.4	7.0	2,321.0	2,314.0	7.0	965.9	–10.9	1,348.1	17.9	3,411.1	512.3
1993	6,389.6	6,368.9	22.1	2,391.5	2,370.7	22.1	1,007.0	15.8	1,363.8	6.2	3,469.5	528.7
1994	6,610.7	6,551.2	60.6	2,514.2	2,453.9	60.6	1,056.7	32.3	1,397.5	28.2	3,542.9	554.9
1995	6,742.1	6,712.7	27.3	2,574.2	2,545.0	27.3	1,124.3	27.3	1,421.9	–.2	3,614.7	555.0
1996	6,928.4	6,901.0	25.0	2,662.6	2,635.5	25.0	1,205.8	15.9	1,433.2	9.1	3,686.6	582.2
1997 ᵖ	7,191.4	7,124.2	62.2	2,808.6	2,739.4	62.2	1,295.0	28.9	1,451.6	33.3	3,790.5	599.4
1992: I	6,175.7	6,175.8	–.5	2,289.2	2,289.3	–.5	945.2	–18.7	1,344.2	18.1	3,379.4	507.1
II	6,214.2	6,203.8	11.0	2,301.2	2,290.7	11.0	953.8	1.2	1,336.9	9.7	3,398.6	514.4
III	6,260.7	6,249.5	12.0	2,327.2	2,316.0	12.0	970.0	–11.4	1,346.0	23.4	3,424.2	509.4
IV	6,327.1	6,320.7	5.6	2,366.4	2,360.1	5.6	994.8	–14.8	1,365.3	20.5	3,442.3	518.5
1993: I	6,327.9	6,297.3	32.3	2,363.6	2,332.9	32.3	977.3	20.7	1,355.6	11.6	3,447.0	517.5
II	6,359.9	6,344.9	16.6	2,383.2	2,368.1	16.6	1,009.0	7.0	1,359.2	9.7	3,454.1	522.8
III	6,393.5	6,379.3	15.3	2,382.7	2,368.6	15.3	1,003.4	13.8	1,365.2	1.4	3,480.4	530.3
IV	6,476.9	6,453.8	24.2	2,436.5	2,413.2	24.2	1,038.2	21.9	1,375.3	2.1	3,496.4	544.5
1994: I	6,524.5	6,473.0	53.1	2,476.7	2,424.5	53.1	1,040.4	28.0	1,384.3	25.0	3,510.4	538.6
II	6,600.3	6,526.7	75.9	2,508.6	2,433.8	75.9	1,044.7	39.1	1,389.3	36.8	3,533.9	559.0
III	6,629.5	6,580.4	49.7	2,508.4	2,458.9	49.7	1,062.1	28.2	1,397.2	21.4	3,559.7	562.1
IV	6,688.6	6,624.8	63.6	2,563.1	2,498.4	63.6	1,079.4	33.8	1,419.3	29.7	3,567.7	560.1
1995: I	6,703.7	6,654.3	48.5	2,563.4	2,513.5	48.5	1,094.9	39.1	1,419.1	9.1	3,583.1	559.0
II	6,708.8	6,685.3	21.6	2,548.5	2,525.3	21.6	1,110.6	25.2	1,415.5	–3.9	3,610.5	550.9
III	6,759.2	6,739.3	17.0	2,576.8	2,557.4	17.0	1,137.2	20.2	1,421.8	–3.4	3,630.6	553.4
IV	6,796.5	6,771.9	22.2	2,608.1	2,583.8	22.2	1,154.3	24.7	1,431.3	–2.8	3,634.5	556.7
1996: I	6,826.4	6,815.0	8.0	2,614.6	2,604.1	8.0	1,171.9	16.3	1,434.5	–8.3	3,648.4	565.7
II	6,926.0	6,902.3	21.3	2,658.8	2,635.5	21.3	1,210.0	17.0	1,429.3	4.3	3,684.9	584.9
III	6,943.8	6,905.0	37.9	2,673.1	2,634.0	37.9	1,211.4	31.3	1,426.5	6.6	3,689.0	585.0
IV	7,017.4	6,981.7	32.9	2,704.1	2,668.4	32.9	1,230.1	–.9	1,442.6	33.8	3,723.9	592.9
1997: I	7,101.6	7,034.1	63.7	2,769.3	2,699.6	63.7	1,245.6	29.9	1,458.3	33.8	3,743.9	595.1
II	7,159.6	7,077.7	77.6	2,796.7	2,711.8	77.6	1,281.4	43.8	1,437.5	33.8	3,774.4	595.7
III	7,214.0	7,160.3	47.5	2,815.4	2,760.7	47.5	1,320.4	17.5	1,449.0	30.1	3,804.8	600.7
IV ᵖ	7,290.3	7,224.6	59.9	2,852.9	2,785.3	59.9	1,332.3	24.5	1,461.8	35.4	3,839.0	606.3

Source: Department of Commerce, Bureau of Economic Analysis.

TABLE B–10.—*Gross domestic product by sector, 1959–97*

[Billions of dollars; quarterly data at seasonally adjusted annual rates]

Year or quarter	Gross domestic product	Business [1]					Households and institutions			General government [2]		
		Total	Nonfarm [1]			Farm	Total	Private households	Non-profit institutions	Total	Federal	State and local
			Total [1]	Nonfarm less housing	Housing							
1959	507.2	436.9	418.0	382.4	35.6	18.9	12.4	3.6	8.9	57.9	31.8	26.1
1960	526.6	451.1	431.3	392.7	38.6	19.8	13.9	3.8	10.1	61.5	32.9	28.6
1961	544.8	464.9	444.8	403.4	41.4	20.1	14.5	3.7	10.7	65.5	34.2	31.3
1962	585.2	499.5	479.3	434.7	44.6	20.2	15.6	3.8	11.8	70.1	36.3	33.8
1963	617.4	525.9	505.5	458.1	47.4	20.4	16.7	3.8	12.8	74.8	38.1	36.7
1964	663.0	564.7	545.5	495.3	50.2	19.3	17.9	3.9	14.0	80.4	40.5	40.0
1965	719.1	613.8	591.9	538.4	53.5	21.9	19.3	4.0	15.3	86.0	42.3	43.7
1966	787.8	670.4	647.5	590.6	57.0	22.9	21.3	4.0	17.2	96.1	47.1	49.0
1967	833.6	703.7	681.5	620.6	60.8	22.2	23.4	4.2	19.2	106.5	51.6	54.9
1968	910.6	766.1	743.4	678.6	64.8	22.7	26.1	4.4	21.7	118.4	56.5	61.9
1969	982.2	823.3	798.1	728.2	69.9	25.2	29.5	4.4	25.0	129.5	60.2	69.3
1970	1,035.6	860.3	834.1	759.2	74.9	26.2	32.4	4.5	27.9	142.9	64.3	78.7
1971	1,125.4	933.9	905.8	824.1	81.7	28.1	35.6	4.6	31.1	155.9	68.2	87.7
1972	1,237.3	1,028.3	995.6	906.9	88.7	32.6	39.0	4.6	34.3	170.1	73.1	96.9
1973	1,382.6	1,154.6	1,104.9	1,007.9	96.9	49.8	43.0	4.8	38.2	185.0	76.9	108.1
1974	1,496.9	1,246.0	1,198.6	1,092.8	105.9	47.4	47.2	4.6	42.6	203.7	83.5	120.3
1975	1,630.6	1,351.5	1,302.7	1,188.4	114.3	48.8	52.0	4.6	47.4	227.1	91.7	135.4
1976	1,819.0	1,516.0	1,469.6	1,344.6	125.0	46.4	57.1	5.4	51.7	245.8	97.9	147.9
1977	2,026.9	1,697.5	1,650.3	1,510.9	139.4	47.2	62.4	5.9	56.5	266.9	106.1	160.9
1978	2,291.4	1,931.9	1,877.1	1,721.3	155.8	54.7	69.8	6.5	63.2	289.7	113.8	175.9
1979	2,557.5	2,164.1	2,099.7	1,923.6	176.1	64.5	77.3	6.4	71.0	316.0	122.3	193.7
1980	2,784.2	2,346.3	2,290.2	2,085.0	205.1	56.1	87.1	6.1	81.0	350.8	135.6	215.2
1981	3,115.9	2,631.8	2,561.9	2,326.6	235.3	69.9	97.6	6.2	91.5	386.4	151.0	235.4
1982	3,242.1	2,714.7	2,649.5	2,390.0	259.5	65.1	108.2	6.3	102.0	419.2	164.0	255.2
1983	3,514.5	2,950.0	2,900.8	2,624.1	276.7	49.2	119.2	6.3	112.9	445.3	173.5	271.8
1984	3,902.4	3,289.6	3,221.1	2,918.6	302.5	68.5	131.2	7.3	123.9	481.7	190.8	290.9
1985	4,180.7	3,520.2	3,453.1	3,121.1	332.0	67.1	140.9	7.3	133.6	519.6	203.6	316.0
1986	4,422.2	3,716.7	3,653.7	3,295.2	358.5	63.0	153.7	7.7	145.9	551.9	211.1	340.7
1987	4,692.3	3,933.1	3,868.0	3,481.6	386.4	65.1	173.3	7.7	165.6	586.0	221.3	364.7
1988	5,049.6	4,233.4	4,169.6	3,750.4	419.2	63.8	195.1	8.3	186.8	621.0	230.0	391.0
1989	5,438.7	4,563.7	4,487.5	4,036.1	451.4	76.2	214.6	8.9	205.7	660.3	240.5	419.8
1990	5,743.8	4,796.9	4,717.3	4,234.1	483.2	79.6	237.9	9.4	228.5	709.0	252.7	456.3
1991	5,916.7	4,908.5	4,835.6	4,325.7	509.9	72.9	257.4	9.1	248.3	750.7	268.1	482.6
1992	6,244.4	5,184.4	5,103.8	4,560.6	543.2	80.6	279.1	10.1	269.0	781.0	274.4	506.6
1993	6,558.1	5,453.1	5,380.1	4,822.9	557.1	73.0	296.5	10.7	285.8	808.5	276.9	531.6
1994	6,947.0	5,801.6	5,718.1	5,123.6	594.4	83.5	312.7	11.0	301.7	832.7	275.2	557.5
1995	7,265.4	6,074.7	6,001.3	5,372.0	629.2	73.5	331.8	11.8	319.9	858.9	275.5	583.4
1996	7,636.0	6,401.0	6,311.6	5,652.8	658.8	89.4	346.0	11.5	334.6	889.0	281.4	607.6
1997 *p*	8,083.4	6,797.4	6,702.6	6,013.2	689.4	94.8	366.3	11.4	355.0	919.7	285.9	633.8
1992: I	6,121.8	5,080.1	5,000.9	4,475.0	525.9	79.2	270.1	9.7	260.4	771.7	274.4	497.3
II	6,201.2	5,143.0	5,062.7	4,531.5	531.2	80.3	278.3	10.0	268.3	780.0	275.8	504.2
III	6,271.7	5,205.2	5,121.0	4,549.7	571.3	84.1	281.7	10.2	271.5	784.8	275.2	509.6
IV	6,383.1	5,309.3	5,230.6	4,686.2	544.4	78.7	286.2	10.4	275.8	787.6	272.1	515.5
1993: I	6,444.5	5,353.0	5,282.0	4,725.6	556.5	71.0	290.1	10.5	279.6	801.4	278.9	522.5
II	6,509.1	5,409.6	5,333.4	4,778.7	554.7	76.2	294.5	10.6	283.9	805.0	276.2	528.9
III	6,574.6	5,463.7	5,398.6	4,841.5	557.1	65.1	298.9	10.7	288.2	812.0	277.2	534.8
IV	6,704.2	5,586.1	5,506.2	4,945.9	560.3	79.9	302.4	10.8	291.6	815.7	275.3	540.4
1994: I	6,794.3	5,663.0	5,572.3	4,984.5	587.8	90.7	305.9	10.8	295.1	825.4	277.5	547.8
II	6,911.4	5,769.9	5,684.9	5,101.6	583.3	85.0	309.6	10.9	298.7	831.8	277.7	554.1
III	6,986.5	5,837.0	5,756.2	5,158.0	598.2	80.8	314.9	11.1	303.8	834.7	273.6	561.1
IV	7,095.7	5,936.3	5,858.8	5,250.4	608.4	77.5	320.5	11.3	309.2	838.9	272.0	566.9
1995: I	7,168.9	5,993.5	5,923.8	5,305.7	618.2	69.6	325.5	11.7	313.8	849.9	275.4	574.5
II	7,209.5	6,023.5	5,952.4	5,326.2	626.2	71.1	330.1	11.8	318.3	855.8	275.2	580.6
III	7,301.3	6,105.5	6,032.2	5,403.0	629.2	73.4	333.5	11.9	321.6	862.2	276.1	586.1
IV	7,381.9	6,176.5	6,096.6	5,453.3	643.3	79.8	337.9	11.9	326.0	867.6	275.3	592.3
1996: I	7,467.5	6,249.0	6,165.6	5,520.5	645.1	83.4	340.3	11.8	328.5	878.3	280.5	597.8
II	7,607.7	6,377.7	6,289.2	5,636.3	652.8	88.6	343.9	11.6	332.3	886.1	281.9	604.2
III	7,676.0	6,434.2	6,341.7	5,677.3	664.4	92.5	347.9	11.4	336.6	893.9	282.1	611.8
IV	7,792.9	6,543.1	6,450.0	5,777.1	673.0	93.0	352.0	11.1	341.0	897.8	281.1	616.7
1997: I	7,933.6	6,666.5	6,573.1	5,892.5	680.6	93.4	357.7	11.1	346.6	909.4	286.2	623.3
II	8,034.3	6,755.0	6,657.9	5,971.0	686.8	97.1	363.6	11.3	352.3	915.8	286.2	629.6
III	8,124.3	6,831.8	6,736.8	6,044.2	692.7	95.0	369.3	11.4	357.9	923.2	286.1	637.1
IV *p*	8,241.5	6,936.2	6,842.5	6,145.2	697.3	93.7	374.7	11.6	363.1	930.5	285.4	645.1

[1] Gross domestic business product equals gross domestic product less gross product of households and institutions and of general government. Nonfarm product equals gross domestic business product less gross farm product.

[2] Equals compensation of general government employees plus general government consumption of fixed capital.

Source: Department of Commerce, Bureau of Economic Analysis.

TABLE B-11.—*Real gross domestic product by sector, 1959-97*

[Billions of chained (1992) dollars; quarterly data at seasonally adjusted annual rates]

Year or quarter	Gross domestic product	Business[1]					Households and institutions			General government[2]		
		Total	Nonfarm[1]			Farm	Total	Private households	Non-profit institutions	Total	Federal	State and local
			Total[1]	Nonfarm less housing	Housing							
1959	2,210.2	1,721.7	1,677.4	1,524.7	149.8	33.7	105.0	18.5	78.6	415.1	232.1	186.4
1960	2,262.9	1,758.2	1,710.8	1,548.3	160.0	35.3	112.1	18.6	85.9	429.3	236.4	196.2
1961	2,314.3	1,795.8	1,748.5	1,576.8	169.4	35.6	113.1	18.1	87.8	444.6	241.5	206.4
1962	2,454.8	1,911.7	1,868.0	1,685.1	180.4	34.9	117.2	17.9	92.3	461.8	251.7	213.6
1963	2,559.4	1,997.7	1,953.4	1,760.9	189.9	35.9	120.1	17.7	95.6	475.7	254.3	224.6
1964	2,708.4	2,122.6	2,083.2	1,881.4	198.9	34.6	123.4	17.5	99.4	492.4	256.8	238.4
1965	2,881.1	2,268.8	2,227.7	2,014.4	210.0	36.5	127.9	16.9	105.0	509.3	258.8	253.0
1966	3,069.2	2,419.3	2,383.8	2,159.8	220.3	35.4	132.6	16.3	110.9	542.1	276.4	268.4
1967	3,147.2	2,470.5	2,430.5	2,195.9	231.2	37.7	136.9	16.3	115.2	571.1	295.1	279.2
1968	3,293.9	2,590.4	2,555.0	2,310.9	240.3	36.5	141.0	15.5	120.6	592.6	300.6	294.8
1969	3,393.6	2,670.8	2,634.6	2,380.0	251.1	37.5	145.5	14.7	126.5	607.3	301.7	307.8
1970	3,397.6	2,673.9	2,635.1	2,373.6	258.7	38.7	144.0	13.8	126.4	609.7	288.9	321.5
1971	3,510.0	2,777.3	2,736.5	2,464.3	269.3	40.4	147.2	13.1	130.6	611.3	276.1	334.9
1972	3,702.3	2,958.2	2,920.6	2,634.3	282.7	40.4	151.4	12.7	135.4	611.5	263.5	347.4
1973	3,916.3	3,159.1	3,127.5	2,827.3	295.9	40.3	154.9	12.4	139.6	614.8	253.8	360.2
1974	3,891.2	3,125.4	3,095.6	2,781.6	311.7	39.3	156.1	10.7	143.2	625.2	252.0	372.6
1975	3,873.9	3,100.1	3,050.3	2,733.9	315.4	46.4	161.2	10.1	149.2	631.1	249.0	381.7
1976	4,082.9	3,298.2	3,256.4	2,929.7	323.4	44.7	163.0	10.4	150.6	634.3	247.5	386.4
1977	4,273.6	3,475.8	3,431.8	3,093.7	333.6	47.0	167.5	10.5	155.0	639.1	246.3	392.6
1978	4,503.0	3,687.8	3,652.2	3,295.2	351.7	44.9	170.3	10.8	157.5	649.2	247.3	401.8
1979	4,630.6	3,804.8	3,763.2	3,388.4	370.7	48.3	173.7	9.4	163.1	654.2	245.1	409.3
1980	4,615.0	3,779.9	3,741.4	3,346.2	395.6	46.7	178.7	8.3	169.8	660.9	246.7	414.5
1981	4,720.7	3,878.4	3,816.7	3,406.8	411.6	60.0	182.7	7.8	174.7	662.3	248.3	414.2
1982	4,620.3	3,772.7	3,705.9	3,291.9	418.7	62.6	188.0	7.6	180.4	666.6	250.3	416.4
1983	4,803.7	3,946.5	3,916.3	3,497.0	421.3	40.2	192.3	7.6	184.8	668.7	254.2	414.4
1984	5,140.1	4,266.0	4,211.8	3,774.7	437.5	56.7	197.1	8.7	188.2	676.0	258.2	417.6
1985	5,323.5	4,425.4	4,357.8	3,906.2	451.9	66.9	203.4	8.7	194.6	693.2	263.9	429.2
1986	5,487.7	4,563.0	4,499.0	4,039.3	459.7	64.2	213.5	9.0	204.3	709.9	266.9	443.0
1987	5,649.5	4,699.8	4,635.1	4,161.0	473.9	65.3	224.1	8.9	215.2	724.2	272.3	452.0
1988	5,865.2	4,882.2	4,826.9	4,335.8	491.0	58.2	240.6	9.5	231.0	741.3	274.1	467.3
1989	6,062.0	5,049.4	4,984.9	4,477.9	506.8	65.9	253.4	10.1	243.3	758.1	276.2	481.9
1990	6,136.3	5,097.0	5,026.5	4,510.5	515.9	70.8	264.1	10.2	253.8	774.7	280.3	494.5
1991	6,079.4	5,026.4	4,954.9	4,428.1	526.8	71.6	272.1	9.4	262.6	781.1	281.0	500.1
1992	6,244.4	5,184.4	5,103.8	4,560.6	543.2	80.6	279.1	10.1	269.0	781.0	274.4	506.6
1993	6,389.6	5,317.2	5,246.2	4,704.1	542.1	71.0	290.1	10.3	279.8	782.3	267.7	514.5
1994	6,610.7	5,530.6	5,446.0	4,883.3	562.7	85.0	297.9	10.4	287.5	782.6	258.4	524.2
1995	6,742.1	5,657.4	5,582.7	5,005.7	577.0	74.2	305.1	10.8	294.3	780.3	248.1	532.2
1996	6,928.4	5,842.9	5,766.8	5,181.4	585.7	75.5	311.2	10.1	301.1	775.9	240.9	535.2
1997 P	7,191.4	6,094.4	6,013.7	5,419.2	595.3	79.9	320.6	9.6	311.0	779.4	236.1	543.8
1992: I	6,175.7	5,119.0	5,039.7	4,508.4	531.3	79.3	277.3	9.9	267.4	779.3	275.8	503.5
II	6,214.2	5,156.7	5,075.3	4,542.4	532.9	81.4	277.2	10.1	267.1	780.3	275.0	505.3
III	6,260.7	5,198.6	5,115.8	4,545.7	570.1	82.8	279.8	10.1	269.6	782.3	274.0	508.4
IV	6,327.1	5,263.1	5,184.4	4,645.9	538.5	78.7	282.0	10.3	271.7	782.0	272.7	509.3
1993: I	6,327.9	5,260.6	5,186.7	4,640.5	546.2	74.0	284.6	10.3	274.2	782.7	271.3	511.4
II	6,359.9	5,287.9	5,213.4	4,672.5	541.0	74.7	289.4	10.4	279.0	782.6	269.2	513.4
III	6,393.5	5,318.5	5,257.1	4,716.5	540.6	61.0	292.5	10.3	282.2	782.5	267.0	515.5
IV	6,476.9	5,401.9	5,327.6	4,787.1	540.6	74.4	293.9	10.3	283.6	781.3	263.5	517.8
1994: I	6,524.5	5,447.5	5,361.7	4,799.8	561.9	86.3	294.9	10.3	284.6	782.4	262.5	519.9
II	6,600.3	5,520.7	5,435.8	4,881.5	554.4	85.4	296.9	10.3	286.6	783.0	259.8	523.2
III	6,629.5	5,547.5	5,461.6	4,897.1	564.5	86.4	298.8	10.4	288.4	783.6	257.6	526.0
IV	6,688.6	5,606.6	5,524.8	4,954.9	569.8	81.9	301.0	10.5	290.5	781.5	253.8	527.8
1995: I	6,703.7	5,618.6	5,542.0	4,968.1	573.9	76.2	302.8	10.8	292.0	782.9	252.0	530.9
II	6,708.8	5,622.1	5,545.6	4,968.8	576.7	76.1	304.3	10.8	293.4	782.9	251.0	531.9
III	6,759.2	5,672.2	5,600.2	5,025.4	574.9	71.5	305.9	10.8	295.1	781.8	249.3	532.6
IV	6,796.5	5,716.7	5,643.0	5,060.6	582.4	73.1	307.4	10.7	296.7	773.6	240.3	533.5
1996: I	6,826.4	5,750.2	5,673.0	5,093.9	579.3	76.6	307.6	10.5	297.1	769.9	240.5	529.6
II	6,926.0	5,838.1	5,761.3	5,179.0	582.6	76.2	310.4	10.3	300.1	778.9	242.8	536.3
III	6,943.8	5,854.9	5,779.8	5,191.3	588.7	74.6	312.5	10.0	302.5	778.1	241.3	537.3
IV	7,017.4	5,928.5	5,853.3	5,261.3	592.3	74.7	314.4	9.6	304.8	776.6	238.9	537.9
1997 I	7,101.6	6,009.6	5,929.7	5,335.3	594.9	79.0	316.9	9.6	307.4	777.7	238.2	539.9
II	7,159.6	6,064.4	5,983.2	5,388.2	595.6	80.4	319.2	9.6	309.6	778.8	237.1	542.1
III	7,214.0	6,114.4	6,034.0	5,439.2	595.7	79.6	321.7	9.7	312.1	781.1	236.3	545.2
IV P	7,290.3	6,189.3	6,108.0	5,514.2	595.1	80.5	324.6	9.7	314.9	780.1	232.7	547.9

[1] Gross domestic business product equals gross domestic product less gross product of households and institutions and of general government. Nonfarm product equals gross domestic business product less gross farm product.

[2] Equals compensation of general government employees plus general government consumption of fixed capital.

Source: Department of Commerce, Bureau of Economic Analysis.

Year	Gross domestic product	Agriculture, forestry, and fishing	Mining	Construction	Manufacturing			Transportation and public utilities	Wholesale trade	Retail trade	Finance, insurance, and real estate	Services	Statistical discrepancy [1]	Government
					Total	Durable goods	Nondurable goods							
Based on 1972 SIC:														
1959	507.2	20.3	12.5	23.7	140.3	81.7	58.6	44.9	36.0	49.1	68.6	48.4	−1.6	64.8
1960	526.6	21.4	12.9	24.2	142.5	82.6	59.8	47.2	37.6	50.4	73.2	51.6	−3.2	68.9
1961	544.8	21.7	13.0	25.2	142.9	81.7	61.3	48.7	38.7	51.7	77.7	55.0	−2.8	73.0
1962	585.2	22.1	13.2	27.0	156.7	92.1	64.6	51.8	41.3	55.4	82.2	59.3	−1.8	78.2
1963	617.4	22.3	13.5	28.8	166.1	98.3	67.8	54.7	43.0	57.9	86.8	63.4	−3.0	83.9
1964	663.0	21.4	13.9	31.5	177.9	105.9	72.0	58.1	46.3	63.5	92.7	69.1	−1.5	90.1
1965	719.1	24.2	14.0	34.6	196.3	118.8	77.5	62.2	49.9	68.0	99.7	74.7	−.8	96.3
1966	787.8	25.4	14.7	37.7	215.3	131.1	84.3	67.1	54.3	72.7	107.8	82.7	3.3	106.9
1967	833.6	24.9	15.2	39.5	220.8	134.1	86.7	70.4	57.7	78.2	117.0	90.8	1.3	117.9
1968	910.6	25.7	16.3	43.3	241.1	146.3	94.8	76.2	63.3	86.6	126.6	99.4	.9	131.2
1969	982.2	28.6	17.1	48.4	254.4	154.4	100.0	82.5	68.4	94.2	136.1	110.8	−1.5	143.3
1970	1,035.6	29.8	18.7	51.1	249.6	146.2	103.4	88.1	72.1	100.2	146.0	120.5	1.9	157.6
1971	1,125.4	32.1	18.9	56.1	263.0	154.2	108.9	97.2	77.9	109.2	162.8	130.4	6.1	171.7
1972	1,237.3	37.3	19.7	62.5	290.5	172.6	117.9	108.3	87.0	118.8	176.2	144.9	4.3	187.8
1973	1,382.6	54.8	23.8	69.7	323.5	195.7	127.8	119.2	97.6	130.9	192.9	163.1	3.4	203.8
1974	1,496.9	53.0	37.1	73.6	337.4	202.2	135.3	129.8	111.0	136.7	208.7	179.3	5.5	224.8
1975	1,630.6	54.7	42.8	75.1	354.9	207.0	147.8	142.2	121.0	152.8	226.6	199.1	12.1	249.3
1976	1,819.0	53.5	47.6	84.9	405.5	239.9	165.6	161.2	129.0	172.2	250.0	223.9	19.9	271.2
1977	2,026.9	54.1	54.1	93.8	462.6	277.6	185.0	179.1	142.2	190.2	283.4	255.5	18.2	293.5
1978	2,291.4	63.1	61.5	110.6	517.1	316.9	200.2	200.2	160.9	215.6	328.0	294.6	18.1	319.8
1979	2,557.5	74.5	71.2	124.7	571.3	343.5	227.9	219.0	182.3	234.2	370.6	333.2	28.2	348.2
1980	2,784.2	66.7	112.7	128.6	584.4	348.7	235.7	242.1	195.2	245.9	418.3	377.3	27.6	385.5
1981	3,115.9	81.1	151.7	129.6	652.1	388.1	264.0	276.2	216.3	270.4	470.9	426.2	14.9	426.5
1982	3,242.1	77.0	149.5	129.8	649.8	377.4	272.4	293.0	219.5	288.1	504.0	471.8	−2.5	461.9
1983	3,514.5	62.5	127.5	138.9	690.2	397.3	292.8	328.1	229.1	321.9	565.3	521.5	37.1	492.4
1984	3,902.4	83.5	134.2	165.0	780.6	469.5	311.1	357.8	264.3	362.2	625.6	590.4	5.0	533.8
1985	4,180.7	84.3	132.8	185.5	803.1	477.1	326.0	376.6	280.7	395.0	690.6	651.1	2.4	578.6
1986	4,422.2	82.0	86.3	207.3	833.2	487.0	346.2	393.8	293.5	415.2	760.4	712.2	23.3	615.0
Based on 1987 SIC:														
1987	4,692.3	88.5	88.3	217.0	889.2	513.3	375.9	420.5	300.8	435.8	829.7	784.6	−15.4	653.2
1988	5,049.6	88.9	99.9	233.4	971.5	556.6	414.8	443.4	336.3	459.3	891.4	877.8	−47.3	694.9
1989	5,438.7	101.9	96.3	242.2	1,013.5	574.9	438.6	460.9	356.3	490.2	959.3	965.5	13.2	739.2
1990	5,743.8	108.7	112.3	245.2	1,031.4	572.8	458.6	482.1	367.2	503.5	1,024.1	1,059.4	17.4	792.5
1991	5,916.7	102.9	101.1	228.8	1,028.1	558.3	469.8	511.6	388.1	517.4	1,081.6	1,107.6	10.1	839.5
1992	6,244.4	112.4	92.2	229.7	1,063.6	573.4	490.3	528.7	406.4	544.3	1,147.9	1,200.8	44.8	873.6
1993	6,558.1	106.1	94.6	242.4	1,116.5	615.7	500.8	561.7	423.3	573.2	1,218.1	1,267.0	52.6	902.7
1994	6,947.0	119.2	94.9	268.7	1,216.1	679.2	536.9	598.7	468.0	615.3	1,267.6	1,350.4	14.6	933.5
1995	7,265.4	111.0	99.8	286.4	1,286.3	716.8	569.5	622.4	484.4	637.6	1,361.3	1,440.3	−28.2	964.1
1996	7,636.0	129.8	113.6	306.1	1,332.1	749.0	583.1	645.3	516.8	667.9	1,448.5	1,539.5	−59.9	996.3

[1] Equals gross domestic product (GDP) measured as the sum of expenditures less gross domestic income.

Source: Department of Commerce, Bureau of Economic Analysis.

TABLE B–13.—*Real gross domestic product by industry, 1977–96*

[Billions of chained (1992) dollars]

Year	Gross domestic product	Private industries													Government	Not allocated by industry[2]
		Agriculture, forestry, and fishing	Mining	Construction	Manufacturing			Transportation and public utilities	Wholesale trade	Retail trade	Finance, insurance, and real estate	Services	Statistical discrepancy[1]			
					Total	Durable goods	Nondurable goods									
Based on 1972 SIC:																
1977	4,273.6	57.3	82.4	213.8	796.5	435.1	361.9	346.8	201.0	364.5	742.7	712.5	37.3	717.4	−4.4
1978	4,503.0	55.2	84.6	221.2	836.5	461.7	374.0	362.8	215.5	389.9	786.0	759.5	34.5	731.6	23.2
1979	4,630.6	59.4	73.6	227.8	864.8	470.5	395.4	378.7	228.2	389.1	830.7	787.3	49.5	739.4	−.9
1980	4,615.0	58.2	82.0	214.7	822.6	451.2	371.5	385.0	226.0	374.5	862.8	810.8	44.5	748.8	−17.0
1981	4,720.7	72.3	81.4	195.4	858.5	468.6	390.5	391.0	241.1	386.2	878.1	830.0	22.0	749.4	11.7
1982	4,620.3	76.0	78.8	172.8	810.0	427.9	386.2	379.6	246.5	387.9	875.8	838.1	−3.4	748.3	3.4
1983	4,803.7	54.6	73.7	181.0	856.7	448.3	413.8	405.2	251.5	422.6	900.0	862.8	49.7	753.0	−15.1
1984	5,140.1	73.2	82.0	210.1	948.1	521.8	426.1	422.1	286.8	465.0	945.0	920.8	6.5	760.1	18.0
1985	5,323.5	85.4	87.1	232.9	976.4	534.6	442.1	423.8	298.1	496.8	968.1	963.9	3.0	777.9	7.3
1986	5,487.7	85.9	83.6	239.0	967.6	527.4	441.0	421.7	333.0	526.6	969.0	996.8	28.6	795.7	35.8
Based on 1987 SIC:																
1987	5,649.5	89.1	86.4	239.6	1,041.7	565.0	477.9	453.9	322.8	509.2	1,015.7	1,041.4	−18.4	810.0	53.4
1988	5,865.2	82.2	104.4	248.8	1,111.0	615.9	494.8	468.2	343.8	537.6	1,069.4	1,099.1	−54.6	829.0	22.9
1989	6,062.0	89.1	92.8	251.9	1,106.0	612.9	492.8	474.5	366.3	553.4	1,101.8	1,149.5	14.7	847.7	9.5
1990	6,136.3	99.4	96.9	247.5	1,090.0	600.4	489.4	491.7	360.5	546.4	1,109.0	1,181.7	18.5	867.0	25.3
1991	6,079.4	101.4	97.5	229.0	1,050.2	568.0	482.2	512.8	381.2	534.1	1,105.7	1,174.2	10.3	873.7	7.8
1992	6,244.4	112.4	92.2	229.7	1,063.6	573.4	490.3	528.7	406.4	544.3	1,147.9	1,200.8	44.8	873.6	.0
1993	6,389.6	102.3	96.4	234.3	1,100.8	608.3	492.5	551.9	416.5	566.2	1,174.3	1,223.5	51.3	875.8	−3.7
1994	6,610.7	119.1	102.5	249.8	1,193.2	671.3	522.0	584.1	448.6	601.2	1,196.9	1,256.5	13.9	878.3	−33.8
1995	6,742.1	111.4	108.4	254.1	1,273.7	731.2	543.2	593.8	457.5	622.5	1,231.1	1,298.8	−26.3	877.4	−61.3
1996	6,928.4	111.7	101.9	264.3	1,323.7	785.5	541.0	608.9	493.3	648.5	1,258.5	1,342.9	−54.7	874.1	−48.1

[1] Equals the current-dollar statistical discrepancy deflated by the implicit price deflator for gross domestic business product.
[2] Equals GDP less the statistical discrepancy and the sum of the most detailed industry groups shown here.

Source: Department of Commerce, Bureau of Economic Analysis.

TABLE B–14.—*Gross domestic product of nonfinancial corporate business, 1959–97*

[Billions of dollars; quarterly data at seasonally adjusted annual rates]

Year or quarter	Gross domestic product of nonfinancial corporate business	Consumption of fixed capital	Net domestic product — Total	Indirect business taxes[1]	Domestic income — Total	Compensation of employees	Corporate profits with inventory valuation and capital consumption adjustments — Total	Profits before tax	Profits tax liability	Profits after tax — Total	Dividends	Undistributed profits	Inventory valuation adjustment	Capital consumption adjustment	Net interest
1959	267.5	23.6	243.8	26.0	217.8	171.5	43.2	43.6	20.7	22.9	10.0	12.9	-0.3	-0.1	3.1
1960	278.1	24.5	253.6	28.3	225.3	181.2	40.7	40.3	19.2	21.1	10.6	10.6	-.2	.5	3.5
1961	285.5	25.1	260.5	29.5	230.9	185.3	41.6	40.1	19.5	20.7	10.6	10.1	.3	1.2	4.0
1962	311.7	26.0	285.7	32.0	253.7	200.1	49.1	45.0	20.6	24.3	11.4	13.0	.0	4.1	4.5
1963	331.8	27.0	304.8	34.0	270.8	211.1	54.9	49.8	22.8	27.0	12.6	14.4	.1	5.0	4.8
1964	358.1	28.4	329.8	36.6	293.2	226.7	61.2	56.0	24.0	32.1	13.7	18.4	-.5	5.7	5.3
1965	393.5	30.3	363.2	39.2	324.0	246.5	71.4	66.2	27.2	39.0	15.6	23.4	-1.2	6.5	6.1
1966	431.0	33.2	397.8	40.5	357.4	274.0	76.1	71.4	29.5	41.9	16.8	25.1	-2.1	6.8	7.4
1967	453.4	36.3	417.2	43.1	374.1	292.3	73.0	67.5	27.8	39.7	17.5	22.2	-1.6	7.0	8.8
1968	500.5	39.9	460.5	49.7	410.8	323.2	77.5	74.0	33.6	40.4	19.1	21.3	-3.7	7.1	10.1
1969	543.3	44.1	499.2	54.7	444.5	358.8	72.5	70.8	33.3	37.5	19.1	18.4	-5.9	7.5	13.2
1970	561.4	48.5	512.8	58.8	454.0	378.7	58.3	58.1	27.2	31.0	18.5	12.5	-6.6	6.7	17.1
1971	606.4	53.0	553.4	64.5	488.9	402.0	68.8	67.1	29.9	37.1	18.5	18.7	-4.6	6.3	18.1
1972	673.3	57.6	615.8	69.2	546.6	447.1	80.4	78.6	33.8	44.8	20.1	24.7	-6.6	8.4	19.2
1973	754.5	62.6	691.8	76.3	615.5	505.9	87.1	98.6	40.2	58.4	21.1	37.3	-20.0	8.6	22.5
1974	814.6	73.3	741.3	81.4	659.9	556.8	74.8	109.2	42.2	67.0	21.7	45.2	-39.5	5.1	28.3
1975	881.2	87.5	793.7	87.4	706.3	580.3	97.3	109.9	41.5	68.4	24.8	43.6	-11.0	-1.6	28.7
1976	995.3	96.9	898.4	95.1	803.3	657.4	118.4	137.3	53.0	84.4	28.0	56.3	-14.9	-4.0	27.5
1977	1,125.4	108.8	1,016.7	104.1	912.6	742.6	139.4	158.6	59.9	98.7	31.5	67.2	-16.6	-2.6	30.6
1978	1,284.1	124.4	1,159.7	116.4	1,043.2	852.9	154.0	183.5	67.1	116.4	36.4	80.0	-25.0	-4.5	36.3
1979	1,429.7	143.9	1,285.8	125.4	1,160.4	968.1	147.2	195.5	69.6	125.9	38.1	87.9	-41.6	-6.8	45.1
1980	1,553.8	165.4	1,388.4	141.6	1,246.8	1,058.5	130.1	181.6	67.0	114.6	45.3	69.2	-43.0	-8.4	58.2
1981	1,767.3	193.2	1,574.1	170.4	1,403.7	1,171.5	160.3	181.4	63.9	117.5	53.3	64.2	-25.7	4.6	71.9
1982	1,823.4	209.7	1,613.7	172.1	1,441.6	1,217.0	142.1	133.7	46.3	87.4	53.3	34.2	-9.9	18.3	82.5
1983	1,950.3	222.7	1,727.6	189.0	1,538.6	1,280.5	181.5	157.4	59.4	97.9	64.2	33.8	-9.1	33.2	76.6
1984	2,187.5	228.7	1,958.8	210.2	1,748.6	1,421.7	239.0	191.0	73.7	117.3	67.8	49.5	-5.6	53.7	87.8
1985	2,319.3	238.9	2,080.4	224.4	1,856.0	1,521.9	243.5	167.6	69.9	97.6	72.3	25.4	.5	75.4	90.6
1986	2,416.3	253.2	2,163.1	235.8	1,927.3	1,603.2	226.0	151.5	75.6	75.9	73.9	2.1	11.4	63.1	98.1
1987	2,589.6	263.6	2,326.1	246.7	2,079.3	1,715.5	258.6	214.9	93.5	121.4	75.9	45.5	-20.7	64.4	105.3
1988	2,805.2	279.7	2,525.5	263.5	2,262.0	1,846.7	294.3	260.6	101.7	158.8	79.4	79.4	-29.3	63.1	121.0
1989	2,950.9	297.4	2,653.5	280.8	2,372.7	1,950.0	276.7	237.0	98.8	138.3	103.5	34.8	-17.5	57.2	145.9
1990	3,084.0	308.4	2,775.6	296.8	2,478.8	2,056.0	275.3	237.3	95.7	141.6	118.4	23.3	-13.5	51.5	147.5
1991	3,132.1	320.2	2,811.9	318.0	2,493.9	2,090.6	269.7	218.1	85.4	132.8	124.6	8.2	4.0	47.6	133.7
1992	3,262.6	330.5	2,932.2	337.0	2,595.1	2,195.3	295.6	257.8	91.1	166.7	133.6	33.1	-7.5	45.3	104.2
1993	3,430.4	340.3	3,090.1	358.5	2,731.6	2,290.7	346.4	308.6	105.0	203.6	147.7	55.9	-8.5	46.3	94.5
1994	3,709.7	360.7	3,349.0	389.0	2,960.1	2,426.7	437.1	392.3	128.8	263.5	158.6	104.9	-16.1	60.8	96.3
1995	3,905.3	373.4	3,531.9	399.8	3,132.1	2,555.5	474.6	438.3	139.4	298.9	188.3	110.6	-24.3	60.5	102.0
1996	4,132.4	393.4	3,739.0	421.8	3,317.2	2,682.9	545.8	477.2	154.8	322.4	196.4	126.0	-2.5	71.1	88.5
1997 ᴾ		413.3		439.7		2,866.5							4.9	79.7	
1992: I	3,202.2	323.3	2,878.9	330.4	2,548.4	2,152.8	285.5	236.3	82.4	153.9	124.0	29.9	.3	48.9	110.2
II	3,236.1	325.1	2,911.0	331.8	2,579.2	2,183.2	290.0	262.6	93.6	169.0	129.7	39.3	-21.9	49.3	106.0
III	3,270.5	343.8	2,926.7	337.8	2,588.9	2,209.3	278.9	254.4	89.9	164.5	134.3	30.2	-8.6	33.0	100.8
IV	3,341.7	329.7	3,012.0	348.0	2,664.0	2,236.1	328.2	277.9	98.4	179.5	146.3	33.2	.2	50.1	99.7
1993: I	3,351.8	335.8	3,015.9	348.2	2,667.7	2,253.5	316.0	275.6	92.5	183.1	143.5	39.6	-12.5	52.9	98.2
II	3,400.3	337.3	3,063.0	353.8	2,709.2	2,279.9	334.4	306.9	104.7	202.2	144.2	58.0	-17.1	44.5	95.0
III	3,444.3	344.5	3,099.8	359.7	2,740.1	2,301.5	345.5	303.1	102.9	200.2	147.6	52.5	.2	42.2	93.1
IV	3,525.2	343.4	3,181.9	372.3	2,809.6	2,327.8	389.9	349.0	120.0	228.9	155.6	73.4	-4.8	45.7	91.9
1994: I	3,624.5	375.1	3,249.3	380.4	2,868.9	2,372.5	405.4	359.1	119.5	239.6	150.4	89.2	-4.3	50.6	91.1
II	3,668.9	351.6	3,317.3	386.1	2,931.1	2,409.8	427.0	380.7	124.6	256.1	158.7	97.4	-15.1	61.4	94.3
III	3,729.1	355.9	3,373.2	392.3	2,980.9	2,439.2	444.1	400.7	130.1	270.6	158.5	112.1	-21.2	64.6	97.6
IV	3,816.4	360.0	3,456.4	397.1	3,059.2	2,485.2	472.0	428.9	141.1	287.8	166.8	121.0	-23.6	66.7	102.1
1995: I	3,833.6	364.4	3,469.2	395.7	3,073.5	2,519.3	449.0	437.6	140.8	296.9	183.4	113.5	-50.3	61.7	105.2
II	3,860.4	370.6	3,489.8	397.1	3,092.7	2,538.4	450.3	428.3	135.3	293.0	189.1	103.9	-37.8	59.8	104.0
III	3,940.4	375.4	3,564.9	401.3	3,163.7	2,568.6	494.3	443.1	140.1	303.0	191.4	111.6	-9.3	60.4	100.8
IV	3,986.8	383.1	3,603.7	405.2	3,198.5	2,595.5	504.8	444.3	141.5	302.9	189.3	113.6	.4	60.1	98.2
1996: I	4,030.7	385.5	3,645.2	413.2	3,232.0	2,613.1	525.4	463.4	149.2	314.2	200.3	113.9	-5.1	67.1	93.5
II	4,112.9	390.2	3,722.7	420.2	3,302.5	2,668.6	542.8	477.4	154.1	323.3	194.3	129.1	-5.4	70.8	91.2
III	4,165.8	396.2	3,769.7	423.7	3,345.9	2,704.7	553.3	483.4	156.8	326.6	191.8	134.8	-2.7	72.6	88.0
IV	4,220.1	401.8	3,818.3	430.0	3,388.3	2,745.3	561.7	484.4	159.0	325.5	199.4	126.1	3.3	74.0	81.3
1997: I	4,299.7	406.3	3,893.4	432.2	3,461.2	2,801.9	575.4	494.5	159.4	335.1	207.0	128.2	3.5	77.4	83.9
II	4,361.1	410.7	3,950.4	437.0	3,513.3	2,840.1	586.7	501.5	161.8	339.8	208.1	131.7	5.9	79.3	86.6
III	4,446.3	415.3	4,031.0	445.3	3,585.7	2,880.6	618.2	534.2	174.1	360.1	207.7	152.4	3.6	80.4	87.0
IV ᴾ		421.0		444.4		2,943.6							6.5	81.6	

[1] Indirect business tax and nontax liability plus business transfer payments less subsidies.

Source: Department of Commerce, Bureau of Economic Analysis.

298

TABLE B–15.—*Output, costs, and profits of nonfinancial corporate business, 1959–97*

[Quarterly data at seasonally adjusted annual rates]

Year or quarter	Gross domestic product of nonfinancial corporate business (billions of dollars)		Current-dollar cost and profit per unit of real output (dollars)[1]							
	Current dollars	Chained (1992) dollars	Total cost and profit[2]	Consumption of fixed capital	Indirect business taxes[3]	Compensation of employees	Corporate profits with inventory valuation and capital consumption adjustments			Net interest
							Total	Profits tax liability	Profits after tax[4]	
1959	267.5	910.3	0.294	0.026	0.029	0.188	0.047	0.023	0.025	0.003
1960	278.1	940.4	.296	.026	.030	.193	.043	.020	.023	.004
1961	285.5	960.5	.297	.026	.031	.193	.043	.020	.023	.004
1962	311.7	1,041.5	.299	.025	.031	.192	.047	.020	.027	.004
1963	331.8	1,101.1	.301	.025	.031	.192	.050	.021	.029	.004
1964	358.1	1,178.5	.304	.024	.031	.192	.052	.020	.032	.005
1965	393.5	1,275.2	.309	.024	.031	.193	.056	.021	.035	.005
1966	431.0	1,364.4	.316	.024	.030	.201	.056	.022	.034	.005
1967	453.4	1,399.1	.324	.026	.031	.209	.052	.020	.032	.006
1968	500.5	1,487.7	.336	.027	.033	.217	.052	.023	.030	.007
1969	543.3	1,546.9	.351	.028	.035	.232	.047	.022	.025	.009
1970	561.4	1,532.5	.366	.032	.038	.247	.038	.018	.020	.011
1971	606.4	1,594.1	.380	.033	.040	.252	.043	.019	.024	.011
1972	673.3	1,719.4	.392	.033	.040	.260	.047	.020	.027	.011
1973	754.5	1,819.7	.415	.034	.042	.278	.048	.022	.026	.012
1974	814.6	1,786.8	.456	.041	.046	.312	.042	.024	.018	.016
1975	881.2	1,759.3	.501	.050	.050	.330	.055	.024	.032	.016
1976	995.3	1,901.3	.524	.051	.050	.346	.062	.028	.034	.014
1977	1,125.4	2,041.8	.551	.053	.051	.364	.068	.029	.039	.015
1978	1,284.1	2,177.1	.590	.057	.053	.392	.071	.031	.040	.017
1979	1,429.7	2,224.2	.643	.065	.056	.435	.066	.031	.035	.020
1980	1,553.8	2,229.9	.697	.074	.064	.475	.058	.030	.028	.026
1981	1,767.3	2,331.9	.758	.083	.073	.502	.069	.027	.041	.031
1982	1,823.4	2,298.8	.793	.091	.075	.529	.062	.020	.042	.036
1983	1,950.3	2,405.1	.811	.093	.079	.532	.075	.025	.051	.032
1984	2,187.5	2,641.2	.828	.087	.080	.538	.090	.028	.063	.033
1985	2,319.3	2,747.3	.844	.087	.082	.554	.089	.025	.063	.033
1986	2,416.3	2,835.4	.852	.089	.083	.565	.080	.027	.053	.035
1987	2,589.6	2,973.9	.871	.089	.083	.577	.087	.031	.056	.035
1988	2,805.2	3,130.1	.896	.089	.084	.590	.094	.033	.062	.039
1989	2,950.9	3,179.8	.928	.094	.088	.613	.087	.031	.056	.046
1990	3,084.0	3,210.2	.961	.096	.092	.640	.086	.030	.056	.046
1991	3,132.1	3,168.8	.988	.101	.100	.660	.085	.027	.058	.042
1992	3,262.6	3,262.6	1.000	.101	.103	.673	.091	.028	.063	.032
1993	3,430.4	3,374.4	1.017	.101	.106	.679	.103	.031	.072	.028
1994	3,709.7	3,586.3	1.034	.101	.108	.677	.122	.036	.086	.027
1995	3,905.3	3,719.7	1.050	.100	.107	.687	.128	.037	.090	.027
1996	4,132.4	3,887.8	1.063	.101	.108	.690	.140	.040	.101	.023
1992: I	3,202.2	3,217.0	.995	.101	.103	.669	.089	.026	.063	.034
II	3,236.1	3,238.4	.999	.100	.102	.674	.090	.029	.061	.033
III	3,270.5	3,267.0	1.001	.105	.103	.676	.085	.028	.058	.031
IV	3,341.7	3,328.2	1.004	.099	.105	.672	.099	.030	.069	.030
1993: I	3,351.8	3,310.2	1.013	.101	.105	.681	.095	.028	.068	.030
II	3,400.3	3,352.5	1.014	.101	.106	.680	.100	.031	.069	.028
III	3,444.3	3,387.2	1.017	.102	.106	.679	.102	.030	.072	.027
IV	3,525.2	3,447.7	1.022	.100	.108	.675	.113	.035	.078	.027
1994: I	3,624.5	3,526.1	1.028	.106	.108	.673	.115	.034	.081	.026
II	3,668.9	3,559.8	1.031	.099	.108	.677	.120	.035	.085	.026
III	3,729.1	3,594.6	1.037	.099	.109	.679	.124	.036	.087	.027
IV	3,816.4	3,664.9	1.041	.098	.108	.678	.129	.038	.090	.028
1995: I	3,833.6	3,664.9	1.046	.099	.108	.687	.123	.038	.084	.029
II	3,860.4	3,683.2	1.048	.101	.108	.689	.122	.037	.086	.028
III	3,940.4	3,747.7	1.051	.100	.107	.685	.132	.037	.094	.027
IV	3,986.8	3,782.9	1.054	.101	.107	.686	.133	.037	.096	.026
1996: I	4,030.7	3,801.8	1.060	.101	.109	.687	.138	.039	.099	.025
II	4,112.9	3,872.4	1.062	.101	.109	.689	.140	.040	.100	.024
III	4,165.8	3,913.7	1.064	.101	.108	.691	.141	.040	.101	.022
IV	4,220.1	3,963.5	1.065	.101	.108	.693	.142	.040	.102	.021
1997: I	4,299.7	4,022.2	1.069	.101	.107	.697	.143	.040	.103	.021
II	4,361.1	4,068.9	1.072	.101	.107	.698	.144	.040	.104	.021
III	4,446.3	4,146.5	1.072	.100	.107	.695	.149	.042	.107	.021

[1] Output is measured by gross domestic product of nonfinancial corporate business in chained (1992) dollars.
[2] This is equal to the deflator for gross domestic product of nonfinancial corporate business with the decimal point shifted two places to the left.
[3] Indirect business tax and nontax liability plus business transfer payments less subsidies.
[4] With inventory valuation and capital consumption adjustments.

Source: Department of Commerce, Bureau of Economic Analysis.

TABLE B-16.—*Personal consumption expenditures, 1959–97*

[Billions of dollars; quarterly data at seasonally adjusted annual rates]

Year or quarter	Personal consumption expenditures	Durable goods			Nondurable goods					Services					
		Total¹	Motor vehicles and parts	Furniture and household equipment	Total¹	Food	Clothing and shoes	Gasoline and oil	Fuel oil and coal	Total¹	Housing²	Household operation		Transportation	Medical care
												Total¹	Electricity and gas		
1959	318.1	42.7	18.9	18.1	148.5	80.7	26.4	11.3	4.0	127.0	45.0	18.7	7.6	10.5	16.4
1960	332.2	43.3	19.7	18.0	152.9	82.3	27.0	12.0	3.8	136.0	48.2	20.3	8.3	11.2	17.6
1961	342.6	41.8	17.8	18.3	156.6	84.0	27.6	12.0	3.8	144.3	51.2	21.2	8.8	11.7	18.7
1962	363.4	46.9	21.5	19.3	162.8	86.1	29.0	12.6	3.8	153.7	54.7	22.4	9.4	12.2	20.8
1963	383.0	51.6	24.4	20.7	168.2	88.3	29.8	13.0	4.0	163.2	58.0	23.6	9.9	12.7	22.6
1964	411.4	56.7	26.0	23.2	178.7	93.6	32.4	13.6	4.1	176.1	61.4	25.0	10.4	13.4	25.8
1965	444.3	63.3	29.9	25.1	191.6	100.7	34.1	14.8	4.4	189.4	65.4	26.5	10.9	14.5	28.0
1966	481.9	68.3	30.3	28.2	208.8	109.3	37.4	16.0	4.7	204.8	69.5	28.2	11.5	15.9	30.7
1967	509.5	70.4	30.0	30.0	217.1	112.5	39.2	17.1	4.8	222.0	74.1	30.2	12.2	17.3	33.9
1968	559.8	80.8	36.1	32.9	235.7	122.2	43.2	18.6	4.7	243.4	79.7	32.3	13.0	18.9	39.2
1969	604.7	85.9	38.4	34.7	253.2	131.5	46.5	20.5	4.6	265.5	86.8	35.1	14.0	20.9	44.7
1970	648.1	85.0	35.5	35.7	272.0	143.8	47.8	21.9	4.4	291.1	94.0	37.8	15.2	23.7	50.4
1971	702.5	96.9	44.5	37.8	285.5	149.7	51.7	23.2	4.6	320.1	102.7	41.0	16.6	27.1	56.9
1972	770.7	110.4	51.1	42.4	308.0	161.4	56.4	24.4	5.1	352.3	112.1	45.3	18.4	29.8	63.8
1973	851.6	123.5	56.1	47.9	343.1	179.6	62.5	28.1	6.3	384.9	122.7	49.8	20.0	31.2	71.6
1974	931.2	122.3	49.5	51.5	384.5	201.8	66.0	36.1	7.8	424.4	134.1	55.5	23.5	33.3	80.6
1975	1,029.1	133.5	54.8	54.5	420.6	223.1	70.8	39.7	8.4	475.0	147.0	63.7	28.5	35.7	93.5
1976	1,148.8	158.9	71.3	60.2	458.2	242.4	76.6	43.0	10.1	531.8	161.5	72.4	32.5	41.3	106.7
1977	1,277.1	181.1	83.5	67.1	496.9	262.4	84.1	46.9	11.1	599.0	179.5	81.9	37.6	49.2	123.0
1978	1,428.8	201.4	93.1	74.0	549.9	289.2	94.3	50.1	11.5	677.4	201.7	91.2	42.1	53.5	140.0
1979	1,593.5	213.9	93.5	82.3	624.0	324.2	101.2	66.2	14.4	755.6	226.6	100.0	46.8	59.1	158.0
1980	1,760.4	213.5	87.0	86.0	695.5	355.4	107.3	86.7	15.4	851.4	255.2	113.0	56.3	64.7	181.2
1981	1,941.3	230.5	95.8	91.3	758.2	382.8	117.2	97.9	15.8	952.6	287.9	126.0	63.4	68.7	213.0
1982	2,076.8	239.3	102.9	92.5	786.8	402.6	120.5	94.1	14.5	1,050.7	313.2	141.4	72.6	70.9	239.4
1983	2,283.4	279.8	126.9	105.3	830.3	422.9	130.9	93.1	13.6	1,173.3	339.0	155.9	80.7	79.4	267.8
1984	2,492.3	325.1	152.5	117.2	883.6	446.3	142.5	94.6	13.9	1,283.6	370.6	168.0	84.7	90.0	294.1
1985	2,704.8	361.1	175.7	126.3	927.6	466.5	152.1	97.2	13.6	1,416.1	407.1	180.3	88.8	100.0	321.8
1986	2,892.7	398.7	192.4	140.3	957.2	490.8	163.1	80.1	11.3	1,536.8	442.2	186.9	87.2	107.3	346.1
1987	3,094.5	416.7	193.1	150.4	1,014.0	513.9	174.4	85.4	11.2	1,663.8	476.6	194.9	88.9	118.2	381.1
1988	3,349.7	451.0	207.5	162.8	1,081.1	551.2	185.9	87.1	11.4	1,817.6	512.9	206.6	94.1	130.5	428.7
1989	3,594.8	472.8	214.4	173.3	1,163.8	588.4	199.9	96.6	11.4	1,958.1	547.4	219.8	98.8	137.8	477.1
1990	3,839.3	476.5	210.3	176.0	1,245.3	630.5	205.9	109.2	12.0	2,117.5	586.3	226.3	98.7	143.7	537.7
1991	3,975.1	455.2	187.6	178.5	1,277.6	650.0	211.3	103.9	11.3	2,242.3	616.5	237.6	104.9	145.3	586.5
1992	4,219.8	488.5	206.9	189.4	1,321.8	660.0	225.5	106.6	10.9	2,409.4	646.8	248.2	106.6	158.1	646.6
1993	4,459.2	530.2	226.2	204.9	1,370.7	686.8	236.5	107.6	10.7	2,558.4	672.8	268.8	115.8	170.2	695.6
1994	4,717.0	579.5	246.6	226.2	1,428.4	714.5	247.8	109.4	10.5	2,709.1	712.7	283.7	116.6	186.2	731.6
1995	4,957.7	608.5	254.8	240.2	1,475.8	735.1	254.7	114.4	10.2	2,873.4	750.3	300.7	119.5	203.1	772.8
1996	5,207.6	634.5	261.3	252.6	1,534.7	756.1	264.3	122.6	11.6	3,038.4	787.2	315.9	125.3	218.4	808.1
1997 ᴾ	5,488.6	659.4	262.9	267.6	1,592.7	776.4	277.6	124.6	10.9	3,236.5	826.4	328.7	127.2	236.3	855.0
1992: I	4,127.6	474.1	199.1	184.8	1,303.1	657.3	219.6	102.3	10.4	2,350.4	636.6	241.5	102.1	154.9	624.2
II	4,183.0	481.3	204.0	186.5	1,308.4	652.3	222.3	105.8	11.8	2,393.3	643.4	248.8	106.2	156.9	640.6
III	4,238.9	492.5	208.3	190.6	1,326.3	657.9	228.1	109.4	10.6	2,420.1	649.9	243.6	106.6	156.0	655.0
IV	4,329.6	506.2	216.1	195.5	1,349.5	672.3	232.1	108.9	10.8	2,473.9	657.4	259.0	111.4	164.5	666.8
1993: I	4,365.4	506.4	212.4	198.0	1,354.4	676.4	231.3	109.7	10.8	2,504.6	662.2	260.3	112.4	166.8	680.8
II	4,428.1	524.2	224.3	202.1	1,366.3	684.1	235.4	107.6	10.5	2,537.6	668.8	264.0	112.6	168.6	690.8
III	4,488.6	537.2	228.5	207.6	1,373.9	690.2	238.0	105.5	10.9	2,577.4	675.8	274.1	119.2	170.7	701.6
IV	4,554.9	553.1	239.6	212.0	1,388.0	696.6	241.6	107.7	10.7	2,613.8	684.4	276.7	118.8	174.5	709.2
1994: I	4,616.6	563.2	241.1	216.2	1,404.4	703.9	244.1	106.2	11.7	2,649.0	698.1	274.8	118.2	179.6	717.8
II	4,680.5	572.4	243.3	223.5	1,416.0	711.8	245.0	105.1	10.1	2,692.2	707.8	287.1	120.0	184.5	726.5
III	4,750.6	583.3	245.4	229.7	1,439.5	718.5	249.0	111.8	10.6	2,727.8	717.7	286.2	115.6	188.3	735.9
IV	4,820.2	599.3	257.3	235.4	1,453.7	723.7	253.2	114.3	9.8	2,767.2	727.2	286.6	112.8	192.6	746.4
1995: I	4,871.7	596.9	249.1	235.8	1,462.7	729.3	252.5	115.3	9.6	2,812.2	736.1	290.6	113.8	196.4	760.5
II	4,934.8	602.8	252.7	237.2	1,472.4	733.0	253.4	115.8	10.3	2,859.6	745.6	299.1	118.8	201.1	768.4
III	4,990.6	616.0	258.9	242.5	1,480.4	737.0	256.4	113.9	10.2	2,894.2	754.7	305.8	123.3	205.7	776.5
IV	5,033.8	618.4	258.5	245.1	1,487.8	741.2	256.5	112.7	10.7	2,927.5	764.6	307.3	122.2	209.2	785.8
1996: I	5,105.8	626.7	262.4	246.5	1,508.1	748.4	259.8	117.1	11.7	2,970.9	773.8	310.7	124.8	212.3	790.3
II	5,189.1	638.6	264.0	253.8	1,532.3	752.2	265.7	125.7	11.3	3,018.2	782.5	317.5	126.7	216.6	803.3
III	5,227.4	634.5	260.0	254.2	1,538.3	757.4	265.7	121.4	11.2	3,054.6	791.8	313.4	122.8	219.7	811.9
IV	5,308.1	638.2	258.9	255.9	1,560.1	766.6	266.2	126.0	12.0	3,109.8	800.7	321.8	126.8	224.8	826.9
1997: I	5,405.7	658.4	265.7	263.8	1,587.4	775.5	275.2	128.5	11.0	3,159.9	810.5	320.8	124.9	228.9	841.0
II	5,432.1	644.5	252.7	265.4	1,578.9	771.4	274.8	121.6	11.0	3,208.7	821.2	326.7	127.2	233.4	849.6
III	5,527.4	667.3	268.7	269.9	1,600.8	779.3	280.5	123.5	10.9	3,259.3	831.9	328.8	125.2	238.5	859.7
IV ᴾ	5,589.3	667.6	264.6	271.5	1,603.9	779.5	279.8	124.6	10.7	3,317.9	842.2	338.6	131.5	244.3	869.7

¹ Includes other items not shown separately.
² Includes imputed rental value of owner-occupied housing.

Source: Department of Commerce, Bureau of Economic Analysis.

TABLE B–17.—*Real personal consumption expenditures, 1982–97*

[Billions of chained (1992) dollars; quarterly data at seasonally adjusted annual rates]

Year or quarter	Personal consumption expenditures	Durable goods			Nondurable goods					Services					
		Total[1]	Motor vehicles and parts	Furniture and household equipment	Total[1]	Food	Clothing and shoes	Gasoline and oil	Fuel oil and coal	Total[1]	Housing[2]	Household operation		Transportation	Medical care
												Total[1]	Electricity and gas		
1982	3,081.5	285.5	133.9	91.3	1,080.6	565.1	157.1	91.0	12.8	1,728.2	500.9	187.0	90.3	109.9	442.2
1983	3,240.6	327.4	160.5	103.5	1,112.4	579.7	167.3	93.0	12.9	1,809.0	511.8	193.0	93.0	117.0	459.7
1984	3,407.6	374.9	187.7	115.5	1,151.8	589.9	179.9	95.9	12.8	1,883.0	531.8	197.7	93.6	128.6	472.4
1985	3,566.5	411.4	211.2	125.3	1,178.3	602.2	186.5	97.8	13.0	1,977.3	551.1	205.6	96.1	140.6	490.7
1986	3,708.7	448.4	224.8	140.6	1,215.9	614.0	199.9	102.5	13.4	2,041.4	565.5	209.8	95.1	145.7	510.3
1987	3,822.3	454.9	216.2	149.9	1,239.3	620.8	205.4	105.3	13.0	2,126.9	583.4	219.4	98.4	151.0	537.3
1988	3,972.7	483.5	229.4	160.8	1,274.4	641.6	210.0	106.5	13.2	2,212.4	600.9	229.2	103.4	159.0	561.3
1989	4,064.6	496.2	230.3	170.9	1,303.5	650.1	220.7	108.1	12.6	2,262.3	614.6	237.6	105.6	160.8	575.8
1990	4,132.2	493.3	224.3	173.5	1,316.1	662.9	217.9	107.3	11.2	2,321.3	627.2	240.1	103.7	159.9	602.8
1991	4,105.8	462.0	193.2	177.0	1,302.9	659.6	215.9	103.4	10.8	2,341.0	635.2	243.4	107.0	152.3	621.6
1992	4,219.8	488.5	206.9	189.4	1,321.8	660.0	225.5	106.6	10.8	2,409.4	646.8	248.2	106.6	158.1	646.6
1993	4,343.6	523.8	218.9	207.8	1,351.0	675.3	234.2	108.7	10.7	2,468.9	654.7	261.5	112.3	163.1	655.3
1994	4,486.0	561.2	230.0	229.4	1,389.9	687.9	247.1	109.8	10.7	2,535.5	674.3	270.5	112.5	175.2	662.1
1995	4,595.3	583.6	229.5	248.4	1,412.6	690.5	257.5	113.1	10.5	2,599.6	688.2	282.9	115.0	185.2	674.9
1996	4,714.1	611.1	231.3	269.5	1,432.3	689.7	267.7	114.1	10.6	2,671.0	700.2	289.6	117.8	194.6	688.1
1997 ᴾ	4,869.7	645.8	232.8	296.7	1,459.3	689.9	278.2	115.9	10.0	2,765.2	713.8	295.3	116.9	202.7	711.8
1992: I	4,173.8	476.1	201.7	183.7	1,314.4	661.0	220.4	104.8	10.5	2,383.2	642.6	243.6	103.2	155.4	638.2
II	4,196.4	481.1	204.5	186.0	1,312.0	653.9	223.2	106.1	11.9	2,403.2	645.5	249.9	106.8	156.7	645.9
III	4,226.7	491.9	207.4	191.3	1,321.1	656.4	227.7	108.2	10.5	2,413.6	648.5	243.3	106.6	160.5	650.3
IV	4,282.3	505.0	213.9	196.4	1,339.8	668.6	230.9	107.3	10.7	2,437.6	650.6	256.1	109.7	159.6	652.2
1993: I	4,286.8	504.0	209.1	200.4	1,337.5	670.1	228.8	107.2	10.8	2,445.3	650.6	256.6	111.0	160.3	653.7
II	4,322.8	519.3	218.4	205.0	1,347.8	674.1	233.4	108.6	10.3	2,455.9	652.4	257.7	109.2	161.9	654.3
III	4,366.6	529.9	219.8	210.9	1,356.8	677.9	235.9	109.8	10.9	2,480.0	655.8	265.2	114.7	163.8	656.4
IV	4,398.0	542.1	228.4	214.8	1,361.8	679.2	238.6	109.0	10.9	2,494.4	660.0	266.3	114.1	166.6	656.7
1994: I	4,439.4	550.7	231.6	219.1	1,378.4	684.3	243.1	109.2	11.9	2,510.9	666.8	263.1	113.8	170.3	658.1
II	4,472.2	555.8	228.4	226.1	1,385.5	689.8	242.7	109.6	10.2	2,531.4	672.2	274.1	115.8	173.6	661.1
III	4,498.2	561.7	227.3	232.2	1,393.2	687.9	248.1	109.9	10.7	2,543.8	677.0	272.3	111.4	176.7	663.2
IV	4,534.1	576.6	232.6	240.3	1,402.5	689.5	254.7	110.7	10.2	2,555.9	681.1	272.4	108.9	180.1	666.0
1995: I	4,551.3	572.2	226.2	241.4	1,408.4	690.8	255.3	112.7	10.0	2,571.2	683.7	274.3	109.7	182.5	669.5
II	4,583.5	577.7	227.5	244.6	1,411.6	690.2	257.0	113.2	10.6	2,594.5	686.7	282.4	114.8	183.8	672.9
III	4,612.9	590.8	232.9	251.5	1,413.9	690.6	259.1	113.0	10.4	2,608.7	689.7	287.5	118.7	185.4	677.0
IV	4,633.5	593.7	231.6	256.2	1,416.3	690.6	258.7	113.6	11.1	2,623.8	692.8	287.5	116.9	189.0	680.4
1996: I	4,669.4	600.7	233.4	259.2	1,422.5	692.4	261.6	112.9	11.1	2,646.5	695.6	288.7	119.0	192.1	679.4
II	4,712.2	614.8	234.2	269.9	1,431.6	690.3	268.4	114.5	10.4	2,666.5	698.7	292.0	119.7	193.8	686.2
III	4,718.2	611.9	229.7	272.3	1,433.9	687.3	270.8	114.1	10.6	2,672.8	701.7	285.8	114.8	195.4	689.8
IV	4,756.4	617.1	228.0	276.8	1,441.2	689.0	270.0	114.8	10.3	2,698.2	704.8	291.7	117.7	197.0	697.1
1997: I	4,818.1	637.8	234.0	287.4	1,457.8	694.6	277.1	114.7	9.4	2,723.9	708.3	288.0	113.8	199.3	704.4
II	4,829.4	629.0	223.1	292.3	1,450.0	688.2	273.8	116.1	10.1	2,749.8	712.0	294.2	117.8	200.9	708.8
III	4,896.2	656.1	238.7	301.1	1,465.5	689.5	281.3	116.2	10.4	2,776.1	715.6	295.7	115.7	203.9	714.2
IV ᴾ	4,935.0	660.3	236.0	305.9	1,464.1	687.3	280.6	116.7	10.1	2,811.0	719.2	303.1	120.3	206.6	719.6

[1] Includes other items not shown separately.
[2] Includes imputed rental value of owner-occupied housing.

Note.—See Table B–2 for data for total personal consumption expenditures for 1959–81.

Source: Department of Commerce, Bureau of Economic Analysis.

TABLE B–18.—*Private gross fixed investment by type, 1959–97*

[Billions of dollars; quarterly data at seasonally adjusted annual rates]

Year or quarter	Private fixed investment	Total nonresidential	Structures				Producers' durable equipment						Residential
			Total[1]	Nonresidential buildings including farm	Utilities	Mining exploration, shafts, and wells	Total[1]	Information processing and related equipment			Industrial equipment	Transportation and related equipment	
								Total	Computers and peripheral equipment[2]	Other			
1959	74.6	46.5	18.1	10.6	4.9	2.5	28.3	4.0	0.0	4.0	8.4	8.3	28.1
1960	75.5	49.2	19.6	12.0	5.0	2.3	29.7	4.7	.2	4.5	9.3	8.5	26.3
1961	75.0	48.6	19.7	12.7	4.6	2.3	28.9	5.1	.3	4.8	8.7	8.0	26.4
1962	81.8	52.8	20.8	13.7	4.6	2.5	32.1	5.4	.3	5.1	9.2	9.8	29.0
1963	87.7	55.6	21.2	13.9	5.0	2.3	34.4	6.1	.7	5.3	10.0	9.4	32.1
1964	96.7	62.4	23.7	15.8	5.4	2.4	38.7	6.8	.9	5.8	11.4	10.6	34.3
1965	108.3	74.1	28.3	19.5	6.1	2.4	45.8	7.8	1.2	6.6	13.6	13.2	34.2
1966	116.7	84.4	31.5	21.3	7.1	2.5	53.0	9.6	1.7	7.9	16.1	14.5	32.3
1967	117.6	85.2	31.5	20.6	7.8	2.4	53.7	10.0	1.9	8.1	16.8	14.3	32.4
1968	130.8	92.1	33.6	21.1	9.2	2.6	58.5	10.6	1.9	8.6	17.2	17.6	38.7
1969	145.5	102.9	37.7	24.4	9.6	2.8	65.2	12.9	2.4	10.4	18.9	18.9	42.6
1970	148.1	106.7	40.3	25.4	11.1	2.8	66.4	14.3	2.7	11.6	20.2	16.2	41.4
1971	167.5	111.7	42.7	27.1	11.9	2.7	69.1	14.9	2.8	12.1	19.4	18.4	55.8
1972	195.7	126.1	47.2	30.1	13.1	3.1	78.9	16.5	3.5	13.1	21.3	21.8	69.7
1973	225.4	150.0	55.0	35.5	15.0	3.5	95.1	19.8	3.5	16.3	25.9	26.6	75.3
1974	231.5	165.6	61.2	38.3	16.5	5.2	104.3	22.9	3.9	19.0	30.5	26.3	66.0
1975	231.7	169.0	61.4	35.6	17.1	7.4	107.6	23.5	3.6	19.9	31.1	25.2	62.7
1976	269.6	187.2	65.9	35.9	20.0	8.6	121.2	27.2	4.4	22.8	33.9	30.0	82.5
1977	333.5	223.2	74.6	39.9	21.5	11.5	148.7	33.1	5.7	27.5	39.2	39.3	110.3
1978	403.6	272.0	91.4	49.7	24.1	15.4	180.6	41.8	7.6	34.2	47.4	47.3	131.6
1979	464.0	323.0	114.9	65.7	27.5	19.0	208.1	49.9	10.2	39.8	55.8	53.6	141.0
1980	473.5	350.3	133.9	73.7	30.2	27.4	216.4	58.9	12.5	46.4	60.4	48.4	123.2
1981	528.1	405.4	164.6	86.3	33.0	42.5	240.9	69.5	17.1	52.3	65.2	50.6	122.6
1982	515.6	409.9	175.0	94.5	32.5	44.8	234.9	72.7	18.9	53.9	62.2	46.8	105.7
1983	552.0	399.4	152.7	90.5	28.7	30.0	246.7	82.0	23.9	58.1	58.2	53.7	152.5
1984	648.1	468.3	176.0	110.0	30.0	31.3	292.3	98.6	31.6	67.0	67.4	64.8	179.8
1985	688.9	502.0	193.3	128.0	30.6	27.9	308.7	104.2	33.7	70.5	71.7	69.7	186.9
1986	712.9	494.8	175.8	123.3	31.2	15.7	319.0	108.8	33.4	75.4	74.6	71.8	218.1
1987	722.9	495.4	172.1	126.0	26.5	13.1	323.3	109.8	35.8	74.0	75.9	70.4	227.6
1988	763.1	530.6	181.3	133.3	27.1	15.7	349.3	118.2	38.1	80.1	82.9	76.0	232.5
1989	797.5	566.2	192.3	142.7	29.4	14.4	373.9	127.1	43.3	83.8	91.5	71.2	231.3
1990	791.6	575.9	200.8	148.9	27.5	17.5	375.1	124.2	38.9	85.2	89.8	75.5	215.7
1991	738.5	547.3	181.7	126.1	31.6	17.1	365.6	122.6	38.1	84.5	86.4	79.5	191.2
1992	783.4	557.9	169.2	113.2	34.5	13.3	388.7	134.2	43.9	90.2	89.3	86.2	225.6
1993	855.7	604.1	176.4	119.2	32.8	16.6	427.7	141.6	48.6	93.0	97.9	99.9	251.6
1994	946.6	660.6	184.5	128.7	32.0	16.7	476.1	152.1	51.8	100.3	109.3	118.6	286.0
1995	1,008.1	723.0	200.6	143.8	33.2	16.3	522.4	172.8	65.6	107.2	121.5	125.7	285.1
1996	1,090.7	781.4	215.2	159.8	33.3	16.1	566.2	195.1	78.7	116.3	127.5	134.5	309.2
1997ᵖ	1,173.0	845.4	230.2	175.3	33.0	16.2	615.2	211.7	85.1	126.6	134.4	150.0	327.5
1992: I	755.4	544.1	171.6	117.2	34.3	12.8	372.5	129.2	41.9	87.3	86.2	79.5	211.3
II ...	780.5	556.8	170.4	114.0	34.8	13.3	386.3	133.0	44.4	88.6	87.7	87.8	223.7
III ..	788.1	561.0	167.6	110.6	34.7	13.3	393.4	137.7	44.6	93.1	90.5	85.5	227.1
IV ..	809.7	569.6	167.1	111.0	34.2	13.8	402.5	136.8	44.9	91.9	92.8	91.9	240.1
1993: I	823.5	580.5	171.7	113.6	33.8	16.0	408.9	137.2	47.1	90.1	94.0	92.9	243.0
II ...	842.9	598.8	175.2	117.6	32.7	16.8	423.6	138.1	47.1	91.0	95.4	102.9	244.1
III ..	858.8	606.4	177.8	121.5	32.2	16.8	428.6	145.0	49.8	95.2	98.1	96.4	252.4
IV ..	897.5	630.6	180.7	124.2	32.5	16.6	449.9	146.0	50.5	95.5	104.1	107.5	266.8
1994: I	911.0	634.6	175.4	120.7	32.1	15.7	459.3	147.6	49.9	97.7	105.4	113.1	276.4
II ...	941.7	652.9	185.2	130.9	31.6	15.8	467.7	149.4	50.6	98.8	107.0	115.5	288.7
III ..	956.9	667.4	186.8	130.0	32.0	17.0	480.6	152.8	51.5	101.2	110.8	119.8	289.5
IV ..	977.0	687.5	190.7	133.2	32.4	18.1	496.8	158.5	55.1	103.4	114.0	126.1	289.5
1995: I	998.7	710.9	197.7	138.9	33.2	18.3	513.2	162.9	57.3	105.6	118.1	129.9	287.8
II ...	999.6	722.5	201.1	144.1	33.5	16.1	521.4	173.0	64.7	108.3	123.0	123.6	277.1
III ..	1,009.4	725.4	202.8	145.6	33.5	15.8	522.6	174.3	67.0	107.3	123.0	122.9	284.0
IV ..	1,024.6	733.1	200.7	146.4	32.7	15.0	532.4	181.1	73.5	107.6	121.8	126.4	291.4
1996: I	1,049.4	750.7	205.7	149.8	33.4	15.7	545.0	188.0	76.4	111.6	124.7	127.1	298.8
II ...	1,082.0	769.3	210.6	155.5	32.9	16.0	558.7	190.9	76.8	114.1	129.2	130.8	312.7
III ..	1,112.0	798.6	217.7	162.5	32.7	16.5	580.9	201.1	80.9	120.3	128.2	140.0	313.5
IV ..	1,119.2	807.2	227.0	171.2	34.1	16.0	580.2	200.3	81.0	119.3	127.9	140.1	312.0
1997: I	1,127.5	811.3	227.4	174.0	32.0	16.1	583.9	202.8	81.8	121.0	127.7	137.7	316.2
II ...	1,160.8	836.3	226.8	172.1	33.7	15.6	609.5	208.4	84.5	123.9	134.9	147.1	324.6
III ..	1,201.3	872.0	232.9	177.5	33.2	16.2	639.1	219.5	88.1	131.3	137.5	159.9	329.3
IVᵖ	1,202.4	862.3	233.7	177.6	33.1	16.8	628.5	216.0	86.0	130.0	137.3	155.3	340.1

[1] Includes other items, not shown separately.
[2] Includes new computers and peripheral equipment only.
Source: Department of Commerce, Bureau of Economic Analysis.

302

TABLE B–19.—*Real private gross fixed investment by type, 1982–97*

[Billions of chained (1992) dollars; quarterly data at seasonally adjusted annual rates]

Year or quarter	Private fixed investment	Total nonresidential	Structures				Producers' durable equipment						Residential
			Total[1]	Nonresidential buildings including farm	Utilities	Mining exploration, shafts, and wells	Total[1]	Information processing and related equipment			Industrial equipment	Transportation and related equipment	
								Total	Computers and peripheral equipment[2]	Other			
1982	610.4	464.3	207.2	126.6	39.5	32.2	260.3	54.5	4.7	67.0	85.5	63.7	140.1
1983	654.2	456.4	185.7	117.6	34.2	26.7	272.4	63.4	7.1	70.4	78.5	71.7	197.6
1984	762.4	535.4	212.2	137.6	35.4	30.3	324.6	79.8	11.6	79.0	89.9	85.1	226.4
1985	799.3	568.4	227.8	155.2	35.6	27.0	342.4	88.0	14.5	81.9	94.1	88.4	229.5
1986	805.0	548.5	203.3	144.5	36.5	15.8	345.9	94.1	16.7	84.6	93.5	85.6	257.0
1987	799.4	542.4	195.9	142.4	30.7	15.5	346.9	97.5	21.0	80.2	91.1	82.1	257.6
1988	818.3	566.0	196.8	145.3	30.0	15.8	369.2	106.6	24.0	85.7	95.3	87.1	252.5
1989	832.0	588.8	201.2	150.2	30.9	13.9	387.6	116.2	29.4	88.1	101.5	78.9	243.2
1990	805.8	585.2	203.3	152.0	28.1	16.1	381.9	116.2	29.4	88.2	95.0	81.2	220.6
1991	741.3	547.7	181.6	126.9	32.0	15.7	366.2	117.8	32.4	85.9	88.3	81.7	193.4
1992	783.4	557.9	169.2	113.2	34.5	13.3	388.7	134.2	43.9	90.2	89.3	86.2	225.6
1993	842.8	600.2	170.8	115.3	31.8	16.0	429.6	147.9	56.1	92.3	96.5	98.3	242.6
1994	915.5	648.4	172.5	119.9	29.9	15.8	476.8	165.1	67.2	99.4	105.5	113.2	267.0
1995	962.1	706.5	179.9	128.8	30.0	14.3	528.3	201.8	102.8	107.0	113.4	118.9	257.0
1996	1,041.7	771.7	188.7	140.0	29.3	13.9	586.0	253.1	160.8	116.3	117.0	125.0	272.1
1997 ᴾ	1,122.3	846.7	195.4	148.9	28.0	13.4	657.4	305.2	224.7	126.9	122.8	138.3	279.7
1992: I	758.3	544.4	172.7	118.1	34.6	12.7	371.7	126.7	39.2	87.7	86.8	79.9	213.9
II ...	782.4	557.5	171.0	114.4	34.8	13.3	386.4	132.4	43.4	88.9	88.1	87.9	224.9
III ..	787.3	560.6	167.4	110.4	34.6	13.4	393.1	138.6	45.7	92.8	89.8	85.4	226.7
IV ..	805.8	569.1	165.6	109.8	33.9	13.7	403.5	138.9	47.5	91.5	92.6	91.5	236.7
1993: I	814.8	577.8	168.0	111.3	33.4	15.2	409.8	140.5	51.0	89.6	93.4	91.9	237.0
II ...	831.1	595.1	170.3	114.4	31.7	16.2	424.9	143.2	53.2	90.3	94.2	101.5	236.1
III ..	844.5	602.3	171.7	117.1	31.0	16.4	430.7	152.5	58.4	94.6	96.5	94.8	242.2
IV ..	880.8	625.6	173.1	118.5	31.0	16.2	452.9	155.5	61.7	94.8	102.0	105.2	255.1
1994: I	887.8	626.2	166.3	114.3	30.3	15.1	460.6	158.1	62.2	96.8	102.8	108.8	261.3
II ...	913.2	641.2	174.5	123.1	29.6	15.1	467.3	160.8	64.1	97.8	103.8	110.0	271.5
III ..	922.7	653.2	174.0	120.6	29.8	16.2	480.0	166.1	67.1	100.2	106.7	113.5	269.4
IV ..	938.5	672.9	175.0	121.8	29.8	16.7	499.1	175.6	75.3	102.8	108.9	120.5	265.9
1995: I	955.8	695.7	179.0	125.5	30.4	16.3	518.1	184.5	82.7	105.1	112.1	124.0	261.2
II ...	954.0	705.4	180.9	129.4	30.4	14.2	525.9	199.3	97.2	107.9	114.9	117.3	250.4
III ..	962.3	708.2	181.2	130.1	30.1	13.8	528.5	205.2	106.8	107.2	114.1	115.7	255.5
IV ..	976.3	716.8	178.6	130.3	29.2	13.1	540.5	218.2	124.4	107.8	112.5	118.6	260.8
1996: I	1,001.5	736.9	182.1	132.7	29.7	13.6	557.4	232.8	138.7	111.7	114.8	119.2	266.1
II ...	1,035.7	759.7	185.6	137.0	29.1	13.9	577.1	244.8	152.0	114.0	118.8	121.8	277.2
III ..	1,060.9	789.3	190.0	141.7	28.7	14.1	602.9	264.3	170.0	120.3	117.6	129.5	274.1
IV ..	1,068.7	800.8	196.9	148.4	29.5	13.8	606.7	270.4	182.4	119.3	116.9	129.7	271.1
1997: I	1,079.0	808.9	195.9	150.1	27.5	13.6	616.6	281.4	195.8	121.5	116.8	127.5	273.3
II ...	1,111.4	837.0	193.5	147.1	28.7	13.0	649.3	296.9	216.1	124.4	123.5	136.0	278.2
III ..	1,149.3	874.5	196.7	150.1	28.0	13.4	685.3	320.5	240.5	131.5	125.6	146.8	280.1
IV ᴾ	1,149.6	866.5	195.3	148.4	27.8	13.6	678.5	322.1	246.6	130.4	125.1	143.0	287.1

[1] Includes other items, not shown separately.
[2] Includes new computers and peripheral equipment only.

Source: Department of Commerce, Bureau of Economic Analysis.

TABLE B-20.—*Government consumption expenditures and gross investment by type, 1959-97*

[Billions of dollars; quarterly data at seasonally adjusted annual rates]

Year or quarter	Total	Federal									State and local			
		Total	National defense				Nondefense				Total	Consumption expenditures	Gross investment	
			Total	Consumption expenditures	Gross investment		Total	Consumption expenditures	Gross investment				Structures	Equipment
					Structures	Equipment			Structures	Equipment				
1959	112.0	67.2	55.7	42.0	2.5	11.2	11.5	9.9	1.5	0.2	44.8	30.9	12.8	1.1
1960	113.2	65.6	54.9	42.5	2.2	10.1	10.8	8.8	1.7	.3	47.6	33.7	12.7	1.2
1961	120.9	69.1	57.7	43.9	2.4	11.5	11.4	9.0	1.9	.5	51.8	36.7	13.8	1.2
1962	131.4	76.5	62.3	47.8	2.0	12.5	14.2	11.3	2.1	.8	55.0	39.1	14.5	1.3
1963	137.7	78.1	62.2	49.6	1.6	11.0	15.9	12.4	2.3	1.1	59.6	42.2	16.0	1.5
1964	144.4	79.4	61.3	49.9	1.3	10.2	18.1	14.0	2.5	1.6	65.0	46.0	17.2	1.7
1965	153.0	81.8	62.0	52.0	1.1	8.9	19.7	15.1	2.8	1.8	71.2	50.5	19.0	1.8
1966	173.6	94.1	73.4	61.2	1.3	11.0	20.7	15.9	2.8	2.0	79.5	56.5	21.0	2.0
1967	194.6	106.6	85.5	71.3	1.2	13.0	21.0	17.0	2.2	1.8	88.1	62.9	23.0	2.2
1968	212.1	113.8	92.0	78.9	1.2	11.8	21.8	18.2	2.1	1.6	98.3	70.8	25.2	2.3
1969	223.8	115.8	92.4	80.0	1.5	10.9	23.4	20.0	1.9	1.5	108.0	79.8	25.6	2.6
1970	236.1	115.9	90.6	78.6	1.3	10.7	25.3	21.9	2.1	1.3	120.2	91.6	25.8	2.8
1971	249.9	117.1	88.7	79.2	1.8	7.7	28.3	24.6	2.5	1.3	132.8	102.9	27.0	2.9
1972	268.9	125.1	93.2	82.3	1.8	9.1	31.9	27.8	2.7	1.3	143.8	113.4	27.1	3.3
1973	287.6	128.2	94.7	83.7	2.1	8.9	33.5	29.2	3.1	1.2	159.4	126.4	29.1	3.8
1974	323.2	139.9	101.9	90.1	2.2	9.7	38.0	33.2	3.4	1.4	183.3	144.0	34.7	4.6
1975	362.6	154.5	110.9	97.0	2.3	11.6	43.6	38.0	4.1	1.4	208.1	164.9	38.1	5.1
1976	385.9	162.7	116.1	101.3	2.1	12.6	46.6	40.4	4.6	1.6	223.1	179.7	38.1	5.3
1977	416.9	178.4	125.8	109.6	2.4	13.8	52.6	45.7	5.0	1.9	238.5	196.1	36.9	5.4
1978	457.9	194.4	135.6	118.4	2.5	14.6	58.9	50.4	6.1	2.3	263.4	214.5	42.8	6.1
1979	507.1	215.0	151.2	130.7	2.5	18.0	63.8	55.2	6.3	2.4	292.0	235.9	49.0	7.1
1980	572.8	248.4	174.2	150.9	3.2	20.1	74.2	64.3	7.1	2.9	324.4	261.3	55.1	8.1
1981	633.4	284.1	202.0	174.3	3.2	24.5	82.2	71.7	7.7	2.8	349.2	285.3	55.4	8.5
1982	684.8	313.2	230.9	197.6	4.0	29.4	82.3	72.3	6.8	3.2	371.6	307.9	54.2	9.4
1983	735.7	344.5	255.0	214.9	4.8	35.4	89.4	78.2	6.7	4.5	391.2	326.2	54.2	10.8
1984	796.6	372.6	282.7	236.3	4.9	41.5	89.9	77.9	7.0	5.0	424.0	350.8	60.5	12.7
1985	875.0	410.1	312.4	257.6	6.2	48.5	97.7	84.9	7.3	5.4	464.9	382.6	67.6	14.8
1986	938.5	435.2	332.4	272.7	6.8	52.9	102.9	89.7	8.0	5.2	503.3	412.7	74.2	16.4
1987	992.8	455.7	350.4	287.6	7.7	55.1	105.3	90.7	9.0	5.6	537.2	441.1	78.8	17.2
1988	1,032.0	457.3	354.0	297.9	7.4	48.7	103.3	89.9	6.8	6.6	574.7	471.3	84.8	18.6
1989	1,095.1	477.2	360.6	303.3	6.4	51.0	116.7	101.9	6.9	7.9	617.9	507.2	88.7	21.9
1990	1,176.1	503.6	373.1	312.7	6.1	54.3	130.4	113.9	8.0	8.6	672.6	550.1	98.5	23.9
1991	1,225.9	522.6	383.5	325.4	4.6	53.5	139.1	120.6	9.2	9.3	703.4	579.4	100.5	23.4
1992	1,263.8	528.0	375.8	319.7	5.2	50.9	152.2	131.4	10.3	10.5	735.8	603.6	108.1	24.0
1993	1,283.4	518.3	360.7	311.1	5.1	44.5	157.7	136.2	11.2	10.2	765.0	631.6	108.7	24.7
1994	1,313.0	510.2	349.2	301.6	5.8	41.8	161.0	141.6	10.4	9.0	802.8	663.8	113.4	25.6
1995	1,355.5	509.6	344.6	298.6	6.4	39.6	165.0	144.9	11.0	9.1	846.0	698.6	121.0	26.4
1996	1,406.7	520.0	352.8	305.7	6.8	40.2	167.3	145.7	11.3	10.2	886.7	730.9	128.5	27.3
1997 P	1,453.9	524.8	350.8	311.2	6.3	33.3	174.0	152.9	10.8	10.3	929.1	762.9	138.6	27.6
1992: I	1,247.9	521.8	372.8	317.2	5.2	50.4	149.0	128.5	10.3	10.1	726.1	592.6	109.9	23.6
II	1,256.4	523.2	374.1	317.3	5.5	51.4	149.1	129.1	10.2	9.9	733.2	600.8	108.6	23.8
III	1,270.7	532.0	380.9	323.5	4.8	52.7	151.1	130.9	9.6	10.5	738.7	607.4	107.1	24.2
IV	1,280.0	535.0	375.3	320.7	5.5	49.1	159.7	137.0	11.0	11.6	745.1	613.6	106.9	24.6
1993: I	1,271.5	521.3	363.6	312.4	4.8	46.4	157.7	134.7	11.5	11.5	750.1	621.4	104.1	24.6
II	1,281.2	517.8	361.7	311.5	4.9	45.4	156.1	134.3	10.9	10.8	763.4	628.9	109.9	24.6
III	1,285.3	515.7	358.0	310.6	5.4	42.0	157.7	136.4	11.3	10.1	769.6	635.0	109.8	24.8
IV	1,295.5	518.5	359.4	309.8	5.3	44.3	159.1	139.4	11.1	8.6	777.0	641.1	111.1	24.8
1994: I	1,291.0	506.9	344.9	299.8	5.4	39.7	162.0	142.6	10.3	9.1	784.1	651.6	107.2	25.3
II	1,300.8	505.3	348.5	300.7	5.5	42.2	156.8	138.5	9.7	8.6	795.5	659.2	110.8	25.5
III	1,332.3	520.4	359.7	308.7	6.1	45.0	160.7	141.8	9.9	8.9	811.9	668.6	117.6	25.8
IV	1,328.0	508.3	343.6	297.3	6.1	40.2	164.7	143.5	11.8	9.4	819.6	676.0	117.9	25.8
1995: I	1,344.7	513.6	346.3	299.9	7.0	39.5	167.3	144.9	12.1	10.3	831.1	686.9	118.1	26.1
II	1,356.0	511.2	348.1	299.8	6.2	42.2	163.0	144.2	10.7	8.2	844.8	696.2	122.3	26.3
III	1,362.2	512.9	347.3	303.2	6.0	38.1	165.5	145.8	10.9	8.8	849.3	702.4	120.5	26.5
IV	1,359.2	500.6	336.5	291.6	6.5	38.4	164.1	144.7	10.1	9.2	858.6	708.8	123.0	26.8
1996: I	1,384.2	516.4	348.4	298.2	6.7	43.5	168.0	146.4	11.1	10.4	867.8	717.6	123.2	27.0
II	1,407.0	524.6	357.3	307.8	7.3	42.2	167.3	145.9	11.6	9.9	882.4	727.0	128.1	27.2
III	1,413.5	521.6	354.8	309.3	6.6	38.8	166.8	144.6	11.3	10.9	891.9	735.9	128.6	27.4
IV	1,422.3	517.6	350.6	307.6	6.6	36.3	167.0	146.0	11.4	9.6	904.7	743.3	133.9	27.4
1997: I	1,433.1	516.1	343.3	306.4	6.3	30.7	172.8	151.7	11.2	9.9	917.0	751.7	137.7	27.5
II	1,449.0	526.1	350.6	311.3	6.2	33.1	175.5	152.9	10.5	12.0	923.0	757.4	138.0	27.7
III	1,457.9	525.7	352.1	311.6	6.2	34.3	173.6	153.1	10.9	9.6	932.3	766.1	138.5	27.7
IV P	1,475.6	531.1	357.1	315.5	6.4	35.2	174.0	153.8	10.6	9.6	944.4	776.5	140.3	27.6

Source: Department of Commerce, Bureau of Economic Analysis.

TABLE B–21.—*Real government consumption expenditures and gross investment by type, 1982–97*

[Billions of chained (1992) dollars; quarterly data at seasonally adjusted annual rates]

Year or quarter	Total	Government consumption expenditures and gross investment												
		Federal									State and local			
		Total	National defense				Nondefense				Total	Con-sumption expend-itures	Gross investment	
			Total	Con-sumption expend-itures	Gross investment		Total	Con-sumption expend-itures	Gross investment				Struc-tures	Equip-ment
					Struc-tures	Equip-ment			Struc-tures	Equip-ment				
1982	960.1	429.4	316.5	282.0	5.6	32.0	113.3	102.3	8.6	3.2	531.4	455.6	67.0	10.7
1983	987.3	452.7	334.6	293.3	6.6	37.0	118.5	105.9	8.4	4.7	534.9	458.2	66.3	12.1
1984	1,018.4	463.7	348.1	301.3	6.4	41.7	115.9	102.3	8.7	5.2	555.0	467.9	73.8	14.2
1985	1,080.1	495.6	374.1	318.2	7.9	48.6	121.8	107.4	8.9	5.7	584.7	487.8	80.9	16.4
1986	1,135.0	518.4	393.4	331.1	8.6	53.7	125.2	110.6	9.4	5.4	616.9	513.3	85.9	18.0
1987	1,165.9	534.4	409.2	341.1	9.2	58.4	125.3	109.2	10.3	5.9	631.8	525.5	87.8	18.8
1988	1,180.9	524.6	405.5	345.3	8.5	51.9	119.1	104.8	7.6	6.8	656.6	545.3	91.6	20.0
1989	1,213.9	531.5	401.6	340.9	6.9	53.8	130.1	114.8	7.4	7.9	682.6	566.3	93.5	23.0
1990	1,250.4	541.9	401.5	338.9	6.4	56.1	140.5	123.8	8.3	8.5	708.6	583.2	100.7	24.7
1991	1,258.0	539.4	397.5	338.7	4.7	54.1	142.0	123.6	9.3	9.2	718.7	593.8	101.3	23.6
1992	1,263.8	528.0	375.8	319.7	5.2	50.9	152.2	131.4	10.3	10.5	735.8	603.6	108.1	24.0
1993	1,252.1	505.7	354.4	306.0	4.7	43.8	151.2	129.9	11.0	10.3	746.4	615.8	106.1	24.5
1994	1,252.3	486.6	336.9	292.2	5.0	39.7	149.5	130.4	9.9	9.1	765.7	633.4	107.1	25.2
1995	1,251.9	470.3	322.6	280.6	5.4	36.5	147.5	128.0	10.0	9.4	781.6	646.0	109.5	26.1
1996	1,257.9	464.2	317.8	275.5	5.6	36.5	146.1	125.3	10.0	11.1	793.7	653.6	112.8	27.4
1997 P	1,270.6	457.8	309.0	273.2	5.0	30.7	148.3	127.6	9.3	11.9	812.9	666.7	117.5	28.8
1992: I	1,258.5	525.1	374.2	318.3	5.2	50.7	150.8	130.4	10.4	10.1	733.5	599.0	110.8	23.6
II	1,257.5	523.3	373.3	316.5	5.5	51.3	150.0	129.9	10.2	9.8	734.2	601.7	108.8	23.8
III	1,266.5	529.6	378.7	321.2	4.8	52.7	150.9	130.7	9.6	10.5	736.9	605.9	106.8	24.2
IV	1,272.5	534.0	376.8	322.6	5.4	48.9	157.1	134.5	10.9	11.7	738.5	607.9	106.1	24.6
1993: I	1,250.1	512.1	359.2	308.5	4.6	46.1	152.9	130.0	11.4	11.5	738.0	610.8	102.7	24.5
II	1,253.1	507.8	356.7	307.1	4.6	44.9	151.1	129.5	10.7	10.9	745.3	613.5	107.4	24.4
III	1,250.5	501.5	351.1	305.0	4.8	41.3	150.3	129.1	11.0	10.2	749.1	617.5	107.0	24.5
IV	1,254.7	501.3	350.8	303.2	4.7	42.9	150.4	130.8	10.8	8.7	753.4	621.5	107.2	24.7
1994: I	1,241.9	487.2	335.1	292.4	4.7	38.1	151.9	132.7	9.9	9.2	754.7	627.2	102.7	24.9
II	1,243.3	481.2	335.9	291.5	4.8	39.6	145.1	127.1	9.3	8.7	762.2	631.6	105.5	25.0
III	1,268.1	496.4	347.0	298.7	5.3	42.9	149.4	130.8	9.4	9.0	771.7	635.9	110.6	25.2
IV	1,255.8	481.7	329.6	286.2	5.2	38.1	151.7	131.1	11.1	9.6	774.1	639.0	109.6	25.4
1995: I	1,257.7	480.4	328.7	285.6	5.9	37.1	151.4	129.8	11.2	10.5	777.3	643.2	108.4	25.7
II	1,257.3	474.9	327.4	283.1	5.3	38.9	147.3	129.0	9.8	8.4	782.3	645.0	111.3	26.0
III	1,255.0	473.4	324.0	283.8	5.1	35.1	149.1	130.0	9.9	9.1	781.5	646.8	108.6	26.2
IV	1,237.7	452.6	310.3	269.7	5.4	35.1	142.1	123.4	9.0	9.6	785.1	648.9	109.8	26.5
1996: I	1,243.2	460.9	314.9	271.3	5.6	37.9	145.7	125.0	9.9	11.0'	782.4	646.6	108.9	26.9
II	1,265.1	470.7	323.2	278.4	6.0	38.7	147.2	126.5	10.2	10.6	794.4	654.2	112.9	27.3
III	1,261.5	465.7	319.4	278.1	5.4	35.8	146.0	124.6	10.0	11.9	795.9	655.7	112.6	27.6
IV	1,261.8	459.6	313.6	274.4	5.4	33.7	145.7	125.1	10.0	10.7	803.2	657.8	116.6	28.0
1997: I	1,260.5	452.8	303.9	270.3	5.0	28.2	148.5	127.7	9.8	11.3	807.7	661.1	118.4	28.3
II	1,270.1	460.1	309.4	273.9	4.9	30.3	150.2	128.2	9.1	13.8	810.1	664.3	117.2	28.6
III	1,273.4	458.8	310.3	273.6	4.9	31.7	148.0	127.8	9.3	11.2	814.7	668.6	117.2	29.1
IV P	1,278.5	459.5	312.6	274.8	5.0	32.6	146.6	126.6	9.0	11.3	819.0	672.6	117.4	29.2

Note.—See Table B–2 for data for total Government consumption expenditures and gross investment for 1959–81.

Source: Department of Commerce, Bureau of Economic Analysis.

TABLE B–22.—*Inventories and final sales of domestic business, 1959–97*

[Billions of dollars, except as noted; seasonally adjusted]

Quarter	Inventories[1]							Final sales of domestic business[3]	Ratio of inventories to final sales of domestic business	
	Total[2]	Farm	Nonfarm						Total	Nonfarm
			Total[2]	Manufacturing	Wholesale trade	Retail trade	Other			
Fourth quarter:										
1959	130.7	31.8	98.9	51.6	18.3	20.0	9.0	36.5	3.58	2.71
1960	134.4	32.6	101.8	52.8	18.6	21.4	8.9	37.7	3.57	2.70
1961	137.6	34.2	103.4	54.3	19.1	20.9	9.2	39.5	3.48	2.62
1962	145.2	36.2	109.0	57.6	19.9	22.3	9.2	41.8	3.47	2.61
1963	147.6	33.3	114.4	59.6	21.3	23.6	9.8	44.5	3.32	2.57
1964	153.3	31.9	121.4	63.2	22.7	24.9	10.6	47.4	3.23	2.56
1965	168.1	36.2	131.9	68.2	24.3	27.7	11.7	52.5	3.20	2.51
1966	185.5	36.8	148.6	78.3	27.7	30.1	12.5	55.6	3.33	2.67
1967	197.7	36.3	161.4	85.2	29.9	31.1	15.3	59.2	3.34	2.73
1968	213.2	39.5	173.8	91.4	31.7	34.4	16.3	65.1	3.28	2.67
1969	232.7	42.7	189.9	99.0	35.2	37.7	18.1	69.1	3.37	2.75
1970	240.9	41.2	199.7	102.8	39.0	38.7	19.3	72.9	3.31	2.74
1971	259.7	48.2	211.5	103.5	42.1	44.9	20.9	79.4	3.27	2.66
1972	287.8	58.9	228.8	109.4	46.0	50.0	23.4	88.5	3.25	2.59
1973	343.1	75.3	267.8	125.1	54.8	58.7	29.2	97.5	3.52	2.75
1974	396.3	66.0	330.3	158.2	69.8	64.2	38.0	105.4	3.76	3.13
1975	408.3	70.0	338.4	164.5	69.3	64.7	39.8	118.0	3.46	2.87
1976	441.7	66.6	375.1	181.1	77.2	73.3	43.5	129.7	3.40	2.89
1977	492.8	71.9	421.0	202.8	86.6	81.2	50.4	145.0	3.40	2.90
1978	580.6	96.6	484.0	228.4	101.9	94.5	59.1	167.6	3.46	2.89
1979	675.5	113.6	561.9	268.7	120.5	105.3	67.5	186.4	3.62	3.01
1980	736.0	113.3	622.8	296.5	138.5	113.7	74.0	204.8	3.59	3.04
1981	781.9	103.7	678.2	318.1	151.4	123.9	84.9	221.8	3.53	3.06
1982	767.2	109.2	658.0	299.5	150.3	123.5	84.6	232.8	3.29	2.83
1983	786.7	105.6	681.1	302.6	154.1	138.0	86.4	255.4	3.08	2.67
1984	860.0	108.5	751.5	333.4	169.0	157.3	91.8	276.7	3.11	2.72
1985	875.0	105.9	769.1	325.3	173.4	171.9	98.4	297.7	2.94	2.58
1986	862.5	94.3	768.2	314.6	177.2	176.8	99.5	315.7	2.73	2.43
1987	927.4	97.9	829.5	332.9	190.6	199.5	106.4	333.1	2.78	2.49
1988	992.8	102.0	890.8	358.8	208.5	213.8	109.6	362.8	2.74	2.46
1989	1,044.6	103.6	941.0	382.1	218.4	232.7	107.8	384.9	2.71	2.44
1990	1,082.4	108.3	974.1	399.7	232.4	237.1	104.8	403.4	2.68	2.41
1991	1,058.1	97.2	961.0	383.4	235.5	240.1	102.0	413.1	2.56	2.33
1992: I	1,065.5	104.9	960.6	379.2	236.9	240.1	104.4	423.4	2.52	2.27
II	1,070.8	104.0	966.8	378.1	240.5	244.1	104.1	427.7	2.50	2.26
III	1,076.2	104.8	971.5	380.1	242.0	246.4	103.0	432.8	2.49	2.24
IV	1,077.9	104.9	973.1	375.5	245.3	249.4	103.0	441.9	2.44	2.20
1993: I	1,099.5	110.1	989.3	378.4	247.8	260.4	102.8	443.5	2.48	2.23
II	1,102.1	105.6	996.5	381.9	248.4	262.2	103.9	449.6	2.45	2.22
III	1,104.9	101.3	1,003.7	383.5	251.9	263.3	105.0	454.1	2.43	2.21
IV	1,114.8	101.5	1,013.4	384.0	254.5	267.3	107.6	463.6	2.40	2.19
1994: I	1,132.2	106.6	1,025.6	388.9	255.9	270.9	110.0	467.6	2.42	2.19
II	1,150.0	100.3	1,049.7	396.4	262.5	279.3	111.6	474.5	2.42	2.21
III	1,168.9	99.9	1,069.0	403.9	268.2	284.2	112.6	482.2	2.42	2.22
IV	1,200.6	104.1	1,096.5	413.3	277.5	290.7	115.0	489.2	2.45	2.24
1995: I	1,234.8	105.2	1,129.6	423.7	287.6	298.5	119.8	495.1	2.49	2.28
II	1,246.5	100.5	1,146.0	428.6	292.9	303.4	121.1	499.9	2.49	2.29
III	1,250.8	97.6	1,153.2	430.8	296.2	304.8	121.4	507.2	2.47	2.27
IV	1,261.5	100.5	1,161.0	431.1	298.0	306.2	125.7	512.7	2.46	2.26
1996: I	1,264.9	97.7	1,167.2	433.2	300.7	303.5	129.8	519.8	2.43	2.25
II	1,276.9	104.3	1,172.6	432.5	303.2	306.0	130.9	529.5	2.41	2.21
III	1,287.1	106.0	1,181.2	436.3	300.3	312.5	132.1	533.1	2.41	2.22
IV	1,294.5	102.6	1,191.9	440.3	300.8	313.0	137.7	542.6	2.39	2.20
1997: I	1,306.1	107.2	1,198.9	443.3	306.2	313.3	136.1	550.0	2.37	2.18
II	1,318.1	107.7	1,210.4	448.0	310.8	313.2	138.3	556.2	2.37	2.18
III	1,334.1	109.1	1,225.0	453.5	316.1	314.7	140.7	565.2	2.36	2.17
IV *p*	1,342.2	108.9	1,233.3	458.3	318.0	316.2	140.8	572.8	2.34	2.15

[1] Inventories at end of quarter. Quarter-to-quarter change calculated from this table is not the current-dollar change in business inventories (CBI) component of GDP. The former is the difference between two inventory stocks, each valued at their respective end-of-quarter prices. The latter is the change in the physical volume of inventories valued at average prices of the quarter. In addition, changes calculated from this table are at quarterly rates, whereas CBI is stated at annual rates.

[2] Inventories of construction establishments are included in "other" nonfarm inventories.

[3] Quarterly totals at monthly rates. Final sales of domestic business equals final sales of domestic product less gross product of households and institutions and of general government and includes a small amount of final sales by farms.

Note.—The industry classification of inventories is on an establishment basis. Estimates for nonfarm industries other than manufacturing and trade for 1986 and earlier periods are based on the 1972 Standard Industrial Classification (SIC). Manufacturing estimates for 1981 and earlier periods and trade estimates for 1966 and earlier periods are based on the 1972 SIC; later estimates for these industries are based on the 1987 SIC. The resulting discontinuities are small.

Source: Department of Commerce, Bureau of Economic Analysis.

TABLE B–23.—*Real inventories and final sales of domestic business, 1959–97*

[Billions of chained (1992) dollars, except as noted; seasonally adjusted]

Quarter	Inventories[1]							Final sales of domestic business[3]	Ratio of inventories to final sales of domestic business	
	Total[2]	Farm	Nonfarm						Total	Nonfarm
			Total[2]	Manu-facturing	Whole-sale trade	Retail trade	Other			
Fourth quarter:										
1959	400.8	89.1	303.6	148.2	56.5	59.4	37.6	144.3	2.78	2.10
1960	411.3	90.7	312.4	150.6	57.9	63.6	38.3	147.0	2.80	2.13
1961	419.9	92.9	318.6	155.1	59.3	62.3	40.1	153.5	2.74	2.08
1962	439.4	94.4	336.7	165.2	61.9	66.7	40.1	160.8	2.73	2.09
1963	457.2	95.7	353.1	171.5	66.3	70.3	42.2	169.5	2.70	2.08
1964	472.7	92.0	372.6	180.4	70.3	74.2	45.0	178.4	2.65	2.09
1965	503.0	94.4	400.3	192.6	74.7	81.7	48.4	194.2	2.59	2.06
1966	545.4	93.1	445.0	217.6	84.6	88.5	49.8	199.4	2.73	2.23
1967	577.5	95.6	474.5	234.4	91.0	88.4	56.9	206.4	2.80	2.30
1968	604.3	99.2	497.5	245.0	94.1	95.8	58.1	217.8	2.77	2.28
1969	631.3	99.2	524.8	256.0	100.6	102.3	61.4	221.7	2.85	2.37
1970	636.7	96.8	533.0	256.0	108.0	102.4	62.6	224.0	2.84	2.38
1971	659.0	100.8	551.1	253.1	113.8	116.1	64.9	234.4	2.81	2.35
1972	683.7	101.1	576.5	259.8	119.0	124.9	69.9	252.7	2.71	2.28
1973	721.5	102.5	615.0	277.7	122.4	134.8	77.4	261.1	2.76	2.36
1974	744.8	97.8	646.8	296.8	133.0	132.9	80.8	254.6	2.93	2.54
1975	734.6	103.9	628.3	289.7	127.5	126.3	81.5	265.6	2.77	2.37
1976	764.4	102.5	660.4	303.4	135.9	136.0	81.7	277.5	2.75	2.38
1977	803.2	109.3	692.1	311.8	146.5	143.7	87.1	291.7	2.75	2.37
1978	846.6	111.8	733.6	325.8	158.8	153.1	93.2	311.9	2.71	2.35
1979	869.9	115.7	752.8	338.5	166.3	153.1	91.5	319.3	2.72	2.36
1980	859.7	108.6	751.3	338.9	171.3	148.9	88.7	319.9	2.69	2.35
1981	892.8	118.2	774.1	343.5	176.0	157.2	94.4	318.9	2.80	2.43
1982	877.2	125.5	751.3	329.5	174.1	153.3	91.7	319.2	2.75	2.35
1983	871.5	108.6	763.4	329.5	173.5	166.2	92.4	338.2	2.58	2.26
1984	946.8	115.0	832.4	358.4	189.6	186.4	96.7	355.7	2.66	2.34
1985	977.0	121.8	855.8	353.9	194.8	201.3	105.1	370.8	2.63	2.31
1986	988.1	120.2	868.2	349.7	201.9	204.4	111.6	384.3	2.57	2.26
1987	1,014.5	111.5	902.5	354.8	208.5	223.9	115.1	393.8	2.58	2.29
1988	1,026.2	98.9	927.2	364.3	217.8	231.3	113.7	411.7	2.49	2.25
1989	1,059.5	98.9	960.7	383.5	223.3	245.0	108.9	420.7	2.52	2.28
1990	1,069.9	101.4	968.4	390.1	231.3	243.5	103.4	421.8	2.54	2.30
1991	1,066.9	99.7	967.2	384.0	236.9	243.3	103.0	419.2	2.55	2.31
1992: I	1,066.8	101.5	965.3	380.7	237.2	242.0	105.4	426.6	2.50	2.26
II	1,069.5	103.8	965.7	377.5	239.8	244.3	104.1	428.9	2.49	2.25
III	1,072.5	105.1	967.4	378.5	241.6	245.1	102.2	432.3	2.48	2.24
IV	1,073.9	104.7	969.2	374.8	244.7	247.2	102.6	438.1	2.45	2.21
1993: I	1,082.0	102.7	979.2	376.1	246.0	256.5	100.6	435.8	2.48	2.25
II	1,086.1	101.1	985.1	378.4	247.1	258.0	101.5	439.4	2.47	2.24
III	1,090.0	98.0	992.0	380.4	249.7	259.6	102.3	442.0	2.47	2.24
IV	1,096.0	97.4	998.7	380.9	250.2	263.0	104.6	448.2	2.45	2.23
1994: I	1,109.3	100.8	1,008.6	384.7	251.2	266.2	106.5	449.7	2.47	2.24
II	1,128.2	105.0	1,023.5	387.3	255.6	272.7	107.9	453.9	2.49	2.25
III	1,140.7	107.9	1,033.1	389.6	259.4	275.8	108.3	458.2	2.49	2.25
IV	1,156.6	109.1	1,047.7	392.0	265.7	279.9	110.1	461.9	2.50	2.27
1995: I	1,168.7	107.3	1,061.4	393.1	271.0	284.5	112.8	464.1	2.52	2.29
II	1,174.1	103.9	1,069.9	395.1	273.9	288.2	112.8	466.6	2.52	2.29
III	1,178.3	100.5	1,077.3	397.8	276.8	288.7	114.0	471.0	2.50	2.29
IV	1,183.9	99.9	1,083.4	399.8	278.4	288.6	116.6	474.3	2.50	2.28
1996: I	1,185.9	98.2	1,087.0	402.9	279.9	285.5	118.7	478.2	2.48	2.27
II	1,191.2	99.3	1,091.4	403.0	281.3	287.4	119.5	484.5	2.46	2.25
III	1,200.7	100.9	1,099.3	406.6	280.1	292.4	120.1	484.7	2.48	2.27
IV	1,208.9	102.5	1,105.9	409.7	282.4	292.7	121.1	491.1	2.46	2.25
1997: I	1,224.8	103.8	1,120.5	414.9	288.1	292.8	124.5	495.1	2.47	2.26
II	1,244.2	105.7	1,138.0	422.1	294.3	294.7	126.7	498.5	2.50	2.28
III	1,256.1	108.0	1,147.6	425.8	298.0	295.4	128.2	505.0	2.49	2.27
IV *p*	1,271.1	110.7	1,160.0	431.1	301.6	297.6	129.6	510.3	2.49	2.27

[1] Inventories at end of quarter. Quarter-to-quarter changes calculated from this table are at quarterly rates, whereas the change in business inventories component of GDP is stated at annual rates.
[2] Inventories of construction establishments are included in "other" nonfarm inventories.
[3] Quarterly totals at monthly rates. Final sales of domestic business equals final sales of domestic product less gross product of households and institutions and of general government and includes a small amount of final sales by farms.

Note.—The industry classification of inventories is on an establishment basis. Estimates for nonfarm industries other than manufacturing and trade for 1986 and earlier periods are based on the 1972 Standard Industrial Classification (SIC). Manufacturing estimates for 1981 and earlier periods and trade estimates for 1966 and earlier periods are based on the 1972 SIC; later estimates for these industries are based on the 1987 SIC. The resulting discontinuities are small.

Source: Department of Commerce, Bureau of Economic Analysis.

307

[Billions of dollars; quarterly data at seasonally adjusted annual rates]

Year or quarter	Receipts from rest of the world					Payments to rest of the world									Net foreign invest-ment
	Total¹	Exports of goods and services			Receipts of factor income	Total	Imports of goods and services			Payments of factor income	Transfer payments (net)				
		Total	Goods²	Services²			Total	Goods²	Services²		Total	From persons (net)	From government (net)	From business	
1959	25.0	20.6	16.5	4.2	4.3	25.0	22.3	15.3	7.0	1.5	2.4	0.4	1.8	0.1	-1.2
1960	30.2	25.3	20.5	4.8	5.0	30.2	22.8	15.2	7.6	1.8	2.4	.5	1.9	.1	3.2
1961	31.4	26.0	20.9	5.1	5.4	31.4	22.7	15.1	7.6	1.8	2.7	.5	2.1	.1	4.3
1962	33.5	27.4	21.7	5.7	6.1	33.5	25.0	16.9	8.1	1.8	2.8	.5	2.1	.1	3.9
1963	36.1	29.4	23.3	6.1	6.6	36.1	26.1	17.7	8.4	2.1	2.8	.6	2.1	.1	5.0
1964	41.0	33.6	26.7	6.9	7.4	41.0	28.1	19.4	8.7	2.4	3.0	.7	2.1	.2	7.5
1965	43.5	35.4	27.8	7.6	8.1	43.5	31.5	22.2	9.3	2.7	3.0	.8	2.1	.2	6.2
1966	47.2	38.9	30.7	8.2	8.3	47.2	37.1	26.3	10.7	3.1	3.2	.8	2.2	.2	3.9
1967	50.2	41.4	32.2	9.2	8.9	50.2	39.9	27.8	12.2	3.4	3.4	1.0	2.1	.2	3.5
1968	55.6	45.3	35.3	10.0	10.3	55.6	46.6	33.9	12.6	4.1	3.2	1.0	1.9	.3	1.7
1969	61.2	49.3	38.3	11.0	11.9	61.2	50.5	36.8	13.7	5.8	3.2	1.1	1.8	.3	1.8
1970	70.8	57.0	44.5	12.4	13.0	70.8	55.8	40.9	14.9	6.6	3.6	1.2	2.0	.4	4.9
1971	74.2	59.3	45.6	13.8	14.1	74.2	62.3	46.6	15.8	6.4	4.1	1.3	2.4	.4	1.3
1972	83.4	66.2	51.8	14.4	16.4	83.4	74.2	56.9	17.3	7.7	4.3	1.3	2.5	.5	-2.9
1973	115.6	91.8	73.9	17.8	23.8	115.6	91.2	71.8	19.3	11.1	4.6	1.4	2.5	.7	8.7
1974	152.6	124.3	101.0	23.3	30.3	152.6	127.5	104.5	22.9	14.6	5.4	1.2	3.2	1.0	5.1
1975	164.4	136.3	109.6	26.7	28.2	164.4	122.7	99.0	23.7	14.9	5.4	1.2	3.5	.7	21.4
1976	181.7	148.9	117.8	31.1	32.9	181.7	151.1	124.6	26.5	15.7	6.0	1.2	3.7	1.1	8.9
1977	196.6	158.8	123.7	35.1	37.9	196.6	182.4	152.6	29.8	17.2	6.0	1.2	3.4	1.4	-9.0
1978	233.5	186.1	145.4	40.7	47.4	233.5	212.3	177.4	34.8	25.3	6.4	1.3	3.8	1.4	-10.4
1979	300.3	228.7	184.0	44.7	70.4	300.3	252.7	212.8	39.9	37.5	7.5	1.4	4.1	2.0	2.6
1980	361.9	278.9	225.8	53.2	81.8	361.9	293.8	248.6	45.3	46.5	9.0	1.6	5.0	2.4	12.5
1981	399.5	302.8	239.1	63.7	95.6	399.5	317.8	267.8	49.9	60.9	13.4	5.2	5.0	3.2	7.4
1982	379.5	282.6	215.0	67.6	96.9	379.5	303.2	250.5	52.6	65.8	16.7	6.2	7.0	3.4	-6.1
1983	374.6	277.0	207.3	69.7	97.6	374.6	328.6	272.7	56.0	65.6	17.7	6.5	7.8	3.4	-37.3
1984	421.8	303.1	225.6	77.5	118.7	421.8	405.1	336.3	68.8	87.6	20.6	7.4	9.7	3.5	-91.5
1985	411.1	303.0	222.2	80.8	108.1	411.1	417.2	343.3	73.9	87.7	23.1	7.8	12.2	3.1	-116.9
1986	427.1	320.7	226.0	94.7	106.5	427.1	452.2	370.0	82.2	93.6	24.3	8.1	12.9	3.3	-142.9
1987	481.8	365.7	257.5	108.2	116.0	481.8	507.9	414.8	93.1	107.1	23.3	8.7	11.2	3.3	-156.4
1988	591.9	447.2	325.8	121.4	144.7	591.9	553.2	452.1	101.1	131.7	25.1	9.1	11.4	4.6	-118.1
1989	678.3	509.3	371.7	137.6	169.0	678.3	589.7	484.5	105.3	154.8	26.1	9.6	11.4	5.1	-92.4
1990	734.8	557.3	398.5	158.8	177.5	734.8	628.6	508.0	120.6	156.4	28.4	9.9	13.3	5.2	-78.6
1991	757.9	601.8	426.4	175.4	156.2	757.9	622.3	500.7	121.6	140.5	-12.1	10.4	-27.9	5.4	7.3
1992	777.3	639.4	448.7	190.7	137.9	777.3	669.0	544.9	124.1	126.8	32.0	9.6	16.6	5.8	-50.5
1993	809.4	658.6	459.7	198.9	150.8	809.4	719.3	592.8	126.5	132.1	36.6	13.3	17.3	6.0	-78.6
1994	897.7	721.2	509.6	211.6	176.5	897.7	812.1	676.8	135.3	168.3	37.3	14.2	16.4	6.8	-120.0
1995	1,041.2	818.4	583.9	234.6	222.8	1,041.2	904.5	757.5	146.9	217.5	33.6	14.8	11.5	7.3	-114.4
1996	1,105.1	870.9	617.5	253.3	234.3	1,105.1	965.7	809.0	156.7	232.6	39.8	15.9	16.3	7.6	-132.9
1997ᵖ	....	958.8	687.1	271.7	....	1,055.5	885.4	170.1			....	39.4	17.9	13.2	8.3
1992: I	773.1	632.4	442.1	190.3	140.7	773.1	641.3	516.8	124.5	124.2	27.5	9.4	12.4	5.7	-19.9
II	779.2	635.9	445.9	190.0	143.3	779.2	664.9	541.1	123.8	132.3	30.7	9.7	15.0	6.0	-48.7
III	774.0	640.2	447.7	192.5	133.8	774.0	677.8	557.2	120.6	124.3	27.8	9.2	12.9	5.8	-56.0
IV	783.0	649.1	459.0	190.1	133.9	783.0	691.8	564.4	127.4	126.4	42.0	9.9	26.1	5.9	-77.2
1993: I	792.7	647.1	451.2	195.8	145.6	792.7	693.7	570.8	122.9	122.1	31.1	13.1	12.6	5.5	-54.2
II	810.0	661.2	462.2	199.0	148.9	810.0	718.7	593.2	125.4	132.7	33.6	13.1	14.8	5.7	-74.9
III	800.0	646.8	447.9	198.9	153.2	800.0	718.9	592.8	126.1	130.9	35.0	13.4	15.5	6.2	-84.9
IV	835.0	679.4	477.7	201.7	155.6	835.0	746.0	614.4	131.6	142.7	46.6	13.7	26.2	6.7	-100.4
1994: I	839.6	678.5	475.7	202.8	161.1	839.6	755.1	622.4	132.8	144.2	31.9	14.0	11.2	6.7	-91.6
II	878.3	710.1	499.2	210.9	168.3	878.3	797.9	663.8	134.1	159.3	33.6	14.1	12.9	6.6	-112.5
III	914.4	732.6	518.9	213.7	181.9	914.4	836.0	699.2	136.9	176.1	36.5	14.2	15.7	6.7	-134.2
IV	958.2	763.7	544.6	219.0	194.6	958.2	859.2	721.7	137.5	193.5	47.3	14.4	25.8	7.1	-141.8
1995: I	998.1	784.5	560.7	223.9	213.6	998.1	882.8	739.3	143.5	207.4	33.8	14.5	12.0	7.2	-125.8
II	1,034.1	807.7	578.6	229.2	226.4	1,034.1	913.1	767.0	146.1	215.3	32.4	14.3	11.0	7.1	-126.7
III	1,054.2	831.6	591.1	240.5	222.6	1,054.2	912.0	762.9	149.1	225.6	33.5	14.9	11.3	7.4	-116.9
IV	1,078.4	849.9	605.1	244.7	228.5	1,078.4	909.9	761.0	149.0	221.9	34.6	15.4	11.8	7.4	-88.0
1996: I	1,076.1	850.2	606.1	244.1	226.0	1,076.1	933.2	778.4	154.8	218.2	41.6	15.4	19.2	7.1	-116.9
II	1,092.0	865.0	613.9	251.1	227.1	1,092.0	958.7	802.9	155.8	224.3	34.7	15.8	11.2	7.6	-125.6
III	1,099.0	863.7	609.7	254.0	235.4	1,099.0	977.6	820.2	157.5	242.3	35.4	15.9	11.9	7.7	-156.4
IV	1,153.4	904.6	640.5	264.2	248.8	1,153.4	993.2	834.6	158.6	245.6	47.4	16.7	22.9	7.8	-132.9
1997: I	1,170.4	922.2	656.2	266.0	248.2	1,170.4	1,021.0	855.8	165.2	262.5	35.2	17.0	10.5	7.7	-148.4
II	1,221.9	960.3	663.0	297.3	261.6	1,221.9	1,049.0	880.1	168.9	282.3	36.5	17.6	10.8	8.1	-146.0
III	1,235.2	965.8	691.1	274.8	269.4	1,235.2	1,077.1	905.6	171.6	290.1	36.9	18.2	10.0	8.7	-168.9
IVᵖ	....	986.9	711.1	275.8	....	1,074.8	900.0	174.8			....	48.9	18.5	21.7	8.7

¹ Includes capital grants received by the United States (net), not shown separately. See Table B-32 for data.
² Certain goods, primarily military equipment purchased and sold by the Federal Government, are included in services. Beginning with 1986, repairs and alterations of equipment were reclassified from goods to services.

Source: Department of Commerce, Bureau of Economic Analysis.

[Billions of chained (1992) dollars; quarterly data at seasonally adjusted annual rates]

Year or quarter	Exports of goods and services					Receipts of factor income	Imports of goods and services					Payments of factor income
	Total	Goods[1]			Services[1]		Total	Goods[1]			Services[1]	
		Total	Durable goods	Nondurable goods				Total	Durable goods	Nondurable goods		
1982	311.4	213.5	117.0	98.4	98.5	143.5	325.5	257.4	138.4	115.6	68.9	100.7
1983	303.3	207.3	114.6	94.4	96.8	138.2	366.6	292.4	166.8	123.1	74.4	95.9
1984	328.4	223.7	127.0	98.1	105.9	160.3	455.7	363.1	221.9	140.2	92.9	121.9
1985	337.3	231.7	137.3	95.3	106.1	140.5	485.2	385.9	244.1	142.0	99.7	116.8
1986	362.2	243.6	145.3	99.1	120.3	134.6	526.1	425.5	266.7	158.8	100.2	120.9
1987	402.0	270.5	165.7	105.0	133.4	141.9	558.2	445.2	278.5	166.8	113.1	133.0
1988	465.8	321.4	205.5	115.8	145.0	170.2	580.2	463.2	290.1	173.2	117.1	157.1
1989	520.2	361.7	236.7	124.9	158.7	189.9	603.0	482.7	302.6	180.1	120.2	176.7
1990	564.4	391.6	260.0	131.6	173.1	190.6	626.3	497.3	310.9	186.4	129.4	170.2
1991	599.9	419.2	279.6	139.6	180.8	161.1	622.2	497.1	312.7	184.4	125.3	145.7
1992	639.4	448.7	300.9	147.8	190.7	137.9	669.0	544.9	346.4	198.4	124.1	126.8
1993	658.2	463.7	317.5	146.2	194.5	147.3	728.4	602.0	389.4	212.5	126.5	128.8
1994	712.4	509.8	356.5	153.5	202.9	168.4	817.0	684.1	456.0	227.8	133.2	160.0
1995	791.2	573.9	411.2	164.1	218.0	207.7	890.1	749.2	511.7	237.2	141.2	200.7
1996	857.0	628.4	463.3	169.1	229.9	214.2	971.5	823.1	569.9	253.5	149.0	210.2
1997ᴾ	964.4	725.8	553.4	181.1	242.5	....	1,106.5	944.1	669.4	277.8	163.5	....
1992: I	633.0	440.3	294.5	145.8	192.8	141.9	647.8	521.2	331.2	190.0	126.7	125.6
II	635.8	445.1	298.4	146.6	190.7	143.5	668.3	543.6	344.6	199.0	124.7	132.6
III	639.7	448.3	299.5	148.8	191.3	133.4	670.5	552.8	351.0	201.8	117.7	123.9
IV	649.1	461.0	311.1	149.9	188.2	132.7	689.1	561.8	359.0	202.8	127.4	125.2
1993: I	647.2	454.1	308.0	146.1	193.1	143.3	701.9	578.7	372.9	205.7	123.3	119.9
II	660.1	465.3	318.3	147.0	194.8	145.6	722.7	597.8	383.5	214.3	124.9	129.6
III	646.3	452.0	309.8	142.1	194.2	149.3	729.4	603.1	389.5	213.5	126.3	127.5
IV	679.1	483.5	334.0	149.6	195.9	150.8	759.7	628.3	411.8	216.4	131.4	138.0
1994: I	676.0	479.1	334.8	144.6	197.0	155.3	773.6	641.4	421.8	219.4	132.3	139.3
II	704.1	501.2	352.6	149.1	203.1	161.3	808.0	674.6	447.6	226.6	133.6	152.3
III	722.1	518.4	361.8	156.8	204.1	173.0	833.2	700.0	464.8	234.8	133.5	166.9
IV	747.3	540.4	376.9	163.6	207.5	184.2	853.2	720.4	489.7	230.4	133.2	181.4
1995: I	760.4	550.4	388.7	162.3	210.6	200.8	873.9	733.5	499.7	233.5	140.7	192.9
II	777.4	567.7	406.4	160.8	212.5	211.4	890.3	751.4	512.7	238.5	139.3	198.9
III	802.4	580.4	416.2	165.5	222.6	207.0	895.4	753.6	511.9	241.2	142.1	207.5
IV	824.6	599.1	433.5	167.8	226.2	211.5	900.7	758.2	522.6	235.7	142.9	203.5
1996: I	828.2	605.2	439.1	168.4	224.0	208.0	929.0	781.4	540.4	241.3	147.8	199.4
II	847.4	619.2	459.1	164.5	229.3	208.1	960.0	811.7	559.8	251.9	148.8	203.7
III	851.4	623.0	460.8	166.4	229.4	214.8	990.2	841.7	582.6	259.4	149.3	218.1
IV	901.1	666.2	494.0	177.0	236.8	226.0	1,006.6	857.5	596.6	261.6	150.0	219.8
1997: I	922.7	686.2	517.0	176.0	238.9	224.6	1,048.9	891.3	630.8	263.3	158.4	234.0
II	962.5	725.8	555.8	179.2	240.8	236.3	1,099.1	938.4	660.7	280.1	161.8	250.8
III	973.0	731.8	559.8	181.1	245.0	242.5	1,137.1	972.7	688.5	287.2	165.8	256.9
IVᴾ	999.3	759.4	580.9	188.0	245.1	....	1,140.8	973.9	697.5	280.8	168.1	....

[1] Certain goods, primarily military equipment purchased and sold by the Federal Government, are included in services. Beginning with 1986, repairs and alterations of equipment were reclassified from goods to services.

Note.—See Table B–2 for data for total exports of goods and services and total imports of goods and services for 1959–81.

Source: Department of Commerce, Bureau of Economic Analysis.

[Billions of dollars; quarterly data at seasonally adjusted annual rates]

Year or quarter	Gross domestic product	Plus: Receipts of factor income from rest of the world	Less: Pay-ments of factor income to rest of the world	Equals: Gross national product	Less: Consumption of fixed capital			Equals: Net na-tional product	Less: Indirect busi-ness tax and nontax liability	Busi-ness trans-fer pay-ments	Statis-tical dis-crepan-cy	Plus: Sub-sidies less cur-rent sur-plus of govern-ment enter-prises	Equals: National income
					Total	Private	Govern-ment						
1959	507.2	4.3	1.5	510.1	54.6	40.5	14.1	455.5	41.9	1.4	−1.6	0.1	413.9
1960	526.6	5.0	1.8	529.8	56.6	42.1	14.5	473.2	45.5	1.4	−3.2	.3	429.8
1961	544.8	5.4	1.8	548.4	58.1	43.1	15.0	490.3	48.1	1.5	−2.8	1.3	444.8
1962	585.2	6.1	1.8	589.4	60.4	44.6	15.8	529.0	51.7	1.6	−1.8	1.5	479.0
1963	617.4	6.6	2.1	621.9	63.0	46.3	16.7	559.0	54.7	1.8	−3.0	.9	506.3
1964	663.0	7.4	2.4	668.0	66.0	48.6	17.4	602.1	58.8	2.0	−1.5	1.4	544.1
1965	719.1	8.1	2.7	724.5	70.2	52.0	18.2	654.3	62.7	2.2	−.8	1.7	592.0
1966	787.8	8.3	3.1	793.0	75.9	56.6	19.3	717.1	65.4	2.3	3.3	3.0	648.9
1967	833.6	8.9	3.4	839.1	82.3	61.5	20.8	756.7	70.4	2.5	1.3	2.9	685.5
1968	910.6	10.3	4.1	916.7	89.8	67.3	22.4	827.0	79.0	2.8	.9	3.1	747.3
1969	982.2	11.9	5.8	988.4	98.3	74.3	24.1	890.0	86.6	3.1	−1.5	3.6	805.4
1970	1,035.6	13.0	6.6	1,042.0	107.0	81.2	25.8	935.0	94.3	3.2	1.9	4.9	840.6
1971	1,125.4	14.1	6.4	1,133.1	116.5	88.9	27.6	1,016.6	103.6	3.4	6.1	5.1	908.6
1972	1,237.3	16.4	7.7	1,246.0	127.6	97.8	29.9	1,118.3	111.4	3.9	4.3	6.4	1,005.3
1973	1,382.6	23.8	11.1	1,395.4	140.0	107.1	32.9	1,255.4	121.0	4.5	3.4	5.9	1,132.3
1974	1,496.9	30.3	14.6	1,512.6	162.5	124.5	38.0	1,350.0	129.3	5.0	5.5	4.5	1,214.9
1975	1,630.6	28.2	14.9	1,643.9	188.7	146.3	42.4	1,455.2	140.0	5.2	12.1	8.1	1,305.9
1976	1,819.0	32.9	15.7	1,836.1	206.0	161.3	44.7	1,630.0	151.6	6.5	19.9	7.4	1,459.4
1977	2,026.9	37.9	17.2	2,047.5	228.6	181.0	47.6	1,818.9	165.5	7.3	18.2	10.1	1,638.0
1978	2,291.4	47.4	25.3	2,313.5	258.3	206.8	51.5	2,055.2	177.8	8.2	18.1	11.1	1,862.3
1979	2,557.5	70.4	37.5	2,590.4	296.7	239.9	56.8	2,293.6	188.7	9.9	28.2	11.7	2,078.5
1980	2,784.2	81.8	46.5	2,819.5	339.4	276.0	63.4	2,480.1	212.0	11.2	27.6	15.2	2,244.5
1981	3,115.9	95.6	60.9	3,150.6	388.5	318.0	70.4	2,762.1	249.3	13.4	14.9	16.9	2,501.4
1982	3,242.1	96.9	65.8	3,273.2	424.3	346.2	78.1	2,848.9	256.4	15.2	−2.5	21.1	2,600.8
1983	3,514.5	97.6	65.6	3,546.5	445.3	365.2	80.1	3,101.3	280.1	16.2	37.1	25.6	2,793.3
1984	3,902.4	118.7	87.6	3,933.5	461.5	378.4	83.1	3,472.0	309.5	18.6	5.0	25.5	3,164.4
1985	4,180.7	108.1	87.7	4,201.0	486.6	399.5	87.1	3,714.5	329.6	20.9	2.4	21.9	3,383.4
1986	4,422.2	106.5	93.6	4,435.1	517.9	424.4	93.5	3,917.2	344.7	23.9	23.3	25.1	3,550.3
1987	4,692.3	116.0	107.1	4,701.3	545.8	447.0	98.7	4,155.5	364.8	24.2	−15.4	31.0	3,813.0
1988	5,049.6	144.7	131.7	5,062.6	582.2	478.0	104.2	4,480.5	385.5	25.4	−47.3	28.5	4,145.3
1989	5,438.7	169.0	154.8	5,452.8	625.4	515.1	110.3	4,827.4	414.7	26.3	13.2	24.2	4,397.3
1990	5,743.8	177.5	156.4	5,764.9	651.5	534.3	117.3	5,113.4	442.6	26.5	17.4	25.3	4,652.1
1991	5,916.7	156.2	140.5	5,932.4	679.9	556.4	123.5	5,252.5	478.1	26.3	10.1	23.6	4,761.6
1992	6,244.4	137.9	126.8	6,255.5	713.5	585.4	128.2	5,542.0	505.6	28.4	44.8	27.1	4,990.4
1993	6,558.1	150.8	132.1	6,576.8	727.9	594.5	133.4	5,848.9	532.5	28.2	52.6	31.1	5,266.8
1994	6,947.0	176.5	168.3	6,955.2	777.5	638.6	138.8	6,177.7	568.5	30.5	14.6	26.6	5,590.7
1995	7,265.4	222.8	217.5	7,270.6	796.8	653.0	143.8	6,473.9	582.8	32.2	−28.2	25.2	5,912.3
1996	7,636.0	234.3	232.6	7,637.7	830.1	682.7	147.4	6,807.6	604.8	33.6	−59.9	25.4	6,254.5
1997 ᴾ	8,083.4	....	....	....	868.0	717.0	151.1	....	619.5	35.4	....	26.1	....
1992: I	6,121.8	140.7	124.2	6,138.3	687.2	560.9	126.3	5,451.1	495.7	27.6	24.5	24.6	4,927.9
II	6,201.2	143.3	132.3	6,212.2	692.4	564.7	127.7	5,519.7	497.9	28.5	37.4	25.4	4,981.5
III	6,271.7	133.8	124.3	6,281.1	770.1	641.5	128.6	5,510.9	507.1	28.6	52.7	26.9	4,949.5
IV	6,383.1	133.9	126.4	6,390.5	704.3	574.3	130.0	5,686.2	521.7	28.8	64.6	31.5	5,102.6
1993: I	6,444.5	145.6	122.1	6,468.1	721.8	590.5	131.3	5,746.2	520.6	27.8	71.0	33.0	5,159.8
II	6,509.1	148.9	132.7	6,525.3	720.7	588.1	132.7	5,804.6	525.9	27.7	46.9	32.8	5,236.9
III	6,574.6	153.2	130.9	6,596.9	735.3	601.1	134.2	5,861.5	534.4	28.2	47.5	30.2	5,281.7
IV	6,704.2	155.6	142.7	6,717.1	733.6	598.1	135.5	5,983.5	549.4	29.0	45.0	28.5	5,388.7
1994: I	6,794.3	161.1	144.2	6,811.2	823.3	685.2	138.1	5,987.9	556.9	29.7	6.3	28.1	5,423.2
II	6,911.4	168.3	159.3	6,920.3	753.1	614.9	138.1	6,167.3	564.4	30.1	42.4	25.9	5,556.3
III	6,986.5	181.9	176.1	6,992.3	762.2	623.3	138.9	6,230.1	573.2	30.7	15.2	25.1	5,636.1
IV	7,095.7	194.6	193.5	7,096.8	771.4	631.2	140.2	6,325.4	579.4	31.5	−5.4	27.4	5,747.3
1995: I	7,168.9	213.6	207.4	7,175.1	780.1	638.3	141.9	6,395.0	578.9	31.8	1.2	24.8	5,807.9
II	7,209.5	226.4	215.3	7,220.6	790.6	647.4	143.2	6,429.9	580.9	32.0	−20.2	25.1	5,862.4
III	7,301.3	222.6	225.6	7,298.3	799.0	654.7	144.3	6,499.2	584.0	32.5	−45.0	25.7	5,953.4
IV	7,381.9	228.5	221.9	7,388.5	817.3	671.7	145.6	6,571.2	587.3	32.7	−48.9	25.5	6,025.5
1996: I	7,467.5	226.0	218.2	7,475.3	815.5	669.2	146.2	6,659.8	594.0	32.7	−50.3	25.3	6,108.8
II	7,607.7	227.1	224.3	7,610.5	824.4	676.8	147.6	6,786.0	599.0	33.5	−50.2	25.2	6,229.4
III	7,676.0	235.4	242.3	7,669.1	835.4	687.7	147.8	6,833.6	600.9	33.8	−79.5	24.9	6,303.3
IV	7,792.9	248.8	245.6	7,796.1	845.6	697.2	148.4	6,950.4	625.3	34.2	−59.5	26.0	6,376.5
1997: I	7,933.6	248.2	262.5	7,919.2	855.0	705.4	149.6	7,064.2	610.2	34.4	−64.3	26.1	6,510.0
II	8,034.3	261.6	282.3	8,013.6	863.0	712.3	150.6	7,150.7	616.2	35.0	−73.5	26.0	6,599.0
III	8,124.3	269.4	290.1	8,103.5	871.6	720.3	151.3	7,231.9	625.4	35.9	−103.2	25.8	6,699.6
IVᴾ	8,241.5	....	....	....	882.5	729.8	152.7	....	626.2	36.2	....	26.4	....

Source: Department of Commerce, Bureau of Economic Analysis.

TABLE B–27.—*Relation of national income and personal income, 1959–97*

[Billions of dollars; quarterly data at seasonally adjusted annual rates]

Year or quarter	National income	Less: Corporate profits with inventory valuation and capital consumption adjustments	Less: Net interest	Less: Contributions for social insurance	Less: Wage accruals less disbursements	Plus: Personal interest income	Plus: Personal dividend income	Plus: Government transfer payments to persons	Plus: Business transfer payments to persons	Equals: Personal income
1959	413.9	52.9	10.2	18.8	0.0	22.7	12.7	25.7	1.3	394.4
1960	429.8	51.4	11.2	21.9	.0	25.0	13.4	27.5	1.3	412.5
1961	444.8	52.5	13.1	22.9	.0	26.9	14.0	31.5	1.4	430.0
1962	479.0	60.5	14.6	25.4	.0	29.3	15.0	32.6	1.5	457.0
1963	506.3	66.3	16.1	28.5	.0	32.4	16.1	34.5	1.7	480.0
1964	544.1	73.3	18.2	30.1	.0	36.1	18.0	36.0	1.8	514.5
1965	592.0	84.1	21.1	31.6	.0	40.3	20.2	39.1	2.0	556.7
1966	648.9	89.8	24.3	40.6	.0	44.9	20.9	43.6	2.1	605.7
1967	685.5	87.4	28.1	45.5	.0	49.5	22.1	52.3	2.3	650.7
1968	747.3	94.2	30.4	50.4	.0	54.6	24.5	60.6	2.5	714.5
1969	805.4	90.9	33.6	57.8	.0	60.8	25.1	67.5	2.8	779.3
1970	840.6	78.7	40.0	62.0	.0	69.2	23.5	81.8	2.8	837.1
1971	908.6	92.0	45.4	69.6	.6	75.7	23.5	97.0	3.0	900.2
1972	1,005.3	106.7	49.3	79.5	.0	81.8	25.5	108.4	3.4	988.8
1973	1,132.3	120.1	56.5	97.9	-.1	94.1	27.7	124.1	3.8	1,107.5
1974	1,214.9	109.2	71.8	111.7	-.5	112.4	29.6	147.4	4.0	1,215.9
1975	1,305.9	128.2	80.0	121.1	.1	123.0	29.2	185.7	4.5	1,319.0
1976	1,459.4	154.9	85.1	137.7	.1	134.6	35.0	202.8	5.5	1,459.4
1977	1,638.0	184.3	100.7	154.4	.1	155.7	39.5	217.5	5.9	1,616.1
1978	1,862.3	209.0	120.5	177.0	.3	184.5	44.3	234.8	6.8	1,825.9
1979	2,078.5	213.1	150.3	204.2	-.2	223.6	50.5	262.8	7.9	2,055.8
1980	2,244.5	188.3	191.9	225.0	.0	274.7	57.5	312.6	8.8	2,293.0
1981	2,501.4	207.0	234.5	261.6	.1	337.2	67.2	355.7	10.2	2,568.5
1982	2,600.8	182.3	264.9	280.6	.0	379.2	66.9	396.3	11.8	2,727.2
1983	2,793.3	235.2	275.9	301.9	-.4	403.2	77.4	426.6	12.8	2,900.8
1984	3,164.4	290.1	318.5	345.5	.2	472.3	79.4	438.5	15.1	3,215.3
1985	3,383.4	304.0	337.2	375.9	-.2	508.4	88.3	468.7	17.8	3,449.8
1986	3,550.3	293.8	363.1	402.0	.0	543.3	105.1	498.0	20.7	3,658.4
1987	3,813.0	333.2	372.2	423.3	.0	560.0	101.1	522.5	20.8	3,888.7
1988	4,145.3	382.1	398.9	462.8	.0	595.5	109.9	556.8	20.8	4,184.6
1989	4,397.3	380.0	456.6	491.2	.0	674.5	130.9	604.9	21.1	4,501.0
1990	4,652.1	397.1	467.3	518.5	.1	704.4	142.9	666.5	21.3	4,804.2
1991	4,761.6	411.3	448.0	543.5	-.1	699.2	153.6	749.1	20.8	4,981.6
1992	4,990.4	428.0	414.3	571.4	-15.8	667.2	159.4	835.7	22.5	5,277.2
1993	5,266.8	492.8	402.5	596.0	4.4	651.0	185.3	889.8	22.1	5,519.2
1994	5,590.7	570.5	412.3	630.5	13.3	668.1	204.8	930.9	23.7	5,791.8
1995	5,912.3	650.0	425.1	659.1	13.1	718.9	251.9	990.0	25.0	6,150.8
1996	6,254.5	735.9	425.1	692.0	1.1	735.7	291.2	1,042.0	26.0	6,495.2
1997 ᵖ	....	....	....	732.0	1.2	768.8	321.5	1,094.1	27.1	6,874.4
1992: I	4,927.9	444.2	419.2	565.1	.0	674.1	152.3	816.4	21.9	5,164.2
II	4,981.5	437.2	417.5	570.1	.0	673.0	154.5	831.0	22.5	5,237.7
III	4,949.5	376.1	408.1	574.8	.0	661.2	160.8	842.5	22.8	5,277.7
IV	5,102.6	454.6	412.4	575.7	-63.0	660.4	170.1	853.0	22.9	5,429.3
1993: I	5,159.8	459.2	411.2	585.3	70.1	660.3	177.8	874.9	22.3	5,369.4
II	5,236.9	478.2	404.6	594.0	-.1	653.7	182.1	886.0	22.0	5,504.1
III	5,281.7	492.8	398.9	598.7	-.1	647.8	187.8	895.3	22.0	5,544.2
IV	5,388.7	541.2	395.4	606.1	-52.2	642.1	193.5	903.1	22.2	5,659.1
1994: I	5,423.2	512.0	397.2	619.2	52.4	641.4	192.1	917.3	23.1	5,616.3
II	5,556.3	562.0	405.6	628.2	.3	656.4	200.3	926.2	23.6	5,766.6
III	5,636.1	590.1	415.6	633.4	.3	674.1	208.5	934.8	24.0	5,838.1
IV	5,747.3	617.7	430.7	641.2	.3	700.4	218.5	945.4	24.4	5,946.1
1995: I	5,807.9	613.2	432.7	650.1	13.1	713.9	243.4	972.4	24.6	6,053.1
II	5,862.4	628.0	429.7	655.1	13.1	719.4	248.6	985.6	24.8	6,114.8
III	5,953.4	672.8	419.5	662.4	13.1	717.9	254.2	996.4	25.1	6,179.1
IV	6,025.5	685.7	418.6	668.6	13.1	724.2	261.5	1,005.7	25.4	6,256.2
1996: I	6,108.8	717.7	416.2	677.3	1.1	722.3	287.4	1,027.6	25.6	6,359.4
II	6,229.4	738.5	422.5	688.7	1.1	727.8	290.0	1,039.0	25.9	6,461.3
III	6,303.3	739.6	430.9	696.8	1.1	742.7	292.0	1,046.3	26.1	6,541.9
IV	6,376.5	747.8	430.6	705.1	1.1	749.8	295.2	1,055.1	26.4	6,618.4
1997: I	6,510.0	779.6	440.5	719.5	1.2	757.2	312.5	1,080.5	26.7	6,746.2
II	6,599.0	795.1	448.1	726.9	1.2	766.1	318.3	1,090.0	26.9	6,829.1
III	6,699.6	827.3	451.8	735.0	1.2	772.6	324.5	1,098.4	27.2	6,906.9
IV ᵖ	....	....	....	746.6	1.2	779.1	330.7	1,107.3	27.5	7,015.4

Source: Department of Commerce, Bureau of Economic Analysis.

311

TABLE B–28.—*National income by type of income, 1959–97*

[Billions of dollars; quarterly data at seasonally adjusted annual rates]

Year or quarter	National income [1]	Compensation of employees							Proprietors' income with inventory valuation and capital consumption adjustments				
		Total	Wages and salaries			Supplements to wages and salaries			Total	Farm		Nonfarm	
			Total	Government	Other	Total	Employer contributions for social insurance	Other labor income		Total	Proprietors' income [2]	Total	Proprietors' income [3]
1959	413.9	281.2	259.8	46.0	213.8	21.4	10.9	10.6	51.9	10.9	11.8	40.9	40.2
1960	429.8	296.7	272.8	49.2	223.7	23.8	12.6	11.2	51.9	11.5	12.3	40.5	39.8
1961	444.8	305.6	280.5	52.4	228.0	25.1	13.3	11.8	54.4	12.1	12.9	42.3	41.8
1962	479.0	327.4	299.3	56.3	243.0	28.1	15.1	13.0	56.5	12.1	12.9	44.4	43.9
1963	506.3	345.5	314.8	60.0	254.8	30.7	16.7	14.0	57.8	11.9	12.7	45.8	45.2
1964	544.1	371.0	337.7	64.9	272.9	33.2	17.5	15.7	60.6	10.8	11.6	49.8	49.2
1965	592.0	399.8	363.7	69.9	293.8	36.1	18.3	17.8	65.1	13.0	13.9	52.1	51.9
1966	648.9	443.0	400.3	78.3	321.9	42.7	22.8	19.9	69.4	14.1	15.0	55.3	55.4
1967	685.5	475.5	428.9	86.4	342.5	46.6	24.9	21.7	71.0	12.7	13.7	58.2	58.3
1968	747.3	524.7	471.9	96.6	375.3	52.8	27.6	25.2	75.3	12.8	13.8	62.5	63.0
1969	805.4	578.3	518.3	105.5	412.7	60.0	31.5	28.5	79.1	14.6	15.8	64.6	65.0
1970	840.6	618.1	551.5	117.1	434.3	66.6	34.1	32.5	80.2	14.8	16.1	65.4	66.0
1971	908.6	660.1	584.5	126.7	457.8	75.6	38.9	36.7	86.5	15.4	16.9	71.1	72.0
1972	1,005.3	726.8	638.7	137.8	500.9	88.1	45.1	43.0	98.3	19.5	21.2	78.8	79.3
1973	1,132.3	813.1	708.6	148.7	560.0	104.4	55.3	49.2	116.8	32.6	34.5	84.2	85.9
1974	1,214.9	892.4	772.2	160.4	611.8	120.3	63.7	56.5	115.7	25.8	28.4	89.8	93.4
1975	1,305.9	951.3	814.7	176.1	638.6	136.6	70.6	65.9	121.8	24.1	27.5	97.7	99.2
1976	1,459.4	1,061.5	899.6	188.7	710.8	162.0	82.2	79.7	133.6	18.6	22.6	115.0	116.3
1977	1,638.0	1,182.9	994.0	202.4	791.6	188.9	94.1	94.7	147.4	17.5	21.8	129.9	131.0
1978	1,862.3	1,338.5	1,121.1	219.8	901.2	217.4	107.3	110.1	169.5	22.2	27.0	147.4	148.7
1979	2,078.5	1,503.3	1,255.7	236.9	1,018.8	247.5	123.2	124.3	185.0	25.3	31.1	159.7	160.9
1980	2,244.5	1,653.9	1,377.6	261.2	1,116.4	276.3	136.4	139.8	176.6	12.2	19.4	164.4	165.2
1981	2,501.4	1,827.8	1,517.6	285.6	1,232.0	310.2	157.1	153.0	187.6	21.9	30.2	165.7	160.7
1982	2,600.8	1,927.6	1,593.9	307.3	1,286.7	333.7	168.3	165.4	179.6	14.5	23.4	165.1	158.2
1983	2,793.3	2,044.2	1,684.8	324.5	1,360.3	359.4	182.2	177.2	191.9	4.1	12.8	187.8	172.2
1984	3,164.4	2,257.0	1,855.3	347.8	1,507.5	401.7	212.8	188.9	248.7	23.2	31.6	225.5	199.7
1985	3,383.4	2,425.7	1,995.7	373.5	1,622.1	430.0	226.9	203.1	268.6	23.6	31.5	245.0	210.5
1986	3,550.3	2,572.4	2,116.5	396.6	1,720.0	455.9	239.9	216.0	279.5	24.2	32.1	255.3	215.9
1987	3,813.0	2,757.7	2,272.7	423.1	1,849.5	485.0	249.7	235.4	305.1	31.5	39.2	273.6	238.2
1988	4,145.3	2,973.9	2,453.6	450.4	2,003.2	520.3	268.6	251.7	335.3	27.5	35.1	307.8	272.0
1989	4,397.3	3,151.6	2,598.1	479.4	2,118.7	553.5	280.4	273.1	357.4	36.3	43.9	321.1	284.8
1990	4,652.1	3,352.8	2,757.5	517.2	2,240.3	595.2	294.6	300.6	374.0	35.4	43.3	338.6	312.7
1991	4,761.6	3,457.9	2,827.6	546.0	2,281.5	630.4	307.7	322.7	376.5	29.3	37.2	347.2	325.0
1992	4,990.4	3,644.9	2,970.6	567.8	2,402.9	674.3	323.0	351.3	423.8	37.1	45.2	386.7	363.1
1993	5,266.8	3,814.9	3,094.0	584.3	2,509.7	720.8	335.7	385.1	450.8	32.4	40.4	418.4	392.7
1994	5,590.7	4,012.0	3,254.0	602.2	2,651.8	758.0	353.0	405.0	471.6	36.9	44.8	434.7	415.0
1995	5,912.3	4,215.4	3,442.6	623.0	2,819.6	772.9	366.0	406.8	489.0	23.4	31.4	465.5	438.8
1996	6,254.5	4,426.9	3,633.6	642.6	2,991.0	793.3	385.7	407.6	520.3	37.2	45.0	483.1	455.3
1997 P	....	4,703.4	3,878.4	665.4	3,213.0	825.0	408.4	416.6	544.7	40.9	48.5	503.8	474.6
1992:I	4,927.9	3,577.1	2,916.5	561.4	2,355.1	660.7	319.9	340.8	410.2	35.9	43.7	374.4	350.8
II	4,981.5	3,626.5	2,956.2	567.2	2,389.0	670.3	322.7	347.6	420.8	37.1	44.9	383.8	360.7
III	4,949.5	3,669.2	2,988.2	569.8	2,418.3	681.0	325.1	355.9	426.6	39.0	47.8	387.6	364.4
IV	5,102.6	3,707.0	3,021.7	572.5	2,449.2	685.3	324.2	361.1	437.4	36.5	44.4	401.0	376.3
1993:I	5,159.8	3,749.3	3,045.5	581.1	2,464.5	703.8	330.0	373.8	440.3	29.7	37.7	410.6	383.5
II	5,236.9	3,796.3	3,079.3	581.5	2,497.7	717.0	334.7	382.3	452.2	36.3	44.2	416.0	389.0
III	5,281.7	3,837.6	3,111.0	586.3	2,524.7	726.6	337.1	389.5	446.2	25.6	33.8	420.6	394.8
IV	5,388.7	3,876.2	3,140.4	588.4	2,552.0	735.8	340.9	394.9	464.4	38.0	46.0	426.5	403.4
1994:I	5,423.2	3,937.4	3,190.7	596.0	2,594.8	746.7	347.1	399.5	463.9	46.4	54.3	417.5	408.1
II	5,556.3	3,988.0	3,232.3	601.3	2,631.0	755.6	352.0	403.7	474.7	38.8	46.7	435.9	410.9
III	5,636.1	4,028.7	3,267.2	603.5	2,663.7	761.5	354.6	406.9	471.6	33.2	41.1	438.4	416.6
IV	5,747.3	4,093.9	3,325.9	608.0	2,717.8	768.1	358.3	409.8	476.1	29.1	37.0	447.0	424.3
1995:I	5,807.9	4,153.2	3,384.3	617.2	2,767.1	768.9	361.0	407.9	478.2	20.6	28.6	457.6	431.3
II	5,862.4	4,187.9	3,417.7	621.1	2,796.7	770.2	363.6	406.6	484.4	21.3	29.3	463.1	436.6
III	5,953.4	4,238.0	3,463.3	625.1	2,838.2	774.6	368.0	406.7	491.7	22.9	30.8	468.7	442.4
IV	6,025.5	4,282.6	3,504.9	628.5	2,876.4	777.7	371.4	406.2	501.5	28.9	36.8	472.6	444.7
1996:I	6,108.8	4,322.2	3,540.3	635.6	2,904.7	781.9	376.8	405.0	509.3	31.9	39.8	477.4	448.8
II	6,229.4	4,403.9	3,612.3	640.3	2,972.0	791.5	383.6	407.9	520.0	36.5	44.3	483.5	456.4
III	6,303.3	4,461.0	3,664.0	645.5	3,018.4	797.0	388.6	408.4	523.8	40.1	47.9	483.7	456.1
IV	6,376.5	4,520.7	3,718.0	648.9	3,069.0	802.7	393.6	409.1	528.3	40.4	48.1	487.9	460.0
1997:I	6,510.0	4,606.3	3,792.7	657.8	3,134.9	813.6	401.3	412.3	534.6	40.2	47.9	494.4	466.3
II	6,599.0	4,663.4	3,842.7	662.0	3,180.8	820.7	405.6	415.1	543.6	43.6	51.2	500.0	470.8
III	6,699.6	4,725.2	3,897.3	667.7	3,229.6	827.9	410.2	417.7	547.2	40.9	48.5	506.3	477.0
IV P	....	4,818.6	3,980.8	674.2	3,306.7	837.7	416.4	421.4	553.3	39.0	46.4	514.4	484.3

[1] National income is the total net income earned in production. It differs from gross domestic product mainly in that it excludes depreciation charges and other allowances for business and institutional consumption of durable capital goods and indirect business taxes. See Table B–26.

See next page for continuation of table.

TABLE B–28.—*National income by type of income, 1959–97*—Continued

[Billions of dollars; quarterly data at seasonally adjusted annual rates]

Year or quarter	Rental income of persons with capital consumption adjustment			Corporate profits with inventory valuation and capital consumption adjustments								Capital consumption adjustment	Net interest
				Profits with inventory valuation adjustment and without capital consumption adjustment									
	Total (Rental income of persons)	Rental income of persons	Capital consumption adjustment	Total	Profits						Inventory valuation adjustment		
					Total	Profits before tax	Profits tax liability	Profits after tax					
								Total	Dividends	Undistributed profits			
1959	17.7	19.8	-2.0	52.9	53.1	53.4	23.6	29.7	12.7	17.0	-0.3	-0.2	10.2
1960	18.6	20.6	-2.1	51.4	51.0	51.1	22.7	28.4	13.4	15.0	-.2	.5	11.2
1961	19.2	21.2	-2.0	52.5	51.3	51.0	22.8	28.2	14.0	14.3	.3	1.2	13.1
1962	20.0	22.0	-2.0	60.5	56.4	56.4	24.0	32.4	15.0	17.4	.0	4.1	14.6
1963	20.7	22.6	-1.9	66.3	61.2	61.2	26.2	34.9	16.1	18.8	.1	5.1	16.1
1964	21.0	23.0	-2.0	73.3	67.5	68.0	28.0	40.0	18.0	22.0	-.5	5.8	18.2
1965	21.8	23.9	-2.2	84.1	77.6	78.8	30.9	47.9	20.2	27.8	-1.2	6.6	21.1
1966	22.5	24.9	-2.5	89.8	83.0	85.1	33.7	51.4	20.9	30.5	-2.1	6.9	24.3
1967	23.6	26.3	-2.7	87.4	80.3	81.8	32.7	49.2	22.1	27.1	-1.6	7.1	28.1
1968	22.7	25.9	-3.2	94.2	86.9	90.6	39.4	51.2	24.6	26.6	-3.7	7.3	30.4
1969	23.4	27.3	-3.9	90.9	83.2	89.0	39.7	49.4	25.2	24.1	-5.9	7.8	33.6
1970	23.6	27.8	-4.2	78.7	71.8	78.4	34.4	44.0	23.7	20.3	-6.6	6.9	40.0
1971	24.6	29.5	-4.9	92.0	85.5	90.1	37.7	52.4	23.7	28.6	-4.6	6.5	45.4
1972	24.3	30.3	-6.0	106.7	97.9	104.5	41.9	62.6	25.8	36.9	-6.6	8.8	49.3
1973	25.8	32.8	-7.0	120.1	110.9	130.9	49.3	81.6	28.1	53.5	-20.0	9.2	56.5
1974	25.7	34.4	-8.6	109.2	103.4	142.8	51.8	91.0	30.4	60.6	-39.5	5.8	71.8
1975	24.7	34.9	-10.2	128.2	129.4	140.4	50.9	89.5	30.1	59.4	-11.0	-1.3	80.0
1976	24.3	35.7	-11.5	154.9	158.9	173.8	64.2	109.6	35.9	73.7	-14.9	-4.0	85.1
1977	22.8	36.4	-13.6	184.3	186.8	203.5	73.0	130.4	40.8	89.6	-16.6	-2.5	100.7
1978	24.8	41.3	-16.5	209.0	213.1	238.1	83.5	154.6	46.0	108.6	-25.0	-4.1	120.5
1979	26.9	46.9	-20.0	213.1	220.2	261.8	88.0	173.8	52.5	121.3	-41.6	-7.1	150.3
1980	33.9	57.5	-23.6	188.3	198.3	241.4	84.8	156.6	59.3	97.3	-43.0	-10.1	191.9
1981	44.5	70.9	-26.5	207.0	204.1	229.8	81.1	148.6	69.5	79.1	-25.7	3.0	234.5
1982	46.5	75.0	-28.5	182.3	166.8	176.7	63.1	113.6	69.8	43.8	-9.9	15.5	264.9
1983	46.1	75.1	-28.9	235.2	203.7	212.8	77.2	135.5	80.8	54.8	-9.1	31.5	275.9
1984	50.1	79.4	-29.4	290.1	238.5	244.2	94.0	150.1	83.2	66.9	-5.6	51.5	318.5
1985	48.1	79.3	-31.2	304.0	230.5	229.9	96.5	133.4	92.8	40.6	.5	73.5	337.2
1986	41.5	73.0	-31.5	293.8	234.0	222.6	106.5	116.1	110.2	5.8	11.4	59.8	363.1
1987	44.8	77.9	-33.1	333.2	272.9	293.6	127.1	166.5	107.0	59.5	-20.7	60.2	372.2
1988	55.1	90.1	-35.0	382.1	325.0	354.3	137.0	217.3	116.8	100.5	-29.3	57.1	398.9
1989	51.7	91.4	-39.7	380.0	330.6	348.1	141.3	206.8	138.9	67.9	-17.5	49.3	456.6
1990	61.0	99.1	-38.1	397.1	358.2	371.7	140.5	231.2	151.9	79.4	-13.5	38.9	467.3
1991	67.9	107.5	-39.6	411.3	378.2	374.2	133.4	240.8	163.1	77.7	4.0	33.1	448.0
1992	79.4	127.5	-48.1	428.0	398.9	406.4	143.0	263.4	169.5	93.9	-7.5	29.1	414.3
1993	105.7	148.5	-42.8	492.8	456.9	465.4	165.2	300.2	195.8	104.5	-8.5	36.0	402.5
1994	124.4	172.0	-47.6	570.5	519.1	535.1	186.6	348.5	216.2	132.3	-16.1	51.4	412.3
1995	132.8	179.8	-47.0	650.0	598.4	622.6	213.2	409.4	264.4	145.0	-24.3	51.6	425.1
1996	146.3	193.3	-47.0	735.9	674.1	676.6	229.0	447.6	304.8	142.8	-2.5	61.8	425.1
1997 *p*	148.1	197.6	-49.5	....	....	....	....	....	336.1	....	4.9	69.7	....
1992: I	77.2	115.3	-38.2	444.2	411.4	411.1	143.9	267.2	162.1	105.2	.3	32.7	419.2
II	79.5	118.1	-38.6	437.2	404.3	426.2	150.9	275.2	164.6	110.6	-21.9	32.9	417.5
III	69.5	145.4	-75.9	376.1	359.4	368.0	127.6	240.4	170.9	69.5	-8.6	16.7	408.1
IV	91.2	131.1	-39.8	454.6	420.5	420.3	149.7	270.6	180.4	90.3	.2	34.1	412.4
1993: I	99.7	144.8	-45.1	459.2	419.2	431.7	149.2	282.5	188.0	94.5	-12.5	40.0	411.2
II	105.6	146.6	-41.0	478.2	444.4	461.5	165.4	296.1	192.5	103.6	-17.1	33.8	404.6
III	106.1	149.4	-43.3	492.8	459.8	459.6	161.2	298.4	198.3	100.1	.2	33.0	398.9
IV	111.5	153.3	-41.9	541.2	504.1	508.9	184.9	324.0	204.2	119.7	-4.8	37.1	395.4
1994: I	112.7	171.2	-58.4	512.0	470.8	475.1	163.0	312.1	203.2	108.9	-4.3	41.2	397.2
II	126.0	169.0	-43.0	562.0	510.2	525.3	182.8	342.5	211.6	131.0	-15.1	51.8	405.6
III	130.1	174.0	-43.9	590.1	535.0	556.2	194.6	361.6	220.0	141.6	-21.2	55.1	415.6
IV	128.9	173.9	-45.0	617.7	560.3	583.9	206.2	377.7	230.2	147.5	-23.6	57.4	430.7
1995: I	130.5	176.2	-45.7	613.2	560.4	610.7	209.6	401.0	255.5	145.6	-50.3	52.9	432.7
II	132.3	178.0	-45.7	628.0	577.2	615.0	209.1	405.9	260.8	145.1	-37.8	50.8	429.7
III	131.5	177.3	-45.9	672.8	621.4	630.6	218.8	411.8	266.8	145.0	-9.3	51.5	419.5
IV	137.1	187.7	-50.6	685.7	634.5	634.1	215.3	418.8	274.4	144.5	.4	51.1	418.6
1996: I	143.4	189.5	-46.1	717.7	659.8	664.9	226.2	438.7	300.7	138.0	-5.1	57.9	416.2
II	144.6	191.0	-46.4	738.5	676.8	682.2	232.2	450.0	303.7	146.4	-5.4	61.6	422.5
III	148.0	195.5	-47.5	739.6	676.4	679.1	231.6	447.5	305.7	141.8	-2.7	63.2	430.9
IV	149.2	197.3	-48.1	747.8	683.4	680.0	226.0	454.0	309.1	144.9	3.3	64.4	430.6
1997: I	149.0	197.9	-48.9	779.6	711.9	708.4	241.2	467.2	326.8	140.3	3.5	67.7	440.5
II	148.7	197.6	-48.9	795.1	725.7	719.8	244.5	475.3	333.0	142.3	5.9	69.4	448.1
III	148.0	197.7	-49.7	827.3	757.1	753.4	258.2	495.2	339.1	156.1	3.6	70.3	451.8
IV *p*	146.6	197.0	-50.4	....	....	....	....	....	345.6	....	6.5	71.3	....

[2] Without capital consumption adjustment.

[3] Without inventory valuation and capital consumption adjustments.

Source: Department of Commerce, Bureau of Economic Analysis.

TABLE B–29.—*Sources of personal income, 1959–97*

[Billions of dollars; quarterly data at seasonally adjusted annual rates]

Year or quarter	Personal income	Wage and salary disbursements[1]							Other labor income[1]	Proprietors' income with inventory valuation and capital consumption adjustments	
		Total	Private industries					Govern-ment		Farm	Nonfarm
			Total	Goods-producing industries		Distrib-utive indus-tries	Service indus-tries				
				Total	Manu-facturing						
1959	394.4	259.8	213.8	109.9	86.9	65.1	38.8	46.0	10.6	10.9	40.9
1960	412.5	272.8	223.7	113.4	89.8	68.6	41.7	49.2	11.2	11.5	40.5
1961	430.0	280.5	228.0	114.0	89.9	69.6	44.4	52.4	11.8	12.1	42.3
1962	457.0	299.3	243.0	122.2	96.8	73.3	47.6	56.3	13.0	12.1	44.4
1963	480.0	314.8	254.8	127.4	100.7	76.8	50.7	60.0	14.0	11.9	45.8
1964	514.5	337.7	272.9	136.0	107.3	82.0	54.9	64.9	15.7	10.8	49.8
1965	556.7	363.7	293.8	146.6	115.7	87.9	59.4	69.9	17.8	13.0	52.1
1966	605.7	400.3	321.9	161.6	128.2	95.1	65.3	78.3	19.9	14.1	55.3
1967	650.7	428.9	342.5	169.0	134.3	101.6	72.0	86.4	21.7	12.7	58.2
1968	714.5	471.9	375.3	184.1	146.0	110.8	80.4	96.6	25.2	12.8	62.5
1969	779.3	518.3	412.7	200.4	157.7	121.7	90.6	105.5	28.5	14.6	64.6
1970	837.1	551.5	434.3	203.7	158.4	131.2	99.4	117.1	32.5	14.8	65.4
1971	900.2	583.9	457.4	209.1	160.5	140.4	107.9	126.5	36.7	15.4	71.1
1972	988.8	638.7	501.2	228.2	175.6	153.3	119.7	137.4	43.0	19.5	78.8
1973	1,107.5	708.7	560.0	255.9	196.6	170.3	133.9	148.7	49.2	32.6	84.2
1974	1,215.9	772.6	611.8	276.5	211.8	186.8	148.6	160.9	56.5	25.8	89.8
1975	1,319.0	814.6	638.6	277.1	211.6	198.1	163.4	176.0	65.9	24.1	97.7
1976	1,459.4	899.5	710.8	309.7	238.0	219.5	181.6	188.6	79.7	18.6	115.0
1977	1,616.1	993.9	791.6	346.1	266.7	242.7	202.8	202.3	94.7	17.5	129.9
1978	1,825.9	1,120.8	901.2	392.6	300.1	274.9	233.7	219.6	110.1	22.2	147.4
1979	2,055.8	1,255.9	1,018.8	442.5	335.3	308.5	267.8	237.1	124.3	25.3	159.7
1980	2,293.0	1,377.7	1,116.4	472.5	356.4	336.7	307.2	261.3	139.8	12.2	164.4
1981	2,568.5	1,517.6	1,232.0	514.9	388.0	368.5	348.6	285.6	153.0	21.9	165.7
1982	2,727.2	1,593.9	1,286.7	515.1	386.2	385.9	385.7	307.3	165.4	14.5	165.1
1983	2,900.8	1,685.3	1,360.3	528.2	401.2	405.7	426.4	325.0	177.2	4.1	187.8
1984	3,215.3	1,855.1	1,507.5	586.6	445.9	445.2	475.6	347.6	188.9	23.2	225.5
1985	3,449.8	1,995.9	1,622.1	620.7	468.9	476.5	525.0	373.8	203.1	23.6	245.0
1986	3,658.4	2,116.5	1,720.0	637.3	481.2	501.6	581.0	396.6	216.0	24.2	255.3
1987	3,888.7	2,272.7	1,849.5	660.4	497.2	535.4	653.7	423.1	235.4	31.5	273.6
1988	4,184.6	2,453.6	2,003.2	707.0	530.1	575.3	720.9	450.4	251.7	27.5	307.8
1989	4,501.0	2,598.1	2,118.7	732.4	548.1	606.8	779.5	479.4	273.1	36.3	321.1
1990	4,804.2	2,757.5	2,240.3	754.2	561.2	634.1	852.1	517.2	300.6	35.4	338.6
1991	4,981.6	2,827.6	2,281.5	746.3	562.5	646.6	888.6	546.1	322.7	29.3	347.2
1992	5,227.2	2,986.4	2,418.6	765.7	583.5	680.3	972.6	567.8	351.3	37.1	386.7
1993	5,519.2	3,089.6	2,505.3	781.2	592.9	699.4	1,024.7	584.3	385.1	32.4	418.4
1994	5,791.8	3,240.7	2,638.5	824.4	620.8	741.4	1,072.7	602.2	405.0	36.9	434.7
1995	6,150.8	3,429.5	2,806.5	864.4	648.4	783.1	1,159.0	623.0	406.8	23.4	465.5
1996	6,495.2	3,632.5	2,989.9	909.1	674.7	823.3	1,257.5	642.6	407.6	37.2	483.1
1997 P	6,874.4	3,877.2	3,211.8	960.1	705.9	876.0	1,375.6	665.4	416.6	40.9	503.8
1992: I	5,164.2	2,916.5	2,355.1	752.7	571.5	666.2	936.2	561.4	340.8	35.9	374.4
II	5,237.7	2,956.2	2,389.0	761.9	579.6	673.6	953.4	567.2	347.6	37.1	383.8
III	5,277.7	2,988.2	2,418.3	764.6	583.0	681.5	972.2	569.8	355.9	39.0	387.6
IV	5,429.3	3,084.7	2,512.2	783.6	599.7	699.9	1,028.6	572.5	361.1	36.5	401.0
1993: I	5,369.4	2,975.4	2,394.4	749.7	566.7	677.5	967.2	581.1	373.8	29.7	410.6
II	5,504.1	3,079.3	2,497.8	779.9	592.8	697.7	1,020.2	581.5	382.3	36.3	416.0
III	5,544.2	3,111.1	2,524.8	786.5	597.2	704.3	1,034.0	586.3	389.5	25.6	420.6
IV	5,659.1	3,192.6	2,604.2	808.6	614.9	718.2	1,077.4	588.4	394.9	38.0	426.5
1994: I	5,616.3	3,138.3	2,542.3	797.1	600.7	715.8	1,029.4	596.0	399.5	46.4	417.5
II	5,766.6	3,232.0	2,630.7	820.5	618.4	737.9	1,072.3	601.3	403.7	38.8	435.9
III	5,838.1	3,266.9	2,663.4	832.9	626.9	748.0	1,082.5	603.5	406.9	33.2	438.4
IV	5,946.1	3,325.6	2,717.5	847.2	637.1	763.6	1,106.7	608.0	409.8	29.1	447.0
1995: I	6,053.1	3,371.2	2,754.0	854.8	643.4	769.9	1,129.3	617.2	407.9	20.6	457.6
II	6,114.8	3,404.6	2,783.5	858.5	644.5	778.7	1,146.3	621.1	406.6	21.3	463.1
III	6,179.1	3,450.2	2,825.1	867.7	650.2	788.4	1,169.0	625.1	406.7	22.9	468.7
IV	6,256.2	3,491.8	2,863.3	876.4	655.3	795.5	1,191.4	628.5	406.2	28.9	472.6
1996: I	6,359.4	3,539.2	2,903.6	884.9	659.1	804.4	1,214.3	635.6	405.0	31.9	477.4
II	6,461.3	3,611.2	2,970.9	906.3	674.1	819.2	1,245.3	640.3	407.9	36.5	483.5
III	6,541.9	3,662.8	3,017.3	917.2	680.1	829.0	1,271.1	645.5	408.4	40.1	483.7
IV	6,618.4	3,716.9	3,067.9	927.8	685.6	840.6	1,299.5	648.9	409.1	40.4	487.9
1997: I	6,746.2	3,791.5	3,133.7	942.9	694.1	856.8	1,334.1	657.8	412.3	40.2	494.4
II	6,829.1	3,841.6	3,179.6	952.8	700.3	867.0	1,359.8	662.0	415.1	43.6	500.0
III	6,906.9	3,896.1	3,228.4	961.4	706.0	880.8	1,386.3	667.7	417.7	40.9	506.3
IV P	7,015.4	3,979.7	3,305.5	983.5	723.1	899.6	1,422.4	674.2	421.4	39.0	514.4

[1] The total of wage and salary disbursements and other labor income differs from compensation of employees in Table B–28 in that it excludes employer contributions for social insurance and the excess of wage accruals over wage disbursements.

See next page for continuation of table.

314

[Billions of dollars; quarterly data at seasonally adjusted annual rates]

Year or quarter	Rental income of persons with capital consumption adjustment	Personal dividend income	Personal interest income	Transfer payments to persons							Less: Personal contributions for social insurance
				Total	Old-age, survivors, disability, and health insurance benefits	Government unemployment insurance benefits	Veterans benefits	Government employees retirement benefits	Family assistance[1]	Other	
1959	17.7	12.7	22.7	27.0	10.2	2.8	4.6	2.8	0.9	5.7	7.9
1960	18.6	13.4	25.0	28.8	11.1	3.0	4.6	3.1	1.0	6.1	9.3
1961	19.2	14.0	26.9	32.8	12.6	4.3	5.0	3.4	1.1	6.5	9.7
1962	20.0	15.0	29.3	34.1	14.3	3.1	4.7	3.7	1.3	7.0	10.3
1963	20.7	16.1	32.4	36.2	15.2	3.0	4.8	4.2	1.4	7.6	11.8
1964	21.0	18.0	36.1	37.9	16.0	2.7	4.7	4.7	1.5	8.2	12.6
1965	21.8	20.2	40.3	41.1	18.1	2.3	4.9	5.2	1.7	9.0	13.3
1966	22.5	20.9	44.9	45.7	20.8	1.9	4.9	6.1	1.9	10.3	17.8
1967	23.6	22.1	49.5	54.6	25.5	2.2	5.6	6.9	2.3	12.2	20.6
1968	22.7	24.5	54.6	63.2	30.2	2.1	5.9	7.6	2.8	14.5	22.9
1969	23.4	25.1	60.8	70.3	32.9	2.2	6.7	8.7	3.5	16.2	26.2
1970	23.6	23.5	69.2	84.6	38.5	4.0	7.7	10.2	4.8	19.4	27.9
1971	24.6	23.5	75.7	100.1	44.5	5.8	8.8	11.8	6.2	23.0	30.7
1972	24.3	25.5	81.8	111.8	49.6	5.7	9.7	13.8	6.9	26.1	34.5
1973	25.8	27.7	94.1	127.9	60.4	4.4	10.4	16.0	7.2	29.5	42.6
1974	25.7	29.6	112.4	151.3	70.1	6.8	11.8	19.0	7.9	35.7	47.9
1975	24.7	29.2	123.0	190.2	81.4	17.6	14.5	22.7	9.2	44.7	50.4
1976	24.3	35.0	134.6	208.3	92.9	15.8	14.4	26.1	10.1	49.1	55.5
1977	22.8	39.5	155.7	223.3	104.9	12.7	13.8	29.0	10.6	52.4	61.2
1978	24.8	44.3	184.5	241.6	116.2	9.7	13.9	32.7	10.7	58.4	69.8
1979	26.9	50.5	223.6	270.7	131.8	9.8	14.4	36.9	11.0	66.8	81.0
1980	33.9	57.5	274.7	321.5	154.2	16.1	15.0	43.0	12.4	80.8	88.6
1981	44.5	67.2	337.2	365.9	182.0	15.9	16.1	49.4	13.0	89.7	104.5
1982	46.5	66.9	379.2	408.1	204.5	25.2	16.4	54.6	13.3	94.1	112.3
1983	46.1	77.4	403.2	439.4	221.7	26.3	16.6	58.0	14.2	102.6	119.7
1984	50.1	79.4	472.3	453.6	235.7	15.9	16.4	60.9	14.8	109.9	132.7
1985	48.1	88.3	508.4	486.5	253.4	15.7	16.7	66.6	15.4	118.7	149.0
1986	41.5	105.1	543.3	518.6	269.2	16.3	16.7	70.7	16.4	129.3	162.1
1987	44.8	101.1	560.0	543.3	282.9	14.5	16.6	76.0	16.7	136.6	173.7
1988	55.1	109.9	595.5	577.6	300.4	13.3	16.9	82.2	17.3	147.6	194.2
1989	51.7	130.9	674.5	626.0	325.1	14.4	17.3	87.6	18.0	163.6	210.8
1990	61.0	142.9	704.4	687.8	352.0	18.1	17.8	94.5	19.8	185.6	223.9
1991	67.9	153.6	699.2	769.9	382.3	26.8	18.3	102.2	22.0	218.2	235.8
1992	79.4	159.4	667.2	858.2	414.0	38.9	19.3	109.0	23.3	253.8	248.4
1993	105.7	185.3	651.0	912.0	444.4	34.0	20.2	116.6	24.0	272.8	260.3
1994	124.4	204.8	668.1	954.7	473.0	23.6	20.2	124.5	24.3	289.3	277.5
1995	132.8	251.9	718.9	1,015.0	507.8	21.4	20.8	133.6	23.3	308.0	293.1
1996	146.3	291.2	735.7	1,068.0	537.6	22.0	21.6	142.5	21.7	322.5	306.3
1997 ᴾ	148.1	321.5	768.8	1,121.1	566.7	21.8	22.4	153.4	18.8	338.2	323.6
1992: I	77.2	152.3	674.1	838.3	405.4	39.2	20.4	107.8	23.0	242.5	245.2
II	79.5	154.5	673.0	853.5	412.2	40.4	18.9	108.6	23.1	250.2	247.4
III	69.5	160.8	661.2	865.3	416.9	38.7	18.8	109.0	23.4	258.5	249.7
IV	91.2	170.1	660.4	875.8	421.5	37.1	19.1	110.5	23.5	264.2	251.4
1993: I	99.7	177.8	660.3	897.2	437.6	34.5	20.0	114.2	23.7	267.3	255.2
II	105.6	182.1	653.7	908.0	441.9	34.4	20.5	115.9	24.0	271.4	259.2
III	106.1	187.8	647.8	917.3	446.4	34.7	20.3	117.4	24.0	274.6	261.6
IV	111.5	193.5	642.1	925.3	451.8	32.6	19.8	119.0	24.2	277.9	265.2
1994: I	112.7	192.1	641.4	940.4	463.3	27.7	20.0	120.5	24.3	284.6	272.0
II	126.0	200.3	656.4	949.8	470.4	23.9	20.1	123.8	24.3	287.3	276.2
III	130.1	208.5	674.1	958.8	475.8	21.6	20.5	125.9	24.4	290.7	278.8
IV	128.9	218.5	700.4	969.8	482.4	20.9	20.1	127.6	24.2	294.5	282.9
1995: I	130.5	243.4	713.9	997.0	498.4	21.0	20.7	130.0	23.9	303.1	289.1
II	132.3	248.6	719.4	1,010.4	505.8	21.0	20.8	132.9	23.5	306.3	291.5
III	131.5	254.2	717.9	1,021.5	511.1	21.8	21.1	134.8	23.2	309.6	294.5
IV	137.1	261.5	724.2	1,031.0	516.0	22.0	20.5	136.6	22.8	313.2	297.2
1996: I	143.4	287.4	722.3	1,053.2	529.5	23.0	21.4	138.3	22.5	318.5	300.5
II	144.6	290.0	727.8	1,064.8	535.4	22.1	21.9	142.2	22.0	321.3	305.0
III	148.0	292.0	742.7	1,072.4	540.0	21.3	21.7	143.7	21.6	324.2	308.2
IV	149.2	295.2	749.8	1,081.5	545.6	21.6	21.4	145.9	20.7	326.2	311.5
1997: I	149.0	312.5	757.2	1,107.2	558.9	22.1	22.4	150.4	19.7	333.8	318.2
II	148.7	318.3	766.1	1,117.0	564.4	21.9	22.4	152.7	19.0	336.6	321.3
III	148.0	324.5	772.6	1,125.7	569.4	21.6	22.5	154.2	18.2	339.8	324.8
IV ᴾ	146.6	330.7	779.1	1,134.8	574.1	21.5	22.3	156.3	18.1	342.5	330.2

[1] Consists of aid to families with dependent children and, beginning with 1996, assistance programs operating under the Personal Responsibility and Work Opportunity Reconciliation Act of 1996.

Note.—The industry classification of wage and salary disbursements and proprietors' income is on an establishment basis and is based on the 1987 Standard Industrial Classification (SIC) beginning 1987 and on the 1972 SIC for earlier years shown.

Source: Department of Commerce, Bureau of Economic Analysis.

TABLE B–30.—*Disposition of personal income, 1959–97*

[Billions of dollars, except as noted; quarterly data at seasonally adjusted annual rates]

Year or quarter	Personal income	Less: Personal tax and nontax payments	Equals: Disposable personal income	Less: Personal outlays				Equals: Personal saving	Percent of disposable personal income [1]		
				Total	Personal consumption expenditures	Interest paid by persons	Personal transfer payments to rest of the world (net)		Personal outlays		Personal saving
									Total	Personal consumption expenditures	
1959	394.4	44.5	349.9	324.7	318.1	6.1	0.4	25.2	92.8	90.9	7.2
1960	412.5	48.7	363.8	339.6	332.2	7.0	.5	24.2	93.4	91.3	6.6
1961	430.0	50.3	379.7	350.5	342.6	7.3	.5	29.2	92.3	90.3	7.7
1962	457.0	54.8	402.2	371.8	363.4	7.8	.5	30.4	92.4	90.4	7.6
1963	480.0	58.0	422.0	392.5	383.0	8.9	.6	29.5	93.0	90.7	7.0
1964	514.5	56.0	458.5	422.1	411.4	10.0	.7	36.4	92.1	89.7	7.9
1965	556.7	61.9	494.8	456.2	444.3	11.1	.8	38.7	92.2	89.8	7.8
1966	605.7	71.0	534.7	494.7	481.9	12.0	.8	40.1	92.5	90.1	7.5
1967	650.7	77.9	572.9	523.0	509.5	12.5	1.0	49.9	91.3	88.9	8.7
1968	714.5	92.1	622.5	574.6	559.8	13.8	1.0	47.8	92.3	89.9	7.7
1969	779.3	109.9	669.4	621.4	604.7	15.7	1.1	47.9	92.8	90.3	7.2
1970	837.1	109.0	728.1	666.1	648.1	16.8	1.2	62.0	91.5	89.0	8.5
1971	900.2	108.7	791.5	721.6	702.5	17.8	1.3	69.9	91.2	88.8	8.8
1972	988.8	132.0	856.8	791.6	770.7	19.6	1.3	65.2	92.4	89.9	7.6
1973	1,107.5	140.6	967.0	875.4	851.6	22.4	1.4	91.5	90.5	88.1	9.5
1974	1,215.9	159.1	1,056.8	956.6	931.2	24.2	1.2	100.2	90.5	88.1	9.5
1975	1,319.0	156.4	1,162.6	1,054.8	1,029.1	24.5	1.2	107.8	90.7	88.5	9.3
1976	1,459.4	182.3	1,277.1	1,176.7	1,148.8	26.7	1.2	100.4	92.1	90.0	7.9
1977	1,616.1	210.0	1,406.1	1,308.9	1,277.1	30.7	1.2	97.2	93.1	90.8	6.9
1978	1,825.9	240.1	1,585.8	1,467.6	1,428.8	37.5	1.3	118.2	92.5	90.1	7.5
1979	2,055.8	280.2	1,775.7	1,639.5	1,593.5	44.5	1.4	136.2	92.3	89.7	7.7
1980	2,293.0	312.4	1,980.5	1,811.5	1,760.4	49.4	1.6	169.1	91.5	88.9	8.5
1981	2,568.5	360.2	2,208.3	2,001.1	1,941.3	54.6	5.2	207.2	90.6	87.9	9.4
1982	2,727.2	371.4	2,355.8	2,141.8	2,076.8	58.8	6.2	214.0	90.9	88.2	9.1
1983	2,900.8	369.3	2,531.5	2,355.5	2,283.4	65.5	6.5	176.1	93.0	90.2	7.0
1984	3,215.3	395.5	2,819.8	2,574.4	2,492.3	74.7	7.4	245.5	91.3	88.4	8.7
1985	3,449.8	437.7	3,012.1	2,795.8	2,704.8	83.2	7.8	216.4	92.8	89.8	7.2
1986	3,658.4	459.9	3,198.5	2,991.1	2,892.7	90.3	8.1	207.4	93.5	90.4	6.5
1987	3,888.7	514.2	3,374.6	3,194.7	3,094.5	91.5	8.7	179.9	94.7	91.7	5.3
1988	4,184.6	532.0	3,652.6	3,451.7	3,349.7	92.9	9.1	200.9	94.5	91.7	5.5
1989	4,501.0	594.9	3,906.1	3,706.7	3,594.8	102.4	9.6	199.4	94.9	92.0	5.1
1990	4,804.2	624.8	4,179.4	3,958.1	3,839.3	108.9	9.9	221.3	94.7	91.9	5.3
1991	4,981.6	624.8	4,356.8	4,097.4	3,975.1	111.9	10.4	259.5	94.0	91.2	6.0
1992	5,277.2	650.5	4,626.7	4,341.0	4,219.8	111.7	9.6	285.6	93.8	91.2	6.2
1993	5,519.2	690.0	4,829.2	4,580.7	4,459.2	108.2	13.3	248.5	94.9	92.3	5.1
1994	5,791.8	739.1	5,052.7	4,842.1	4,717.0	110.9	14.2	210.6	95.8	93.4	4.2
1995	6,150.8	795.1	5,355.7	5,101.1	4,957.7	128.5	14.8	254.6	95.2	92.6	4.8
1996	6,495.2	886.9	5,608.3	5,368.8	5,207.6	145.2	15.9	239.6	95.7	92.9	4.3
1997 ᵖ	6,874.4	987.9	5,886.6	5,661.0	5,488.6	154.5	17.9	225.6	96.2	93.2	3.8
1992: I	5,164.2	636.7	4,527.5	4,250.0	4,127.6	112.9	9.4	277.5	93.9	91.2	6.1
II	5,237.7	640.0	4,597.7	4,304.8	4,183.0	112.1	9.7	292.9	93.6	91.0	6.4
III	5,277.7	650.6	4,627.1	4,359.5	4,238.9	111.4	9.2	267.6	94.2	91.6	5.8
IV	5,429.3	674.8	4,754.5	4,450.0	4,329.6	110.4	9.9	304.5	93.6	91.1	6.4
1993: I	5,369.4	662.5	4,707.0	4,488.4	4,365.4	110.0	13.1	218.6	95.4	92.7	4.6
II	5,504.1	685.6	4,818.5	4,549.5	4,428.1	108.3	13.1	269.0	94.4	91.9	5.6
III	5,544.2	695.5	4,848.7	4,609.8	4,488.6	107.9	13.4	239.0	95.1	92.6	4.9
IV	5,659.1	716.4	4,942.8	4,675.2	4,554.9	106.6	13.7	267.6	94.6	92.2	5.4
1994: I	5,616.3	712.9	4,903.4	4,738.2	4,616.6	107.6	14.0	165.2	96.6	94.2	3.4
II	5,766.6	750.5	5,016.1	4,803.3	4,680.5	108.7	14.1	212.8	95.8	93.3	4.2
III	5,838.1	739.9	5,098.2	4,876.1	4,750.6	111.4	14.2	222.1	95.6	93.2	4.4
IV	5,946.1	753.0	5,193.1	4,950.7	4,820.2	116.1	14.4	242.4	95.3	92.8	4.7
1995: I	6,053.1	766.5	5,286.6	5,007.3	4,871.7	121.1	14.5	279.2	94.7	92.2	5.3
II	6,114.8	795.1	5,319.6	5,074.3	4,934.8	125.1	14.3	245.4	95.4	92.8	4.6
III	6,179.1	798.9	5,380.2	5,136.4	4,990.6	130.9	14.9	243.8	95.5	92.8	4.5
IV	6,256.2	820.0	5,436.2	5,186.3	5,033.8	137.1	15.4	249.9	95.4	92.6	4.6
1996: I	6,359.4	840.0	5,519.4	5,261.3	5,105.8	140.1	15.4	258.1	95.3	92.5	4.7
II	6,461.3	887.8	5,573.5	5,347.8	5,189.1	143.0	15.8	225.7	95.9	93.1	4.1
III	6,541.9	897.3	5,644.6	5,390.6	5,227.4	147.4	15.9	254.0	95.5	92.6	4.5
IV	6,618.4	922.6	5,695.8	5,475.4	5,308.1	150.5	16.7	220.4	96.1	93.2	3.9
1997: I	6,746.2	955.7	5,790.5	5,574.6	5,405.7	151.9	17.0	215.9	96.3	93.4	3.7
II	6,829.1	979.2	5,849.9	5,602.8	5,432.1	153.1	17.6	247.0	95.8	92.9	4.2
III	6,906.9	998.0	5,908.9	5,700.8	5,527.4	155.1	18.2	208.2	96.5	93.5	3.5
IV ᵖ	7,015.4	1,018.5	5,996.9	5,765.8	5,589.3	157.9	18.5	231.1	96.1	93.2	3.9

[1] Percents based on data in millions of dollars.

Source: Department of Commerce, Bureau of Economic Analysis.

316

TABLE B-31.—*Total and per capita disposable personal income and personal consumption expenditures in current and real dollars, 1959–97*

[Quarterly data at seasonally adjusted annual rates, except as noted]

Year or quarter	Disposable personal income				Personal consumption expenditures				Gross domestic product per capita		Popula-tion (thou-sands)[1]
	Total (billions of dollars)		Per capita (dollars)		Total (billions of dollars)		Per capita (dollars)				
	Current dollars	Chained (1992) dollars	Current dollars	Chained (1992) dollars	Current dollars	Chained (1992) dollars	Current dollars	Chained (1992) dollars	Current dollars	Chained (1992) dollars	
1959	349.9	1,533.9	1,975	8,660	318.1	1,394.6	1,796	7,873	2,864	12,478	177,130
1960	363.8	1,569.2	2,013	8,681	332.2	1,432.6	1,838	7,926	2,913	12,519	180,760
1961	379.7	1,619.4	2,066	8,814	342.6	1,461.5	1,865	7,954	2,965	12,595	183,742
1962	402.2	1,697.5	2,156	9,098	363.4	1,533.8	1,948	8,220	3,136	13,156	186,590
1963	422.0	1,759.3	2,229	9,294	383.0	1,596.6	2,023	8,434	3,261	13,520	189,300
1964	458.5	1,885.8	2,389	9,825	411.4	1,692.3	2,144	8,817	3,455	14,112	191,927
1965	494.8	2,003.9	2,546	10,311	444.3	1,799.1	2,286	9,257	3,700	14,825	194,347
1966	534.7	2,110.6	2,720	10,735	481.9	1,902.0	2,451	9,674	4,007	15,612	196,599
1967	572.9	2,202.3	2,882	11,081	509.5	1,958.6	2,563	9,854	4,194	15,835	198,752
1968	622.5	2,302.1	3,101	11,468	559.8	2,070.2	2,789	10,313	4,536	16,408	200,745
1969	669.4	2,377.2	3,302	11,726	604.7	2,147.5	2,982	10,593	4,845	16,739	202,736
1970	728.1	2,469.0	3,550	12,039	648.1	2,197.8	3,160	10,717	5,050	16,566	205,089
1971	791.5	2,568.3	3,811	12,366	702.5	2,279.5	3,383	10,975	5,419	16,900	207,692
1972	856.8	2,685.7	4,082	12,794	770.7	2,415.9	3,671	11,508	5,894	17,637	209,924
1973	967.0	2,875.2	4,562	13,566	851.6	2,532.6	4,018	11,950	6,524	18,479	211,939
1974	1,056.8	2,854.2	4,941	13,344	931.2	2,514.7	4,353	11,756	6,998	18,192	213,898
1975	1,162.6	2,903.6	5,383	13,444	1,029.1	2,570.0	4,765	11,899	7,550	17,936	215,981
1976	1,277.1	3,017.6	5,856	13,837	1,148.8	2,714.3	5,268	12,446	8,341	18,721	218,086
1977	1,406.1	3,115.4	6,383	14,142	1,277.1	2,829.8	5,797	12,846	9,201	19,400	220,289
1978	1,585.8	3,276.0	7,123	14,715	1,428.8	2,951.6	6,418	13,258	10,292	20,226	222,629
1979	1,775.7	3,365.5	7,888	14,951	1,593.5	3,020.2	7,079	13,417	11,361	20,571	225,106
1980	1,980.5	3,385.7	8,697	14,867	1,760.4	3,009.7	7,730	13,216	12,226	20,265	227,726
1981	2,208.3	3,464.9	9,601	15,064	1,941.3	3,046.4	8,440	13,245	13,547	20,524	230,008
1982	2,355.8	3,495.6	10,145	15,053	2,076.8	3,081.5	8,943	13,270	13,961	19,896	232,218
1983	2,531.5	3,592.8	10,803	15,332	2,283.4	3,240.6	9,744	13,829	14,998	20,499	234,332
1984	2,819.8	3,855.4	11,929	16,309	2,492.3	3,407.6	10,543	14,415	16,508	21,744	236,394
1985	3,012.1	3,972.0	12,629	16,654	2,704.8	3,566.5	11,341	14,954	17,529	22,320	238,506
1986	3,198.5	4,101.0	13,289	17,039	2,892.7	3,708.7	12,019	15,409	18,374	22,801	240,682
1987	3,374.6	4,168.2	13,896	17,164	3,094.5	3,822.3	12,743	15,740	19,323	23,264	242,842
1988	3,652.6	4,332.1	14,905	17,678	3,349.7	3,972.7	13,669	16,211	20,605	23,934	245,061
1989	3,906.1	4,416.8	15,790	17,854	3,594.8	4,064.6	14,531	16,430	21,984	24,504	247,387
1990	4,179.4	4,498.2	16,721	17,996	3,839.3	4,132.2	15,360	16,532	22,979	24,549	249,956
1991	4,356.8	4,500.0	17,242	17,809	3,975.1	4,105.8	15,732	16,249	23,416	24,060	252,680
1992	4,626.7	4,626.7	18,113	18,113	4,219.8	4,219.8	16,520	16,520	24,447	24,447	255,432
1993	4,829.2	4,703.9	18,706	18,221	4,459.2	4,343.6	17,273	16,825	25,403	24,750	258,161
1994	5,052.7	4,805.1	19,381	18,431	4,717.0	4,486.0	18,093	17,207	26,647	25,357	260,705
1995	5,355.7	4,964.2	20,349	18,861	4,957.7	4,595.3	18,837	17,460	27,605	25,616	263,194
1996	5,608.3	5,076.9	21,117	19,116	5,207.6	4,714.1	19,608	17,750	28,752	26,088	265,579
1997 ᴾ	5,886.6	5,222.7	21,976	19,497	5,488.6	4,869.7	20,490	18,179	30,177	26,847	267,869
1992: I	4,527.5	4,578.1	17,801	18,000	4,127.6	4,173.8	16,229	16,410	24,070	24,281	254,338
II	4,597.7	4,612.4	18,028	18,085	4,183.0	4,196.4	16,402	16,454	24,315	24,366	255,032
III	4,627.1	4,613.8	18,088	18,036	4,238.9	4,226.7	16,570	16,522	24,516	24,474	255,815
IV	4,754.5	4,702.5	18,533	18,330	4,329.6	4,282.3	16,877	16,692	24,881	24,663	256,543
1993: I	4,707.0	4,622.3	18,304	17,975	4,365.4	4,286.8	16,976	16,671	25,061	24,608	257,151
II	4,818.5	4,703.9	18,692	18,247	4,428.1	4,322.8	17,177	16,769	25,250	24,671	257,785
III	4,848.7	4,716.9	18,756	18,246	4,488.6	4,366.6	17,363	16,891	25,432	24,732	258,516
IV	4,942.8	4,772.5	19,070	18,413	4,554.9	4,398.0	17,574	16,968	25,866	24,989	259,191
1994: I	4,903.4	4,715.3	18,878	18,154	4,616.6	4,439.4	17,774	17,092	26,158	25,120	259,738
II	5,016.1	4,792.8	19,267	18,409	4,680.5	4,472.2	17,978	17,178	26,546	25,352	260,351
III	5,098.2	4,827.3	19,530	18,493	4,750.6	4,498.2	18,199	17,232	26,764	25,396	261,040
IV	5,193.1	4,884.9	19,844	18,667	4,820.2	4,534.1	18,419	17,326	27,115	25,559	261,692
1995: I	5,286.6	4,938.9	20,160	18,834	4,871.7	4,551.3	18,578	17,356	27,338	25,564	262,235
II	5,319.6	4,940.9	20,239	18,798	4,934.8	4,583.5	18,774	17,438	27,428	25,524	262,847
III	5,380.2	4,973.0	20,416	18,871	4,990.6	4,612.9	18,938	17,505	27,706	25,649	263,527
IV	5,436.2	5,003.9	20,579	18,942	5,033.8	4,633.5	19,055	17,540	27,944	25,728	264,169
1996: I	5,519.4	5,047.6	20,853	19,071	5,105.8	4,669.4	19,291	17,642	28,213	25,791	264,680
II	5,573.5	5,061.3	21,012	19,081	5,189.1	4,712.2	19,562	17,765	28,680	26,111	265,258
III	5,644.6	5,094.8	21,229	19,161	5,227.4	4,718.2	19,660	17,745	28,869	26,116	265,887
IV	5,695.8	5,103.8	21,373	19,152	5,308.1	4,756.4	19,919	17,848	29,243	26,333	266,491
1997: I	5,790.5	5,161.1	21,689	19,331	5,405.7	4,818.1	20,247	18,046	29,715	26,599	266,987
II	5,849.9	5,200.9	21,865	19,439	5,432.1	4,829.4	20,303	18,051	30,030	26,760	267,545
III	5,908.9	5,234.1	22,034	19,518	5,527.4	4,896.2	20,612	18,258	30,295	26,901	268,171
IV ᴾ	5,996.9	5,294.8	22,312	19,700	5,589.3	4,935.0	20,796	18,361	30,664	27,124	268,772

[1] Population of the United States including Armed Forces overseas; includes Alaska and Hawaii beginning 1960. Annual data are averages of quarterly data. Quarterly data are averages for the period.

Source: Department of Commerce (Bureau of Economic Analysis and Bureau of the Census).

[Billions of dollars, except as noted; quarterly data at seasonally adjusted annual rates]

Year or quarter	Gross saving														Capital grants received by the United States (net)[3]
		Gross private saving					Gross government saving								
				Gross business saving				Federal			State and local			
	Total	Total	Personal saving	Total[1]	Undistributed corporate profits[2]	Corporate and noncorporate consumption of fixed capital	Total	Total	Consumption of fixed capital	Current surplus or deficit (−)(NIPA)	Total	Consumption of fixed capital	Current surplus or deficit (−)(NIPA)	
1959	108.5	82.3	25.2	57.1	16.5	40.5	26.2	12.8	10.2	2.6	13.5	3.9	9.6	....
1960	113.4	81.6	24.2	57.4	15.3	42.1	31.8	17.8	10.5	7.4	14.0	4.0	9.9	....
1961	116.3	88.0	29.2	58.8	15.7	43.1	28.3	13.6	10.7	2.9	14.7	4.3	10.4	....
1962	126.8	96.5	30.4	66.1	21.5	44.6	30.3	14.0	11.2	2.8	16.3	4.6	11.7	....
1963	134.9	99.8	29.5	70.2	24.0	46.2	35.1	17.2	11.8	5.4	17.9	4.9	13.0	....
1964	145.3	112.3	36.4	75.9	27.3	48.7	32.9	13.0	12.1	.9	19.9	5.2	14.7	....
1965	160.4	123.8	38.7	85.1	33.1	52.0	36.6	15.9	12.5	3.4	20.8	5.7	15.1	....
1966	171.1	131.9	40.1	91.9	35.2	56.7	39.2	15.6	13.0	2.6	23.5	6.3	17.3	....
1967	173.8	144.1	49.9	94.2	32.7	61.5	29.7	5.6	13.9	−8.3	24.1	6.8	17.3	....
1968	185.1	145.4	47.8	97.6	30.2	67.3	39.7	12.0	14.9	−2.8	27.6	7.6	20.0	....
1969	202.1	148.2	47.9	100.3	26.0	74.2	53.9	24.3	15.6	8.7	29.6	8.5	21.1	....
1970	197.3	163.8	62.0	101.8	20.7	81.2	32.6	2.2	16.2	−14.1	30.4	9.6	20.8	0.9
1971	214.3	189.7	69.9	119.8	30.5	88.9	23.9	−8.5	16.9	−25.3	32.4	10.7	21.7	.7
1972	243.9	201.7	65.2	136.5	39.0	97.8	41.5	−2.4	18.2	−20.5	43.9	11.7	32.2	.7
1973	296.4	241.3	91.5	149.7	42.7	107.1	55.1	8.7	19.9	−11.1	46.4	13.0	33.4	0
1974	301.2	251.7	100.2	151.5	27.0	124.5	51.5	5.1	22.0	−16.9	46.5	16.0	30.5	6−2.0
1975	297.3	301.2	107.8	193.5	47.2	146.3	−3.9	−49.9	24.0	−73.9	46.0	18.4	27.6	0
1976	340.0	316.5	100.4	216.1	54.8	161.3	23.5	−31.9	25.4	−57.2	55.3	19.4	35.9	0
1977	394.7	348.6	97.2	251.4	70.5	181.0	46.1	−19.3	27.0	−46.3	65.4	20.7	44.7	0
1978	476.9	404.5	118.2	286.3	79.5	206.8	72.4	−2.8	28.9	−31.7	75.1	22.5	52.6	0
1979	540.6	448.8	136.2	312.5	72.6	239.9	90.7	13.0	31.5	−18.4	77.7	25.4	52.3	1.1
1980	547.2	489.2	169.1	320.1	44.1	276.0	56.8	−26.8	34.1	−61.0	83.6	29.2	54.4	1.2
1981	650.8	581.7	207.2	374.4	56.4	318.1	68.1	−20.6	37.1	−57.8	88.7	33.3	55.4	1.1
1982	604.3	609.6	214.0	395.6	49.4	346.2	−5.3	−92.8	41.9	−134.7	87.5	36.2	51.3	0
1983	589.0	618.4	176.1	442.4	77.2	365.2	−29.4	−131.8	42.6	−174.4	102.4	37.5	64.9	0
1984	750.7	736.7	245.5	491.2	112.8	378.4	14.0	−111.9	44.1	−156.0	125.9	39.0	86.9	0
1985	745.6	730.5	216.4	514.1	114.7	399.4	15.2	−116.9	46.1	−162.9	132.0	41.0	91.0	0
1986	719.8	708.9	207.4	501.5	77.1	424.4	10.8	−127.9	49.6	−177.5	138.8	43.9	94.9	0
1987	779.6	726.0	179.9	546.1	99.1	447.1	53.6	−77.2	51.7	−128.9	130.8	47.1	83.8	0
1988	876.0	807.2	200.9	606.3	128.3	478.0	68.8	−67.0	54.3	−121.3	135.8	49.9	85.9	0
1989	906.3	814.3	199.4	614.8	99.7	515.1	92.0	−56.4	57.0	−113.4	148.4	53.3	95.1	0
1990	903.1	860.3	221.3	639.0	104.7	534.3	42.7	−94.0	60.7	−154.7	136.7	56.6	80.1	0
1991	934.0	930.6	259.5	671.2	114.8	556.4	3.3	−132.2	63.9	−196.0	135.5	59.6	75.8	0
1992	904.3	970.7	285.6	685.1	115.5	585.4	−66.5	−215.0	65.9	−280.9	148.6	62.3	86.3	0
1993	949.5	979.3	248.5	730.8	131.9	594.5	−29.8	−182.7	67.9	−250.7	152.9	65.5	87.4	0
1994	1,079.2	1,030.2	210.6	819.6	167.6	638.6	49.0	−117.2	69.5	−186.7	166.2	69.4	96.8	0
1995	1,165.5	1,093.1	254.6	838.5	172.4	653.0	72.4	−103.6	70.9	−174.4	176.0	72.9	103.1	0
1996	1,267.8	1,125.5	239.6	885.9	202.1	682.8	142.3	−39.2	71.2	−110.5	181.5	76.2	105.3	0
1997 ᴾ	....	....	225.6	....	....	717.0	....	....	71.6	....	....	79.5	....	0
1992: I	920.3	976.6	277.5	699.1	138.2	560.9	−56.3	−202.2	65.2	−267.4	145.9	61.1	84.8	0
II	914.0	979.3	292.9	686.4	121.7	564.7	−65.3	−213.9	65.8	−279.6	148.5	62.0	86.6	0
III ...	899.9	986.7	267.6	719.1	77.6	641.5	−86.9	−231.5	66.0	−297.5	144.6	62.7	82.0	0
IV ...	883.0	940.3	304.5	635.8	124.5	574.3	−57.3	−212.5	66.5	−279.0	155.2	63.5	91.7	0
1993: I	932.0	1,001.1	218.6	782.5	121.9	590.5	−69.1	−211.2	67.0	−278.2	142.1	64.3	77.8	0
II	942.1	977.3	269.0	708.3	120.3	588.0	−35.2	−181.7	67.5	−249.2	146.5	65.2	81.3	0
III ...	943.8	973.3	239.0	734.3	133.2	601.1	−29.4	−182.2	68.4	−250.6	152.7	65.8	86.9	0
IV ...	980.1	965.6	267.6	698.0	152.1	598.1	14.5	−155.8	68.8	−224.6	170.4	66.6	103.7	0
1994: I	1,062.4	1,048.6	165.2	883.4	145.8	685.2	13.8	−139.9	69.1	−209.0	153.7	69.0	84.7	0
II	1,065.5	995.7	212.8	782.9	167.7	614.9	69.7	−93.6	69.6	−163.2	163.3	68.5	94.8	0
III ...	1,071.0	1,021.2	222.1	799.1	175.5	623.3	49.7	−118.3	69.3	−187.6	168.0	69.6	98.4	0
IV ...	1,118.0	1,055.3	242.4	812.9	181.3	631.2	62.7	−117.0	69.8	−186.8	179.7	70.4	109.3	0
1995: I	1,136.8	1,078.7	279.2	799.5	148.1	638.2	58.0	−121.2	70.3	−191.5	179.2	71.5	107.7	0
II	1,133.4	1,064.0	245.4	818.6	158.1	647.4	69.4	−108.6	70.9	−179.5	178.0	72.4	105.6	0
III ...	1,167.7	1,098.8	243.8	855.0	187.2	654.7	68.9	−105.5	71.0	−176.5	174.5	73.3	101.1	0
IV ...	1,224.0	1,130.7	249.9	880.8	196.0	671.7	93.3	−78.9	71.3	−150.2	172.1	74.3	97.8	0
1996: I	1,215.9	1,119.3	258.1	861.2	190.8	669.2	96.7	−82.6	71.0	−153.6	179.3	75.2	104.1	0
II	1,256.3	1,106.3	225.7	880.5	202.6	676.8	150.0	−40.2	71.4	−111.6	190.2	75.8	114.4	0
III ...	1,295.9	1,145.1	254.0	891.1	202.3	687.7	150.8	−28.3	71.2	−99.5	179.1	76.5	102.6	0
IV ...	1,303.0	1,131.4	220.4	911.0	212.6	697.2	171.6	−5.9	71.3	−77.1	177.5	77.2	100.4	0
1997: I	1,332.9	1,134.0	215.9	918.1	211.5	705.4	198.9	15.9	71.4	−55.5	182.9	78.2	104.7	0
II	1,396.9	1,178.1	247.0	931.1	217.6	712.3	218.8	34.7	71.5	−36.8	184.1	79.2	104.9	0
III ...	1,411.6	1,159.6	208.2	951.4	230.0	720.4	251.9	60.8	71.6	−10.8	191.1	79.7	111.4	0
IV ᴾ	....	....	231.1	....	....	729.9	....	....	71.9	....	....	80.8	....	0

[1] Includes private wage accruals less disbursements not shown separately.
[2] With inventory valuation and capital consumption adjustments.
[3] Consists mainly of allocations of special drawing rights (SDRs).

See next page for continuation of table.

[Billions of dollars except as noted; quarterly data at seasonally adjusted annual rates]

Year or quarter	Gross investment				Statistical discrepancy	Addenda:	
	Total	Gross private domestic investment	Gross government investment[4]	Net foreign investment[5]		Gross saving as a percent of gross national product	Personal saving as a percent of disposable personal income
1959	106.9	78.8	29.3	-1.2	-1.6	21.3	7.2
1960	110.2	78.8	28.2	3.2	-3.2	21.4	6.6
1961	113.5	77.9	31.3	4.3	-2.8	21.2	7.7
1962	125.0	87.9	33.2	3.9	-1.8	21.5	7.6
1963	131.9	93.4	33.5	5.0	-3.0	21.7	7.0
1964	143.8	101.7	34.5	7.5	-1.5	21.7	7.9
1965	159.6	118.0	35.4	6.2	-.8	22.1	7.8
1966	174.4	130.4	40.1	3.9	3.3	21.6	7.5
1967	175.1	128.0	43.5	3.5	1.3	20.7	8.7
1968	186.0	139.9	44.3	1.7	.9	20.2	7.7
1969	200.7	155.0	43.9	1.8	-1.5	20.5	7.2
1970	199.1	150.2	44.0	4.9	1.9	18.9	8.5
1971	220.4	176.0	43.1	1.3	6.1	18.9	8.8
1972	248.1	205.6	45.4	-2.9	4.3	19.6	7.6
1973	299.9	242.9	48.3	8.7	3.4	21.2	9.5
1974	306.7	245.6	56.0	5.1	5.5	19.9	9.5
1975	309.5	225.4	62.7	21.4	12.1	18.1	9.3
1976	359.9	286.6	64.4	8.9	19.9	18.5	7.9
1977	413.0	356.6	65.4	-9.0	18.2	19.3	6.9
1978	494.9	430.8	74.6	-10.4	18.1	20.6	7.5
1979	568.7	480.9	85.3	2.6	28.2	20.9	7.7
1980	574.8	465.9	96.4	12.5	27.6	19.4	8.5
1981	665.7	556.2	102.1	7.4	14.9	20.7	9.4
1982	601.8	501.1	106.9	-6.1	-2.5	18.5	9.1
1983	626.2	547.1	116.5	-37.3	37.1	16.6	7.0
1984	755.7	715.6	131.7	-91.5	5.0	19.1	8.7
1985	748.0	715.1	149.9	-116.9	2.4	17.7	7.2
1986	743.1	722.5	163.5	-142.9	23.3	16.2	6.5
1987	764.2	747.2	173.5	-156.4	-15.4	16.6	5.3
1988	828.7	773.9	172.9	-118.1	-47.3	17.3	5.5
1989	919.5	829.2	182.7	-92.4	13.2	16.6	5.1
1990	920.5	799.7	199.4	-78.6	17.4	15.7	5.3
1991	944.0	736.2	200.5	7.3	10.1	15.7	6.0
1992	949.1	790.4	209.1	-50.5	44.8	14.5	6.2
1993	1,002.1	876.2	204.5	-78.6	52.6	14.4	5.1
1994	1,093.8	1,007.9	205.9	-120.0	14.6	15.5	4.2
1995	1,137.2	1,038.2	213.4	-114.4	-28.2	16.0	4.8
1996	1,207.9	1,116.5	224.3	-132.9	-59.9	16.6	4.3
1997 ᴾ	....	1,237.6	226.9	....	....	....	3.8
1992: I	944.8	755.2	209.5	-19.9	24.5	15.0	6.1
II	951.3	790.7	209.3	-48.7	37.4	14.7	6.4
III	952.5	799.7	208.9	-56.0	52.7	14.3	5.8
IV	947.7	816.1	208.8	-77.2	64.6	13.8	6.4
1993: I	1,003.0	854.3	202.9	-54.2	71.0	14.4	4.6
II	989.0	857.4	206.5	-74.9	46.9	14.4	5.6
III	991.3	872.8	203.4	-84.9	47.5	14.3	4.9
IV	1,025.1	920.3	205.2	-100.4	45.0	14.6	5.4
1994: I	1,068.7	963.4	197.0	-91.6	6.3	15.6	3.4
II	1,107.8	1,017.9	202.4	-112.5	42.4	15.4	4.2
III	1,086.2	1,007.1	213.2	-134.2	15.2	15.3	4.4
IV	1,112.6	1,043.1	211.2	-141.8	-5.4	15.8	4.7
1995: I	1,138.0	1,050.8	213.0	-125.8	1.2	15.8	5.3
II	1,113.2	1,024.0	215.8	-126.7	-20.2	15.7	4.6
III	1,122.7	1,028.8	210.8	-116.9	-45.0	16.0	4.5
IV	1,175.1	1,049.1	214.1	-88.0	-48.9	16.6	4.6
1996: I	1,165.6	1,060.5	222.0	-116.9	-50.3	16.3	4.7
II	1,206.0	1,105.4	226.3	-125.6	-50.2	16.5	4.1
III	1,216.4	1,149.2	223.6	-156.4	-79.5	16.9	4.5
IV	1,243.5	1,151.1	225.3	-132.9	-59.5	16.7	3.9
1997: I	1,268.6	1,193.6	223.3	-148.4	-64.3	16.8	3.7
II	1,323.4	1,242.0	227.4	-146.0	-73.5	17.4	4.2
III	1,308.4	1,250.2	227.1	-168.9	-103.2	17.4	3.5
IV ᴾ	....	1,264.5	229.7	....	....	....	3.9

[4] For details on government investment, see Table B–20.

[5] Net exports of goods and services plus net receipts of factor income from rest of the world less net transfers plus net capital grants received by the United States. See also Table B–24.

[6] Consists of a U.S. payment to India under the Agricultural Trade Development and Assistance Act. This payment is included in capital grants received by the United States, net.

Source: Department of Commerce, Bureau of Economic Analysis.

TABLE B–33.—*Median money income (in 1996 dollars) and poverty status of families and persons, by race, selected years, 1978–96*

Year	Families[1] Number (millions)	Families Median money income (in 1996 dollars)[2]	Below poverty level Total Number (millions)	Below poverty level Total Percent	Below poverty level Female householder Number (millions)	Below poverty level Female householder Percent	Persons below poverty level Number (millions)	Persons below poverty level Percent	Males All persons	Males Year-round full-time workers	Females All persons	Females Year-round full-time workers
ALL RACES												
1978	57.8	$41,003	5.3	9.1	2.7	31.4	24.5	11.4	$25,418	$37,335	$9,456	$22,410
1979[4]	59.6	41,530	5.5	9.2	2.6	30.4	26.1	11.7	24,975	37,060	9,227	22,329
1980	60.3	40,079	6.2	10.3	3.0	32.7	29.3	13.0	23,888	36,552	9,380	22,098
1981	61.0	38,986	6.9	11.2	3.3	34.6	31.8	14.0	23,462	36,033	9,505	21,693
1982	61.4	38,459	7.5	12.2	3.4	36.3	34.4	15.0	22,895	35,540	9,662	22,424
1983[5]	62.0	38,869	7.6	12.3	3.6	36.0	35.3	15.2	23,095	35,454	10,090	22,823
1984	62.7	39,917	7.3	11.6	3.5	34.5	33.7	14.4	23,558	36,249	10,371	23,289
1985	63.6	40,443	7.2	11.4	3.5	34.0	33.1	14.0	23,784	36,453	10,524	23,698
1986	64.5	42,171	7.0	10.9	3.6	34.6	32.4	13.6	24,500	37,069	10,894	24,112
1987[6]	65.2	42,775	7.0	10.7	3.7	34.2	32.2	13.4	24,565	36,851	11,457	24,259
1988	65.8	42,695	6.9	10.4	3.6	33.4	31.7	13.0	25,077	36,263	11,783	24,596
1989	66.1	43,290	6.8	10.3	3.5	32.2	31.5	12.8	25,171	35,959	12,177	24,848
1990	66.3	42,440	7.1	10.7	3.8	33.4	33.6	13.5	24,361	34,788	12,089	24,719
1991	67.2	41,401	7.7	11.5	4.2	35.6	35.7	14.2	23,580	34,941	12,068	24,474
1992[7]	68.2	40,900	8.1	11.9	4.3	35.4	38.0	14.8	22,875	34,480	11,982	24,707
1993	68.5	40,131	8.4	12.3	4.4	35.6	39.3	15.1	22,913	33,744	11,994	24,397
1994	69.3	41,059	8.1	11.6	4.2	34.6	38.1	14.5	22,995	33,468	12,139	24,631
1995	69.6	41,810	7.5	10.8	4.1	32.4	36.4	13.8	23,228	33,150	12,488	24,479
1996	70.2	42,300	7.7	11.0	4.2	32.6	36.5	13.7	23,834	33,538	12,815	24,935
WHITE												
1978	50.9	42,695	3.5	6.9	1.4	23.5	16.3	8.7	26,622	38,028	9,570	22,621
1979[4]	52.2	43,336	3.6	6.9	1.4	22.3	17.2	9.0	26,090	38,131	9,314	22,524
1980	52.7	41,759	4.2	8.0	1.6	25.7	19.7	10.2	25,409	37,595	9,431	22,311
1981	53.3	40,952	4.7	8.8	1.8	27.4	21.6	11.1	24,895	36,879	9,611	22,055
1982	53.4	40,379	5.1	9.6	1.8	27.9	23.5	12.0	24,205	36,487	9,793	22,726
1983[5]	53.9	40,701	5.2	9.7	1.9	28.3	24.0	12.1	24,297	36,400	10,266	23,129
1984	54.4	41,809	4.9	9.1	1.9	27.1	23.0	11.5	24,867	37,490	10,494	23,520
1985	55.0	42,509	5.0	9.1	2.0	27.4	22.9	11.4	24,951	37,465	10,728	24,034
1986	55.7	44,105	4.8	8.6	2.0	28.2	22.2	11.0	25,854	38,104	11,109	24,481
1987[6]	56.1	44,729	4.6	8.1	2.0	26.9	21.2	10.4	26,111	37,710	11,750	24,708
1988	56.5	44,981	4.5	7.9	1.9	26.5	20.7	10.1	26,471	37,484	12,073	24,965
1989	56.6	45,520	4.4	7.8	1.9	25.4	20.8	10.0	26,398	37,545	12,415	25,143
1990	56.8	44,315	4.6	8.1	2.0	26.8	22.3	10.7	25,414	36,111	12,385	25,016
1991	57.2	43,525	5.0	8.8	2.2	28.4	23.7	11.3	24,647	35,657	12,350	24,831
1992[7]	57.7	43,245	5.3	9.1	2.2	28.5	25.3	11.9	23,939	35,300	12,260	24,993
1993	57.9	42,672	5.5	9.4	2.4	29.2	26.2	12.2	23,867	34,564	12,233	24,951
1994	58.4	43,284	5.3	9.1	2.3	29.0	25.4	11.7	24,000	34,344	12,313	25,297
1995	58.9	43,905	5.0	8.5	2.2	26.6	24.4	11.2	24,601	34,505	12,680	24,980
1996	58.9	44,756	5.1	8.6	2.3	27.3	24.7	11.2	24,949	34,741	12,961	25,358
BLACK												
1978	5.9	25,288	1.6	27.5	1.2	50.6	7.6	30.6	15,948	29,125	8,617	20,966
1979[4]	6.2	24,540	1.7	27.8	1.2	49.4	8.1	31.0	16,150	27,481	8,477	20,639
1980	6.3	24,162	1.8	28.9	1.3	49.4	8.6	32.5	15,269	26,452	8,731	20,809
1981	6.4	23,101	2.0	30.8	1.4	52.9	9.2	34.2	14,804	26,093	8,538	19,918
1982	6.5	22,317	2.2	33.0	1.5	56.2	9.7	35.6	14,505	25,915	8,638	20,312
1983[5]	6.7	22,938	2.2	32.3	1.5	53.7	9.9	35.7	14,209	25,953	8,773	20,531
1984	6.8	23,302	2.1	30.9	1.5	51.7	9.5	33.8	14,267	25,586	9,308	21,196
1985	6.9	24,477	2.0	28.7	1.5	50.5	8.9	31.3	15,702	26,205	9,153	21,275
1986	7.1	25,201	2.0	28.0	1.5	50.1	9.0	31.1	15,492	26,865	9,400	21,422
1987[6]	7.2	25,422	2.1	29.4	1.6	51.1	9.5	32.4	15,490	26,963	9,598	22,068
1988	7.4	25,636	2.1	28.2	1.6	49.0	9.4	31.3	15,974	27,475	9,747	22,371
1989	7.5	25,571	2.1	27.8	1.5	46.5	9.3	30.7	15,954	26,197	9,964	22,613
1990	7.5	25,717	2.2	29.3	1.6	48.1	9.8	31.9	15,448	25,787	9,997	22,261
1991	7.7	24,823	2.3	30.4	1.8	51.2	10.2	32.7	14,932	26,067	10,156	22,042
1992[7]	8.0	23,600	2.5	31.1	1.9	50.2	10.8	33.4	14,610	25,711	9,938	22,655
1993	8.0	23,391	2.5	31.3	1.9	49.9	10.9	33.1	15,858	25,588	10,324	22,058
1994	8.1	26,148	2.2	27.3	1.7	46.2	10.2	30.6	15,862	25,838	11,163	21,839
1995	8.1	26,737	2.1	26.4	1.7	45.1	9.9	29.3	16,479	25,530	11,285	21,701
1996	8.5	26,522	2.2	26.1	1.7	43.7	9.7	28.4	16,491	27,136	11,772	21,990

[1] The term "family" refers to a group of two or more persons related by birth, marriage, or adoption and residing together. Every family must include a reference person. Beginning 1979, based on householder concept and restricted to primary families.
[2] Current dollar median money income adjusted by CPI-U-X1.
[3] Prior to 1979, data are for persons 14 years and over.
[4] Based on 1980 census population controls; comparable with succeeding years.
[5] Reflects implementation of Hispanic population controls; comparable with succeeding years.
[6] Based on revised methodology; comparable with succeeding years.
[7] Based on 1990 census adjusted population controls; comparable with succeeding years.

Note.—Poverty rates (percent of persons below poverty level) for all races for years not shown above are: 1959, 22.4; 1960, 22.2; 1961, 21.9; 1962, 21.0; 1963, 19.5; 1964, 19.0; 1965, 17.3; 1966, 14.7; 1967, 14.2; 1968, 12.8; 1969, 12.1; 1970, 12.6; 1971, 12.5; 1972, 11.9; 1973, 11.1; 1974, 11.2; 1975, 12.3; 1976, 11.8; and 1977, 11.6.

Poverty thresholds are updated each year to reflect changes in the consumer price index (CPI–U).

For details see "Current Population Reports," Series P–60.

Source: Department of Commerce, Bureau of the Census.

TABLE B–34.—*Population by age group, 1929–97*

[Thousands of persons]

July 1	Total	Age (years)						
		Under 5	5–15	16–19	20–24	25–44	45–64	65 and over
1929	121,767	11,734	26,800	9,127	10,694	35,862	21,076	6,474
1933	125,579	10,612	26,897	9,302	11,152	37,319	22,933	7,363
1939	130,880	10,418	25,179	9,822	11,519	39,354	25,823	8,764
1940	132,122	10,579	24,811	9,895	11,690	39,868	26,249	9,031
1941	133,402	10,850	24,516	9,840	11,807	40,383	26,718	9,288
1942	134,860	11,301	24,231	9,730	11,955	40,861	27,196	9,584
1943	136,739	12,016	24,093	9,607	12,064	41,420	27,671	9,867
1944	138,397	12,524	23,949	9,561	12,062	42,016	28,138	10,147
1945	139,928	12,979	23,907	9,361	12,036	42,521	28,630	10,494
1946	141,389	13,244	24,103	9,119	12,004	43,027	29,064	10,828
1947	144,126	14,406	24,468	9,097	11,814	43,657	29,498	11,185
1948	146,631	14,919	25,209	8,952	11,794	44,288	29,931	11,538
1949	149,188	15,607	25,852	8,788	11,700	44,916	30,405	11,921
1950	152,271	16,410	26,721	8,542	11,680	45,672	30,849	12,397
1951	154,878	17,333	27,279	8,446	11,552	46,103	31,362	12,803
1952	157,553	17,312	28,894	8,414	11,350	46,495	31,884	13,203
1953	160,184	17,638	30,227	8,460	11,062	46,786	32,394	13,617
1954	163,026	18,057	31,480	8,637	10,832	47,001	32,942	14,076
1955	165,931	18,566	32,682	8,744	10,714	47,194	33,506	14,525
1956	168,903	19,003	33,994	8,916	10,616	47,379	34,057	14,938
1957	171,984	19,494	35,272	9,195	10,603	47,440	34,591	15,388
1958	174,882	19,887	36,445	9,543	10,756	47,337	35,109	15,806
1959	177,830	20,175	37,368	10,215	10,969	47,192	35,663	16,248
1960	180,671	20,341	38,494	10,683	11,134	47,140	36,203	16,675
1961	183,691	20,522	39,765	11,025	11,483	47,084	36,722	17,089
1962	186,538	20,469	41,205	11,180	11,959	47,013	37,255	17,457
1963	189,242	20,342	41,626	12,007	12,714	46,994	37,782	17,778
1964	191,889	20,165	42,297	12,736	13,269	46,958	38,338	18,127
1965	194,303	19,824	42,938	13,516	13,746	46,912	38,916	18,451
1966	196,560	19,208	43,702	14,311	14,050	47,001	39,534	18,755
1967	198,712	18,563	44,244	14,200	15,248	47,194	40,193	19,071
1968	200,706	17,913	44,622	14,452	15,786	47,721	40,846	19,365
1969	202,677	17,376	44,840	14,800	16,480	48,064	41,437	19,680
1970	205,052	17,166	44,816	15,289	17,202	48,473	41,999	20,107
1971	207,661	17,244	44,591	15,688	18,159	48,936	42,482	20,561
1972	209,896	17,101	44,203	16,039	18,153	50,482	42,898	21,020
1973	211,909	16,851	43,582	16,446	18,521	51,749	43,235	21,525
1974	213,854	16,487	42,989	16,769	18,975	53,051	43,522	22,061
1975	215,973	16,121	42,508	17,017	19,527	54,302	43,801	22,696
1976	218,035	15,617	42,099	17,194	19,986	55,852	44,008	23,278
1977	220,239	15,564	41,298	17,276	20,499	57,561	44,150	23,892
1978	222,585	15,735	40,428	17,288	20,946	59,400	44,286	24,502
1979	225,055	16,063	39,552	17,242	21,297	61,379	44,390	25,134
1980	227,726	16,451	38,838	17,167	21,590	63,470	44,504	25,707
1981	229,966	16,893	38,144	16,812	21,869	65,528	44,500	26,221
1982	232,188	17,228	37,784	16,332	21,902	67,692	44,462	26,787
1983	234,307	17,547	37,526	15,823	21,844	69,733	44,474	27,361
1984	236,348	17,695	37,461	15,295	21,737	71,735	44,547	27,878
1985	238,466	17,842	37,450	15,005	21,478	73,673	44,602	28,416
1986	240,651	17,963	37,404	15,024	20,942	75,651	44,660	29,008
1987	242,804	18,052	37,333	15,215	20,385	77,338	44,854	29,626
1988	245,021	18,195	37,593	15,198	19,846	78,595	45,471	30,124
1989	247,342	18,508	37,972	14,913	19,442	79,943	45,882	30,682
1990	249,949	18,851	38,588	14,461	19,309	81,207	46,294	31,237
1991	252,636	19,187	39,146	13,970	19,357	82,444	46,766	31,766
1992	255,382	19,489	39,802	13,736	19,211	82,516	48,355	32,273
1993	258,089	19,670	40,386	13,879	18,949	82,831	49,595	32,779
1994	260,602	19,694	41,009	14,122	18,553	83,155	50,906	33,164
1995	263,039	19,526	41,666	14,379	18,136	83,513	52,258	33,560
1996	265,453	19,324	42,157	14,874	17,650	83,847	53,734	33,867
1997	267,901	19,150	42,648	15,211	17,594	83,771	55,452	34,076

Note.—Includes Armed Forces overseas beginning 1940. Includes Alaska and Hawaii beginning 1950.
All estimates are consistent with decennial census enumerations.
Source: Department of Commerce, Bureau of the Census.

[Monthly data seasonally adjusted, except as noted]

Year or month	Civilian noninstitutional population[1]	Civilian labor force					Not in labor force	Civilian labor force participation rate[2]	Civilian employment/population ratio[3]	Unemployment rate, civilian workers[4]
		Total	Employment			Unemployment				
			Total	Agricultural	Nonagricultural					
		Thousands of persons 14 years of age and over							Percent	
1929	....	49,180	47,630	10,450	37,180	1,550	....	....	....	3.2
1933	....	51,590	38,760	10,090	28,670	12,830	....	....	....	24.9
1939	....	55,230	45,750	9,610	36,140	9,480	....	....	....	17.2
1940	99,840	55,640	47,520	9,540	37,980	8,120	44,200	55.7	47.6	14.6
1941	99,900	55,910	50,350	9,100	41,250	5,560	43,990	56.0	50.4	9.9
1942	98,640	56,410	53,750	9,250	44,500	2,660	42,230	57.2	54.5	4.7
1943	94,640	55,540	54,470	9,080	45,390	1,070	39,100	58.7	57.6	1.9
1944	93,220	54,630	53,960	8,950	45,010	670	38,590	58.6	57.9	1.2
1945	94,090	53,860	52,820	8,580	44,240	1,040	40,230	57.2	56.1	1.9
1946	103,070	57,520	55,250	8,320	46,930	2,270	45,550	55.8	53.6	3.9
1947	106,018	60,168	57,812	8,256	49,557	2,356	45,850	56.8	54.5	3.9
		Thousands of persons 16 years of age and over								
1947	101,827	59,350	57,038	7,890	49,148	2,311	42,477	58.3	56.0	3.9
1948	103,068	60,621	58,343	7,629	50,714	2,276	42,447	58.8	56.6	3.8
1949	103,994	61,286	57,651	7,658	49,993	3,637	42,708	58.9	55.4	5.9
1950	104,995	62,208	58,918	7,160	51,758	3,288	42,787	59.2	56.1	5.3
1951	104,621	62,017	59,961	6,726	53,235	2,055	42,604	59.2	57.3	3.3
1952	105,231	62,138	60,250	6,500	53,749	1,883	43,093	59.0	57.3	3.0
1953[5]	107,056	63,015	61,179	6,260	54,919	1,834	44,041	58.9	57.1	2.9
1954	108,321	63,643	60,109	6,205	53,904	3,532	44,678	58.8	55.5	5.5
1955	109,683	65,023	62,170	6,450	55,722	2,852	44,660	59.3	56.7	4.4
1956	110,954	66,552	63,799	6,283	57,514	2,750	44,402	60.0	57.5	4.1
1957	112,265	66,929	64,071	5,947	58,123	2,859	45,336	59.6	57.1	4.3
1958	113,727	67,639	63,036	5,586	57,450	4,602	46,088	59.5	55.4	6.8
1959	115,329	68,369	64,630	5,565	59,065	3,740	46,960	59.3	56.0	5.5
1960[5]	117,245	69,628	65,778	5,458	60,318	3,852	47,617	59.4	56.1	5.5
1961	118,771	70,459	65,746	5,200	60,546	4,714	48,312	59.3	55.4	6.7
1962[5]	120,153	70,614	66,702	4,944	61,759	3,911	49,539	58.8	55.5	5.5
1963	122,416	71,833	67,762	4,687	63,076	4,070	50,583	58.7	55.4	5.7
1964	124,485	73,091	69,305	4,523	64,782	3,786	51,394	58.7	55.7	5.2
1965	126,513	74,455	71,088	4,361	66,726	3,366	52,058	58.9	56.2	4.5
1966	128,058	75,770	72,895	3,979	68,915	2,875	52,288	59.2	56.9	3.8
1967	129,874	77,347	74,372	3,844	70,527	2,975	52,527	59.6	57.3	3.8
1968	132,028	78,737	75,920	3,817	72,103	2,817	53,291	59.6	57.5	3.6
1969	134,335	80,734	77,902	3,606	74,296	2,832	53,602	60.1	58.0	3.5
1970	137,085	82,771	78,678	3,463	75,215	4,093	54,315	60.4	57.4	4.9
1971	140,216	84,382	79,367	3,394	75,972	5,016	55,834	60.2	56.6	5.9
1972[5]	144,126	87,034	82,153	3,484	78,669	4,882	57,091	60.4	57.0	5.6
1973[5]	147,096	89,429	85,064	3,470	81,594	4,365	57,667	60.8	57.8	4.9
1974	150,120	91,949	86,794	3,515	83,279	5,156	58,171	61.3	57.8	5.6
1975	153,153	93,775	85,846	3,408	82,438	7,929	59,377	61.2	56.1	8.5
1976	156,150	96,158	88,752	3,331	85,421	7,406	59,991	61.6	56.8	7.7
1977	159,033	99,009	92,017	3,283	88,734	6,991	60,025	62.3	57.9	7.1
1978[5]	161,910	102,251	96,048	3,387	92,661	6,202	59,659	63.2	59.3	6.1
1979	164,863	104,962	98,824	3,347	95,477	6,137	59,900	63.7	59.9	5.8
1980	167,745	106,940	99,303	3,364	95,938	7,637	60,806	63.8	59.2	7.1
1981	170,130	108,670	100,397	3,368	97,030	8,273	61,460	63.9	59.0	7.6
1982	172,271	110,204	99,526	3,401	96,125	10,678	62,067	64.0	57.8	9.7
1983	174,215	111,550	100,834	3,383	97,450	10,717	62,665	64.0	57.9	9.6
1984	176,383	113,544	105,005	3,321	101,685	8,539	62,839	64.4	59.5	7.5
1985	178,206	115,461	107,150	3,179	103,971	8,312	62,744	64.8	60.1	7.2
1986[5]	180,587	117,834	109,597	3,163	106,434	8,237	62,752	65.3	60.7	7.0
1987	182,753	119,865	112,440	3,208	109,232	7,425	62,888	65.6	61.5	6.2
1988	184,613	121,669	114,968	3,169	111,800	6,701	62,944	65.9	62.3	5.5
1989	186,393	123,869	117,342	3,199	114,142	6,528	62,523	66.5	63.0	5.3
1990[5]	189,164	125,840	118,793	3,223	115,570	7,047	63,324	66.5	62.8	5.6
1991	190,925	126,346	117,718	3,269	114,449	8,628	64,578	66.2	61.7	6.8
1992	192,805	128,105	118,492	3,247	115,245	9,613	64,700	66.4	61.5	7.5
1993	194,838	129,200	120,259	3,115	117,144	8,940	65,638	66.3	61.7	6.9
1994[5]	196,814	131,056	123,060	3,409	119,651	7,996	65,758	66.6	62.5	6.1
1995	198,584	132,304	124,900	3,440	121,460	7,404	66,280	66.6	62.9	5.6
1996	200,591	133,943	126,708	3,443	123,264	7,236	66,647	66.8	63.2	5.4
1997[5]	203,133	136,297	129,558	3,399	126,159	6,739	66,837	67.1	63.8	4.9

[1] Not seasonally adjusted.
[2] Civilian labor force as percent of civilian noninstitutional population.
[3] Civilian employment as percent of civilian noninstitutional population.
[4] Unemployed as percent of civilian labor force.

See next page for continuation of table.

TABLE B–35.—*Civilian population and labor force, 1929–97*—Continued

[Monthly data seasonally adjusted, except as noted]

Year or month	Civilian noninstitutional population[1]	Civilian labor force					Not in labor force	Civilian labor force participation rate[2]	Civilian employment/population ratio[3]	Unemployment rate, civilian workers[4]
		Total	Employment			Unemployment				
			Total	Agricultural	Nonagricultural					
	Thousands of persons 16 years of age and over							Percent		
1994: Jan[5]	195,953	130,638	121,971	3,306	118,665	8,667	65,315	66.7	62.2	6.6
Feb	196,090	130,698	122,118	3,343	118,775	8,580	65,392	66.7	62.3	6.6
Mar	196,213	130,441	121,955	3,351	118,604	8,486	65,772	66.5	62.2	6.5
Apr	196,363	130,638	122,303	3,411	118,892	8,335	65,725	66.5	62.3	6.4
May	196,510	130,782	122,907	3,408	119,499	7,875	65,728	66.6	62.5	6.0
June	196,693	130,567	122,643	3,296	119,347	7,924	66,126	66.4	62.4	6.1
July	196,859	130,669	122,714	3,339	119,375	7,955	66,190	66.4	62.3	6.1
Aug	197,043	131,221	123,271	3,457	119,814	7,950	65,822	66.6	62.6	6.1
Sept	197,248	131,318	123,601	3,435	120,166	7,717	65,930	66.6	62.7	5.9
Oct	197,430	131,754	124,085	3,494	120,591	7,669	65,676	66.7	62.9	5.8
Nov	197,607	131,916	124,531	3,581	120,950	7,385	65,691	66.8	63.0	5.6
Dec	197,765	131,893	124,729	3,573	121,156	7,164	65,872	66.7	63.1	5.4
1995: Jan	197,753	132,100	124,716	3,525	121,191	7,384	65,653	66.8	63.1	5.6
Feb	197,886	132,167	124,976	3,612	121,364	7,191	65,719	66.8	63.2	5.4
Mar	198,007	132,171	125,000	3,626	121,374	7,171	65,836	66.8	63.1	5.4
Apr	198,148	132,598	124,975	3,548	121,427	7,623	65,550	66.9	63.1	5.7
May	198,286	131,873	124,496	3,344	121,152	7,377	66,413	66.5	62.8	5.6
June	198,453	131,951	124,526	3,458	121,068	7,425	66,502	66.5	62.7	5.6
July	198,615	132,335	124,791	3,389	121,402	7,544	66,280	66.6	62.8	5.7
Aug	198,801	132,256	124,735	3,385	121,350	7,521	66,545	66.5	62.7	5.7
Sept	199,005	132,490	125,002	3,297	121,705	7,488	66,515	66.6	62.8	5.7
Oct	199,192	132,684	125,303	3,445	121,858	7,381	66,508	66.6	62.9	5.6
Nov	199,355	132,640	125,203	3,346	121,857	7,437	66,715	66.5	62.8	5.6
Dec	199,508	132,470	125,116	3,347	121,769	7,354	67,038	66.4	62.7	5.6
1996: Jan	199,634	132,768	125,246	3,488	121,758	7,522	66,866	66.5	62.7	5.7
Feb	199,773	133,116	125,771	3,544	122,227	7,345	66,657	66.6	63.0	5.5
Mar	199,921	133,306	125,951	3,472	122,479	7,355	66,615	66.7	63.0	5.5
Apr	200,101	133,405	126,057	3,382	122,675	7,348	66,696	66.7	63.0	5.5
May	200,278	133,680	126,321	3,466	122,855	7,359	66,598	66.7	63.1	5.5
June	200,459	133,686	126,591	3,412	123,179	7,095	66,773	66.7	63.2	5.3
July	200,641	134,214	126,867	3,454	123,413	7,347	66,427	66.9	63.2	5.5
Aug	200,847	133,911	126,995	3,415	123,580	6,916	66,936	66.7	63.2	5.2
Sept	201,061	134,341	127,338	3,466	123,872	7,003	66,720	66.8	63.3	5.2
Oct	201,273	134,794	127,715	3,477	124,238	7,079	66,479	67.0	63.5	5.3
Nov	201,463	134,977	127,746	3,363	124,383	7,231	66,486	67.0	63.4	5.4
Dec	201,636	135,060	127,899	3,423	124,476	7,161	66,576	67.0	63.4	5.3
1997: Jan[5]	202,285	135,729	128,541	3,453	125,088	7,188	66,556	67.1	63.5	5.3
Feb	202,389	135,689	128,515	3,340	125,175	7,174	66,700	67.0	63.5	5.3
Mar	202,513	136,115	129,035	3,387	125,648	7,080	66,398	67.2	63.7	5.2
Apr	202,674	136,043	129,275	3,462	125,813	6,768	66,631	67.1	63.8	5.0
May	202,832	136,060	129,494	3,418	126,076	6,566	66,772	67.1	63.8	4.8
June	203,000	136,206	129,392	3,389	126,003	6,814	66,794	67.1	63.7	5.0
July	203,166	136,294	129,661	3,452	126,209	6,633	66,872	67.1	63.8	4.9
Aug	203,364	136,404	129,747	3,379	126,368	6,657	66,960	67.1	63.8	4.9
Sept	203,570	136,439	129,761	3,422	126,339	6,678	67,131	67.0	63.7	4.9
Oct	203,767	136,406	129,910	3,327	126,583	6,496	67,361	66.9	63.8	4.8
Nov	203,941	136,864	130,575	3,384	127,191	6,289	67,077	67.1	64.0	4.6
Dec	204,098	137,169	130,777	3,385	127,392	6,392	66,929	67.2	64.1	4.7

[5] Not strictly comparable with earlier data due to population adjustments as follows: Beginning 1953, introduction of 1950 census data added about 600,000 to population and 350,000 to labor force, total employment, and agricultural employment. Beginning 1960, inclusion of Alaska and Hawaii added about 500,000 to population, 300,000 to labor force, and 240,000 to nonagricultural employment. Beginning 1962, introduction of 1960 census data reduced population by about 50,000 and labor force and employment by 200,000. Beginning 1972, introduction of 1970 census data added about 800,000 to civilian noninstitutional population and 333,000 to labor force and employment. A subsequent adjustment based on 1970 census in March 1973 added 60,000 to labor force and to employment. Beginning 1978, changes in sampling and estimation procedures introduced into the household survey added about 250,000 to labor force and to employment. Unemployment levels and rates were not significantly affected. Beginning 1986, the introduction of revised population controls added about 400,000 to the civilian population and labor force and 350,000 to civilian employment. Unemployment levels and rates were not significantly affected. Beginning 1990, the introduction of 1990 census-based population controls, adjusted for the estimated undercount, added about 1.1 million to the civilian population and labor force, 880,000 to civilian employment, and 175,000 to unemployment. The overall unemployment rate rose by about 0.1 percentage point.

Beginning 1994, data are not strictly comparable with earlier data because of the introduction of a major redesign of the Current Population Survey and collection methodology.

Beginning 1997, data are not strictly comparable with earlier data due to the introduction of revised population controls which added about 470,000 to the civilian population, 320,000 to the labor force, and 290,000 to employment. Unemployment rates and other percentages of labor market participation were not affected.

Note.—Labor force data in Tables B–35 through B–44 are based on household interviews and relate to the calendar week including the 12th of the month. For definitions of terms, area samples used, historical comparability of the data, comparability with other series, etc., see "Employment and Earnings."

Source: Department of Labor, Bureau of Labor Statistics.

TABLE B-36.—*Civilian employment and unemployment by sex and age, 1950–97*

[Thousands of persons 16 years of age and over; monthly data seasonally adjusted]

Year or month	Civilian employment Total	Males Total	Males 16–19 years	Males 20 years and over	Females Total	Females 16–19 years	Females 20 years and over	Unemployment Total	Males Total	Males 16–19 years	Males 20 years and over	Females Total	Females 16–19 years	Females 20 years and over
1950	58,918	41,578	2,186	39,394	17,340	1,517	15,824	3,288	2,239	318	1,922	1,049	195	854
1951	59,961	41,780	2,156	39,626	18,181	1,611	16,570	2,055	1,221	191	1,029	834	145	689
1952	60,250	41,682	2,107	39,578	18,568	1,612	16,958	1,883	1,185	205	980	698	140	559
1953	61,179	42,430	2,136	40,296	18,749	1,584	17,164	1,834	1,202	184	1,019	632	123	510
1954	60,109	41,619	1,985	39,634	18,490	1,490	17,000	3,532	2,344	310	2,035	1,188	191	997
1955	62,170	42,621	2,095	40,526	19,551	1,547	18,002	2,852	1,854	274	1,580	998	176	823
1956	63,799	43,379	2,164	41,216	20,419	1,654	18,767	2,750	1,711	269	1,442	1,039	209	832
1957	64,071	43,357	2,115	41,239	20,714	1,663	19,052	2,859	1,841	300	1,541	1,018	197	821
1958	63,036	42,423	2,012	40,411	20,613	1,570	19,043	4,602	3,098	416	2,681	1,504	262	1,242
1959	64,630	43,466	2,198	41,267	21,164	1,640	19,524	3,740	2,420	398	2,022	1,320	256	1,063
1960	65,778	43,904	2,361	41,543	21,874	1,768	20,105	3,852	2,486	426	2,060	1,366	286	1,080
1961	65,746	43,656	2,315	41,342	22,090	1,793	20,296	4,714	2,997	479	2,518	1,717	349	1,368
1962	66,702	44,177	2,362	41,815	22,525	1,833	20,693	3,911	2,423	408	2,016	1,488	313	1,175
1963	67,762	44,657	2,406	42,251	23,105	1,849	21,257	4,070	2,472	501	1,971	1,598	383	1,216
1964	69,305	45,474	2,587	42,886	23,831	1,929	21,903	3,786	2,205	487	1,718	1,581	385	1,195
1965	71,088	46,340	2,918	43,422	24,748	2,118	22,630	3,366	1,914	479	1,435	1,452	395	1,056
1966	72,895	46,919	3,253	43,668	25,976	2,468	23,510	2,875	1,551	432	1,120	1,324	405	921
1967	74,372	47,479	3,186	44,294	26,893	2,496	24,397	2,975	1,508	448	1,060	1,468	391	1,078
1968	75,920	48,114	3,255	44,859	27,807	2,526	25,281	2,817	1,419	426	993	1,397	412	985
1969	77,902	48,818	3,430	45,388	29,084	2,687	26,397	2,832	1,403	440	963	1,429	413	1,015
1970	78,678	48,990	3,409	45,581	29,688	2,735	26,952	4,093	2,238	599	1,638	1,855	506	1,349
1971	79,367	49,390	3,478	45,912	29,976	2,730	27,246	5,016	2,789	693	2,097	2,227	568	1,658
1972	82,153	50,896	3,765	47,130	31,257	2,980	28,276	4,882	2,659	711	1,948	2,222	598	1,625
1973	85,064	52,349	4,039	48,310	32,715	3,231	29,484	4,365	2,275	653	1,624	2,089	583	1,507
1974	86,794	53,024	4,103	48,922	33,769	3,345	30,424	5,156	2,714	757	1,957	2,441	665	1,777
1975	85,846	51,857	3,839	48,018	33,989	3,263	30,726	7,929	4,442	966	3,476	3,486	802	2,684
1976	88,752	53,138	3,947	49,190	35,615	3,389	32,226	7,406	4,036	939	3,098	3,369	780	2,588
1977	92,017	54,728	4,174	50,555	37,289	3,514	33,775	6,991	3,667	874	2,794	3,324	789	2,535
1978	96,048	56,479	4,336	52,143	39,569	3,734	35,836	6,202	3,142	813	2,328	3,061	769	2,292
1979	98,824	57,607	4,300	53,308	41,217	3,783	37,434	6,137	3,120	811	2,308	3,018	743	2,276
1980	99,303	57,186	4,085	53,101	42,117	3,625	38,492	7,637	4,267	913	3,353	3,370	755	2,615
1981	100,397	57,397	3,815	53,582	43,000	3,411	39,590	8,273	4,577	962	3,615	3,696	800	2,895
1982	99,526	56,271	3,379	52,891	43,256	3,170	40,086	10,678	6,179	1,090	5,089	4,499	886	3,613
1983	100,834	56,787	3,300	53,487	44,047	3,043	41,004	10,717	6,260	1,003	5,257	4,457	825	3,632
1984	105,005	59,091	3,322	55,769	45,915	3,122	42,793	8,539	4,744	812	3,932	3,794	687	3,107
1985	107,150	59,891	3,328	56,562	47,259	3,105	44,154	8,312	4,521	806	3,715	3,791	661	3,129
1986	109,597	60,892	3,323	57,569	48,706	3,149	45,556	8,237	4,530	779	3,751	3,707	675	3,032
1987	112,440	62,107	3,381	58,726	50,334	3,260	47,074	7,425	4,101	732	3,369	3,324	616	2,709
1988	114,968	63,273	3,492	59,781	51,696	3,313	48,383	6,701	3,655	667	2,987	3,046	558	2,487
1989	117,342	64,315	3,477	60,837	53,027	3,282	49,745	6,528	3,525	658	2,867	3,003	536	2,467
1990	118,793	65,104	3,427	61,678	53,689	3,154	50,535	7,047	3,906	667	3,239	3,140	544	2,596
1991	117,718	64,223	3,044	61,178	53,496	2,862	50,634	8,628	4,946	751	4,195	3,683	608	3,074
1992	118,492	64,440	2,944	61,496	54,052	2,724	51,328	9,613	5,523	806	4,717	4,090	621	3,469
1993	120,259	65,349	2,994	62,355	54,910	2,811	52,099	8,940	5,055	768	4,287	3,885	597	3,288
1994	123,060	66,450	3,156	63,294	56,610	3,005	53,606	7,996	4,367	740	3,627	3,629	580	3,049
1995	124,900	67,377	3,292	64,085	57,523	3,127	54,396	7,404	3,983	744	3,239	3,421	602	2,819
1996	126,708	68,207	3,310	64,897	58,501	3,190	55,311	7,236	3,880	733	3,146	3,356	573	2,783
1997	129,558	69,685	3,401	66,284	59,873	3,260	56,613	6,739	3,577	694	2,882	3,162	577	2,585
1996: Jan	125,246	67,538	3,270	64,268	57,708	3,101	54,607	7,522	3,972	757	3,215	3,550	615	2,935
Feb	125,771	67,765	3,309	64,456	58,006	3,121	54,885	7,345	4,004	727	3,277	3,341	581	2,760
Mar	125,951	67,817	3,268	64,549	58,134	3,118	55,016	7,355	4,054	755	3,299	3,301	573	2,728
Apr	126,057	67,888	3,345	64,543	58,169	3,109	55,060	7,348	4,002	741	3,261	3,346	570	2,776
May	126,321	68,079	3,359	64,720	58,242	3,182	55,060	7,359	3,976	733	3,243	3,383	570	2,813
June	126,591	68,266	3,340	64,926	58,325	3,156	55,169	7,095	3,827	673	3,154	3,268	559	2,709
July	126,867	68,362	3,323	65,039	58,505	3,192	55,313	7,347	3,990	796	3,194	3,357	491	2,866
Aug	126,995	68,374	3,259	65,115	58,621	3,128	55,493	6,916	3,608	709	2,899	3,308	590	2,718
Sept	127,338	68,373	3,376	64,997	58,965	3,320	55,645	7,003	3,801	702	3,099	3,202	550	2,652
Oct	127,715	68,686	3,346	65,340	59,029	3,308	55,721	7,079	3,739	746	2,993	3,340	578	2,762
Nov	127,746	68,590	3,212	65,378	59,156	3,297	55,859	7,231	3,809	739	3,070	3,422	597	2,825
Dec	127,899	68,773	3,318	65,455	59,126	3,256	55,870	7,161	3,691	722	2,969	3,470	609	2,861
1997: Jan	128,541	69,209	3,353	65,856	59,332	3,254	56,078	7,188	3,843	750	3,093	3,345	591	2,754
Feb	128,515	69,248	3,388	65,860	59,267	3,246	56,021	7,174	3,753	741	3,012	3,421	651	2,770
Mar	129,035	69,415	3,384	66,031	59,620	3,298	56,322	7,080	3,749	740	3,009	3,331	583	2,748
Apr	129,275	69,565	3,367	66,198	59,710	3,353	56,357	6,768	3,619	710	2,909	3,149	531	2,618
May	129,494	69,765	3,456	66,309	59,729	3,241	56,488	6,566	3,324	643	2,681	3,242	601	2,641
June	129,392	69,586	3,328	66,258	59,806	3,231	56,575	6,814	3,639	740	2,899	3,175	555	2,620
July	129,661	69,711	3,350	66,361	59,950	3,257	56,693	6,633	3,507	697	2,810	3,126	587	2,539
Aug	129,747	69,748	3,362	66,386	59,999	3,210	56,789	6,657	3,517	705	2,812	3,140	567	2,573
Sept	129,761	69,656	3,358	66,298	60,105	3,222	56,883	6,678	3,536	698	2,838	3,142	593	2,549
Oct	129,910	69,785	3,448	66,337	60,125	3,206	56,919	6,496	3,526	670	2,856	2,970	551	2,419
Nov	130,575	70,352	3,528	66,824	60,223	3,270	56,953	6,289	3,330	654	2,676	2,959	564	2,395
Dec	130,777	70,195	3,519	66,676	60,582	3,327	57,255	6,392	3,467	582	2,885	2,925	556	2,369

Note.—See footnote 5 and Note, Table B–35.

Source: Department of Labor, Bureau of Labor Statistics.

TABLE B–37.—*Civilian employment by demographic characteristic, 1954–97*

[Thousands of persons 16 years of age and over; monthly data seasonally adjusted]

Year or month	All civilian workers	White				Black and other				Black			
		Total	Males	Females	Both sexes 16–19	Total	Males	Females	Both sexes 16–19	Total	Males	Females	Both sexes 16–19
1954	60,109	53,957	37,846	16,111	3,078	6,152	3,773	2,379	396				
1955	62,170	55,833	38,719	17,114	3,225	6,341	3,904	2,437	418				
1956	63,799	57,269	39,368	17,901	3,389	6,534	4,013	2,521	430				
1957	64,071	57,465	39,349	18,116	3,374	6,604	4,006	2,598	407				
1958	63,036	56,613	38,591	18,022	3,216	6,423	3,833	2,590	365				
1959	64,630	58,006	39,494	18,512	3,475	6,623	3,971	2,652	362				
1960	65,778	58,850	39,755	19,095	3,700	6,928	4,149	2,779	430				
1961	65,746	58,913	39,588	19,325	3,693	6,833	4,068	2,765	414				
1962	66,702	59,698	40,016	19,682	3,774	7,003	4,160	2,843	420				
1963	67,762	60,622	40,428	20,194	3,851	7,140	4,229	2,911	404				
1964	69,305	61,922	41,115	20,807	4,076	7,383	4,359	3,024	440				
1965	71,088	63,446	41,844	21,602	4,562	7,643	4,496	3,147	474				
1966	72,895	65,021	42,331	22,690	5,176	7,877	4,588	3,289	545				
1967	74,372	66,361	42,833	23,528	5,114	8,011	4,646	3,365	568				
1968	75,920	67,750	43,411	24,339	5,195	8,169	4,702	3,467	584				
1969	77,902	69,518	44,048	25,470	5,508	8,384	4,770	3,614	609				
1970	78,678	70,217	44,178	26,039	5,571	8,464	4,813	3,650	574				
1971	79,367	70,878	44,595	26,283	5,670	8,488	4,796	3,692	538				
1972	82,153	73,370	45,944	27,426	6,173	8,783	4,952	3,832	573	7,802	4,368	3,433	509
1973	85,064	75,708	47,085	28,623	6,623	9,356	5,265	4,092	647	8,128	4,527	3,601	570
1974	86,794	77,184	47,674	29,511	6,796	9,610	5,352	4,258	652	8,203	4,527	3,677	554
1975	85,846	76,411	46,697	29,714	6,487	9,435	5,161	4,275	615	7,894	4,275	3,618	507
1976	88,752	78,853	47,775	31,078	6,724	9,899	5,363	4,536	611	8,227	4,404	3,823	508
1977	92,017	81,700	49,150	32,550	7,068	10,317	5,579	4,739	619	8,540	4,565	3,975	508
1978	96,048	84,936	50,544	34,392	7,367	11,112	5,936	5,177	703	9,102	4,796	4,307	571
1979	98,824	87,259	51,452	35,807	7,356	11,565	6,156	5,409	727	9,359	4,923	4,436	579
1980	99,303	87,715	51,127	36,587	7,021	11,588	6,059	5,529	689	9,313	4,798	4,515	547
1981	100,397	88,709	51,315	37,394	6,588	11,688	6,083	5,606	637	9,355	4,794	4,561	505
1982	99,526	87,903	50,287	37,615	5,984	11,624	5,983	5,641	565	9,189	4,637	4,552	428
1983	100,834	88,893	50,621	38,272	5,799	11,941	6,166	5,775	543	9,375	4,753	4,622	416
1984	105,005	92,120	52,462	39,659	5,836	12,885	6,629	6,256	607	10,119	5,124	4,995	474
1985	107,150	93,736	53,046	40,690	5,768	13,414	6,845	6,569	666	10,501	5,270	5,231	532
1986	109,597	95,660	53,785	41,876	5,792	13,937	7,107	6,830	681	10,814	5,428	5,386	536
1987	112,440	97,789	54,647	43,142	5,898	14,652	7,459	7,192	742	11,309	5,661	5,648	587
1988	114,968	99,812	55,550	44,262	6,030	15,156	7,722	7,434	774	11,658	5,824	5,834	601
1989	117,342	101,584	56,352	45,232	5,946	15,757	7,963	7,795	813	11,953	5,928	6,025	625
1990	118,793	102,261	56,703	45,558	5,779	16,533	8,401	8,131	801	12,175	5,995	6,180	598
1991	117,718	101,182	55,797	45,385	5,216	16,536	8,426	8,110	690	12,074	5,961	6,113	494
1992	118,492	101,669	55,959	45,710	4,985	16,823	8,482	8,342	684	12,151	5,930	6,221	492
1993	120,259	103,045	56,656	46,390	5,113	17,214	8,693	8,521	691	12,382	6,047	6,334	494
1994	123,060	105,190	57,452	47,738	5,398	17,870	8,998	8,872	763	12,835	6,241	6,595	552
1995	124,900	106,490	58,146	48,344	5,593	18,409	9,231	9,179	826	13,279	6,422	6,857	586
1996	126,708	107,808	58,888	48,920	5,667	18,900	9,319	9,580	832	13,542	6,456	7,086	613
1997	129.558	109,856	59,998	49,859	5,807	19,701	9,687	10,014	853	13,969	6,607	7,362	631
1996: Jan	125,246	106,594	58,350	48,244	5,555	18,579	9,151	9,428	822	13,410	6,412	6,998	601
Feb	125,771	107,237	58,631	48,606	5,627	18,503	9,119	9,384	782	13,360	6,391	6,969	581
Mar	125,951	107,313	58,576	48,737	5,570	18,626	9,213	9,413	822	13,420	6,406	7,014	623
Apr	126,057	107,289	58,639	48,650	5,597	18,728	9,227	9,501	855	13,434	6,409	7,025	641
May	126,321	107,446	58,731	48,715	5,671	18,860	9,311	9,549	874	13,587	6,490	7,097	674
June	126,591	107,698	58,929	48,769	5,683	18,884	9,307	9,577	823	13,512	6,425	7,087	615
July	126,867	107,860	58,988	48,872	5,686	19,003	9,366	9,637	843	13,604	6,478	7,126	607
Aug	126,995	107,936	58,966	48,970	5,526	19,133	9,482	9,651	818	13,629	6,544	7,085	590
Sept	127,338	108,377	59,094	49,283	5,826	19,037	9,373	9,664	857	13,511	6,421	7,090	609
Oct	127,715	108,597	59,284	49,313	5,811	19,112	9,406	9,706	850	13,653	6,483	7,170	622
Nov	127,746	108,594	59,159	49,435	5,732	19,162	9,437	9,725	808	13,680	6,495	7,185	582
Dec	127,899	108,752	59,337	49,415	5,736	19,154	9,434	9,720	832	13,692	6,515	7,177	615
1997: Jan	128,541	109,154	59,631	49,523	5,742	19,316	9,523	9,793	856	13,736	6,501	7,235	633
Feb	128,515	109,211	59,686	49,525	5,755	19,296	9,569	9,727	875	13,722	6,506	7,216	658
Mar	129,035	109,528	59,855	49,673	5,776	19,508	9,528	9,980	912	13,816	6,487	7,329	665
Apr	129,275	109,721	59,955	49,766	5,849	19,512	9,583	9,929	863	13,864	6,535	7,329	624
May	129,494	109,906	60,093	49,813	5,851	19,563	9,631	9,932	850	13,837	6,565	7,272	596
June	129,392	109,779	59,893	49,886	5,735	19,584	9,649	9,935	815	13,836	6,571	7,265	599
July	129,661	109,851	59,967	49,884	5,768	19,786	9,714	10,072	831	14,040	6,641	7,399	621
Aug	129,747	109,832	59,949	49,883	5,699	19,989	9,869	10,120	832	14,237	6,766	7,471	642
Sept	129,761	109,904	59,981	49,923	5,750	19,955	9,786	10,169	823	14,180	6,690	7,490	621
Oct	129,910	110,063	60,025	50,038	5,813	19,857	9,780	10,077	857	14,067	6,680	7,387	656
Nov	130,575	110,604	60,545	50,059	5,976	19,984	9,818	10,166	855	14,128	6,700	7,428	628
Dec	130,777	110,729	60,416	50,313	5,983	20,061	9,790	10,271	872	14,149	6,628	7,521	630

Note.—See footnote 5 and Note, Table B–35.

Source: Department of Labor, Bureau of Labor Statistics.

[Thousands of persons 16 years of age and over; monthly data seasonally adjusted]

Year or month	All civilian workers	White				Black and other				Black			
		Total	Males	Females	Both sexes 16–19	Total	Males	Females	Both sexes 16–19	Total	Males	Females	Both sexes 16–19
1954	3,532	2,859	1,913	946	423	673	431	242	79	....	....	....	....
1955	2,852	2,252	1,478	774	373	601	376	225	77	....	....	....	....
1956	2,750	2,159	1,366	793	382	591	345	246	95	....	....	....	....
1957	2,859	2,289	1,477	812	401	570	364	206	96	....	....	....	....
1958	4,602	3,680	2,489	1,191	541	923	610	313	138	....	....	....	....
1959	3,740	2,946	1,903	1,043	525	793	517	276	128	....	....	....	....
1960	3,852	3,065	1,988	1,077	575	788	498	290	138	....	....	....	....
1961	4,714	3,743	2,398	1,345	669	971	599	372	159	....	....	....	....
1962	3,911	3,052	1,915	1,137	580	861	509	352	142	....	....	....	....
1963	4,070	3,208	1,976	1,232	708	863	496	367	176	....	....	....	....
1964	3,786	2,999	1,779	1,220	708	787	426	361	165	....	....	....	....
1965	3,366	2,691	1,556	1,135	705	678	360	318	171	....	....	....	....
1966	2,875	2,255	1,241	1,014	651	622	310	312	186	....	....	....	....
1967	2,975	2,338	1,208	1,130	635	638	300	338	203	....	....	....	....
1968	2,817	2,226	1,142	1,084	644	590	277	313	194	....	....	....	....
1969	2,832	2,260	1,137	1,123	660	571	267	304	193	....	....	....	....
1970	4,093	3,339	1,857	1,482	871	754	380	374	235	....	....	....	....
1971	5,016	4,085	2,309	1,777	1,011	930	481	450	249	....	....	....	....
1972	4,882	3,906	2,173	1,733	1,021	977	486	491	288	906	448	458	279
1973	4,365	3,442	1,836	1,606	955	924	440	484	280	846	395	451	262
1974	5,156	4,097	2,169	1,927	1,104	1,058	544	514	318	965	494	470	297
1975	7,929	6,421	3,627	2,794	1,413	1,507	815	692	355	1,369	741	629	330
1976	7,406	5,914	3,258	2,656	1,364	1,492	779	713	355	1,334	698	637	330
1977	6,991	5,441	2,883	2,558	1,284	1,550	784	766	379	1,393	698	695	354
1978	6,202	4,698	2,411	2,287	1,189	1,505	731	774	394	1,330	641	690	360
1979	6,137	4,664	2,405	2,260	1,193	1,473	714	759	362	1,319	636	683	333
1980	7,637	5,884	3,345	2,540	1,291	1,752	922	830	377	1,553	815	738	343
1981	8,273	6,343	3,580	2,762	1,374	1,930	997	933	388	1,731	891	840	357
1982	10,678	8,241	4,846	3,395	1,534	2,437	1,334	1,104	443	2,142	1,167	975	396
1983	10,717	8,128	4,859	3,270	1,387	2,588	1,401	1,187	441	2,272	1,213	1,059	392
1984	8,539	6,372	3,600	2,772	1,116	2,167	1,144	1,022	384	1,914	1,003	911	353
1985	8,312	6,191	3,426	2,765	1,074	2,121	1,095	1,026	394	1,864	951	913	357
1986	8,237	6,140	3,433	2,708	1,070	2,097	1,097	999	383	1,840	946	894	347
1987	7,425	5,501	3,132	2,369	995	1,924	969	955	353	1,684	826	858	312
1988	6,701	4,944	2,766	2,177	910	1,757	888	869	316	1,547	771	776	288
1989	6,528	4,770	2,636	2,135	863	1,757	889	868	331	1,544	773	772	300
1990	7,047	5,186	2,935	2,251	903	1,860	971	889	308	1,565	806	758	268
1991	8,628	6,560	3,859	2,701	1,029	2,068	1,087	981	330	1,723	890	833	280
1992	9,613	7,169	4,209	2,959	1,037	2,444	1,314	1,130	390	2,011	1,067	944	324
1993	8,940	6,655	3,828	2,827	992	2,285	1,227	1,058	373	1,844	971	872	313
1994	7,996	5,892	3,275	2,617	960	2,104	1,092	1,011	360	1,666	848	818	300
1995	7,404	5,459	2,999	2,460	952	1,945	984	961	394	1,538	762	777	325
1996	7,236	5,300	2,896	2,404	939	1,936	984	952	367	1,592	808	784	310
1997	6,739	4,836	2,641	2,195	912	1,903	935	967	359	1,560	747	813	302
1996:Jan	7,522	5,520	2,982	2,538	1,011	1,956	971	985	354	1,578	779	799	304
Feb	7,345	5,444	2,974	2,470	954	1,878	1,009	869	344	1,509	798	711	276
Mar	7,355	5,397	3,006	2,391	956	1,940	1,033	907	367	1,590	841	749	301
Apr	7,348	5,407	2,972	2,435	950	1,933	1,024	909	375	1,589	816	773	320
May	7,359	5,538	3,028	2,510	951	1,905	998	907	356	1,547	802	745	292
June	7,095	5,214	2,889	2,325	911	1,875	941	934	325	1,520	768	752	279
July	7,347	5,297	2,933	2,364	921	1,992	1,035	957	364	1,624	859	765	318
Aug	6,916	5,027	2,710	2,317	911	1,895	905	990	392	1,627	779	848	356
Sept	7,003	5,057	2,808	2,249	886	1,950	985	965	366	1,616	833	783	308
Oct	7,079	5,097	2,779	2,318	915	2,003	986	1,017	404	1,650	827	823	336
Nov	7,231	5,302	2,839	2,463	964	1,952	985	967	376	1,645	847	798	310
Dec	7,161	5,266	2,761	2,505	946	1,938	925	1,013	381	1,607	746	861	315
1997:Jan	7,188	5,157	2,842	2,315	944	1,991	988	1,003	389	1,644	805	839	328
Feb	7,174	5,115	2,766	2,349	985	2,037	962	1,075	398	1,698	782	916	333
Mar	7,080	5,069	2,746	2,323	945	1,996	995	1,001	373	1,622	795	827	314
Apr	6,768	4,846	2,657	2,189	909	1,915	960	955	347	1,525	745	780	292
May	6,566	4,656	2,427	2,229	865	1,975	931	1,044	387	1,587	732	855	306
June	6,814	4,880	2,669	2,211	961	1,923	973	950	339	1,590	791	799	285
July	6,633	4,771	2,607	2,164	968	1,814	882	932	313	1,484	718	766	266
Aug	6,657	4,837	2,631	2,206	942	1,824	891	933	334	1,491	702	789	280
Sept	6,678	4,854	2,626	2,228	943	1,835	907	928	350	1,511	714	797	302
Oct	6,496	4,721	2,642	2,079	897	1,781	900	881	319	1,488	713	775	274
Nov	6,289	4,469	2,460	2,009	836	1,843	884	959	378	1,510	696	814	314
Dec	6,392	4,534	2,518	2,016	757	1,892	943	949	376	1,560	755	805	331

Note.—See footnote 5 and Note, Table B–35.

Source: Department of Labor, Bureau of Labor Statistics.

TABLE B–39.—*Civilian labor force participation rate and employment/population ratio, 1950–97*

[Percent;[1] monthly data seasonally adjusted]

Year or month	Labor force participation rate							Employment/population ratio						
	All civilian workers	Males	Fe-males	Both sexes 16–19 years	White	Black and other	Black	All civilian workers	Males	Fe-males	Both sexes 16–19 years	White	Black and other	Black
1950	59.2	86.4	33.9	51.8	......	......	......	56.1	82.0	32.0	45.5	......	......	......
1951	59.2	86.3	34.6	52.2	......	......	......	57.3	84.0	33.1	47.9	......	......	......
1952	59.0	86.3	34.7	51.3	......	......	......	57.3	83.9	33.4	46.9	......	......	......
1953	58.9	86.0	34.4	50.2	......	......	......	57.1	83.6	33.3	46.4	......	......	......
1954	58.8	85.5	34.6	48.3	58.2	64.0	......	55.5	81.0	32.5	42.3	55.2	58.0	......
1955	59.3	85.4	35.7	48.9	58.7	64.2	......	56.7	81.8	34.0	43.5	56.5	58.7	......
1956	60.0	85.5	36.9	50.9	59.4	64.9	......	57.5	82.3	35.1	45.3	57.3	59.5	......
1957	59.6	84.8	36.9	49.6	59.1	64.4	......	57.1	81.3	35.1	43.9	56.8	59.3	......
1958	59.5	84.2	37.1	47.4	58.9	64.8	......	55.4	78.5	34.5	39.9	55.3	56.7	......
1959	59.3	83.7	37.1	46.7	58.7	64.3	......	56.0	79.3	35.0	39.9	55.9	57.5	......
1960	59.4	83.3	37.7	47.5	58.8	64.5	......	56.1	78.9	35.5	40.5	55.9	57.9	......
1961	59.3	82.9	38.1	46.9	58.8	64.1	......	55.4	77.6	35.4	39.1	55.3	56.2	......
1962	58.8	82.0	37.9	46.1	58.3	63.2	......	55.5	77.7	35.6	39.4	55.4	56.3	......
1963	58.7	81.4	38.3	45.2	58.2	63.0	......	55.4	77.1	35.8	37.4	55.3	56.2	......
1964	58.7	81.0	38.7	44.5	58.2	63.1	......	55.7	77.3	36.3	37.3	55.5	57.0	......
1965	58.9	80.7	39.3	45.7	58.4	62.9	......	56.2	77.5	37.1	38.9	56.0	57.8	......
1966	59.2	80.4	40.3	48.2	58.7	63.0	......	56.9	77.9	38.3	42.1	56.8	58.4	......
1967	59.6	80.4	41.1	48.4	59.2	62.8	......	57.3	78.0	39.0	42.2	57.2	58.2	......
1968	59.6	80.1	41.6	48.3	59.3	62.2	......	57.5	77.8	39.6	42.2	57.4	58.0	......
1969	60.1	79.8	42.7	49.4	59.9	62.1	......	58.0	77.6	40.7	43.4	58.0	58.1	......
1970	60.4	79.7	43.3	49.9	60.2	61.8	......	57.4	76.2	40.8	42.3	57.5	56.8	......
1971	60.2	79.1	43.4	49.7	60.1	60.9	......	56.6	74.9	40.4	41.3	56.8	54.9	......
1972	60.4	78.9	43.9	51.9	60.4	60.2	59.9	57.0	75.0	41.0	43.5	57.4	54.1	53.7
1973	60.8	78.8	44.7	53.7	60.8	60.5	60.2	57.8	75.5	42.0	45.9	58.2	55.0	54.5
1974	61.3	78.7	45.7	54.8	61.4	60.3	59.8	57.8	74.9	42.6	46.0	58.3	54.3	53.5
1975	61.2	77.9	46.3	54.0	61.5	59.6	58.8	56.1	71.7	42.0	43.3	56.7	51.4	50.1
1976	61.6	77.5	47.3	54.5	61.8	59.8	59.0	56.8	72.0	43.2	44.2	57.5	52.0	50.8
1977	62.3	77.7	48.4	56.0	62.5	60.4	59.8	57.9	72.8	44.5	46.1	58.6	52.5	51.4
1978	63.2	77.9	50.0	57.8	63.3	62.2	61.5	59.3	73.8	46.4	48.3	60.0	54.7	53.6
1979	63.7	77.8	50.9	57.9	63.9	62.2	61.4	59.9	73.8	47.5	48.5	60.6	55.2	53.8
1980	63.8	77.4	51.5	56.7	64.1	61.7	61.0	59.2	72.0	47.7	46.6	60.0	53.6	52.3
1981	63.9	77.0	52.1	55.4	64.3	61.3	60.8	59.0	71.3	48.0	44.6	60.0	52.6	51.3
1982	64.0	76.6	52.6	54.1	64.3	61.6	61.0	57.8	69.0	47.7	41.5	58.8	50.9	49.4
1983	64.0	76.4	52.9	53.5	64.3	62.1	61.5	57.9	68.8	48.0	41.5	58.9	51.0	49.5
1984	64.4	76.4	53.6	53.9	64.6	62.6	62.2	59.5	70.7	49.5	43.7	60.5	53.6	52.3
1985	64.8	76.3	54.5	54.5	65.0	63.3	62.9	60.1	70.9	50.4	44.4	61.0	54.7	53.4
1986	65.3	76.3	55.3	54.7	65.5	63.7	63.3	60.7	71.0	51.4	44.6	61.5	55.4	54.1
1987	65.6	76.2	56.0	54.7	65.8	64.3	63.8	61.5	71.5	52.5	45.5	62.3	56.8	55.6
1988	65.9	76.2	56.6	55.3	66.2	64.0	63.8	62.3	72.0	53.4	46.8	63.1	57.4	56.3
1989	66.5	76.4	57.4	55.9	66.7	64.7	64.2	63.0	72.5	54.3	47.5	63.8	58.2	56.9
1990	66.5	76.4	57.5	53.7	66.9	64.4	64.0	62.8	72.0	54.3	45.3	63.7	57.9	56.7
1991	66.2	75.8	57.4	51.6	66.6	63.8	63.3	61.7	70.4	53.7	42.0	62.6	56.7	55.4
1992	66.4	75.8	57.8	51.3	66.8	64.6	63.9	61.5	69.8	53.8	41.0	62.4	56.4	54.9
1993	66.3	75.4	57.9	51.5	66.8	63.8	63.2	61.7	70.0	54.1	41.7	62.7	56.3	55.0
1994	66.6	75.1	58.8	52.7	67.1	63.9	63.4	62.5	70.4	55.3	43.4	63.5	57.2	56.1
1995	66.6	75.0	58.9	53.5	67.1	64.3	63.7	62.9	70.8	55.6	44.2	63.8	58.1	57.1
1996	66.8	74.9	59.3	52.3	67.2	64.6	64.1	63.2	70.9	56.0	43.5	64.1	58.6	57.4
1997	67.1	75.0	59.8	51.6	67.5	65.2	64.7	63.8	71.3	56.8	43.4	64.6	59.4	58.2
1996:Jan	66.5	74.7	58.9	52.7	66.9	64.2	64.0	62.7	70.6	55.5	43.4	63.6	58.1	57.2
Feb	66.6	74.9	59.0	52.6	67.2	63.7	63.4	63.0	70.7	55.8	43.7	63.9	57.8	57.0
Mar	66.7	75.0	59.0	52.3	67.1	64.1	63.9	63.0	70.7	55.9	43.3	63.9	58.1	57.1
Apr	66.7	74.9	59.1	52.4	67.1	64.3	63.9	63.0	70.7	55.9	43.6	63.9	58.3	57.1
May	66.7	75.0	59.1	52.9	67.2	64.5	64.3	63.1	70.9	55.9	44.1	63.9	58.6	57.7
June	66.7	75.0	59.0	51.9	67.1	64.4	63.8	63.2	71.0	55.9	43.6	64.0	58.6	57.3
July	66.9	75.2	59.2	52.1	67.2	65.0	64.5	63.2	71.0	56.0	43.5	64.1	58.8	57.6
Aug	66.7	74.7	59.3	51.1	67.0	65.0	64.5	63.2	71.0	56.1	42.4	64.1	59.1	57.6
Sept	66.8	74.8	59.4	52.6	67.3	64.7	63.9	63.3	70.9	56.4	44.3	64.3	58.7	57.0
Oct	67.0	75.0	59.6	52.7	67.4	65.0	64.5	63.5	71.1	56.4	43.9	64.3	58.8	57.5
Nov	67.0	74.9	59.7	51.9	67.4	64.9	64.5	63.4	71.0	56.4	43.0	64.3	58.9	57.6
Dec	67.0	74.9	59.7	52.2	67.4	64.7	64.3	63.4	71.1	56.4	43.4	64.3	58.8	57.5
1997:Jan	67.1	75.1	59.7	51.9	67.5	64.9	64.5	63.5	71.2	56.5	43.1	64.4	58.8	57.6
Feb	67.0	75.0	59.7	52.6	67.5	64.8	64.6	63.5	71.2	56.4	43.5	64.4	58.7	57.5
Mar	67.2	75.1	59.9	52.4	67.6	65.3	64.6	63.7	71.3	56.7	43.8	64.6	59.2	57.8
Apr	67.1	75.1	59.8	52.0	67.5	64.9	64.3	63.8	71.4	56.8	43.9	64.7	59.1	58.0
May	67.1	74.9	59.8	51.9	67.5	65.2	64.4	63.8	71.5	56.7	43.8	64.7	59.2	57.8
June	67.1	75.0	59.8	51.2	67.5	65.0	64.3	63.7	71.3	56.8	42.8	64.6	59.2	57.7
July	67.1	74.9	59.8	51.4	67.4	65.1	64.7	63.8	71.3	56.9	43.0	64.6	59.7	58.5
Aug	67.1	74.9	59.8	51.0	67.4	65.7	65.4	63.8	71.3	56.9	42.7	64.6	60.2	59.2
Sept	67.0	74.7	59.9	51.0	67.4	65.5	65.2	63.7	71.1	56.9	42.7	64.5	60.0	58.9
Oct	66.9	74.8	59.7	50.9	67.4	64.9	64.5	63.8	71.2	56.9	43.0	64.6	59.6	58.3
Nov	67.1	75.1	59.7	51.8	67.5	65.4	64.8	64.0	71.7	56.9	43.9	64.9	59.8	58.5
Dec	67.2	75.0	60.0	51.6	67.5	65.6	65.0	64.1	71.5	57.2	44.3	64.9	60.0	58.5

[1] Civilian labor force or civilian employment as percent of civilian noninstitutional population in group specified.

Note.—Data relate to persons 16 years of age and over.
See footnote 5 and Note, Table B–35.

Source: Department of Labor, Bureau of Labor Statistics.

TABLE B–40.—*Civilian labor force participation rate by demographic characteristic, 1954–97*

[Percent;[1] monthly data seasonally adjusted]

Year or month	All civilian workers	White Total	White Males Total	White Males 16–19 years	White Males 20 years and over	White Females Total	White Females 16–19 years	White Females 20 years and over	Black and other/Black Total	Males Total	Males 16–19 years	Males 20 years and over	Females Total	Females 16–19 years	Females 20 years and over
									Black and other						
1954	58.8	58.2	85.6	57.6	87.8	33.3	40.6	32.7	64.0	85.2	61.2	87.1	46.1	31.0	47.7
1955	59.3	58.7	85.4	58.6	87.5	34.5	40.7	34.0	64.2	85.1	60.8	87.8	46.1	32.7	47.5
1956	60.0	59.4	85.6	60.4	87.6	35.7	43.1	35.1	64.9	85.1	61.5	87.8	47.3	36.3	48.4
1957	59.6	59.1	84.8	59.2	86.9	35.7	42.2	35.2	64.4	84.2	58.8	87.0	47.1	33.2	48.6
1958	59.5	58.9	84.3	56.5	86.6	35.8	40.1	35.5	64.8	84.1	57.3	87.1	48.0	31.9	49.8
1959	59.3	58.7	83.8	55.9	86.3	36.0	39.6	35.6	64.3	83.4	55.5	86.7	47.7	28.2	49.8
1960	59.4	58.8	83.4	55.9	86.0	36.5	40.3	36.2	64.5	83.0	57.6	86.2	48.2	32.9	49.9
1961	59.3	58.8	83.0	54.5	85.7	36.9	40.6	36.6	64.1	82.2	55.8	85.5	48.3	32.8	50.1
1962	58.8	58.3	82.1	53.8	84.9	36.7	39.8	36.5	63.2	80.8	53.5	84.2	48.0	33.1	49.6
1963	58.7	58.2	81.5	53.1	84.4	37.2	38.7	37.0	63.0	80.2	51.5	83.9	48.1	32.6	49.9
1964	58.7	58.2	81.1	52.7	84.2	37.5	37.8	37.5	63.1	80.1	49.9	84.1	48.6	31.7	50.7
1965	58.9	58.4	80.8	54.1	83.9	38.1	39.2	38.0	62.9	79.6	51.3	83.7	48.6	29.5	51.1
1966	59.2	58.7	80.6	55.9	83.6	39.2	42.6	38.8	63.0	79.0	51.4	83.3	49.4	33.5	51.6
1967	59.6	59.2	80.6	56.3	83.5	40.1	42.5	39.8	62.8	78.5	51.1	82.9	49.5	35.2	51.6
1968	59.6	59.3	80.4	55.9	83.2	40.7	43.0	40.4	62.2	77.7	49.7	82.2	49.3	34.8	51.4
1969	60.1	59.9	80.2	56.8	83.0	41.8	44.6	41.5	62.1	76.9	49.6	81.4	49.8	34.6	52.0
1970	60.4	60.2	80.0	57.5	82.8	42.6	45.6	42.2	61.8	76.5	47.4	81.4	49.5	34.1	51.8
1971	60.2	60.1	79.6	57.9	82.3	42.6	45.4	42.3	60.9	74.9	44.7	80.0	49.2	31.2	51.8
1972	60.4	60.4	79.6	60.1	82.0	43.2	48.1	42.7	60.2	73.9	46.0	78.6	48.8	32.3	51.2
									Black						
1972	60.4	60.4	79.6	60.1	82.0	43.2	48.1	42.7	59.9	73.6	46.3	78.5	48.7	32.2	51.2
1973	60.8	60.8	79.4	62.0	81.6	44.1	50.1	43.5	60.2	73.4	45.7	78.4	49.3	34.2	51.6
1974	61.3	61.4	79.4	62.9	81.4	45.2	51.7	44.4	59.8	72.9	46.7	77.6	49.0	33.4	51.4
1975	61.2	61.5	78.7	61.9	80.7	45.9	51.5	45.3	58.8	70.9	42.6	76.0	48.8	34.2	51.1
1976	61.6	61.8	78.4	62.3	80.3	46.9	52.8	46.2	59.0	70.0	41.3	75.4	49.8	32.9	52.5
1977	62.3	62.5	78.5	64.0	80.2	48.0	54.5	47.3	59.8	70.6	43.2	75.6	50.8	32.9	53.6
1978	63.2	63.3	78.6	65.0	80.1	49.4	56.7	48.7	61.5	71.5	44.9	76.2	53.1	37.3	55.5
1979	63.7	63.9	78.6	64.8	80.1	50.5	57.4	49.8	61.4	71.3	43.6	76.3	53.1	36.8	55.4
1980	63.8	64.1	78.2	63.7	79.8	51.2	56.2	50.6	61.0	70.3	43.2	75.1	53.1	34.9	55.6
1981	63.9	64.3	77.9	62.4	79.5	51.9	55.4	51.5	60.8	70.0	41.6	74.5	53.5	34.0	56.0
1982	64.0	64.3	77.4	60.0	79.2	52.4	55.0	52.2	61.0	70.1	39.8	74.7	53.7	33.5	56.2
1983	64.0	64.3	77.1	59.4	78.9	52.7	54.5	52.5	61.5	70.6	39.9	75.2	54.2	33.0	56.8
1984	64.4	64.6	77.1	59.0	78.7	53.3	55.4	53.1	62.2	70.8	41.7	74.8	55.2	35.0	57.6
1985	64.8	65.0	77.0	59.7	78.5	54.1	55.2	54.0	62.9	70.8	44.6	74.4	56.5	37.9	58.6
1986	65.3	65.5	76.9	59.3	78.5	55.0	56.3	54.9	63.3	71.2	43.7	74.8	56.9	39.1	58.9
1987	65.6	65.8	76.8	59.0	78.4	55.7	56.5	55.6	63.8	71.1	43.6	74.7	58.0	39.6	60.0
1988	65.9	66.2	76.9	60.0	78.3	56.4	57.2	56.3	63.8	71.0	43.8	74.6	58.0	37.9	60.1
1989	66.5	66.7	77.1	61.0	78.5	57.2	57.1	57.2	64.2	71.0	44.6	74.4	58.7	40.4	60.6
1990	66.5	66.9	77.1	59.6	78.5	57.4	55.3	57.6	64.0	71.0	40.7	75.0	58.3	36.8	60.6
1991	66.2	66.6	76.5	57.3	78.0	57.4	54.1	57.6	63.3	70.4	37.3	74.6	57.5	33.5	60.0
1992	66.4	66.8	76.5	56.9	78.0	57.7	52.5	58.1	63.9	70.7	40.6	74.3	58.5	35.2	60.8
1993	66.3	66.8	76.2	56.6	77.7	58.0	53.5	58.3	63.2	69.6	39.5	73.2	57.9	34.6	60.2
1994	66.6	67.1	75.9	57.7	77.3	58.9	55.1	59.2	63.4	69.1	40.8	72.5	58.7	36.3	60.9
1995	66.6	67.1	75.7	58.5	77.1	59.0	55.5	59.2	63.7	69.0	40.1	72.5	59.5	39.8	61.4
1996	66.8	67.2	75.8	57.1	77.3	59.1	54.7	59.4	64.1	68.7	39.5	72.3	60.4	38.9	62.6
1997	67.1	67.5	75.9	56.1	77.5	59.5	54.1	59.9	64.7	68.3	37.4	72.2	61.7	39.9	64.0
1996:Jan	66.5	66.9	75.6	58.1	77.0	58.7	54.8	59.0	64.0	68.6	38.8	72.2	60.3	39.6	62.3
Feb	66.6	67.2	75.9	58.0	77.3	59.0	54.9	59.3	63.4	68.4	37.3	72.2	59.3	36.9	61.5
Mar	66.7	67.1	75.8	57.1	77.3	59.0	54.5	59.4	63.9	68.9	40.3	72.4	59.9	39.3	61.9
Apr	66.7	67.1	75.8	57.9	77.2	58.9	53.7	59.3	63.9	68.6	42.2	71.8	60.1	40.3	62.0
May	66.7	67.2	75.9	58.1	77.3	59.1	54.3	59.4	64.3	69.1	41.9	72.4	60.3	40.7	62.3
June	66.7	67.1	75.9	57.3	77.4	58.9	54.3	59.2	63.8	68.1	37.5	71.8	60.2	38.6	62.4
July	66.9	67.2	76.0	57.4	77.5	59.0	54.1	59.4	64.5	69.4	43.3	72.6	60.5	35.3	63.1
Aug	66.7	67.0	75.6	54.6	77.3	59.0	53.7	59.4	64.5	69.1	39.9	72.8	60.8	39.3	63.0
Sept	66.8	67.3	75.8	57.1	77.3	59.2	55.5	59.5	63.9	68.3	37.6	72.2	60.2	38.6	62.4
Oct	67.0	67.4	75.9	57.0	77.5	59.3	55.5	59.6	64.5	68.7	40.1	72.3	61.0	39.7	63.2
Nov	67.0	67.4	75.8	56.0	77.4	59.6	55.8	59.9	64.5	68.9	37.4	72.8	60.9	37.6	63.3
Dec	67.0	67.4	75.8	56.4	77.4	59.6	54.9	59.9	64.3	68.1	37.6	71.8	61.2	40.2	63.4
1997:Jan	67.1	67.5	75.9	55.8	77.6	59.5	54.5	59.8	64.5	68.4	39.7	71.9	61.4	40.5	63.5
Feb	67.0	67.5	75.9	56.1	77.5	59.5	55.1	59.8	64.6	68.1	42.0	71.3	61.7	40.8	63.9
Mar	67.2	67.6	76.0	56.5	77.6	59.6	54.3	60.0	64.6	68.0	38.0	71.8	61.9	42.7	63.8
Apr	67.1	67.5	76.0	56.0	77.6	59.5	55.4	59.8	64.3	67.9	37.4	71.7	61.4	38.5	63.8
May	67.1	67.5	75.8	56.4	77.4	59.6	54.1	60.0	64.4	68.0	37.6	71.7	61.5	37.5	63.9
June	67.1	67.5	75.8	55.6	77.5	59.6	54.4	60.0	64.3	68.5	37.0	72.4	61.0	36.0	63.5
July	67.1	67.4	75.8	55.5	77.4	59.5	55.0	59.9	64.7	68.4	34.9	72.5	61.7	38.4	64.1
Aug	67.1	67.4	75.7	55.2	77.4	59.5	53.6	60.0	65.4	69.3	36.6	73.3	62.3	39.8	64.6
Sept	67.0	67.4	75.7	55.7	77.3	59.6	53.8	60.0	65.2	68.6	36.0	72.6	62.4	40.6	64.6
Oct	66.9	67.4	75.7	56.8	77.2	59.5	52.8	60.0	64.5	68.3	37.0	72.3	61.4	39.4	63.6
Nov	67.1	67.5	76.0	58.1	77.5	59.4	53.1	59.9	64.8	68.3	36.6	72.1	61.9	41.7	63.9
Dec	67.2	67.5	75.9	56.3	77.5	59.7	53.6	60.1	65.0	68.1	35.8	72.0	62.4	43.6	64.4

[1] Civilian labor force as percent of civilian noninstitutional population in group specified.

Note.—See Note, Table B–39.

Source: Department of Labor, Bureau of Labor Statistics.

TABLE B–41.—*Civilian employment/population ratio by demographic characteristic, 1954–97*

[Percent;[1] monthly data seasonally adjusted]

Year or month	All civilian workers	White							Black and other or black						
		Total	Males			Females			Total	Males			Females		
			Total	16–19 years	20 years and over	Total	16–19 years	20 years and over		Total	16–19 years	20 years and over	Total	16–19 years	20 years and over
									Black and other						
1954	55.5	55.2	81.5	49.9	84.0	31.4	36.4	31.1	58.0	76.5	52.4	79.2	41.9	24.7	43.7
1955	56.7	56.5	82.2	52.0	84.7	33.0	37.0	32.7	58.7	77.6	52.7	80.4	42.2	26.4	43.9
1956	57.5	57.3	82.7	54.1	85.0	34.2	38.9	33.8	59.5	78.4	52.2	81.3	43.0	28.0	44.7
1957	57.1	56.8	81.8	52.4	84.1	34.2	38.2	33.9	59.3	77.2	48.0	80.5	43.7	26.5	45.5
1958	55.4	55.3	79.2	47.6	81.8	33.6	35.0	33.5	56.7	72.5	42.0	76.0	42.8	22.8	45.0
1959	56.0	55.9	79.9	48.1	82.8	34.0	34.8	34.0	57.5	73.8	41.4	77.6	43.2	20.3	45.7
1960	56.1	55.9	79.4	48.1	82.4	34.6	35.1	34.5	57.9	74.1	43.8	77.9	43.6	24.8	45.8
1961	55.4	55.3	78.2	45.9	81.4	34.5	34.6	34.5	56.2	71.7	41.0	75.5	42.6	23.2	44.8
1962	55.5	55.4	78.4	46.4	81.5	34.7	34.8	34.7	56.3	72.0	41.7	75.7	42.7	23.1	44.9
1963	55.4	55.3	77.7	44.7	81.1	35.0	32.9	35.2	56.2	71.8	37.4	76.2	42.7	21.3	45.2
1964	55.7	55.5	77.8	45.0	81.3	35.5	32.2	35.8	57.0	72.9	37.8	77.7	43.4	21.8	46.1
1965	56.2	56.0	77.9	47.1	81.5	36.2	33.7	36.5	57.8	73.7	39.4	78.7	44.1	20.2	47.3
1966	56.9	56.8	78.3	50.1	81.7	37.5	37.5	37.5	58.4	74.0	40.5	79.2	45.1	23.1	48.2
1967	57.3	57.2	78.4	50.2	81.7	38.3	37.7	38.3	58.2	73.8	38.8	79.4	45.0	24.8	47.9
1968	57.5	57.4	78.3	50.3	81.6	38.9	37.8	39.1	58.0	73.3	38.7	78.9	45.2	24.7	48.2
1969	58.0	58.0	78.2	51.1	81.4	40.1	39.5	40.1	58.1	72.8	39.0	78.4	45.9	25.1	48.9
1970	57.4	57.5	76.8	49.6	80.1	40.3	39.5	40.4	56.8	70.9	35.5	76.8	44.9	22.4	48.2
1971	56.6	56.8	75.7	49.2	79.0	39.9	38.6	40.1	54.9	68.1	31.8	74.2	43.9	20.2	47.3
1972	57.0	57.4	76.0	51.5	79.0	40.7	41.3	40.6	54.1	67.3	32.4	73.2	43.3	19.9	46.7
									Black						
1972	57.0	57.4	76.0	51.5	79.0	40.7	41.3	40.6	53.7	66.8	31.6	73.0	43.0	19.2	46.5
1973	57.8	58.2	76.5	54.3	79.2	41.8	43.6	41.6	54.5	67.5	32.8	73.7	43.8	22.0	47.2
1974	57.8	58.3	75.9	54.4	78.6	42.4	44.3	42.2	53.5	65.8	31.4	71.9	43.5	20.9	46.9
1975	56.1	56.7	73.0	50.6	75.7	42.0	42.5	41.9	50.1	60.6	26.3	66.5	41.6	20.2	44.9
1976	56.8	57.5	73.4	51.5	76.0	43.2	44.2	43.1	50.8	60.6	25.8	66.8	42.8	19.2	46.4
1977	57.9	58.6	74.1	54.4	76.5	44.5	45.9	44.4	51.4	61.4	26.4	67.5	43.3	18.5	47.0
1978	59.3	60.0	75.0	56.3	77.2	46.3	48.5	46.1	53.6	63.3	28.5	69.1	45.8	22.1	49.3
1979	59.9	60.6	75.1	55.7	77.3	47.5	49.4	47.3	53.8	63.4	28.7	69.1	46.0	22.4	49.3
1980	59.2	60.0	73.4	53.4	75.6	47.8	47.9	47.8	52.3	60.4	27.0	65.8	45.7	21.0	49.1
1981	59.0	60.0	72.8	51.3	75.1	48.3	46.2	48.5	51.3	59.1	24.6	64.5	45.1	19.7	48.5
1982	57.8	58.8	70.6	47.0	73.0	48.1	44.6	48.4	49.4	56.0	20.3	61.4	44.2	17.7	47.5
1983	57.9	58.9	70.4	47.4	72.6	48.5	44.5	48.9	49.5	56.3	20.4	61.6	44.1	17.0	47.4
1984	59.5	60.5	72.1	49.1	74.3	49.8	47.0	50.0	52.3	59.2	23.9	64.1	46.7	20.1	49.8
1985	60.1	61.0	72.3	49.9	74.3	50.7	47.1	51.0	53.4	60.0	26.3	64.6	48.1	23.1	50.9
1986	60.7	61.5	72.3	49.6	74.3	51.7	47.9	52.0	54.1	60.6	26.5	65.1	48.8	23.8	51.6
1987	61.5	62.3	72.7	49.9	74.7	52.8	49.0	53.1	55.6	62.0	28.5	66.4	50.3	25.8	53.0
1988	62.3	63.1	73.2	51.7	75.1	53.8	50.2	54.0	56.3	62.7	29.4	67.1	51.2	25.8	53.9
1989	63.0	63.8	73.7	52.6	75.4	54.6	50.5	54.9	56.9	62.8	30.4	67.0	52.0	27.1	54.6
1990	62.8	63.7	73.3	51.0	75.1	54.7	48.3	55.2	56.7	62.6	27.7	67.1	51.9	25.8	54.7
1991	61.7	62.6	71.6	47.2	73.5	54.2	45.9	54.8	55.4	61.3	23.8	65.9	50.6	21.5	53.6
1992	61.5	62.4	71.1	46.4	73.1	54.2	44.2	54.9	54.9	59.9	23.6	64.3	50.8	22.1	53.6
1993	61.7	62.7	71.4	46.6	73.3	54.6	45.7	55.2	55.0	60.0	23.6	64.3	50.9	21.6	53.8
1994	62.5	63.5	71.8	48.3	73.6	55.8	47.5	56.4	56.1	60.8	25.4	65.0	52.3	24.5	55.0
1995	62.9	63.8	72.0	49.4	73.8	56.1	48.1	56.7	57.1	61.7	25.2	66.1	53.4	26.1	56.1
1996	63.2	64.1	72.3	48.2	74.2	56.3	47.6	57.0	57.4	61.1	24.9	65.5	54.4	27.1	57.1
1997	63.8	64.6	72.7	48.1	74.7	57.0	47.2	57.8	58.2	61.4	23.7	66.1	55.6	28.5	58.4
1996: Jan	62.7	63.6	71.9	48.6	73.8	55.8	47.0	56.4	57.2	61.1	24.6	65.6	54.1	27.4	56.8
Feb	63.0	63.9	72.2	49.0	74.1	56.1	47.6	56.8	57.0	60.8	25.4	65.2	53.8	24.9	56.7
Mar	63.0	63.9	72.1	48.0	74.0	56.3	47.3	56.9	57.1	60.9	26.1	65.1	54.1	27.6	56.7
Apr	63.0	63.9	72.1	48.9	74.0	56.1	46.5	56.8	57.1	60.8	27.3	64.9	54.1	27.7	56.8
May	63.1	63.9	72.2	49.0	74.0	56.2	47.3	56.8	57.7	61.5	28.8	65.5	54.6	28.8	57.2
June	63.2	64.0	72.4	49.0	74.2	56.2	47.2	56.8	57.3	60.8	24.3	65.3	54.4	28.0	57.1
July	63.2	64.1	72.4	48.3	74.3	56.3	47.7	56.9	57.6	61.2	24.3	65.8	54.7	27.1	57.5
Aug	63.2	64.1	72.3	46.3	74.4	56.3	46.7	57.0	57.6	61.8	24.5	66.4	54.3	24.9	57.3
Sept	63.4	64.3	72.4	48.7	74.3	56.7	49.0	57.2	57.0	60.5	23.9	65.1	54.2	26.8	57.0
Oct	63.5	64.3	72.5	48.4	74.5	56.7	48.9	57.2	57.5	61.0	24.6	65.5	54.8	27.2	57.6
Nov	63.4	64.3	72.3	47.1	74.3	56.8	48.6	57.3	57.6	61.0	22.0	65.8	54.8	26.9	57.7
Dec	63.4	64.3	72.5	47.9	74.5	56.7	47.6	57.3	57.5	61.1	23.3	65.7	54.7	28.1	57.4
1997: Jan	63.5	64.4	72.5	47.4	74.5	56.8	47.3	57.5	57.6	60.8	23.4	65.5	55.0	29.3	57.6
Feb	63.5	64.4	72.5	47.7	74.6	56.8	47.2	57.5	57.5	60.8	26.5	65.0	54.8	28.4	57.5
Mar	63.7	64.6	72.7	48.0	74.7	56.9	47.3	57.6	57.8	60.6	22.6	65.4	55.6	32.2	58.0
Apr	63.8	64.7	72.8	47.8	74.8	57.0	48.6	57.6	58.0	60.9	23.3	65.7	55.5	28.4	58.3
May	63.8	64.7	72.9	49.0	74.8	57.0	47.2	57.8	57.8	61.1	24.6	65.7	55.0	25.0	58.1
June	63.7	64.6	72.6	46.8	74.7	57.1	47.5	57.8	57.7	61.1	22.5	65.9	54.9	26.8	57.8
July	63.8	64.6	72.6	47.2	74.7	57.1	47.5	57.8	58.5	61.7	22.8	66.5	55.9	28.4	58.7
Aug	63.8	64.6	72.5	46.8	74.6	57.0	46.5	57.8	59.2	62.8	24.2	67.5	56.3	29.0	59.1
Sept	63.7	64.5	72.5	47.7	74.5	57.0	46.4	57.8	58.9	61.9	22.5	66.8	56.4	29.0	59.2
Oct	63.8	64.6	72.5	48.7	74.4	57.1	46.3	57.9	58.3	61.8	25.9	66.3	55.5	28.0	58.3
Nov	64.0	64.9	73.0	50.6	74.9	57.1	46.9	57.8	58.5	61.9	23.8	66.5	55.8	28.4	58.6
Dec	64.1	64.9	72.8	50.0	74.7	57.4	47.6	58.1	58.5	61.1	22.9	65.8	56.4	29.2	59.2

[1] Civilian employment as percent of civilian noninstitutional population in group specified.

Note.—Data relate to persons 16 years of age and over.

See footnote 5 and Note, Table B–35.

Source: Department of Labor, Bureau of Labor Statistics.

TABLE B–42.—*Civilian unemployment rate, 1950–97*

[Percent;[1] monthly data seasonally adjusted]

Year or month	All civilian workers	Males			Females			Both sexes 16–19 years	White	Black and other	Black	Experienced wage and salary workers	Married men, spouse present[2]	Women who maintain families
		Total	16–19 years	20 years and over	Total	16–19 years	20 years and over							
1950	5.3	5.1	12.7	4.7	5.7	11.4	5.1	12.2	4.9	9.0	....	6.0	4.6	....
1951	3.3	2.8	8.1	2.5	4.4	8.3	4.0	8.2	3.1	5.3	....	3.7	1.5	....
1952	3.0	2.8	8.9	2.4	3.6	8.0	3.2	8.5	2.8	5.4	....	3.4	1.4	....
1953	2.9	2.8	7.9	2.5	3.3	7.2	2.9	7.6	2.7	4.5	....	3.2	1.7	....
1954	5.5	5.3	13.5	4.9	6.0	11.4	5.5	12.6	5.0	9.9	....	6.2	4.0	....
1955	4.4	4.2	11.6	3.8	4.9	10.2	4.4	11.0	3.9	8.7	....	4.8	2.6	....
1956	4.1	3.8	11.1	3.4	4.8	11.2	4.2	11.1	3.6	8.3	....	4.4	2.3	....
1957	4.3	4.1	12.4	3.6	4.7	10.6	4.1	11.6	3.8	7.9	....	4.6	2.8	....
1958	6.8	6.8	17.1	6.2	6.8	14.3	6.1	15.9	6.1	12.6	....	7.3	5.1	....
1959	5.5	5.2	15.3	4.7	5.9	13.5	5.2	14.6	4.8	10.7	....	5.7	3.6	....
1960	5.5	5.4	15.3	4.7	5.9	13.9	5.1	14.7	5.0	10.2	....	5.7	3.7	....
1961	6.7	6.4	17.1	5.7	7.2	16.3	6.3	16.8	6.0	12.4	....	6.8	4.6	....
1962	5.5	5.2	14.7	4.6	6.2	14.6	5.4	14.7	4.9	10.9	....	5.6	3.6	....
1963	5.7	5.2	17.2	4.5	6.5	17.2	5.4	17.2	5.0	10.8	....	5.6	3.4	....
1964	5.2	4.6	15.8	3.9	6.2	16.6	5.2	16.2	4.6	9.6	....	5.0	2.8	....
1965	4.5	4.0	14.1	3.2	5.5	15.7	4.5	14.8	4.1	8.1	....	4.3	2.4	....
1966	3.8	3.2	11.7	2.5	4.8	14.1	3.8	12.8	3.4	7.3	....	3.5	1.9	....
1967	3.8	3.1	12.3	2.3	5.2	13.5	4.2	12.9	3.4	7.4	....	3.6	1.8	4.9
1968	3.6	2.9	11.6	2.2	4.8	14.0	3.8	12.7	3.2	6.7	....	3.4	1.6	4.4
1969	3.5	2.8	11.4	2.1	4.7	13.3	3.7	12.2	3.1	6.4	....	3.3	1.5	4.4
1970	4.9	4.4	15.0	3.5	5.9	15.6	4.8	15.3	4.5	8.2	....	4.8	2.6	5.4
1971	5.9	5.3	16.6	4.4	6.9	17.2	5.7	16.9	5.4	9.9	....	5.7	3.2	7.3
1972	5.6	5.0	15.9	4.0	6.6	16.7	5.4	16.2	5.1	10.0	10.4	5.3	2.8	7.2
1973	4.9	4.2	13.9	3.3	6.0	15.3	4.9	14.5	4.3	9.0	9.4	4.5	2.3	7.1
1974	5.6	4.9	15.6	3.8	6.7	16.6	5.5	16.0	5.0	9.9	10.5	5.3	2.7	7.0
1975	8.5	7.9	20.1	6.8	9.3	19.7	8.0	19.9	7.8	13.8	14.8	8.2	5.1	10.0
1976	7.7	7.1	19.2	5.9	8.6	18.7	7.4	19.0	7.0	13.1	14.0	7.3	4.2	10.1
1977	7.1	6.3	17.3	5.2	8.2	18.3	7.0	17.8	6.2	13.1	14.0	6.6	3.6	9.4
1978	6.1	5.3	15.8	4.3	7.2	17.1	6.0	16.4	5.2	11.9	12.8	5.6	2.8	8.5
1979	5.8	5.1	15.9	4.2	6.8	16.4	5.7	16.1	5.1	11.3	12.3	5.5	2.8	8.3
1980	7.1	6.9	18.3	5.9	7.4	17.2	6.4	17.8	6.3	13.1	14.3	6.9	4.2	9.2
1981	7.6	7.4	20.1	6.3	7.9	19.0	6.8	19.6	6.7	14.2	15.6	7.3	4.3	10.4
1982	9.7	9.9	24.4	8.8	9.4	21.9	8.3	23.2	8.6	17.3	18.9	9.3	6.5	11.7
1983	9.6	9.9	23.3	8.9	9.2	21.3	8.1	22.4	8.4	17.8	19.5	9.2	6.5	12.2
1984	7.5	7.4	19.6	6.6	7.6	18.0	6.8	18.9	6.5	14.4	15.9	7.1	4.6	10.3
1985	7.2	7.0	19.5	6.2	7.4	17.6	6.6	18.6	6.2	13.7	15.1	6.8	4.3	10.4
1986	7.0	6.9	19.0	6.1	7.1	17.6	6.2	18.3	6.0	13.1	14.5	6.6	4.4	9.8
1987	6.2	6.2	17.8	5.4	6.2	15.9	5.4	16.9	5.3	11.6	13.0	5.8	3.9	9.2
1988	5.5	5.5	16.0	4.8	5.6	14.4	4.9	15.3	4.7	10.4	11.7	5.2	3.3	8.1
1989	5.3	5.2	15.9	4.5	5.4	14.0	4.7	15.0	4.5	10.0	11.4	5.0	3.0	8.1
1990	5.6	5.7	16.3	5.0	5.5	14.7	4.9	15.5	4.8	10.1	11.4	5.3	3.4	8.3
1991	6.8	7.2	19.8	6.4	6.4	17.5	5.7	18.7	6.1	11.1	12.5	6.6	4.4	9.3
1992	7.5	7.9	21.5	7.1	7.0	18.6	6.3	20.1	6.6	12.7	14.2	7.2	5.1	10.0
1993	6.9	7.2	20.4	6.4	6.6	17.5	5.9	19.0	6.1	11.7	13.0	6.6	4.4	9.7
1994	6.1	6.2	19.0	5.4	6.0	16.2	5.4	17.6	5.3	10.5	11.5	5.9	3.7	8.9
1995	5.6	5.6	18.4	4.8	5.6	16.1	4.9	17.3	4.9	9.6	10.4	5.4	3.3	8.0
1996	5.4	5.4	18.1	4.6	5.4	15.2	4.8	16.7	4.7	9.3	10.5	5.2	3.0	8.2
1997	4.9	4.9	16.9	4.2	5.0	15.0	4.4	16.0	4.2	8.8	10.0	4.7	2.7	8.1
1996: Jan	5.7	5.6	18.8	4.8	5.8	16.6	5.1	17.7	4.9	9.5	10.5	5.4	3.2	7.9
Feb	5.5	5.6	18.0	4.8	5.4	15.7	4.8	16.9	4.8	9.2	10.1	5.3	3.1	7.4
Mar	5.5	5.6	18.8	4.9	5.4	15.5	4.7	17.2	4.8	9.4	10.6	5.4	3.1	7.4
Apr	5.5	5.6	18.1	4.8	5.4	15.5	4.8	16.9	4.8	9.4	10.6	5.3	3.0	7.6
May	5.5	5.5	17.9	4.8	5.5	15.2	4.9	16.6	4.9	9.2	10.2	5.5	3.0	8.7
June	5.3	5.3	16.8	4.6	5.3	15.0	4.7	15.9	4.6	9.0	10.1	5.1	3.0	7.7
July	5.5	5.5	19.3	4.7	5.4	13.3	4.9	16.5	4.7	9.5	10.7	5.3	3.0	9.0
Aug	5.2	5.0	17.9	4.3	5.3	15.9	4.7	16.9	4.5	9.0	10.7	5.0	2.9	8.5
Sept	5.2	5.3	17.2	4.6	5.2	14.2	4.5	15.8	4.5	9.3	10.7	5.0	3.0	8.4
Oct	5.3	5.2	18.2	4.4	5.4	14.9	4.7	16.6	4.5	9.5	10.8	5.1	2.9	8.5
Nov	5.4	5.3	18.7	4.5	5.5	15.3	4.8	17.0	4.7	9.2	10.7	5.2	3.1	8.7
Dec	5.3	5.1	17.9	4.3	5.5	15.8	4.9	16.8	4.6	9.2	10.5	5.1	2.9	8.5
1997: Jan	5.3	5.3	18.3	4.5	5.3	15.4	4.7	16.9	4.5	9.3	10.7	5.1	2.8	8.7
Feb	5.3	5.1	17.9	4.4	5.5	16.7	4.7	17.3	4.5	9.5	11.0	5.0	2.8	8.8
Mar	5.2	5.1	17.9	4.4	5.3	15.0	4.7	16.5	4.4	9.3	10.5	4.9	2.8	8.7
Apr	5.0	4.9	17.4	4.2	5.0	13.7	4.4	15.6	4.2	8.9	9.9	4.7	2.7	7.9
May	4.8	4.5	15.7	3.9	5.1	15.6	4.5	15.7	4.1	9.2	10.3	4.7	2.7	7.9
June	5.0	5.0	18.2	4.2	5.0	14.7	4.4	16.5	4.3	8.9	10.3	4.8	2.7	8.0
July	4.9	4.8	17.2	4.1	5.0	15.3	4.3	16.3	4.2	8.4	9.6	4.6	2.6	7.6
Aug	4.9	4.8	17.3	4.1	5.0	15.0	4.3	16.2	4.2	8.4	9.5	4.7	2.6	8.0
Sept	4.9	4.8	17.2	4.1	5.0	15.5	4.3	16.4	4.2	8.4	9.6	4.7	2.6	7.8
Oct	4.8	4.8	16.3	4.1	4.7	14.7	4.1	15.5	4.1	8.2	9.6	4.5	2.6	7.8
Nov	4.6	4.5	15.6	3.9	4.7	14.7	4.0	15.2	3.9	8.4	9.7	4.4	2.4	8.1
Dec	4.7	4.7	14.2	4.1	4.6	14.3	4.0	14.3	3.9	8.6	9.9	4.5	2.6	7.7

[1] Unemployed as percent of civilian labor force in group specified.
[2] Data for 1950 are for March; data for 1951–54 are for April.

Note.—Data relate to persons 16 years of age and over.
See footnote 5 and Note, Table B–35.

Source: Department of Labor, Bureau of Labor Statistics.

TABLE B–43.—*Civilian unemployment rate by demographic characteristic, 1954–97*

[Percent;[1] monthly data seasonally adjusted]

Year or month	All civil- ian work- ers	White							Black and other or black						
		Total	Males			Females			Total	Males			Females		
			Total	16–19 years	20 years and over	Total	16–19 years	20 years and over		Total	16–19 years	20 years and over	Total	16–19 years	20 years and over
									Black and other						
1954	5.5	5.0	4.8	13.4	4.4	5.5	10.4	5.1	9.9	10.3	14.4	9.9	9.2	20.6	8.4
1955	4.4	3.9	3.7	11.3	3.3	4.3	9.1	3.9	8.7	8.8	13.4	8.4	8.5	19.2	7.7
1956	4.1	3.6	3.4	10.5	3.0	4.2	9.7	3.7	8.3	7.9	15.0	7.4	8.9	22.8	7.8
1957	4.3	3.8	3.6	11.5	3.2	4.3	9.5	3.8	7.9	8.3	18.4	7.6	7.3	20.2	6.4
1958	6.8	6.1	6.1	15.7	5.5	6.2	12.7	5.6	12.6	13.7	26.8	12.7	10.8	28.4	9.5
1959	5.5	4.8	4.6	14.0	4.1	5.3	12.0	4.7	10.7	11.5	25.2	10.5	9.4	27.7	8.3
1960	5.5	5.0	4.8	14.0	4.2	5.3	12.7	4.6	10.2	10.7	24.0	9.6	9.4	24.8	8.3
1961	6.7	6.0	5.7	15.7	5.1	6.5	14.8	5.7	12.4	12.8	26.8	11.7	11.9	29.2	10.6
1962	5.5	4.9	4.6	13.7	4.0	5.5	12.8	4.7	10.9	10.9	22.0	10.0	11.0	30.2	9.6
1963	5.7	5.0	4.7	15.9	3.9	5.8	15.1	4.8	10.8	10.5	27.3	9.2	11.2	34.7	9.4
1964	5.2	4.6	4.1	14.7	3.4	5.5	14.9	4.6	9.6	8.9	24.3	7.7	10.7	31.6	9.0
1965	4.5	4.1	3.6	12.9	2.9	5.0	14.0	4.0	8.1	7.4	23.3	6.0	9.2	31.7	7.5
1966	3.8	3.4	2.8	10.5	2.2	4.3	12.1	3.3	7.3	6.3	21.3	4.9	8.7	31.3	6.6
1967	3.8	3.4	2.7	10.7	2.1	4.6	11.5	3.8	7.4	6.0	23.9	4.3	9.1	29.6	7.1
1968	3.6	3.2	2.6	10.1	2.0	4.3	12.1	3.4	6.7	5.6	22.1	3.9	8.3	28.7	6.3
1969	3.5	3.1	2.5	10.0	1.9	4.2	11.5	3.4	6.4	5.3	21.4	3.7	7.8	27.6	5.8
1970	4.9	4.5	4.0	13.7	3.2	5.4	13.4	4.4	8.2	7.3	25.0	5.6	9.3	34.5	6.9
1971	5.9	5.4	4.9	15.1	4.0	6.3	15.1	5.3	9.9	9.1	28.8	7.3	10.9	35.4	8.7
1972	5.6	5.1	4.5	14.2	3.6	5.9	14.2	4.9	10.0	8.9	29.7	6.9	11.4	38.4	8.8
									Black						
1972	5.6	5.1	4.5	14.2	3.6	5.9	14.2	4.9	10.4	9.3	31.7	7.0	11.8	40.5	9.0
1973	4.9	4.3	3.8	12.3	3.0	5.3	13.0	4.3	9.4	8.0	27.8	6.0	11.1	36.1	8.6
1974	5.6	5.0	4.4	13.5	3.5	6.1	14.5	5.1	10.5	9.8	33.1	7.4	11.3	37.4	8.8
1975	8.5	7.8	7.2	18.3	6.2	8.6	17.4	7.5	14.8	14.8	38.1	12.5	14.8	41.0	12.2
1976	7.7	7.0	6.4	17.3	5.4	7.9	16.4	6.8	14.0	13.7	37.5	11.4	14.3	41.6	11.7
1977	7.1	6.2	5.5	15.0	4.7	7.3	15.9	6.2	14.0	13.3	39.2	10.7	14.9	43.4	12.3
1978	6.1	5.2	4.6	13.5	3.7	6.2	14.4	5.2	12.8	11.8	36.7	9.3	13.8	40.8	11.2
1979	5.8	5.1	4.5	13.9	3.6	5.9	14.0	5.0	12.3	11.4	34.2	9.3	13.3	39.1	10.9
1980	7.1	6.3	6.1	16.2	5.3	6.5	14.8	5.6	14.3	14.5	37.5	12.4	14.0	39.8	11.9
1981	7.6	6.7	6.5	17.9	5.6	6.9	16.6	5.9	15.6	15.7	40.7	13.5	15.6	42.2	13.4
1982	9.7	8.6	8.8	21.7	7.8	8.3	19.0	7.3	18.9	20.1	48.9	17.8	17.6	47.1	15.4
1983	9.6	8.4	8.8	20.2	7.9	7.9	18.3	6.9	19.5	20.3	48.8	18.1	18.6	48.2	16.5
1984	7.5	6.5	6.4	16.8	5.7	6.5	15.2	5.8	15.9	16.4	42.7	14.3	15.4	42.6	13.5
1985	7.2	6.2	6.1	16.5	5.4	6.4	14.8	5.7	15.1	15.3	41.0	13.2	14.9	39.2	13.1
1986	7.0	6.0	6.0	16.3	5.3	6.1	14.9	5.4	14.5	14.8	39.3	12.9	14.2	39.2	12.4
1987	6.2	5.3	5.4	15.5	4.8	5.2	13.4	4.6	13.0	12.7	34.4	11.1	13.2	34.9	11.6
1988	5.5	4.7	4.7	13.9	4.1	4.7	12.3	4.1	11.7	11.7	32.7	10.1	11.7	32.0	10.4
1989	5.3	4.5	4.5	13.7	3.9	4.5	11.5	4.0	11.4	11.5	31.9	10.0	11.4	33.0	9.8
1990	5.6	4.8	4.9	14.3	4.3	4.7	12.6	4.1	11.4	11.9	31.9	10.4	10.9	29.9	9.7
1991	6.8	6.1	6.5	17.6	5.8	5.6	15.2	5.0	12.5	13.0	36.3	11.5	12.0	36.0	10.6
1992	7.5	6.6	7.0	18.5	6.4	6.1	15.8	5.5	14.2	15.2	42.0	13.5	13.2	37.2	11.8
1993	6.9	6.1	6.3	17.7	5.7	5.7	14.7	5.2	13.0	13.8	40.1	12.1	12.1	37.4	10.7
1994	6.1	5.3	5.4	16.3	4.8	5.2	13.8	4.6	11.5	12.0	37.6	10.3	11.0	32.6	9.8
1995	5.6	4.9	4.9	15.6	4.3	4.8	13.4	4.3	10.4	10.6	37.1	8.8	10.2	34.3	8.6
1996	5.4	4.7	4.7	15.5	4.1	4.7	12.9	4.1	10.5	11.1	36.9	9.4	10.0	30.3	8.7
1997	4.9	4.2	4.2	14.3	3.6	4.2	12.8	3.7	10.0	10.2	36.5	8.5	9.9	28.7	8.8
1996:Jan	5.7	4.9	4.9	16.4	4.2	5.0	14.3	4.4	10.5	10.8	36.7	9.1	10.2	30.7	9.0
Feb	5.5	4.8	4.8	15.6	4.2	4.8	13.3	4.3	10.1	11.1	31.8	9.8	9.3	32.6	7.9
Mar	5.5	4.8	4.9	16.0	4.2	4.7	13.2	4.1	10.6	11.6	35.2	10.0	9.6	30.0	8.4
Apr	5.5	4.8	4.8	15.6	4.2	4.8	13.3	4.2	10.6	11.3	35.2	9.6	9.9	31.4	8.5
May	5.5	4.9	4.9	15.6	4.3	4.9	12.9	4.4	10.2	11.0	31.3	9.6	9.5	29.1	8.2
June	5.3	4.6	4.7	14.6	4.1	4.6	12.9	4.0	10.1	10.7	35.1	9.1	9.6	27.5	8.5
July	5.5	4.7	4.7	15.9	4.1	4.6	11.8	4.1	10.7	11.7	43.8	9.3	9.7	23.2	8.9
Aug	5.2	4.5	4.4	15.3	3.8	4.5	13.0	4.0	10.7	10.6	38.7	8.7	10.7	36.6	9.0
Sept	5.2	4.5	4.5	14.6	3.9	4.4	11.7	3.9	10.7	11.5	36.6	9.8	9.9	30.7	8.6
Oct	5.3	4.5	4.5	15.1	3.8	4.5	12.0	4.0	10.8	11.3	38.6	9.4	10.3	31.6	8.9
Nov	5.4	4.7	4.6	15.8	3.9	4.7	13.0	4.2	10.7	11.5	41.1	9.7	10.0	28.7	8.9
Dec	5.3	4.6	4.4	15.0	3.8	4.8	13.2	4.3	10.5	10.3	38.1	8.5	10.7	30.1	9.5
1997:Jan	5.3	4.5	4.5	15.1	3.9	4.5	13.1	3.9	10.7	11.0	40.9	9.0	10.4	27.7	9.3
Feb	5.3	4.5	4.4	14.8	3.8	4.5	14.4	3.9	11.0	10.7	36.8	8.8	11.3	30.4	10.0
Mar	5.2	4.4	4.4	15.1	3.8	4.5	13.0	3.9	10.5	10.9	40.5	8.9	10.1	24.6	9.2
Apr	5.0	4.2	4.2	14.6	3.6	4.2	12.2	3.7	9.9	10.2	37.7	8.4	9.6	26.3	8.6
May	4.8	4.1	3.9	13.0	3.3	4.3	12.7	3.7	10.3	10.0	34.5	8.4	10.5	33.3	9.2
June	5.0	4.3	4.3	15.8	3.6	4.2	12.8	3.7	10.3	10.7	39.1	9.0	9.9	25.5	9.0
July	4.9	4.2	4.2	15.0	3.5	4.2	13.7	3.5	9.6	9.8	34.6	8.3	9.4	25.9	8.4
Aug	4.9	4.2	4.2	15.1	3.6	4.2	13.1	3.7	9.5	9.4	33.9	7.9	9.6	28.4	8.4
Sept	4.9	4.2	4.2	14.4	3.6	4.3	13.7	3.7	9.6	9.6	37.6	7.9	9.6	28.6	8.5
Oct	4.8	4.1	4.2	14.3	3.6	4.0	12.3	3.5	9.6	9.6	30.1	8.3	9.5	28.8	8.3
Nov	4.6	3.9	3.9	12.8	3.4	3.9	11.6	3.4	9.7	9.4	35.0	7.8	9.9	31.9	8.8
Dec	4.7	3.9	4.0	11.3	3.6	3.9	11.1	3.4	9.9	10.2	36.2	8.6	9.7	33.1	8.1

[1] Unemployed as percent of civilian labor force in group specified.

Note.—See Note, Table B–42.

Source: Department of Labor, Bureau of Labor Statistics.

[Thousands of persons, except as noted; monthly data seasonally adjusted[1]]

Year or month	Unemployment	Duration of unemployment						Reason for unemployment					
		Less than 5 weeks	5–14 weeks	15–26 weeks	27 weeks and over	Average (mean) duration (weeks)	Median duration (weeks)	Job losers[3]			Job leavers	Reentrants	New entrants
								Total	On layoff	Other			
1950	3,288	1,450	1,055	425	357	12.1	....	....	....	....	....	....	....
1951	2,055	1,177	574	166	137	9.7	....	....	....	....	....	....	....
1952	1,883	1,135	516	148	84	8.4	....	....	....	....	....	....	....
1953	1,834	1,142	482	132	78	8.0	....	....	....	....	....	....	....
1954	3,532	1,605	1,116	495	317	11.8	....	....	....	....	....	....	....
1955	2,852	1,335	815	366	336	13.0	....	....	....	....	....	....	....
1956	2,750	1,412	805	301	232	11.3	....	....	....	....	....	....	....
1957	2,859	1,408	891	321	239	10.5	....	....	....	....	....	....	....
1958	4,602	1,753	1,396	785	667	13.9	....	....	....	....	....	....	....
1959	3,740	1,585	1,114	469	571	14.4	....	....	....	....	....	....	....
1960	3,852	1,719	1,176	503	454	12.8	....	....	....	....	....	....	....
1961	4,714	1,806	1,376	728	804	15.6	....	....	....	....	....	....	....
1962	3,911	1,663	1,134	534	585	14.7	....	....	....	....	....	....	....
1963	4,070	1,751	1,231	535	553	14.0	....	....	....	....	....	....	....
1964	3,786	1,697	1,117	491	482	13.3	....	....	....	....	....	....	....
1965	3,366	1,628	983	404	351	11.8	....	....	....	....	....	....	....
1966	2,875	1,573	779	287	239	10.4	....	....	....	....	....	....	....
1967[2]	2,975	1,634	893	271	177	8.7	2.3	1,229	394	836	438	945	396
1968	2,817	1,594	810	256	156	8.4	4.5	1,070	334	736	431	909	407
1969	2,832	1,629	827	242	133	7.8	4.4	1,017	339	678	436	965	413
1970	4,093	2,139	1,290	428	235	8.6	4.9	1,811	675	1,137	550	1,228	504
1971	5,016	2,245	1,585	668	519	11.3	6.3	2,323	735	1,588	590	1,472	630
1972	4,882	2,242	1,472	601	566	12.0	6.2	2,108	582	1,526	641	1,456	677
1973	4,365	2,224	1,314	483	343	10.0	5.2	1,694	472	1,221	683	1,340	649
1974	5,156	2,604	1,597	574	381	9.8	5.2	2,242	746	1,495	768	1,463	681
1975	7,929	2,940	2,484	1,303	1,203	14.2	8.4	4,386	1,671	2,714	827	1,892	823
1976	7,406	2,844	2,196	1,018	1,348	15.8	8.2	3,679	1,050	2,628	903	1,928	895
1977	6,991	2,919	2,132	913	1,028	14.3	7.0	3,166	865	2,300	909	1,963	953
1978	6,202	2,865	1,923	766	648	11.9	5.9	2,585	712	1,873	874	1,857	885
1979	6,137	2,950	1,946	706	535	10.8	5.4	2,635	851	1,784	880	1,806	817
1980	7,637	3,295	2,470	1,052	820	11.9	6.5	3,947	1,488	2,459	891	1,927	872
1981	8,273	3,449	2,539	1,122	1,162	13.7	6.9	4,267	1,430	2,837	923	2,102	981
1982	10,678	3,883	3,311	1,708	1,776	15.6	8.7	6,268	2,127	4,141	840	2,384	1,185
1983	10,717	3,570	2,937	1,652	2,559	20.0	10.1	6,258	1,780	4,478	830	2,412	1,216
1984	8,539	3,350	2,451	1,104	1,634	18.2	7.9	4,421	1,171	3,250	823	2,184	1,110
1985	8,312	3,498	2,509	1,025	1,280	15.6	6.8	4,139	1,157	2,982	877	2,256	1,039
1986	8,237	3,448	2,557	1,045	1,187	15.0	6.9	4,033	1,090	2,943	1,015	2,160	1,029
1987	7,425	3,246	2,196	943	1,040	14.5	6.5	3,566	943	2,623	965	1,974	920
1988	6,701	3,084	2,007	801	809	13.5	5.9	3,092	851	2,241	983	1,809	816
1989	6,528	3,174	1,978	730	646	11.9	4.8	2,983	850	2,133	1,024	1,843	677
1990	7,047	3,265	2,257	822	703	12.0	5.3	3,387	1,028	2,359	1,041	1,930	688
1991	8,628	3,480	2,791	1,246	1,111	13.7	6.8	4,694	1,292	3,402	1,004	2,139	792
1992	9,613	3,376	2,830	1,453	1,954	17.7	8.7	5,389	1,260	4,129	1,002	2,285	937
1993	8,940	3,262	2,584	1,297	1,798	18.0	8.3	4,848	1,115	3,733	976	2,198	919
1994	7,996	2,728	2,408	1,237	1,623	18.8	9.2	3,815	977	2,838	791	2,786	604
1995	7,404	2,700	2,342	1,085	1,278	16.6	8.3	3,476	1,030	2,446	824	2,525	579
1996	7,236	2,633	2,287	1,053	1,262	16.7	8.3	3,370	1,021	2,349	774	2,512	580
1997	6,739	2,538	2,138	995	1,067	15.8	8.0	3,037	931	2,106	775	2,338	569
1996:Jan	7,522	2,673	2,397	1,133	1,233	16.1	8.3	3,539	1,108	2,431	817	2,477	619
Feb	7,345	2,731	2,259	1,107	1,212	16.5	7.9	3,532	1,043	2,489	759	2,470	586
Mar	7,355	2,606	2,264	1,103	1,318	17.2	8.3	3,474	1,008	2,466	792	2,506	569
Apr	7,348	2,538	2,351	1,073	1,312	17.4	8.5	3,601	1,078	2,523	739	2,492	558
May	7,359	2,778	2,350	1,027	1,336	17.0	8.5	3,459	1,112	2,347	690	2,747	545
June	7,095	2,542	2,177	1,033	1,323	17.4	8.2	3,357	1,002	2,355	699	2,409	568
July	7,347	2,711	2,342	974	1,326	16.8	8.2	3,386	993	2,393	751	2,546	609
Aug	6,916	2,516	2,190	1,020	1,262	17.1	8.5	3,079	953	2,126	762	2,495	562
Sept	7,003	2,535	2,227	1,039	1,223	16.8	8.4	3,226	1,002	2,224	785	2,444	559
Oct	7,079	2,473	2,292	1,085	1,216	16.5	8.4	3,186	936	2,250	802	2,491	581
Nov	7,231	2,879	2,224	1,025	1,170	16.1	7.8	3,333	999	2,334	829	2,518	587
Dec	7,161	2,622	2,382	989	1,189	15.8	7.9	3,174	960	2,214	849	2,567	627
1997:Jan	7,188	2,678	2,251	964	1,186	15.9	7.9	3,191	953	2,238	861	2,499	596
Feb	7,174	2,580	2,341	1,031	1,127	15.9	8.2	3,147	949	2,198	804	2,608	623
Mar	7,080	2,618	2,325	1,003	1,076	15.4	7.9	3,148	993	2,155	797	2,497	617
Apr	6,768	2,471	2,177	1,033	1,055	15.4	8.1	3,038	958	2,080	776	2,422	569
May	6,566	2,542	2,067	1,054	1,022	15.3	7.8	2,961	909	2,052	808	2,338	573
June	6,814	2,541	2,188	1,031	1,038	15.3	7.9	3,094	928	2,166	827	2,333	510
July	6,633	2,446	2,097	1,061	1,067	16.5	8.2	2,954	894	2,060	812	2,263	564
Aug	6,657	2,564	2,121	950	1,077	15.8	7.9	3,010	891	2,119	894	2,173	554
Sept	6,678	2,484	2,115	1,031	1,078	15.9	8.1	3,007	893	2,114	853	2,263	560
Oct	6,496	2,558	1,912	919	1,071	16.3	7.7	2,934	963	1,971	732	2,247	555
Nov	6,289	2,423	2,048	899	966	15.6	7.8	2,886	815	2,071	655	2,229	560
Dec	6,392	2,531	1,922	936	1,028	15.2	7.7	2,991	961	2,030	692	2,170	552

[1] Because of independent seasonal adjustment of the various series, detail will not add to totals.
[2] Data for 1967 by reason for unemployment are not equal to total unemployment.
[3] Beginning January 1994, job losers and persons who completed temporary jobs.

Note.—Data relate to persons 16 years of age and over.
See footnote 5 and Note, Table B–35.

Source: Department of Labor, Bureau of Labor Statistics.

TABLE B–45.—*Unemployment insurance programs, selected data, 1965–97*

Year or month	All programs			State programs					
	Covered employ- ment[1]	Insured unemploy- ment (weekly aver- age)[2][3]	Total benefits paid (millions of dollars)[2][4]	Insured unem- ploy- ment[3]	Initial claims	Exhaus- tions[5]	Insured unemploy- ment as percent of covered employ- ment	Benefits paid	
								Total (millions of dollars)[4]	Average weekly check (dollars)[6]
	Thousands			Weekly average; thousands					
1965	51,580	1,450	2,360	1,328	232	21	3.0	2,166	37.19
1966	54,739	1,129	1,891	1,061	203	15	2.3	1,771	39.75
1967	56,342	1,270	2,222	1,205	226	17	2.5	2,092	41.25
1968	57,977	1,187	2,191	1,111	201	16	2.2	2,032	43.43
1969	59,999	1,177	2,299	1,101	200	16	2.1	2,128	46.17
1970	59,526	2,070	4,209	1,805	296	25	3.4	3,849	50.34
1971	59,375	2,608	6,154	2,150	295	39	4.1	4,957	54.02
1972	66,458	2,192	5,491	1,848	261	35	3.5	4,471	56.76
1973	69,897	1,793	4,517	1,632	247	29	2.7	4,008	59.00
1974	72,451	2,558	6,934	2,262	363	37	3.5	5,975	64.25
1975	71,037	4,937	16,802	3,986	478	81	6.0	11,755	70.23
1976	73,459	3,846	12,345	2,991	386	63	4.6	8,975	75.16
1977	76,419	3,308	10,999	2,655	375	55	3.9	8,357	78.79
1978	88,804	2,645	9,007	2,359	346	39	3.3	7,717	83.67
1979	92,062	2,592	9,401	2,434	388	39	2.9	8,613	89.67
1980	92,659	3,837	16,175	3,350	488	59	3.9	13,761	98.95
1981	93,300	3,410	15,287	3,047	460	57	3.5	13,262	106.70
1982	91,628	4,592	24,491	4,059	583	80	4.6	20,649	119.34
1983	91,898	3,774	21,000	3,395	438	80	3.9	17,787	123.59
1984	96,474	2,560	13,838	2,475	377	50	2.8	12,610	123.47
1985	99,186	2,699	15,283	2,617	397	49	2.9	14,131	128.14
1986	101,099	2,739	16,670	2,643	378	52	2.8	15,329	135.65
1987	103,936	2,369	14,929	2,300	328	46	2.4	13,607	140.55
1988	107,156	2,135	13,694	2,081	310	38	2.0	12,565	144.97
1989	109,929	2,205	14,948	2,158	330	37	2.1	13,760	151.73
1990	111,500	2,575	18,721	2,522	388	45	2.4	17,356	161.56
1991	109,606	3,406	26,717	3,342	447	67	3.2	24,526	169.88
1992	110,167	3,348	8 26,460	3,245	408	74	3.1	23,869	173.64
1993	112,146	2,845	8 22,950	2,751	341	62	2.6	20,539	179.62
1994	115,255	2,746	22,844	2,670	340	57	2.5	20,401	182.16
1995	118,068	2,639	22,386	2,572	357	51	2.3	20,125	187.29
1996	7 120,567	2,656	22,915	2,595	356	53	2.3	20,645	189.51
1997 P	....	2,369	....	2,321	324	48	....	....	192.73
		**		**	**		**		
1996: Jan	....	3,507	2,568.1	2,642	371	58	2.4	2,488.2	191.92
Feb	....	3,343	2,371.7	2,652	369	53	2.4	2,305.3	193.85
Mar	....	3,170	2,247.9	2,639	389	55	2.4	2,188.1	193.45
Apr	....	2,941	2,130.0	2,584	356	61	2.3	2,073.8	192.11
May	....	2,358	1,793.7	2,554	349	53	2.3	1,744.3	189.02
June	....	2,387	1,550.6	2,573	355	52	2.3	1,504.0	187.70
July	....	2,554	1,838.7	2,535	334	56	2.2	1,782.3	176.96
Aug	....	2,258	1,599.6	2,524	325	49	2.2	1,549.1	184.79
Sept	....	2,188	1,452.0	2,468	335	47	2.2	1,405.4	188.92
Oct	....	2,050	1,520.0	2,470	334	46	2.2	1,467.3	189.07
Nov	....	2,108	1,418.6	2,444	338	44	2.1	1,371.3	190.43
Dec	....	2,754	1,928.8	2,518	355	53	2.2	1,871.7	192.30
1997: Jan	....	3,041	2,299.5	2,453	334	53	2.1	2,242.0	194.44
Feb	....	3,039	2,072.9	2,375	311	51	2.1	2,020.2	196.38
Mar	....	2,936	2,111.1	2,294	312	52	2.0	2,058.1	196.75
Apr	....	2,508	1,885.9	2,274	333	55	2.0	1,837.3	194.50
May	....	2,073	1,534.5	2,263	326	47	2.0	1,495.9	193.43
June	....	2,211	1,495.5	2,326	341	47	2.0	1,457.8	191.22
July	....	2,232	1,649.8	2,300	319	50	2.0	1,608.3	188.09
Aug	....	2,110	1,424.8	2,308	325	44	2.0	1,385.0	184.69
Sept	....	1,973	1,416.0	2,233	308	43	1.9	1,369.6	191.35
Oct	....	1,759	1,333.5	2,229	308	41	1.9	1,283.7	191.80
Nov	....	2,021	1,284.7	2,241	318	43	1.9	1,236.8	191.80
Dec P	....	2,450	1,844.8	2,282	317	48	2.0	1,787.7	193.99

** Monthly data are seasonally adjusted.

[1] Includes persons under the State, UCFE (Federal employee, effective January 1955), RRB (Railroad Retirement Board) programs, and UCX (unemployment compensation for ex-servicemembers, effective October 1958) programs.

[2] Includes State, UCFE, RR, UCX, UCV (unemployment compensation for veterans, October 1952–January 1960), and SRA (Servicemen's Readjustment Act, September 1944–September 1951) programs. Also includes Federal and State extended benefit programs. Does not include FSB (Federal supplemental benefits), SUA (special unemployment assistance), Federal Supplemental Compensation, and Emergency Unemployment Compensation programs, except as noted in footnote 8.

[3] Covered workers who have completed at least 1 week of unemployment.

[4] Annual data are net amounts and monthly data are gross amounts.

[5] Individuals receiving final payments in benefit year.

[6] For total unemployment only.

[7] Latest data available for all programs combined. Workers covered by State programs account for about 97 percent of wage and salary earners.

[8] Including Emergency Unemployment Compensation and Federal Supplemental Compensation, total benefits paid for 1992 and 1993 would be approximately (in millions of dollars): for 1992, 39,990 and for 1993, 34,876.

Note.—Insured unemployment and initial claims programs include Puerto Rican sugar cane workers beginning 1963.

Source: Department of Labor, Employment and Training Administration.

TABLE B–46.—*Employees on nonagricultural payrolls, by major industry, 1950–97*

[Thousands of persons; monthly data seasonally adjusted]

Year or month	Total	Goods-producing industries					
		Total	Mining	Construc-tion	Manufacturing		
					Total	Durable goods	Nondura-ble goods
1950	45,197	18,506	901	2,364	15,241	8,066	7,175
1951	47,819	19,959	929	2,637	16,393	9,059	7,334
1952	48,793	20,198	898	2,668	16,632	9,320	7,313
1953	50,202	21,074	866	2,659	17,549	10,080	7,468
1954	48,990	19,751	791	2,646	16,314	9,101	7,213
1955	50,641	20,513	792	2,839	16,882	9,511	7,370
1956	52,369	21,104	822	3,039	17,243	9,802	7,442
1957	52,855	20,967	828	2,962	17,176	9,825	7,351
1958	51,322	19,513	751	2,817	15,945	8,801	7,144
1959	53,270	20,411	732	3,004	16,675	9,342	7,333
1960	54,189	20,434	712	2,926	16,796	9,429	7,367
1961	53,999	19,857	672	2,859	16,326	9,041	7,285
1962	55,549	20,451	650	2,948	16,853	9,450	7,403
1963	56,653	20,640	635	3,010	16,995	9,586	7,410
1964	58,283	21,005	634	3,097	17,274	9,785	7,489
1965	60,763	21,926	632	3,232	18,062	10,374	7,688
1966	63,901	23,158	627	3,317	19,214	11,250	7,963
1967	65,803	23,308	613	3,248	19,447	11,408	8,039
1968	67,897	23,737	606	3,350	19,781	11,594	8,187
1969	70,384	24,361	619	3,575	20,167	11,862	8,304
1970	70,880	23,578	623	3,588	19,367	11,176	8,190
1971	71,211	22,935	609	3,704	18,623	10,604	8,019
1972	73,675	23,668	628	3,889	19,151	11,022	8,129
1973	76,790	24,893	642	4,097	20,154	11,863	8,291
1974	78,265	24,794	697	4,020	20,077	11,897	8,181
1975	76,945	22,600	752	3,525	18,323	10,662	7,661
1976	79,382	23,352	779	3,576	18,997	11,051	7,946
1977	82,471	24,346	813	3,851	19,682	11,570	8,112
1978	86,697	25,585	851	4,229	20,505	12,245	8,259
1979	89,823	26,461	958	4,463	21,040	12,730	8,310
1980	90,406	25,658	1,027	4,346	20,285	12,159	8,127
1981	91,152	25,497	1,139	4,188	20,170	12,082	8,089
1982	89,544	23,812	1,128	3,904	18,780	11,014	7,766
1983	90,152	23,330	952	3,946	18,432	10,707	7,725
1984	94,408	24,718	966	4,380	19,372	11,476	7,896
1985	97,387	24,842	927	4,668	19,248	11,458	7,790
1986	99,344	24,533	777	4,810	18,947	11,195	7,752
1987	101,958	24,674	717	4,958	18,999	11,154	7,845
1988	105,209	25,125	713	5,098	19,314	11,363	7,951
1989	107,884	25,254	692	5,171	19,391	11,394	7,997
1990	109,403	24,905	709	5,120	19,076	11,109	7,968
1991	108,249	23,745	689	4,650	18,406	10,569	7,837
1992	108,601	23,231	635	4,492	18,104	10,277	7,827
1993	110,713	23,352	610	4,668	18,075	10,221	7,854
1994	114,163	23,908	601	4,986	18,321	10,448	7,873
1995	117,191	24,265	581	5,160	18,524	10,683	7,841
1996	119,523	24,431	574	5,400	18,457	10,766	7,691
1997 ᴾ	122,257	24,738	573	5,627	18,538	10,915	7,622
1996: Jan	118,058	24,247	573	5,214	18,460	10,724	7,736
Feb	118,550	24,383	576	5,309	18,498	10,749	7,749
Mar	118,804	24,377	577	5,340	18,460	10,718	7,742
Apr	118,966	24,398	577	5,356	18,465	10,749	7,716
May	119,263	24,432	579	5,384	18,469	10,762	7,707
June	119,516	24,453	577	5,408	18,468	10,778	7,690
July	119,691	24,433	574	5,417	18,442	10,766	7,676
Aug	119,983	24,468	574	5,433	18,461	10,788	7,673
Sept	120,019	24,439	571	5,441	18,427	10,771	7,656
Oct	120,248	24,479	570	5,467	18,442	10,780	7,662
Nov	120,450	24,508	571	5,495	18,442	10,791	7,651
Dec	120,659	24,540	571	5,521	18,448	10,803	7,645
1997: Jan	120,909	24,581	574	5,542	18,465	10,821	7,644
Feb	121,162	24,653	574	5,604	18,475	10,836	7,639
Mar	121,344	24,670	572	5,609	18,489	10,848	7,641
Apr	121,671	24,667	573	5,599	18,495	10,856	7,639
May	121,834	24,702	576	5,628	18,498	10,864	7,634
June	122,056	24,714	574	5,622	18,518	10,891	7,627
July	122,440	24,713	574	5,625	18,514	10,910	7,604
Aug	122,492	24,765	573	5,637	18,555	10,957	7,598
Sept	122,792	24,771	576	5,642	18,553	10,952	7,601
Oct	123,083	24,814	574	5,650	18,590	10,985	7,605
Nov ᴾ	123,495	24,891	572	5,680	18,639	11,019	7,620
Dec ᴾ	123,865	24,980	572	5,730	18,678	11,050	7,628

Note.—Data in Tables B–46 and B–47 are based on reports from employing establishments and relate to full- and part-time wage and salary workers in nonagricultural establishments who received pay for any part of the pay period which includes the 12th of the month. Not comparable with labor force data (Tables B–35 through B–44), which include proprietors, self-employed persons, domestic servants,

See next page for continuation of table.

334

[Thousands of persons; monthly data seasonally adjusted]

Year or month	Total	Service-producing industries							
		Transportation and public utilities	Wholesale trade	Retail trade	Finance, insurance, and real estate	Services	Government		
							Total	Federal	State and local
1950	26,691	4,034	2,643	6,743	1,888	5,356	6,026	1,928	4,098
1951	27,860	4,226	2,735	7,007	1,956	5,547	6,389	2,302	4,087
1952	28,595	4,248	2,821	7,184	2,035	5,699	6,609	2,420	4,188
1953	29,128	4,290	2,862	7,385	2,111	5,835	6,645	2,305	4,340
1954	29,239	4,084	2,875	7,360	2,200	5,969	6,751	2,188	4,563
1955	30,128	4,141	2,934	7,601	2,298	6,240	6,914	2,187	4,727
1956	31,264	4,244	3,027	7,831	2,389	6,497	7,278	2,209	5,069
1957	31,889	4,241	3,037	7,848	2,438	6,708	7,616	2,217	5,399
1958	31,811	3,976	2,989	7,761	2,481	6,765	7,839	2,191	5,648
1959	32,857	4,011	3,092	8,035	2,549	7,087	8,083	2,233	5,850
1960	33,755	4,004	3,153	8,238	2,628	7,378	8,353	2,270	6,083
1961	34,142	3,903	3,142	8,195	2,688	7,619	8,594	2,279	6,315
1962	35,098	3,906	3,207	8,359	2,754	7,982	8,890	2,340	6,550
1963	36,013	3,903	3,258	8,520	2,830	8,277	9,225	2,358	6,868
1964	37,278	3,951	3,347	8,812	2,911	8,660	9,596	2,348	7,248
1965	38,839	4,036	3,477	9,239	2,977	9,036	10,074	2,378	7,696
1966	40,743	4,158	3,608	9,637	3,058	9,498	10,784	2,564	8,220
1967	42,495	4,268	3,700	9,906	3,185	10,045	11,391	2,719	8,672
1968	44,158	4,318	3,791	10,308	3,337	10,567	11,839	2,737	9,102
1969	46,023	4,442	3,919	10,785	3,512	11,169	12,195	2,758	9,437
1970	47,302	4,515	4,006	11,034	3,645	11,548	12,554	2,731	9,823
1971	48,276	4,476	4,014	11,338	3,772	11,797	12,881	2,696	10,185
1972	50,007	4,541	4,127	11,822	3,908	12,276	13,334	2,684	10,649
1973	51,897	4,656	4,291	12,315	4,046	12,857	13,732	2,663	11,068
1974	53,471	4,725	4,447	12,539	4,148	13,441	14,170	2,724	11,446
1975	54,345	4,542	4,430	12,630	4,165	13,892	14,686	2,748	11,937
1976	56,030	4,582	4,562	13,193	4,271	14,551	14,871	2,733	12,138
1977	58,125	4,713	4,723	13,792	4,467	15,302	15,127	2,727	12,399
1978	61,113	4,923	4,985	14,556	4,724	16,252	15,672	2,753	12,919
1979	63,363	5,136	5,221	14,972	4,975	17,112	15,947	2,773	13,174
1980	64,748	5,146	5,292	15,018	5,160	17,890	16,241	2,866	13,375
1981	65,655	5,165	5,375	15,171	5,298	18,615	16,031	2,772	13,259
1982	65,732	5,081	5,295	15,158	5,340	19,021	15,837	2,739	13,098
1983	66,821	4,952	5,283	15,587	5,466	19,664	15,869	2,774	13,096
1984	69,690	5,156	5,568	16,512	5,684	20,746	16,024	2,807	13,216
1985	72,544	5,233	5,727	17,315	5,948	21,927	16,394	2,875	13,519
1986	74,811	5,247	5,761	17,880	6,273	22,957	16,693	2,899	13,794
1987	77,284	5,362	5,848	18,422	6,533	24,110	17,010	2,943	14,067
1988	80,084	5,512	6,030	19,023	6,630	25,504	17,386	2,971	14,415
1989	82,630	5,614	6,187	19,475	6,668	26,907	17,779	2,988	14,791
1990	84,497	5,777	6,173	19,601	6,709	27,934	18,304	3,085	15,219
1991	84,504	5,755	6,081	19,284	6,646	28,336	18,402	2,966	15,436
1992	85,370	5,718	5,997	19,356	6,602	29,052	18,645	2,969	15,676
1993	87,361	5,811	5,981	19,773	6,757	30,197	18,841	2,915	15,926
1994	90,256	5,984	6,162	20,507	6,896	31,579	19,128	2,870	16,258
1995	92,925	6,132	6,378	21,187	6,806	33,117	19,305	2,822	16,484
1996	95,092	6,261	6,483	21,625	6,899	34,377	19,447	2,757	16,690
1997 ᵖ	97,519	6,426	6,657	22,131	7,053	35,597	19,655	2,700	16,956
1996: Jan	93,811	6,195	6,421	21,340	6,831	33,698	19,326	2,782	16,544
Feb	94,167	6,203	6,429	21,393	6,848	33,938	19,356	2,782	16,574
Mar	94,427	6,211	6,437	21,463	6,856	34,064	19,396	2,779	16,617
Apr	94,568	6,229	6,443	21,479	6,867	34,150	19,400	2,774	16,626
May	94,831	6,246	6,457	21,547	6,888	34,277	19,416	2,770	16,646
June	95,063	6,270	6,469	21,600	6,897	34,390	19,437	2,757	16,680
July	95,258	6,296	6,481	21,651	6,910	34,465	19,455	2,752	16,703
Aug	95,515	6,299	6,497	21,692	6,917	34,560	19,550	2,743	16,807
Sept	95,580	6,290	6,513	21,718	6,925	34,621	19,513	2,740	16,773
Oct	95,769	6,293	6,538	21,791	6,941	34,717	19,489	2,732	16,757
Nov	95,942	6,303	6,549	21,847	6,949	34,800	19,494	2,732	16,762
Dec	96,119	6,288	6,559	21,912	6,962	34,884	19,514	2,728	16,786
1997: Jan	96,328	6,351	6,570	21,917	6,971	34,990	19,529	2,723	16,806
Feb	96,509	6,376	6,593	21,922	6,980	35,091	19,547	2,716	16,831
Mar	96,674	6,405	6,611	21,945	6,992	35,176	19,545	2,709	16,836
Apr	97,004	6,421	6,622	22,029	7,019	35,334	19,579	2,708	16,871
May	97,132	6,431	6,630	22,026	7,029	35,451	19,565	2,703	16,862
June	97,342	6,434	6,634	22,079	7,034	35,522	19,639	2,694	16,945
July	97,727	6,443	6,664	22,159	7,058	35,684	19,719	2,689	17,030
Aug	97,727	6,289	6,675	22,189	7,068	35,702	19,804	2,690	17,114
Sept	98,021	6,473	6,687	22,215	7,082	35,850	19,714	2,680	17,034
Oct	98,269	6,497	6,712	22,258	7,108	35,945	19,749	2,687	17,062
Nov ᵖ	98,604	6,498	6,730	22,373	7,132	36,109	19,762	2,696	17,066
Dec ᵖ	98,885	6,488	6,743	22,425	7,155	36,290	19,784	2,689	17,095

Note (cont'd).—which count persons as employed when they are not at work because of industrial disputes, bad weather, etc., even if they are not paid for the time off; and which are based on a sample of the working-age population. For description and details of the various establishment data, see "Employment and Earnings."

Source: Department of Labor, Bureau of Labor Statistics.

[Monthly data seasonally adjusted, except as noted]

Year or month	Average weekly hours			Average hourly earnings			Average weekly earnings, total private			
	Total private	Manufacturing		Total private		Manu-facturing (current dollars)	Level		Percent change from year earlier[3]	
		Total	Over-time	Current dollars	1982 dollars[2]		Current dollars	1982 dollars[2]	Current dollars	1982 dollars[2]
1959	39.0	40.3	2.7	$2.02	$6.69	$2.19	$78.78	$260.86	4.9	4.2
1960	38.6	39.7	2.5	2.09	6.79	2.26	80.67	261.92	2.4	.4
1961	38.6	39.8	2.4	2.14	6.88	2.32	82.60	265.59	2.4	1.4
1962	38.7	40.4	2.8	2.22	7.07	2.39	85.91	273.60	4.0	3.0
1963	38.8	40.5	2.8	2.28	7.17	2.45	88.46	278.18	3.0	1.7
1964	38.7	40.7	3.1	2.36	7.33	2.53	91.33	283.63	3.2	2.0
1965	38.8	41.2	3.6	2.46	7.52	2.61	95.45	291.90	4.5	2.9
1966	38.6	41.4	3.9	2.56	7.62	2.71	98.82	294.11	3.5	.8
1967	38.0	40.6	3.4	2.68	7.72	2.82	101.84	293.49	3.1	-.2
1968	37.8	40.7	3.6	2.85	7.89	3.01	107.73	298.42	5.8	1.7
1969	37.7	40.6	3.6	3.04	7.98	3.19	114.61	300.81	6.4	.8
1970	37.1	39.8	3.0	3.23	8.03	3.35	119.83	298.08	4.6	-.9
1971	36.9	39.9	2.9	3.45	8.21	3.57	127.31	303.12	6.2	1.7
1972	37.0	40.5	3.5	3.70	8.53	3.82	136.90	315.44	7.5	4.1
1973	36.9	40.7	3.8	3.94	8.55	4.09	145.39	315.38	6.2	-.0
1974	36.5	40.0	3.3	4.24	8.28	4.42	154.76	302.27	6.4	-4.2
1975	36.1	39.5	2.6	4.53	8.12	4.83	163.53	293.06	5.7	-3.0
1976	36.1	40.1	3.1	4.86	8.24	5.22	175.45	297.37	7.3	1.5
1977	36.0	40.3	3.5	5.25	8.36	5.68	189.00	300.96	7.7	1.2
1978	35.8	40.4	3.6	5.69	8.40	6.17	203.70	300.89	7.8	-.0
1979	35.7	40.2	3.3	6.16	8.17	6.70	219.91	291.66	8.0	-3.1
1980	35.3	39.7	2.8	6.66	7.78	7.27	235.10	274.65	6.9	-5.8
1981	35.2	39.8	2.8	7.25	7.69	7.99	255.20	270.63	8.5	-1.5
1982	34.8	38.9	2.3	7.68	7.68	8.49	267.26	267.26	4.7	-1.2
1983	35.0	40.1	3.0	8.02	7.79	8.83	280.70	272.52	5.0	2.0
1984	35.2	40.7	3.4	8.32	7.80	9.19	292.86	274.73	4.3	.8
1985	34.9	40.5	3.3	8.57	7.77	9.54	299.09	271.16	2.1	-1.3
1986	34.8	40.7	3.4	8.76	7.81	9.73	304.85	271.94	1.9	.3
1987	34.8	41.0	3.7	8.98	7.73	9.91	312.50	269.16	2.5	-1.0
1988	34.7	41.1	3.9	9.28	7.69	10.19	322.02	266.79	3.0	-.9
1989	34.6	41.0	3.8	9.66	7.64	10.48	334.24	264.22	3.8	-1.0
1990	34.5	40.8	3.6	10.01	7.52	10.83	345.35	259.47	3.3	-1.8
1991	34.3	40.7	3.6	10.32	7.45	11.18	353.98	255.40	2.5	-1.6
1992	34.4	41.0	3.8	10.57	7.41	11.46	363.61	254.99	2.7	-.2
1993	34.5	41.4	4.1	10.83	7.39	11.74	373.64	254.87	2.8	-.0
1994	34.7	42.0	4.7	11.12	7.40	12.07	385.86	256.73	3.3	.7
1995	34.5	41.6	4.4	11.43	7.39	12.37	394.34	255.07	2.2	-.6
1996	34.4	41.6	4.5	11.81	7.43	12.78	406.26	255.51	3.0	.2
1997 *p*	34.6	42.0	4.8	12.26	7.54	13.17	424.20	260.89	4.4	2.1
1996: Jan	33.9	40.1	4.2	11.62	7.41	12.64	393.92	251.06	.1	-2.5
Feb	34.4	41.4	4.4	11.64	7.40	12.60	400.42	254.72	2.6	-.1
Mar	34.4	41.3	4.3	11.66	7.39	12.54	401.10	254.18	3.0	.2
Apr	34.3	41.5	4.5	11.71	7.40	12.71	401.65	253.73	2.6	-.3
May	34.3	41.6	4.6	11.74	7.40	12.73	402.68	253.74	3.6	.6
June	34.7	41.7	4.5	11.81	7.44	12.77	409.81	258.07	4.6	1.8
July	34.3	41.6	4.5	11.81	7.42	12.80	405.08	254.45	2.4	-.5
Aug	34.5	41.7	4.5	11.86	7.44	12.85	409.17	256.69	3.5	.7
Sept	34.7	41.7	4.5	11.91	7.45	12.87	413.28	258.46	4.5	1.4
Oct	34.4	41.7	4.5	11.91	7.42	12.87	409.70	255.26	2.5	-.5
Nov	34.5	41.7	4.6	11.98	7.44	12.93	413.31	256.71	3.9	.6
Dec	34.7	42.0	4.7	12.03	7.45	12.99	417.44	258.64	5.5	2.1
1997: Jan	34.4	41.8	4.7	12.05	7.46	13.02	414.52	256.51	5.1	2.0
Feb	34.8	41.9	4.7	12.10	7.47	13.03	421.08	260.09	5.2	2.1
Mar	34.8	42.1	4.9	12.14	7.49	13.07	422.47	260.78	5.4	2.7
Apr	34.5	42.1	4.9	12.14	7.49	13.07	418.83	258.54	4.6	2.2
May	34.5	42.0	4.8	12.19	7.52	13.11	420.56	259.60	4.4	2.3
June	34.6	41.8	4.6	12.23	7.54	13.12	423.16	260.89	3.6	1.4
July	34.4	41.8	4.7	12.24	7.53	13.11	421.06	259.11	3.9	1.8
Aug	34.6	41.8	4.7	12.31	7.56	13.20	425.93	261.63	4.4	2.2
Sept	34.5	41.9	4.7	12.35	7.56	13.22	426.08	260.92	3.1	1.0
Oct	34.5	42.0	4.8	12.40	7.58	13.35	427.80	261.49	4.3	2.3
Nov *p*	34.8	42.1	4.9	12.47	7.62	13.36	433.96	265.09	5.2	3.4
Dec *p*	34.6	42.3	4.9	12.48	7.62	13.37	431.81	263.62	3.4	1.9

[1] For production or nonsupervisory workers; total includes private industry groups shown in Table B–46.
[2] Current dollars divided by the consumer price index for urban wage earners and clerical workers on a 1982=100 base.
[3] Percent changes are based on data that are not seasonally adjusted.

Note.—See Note, Table B–46.

Source: Department of Labor, Bureau of Labor Statistics.

TABLE B–48.—*Employment cost index, private industry, 1980–97*

Year and month	Total private			Goods-producing			Service-producing			Manufacturing			Nonmanufacturing		
	Total compensation	Wages and salaries	Benefits[1]	Total compensation	Wages and salaries	Benefits[1]	Total compensation	Wages and salaries	Benefits[1]	Total compensation	Wages and salaries	Benefits[1]	Total compensation	Wages and salaries	Benefits[1]
	Index, June 1989=100; not seasonally adjusted														
December:															
1980	64.8	67.1	59.4	66.7	69.7	60.5	63.3	65.3	58.4	66.0	68.9	59.9	64.2	66.2	59.1
1981	71.2	73.0	66.6	73.3	75.7	68.2	69.5	71.1	65.1	72.5	74.9	67.5	70.4	72.1	66.1
1982	75.8	77.6	71.4	77.8	80.0	73.2	74.1	75.9	69.6	76.9	79.1	72.4	75.1	76.8	70.6
1983	80.1	81.4	76.7	81.6	83.2	78.3	78.9	80.2	75.2	80.8	82.5	77.5	79.6	81.0	76.2
1984	84.0	84.8	81.7	85.4	86.4	83.2	82.9	83.7	80.4	85.0	86.1	82.7	83.4	84.2	81.1
1985	87.3	88.3	84.6	88.2	89.4	85.7	86.6	87.7	83.6	87.8	89.2	85.0	87.0	88.0	84.4
1986	90.1	91.1	87.5	91.0	92.3	88.3	89.3	90.3	86.8	90.7	92.1	87.5	89.7	90.6	87.5
1987	93.1	94.1	90.5	93.8	95.2	90.9	92.6	93.4	90.2	93.4	95.2	89.8	92.9	93.7	91.0
1988	97.6	98.0	96.7	97.9	98.2	97.3	97.3	97.8	96.1	97.6	98.1	96.6	97.5	97.8	96.8
1989	102.3	102.0	102.6	102.1	102.0	102.6	102.3	102.2	102.6	102.0	101.9	102.3	102.3	102.2	102.8
1990	107.0	106.1	109.4	107.0	105.8	109.9	107.0	106.3	109.0	107.2	106.2	109.5	106.9	106.1	109.3
1991	111.7	110.0	116.2	111.9	109.7	116.7	111.6	110.2	115.7	112.2	110.3	116.1	111.5	109.8	116.2
1992	115.6	112.9	122.2	116.1	112.8	123.4	115.2	113.0	121.2	116.5	113.7	122.6	115.1	112.6	122.0
1993	119.8	116.4	128.3	120.6	116.1	130.3	119.3	116.6	126.7	121.3	117.3	130.0	119.0	116.0	127.4
1994	123.5	119.7	133.0	124.3	119.6	134.8	122.8	119.7	131.5	125.1	120.8	134.3	122.6	119.1	132.3
1995	126.7	123.1	135.9	127.3	122.9	137.1	126.2	123.2	134.7	128.3	124.3	136.7	125.9	122.5	135.3
1996: Mar	127.9	124.4	136.6	128.2	123.9	137.7	127.6	124.7	135.5	129.3	125.4	137.5	127.2	123.9	136.0
June	129.0	125.6	137.4	129.3	125.1	138.6	128.6	125.8	136.2	130.4	126.5	138.5	128.2	125.1	136.7
Sept	129.8	126.5	138.1	130.1	126.1	138.8	129.5	126.7	137.2	131.3	127.7	138.8	129.1	125.9	137.5
Dec	130.6	127.3	138.6	130.9	126.8	139.7	130.2	127.5	137.4	132.1	128.4	139.8	129.8	126.8	137.9
1997: Mar	131.7	128.6	139.4	131.4	127.5	139.9	131.6	129.0	138.5	132.6	129.1	139.9	131.1	128.2	138.9
June	132.8	129.7	140.1	132.7	128.9	140.9	132.5	130.1	139.2	133.8	130.3	141.0	132.1	129.3	139.5
Sept	133.9	131.0	140.8	133.6	129.9	141.5	133.8	131.5	139.8	134.6	131.3	141.4	133.3	130.7	140.2
Dec	135.1	132.3	141.8	134.1	130.6	141.5	135.3	133.1	141.4	135.3	132.2	141.7	134.7	132.1	141.5
	Index, June 1989=100; seasonally adjusted														
1996: Mar	127.7	124.4	136.0	128.2	123.9	137.3	127.5	124.7	135.3	129.1	125.4	137.0	127.1	123.9	135.9
June	128.8	125.5	137.0	129.4	125.1	138.4	128.5	125.7	136.1	130.2	126.5	138.3	128.1	125.0	136.6
Sept	129.7	126.4	137.7	130.3	126.1	139.0	129.4	126.6	137.0	131.3	127.7	139.1	129.0	125.8	137.3
Dec	130.6	127.4	138.7	131.1	126.8	140.2	130.4	127.7	137.8	132.2	128.4	140.2	130.1	127.0	138.3
1997: Mar	131.4	128.5	138.7	131.4	127.5	139.4	131.5	129.0	138.3	132.4	129.1	139.4	131.0	128.2	138.8
June	132.5	129.7	139.7	132.7	128.9	140.7	132.4	130.0	139.1	133.6	130.3	140.8	132.0	129.2	139.4
Sept	133.6	130.9	140.4	133.7	129.9	141.7	133.6	131.4	139.6	134.6	131.3	141.7	133.1	130.6	140.0
Dec	135.2	132.5	141.9	134.3	130.6	142.0	135.6	133.3	141.8	135.4	132.2	142.1	135.0	132.3	141.9
	Percent change from 12 months earlier, not seasonally adjusted														
December:															
1980	9.6	9.1	11.7	9.9	9.4	10.8	9.7	8.8	12.5	9.8	9.4	10.5	9.7	8.9	12.6
1981	9.9	8.8	12.1	9.9	8.6	12.7	9.8	8.9	11.5	9.8	8.7	12.7	9.7	8.9	11.8
1982	6.5	6.3	7.2	6.1	5.7	7.3	6.6	6.8	6.9	6.1	5.6	7.3	6.7	6.5	6.8
1983	5.7	4.9	7.4	4.9	4.0	7.0	6.5	5.7	8.0	5.1	4.3	7.0	6.0	5.5	7.9
1984	4.9	4.2	6.5	4.7	3.8	6.3	5.1	4.4	6.9	5.2	4.4	6.7	4.8	4.0	6.4
1985	3.9	4.1	3.5	3.3	3.5	3.0	4.5	4.8	4.0	3.3	3.6	2.8	4.3	4.5	4.1
1986	3.2	3.2	3.4	3.2	3.2	3.0	3.1	3.0	3.8	3.3	3.3	2.9	3.1	3.0	3.7
1987	3.3	3.3	3.4	3.1	3.1	2.9	3.7	3.4	3.9	3.0	3.4	2.6	3.6	3.4	4.0
1988	4.8	4.1	6.9	4.4	3.2	7.0	5.1	4.7	6.5	4.5	3.0	7.6	5.0	4.4	6.4
1989	4.8	4.1	6.1	4.3	3.9	5.4	5.1	4.5	6.8	4.5	3.9	5.9	4.9	4.5	6.2
1990	4.6	4.0	6.6	4.8	3.7	7.1	4.6	4.0	6.2	5.1	4.2	7.0	4.5	3.8	6.3
1991	4.4	3.7	6.2	4.6	3.7	6.2	4.3	3.7	6.1	4.7	3.9	6.0	4.3	3.5	6.3
1992	3.5	2.6	5.2	3.8	2.8	5.7	3.2	2.5	4.8	3.8	3.1	5.6	3.2	2.6	5.0
1993	3.6	3.1	5.0	3.9	2.9	5.6	3.6	3.2	4.5	4.1	3.2	6.0	3.4	3.0	4.4
1994	3.1	2.8	3.7	3.1	3.0	3.5	2.9	2.7	3.8	3.1	3.0	3.3	3.0	2.7	3.8
1995	2.6	2.8	2.2	2.4	2.8	1.7	2.8	2.9	2.4	2.6	2.9	1.8	2.7	2.9	2.3
1996: Mar	2.7	3.2	1.6	2.3	2.9	1.3	3.0	3.3	1.7	2.5	2.9	1.6	2.8	3.3	1.6
June	2.9	3.4	1.7	2.7	3.0	2.0	3.0	3.5	1.6	2.8	2.9	2.4	2.9	3.5	1.5
Sept	2.9	3.3	1.8	2.8	3.3	1.9	2.9	3.3	1.8	3.1	3.4	2.4	2.9	3.3	1.6
Dec	3.1	3.4	2.0	2.8	3.2	1.9	3.2	3.5	2.0	3.0	3.3	2.3	3.1	3.5	1.9
1997: Mar	3.0	3.4	2.0	2.5	2.9	1.6	3.1	3.4	2.2	2.6	3.0	1.7	3.1	3.5	2.1
June	2.9	3.3	2.0	2.6	3.0	1.7	3.0	3.4	2.2	2.6	3.0	1.8	3.0	3.4	2.0
Sept	3.2	3.6	2.0	2.7	3.0	1.9	3.3	3.8	1.9	2.5	2.8	1.9	3.3	3.8	2.0
Dec	3.4	3.9	2.3	2.4	3.0	1.3	3.9	4.4	2.9	2.4	3.0	1.4	3.8	4.2	2.6
	Percent change from 3 months earlier, seasonally adjusted														
1996: Mar	0.6	1.0	0	0.4	0.8	-0.2	0.8	1.1	0.1	0.5	0.9	-0.1	0.7	1.0	0.1
June	.9	.9	.7	.9	1.0	.8	.8	.8	.6	.9	.9	.9	.8	.9	.5
Sept	.7	.7	.5	.7	.7	.8	.7	.7	.7	.9	.9	.6	.7	.6	.5
Dec	.7	.8	.7	.6	.6	.9	.8	.9	.6	.7	.5	.8	.9	1.0	.7
1997: Mar	.6	.9	0	.2	.6	-.6	.8	1.0	.4	.2	.5	-.6	.7	.9	.4
June	.8	.9	.7	1.0	1.1	.9	.7	.8	.6	.9	.9	1.0	.8	.8	.4
Sept	.8	.9	.5	.8	.8	.7	.9	1.1	.4	.7	.8	.6	.8	1.1	.4
Dec	1.2	1.2	1.1	.4	.5	.2	1.5	1.4	1.6	.6	.7	.3	1.4	1.3	1.4

[1] Employer costs for employee benefits.

Note.—The employment cost index is a measure of the change in the cost of labor, free from the influence of employment shifts among occupations and industries.

Data exclude farm and household workers.

Source: Department of Labor, Bureau of Labor Statistics.

337

[Index numbers, 1992=100; quarterly data seasonally adjusted]

Year or quarter	Output per hour of all persons		Output[1]		Hours of all persons[2]		Compensation per hour[3]		Real compensation per hour[4]		Unit labor costs		Implicit price deflator[5]	
	Business sector	Nonfarm business sector	Business sector	Nonfarm business sector	Business sector	Nonfarm business sector	Business sector	Nonfarm business sector	Business sector	Nonfarm business sector	Business sector	Nonfarm business sector	Business sector	Nonfarm business sector
1959	50.5	54.2	33.7	33.5	66.7	61.7	13.1	13.7	63.1	66.0	25.9	25.3	25.6	25.0
1960	51.4	54.8	34.3	34.0	66.7	62.0	13.6	14.3	64.7	67.7	26.6	26.1	25.8	25.3
1961	53.2	56.5	34.9	34.7	65.7	61.3	14.2	14.8	66.6	69.3	26.7	26.1	26.1	25.6
1962	55.7	59.1	37.2	37.0	66.8	62.6	14.8	15.4	68.9	71.5	26.6	26.0	26.3	25.8
1963	57.9	61.2	38.9	38.7	67.2	63.3	15.4	15.9	70.5	73.0	26.6	26.0	26.5	26.0
1964	60.5	63.8	41.4	41.3	68.3	64.8	16.2	16.7	73.2	75.4	26.7	26.1	26.8	26.3
1965	62.7	65.7	44.2	44.2	70.6	67.3	16.8	17.2	74.8	76.7	26.8	26.2	27.2	26.7
1966	65.2	68.0	47.2	47.4	72.5	69.7	17.9	18.2	77.5	78.8	27.5	26.8	27.9	27.3
1967	66.6	69.2	48.1	48.2	72.3	69.7	18.9	19.3	79.5	80.9	28.4	27.8	28.7	28.2
1968	68.9	71.6	50.5	50.7	73.3	70.9	20.5	20.8	82.5	83.8	29.7	29.0	29.8	29.3
1969	69.2	71.6	52.0	52.3	75.2	72.9	21.9	22.2	83.7	84.9	31.7	31.0	31.1	30.5
1970	70.5	72.6	52.0	52.1	73.7	71.8	23.6	23.8	85.4	86.1	33.5	32.8	32.4	31.9
1971	73.6	75.6	54.0	54.1	73.3	71.5	25.1	25.4	87.0	87.8	34.1	33.5	33.9	33.3
1972	76.0	78.2	57.6	57.8	75.7	73.9	26.7	27.0	89.6	90.6	35.1	34.5	35.0	34.3
1973	78.4	80.7	61.6	62.0	78.5	76.9	29.0	29.2	91.6	92.3	37.0	36.2	36.8	35.5
1974	77.1	79.4	60.6	61.1	78.6	77.0	31.8	32.1	90.5	91.3	41.3	40.4	40.3	39.1
1975	79.8	81.5	60.0	60.0	75.2	73.6	35.1	35.3	91.5	92.1	44.0	43.3	44.2	43.2
1976	82.5	84.5	64.0	64.3	77.6	76.1	38.2	38.4	94.1	94.6	46.2	45.4	46.5	45.6
1977	83.9	85.8	67.6	67.9	80.6	79.2	41.2	41.5	95.3	96.0	49.0	48.3	49.4	48.6
1978	84.9	86.9	71.7	72.3	84.5	83.1	44.8	45.2	96.5	97.3	52.8	52.0	53.0	51.9
1979	84.5	86.3	73.9	74.3	87.4	86.1	49.2	49.5	95.0	95.7	58.2	57.4	57.6	56.4
1980	84.2	86.0	73.0	73.4	86.6	85.4	54.5	54.8	92.7	93.3	64.7	63.8	62.8	61.9
1981	85.7	86.9	74.8	74.8	87.2	86.1	59.6	60.1	92.0	92.8	69.5	69.2	68.7	67.9
1982	85.3	86.3	72.5	72.4	85.0	83.9	64.1	64.6	93.1	93.9	75.1	74.8	72.7	72.2
1983	88.0	89.9	76.1	76.8	86.5	85.5	66.7	67.3	94.0	94.8	75.8	74.9	75.4	74.7
1984	90.2	91.4	82.5	82.8	91.5	90.6	69.6	70.1	94.0	94.7	77.2	76.7	77.7	77.0
1985	91.7	92.3	85.7	85.8	93.5	92.9	73.0	73.4	95.2	95.7	79.7	79.5	80.0	79.6
1986	94.0	94.7	88.5	88.7	94.1	93.7	76.8	77.2	98.3	98.8	81.7	81.5	81.7	81.4
1987	94.0	94.5	91.1	91.3	97.0	96.7	79.8	80.1	98.5	98.9	84.9	84.7	83.8	83.6
1988	94.6	95.2	94.6	95.1	100.0	99.9	83.5	83.6	99.0	99.1	88.2	87.8	86.8	86.4
1989	95.4	95.7	97.8	98.1	102.5	102.5	85.8	85.8	97.1	97.1	89.9	89.7	90.4	90.0
1990	96.1	96.2	98.6	98.8	102.6	102.7	90.7	90.6	97.4	97.3	94.4	94.1	94.1	93.8
1991	96.7	96.9	96.9	97.1	100.2	100.2	95.1	95.1	97.9	97.9	98.3	98.1	97.7	97.6
1992	100.0	100.0	100.0	100.0	100.0	100.0	100.0	100.0	100.0	100.0	100.0	100.0	100.0	100.0
1993	100.2	100.1	102.7	103.0	102.6	102.8	102.6	102.3	99.6	99.3	102.4	102.2	102.5	102.5
1994	100.6	100.5	107.0	107.0	106.3	106.4	104.3	104.1	98.7	98.5	103.7	103.6	104.8	104.9
1995	100.5	100.7	109.5	109.8	108.9	109.0	106.9	106.7	98.4	98.3	106.3	106.0	107.2	107.3
1996	102.0	102.0	113.3	113.6	111.0	111.3	110.4	110.1	98.7	98.4	108.2	107.9	109.2	109.1
1992:I	99.4	99.3	98.8	98.8	99.5	99.5	98.6	98.6	99.7	99.7	99.3	99.2	99.3	99.2
II	99.9	100.0	99.6	99.6	99.7	99.6	99.5	99.6	99.8	99.9	99.6	99.6	99.7	99.8
III	99.7	99.7	99.8	99.8	100.1	100.1	100.7	100.7	100.2	100.2	101.0	101.0	100.1	100.1
IV	101.0	101.1	101.7	101.8	100.7	100.7	101.2	101.2	99.9	99.9	100.1	100.1	100.9	100.9
1993:I	100.1	100.1	101.4	101.6	101.4	101.5	101.8	101.6	99.8	99.6	101.7	101.6	101.7	101.8
II	99.7	99.6	102.1	102.3	102.4	102.6	102.4	102.1	99.7	99.4	102.7	102.5	102.3	102.3
III	99.9	100.0	102.8	103.2	102.9	103.2	102.9	102.5	99.6	99.3	103.0	102.5	102.7	102.6
IV	101.0	100.8	104.6	104.8	103.6	103.9	103.3	103.0	99.2	98.9	102.3	102.1	103.4	103.3
1994:I	100.7	100.6	105.2	105.2	104.5	104.6	104.0	103.8	99.5	99.2	103.3	103.2	103.9	103.8
II	100.7	100.7	106.9	106.9	106.1	106.1	104.0	103.9	98.8	98.7	103.2	103.1	104.4	104.5
III	100.5	100.4	107.3	107.3	106.7	106.8	104.4	104.2	98.3	98.1	103.9	103.8	105.1	105.3
IV	100.7	100.8	108.5	108.6	107.7	107.8	105.1	105.0	98.3	98.2	104.3	104.2	105.8	106.0
1995:I	100.2	100.3	108.7	108.9	108.5	108.5	105.8	105.6	98.3	98.2	105.6	105.3	106.5	106.8
II	100.4	100.5	108.7	108.9	108.3	108.4	106.6	106.4	98.3	98.1	106.1	105.8	107.0	107.2
III	100.6	100.8	109.8	110.2	109.2	109.3	107.3	107.1	98.4	98.3	106.7	106.3	107.4	107.5
IV	101.1	101.2	110.7	111.0	109.5	109.7	108.1	107.9	98.6	98.4	107.0	106.6	107.8	107.8
1996:I	101.6	101.7	111.4	111.7	109.6	109.8	108.9	108.7	98.4	98.3	107.1	106.9	108.4	108.4
II	102.3	102.2	113.2	113.5	110.7	111.0	110.1	109.8	98.8	98.5	107.7	107.4	108.9	108.8
III	102.0	102.0	113.5	113.8	111.3	111.6	111.0	110.6	98.9	98.6	108.8	108.5	109.6	109.4
IV	102.5	102.4	115.0	115.3	112.2	112.6	111.9	111.5	98.9	98.5	109.2	108.9	110.0	109.8
1997:I	102.9	102.8	116.6	116.9	113.3	113.8	113.1	112.8	99.4	99.1	109.9	109.7	110.6	110.5
II	103.5	103.4	117.8	118.0	113.7	114.2	114.0	113.7	99.9	99.6	110.1	110.0	111.0	110.9
III	104.6	104.4	118.9	119.2	113.7	114.1	115.2	114.8	100.5	100.1	110.2	109.9	111.3	111.2

[1] Output refers to real gross domestic product in the sector.
[2] Hours at work of all persons engaged in the sector, including hours of proprietors and unpaid family workers. Estimates based primarily on establishment data.
[3] Wages and salaries of employees plus employers' contributions for social insurance and private benefit plans. Also includes an estimate of wages, salaries, and supplemental payments for the self-employed.
[4] Hourly compensation divided by the consumer price index for all urban consumers.
[5] Current dollar output divided by the output index.

Source: Department of Labor, Bureau of Labor Statistics.

TABLE B–50.—*Changes in productivity and related data, business sector, 1959–97*

[Percent change from preceding period; quarterly data at seasonally adjusted annual rates]

Year or quarter	Output per hour of all persons — Business sector	Nonfarm business sector	Output[1] — Business sector	Nonfarm business sector	Hours of all persons[2] — Business sector	Nonfarm business sector	Compensation per hour[3] — Business sector	Nonfarm business sector	Real compensation per hour[4] — Business sector	Nonfarm business sector	Unit labor costs — Business sector	Nonfarm business sector	Implicit price deflator[5] — Business sector	Nonfarm business sector
1959	4.2	4.2	8.5	9.0	4.1	4.6	4.2	4.0	3.5	3.2	0	-0.2	0.6	1.1
1960	1.7	1.2	1.8	1.6	.1	.5	4.3	4.4	2.6	2.7	2.5	3.2	1.1	1.1
1961	3.5	3.1	1.9	1.9	-1.6	-1.2	4.0	3.4	2.9	2.4	.4	.3	.9	.9
1962	4.7	4.6	6.5	6.9	1.7	2.1	4.5	4.1	3.5	3.0	-.2	-.5	.9	.8
1963	3.9	3.4	4.5	4.5	.6	1.1	3.7	3.5	2.3	2.2	-.2	.1	.7	.8
1964	4.6	4.3	6.4	6.8	1.7	2.4	5.2	4.6	3.8	3.3	.5	.3	1.0	1.2
1965	3.5	3.0	7.0	7.0	3.4	3.9	3.7	3.3	2.1	1.7	.2	.3	1.7	1.5
1966	4.0	3.5	6.7	7.1	2.6	3.6	6.7	5.8	3.7	2.8	2.6	2.3	2.5	2.3
1967	2.2	1.7	1.9	1.7	-.3	-.0	5.7	5.8	2.5	2.7	3.4	4.0	2.9	3.3
1968	3.4	3.4	4.9	5.2	1.4	1.7	8.1	7.9	3.8	3.5	4.6	4.3	3.9	3.9
1969	.4	.1	3.0	3.0	2.5	2.9	7.0	6.8	1.5	1.3	6.6	6.7	4.3	4.2
1970	2.0	1.4	-.1	-.2	-2.0	-1.6	7.8	7.2	1.9	1.4	5.7	5.7	4.4	4.5
1971	4.3	4.1	3.8	3.8	-.4	-.3	6.4	6.5	1.9	2.0	2.0	2.3	4.5	4.5
1972	3.3	3.4	6.7	6.9	3.3	3.4	6.3	6.4	3.0	3.1	2.9	2.9	3.3	2.9
1973	3.2	3.1	7.0	7.3	3.7	4.0	8.6	8.2	2.2	1.9	5.2	4.9	5.2	3.6
1974	-1.7	-1.6	-1.5	-1.5	.1	.1	9.7	9.9	-1.2	-1.1	11.6	11.6	9.4	10.0
1975	3.5	2.7	-1.0	-1.7	-4.3	-4.3	10.3	10.1	1.0	.9	6.6	7.2	9.5	10.6
1976	3.4	3.6	6.7	7.1	3.1	3.4	8.8	8.6	2.9	2.7	5.2	4.9	5.4	5.6
1977	1.7	1.6	5.7	5.7	3.9	4.0	7.9	8.0	1.3	1.4	6.0	6.3	6.1	6.4
1978	1.1	1.3	6.1	6.4	4.9	5.0	8.9	9.1	1.3	1.4	7.7	7.6	7.3	6.9
1979	-.4	-.8	2.9	2.8	3.4	3.6	9.7	9.5	-1.5	-1.7	10.1	10.3	8.6	8.6
1980	-.3	-.4	-1.2	-1.2	-.9	-.8	10.8	10.8	-2.4	-2.4	11.1	11.2	9.1	9.8
1981	1.8	1.1	2.5	1.9	.7	.7	9.5	9.7	-.8	-.6	7.6	8.5	9.3	9.6
1982	-.5	-.8	-3.1	-3.2	-2.5	-2.5	7.5	7.4	1.2	1.1	8.0	8.2	5.9	6.4
1983	3.2	4.2	4.9	6.1	1.7	1.9	4.2	4.2	.9	1.0	.9	.1	3.7	3.4
1984	2.5	1.7	8.5	7.9	5.8	6.0	4.4	4.2	.0	-.1	1.8	2.5	3.0	3.1
1985	1.6	1.0	3.9	3.6	2.2	2.5	4.9	4.6	1.3	1.0	3.2	3.6	3.0	3.4
1986	2.6	2.6	3.3	3.4	.7	.8	5.2	5.2	3.3	3.2	2.5	2.5	2.1	2.2
1987	-.1	-.2	2.9	3.0	3.0	3.2	3.9	3.8	.2	.1	3.9	4.0	2.6	2.6
1988	.6	.7	3.8	4.1	3.2	3.3	4.6	4.4	.5	.3	4.0	3.6	3.5	3.4
1989	.8	.6	3.4	3.2	2.5	2.6	2.8	2.7	-1.9	-2.0	1.9	2.1	4.2	4.2
1990	.7	.5	.8	.7	.1	.2	5.7	5.5	.3	.1	5.0	5.0	4.0	4.2
1991	.7	.7	-1.7	-1.8	-2.3	-2.5	4.8	4.9	.6	.7	4.1	4.2	3.8	4.1
1992	3.4	3.2	3.2	3.0	-.2	-.2	5.2	5.2	2.1	2.1	1.7	1.9	2.4	2.4
1993	.2	.1	2.7	3.0	2.6	2.8	2.6	2.3	-.4	-.7	2.4	2.2	2.5	2.5
1994	.4	.4	4.1	3.9	3.7	3.5	1.6	1.7	-.9	-.8	1.2	1.4	2.2	2.3
1995	-.0	.2	2.3	2.6	2.4	2.4	2.5	2.5	-.3	-.3	2.6	2.4	2.3	2.3
1996	1.5	1.3	3.5	3.5	2.0	2.2	3.3	3.1	.3	.2	1.8	1.8	1.9	1.7
1992:I	8.0	7.1	6.2	5.6	-1.6	-1.4	7.9	7.7	5.0	4.8	0	.5	2.8	3.0
II	2.2	2.6	3.2	3.0	.9	.4	3.6	4.3	.5	1.1	1.4	1.6	2.0	2.1
III	-.7	-1.2	.8	.7	1.5	1.9	4.7	4.4	1.6	1.2	5.5	5.6	1.5	1.4
IV	5.4	5.9	7.9	8.4	2.3	2.4	2.0	2.0	-1.5	-1.5	-3.2	-3.7	3.0	3.2
1993:I	-3.8	-4.0	-1.2	-.8	2.7	3.3	2.5	1.9	-.4	-1.0	6.6	6.1	3.5	3.8
II	-1.3	-1.8	2.7	2.6	4.0	4.5	2.5	2.0	-.4	-.9	3.9	3.9	2.1	1.7
III	.7	1.7	2.8	3.9	2.0	2.2	1.8	1.6	-.1	-.3	1.0	-.1	1.6	1.5
IV	4.3	3.3	7.1	6.1	2.7	2.7	1.6	1.7	-1.6	-1.6	-2.6	-1.5	2.7	2.6
1994:I	-.9	-1.1	2.6	1.6	3.5	2.8	3.0	3.2	.9	1.2	3.9	4.4	2.0	2.1
II	0	.6	6.4	6.6	6.3	5.9	-.2	.3	-2.5	-2.0	-.2	-.2	2.1	2.5
III	-.7	-1.1	1.5	1.5	2.3	2.6	1.7	1.3	-2.0	-2.3	2.4	2.4	2.7	3.2
IV	.7	1.3	4.5	5.0	3.8	3.7	2.5	2.8	.0	.3	1.8	1.6	2.5	2.4
1995:I	-2.1	-1.6	.8	1.2	2.9	2.9	2.6	2.6	-.2	-.2	4.8	4.2	2.9	3.1
II	.9	.8	.2	.2	-.7	-.6	3.2	3.1	.1	-.1	2.3	2.3	1.6	1.5
III	.7	1.1	4.2	4.6	3.5	3.5	2.6	2.7	.5	.6	1.9	1.6	1.7	1.2
IV	2.0	1.6	3.0	3.0	1.0	1.4	3.2	2.9	.7	.5	1.2	1.3	1.3	1.0
1996:I	2.2	1.9	2.8	2.6	.6	.6	2.7	2.8	-.6	-.5	.5	.9	2.3	2.3
II	2.5	2.2	6.6	6.8	4.0	4.4	4.7	4.4	1.3	1.0	2.2	2.1	2.1	1.7
III	-1.1	-1.0	.9	1.0	2.0	2.1	3.3	2.9	.6	.2	4.4	3.9	2.4	2.0
IV	1.9	1.8	5.4	5.4	3.4	3.6	3.3	3.3	-.1	-.1	1.4	1.5	1.7	1.7
1997:I	1.8	1.4	5.9	5.6	4.0	4.2	4.4	4.5	1.9	2.1	2.5	3.1	2.0	2.4
II	2.4	2.4	3.9	3.8	1.5	1.4	3.3	3.3	2.2	2.2	.9	.9	1.5	1.4
III	4.0	4.1	3.8	4.0	-.2	-.1	4.3	3.9	2.3	1.9	.3	-.2	1.1	1.2

[1] Output refers to real gross domestic product in the sector.
[2] Hours at work of all persons engaged in the sector, including hours of proprietors and unpaid family workers. Estimates based primarily on establishment data.
[3] Wages and salaries of employees plus employers' contributions for social insurance and private benefit plans. Also includes an estimate of wages, salaries, and supplemental payments for the self-employed.
[4] Hourly compensation divided by the consumer price index for all urban consumers.
[5] Current dollar output divided by the output index.

Note.—Percent changes are based on original data and may differ slightly from percent changes based on indexes in Table B-49.

Source: Department of Labor, Bureau of Labor Statistics.

PRODUCTION AND BUSINESS ACTIVITY

Table B–51.—*Industrial production indexes, major industry divisions, 1947–97*

[1992=100; monthly data seasonally adjusted]

Year or month	Total industrial production	Manufacturing			Mining	Utilities
		Total	Durable	Nondurable		
1947	21.7	20.6	19.7	21.4	56.4	10.7
1948	22.6	21.3	20.6	22.1	59.3	11.9
1949	21.4	20.2	18.7	21.7	52.6	12.7
1950	24.7	23.5	22.7	24.2	58.7	14.5
1951	26.8	25.4	25.6	25.0	64.4	16.5
1952	27.8	26.4	27.2	25.4	63.9	17.9
1953	30.2	28.8	30.7	26.5	65.6	19.4
1954	28.6	26.9	27.1	26.7	64.3	20.9
1955	32.2	30.3	31.0	29.6	71.7	23.3
1956	33.6	31.6	32.0	31.1	75.4	25.6
1957	34.1	31.9	32.2	31.6	75.5	27.3
1958	31.9	29.7	28.2	31.9	69.3	28.6
1959	35.7	33.5	32.4	35.1	72.5	31.5
1960	36.5	34.1	32.9	35.9	73.9	33.7
1961	36.7	34.2	32.3	37.0	74.4	35.6
1962	39.8	37.3	35.9	39.3	76.5	38.2
1963	42.1	39.5	38.3	41.4	79.5	40.9
1964	45.0	42.2	41.0	44.1	82.7	44.4
1965	49.5	46.8	46.6	47.1	85.8	47.1
1966	53.8	51.0	51.8	50.0	90.4	50.7
1967	55.0	52.0	52.3	51.6	92.1	53.3
1968	58.1	54.9	54.9	54.9	95.6	57.6
1969	60.7	57.4	57.1	57.8	99.5	62.7
1970	58.7	54.8	52.7	57.8	102.0	66.5
1971	59.5	55.6	52.5	60.2	99.5	69.7
1972	65.3	61.5	58.6	65.5	101.5	74.2
1973	70.6	66.9	65.4	68.8	102.5	77.1
1974	69.6	65.9	64.1	68.3	101.9	76.1
1975	63.4	59.3	56.1	64.0	99.7	76.9
1976	69.3	65.4	61.9	70.5	100.5	79.9
1977	74.9	71.2	68.1	75.7	103.4	82.0
1978	79.3	75.8	73.6	78.9	106.5	84.4
1979	82.0	78.5	77.4	79.9	108.3	86.8
1980	79.7	75.5	73.4	78.3	111.5	87.3
1981	81.0	76.7	74.6	79.5	115.6	85.0
1982	76.7	72.1	68.2	77.7	111.2	82.3
1983	79.5	76.3	72.2	81.9	106.6	83.7
1984	86.6	83.8	82.7	85.3	113.9	86.7
1985	88.0	85.7	85.6	86.0	111.0	88.8
1986	89.0	88.1	87.4	89.1	102.6	86.4
1987	93.2	92.8	92.0	93.8	102.1	89.4
1988	97.4	97.1	98.1	96.0	104.7	93.9
1989	99.1	99.0	100.5	97.3	103.2	97.1
1990	98.9	98.5	99.0	97.9	104.8	98.3
1991	97.0	96.2	95.5	97.0	102.6	100.4
1992	100.0	100.0	100.0	100.0	100.0	100.0
1993	103.6	103.8	105.7	101.7	100.1	103.9
1994	109.2	110.0	114.4	105.2	102.6	105.3
1995	114.5	116.0	123.9	107.4	102.3	109.0
1996	118.5	120.2	131.7	108.0	103.9	112.5
1997 ᴾ	124.5	127.0	142.4	111.1	106.0	112.5
1996: Jan	115.3	116.7	126.7	106.0	100.6	112.3
Feb	116.7	118.1	128.9	106.7	102.2	113.5
Mar	116.3	117.4	127.1	107.1	103.9	114.5
Apr	117.5	119.0	130.4	106.9	104.5	112.5
May	118.3	119.7	131.3	107.5	104.4	113.7
June	118.9	120.4	132.4	107.9	105.5	113.0
July	118.9	120.9	132.8	108.3	105.2	109.4
Aug	119.3	121.1	133.5	108.0	104.9	111.3
Sept	119.6	121.5	133.4	108.9	105.0	111.5
Oct	119.7	121.5	133.3	109.1	104.4	112.1
Nov	120.6	122.5	134.9	109.6	103.6	113.6
Dec	120.9	123.1	135.3	110.3	102.9	112.7
1997: Jan	121.3	123.5	136.1	110.2	103.7	112.5
Feb	122.1	124.4	137.8	110.4	106.0	110.3
Mar	122.5	124.9	138.7	110.5	106.7	109.6
Apr	123.1	125.4	139.5	110.8	105.5	112.5
May	123.3	125.7	140.1	110.7	106.7	111.8
June	123.5	126.1	141.2	110.5	105.7	110.9
July	124.5	126.9	142.4	110.9	106.5	113.8
Aug	125.2	127.9	144.3	111.0	106.3	113.0
Sept	125.6	128.0	144.4	111.3	106.5	115.1
Oct ᴾ	126.5	128.9	145.4	112.0	106.2	116.7
Nov ᴾ	127.5	130.5	147.8	112.7	105.8	114.5
Dec ᴾ	128.1	131.1	148.8	113.1	106.1	114.9

Source: Board of Governors of the Federal Reserve System.

340

TABLE B–52.—*Industrial production indexes, market groupings, 1947–97*

[1992=100; monthly data seasonally adjusted]

Year or month	Total indus-trial pro-duc-tion	Final products								Inter-mediate prod-ucts	Materials			
		Total	Consumer goods				Equipment				Total	Dura-ble	Non-dur-able	Ener-gy
			Total	Auto-motive prod-ucts	Other dura-ble goods	Non-durable goods	Total[1]	Busi-ness	De-fense and space					
1947	21.7	21.0	23.7	22.3	18.6	25.5	16.3	16.0	8.3	22.6	22.1	18.4		
1948	22.6	21.7	24.4	23.4	19.4	26.2	17.2	16.7	9.7	23.9	23.0	18.9		
1949	21.4	21.1	24.3	23.2	18.0	26.4	15.3	14.6	10.2	22.6	21.0	16.9		
1950	24.7	23.8	27.8	29.2	24.8	28.6	16.6	15.6	11.9	26.3	25.1	21.3		
1951	26.8	25.7	27.5	25.8	21.4	29.6	23.1	19.1	29.3	27.6	27.8	24.3		
1952	27.8	27.5	28.1	23.2	21.4	30.8	27.7	21.6	41.2	27.5	28.2	24.8		
1953	30.2	29.4	29.8	29.3	24.2	31.7	30.1	22.5	49.4	29.4	31.3	28.9		
1954	28.6	27.9	29.6	27.3	22.3	32.1	26.3	19.8	43.5	29.3	28.9	25.0	23.0	51.4
1955	32.2	30.1	33.0	36.3	26.3	34.5	26.9	21.4	39.8	33.2	34.2	30.6	26.3	57.8
1956	33.6	31.9	34.2	29.9	27.7	36.8	29.5	24.8	38.9	34.7	35.1	30.7	27.6	61.1
1957	34.1	32.8	35.1	31.3	27.1	37.9	30.7	25.8	40.6	34.7	35.1	30.6	27.4	61.8
1958	31.9	31.3	34.8	24.9	25.6	39.0	27.5	21.8	40.8	33.9	31.6	25.8	27.3	57.3
1959	35.7	34.3	38.1	31.2	29.4	41.7	30.2	24.5	43.0	37.5	36.4	30.7	31.2	60.7
1960	36.5	35.5	39.6	35.7	29.6	43.1	31.0	25.1	44.2	37.7	36.9	31.1	31.7	61.5
1961	36.7	35.8	40.4	32.6	30.5	44.5	30.6	24.4	44.9	38.5	36.9	30.4	33.0	62.0
1962	39.8	38.8	43.1	39.5	33.1	46.6	34.0	26.5	52.0	40.8	40.2	33.8	35.8	64.1
1963	42.1	41.0	45.5	43.2	35.7	48.7	36.1	27.8	56.1	43.1	42.8	36.0	37.9	67.9
1964	45.0	43.3	48.1	45.3	39.0	51.1	38.1	31.1	54.3	45.9	46.3	39.3	41.3	70.7
1965	49.5	47.6	51.8	55.8	44.2	53.3	43.1	35.6	60.1	48.9	51.6	45.0	45.3	73.9
1966	53.8	52.1	54.5	55.6	48.7	55.8	50.2	41.3	70.6	51.9	56.2	49.6	48.9	78.6
1967	55.0	54.2	55.8	48.9	49.3	58.7	53.4	42.1	80.6	54.0	55.7	47.8	49.8	81.3
1968	58.1	56.8	59.2	58.2	52.8	61.0	54.9	43.9	80.7	57.1	59.4	50.7	54.7	85.0
1969	60.7	58.6	61.4	58.5	56.3	63.1	56.4	46.8	76.8	60.2	62.9	53.3	59.2	89.4
1970	58.7	56.5	60.7	49.2	54.6	64.1	52.4	45.1	65.1	59.3	60.7	48.4	59.5	93.8
1971	59.5	57.0	64.2	62.7	57.8	66.0	49.1	42.9	58.5	61.1	61.6	48.6	62.0	94.6
1972	65.3	61.9	69.3	67.7	66.2	70.2	53.7	48.9	56.8	68.2	67.9	54.9	68.4	98.2
1973	70.6	66.5	72.4	74.7	70.0	72.4	59.9	57.2	55.5	72.6	74.3	62.8	73.4	98.9
1974	69.6	66.3	70.2	64.6	64.7	72.4	61.9	59.7	54.7	70.0	72.8	61.0	73.7	96.3
1975	63.4	62.4	67.4	60.8	57.0	70.9	56.7	53.3	53.7	63.2	63.9	50.8	65.6	94.2
1976	69.3	66.8	74.1	75.5	63.9	76.1	58.6	55.3	54.6	69.6	71.4	58.5	74.3	96.5
1977	74.9	72.4	79.5	87.2	71.8	79.8	64.3	62.0	54.4	75.7	76.9	64.6	78.9	97.9
1978	79.3	77.2	82.6	89.6	74.9	82.9	71.0	69.3	55.9	79.9	81.0	70.2	81.6	98.9
1979	82.0	79.7	81.5	81.4	73.6	82.9	77.6	77.3	57.7	82.0	83.9	73.3	84.4	101.4
1980	79.7	79.3	79.6	62.3	69.7	83.8	79.1	76.7	63.2	77.7	80.3	67.7	80.7	102.2
1981	81.0	81.2	80.1	61.6	70.7	84.3	82.8	78.0	64.5	77.6	81.4	70.4	82.3	100.2
1982	76.7	78.3	78.8	59.1	64.4	84.2	77.7	70.6	72.6	75.8	75.1	62.6	74.6	96.7
1983	79.5	80.0	83.2	74.3	73.1	86.2	76.4	68.3	80.4	81.0	78.3	68.2	81.0	94.7
1984	86.6	87.0	86.7	89.4	80.1	87.5	87.6	79.2	89.5	86.9	85.9	79.5	84.5	99.5
1985	88.0	89.3	87.6	95.4	77.3	88.5	91.8	82.5	103.8	89.1	86.3	80.9	83.2	99.1
1986	89.0	90.3	90.7	97.5	82.6	91.3	90.0	82.0	113.0	92.7	86.3	82.3	85.7	95.2
1987	93.2	93.3	93.7	100.7	89.1	93.6	92.9	85.1	117.5	100.7	90.4	87.5	90.9	96.2
1988	97.4	97.9	96.7	107.1	94.5	95.9	99.9	93.5	117.1	102.5	95.1	93.6	94.8	98.5
1989	99.1	99.9	97.7	108.9	95.9	96.7	103.7	98.8	117.4	102.9	97.0	95.7	97.2	99.5
1990	98.9	99.5	97.3	100.9	96.0	97.1	103.2	98.2	115.9	101.9	97.2	95.3	98.1	100.6
1991	97.0	97.7	97.0	90.3	95.2	98.1	98.8	95.7	106.7	97.5	95.9	93.2	96.9	100.8
1992	100.0	100.0	100.0	100.0	100.0	100.0	100.0	100.0	100.0	100.0	100.0	100.0	100.0	100.0
1993	103.6	103.4	103.0	111.0	108.0	101.5	104.1	105.8	93.8	102.5	104.1	107.1	101.8	99.6
1994	109.2	107.5	107.1	122.7	117.2	104.0	108.1	112.5	86.9	106.3	112.3	119.5	106.9	101.4
1995	114.5	111.3	109.9	122.3	121.1	106.9	113.8	121.5	81.4	108.3	120.8	134.4	108.6	102.6
1996	118.5	114.6	111.8	123.9	127.3	108.3	119.6	129.7	76.9	110.8	126.2	144.7	108.3	103.5
1997 *P*	124.5	119.6	114.4	130.0	132.3	110.1	128.7	141.8	75.3	115.0	134.2	158.3	112.9	104.1
1996: Jan	115.3	111.7	109.7	118.3	121.7	107.1	115.1	124.4	75.4	107.6	122.6	139.9	105.1	102.0
Feb	116.7	113.5	111.2	123.2	124.0	108.0	117.5	127.1	76.6	108.7	123.7	141.3	105.9	103.1
Mar	116.3	112.7	110.7	111.2	124.8	108.6	116.3	125.2	77.8	109.5	123.2	139.6	105.9	104.4
Apr	117.5	114.0	111.2	125.7	126.1	107.5	118.8	128.4	77.3	109.0	125.1	142.9	107.2	103.9
May	118.3	114.3	111.6	125.8	128.2	107.7	119.1	128.6	77.5	110.4	126.1	144.3	107.8	104.4
June	118.9	115.0	112.1	128.3	130.6	107.8	119.9	130.1	76.5	111.4	126.5	145.0	108.0	104.6
July	118.9	115.3	112.1	130.8	127.8	107.8	121.0	131.3	77.2	110.8	126.5	145.1	109.1	103.2
Aug	119.3	115.0	111.7	127.4	128.8	107.6	120.7	131.0	77.3	111.4	127.4	147.1	108.6	103.6
Sept	119.6	115.6	112.4	125.5	128.6	108.7	121.1	131.5	77.5	111.9	127.5	146.5	109.6	103.9
Oct	119.7	115.3	112.1	120.7	127.4	108.9	121.0	131.6	76.9	111.9	127.9	147.2	110.1	103.8
Nov	120.6	116.3	113.1	124.5	128.8	109.7	121.8	133.0	76.5	113.7	128.4	148.4	110.4	103.0
Dec	120.9	116.8	113.6	125.9	130.4	109.9	122.4	134.0	76.2	113.0	129.0	149.3	111.4	102.7
1997: Jan	121.3	116.8	113.2	127.4	128.5	109.4	123.1	134.9	75.5	113.5	129.7	150.2	111.6	103.6
Feb	122.1	117.2	113.1	128.5	130.1	109.0	124.6	136.5	75.6	114.1	131.0	152.2	112.6	103.8
Mar	122.5	117.9	113.4	129.0	132.0	109.1	125.8	137.5	75.7	114.1	131.3	153.0	112.5	103.4
Apr	123.1	118.0	113.4	122.3	131.4	109.9	126.0	137.9	75.4	114.7	132.5	155.1	113.0	103.7
May	123.3	118.6	113.9	124.6	132.1	110.1	126.8	139.0	75.6	114.9	132.4	155.4	111.8	103.7
June	123.5	118.6	113.5	126.7	132.3	109.4	127.7	140.2	76.0	114.7	133.0	156.9	111.9	103.2
July	124.5	119.2	113.9	120.3	134.4	110.3	128.6	141.6	74.9	114.6	134.9	159.3	113.5	104.6
Aug	125.2	120.5	114.6	131.6	132.5	110.3	130.9	144.6	75.0	115.3	134.9	160.3	112.3	103.9
Sept	125.6	120.3	114.5	132.8	131.1	110.2	130.6	144.4	74.7	115.2	136.1	161.3	113.3	105.5
Oct *P*	126.5	121.1	115.4	131.2	131.0	111.4	131.3	145.4	74.7	116.4	136.9	163.2	113.2	105.3
Nov *P*	127.5	122.2	116.3	138.5	134.1	111.5	132.5	147.1	75.1	116.6	138.3	166.0	114.3	104.5
Dec *P*	128.1	122.6	116.6	135.0	136.6	111.9	133.1	147.8	75.2	117.2	139.3	167.4	114.8	105.0

[1] Two components—oil and gas well drilling and manufactured homes—are included in total equipment, but not in detail shown.

Source: Board of Governors of the Federal Reserve System.

341

Year or month	Durable manufactures								Nondurable manufactures				
	Primary metals		Fabricated metal products	Industrial machinery and equipment	Electrical machinery	Transportation equipment		Lumber and products	Apparel products	Textile mill products	Printing and publishing	Chemicals and products	Foods
	Total	Iron and steel				Total	Motor vehicles and parts						
1947	68.6	97.1	38.2	15.1	5.5	19.0	26.5	40.6	47.2	34.1	22.7	7.5	31.1
1948	71.3	101.6	38.9	15.1	5.7	20.7	28.8	42.2	49.2	36.5	23.9	8.2	30.8
1949	60.0	86.7	35.1	12.9	5.4	20.8	29.5	37.3	48.8	33.7	24.5	8.0	31.1
1950	75.5	106.9	43.0	14.5	7.4	24.9	38.0	45.3	52.5	38.3	25.7	10.1	32.2
1951	82.1	119.5	45.9	18.4	7.4	27.8	34.8	45.2	51.5	38.0	26.2	11.4	32.8
1952	75.0	105.2	44.8	20.0	8.5	32.3	29.8	44.6	54.2	37.6	26.1	11.9	33.5
1953	85.0	121.3	50.6	20.9	9.7	40.6	37.6	47.1	54.9	38.6	27.3	12.9	34.2
1954	68.8	94.3	45.5	17.8	8.6	35.3	32.4	46.8	54.2	36.1	28.4	13.1	34.9
1955	89.4	125.3	52.0	19.5	9.9	40.6	43.4	52.3	59.9	41.2	31.3	15.3	36.9
1956	88.8	123.0	52.7	22.4	10.7	39.4	35.2	51.7	61.3	42.3	33.2	16.4	39.0
1957	85.0	118.5	54.1	22.3	10.6	42.2	36.9	47.4	61.1	40.3	34.4	17.3	39.6
1958	67.4	89.3	48.5	18.8	9.7	33.3	27.3	48.2	59.4	39.8	33.6	17.9	40.6
1959	78.8	102.8	54.4	21.9	11.8	37.7	35.4	54.6	65.4	45.0	35.9	20.8	42.6
1960	78.5	104.5	54.5	22.0	12.8	39.0	40.0	51.5	66.7	44.1	37.3	21.6	43.8
1961	77.0	99.8	53.1	21.4	13.6	36.7	35.1	53.9	67.1	45.4	37.5	22.7	45.0
1962	82.6	104.0	57.7	24.0	15.7	42.4	42.7	56.8	69.9	48.5	38.9	25.2	46.4
1963	89.1	113.3	59.6	25.6	16.1	46.5	47.3	59.5	72.7	50.3	40.9	27.6	48.1
1964	100.5	128.9	63.3	29.2	17.0	47.7	48.5	63.9	75.3	54.3	43.4	30.2	50.3
1965	110.6	141.4	69.6	32.8	20.3	56.7	62.0	66.4	79.5	59.1	46.2	33.7	51.5
1966	117.4	145.7	74.5	38.1	24.4	60.8	60.9	68.9	81.6	62.7	49.7	36.7	53.4
1967	108.5	134.6	77.9	38.9	24.5	59.5	53.6	68.2	81.2	62.7	52.4	38.4	55.8
1968	112.4	139.0	82.1	39.2	25.8	64.6	64.2	70.2	83.2	70.0	53.3	43.2	57.3
1969	120.9	151.4	83.5	42.4	27.5	64.1	64.5	70.1	85.9	73.6	55.9	46.7	59.2
1970	112.5	140.9	77.4	41.1	26.3	53.8	51.9	69.7	82.5	72.0	54.3	48.6	60.1
1971	106.7	128.9	77.0	38.2	26.4	58.2	65.0	71.5	83.5	76.0	54.8	51.7	62.0
1972	119.5	143.3	84.5	44.3	30.2	62.2	71.0	81.9	88.6	83.3	58.5	58.2	65.3
1973	135.6	163.1	93.9	51.8	34.4	70.8	82.7	82.2	89.3	86.7	60.0	63.6	66.6
1974	131.4	158.0	90.1	55.1	34.1	64.4	71.4	74.6	85.3	78.9	59.1	65.9	67.5
1975	104.7	127.0	78.1	47.7	29.3	57.9	60.5	69.5	77.9	75.2	55.3	60.1	67.1
1976	117.1	139.9	86.5	50.1	32.9	65.9	79.7	79.0	91.8	83.5	60.4	67.2	70.9
1977	119.0	138.0	94.7	56.6	38.1	71.9	92.4	86.1	98.0	88.3	66.3	72.4	74.6
1978	128.0	147.5	98.2	63.3	42.2	77.5	96.8	87.5	100.4	88.6	70.1	76.4	77.2
1979	130.0	148.4	101.6	70.2	46.9	78.7	89.0	86.3	95.3	91.5	72.0	79.2	77.9
1980	108.0	119.0	94.4	70.5	48.6	70.3	65.8	80.4	95.4	89.0	72.4	75.9	79.7
1981	113.9	126.6	93.0	74.7	51.0	66.9	62.8	78.1	97.3	86.3	74.3	77.3	81.4
1982	80.5	80.5	84.9	65.8	51.7	63.0	56.9	70.3	96.3	80.1	77.5	71.0	82.4
1983	88.2	90.0	87.2	65.2	55.9	70.5	72.1	83.3	100.3	89.9	81.4	76.0	84.6
1984	98.7	98.9	95.2	78.9	66.7	80.5	87.3	89.8	102.2	90.4	87.0	79.3	86.4
1985	98.4	98.8	96.5	81.2	68.4	88.8	95.0	92.0	98.6	86.5	90.2	79.4	88.9
1986	91.2	86.8	95.6	81.8	71.0	94.1	94.2	99.6	101.8	90.5	93.4	82.4	91.2
1987	97.8	95.4	101.9	86.0	75.6	96.1	94.9	104.9	105.5	96.3	102.5	87.0	93.5
1988	106.2	107.6	106.1	97.1	82.5	101.1	100.2	105.1	103.5	95.0	103.4	92.2	94.9
1989	104.9	106.2	104.8	103.0	85.8	105.1	101.2	104.3	100.3	96.5	103.5	95.1	95.9
1990	104.0	106.4	101.2	100.1	87.7	102.3	95.3	101.6	97.2	93.2	103.1	97.3	97.0
1991	96.7	96.0	96.2	95.4	89.6	96.5	88.5	94.5	97.8	92.7	99.1	96.4	98.4
1992	100.0	100.0	100.0	100.0	100.0	100.0	100.0	100.0	100.0	100.0	100.0	100.0	100.0
1993	105.7	107.1	104.4	109.9	110.7	103.8	113.6	100.8	102.4	105.2	100.6	101.4	102.0
1994	113.4	113.7	112.2	124.8	133.2	107.1	129.8	105.9	106.5	110.6	100.7	104.7	103.7
1995	117.2	117.7	116.6	142.7	170.9	105.7	131.0	107.8	107.1	109.9	101.5	107.5	106.8
1996	118.9	117.6	119.6	155.3	199.3	106.5	130.2	111.8	102.2	106.7	101.5	110.5	107.3
1997 *P*	124.6	123.1	123.0	171.4	231.6	115.5	136.9	114.8	99.7	109.8	104.8	115.1	109.6
1996: Jan	115.8	116.7	117.7	148.7	185.6	103.1	128.8	107.5	100.7	102.4	99.7	107.9	106.6
Feb	116.0	114.3	118.7	151.3	192.5	104.9	130.2	108.3	103.6	104.6	101.0	108.0	107.0
Mar	117.6	116.3	118.5	152.2	192.6	94.7	108.7	111.5	102.4	107.7	100.3	108.0	107.4
Apr	118.0	116.4	118.4	152.4	194.8	107.8	135.1	112.3	103.4	105.7	100.5	108.1	107.1
May	117.7	115.6	119.2	153.8	197.1	108.2	135.2	112.4	103.2	106.9	101.7	109.1	106.8
June	119.1	118.4	119.5	155.1	200.0	108.3	134.6	114.7	102.9	108.9	101.2	109.5	107.1
July	117.7	116.7	120.0	155.8	200.4	110.3	137.9	111.6	102.2	107.6	101.4	110.8	107.2
Aug	120.1	118.9	120.1	157.8	201.9	109.6	135.8	113.5	102.9	108.2	101.4	110.8	105.9
Sept	121.3	118.5	120.4	157.3	203.9	107.7	130.1	112.6	102.3	107.3	102.1	112.0	107.0
Oct	121.9	121.9	120.8	157.6	204.8	105.9	125.4	111.6	101.6	107.5	102.6	113.2	107.8
Nov	120.8	119.3	120.9	159.9	207.7	108.8	130.7	115.2	101.2	108.0	103.1	113.5	108.2
Dec	120.5	118.0	120.6	161.3	210.5	109.1	130.1	110.2	100.0	105.9	103.2	114.9	109.0
1997: Jan	119.4	118.8	120.6	162.8	211.1	110.9	133.4	111.4	100.5	107.0	103.2	115.2	109.3
Feb	121.6	119.9	121.7	164.0	217.4	111.4	133.3	114.2	99.5	107.0	103.3	114.6	109.4
Mar	121.8	119.6	122.1	165.1	220.8	112.3	134.0	114.9	100.1	108.0	103.6	113.6	110.0
Apr	122.3	121.2	122.5	167.8	223.7	110.7	129.7	115.9	99.8	109.2	104.4	115.2	109.2
May	124.2	123.9	122.7	168.0	226.3	110.8	129.2	116.4	99.8	107.2	104.5	114.5	109.2
June	124.9	122.6	121.9	168.8	229.7	113.0	132.5	117.0	99.6	109.1	104.1	114.6	108.8
July	125.2	122.2	122.4	172.2	235.5	112.2	130.0	116.1	99.7	110.7	104.1	114.3	110.0
Aug	125.5	121.8	122.8	175.9	236.8	117.0	138.9	115.4	99.1	110.7	104.4	114.5	108.9
Sept	125.9	124.5	122.7	173.7	237.5	118.8	141.2	113.3	99.1	111.4	105.1	115.6	108.6
Oct *P*	127.4	126.5	124.2	176.3	240.8	118.2	139.6	112.5	99.3	111.7	106.7	116.1	109.3
Nov *P*	128.5	127.9	125.4	177.5	247.0	122.2	146.9	115.2	98.8	112.9	107.4	115.8	111.0
Dec *P*	129.6	128.8	127.1	179.3	251.5	121.0	141.6	114.8	100.0	113.1	106.8	116.6	111.1

Source: Board of Governors of the Federal Reserve System.

TABLE B–54.—*Capacity utilization rates, 1948–97*

[Percent;[1] monthly data seasonally adjusted]

Year or month	Total industry	Manufacturing					Mining	Utilities
		Total	Durable goods	Non-durable goods	Primary processing	Advanced processing		
1948		82.5			87.3	80.0		
1949		74.2			76.2	73.2		
1950		82.8			88.5	79.8		
1951		85.8			90.2	83.4		
1952		85.4			84.9	85.9		
1953		89.3			89.4	89.3		
1954		80.1			80.6	80.0		
1955		87.0			92.0	84.2		
1956		86.1			89.4	84.4		
1957		83.6			84.7	83.1		
1958		75.0			75.4	74.9		
1959		81.6			83.0	81.1		
1960		80.1			79.8	80.5		
1961		77.3			77.9	77.2		
1962		81.4			81.5	81.6		
1963		83.5			83.8	83.4		
1964		85.6			87.8	84.6		
1965		89.5			91.0	88.8		
1966		91.1			91.4	91.1		
1967	87.0	87.2	87.5	86.3	85.3	88.0	81.2	94.5
1968	87.3	87.1	87.2	86.6	86.1	87.3	83.5	95.1
1969	87.3	86.6	86.7	86.5	86.5	86.4	86.5	96.7
1970	81.1	79.4	77.2	82.8	79.9	78.9	88.8	96.2
1971	79.4	77.9	74.7	82.6	78.7	77.1	87.3	94.6
1972	84.4	83.4	81.4	86.4	85.5	82.2	90.3	95.2
1973	88.4	87.7	88.0	87.3	90.5	86.2	92.3	93.5
1974	84.3	83.4	83.1	83.9	85.1	82.5	92.3	87.3
1975	74.6	72.9	70.6	76.3	72.1	73.3	89.7	84.4
1976	79.3	78.2	75.7	81.8	79.2	77.6	89.8	85.2
1977	83.5	82.6	80.8	85.3	83.8	81.9	90.9	85.0
1978	85.8	85.2	84.4	86.4	85.9	84.8	90.9	85.4
1979	86.0	85.3	85.6	84.9	86.0	84.9	91.4	86.6
1980	81.5	79.5	78.4	81.0	77.2	80.8	93.4	85.9
1981	80.8	78.3	76.8	80.4	77.2	78.8	93.9	82.5
1982	74.5	71.8	68.0	77.5	68.6	73.5	86.3	79.3
1983	75.7	74.4	70.1	80.8	74.5	74.4	80.4	79.7
1984	80.8	79.8	77.6	82.9	80.0	79.7	86.0	81.9
1985	79.8	78.8	76.8	81.5	79.1	78.6	84.3	83.5
1986	78.7	78.7	75.7	82.8	79.9	78.1	77.6	80.6
1987	81.3	81.3	77.9	85.9	84.5	79.9	80.3	82.5
1988	84.0	83.8	81.7	86.4	86.8	82.3	85.2	84.9
1989	84.1	83.6	82.0	85.7	86.1	82.5	86.9	86.3
1990	82.3	81.4	79.0	84.4	83.9	80.3	89.8	85.7
1991	79.3	77.9	74.7	81.9	79.6	77.2	88.4	86.3
1992	80.2	79.4	76.6	82.7	82.3	78.2	86.5	84.6
1993	81.3	80.5	78.8	82.4	84.1	78.9	86.2	87.2
1994	83.1	82.5	81.5	83.6	87.4	80.4	87.6	87.3
1995	83.4	82.8	82.1	83.5	87.1	80.8	87.1	89.0
1996	82.4	81.4	80.8	82.0	85.6	79.5	88.8	90.2
1997 ᵖ	82.7	81.7	81.0	82.6	86.0	79.8	89.8	89.3
1996: Jan	81.8	80.8	80.4	81.4	84.8	79.1	86.1	90.6
Feb	82.5	81.5	81.3	81.8	84.8	80.0	87.4	91.6
Mar	81.9	80.6	79.6	81.9	85.2	78.6	88.8	92.2
Apr	82.5	81.4	81.2	81.6	85.1	79.8	89.3	90.5
May	82.7	81.6	81.3	81.8	85.4	79.9	89.3	91.4
June	82.8	81.7	81.5	81.9	86.0	79.8	90.2	90.7
July	82.6	81.7	81.3	82.1	85.8	79.9	89.9	87.7
Aug	82.5	81.5	81.3	81.8	85.9	79.6	89.6	89.2
Sept	82.4	81.4	80.7	82.3	86.0	79.4	89.6	89.1
Oct	82.2	81.1	80.2	82.3	86.0	79.0	89.0	89.5
Nov	82.5	81.5	80.7	82.5	86.0	79.5	88.3	90.6
Dec	82.5	81.5	80.4	82.9	85.7	79.7	87.6	89.8
1997: Jan	82.4	81.4	80.4	82.6	85.5	79.6	88.2	89.5
Feb	82.6	81.7	80.9	82.6	86.1	79.7	90.1	87.7
Mar	82.5	81.6	80.9	82.6	86.1	79.7	90.6	87.0
Apr	82.6	81.6	80.8	82.7	86.2	79.6	89.5	89.2
May	82.4	81.4	80.6	82.5	86.0	79.4	90.5	88.5
June	82.3	81.3	80.7	82.1	85.8	79.4	89.6	87.7
July	82.6	81.5	80.8	82.3	86.0	79.6	90.3	89.9
Aug	82.8	81.8	81.4	82.2	85.8	80.0	90.0	89.2
Sept	82.7	81.6	81.0	82.3	85.7	79.7	90.1	90.8
Oct ᵖ	83.0	81.8	81.0	82.7	85.7	80.0	89.8	92.0
Nov ᵖ	83.3	82.4	81.9	83.0	86.3	80.6	89.5	90.1
Dec ᵖ	83.4	82.5	81.8	83.2	86.7	80.6	89.7	90.3

[1] Output as percent of capacity.

Source: Board of Governors of the Federal Reserve System.

343

TABLE B–55.—*New construction activity, 1959–97*

[Value put in place, billions of dollars; monthly data at seasonally adjusted annual rates]

Year or month	Total new construction	Private construction							Public construction		
		Total	Residential buildings[1]		Nonresidential buildings and other construction[1]				Total	Federal	State and local[5]
			Total[2]	New housing units	Total	Commercial[3]	Industrial	Other[4]			
1959	55.4	39.3	24.3	19.2	15.1	3.9	2.1	9.0	16.1	3.7	12.3
1960	54.7	38.9	23.0	17.3	15.9	4.2	2.9	8.9	15.9	3.6	12.2
1961	56.4	39.3	23.1	17.1	16.2	4.7	2.8	8.7	17.1	3.9	13.3
1962	60.2	42.3	25.2	19.4	17.2	5.1	2.8	9.2	17.9	3.9	14.0
1963	64.8	45.5	27.9	21.7	17.6	5.0	2.9	9.7	19.4	4.0	15.4
New series											
1964	75.1	54.9	30.5	24.1	24.4	7.9	5.0	11.5	20.2	3.7	16.5
1965	81.9	60.0	30.2	23.8	29.7	9.4	7.2	13.1	21.9	3.9	18.0
1966	85.8	61.9	28.6	21.8	33.3	9.4	9.3	14.6	23.8	3.8	20.0
1967	87.2	61.8	28.7	21.5	33.1	9.3	8.4	15.4	25.4	3.3	22.1
1968	96.8	69.4	34.2	26.7	35.2	10.4	8.5	16.3	27.4	3.2	24.2
1969	104.9	77.2	37.2	29.2	39.9	12.5	9.6	17.8	27.8	3.2	24.6
1970	105.9	78.0	35.9	27.1	42.1	13.0	9.3	19.8	27.9	3.1	24.8
1971	122.4	92.7	48.5	38.7	44.2	15.3	7.8	21.1	29.7	3.8	25.9
1972	139.1	109.1	60.7	50.1	48.4	18.8	6.7	22.9	30.0	4.2	25.8
1973	153.8	121.4	65.1	54.6	56.3	21.7	9.0	25.6	32.3	4.7	27.6
1974	155.2	117.0	56.0	43.4	61.1	21.7	11.5	27.9	38.1	5.1	33.0
1975	152.6	109.3	51.6	36.3	57.8	17.2	11.7	28.9	43.3	6.1	37.2
1976	172.1	128.2	68.3	50.8	59.9	17.0	10.5	32.4	44.0	6.8	37.2
1977	200.5	157.4	92.0	72.2	65.4	19.7	11.3	34.5	43.1	7.1	36.0
1978	239.9	189.7	109.8	85.6	79.9	24.7	16.2	39.0	50.1	8.1	42.0
1979	272.9	216.2	116.4	89.3	99.8	34.0	22.0	43.7	56.6	8.6	48.1
1980	273.9	210.3	100.4	69.6	109.9	41.7	20.5	47.7	63.6	9.6	54.0
1981	289.1	224.4	99.2	69.4	125.1	48.7	25.4	51.0	64.7	10.4	54.3
1982	279.3	216.3	84.7	57.0	131.6	53.9	26.1	51.6	63.1	10.0	53.1
1983	311.6	248.1	125.5	94.6	122.6	53.4	19.5	49.8	63.5	10.6	52.9
1984	369.0	298.8	153.8	113.8	144.9	71.6	20.9	52.4	70.2	11.2	59.0
1985	401.4	323.6	158.5	114.7	165.1	88.1	24.1	52.9	77.8	12.0	65.8
1986	429.9	345.3	187.1	133.2	158.2	84.0	21.0	53.2	84.6	12.4	72.2
1987	441.6	351.0	194.7	139.9	156.3	83.2	21.2	52.0	90.6	14.1	76.6
1988	455.6	360.9	198.1	138.9	162.8	86.4	23.2	53.2	94.7	12.3	82.5
1989	469.8	371.6	196.6	139.2	175.1	89.2	28.8	57.1	98.2	12.2	86.0
1990	468.5	361.1	182.9	128.0	178.2	85.8	33.6	58.8	107.5	12.1	95.4
1991	424.2	314.1	157.8	110.6	156.2	62.2	31.4	62.6	110.1	12.8	97.3
1992	452.1	336.2	187.8	129.6	148.4	53.2	29.0	66.2	115.8	14.4	101.5
1993	478.6	362.7	210.5	144.1	152.2	57.9	26.5	67.8	116.0	14.4	101.5
1994	519.9	399.4	238.9	167.9	160.5	64.4	28.9	67.2	120.5	14.4	106.1
1995	534.1	406.8	230.7	162.9	176.1	75.4	32.5	68.2	127.3	15.9	111.4
1996	568.6	437.1	247.2	179.4	189.9	86.7	32.1	71.1	131.5	15.6	115.9
1997 ᴾ	600.7	461.9	260.2	185.5	201.8	93.6	30.6	77.5	138.8	15.3	123.4
1996: Jan	550.7	420.3	237.4	171.1	182.9	79.3	33.4	70.2	130.4	15.7	114.8
Feb	546.1	421.7	239.3	173.5	182.5	80.1	32.1	70.3	124.3	15.7	108.6
Mar	548.6	421.2	243.0	176.5	178.3	79.5	31.4	67.5	127.3	15.4	111.9
Apr	562.9	431.1	248.8	181.4	182.3	83.1	31.9	67.3	131.8	16.2	115.7
May	562.3	428.5	249.7	181.8	178.8	82.7	30.2	65.9	133.8	16.2	117.6
June	568.2	438.6	250.2	182.4	188.4	87.9	32.0	68.5	129.6	15.3	114.3
July	567.0	436.8	249.4	181.2	187.4	85.8	30.5	71.1	130.2	14.9	115.2
Aug	571.0	443.6	249.2	181.1	194.3	90.5	31.0	72.9	127.4	14.4	113.0
Sept	580.0	444.4	249.0	180.6	195.4	89.4	32.8	73.2	135.6	16.9	118.7
Oct	584.1	449.0	247.9	179.9	201.1	92.5	34.7	73.8	135.2	15.5	119.7
Nov	586.2	448.9	248.3	180.0	200.6	93.2	33.2	74.2	137.3	16.0	121.3
Dec	579.1	447.0	247.9	179.1	199.1	92.2	30.8	76.2	132.1	14.1	117.9
1997: Jan	577.1	444.4	246.7	178.3	197.7	94.9	31.9	70.9	132.7	14.8	118.0
Feb	592.4	452.0	251.4	183.4	200.6	96.0	32.2	72.5	140.3	15.9	124.4
Mar	593.9	452.7	254.0	184.1	198.8	94.0	30.5	74.2	141.2	14.9	126.3
Apr	596.9	457.6	259.9	185.2	197.7	89.0	29.3	79.4	139.3	14.7	124.6
May	595.8	459.9	259.7	185.3	200.2	91.8	30.5	77.9	135.9	14.1	121.8
June	594.2	456.9	257.3	182.8	199.7	92.3	31.0	76.3	137.3	14.1	123.2
July	603.0	464.3	258.8	182.9	205.5	96.0	31.8	77.7	138.7	14.9	123.8
Aug	603.7	465.2	260.0	183.8	205.3	94.7	31.5	79.1	138.4	14.6	123.9
Sept	605.7	468.8	263.8	186.7	205.0	93.9	30.7	80.5	136.9	15.5	121.4
Oct	611.8	469.6	265.7	189.9	203.9	94.3	30.0	79.6	142.2	16.8	125.4
Nov	611.3	469.4	268.1	190.1	201.3	92.4	29.4	79.4	141.9	17.1	124.9
Dec ᴾ	611.8	472.9	271.9	193.5	200.9	93.8	28.1	79.0	138.9	16.9	121.9

[1] Beginning 1960, farm residential buildings included in residential buildings; prior to 1960, included in nonresidential buildings and other construction.
[2] Includes residential improvements, not shown separately. Prior to 1964, also includes nonhousekeeping units (hotels, motels, etc.).
[3] Office buildings, warehouses, stores, restaurants, garages, etc., and, beginning 1964, hotels and motels; prior to 1964 hotels and motels are included in total residential.
[4] Religious, educational, hospital and institutional, miscellaneous nonresidential, farm (see also footnote 1), public utilities (telecommunications, gas, electric, railroad, and petroleum pipelines), and all other private.
[5] Includes Federal grants-in-aid for State and local projects.

Source: Department of Commerce, Bureau of the Census.

344

TABLE B–56.—*New housing units started and authorized, 1959–97*

[Thousands of units; monthly data at seasonally adjusted annual rates]

Year or month	New housing units started — Private and public¹ Total (farm and nonfarm)	New housing units started — Private and public¹ Nonfarm	New housing units started — Private (farm and nonfarm)¹ Total	New housing units started — Private (farm and nonfarm)¹ Type of structure 1 unit	New housing units started — Private (farm and nonfarm)¹ Type of structure 2 to 4 units	New housing units started — Private (farm and nonfarm)¹ Type of structure 5 units or more	New private housing units authorized² Total	New private housing units authorized² Type of structure 1 unit	New private housing units authorized² Type of structure 2 to 4 units	New private housing units authorized² Type of structure 5 units or more
1959	1,553.7	1,531.3	1,517.0	1,234.0	282.9		1,208.3	938.3	77.1	192.9
1960	1,296.1	1,274.0	1,252.2	994.7	257.5		998.0	746.1	64.6	187.4
1961	1,365.0	1,336.8	1,313.0	974.3	338.7		1,064.2	722.8	67.6	273.8
1962	1,492.5	1,468.7	1,462.9	991.4	471.5		1,186.6	716.2	87.1	383.3
1963	1,634.9	1,614.8	1,603.2	1,012.4	590.7		1,334.7	750.2	118.9	465.6
1964	1,561.0	1,534.0	1,528.8	970.5	108.4	450.0	1,285.8	720.1	100.8	464.9
1965	1,509.7	1,487.5	1,472.8	963.7	86.6	422.5	1,239.8	709.9	84.8	445.1
1966	1,195.8	1,172.8	1,164.9	778.6	61.1	325.1	971.9	563.2	61.0	347.7
1967	1,321.9	1,298.8	1,291.6	843.9	71.6	376.1	1,141.0	650.6	73.0	417.5
1968	1,545.4	1,521.4	1,507.6	899.4	80.9	527.3	1,353.4	694.7	84.3	574.4
1969	1,499.5	1,482.3	1,466.8	810.6	85.0	571.2	1,323.7	625.9	85.2	612.7
1970	1,469.0	(³)	1,433.6	812.9	84.8	535.9	1,351.5	646.8	88.1	616.7
1971	2,084.5	(³)	2,052.2	1,151.0	120.3	780.9	1,924.6	906.1	132.9	885.7
1972	2,378.5	(³)	2,356.6	1,309.2	141.3	906.2	2,218.9	1,033.1	148.6	1,037.2
1973	2,057.5	(³)	2,045.3	1,132.0	118.3	795.0	1,819.5	882.1	117.0	820.5
1974	1,352.5	(³)	1,337.7	888.1	68.1	381.6	1,074.4	643.8	64.3	366.2
1975	1,171.4	(³)	1,160.4	892.2	64.0	204.3	939.2	675.5	63.9	199.8
1976	1,547.6	(³)	1,537.5	1,162.4	85.9	289.2	1,296.2	893.6	93.1	309.5
1977	2,001.7	(³)	1,987.1	1,450.9	121.7	414.4	1,690.0	1,126.1	121.3	442.7
1978	2,036.1	(³)	2,020.3	1,433.3	125.0	462.0	1,800.5	1,182.6	130.6	487.3
1979	1,760.0	(³)	1,745.1	1,194.1	122.0	429.0	1,551.8	981.5	125.4	444.8
1980	1,312.6	(³)	1,292.2	852.2	109.5	330.5	1,190.6	710.4	114.5	365.7
1981	1,100.3	(³)	1,084.2	705.4	91.1	287.7	985.5	564.3	101.8	319.4
1982	1,072.1	(³)	1,062.2	662.6	80.0	319.6	1,000.5	546.4	88.3	365.8
1983	1,712.5	(³)	1,703.0	1,067.6	113.5	522.0	1,605.2	901.5	133.6	570.1
1984	1,755.8	(³)	1,749.5	1,084.2	121.4	544.0	1,681.8	922.4	142.6	616.8
1985	1,745.0	(³)	1,741.8	1,072.4	93.4	576.1	1,733.3	956.6	120.1	656.6
1986	1,807.1	(³)	1,805.4	1,179.4	84.0	542.0	1,769.4	1,077.6	108.4	583.5
1987	1,622.7	(³)	1,620.5	1,146.4	65.3	408.7	1,534.8	1,024.4	89.3	421.1
1988	(⁴)	(³)	1,488.1	1,081.3	58.8	348.0	1,455.6	993.8	75.7	386.1
1989	(⁴)	(³)	1,376.1	1,003.3	55.2	317.6	1,338.4	931.7	67.0	339.8
1990	(⁴)	(³)	1,192.7	894.8	37.5	260.4	1,110.8	793.9	54.3	262.6
1991	(⁴)	(³)	1,013.9	840.4	35.6	137.9	948.8	753.5	43.1	152.1
1992	(⁴)	(³)	1,199.7	1,029.9	30.7	139.0	1,094.9	910.7	45.8	138.4
1993	(⁴)	(³)	1,287.6	1,125.7	29.4	132.6	1,199.1	986.5	52.3	160.2
1994	(⁴)	(³)	1,457.0	1,198.4	35.0	223.5	1,371.6	1,068.5	62.2	241.0
1995	(⁴)	(³)	1,354.1	1,076.2	33.7	244.1	1,332.5	997.3	63.7	271.5
1996	(⁴)	(³)	1,476.8	1,160.9	45.2	270.8	1,425.6	1,069.5	65.8	290.3
1997 ᵖ	(⁴)	(³)	1,475.9	1,133.6	44.2	298.1	1,442.3	1,055.6	70.5	316.1
1996: Jan	(⁴)	(³)	1,444	1,138	22	284	1,385	1,047	64	274
Feb	(⁴)	(³)	1,520	1,188	35	297	1,425	1,083	60	282
Mar	(⁴)	(³)	1,429	1,156	24	249	1,438	1,119	60	259
Apr	(⁴)	(³)	1,522	1,215	55	252	1,486	1,128	74	284
May	(⁴)	(³)	1,476	1,142	48	286	1,457	1,101	64	292
June	(⁴)	(³)	1,488	1,214	46	228	1,432	1,094	64	274
July	(⁴)	(³)	1,492	1,164	44	284	1,454	1,077	67	310
Aug	(⁴)	(³)	1,515	1,222	37	256	1,405	1,061	62	282
Sept	(⁴)	(³)	1,470	1,148	45	277	1,391	1,029	70	292
Oct	(⁴)	(³)	1,407	1,104	58	245	1,349	1,003	68	278
Nov	(⁴)	(³)	1,486	1,133	60	293	1,391	1,016	65	310
Dec	(⁴)	(³)	1,353	1,024	48	281	1,405	999	65	341
1997: Jan	(⁴)	(³)	1,375	1,125	43	207	1,395	1,052	62	281
Feb	(⁴)	(³)	1,554	1,237	44	273	1,438	1,069	68	301
Mar	(⁴)	(³)	1,479	1,142	45	292	1,457	1,034	71	352
Apr	(⁴)	(³)	1,483	1,133	40	310	1,442	1,060	68	314
May	(⁴)	(³)	1,402	1,098	34	270	1,432	1,053	66	313
June	(⁴)	(³)	1,503	1,134	37	332	1,402	1,049	70	283
July	(⁴)	(³)	1,465	1,149	37	279	1,414	1,030	77	307
Aug	(⁴)	(³)	1,395	1,091	42	262	1,397	1,027	66	304
Sept	(⁴)	(³)	1,507	1,181	46	280	1,460	1,065	69	326
Oct	(⁴)	(³)	1,527	1,122	63	342	1,487	1,087	77	323
Nov ᵖ	(⁴)	(³)	1,531	1,161	40	330	1,440	1,061	58	321
Dec ᵖ	(⁴)	(³)	1,519	1,092	55	372	1,440	1,071	92	319

¹ Units in structures built by private developers for sale upon completion to local public housing authorities under the Department of Housing and Urban Development "Turnkey" program are classified as private housing. Military housing starts, including those financed with mortgages insured by FHA under Section 803 of the National Housing Act, are included in publicly owned starts and excluded from total private starts.

² Authorized by issuance of local building permit: in 19,000 permit-issuing places beginning 1994; in 17,000 places for 1984–93; in 16,000 places for 1978–83; in 14,000 places for 1972–77; in 13,000 places for 1967–71; in 12,000 places for 1963–66; and in 10,000 places prior to 1963.

³ Not available separately beginning January 1970.

⁴ Series discontinued December 1988.

Source: Department of Commerce, Bureau of the Census.

345

[Amounts in millions of dollars; monthly data seasonally adjusted]

Year or month	Total manufacturing and trade			Manufacturing			Merchant wholesalers			Retail trade		
	Sales [1]	Inventories [2]	Ratio [3]	Sales [1]	Inventories [2]	Ratio [3]	Sales [1]	Inventories [2]	Ratio [3]	Sales [1]	Inventories [2]	Ratio [3]
1954	46,443	73,175	1.60	23,355	41,612	1.81	8,993	10,637	1.18	14,095	20,926	1.51
1955	51,694	79,516	1.47	26,480	45,069	1.62	9,893	11,678	1.13	15,321	22,769	1.43
1956	54,063	87,304	1.55	27,740	50,642	1.73	10,513	13,260	1.19	15,811	23,402	1.47
1957	55,879	89,052	1.59	28,736	51,871	1.80	10,475	12,730	1.23	16,667	24,451	1.44
1958	54,201	87,055	1.61	27,248	50,203	1.84	10,257	12,739	1.24	16,696	24,113	1.44
1959	59,729	92,097	1.54	30,286	52,913	1.75	11,491	13,879	1.21	17,951	25,305	1.41
1960	60,827	94,719	1.56	30,878	53,786	1.74	11,656	14,120	1.21	18,294	26,813	1.47
1961	61,159	95,580	1.56	30,922	54,871	1.77	11,988	14,488	1.21	18,249	26,221	1.44
1962	65,662	101,049	1.54	33,358	58,172	1.74	12,674	14,936	1.18	19,630	27,941	1.42
1963	68,995	105,463	1.53	35,058	60,029	1.71	13,382	16,048	1.20	20,556	29,386	1.43
1964	73,682	111,504	1.51	37,331	63,410	1.70	14,529	17,000	1.17	21,823	31,094	1.42
1965	80,283	120,929	1.51	40,995	68,207	1.66	15,611	18,317	1.17	23,677	34,405	1.45
1966	87,187	136,824	1.57	44,870	77,986	1.74	16,987	20,765	1.22	25,330	38,073	1.50
1967	90,820	145,681	1.60	46,486	84,646	1.82	19,576	25,786	1.32	24,757	35,249	1.42
1968	98,685	156,611	1.59	50,229	90,560	1.80	21,012	27,166	1.29	27,445	38,885	1.42
1969	105,690	170,400	1.61	53,501	98,145	1.83	22,818	29,800	1.31	29,371	42,455	1.45
1970	108,221	178,594	1.65	52,805	101,599	1.92	24,167	33,354	1.38	31,249	43,641	1.40
1971	116,895	188,991	1.62	55,906	102,567	1.83	26,492	36,568	1.38	34,497	49,856	1.45
1972	131,081	203,227	1.55	63,027	108,121	1.72	29,866	40,297	1.35	38,189	54,809	1.44
1973	153,677	234,406	1.53	72,931	124,499	1.71	38,115	46,918	1.23	42,631	62,989	1.48
1974	177,912	287,144	1.61	84,790	157,625	1.86	47,982	58,667	1.22	45,141	70,852	1.57
1975	182,198	288,992	1.59	86,589	159,708	1.84	46,634	57,774	1.24	48,975	71,510	1.46
1976	204,150	318,345	1.56	98,797	174,636	1.77	50,698	64,622	1.27	54,655	79,087	1.45
1977	229,513	350,706	1.53	113,201	188,378	1.66	56,136	73,179	1.30	60,176	89,149	1.48
1978	260,320	400,931	1.54	126,905	211,691	1.67	66,413	86,934	1.31	67,002	102,306	1.53
1979	297,701	452,640	1.52	143,936	242,157	1.68	79,051	99,679	1.26	74,713	110,804	1.48
1980	327,233	508,924	1.56	154,391	265,215	1.72	93,099	122,631	1.32	79,743	121,078	1.52
1981	355,822	545,786	1.53	168,129	283,413	1.69	101,180	129,654	1.28	86,514	132,719	1.53
1982	347,625	573,908	1.67	163,351	311,852	1.95	95,211	127,428	1.36	89,062	134,628	1.49
1983	369,286	590,287	1.56	172,547	312,379	1.78	99,225	130,075	1.28	97,514	147,833	1.44
1984	410,124	649,780	1.53	190,682	339,516	1.73	112,199	142,452	1.23	107,243	167,812	1.49
1985	422,583	664,039	1.56	194,538	334,749	1.73	113,459	147,409	1.28	114,586	181,881	1.52
1986	430,419	662,738	1.55	194,657	322,654	1.68	114,960	153,574	1.32	120,803	186,510	1.56
1987	457,735	709,848	1.50	206,326	338,109	1.59	122,968	163,903	1.29	128,442	207,836	1.55
1988	497,157	767,222	1.49	224,619	369,374	1.57	134,521	178,801	1.30	138,017	219,047	1.54
1989	527,039	815,455	1.52	236,698	391,212	1.63	143,760	187,009	1.28	146,581	237,234	1.58
1990	545,909	840,396	1.52	242,686	405,073	1.65	149,506	195,550	1.29	153,718	239,773	1.55
1991	542,815	834,287	1.53	239,847	390,950	1.65	148,306	200,062	1.33	154,661	243,275	1.54
1992	567,176	842,204	1.48	250,394	382,547	1.54	154,150	207,663	1.32	162,632	251,994	1.52
1993	595,049	867,513	1.44	260,635	384,138	1.48	161,681	215,878	1.31	172,732	267,497	1.51
1994	637,585	930,049	1.41	279,002	405,028	1.41	172,973	234,893	1.30	185,610	290,128	1.50
1995	681,597	985,905	1.42	299,116	429,089	1.41	188,811	253,066	1.31	193,670	303,750	1.55
1996	716,763	1,004,425	1.39	311,265	434,434	1.39	201,723	255,808	1.27	203,775	314,183	1.52
1996: Jan	693,216	990,600	1.43	300,439	431,192	1.44	195,063	254,314	1.30	197,714	305,094	1.54
Feb	699,473	990,843	1.42	303,090	431,462	1.42	195,298	254,045	1.30	201,085	305,336	1.52
Mar	700,685	989,251	1.41	301,666	431,363	1.43	197,334	254,151	1.29	201,685	303,737	1.51
Apr	711,826	993,660	1.40	309,477	431,352	1.39	199,853	257,612	1.29	202,496	304,696	1.50
May	717,503	992,630	1.38	313,247	430,298	1.37	200,079	256,740	1.28	204,177	305,592	1.50
June	712,727	992,101	1.39	310,052	429,802	1.39	199,977	256,122	1.28	202,698	306,177	1.51
July	720,755	996,582	1.38	313,851	430,543	1.37	203,814	256,053	1.26	203,090	309,986	1.53
Aug	719,660	998,876	1.39	313,854	431,647	1.38	202,719	256,189	1.26	203,087	311,040	1.53
Sept	724,357	999,312	1.38	315,971	432,674	1.37	203,437	254,654	1.25	204,949	311,984	1.52
Oct	728,644	1,003,742	1.38	316,461	434,038	1.37	205,490	255,526	1.24	206,693	314,178	1.52
Nov	730,974	1,003,740	1.37	319,296	435,200	1.36	205,712	255,670	1.24	205,966	312,870	1.52
Dec	728,394	1,004,425	1.38	316,306	434,434	1.37	205,560	255,808	1.24	206,528	314,183	1.52
1997: Jan	737,464	1,007,618	1.37	319,725	435,743	1.36	207,506	257,895	1.24	210,233	313,980	1.49
Feb	747,790	1,011,899	1.35	322,967	437,873	1.36	211,801	258,088	1.22	213,022	315,938	1.48
Mar	745,460	1,013,376	1.36	322,923	438,560	1.36	210,195	259,389	1.23	212,342	315,427	1.49
Apr	746,769	1,017,150	1.36	326,909	441,508	1.35	209,926	258,046	1.23	209,934	317,596	1.51
May	742,945	1,019,025	1.37	323,567	443,460	1.37	210,008	259,029	1.23	209,370	316,536	1.51
June	750,027	1,026,255	1.37	328,315	444,823	1.35	210,772	264,154	1.25	210,940	317,278	1.50
July	757,485	1,027,787	1.36	332,895	446,602	1.34	211,041	262,314	1.24	213,549	318,871	1.49
Aug	752,886	1,030,243	1.37	330,178	448,447	1.36	208,336	264,899	1.27	214,372	316,897	1.48
Sept	762,543	1,037,172	1.36	335,366	449,152	1.34	213,372	268,112	1.26	213,805	319,908	1.50
Oct *p*	759,880	1,040,265	1.37	334,064	452,139	1.35	212,299	268,183	1.26	213,517	319,943	1.50
Nov *p*	757,296	1,044,312	1.38	332,339	453,955	1.37	210,864	270,627	1.28	214,093	319,730	1.49

[1] Annual data are averages of monthly not seasonally adjusted figures.
[2] Seasonally adjusted, end of period. Inventories beginning January 1982 for manufacturing and December 1980 for wholesale and retail trade are not comparable with earlier periods.
[3] Inventory/sales ratio. Annual data are: beginning 1982, averages of monthly ratios; for 1958–81, ratio of December inventories to monthly average sales for the year; and for earlier years, weighted averages. Monthly data are ratio of inventories at end of month to sales for month.

Note.—Earlier data are not strictly comparable with data beginning 1958 for manufacturing and beginning 1967 for wholesale and retail trade.

Source: Department of Commerce, Bureau of the Census.

[Millions of dollars; monthly data seasonally adjusted]

Year or month	Shipments[1]			Inventories[2]								
					Durable goods industries				Nondurable goods industries			
	Total	Durable goods industries	Nondurable goods industries	Total	Total	Materials and supplies	Work in process	Finished goods	Total	Materials and supplies	Work in process	Finished goods
1954	23,355	11,828	11,527	41,612	23,710	7,894	9,721	6,040	17,902	8,167	2,440	7,415
1955	26,480	14,071	12,409	45,069	26,405	9,194	10,756	6,348	18,664	8,556	2,571	7,666
1956	27,740	14,715	13,025	50,642	30,447	10,417	12,317	7,565	20,195	8,971	2,721	8,622
1957	28,736	15,237	13,499	51,871	31,728	10,608	12,837	8,125	20,143	8,775	2,864	8,624
1958	27,248	13,553	13,695	50,203	30,194	9,970	12,408	7,816	20,009	8,676	2,827	8,506
1959	30,286	15,597	14,689	52,913	32,012	10,709	13,086	8,217	20,901	9,094	2,942	8,865
1960	30,878	15,870	15,008	53,786	32,337	10,306	12,809	9,222	21,449	9,097	2,947	9,405
1961	30,922	15,601	15,321	54,871	32,496	10,246	13,211	9,039	22,375	9,505	3,108	9,762
1962	33,358	17,247	16,111	58,172	34,565	10,794	14,124	9,647	23,607	9,836	3,304	10,467
1963	35,058	18,255	16,803	60,029	35,776	11,053	14,835	9,888	24,253	10,009	3,420	10,824
1964	37,331	19,611	17,720	63,410	38,421	11,946	16,158	10,317	24,989	10,167	3,531	11,291
1965	40,995	22,193	18,802	68,207	42,189	13,298	18,055	10,836	26,018	10,487	3,825	11,706
1966	44,870	24,617	20,253	77,986	49,852	15,464	21,908	12,480	28,134	11,197	4,226	12,711
1967	46,486	25,233	21,253	84,646	54,896	16,423	24,933	13,540	29,750	11,760	4,431	13,559
1968	50,229	27,624	22,605	90,560	58,732	17,344	27,213	14,175	31,828	12,328	4,852	14,648
1969	53,501	29,403	24,098	98,145	64,598	18,636	30,282	15,680	33,547	12,753	5,120	15,674
1970	52,805	28,156	24,649	101,599	66,651	19,149	29,745	17,757	34,948	13,168	5,271	16,509
1971	55,906	29,924	25,982	102,567	66,136	19,679	28,550	17,907	36,431	13,686	5,678	17,067
1972	63,027	33,987	29,040	108,121	70,067	20,807	30,713	18,547	38,054	14,677	5,998	17,379
1973	72,931	39,635	33,296	124,499	81,192	25,944	35,490	19,758	43,307	18,147	6,729	18,431
1974	84,790	44,173	40,617	157,625	101,493	35,070	42,530	23,893	56,132	23,744	8,189	24,199
1975	86,589	43,598	42,991	159,708	102,590	33,903	43,227	25,460	57,118	23,565	8,834	24,719
1976	98,797	50,623	48,174	174,636	111,988	37,457	46,074	28,457	62,648	25,847	9,929	26,872
1977	113,201	59,168	54,033	188,378	120,877	40,186	50,226	30,465	67,501	27,387	10,961	29,153
1978	126,905	67,731	59,174	211,691	138,181	45,198	58,848	34,135	73,510	29,619	12,085	31,806
1979	143,936	75,927	68,009	242,157	160,734	52,670	69,325	38,739	81,423	32,814	13,910	34,699
1980	154,391	77,419	76,972	265,215	174,788	55,173	76,945	42,670	90,427	36,606	15,884	37,937
1981	168,129	83,727	84,402	283,413	186,443	57,998	80,998	47,447	96,970	38,165	16,194	42,611
1982	163,351	79,212	84,139	311,852	200,444	59,136	86,707	54,601	111,408	44,039	18,612	48,757
1983	172,547	85,481	87,066	312,379	199,854	60,325	86,899	52,630	112,525	44,816	18,691	49,018
1984	190,682	97,940	92,742	339,516	221,330	66,031	98,251	57,048	118,186	45,692	19,328	53,166
1985	194,538	101,279	93,259	334,749	218,193	63,904	98,162	56,127	116,556	44,106	19,442	53,008
1986	194,657	103,238	91,419	322,654	211,997	61,331	97,000	53,666	110,657	42,335	18,124	50,198
1987	206,326	108,128	98,198	338,109	220,799	63,562	102,393	54,844	117,310	45,319	19,270	52,721
1988	224,619	118,458	106,161	369,374	242,468	69,611	112,958	59,899	126,906	49,396	20,559	56,951
1989	236,698	123,158	113,540	391,212	257,513	72,435	122,251	62,827	133,699	50,674	21,653	61,372
1990	242,686	123,776	118,910	405,073	263,209	73,559	124,130	65,520	141,864	52,645	22,817	66,402
1991	239,847	121,000	118,847	390,950	250,019	70,834	114,960	64,225	140,931	53,011	22,815	65,105
1992	250,394	128,489	121,905	382,547	238,166	69,427	104,572	64,167	144,381	53,995	23,536	66,850
1993	260,635	135,886	124,749	384,138	239,404	72,544	102,632	64,228	144,734	55,069	23,394	66,271
1994	279,002	149,131	129,870	405,028	253,691	78,401	107,244	68,046	151,337	58,163	24,685	68,489
1995	299,116	160,101	139,015	429,089	265,915	85,040	105,810	75,065	163,174	62,530	26,185	74,459
1996	311,265	167,166	144,099	434,434	271,329	83,846	110,559	76,924	163,105	60,741	26,668	75,696
1996: Jan	300,439	160,363	140,076	431,192	267,964	85,722	106,519	75,723	163,228	62,561	26,358	74,309
Feb	303,090	162,473	140,617	431,462	268,245	86,049	106,456	75,740	163,217	62,422	26,253	74,542
Mar	301,666	160,768	140,898	431,363	268,392	85,891	107,003	75,498	162,971	61,779	26,266	74,926
Apr	309,477	165,496	143,981	431,352	268,648	85,844	107,500	75,304	162,704	61,682	26,334	74,688
May	313,247	168,781	144,466	430,298	268,657	85,483	107,734	75,440	161,641	61,187	26,318	74,136
June	310,052	167,524	142,528	429,802	268,294	84,397	108,228	75,669	161,508	60,727	26,373	74,408
July	313,851	168,762	145,089	430,543	269,493	85,307	108,368	75,818	161,050	60,635	26,240	74,175
Aug	313,854	168,960	144,894	431,647	270,537	84,805	108,874	76,858	161,110	60,506	26,568	74,036
Sept	315,971	171,415	144,556	432,674	270,794	85,018	108,712	77,064	161,880	60,638	26,489	74,753
Oct	316,461	169,368	147,093	434,038	271,616	84,227	109,806	77,583	162,422	61,028	26,652	74,742
Nov	319,296	171,426	147,870	435,200	272,198	84,154	110,655	77,389	163,002	60,852	26,728	75,422
Dec	316,306	169,504	146,802	434,434	271,329	83,846	110,559	76,924	163,105	60,741	26,668	75,696
1997: Jan	319,725	171,403	148,322	435,743	272,652	84,033	110,804	77,815	163,091	60,706	26,788	75,597
Feb	322,967	174,862	148,105	437,873	274,170	84,147	111,395	78,628	163,703	61,191	27,032	75,480
Mar	322,923	176,224	146,699	438,560	274,633	84,982	111,780	77,871	163,927	61,157	27,076	75,694
Apr	326,909	178,482	148,427	441,508	276,992	85,066	112,555	79,371	164,516	61,067	27,363	76,086
May	323,567	175,900	147,667	443,460	278,084	85,373	112,939	79,772	165,376	61,160	27,785	76,431
June	328,315	180,687	147,628	444,823	279,166	86,081	113,043	80,042	165,657	60,837	27,580	77,090
July	332,895	183,827	149,068	446,602	280,800	86,461	113,931	80,408	165,802	60,906	27,744	77,152
Aug	330,178	181,131	149,047	448,447	281,878	86,360	114,626	80,892	166,569	60,944	28,149	77,476
Sept	335,366	185,496	149,870	449,152	281,762	87,175	113,995	80,592	167,390	61,491	28,358	77,541
Oct	334,064	183,602	150,462	452,139	283,477	87,261	115,099	81,117	168,662	61,545	28,928	78,189
Nov[P]	332,339	182,797	149,542	453,955	284,463	87,163	116,275	81,025	169,492	60,872	29,319	79,301

[1] Annual data are averages of monthly not seasonally adjusted figures.
[2] Seasonally adjusted, end of period. Data beginning 1982 are not comparable with data for prior periods.

Note.—Data beginning 1958 are not strictly comparable with earlier data.

Source: Department of Commerce, Bureau of the Census.

Table B–59.—*Manufacturers' new and unfilled orders, 1954–97*

[Amounts in millions of dollars; monthly data seasonally adjusted]

Year or month	New orders[1]				Unfilled orders[2]			Unfilled orders—shipments ratio[3]		
	Total	Durable goods industries		Non-durable goods industries	Total	Durable goods industries	Non-durable goods industries	Total	Durable goods industries	Non-durable goods industries
		Total	Capital goods industries, non-defense							
1954	22,335	10,768		11,566	48,266	45,250	3,016	3.42	4.12	0.96
1955	27,465	14,996		12,469	60,004	56,241	3,763	3.63	4.27	1.12
1956	28,368	15,365		13,003	67,375	63,880	3,495	3.87	4.55	1.04
1957	27,559	14,111		13,448	53,183	50,352	2,831	3.35	4.00	.85
1958	27,193	13,387		13,805	46,609	43,807	2,802	3.02	3.62	.85
1959	30,711	15,979		14,732	51,717	48,369	3,348	2.94	3.47	.92
1960	30,232	15,288		14,944	44,213	41,650	2,563	2.71	3.29	.71
1961	31,112	15,753		15,359	46,624	43,582	3,042	2.58	3.08	.78
1962	33,440	17,363		16,078	47,798	45,170	2,628	2.64	3.18	.68
1963	35,511	18,671		16,840	53,417	50,346	3,071	2.74	3.31	.72
1964	38,240	20,507		17,732	64,518	61,315	3,203	2.99	3.59	.71
1965	42,137	23,286		18,851	78,249	74,459	3,790	3.25	3.86	.79
1966	46,420	26,163		20,258	96,846	93,002	3,844	3.74	4.48	.75
1967	47,067	25,803		21,265	103,711	99,735	3,976	3.66	4.37	.73
1968	50,657	28,051	6,314	22,606	108,377	104,393	3,984	3.79	4.58	.69
1969	53,990	29,876	7,046	24,114	114,341	110,161	4,180	3.71	4.45	.69
1970	52,022	27,340	6,072	24,682	105,008	100,412	4,596	3.61	4.36	.76
1971	55,921	29,905	6,682	26,016	105,247	100,225	5,022	3.32	4.00	.76
1972	64,182	35,038	7,745	29,144	119,349	113,034	6,315	3.26	3.85	.86
1973	76,003	42,627	9,926	33,376	156,561	149,204	7,357	3.80	4.51	.91
1974	87,327	46,862	11,594	40,465	187,043	181,519	5,524	4.09	4.93	.62
1975	85,139	41,957	9,886	43,181	169,546	161,664	7,882	3.69	4.45	.82
1976	99,513	51,307	11,490	48,206	178,128	169,857	8,271	3.24	3.88	.74
1977	115,109	61,035	13,681	54,073	202,024	193,323	8,701	3.24	3.85	.71
1978	131,629	72,278	17,588	59,351	259,169	248,281	10,888	3.57	4.20	.81
1979	147,604	79,483	21,154	68,121	303,593	291,321	12,272	3.89	4.62	.82
1980	156,359	79,392	21,135	76,967	327,416	315,202	12,214	3.85	4.58	.75
1981	168,025	83,654	21,806	84,371	326,547	314,707	11,840	3.87	4.68	.69
1982	162,140	78,064	19,213	84,077	311,887	300,798	11,089	3.84	4.74	.62
1983	175,451	88,140	19,624	87,311	347,273	333,114	14,159	3.53	4.29	.69
1984	192,879	100,164	23,669	92,715	373,529	359,651	13,878	3.60	4.37	.64
1985	195,706	102,356	24,545	93,351	387,196	372,097	15,099	3.67	4.47	.68
1986	195,204	103,647	23,982	91,557	393,515	376,699	16,816	3.59	4.41	.70
1987	209,389	110,809	26,094	98,579	430,426	408.688	21,738	3.63	4.43	.83
1988	228,270	122,076	31,108	106,194	474,154	452.150	22,004	3.64	4.46	.76
1989	239,572	126,055	32,988	113,516	508,849	487,098	21,751	3.96	4.85	.77
1990	244,507	125,583	33,331	118,924	531,131	509,124	22,007	4.15	5.15	.76
1991	238,805	119,849	30,471	118,957	519,199	495,802	23,397	4.08	5.07	.79
1992	248,212	126,308	31,524	121,905	493,184	469,654	23,530	3.51	4.30	.75
1993	257,698	133,081	31,694	124,617	458,245	436,442	21,803	3.15	3.80	.70
1994	279,733	149,542	35,697	130,191	467,369	441,677	25,692	2.93	3.51	.75
1995	300,353	161,469	40,561	138,885	482,605	458,520	24,085	2.84	3.43	.67
1996	314,197	169,963	43,913	144,234	517,647	491,911	25,736	2.96	3.54	.71
1996:Jan	308,892	168,420	45,260	140,472	491,058	466,577	24,481	2.94	3.56	.69
Feb	303,957	163,553	43,748	140,404	491,925	467,657	24,268	2.92	3.52	.68
Mar	306,561	166,267	45,608	140,294	496,820	473,156	23,664	2.96	3.58	.66
Apr	308,467	164,329	39,593	144,138	495,810	471,989	23,821	2.91	3.51	.66
May	315,764	171,209	44,488	144,555	498,327	474,417	23,910	2.88	3.46	.67
June	313,081	170,382	41,982	142,699	501,356	477,275	24,081	2.91	3.51	.67
July	318,488	173,087	45,044	145,401	505,993	481,600	24,393	2.94	3.53	.68
Aug	311,958	167,204	40,314	144,754	504,097	479,844	24,253	2.91	3.50	.67
Sept	319,894	175,113	46,931	144,781	508,020	483,542	24,478	2.92	3.50	.68
Oct	322,392	175,015	46,293	147,377	513,951	489,189	24,762	2.97	3.56	.70
Nov	322,400	173,636	43,081	148,764	517,055	491,399	25,656	2.94	3.52	.71
Dec	316,898	170,016	43,162	146,882	517,647	491,911	25,736	2.96	3.54	.71
1997:Jan	323,864	175,803	45,094	148,061	521,786	496,311	25,475	2.98	3.57	.71
Feb	326,537	178,872	46,264	147,665	525,356	500,321	25,035	2.93	3.49	.69
Mar	321,146	173,944	44,505	147,202	523,579	498,041	25,538	2.90	3.44	.71
Apr	325,544	177,112	43,751	148,432	522,214	496,671	25,543	2.86	3.40	.71
May	324,042	176,443	44,211	147,599	522,689	497,214	25,475	2.89	3.44	.71
June	329,554	181,584	47,211	147,970	523,928	498,111	25,817	2.84	3.36	.71
July	331,138	181,679	47,412	149,459	522,171	495,963	26,208	2.80	3.32	.71
Aug	335,040	186,195	47,987	148,845	527,033	501,027	26,006	2.85	3.38	.71
Sept	336,264	186,210	48,625	150,054	527,931	501,741	26,190	2.78	3.30	.70
Oct	336,631	186,028	49,930	150,603	530,498	504,167	26,331	2.82	3.35	.70
Nov ᵖ	345,136	195,518	58,770	149,618	543,295	516,888	26,407	2.89	3.44	.70

[1] Annual data are averages of monthly not seasonally adjusted figures.
[2] Seasonally adjusted, end of period.
[3] Ratio of unfilled orders at end of period to shipments for period; excludes industries with no unfilled orders. Annual figures relate to seasonally adjusted data for December.

Note.—Data beginning 1958 are not strictly comparable with earlier data.

Source: Department of Commerce, Bureau of the Census.

348

TABLE B–60.—*Consumer price indexes for major expenditure classes, 1954–97*

[For all urban consumers; 1982–84=100]

Year or month	All items (CPI–U)	Food and beverages Total[1]	Food	Housing Total	Shelter	Fuel and other utilities	Household furnishings and operation	Apparel and upkeep	Transportation	Medical care	Entertainment	Other goods and services	Energy[2]
1954	26.9		28.2		22.5	22.6		43.1	26.1	17.8			
1955	26.8		27.8		22.7	23.0		42.9	25.8	18.2			
1956	27.2		28.0		23.1	23.6		43.7	26.2	18.9			
1957	28.1		28.9		24.0	24.3		44.5	27.7	19.7			21.5
1958	28.9		30.2		24.5	24.8		44.6	28.6	20.6			21.5
1959	29.1		29.7		24.7	25.4		45.0	29.8	21.5			21.9
1960	29.6		30.0		25.2	26.0		45.7	29.8	22.3			22.4
1961	29.9		30.4		25.4	26.3		46.1	30.1	22.9			22.5
1962	30.2		30.6		25.8	26.3		46.3	30.8	23.5			22.6
1963	30.6		31.1		26.1	26.6		46.9	30.9	24.1			22.6
1964	31.0		31.5		26.5	26.6		47.3	31.4	24.6			22.5
1965	31.5		32.2		27.0	26.6		47.8	31.9	25.2			22.9
1966	32.4		33.8		27.8	26.7		49.0	32.3	26.3			23.3
1967	33.4	35.0	34.1	30.8	28.8	27.1	42.0	51.0	33.3	28.2	40.7	35.1	23.8
1968	34.8	36.2	35.3	32.0	30.1	27.4	43.6	53.7	34.3	29.9	43.0	36.9	24.2
1969	36.7	38.1	37.1	34.0	32.6	28.0	45.2	56.8	35.7	31.9	45.2	38.7	24.8
1970	38.8	40.1	39.2	36.4	35.5	29.1	46.8	59.2	37.5	34.0	47.5	40.9	25.5
1971	40.5	41.4	40.4	38.0	37.0	31.1	48.6	61.1	39.5	36.1	50.0	42.9	26.5
1972	41.8	43.1	42.1	39.4	38.7	32.5	49.7	62.3	39.9	37.3	51.5	44.7	27.2
1973	44.4	48.8	48.2	41.2	40.5	34.3	51.1	64.6	41.2	38.8	52.9	46.4	29.4
1974	49.3	55.5	55.1	45.8	44.4	40.7	56.8	69.4	45.8	42.4	56.9	49.8	38.1
1975	53.8	60.2	59.8	50.7	48.8	45.4	63.4	72.5	50.1	47.5	62.0	53.9	42.1
1976	56.9	62.1	61.6	53.8	51.5	49.4	67.3	75.2	55.1	52.0	65.1	57.0	45.1
1977	60.6	65.8	65.5	57.4	54.9	54.7	70.4	78.6	59.0	57.0	68.3	60.4	49.4
1978	65.2	72.2	72.0	62.4	60.5	58.5	74.7	81.4	61.7	61.8	71.9	64.3	52.5
1979	72.6	79.9	79.9	70.1	68.9	64.8	79.9	84.9	70.5	67.5	76.7	68.9	65.7
1980	82.4	86.7	86.8	81.1	81.0	75.4	86.3	90.9	83.1	74.9	83.6	75.2	86.0
1981	90.9	93.5	93.6	90.4	90.5	86.4	93.0	95.3	93.2	82.9	90.1	82.6	97.7
1982	96.5	97.3	97.4	96.9	96.9	94.9	98.0	97.8	97.0	92.5	96.0	91.1	99.2
1983	99.6	99.5	99.4	99.5	99.1	100.2	100.2	100.2	99.3	100.6	100.1	101.1	99.9
1984	103.9	103.2	103.2	103.6	104.0	104.8	101.9	102.1	103.7	106.8	103.8	107.9	100.9
1985	107.6	105.6	105.6	107.7	109.8	106.5	103.8	105.0	106.4	113.5	107.9	114.5	101.6
1986	109.6	109.1	109.0	110.9	115.8	104.1	105.2	105.9	102.3	122.0	111.6	121.4	88.2
1987	113.6	113.5	113.5	114.2	121.3	103.0	107.1	110.6	105.4	130.1	115.3	128.5	88.6
1988	118.3	118.2	118.2	118.5	127.1	104.4	109.4	115.4	108.7	138.6	120.3	137.0	89.3
1989	124.0	124.9	125.1	123.0	132.8	107.8	111.2	118.6	114.1	149.3	126.5	147.7	94.3
1990	130.7	132.1	132.4	128.5	140.0	111.6	113.3	124.1	120.5	162.8	132.4	159.0	102.1
1991	136.2	136.8	136.3	133.6	146.3	115.3	116.0	128.7	123.8	177.0	138.4	171.6	102.5
1992	140.3	138.7	137.9	137.5	151.2	117.8	118.0	131.9	126.5	190.1	142.3	183.3	103.0
1993	144.5	141.6	140.9	141.2	155.7	121.3	119.3	133.7	130.4	201.4	145.8	192.9	104.2
1994	148.2	144.9	144.3	144.8	160.5	122.8	121.0	133.4	134.3	211.0	150.1	198.5	104.6
1995	152.4	148.9	148.4	148.5	165.7	123.7	123.0	132.0	139.1	220.5	153.9	206.9	105.2
1996	156.9	153.7	153.3	152.8	171.0	127.5	124.7	131.7	143.0	228.2	159.1	215.4	110.1
1997	160.5	157.7	157.3	156.8	176.3	130.8	125.4	132.9	144.3	234.6	162.5	224.8	111.5
1996: Jan	154.4	151.4	151.0	150.6	168.6	124.7	124.1	130.0	139.9	225.2	157.0	212.0	105.0
Feb	154.9	151.3	150.8	151.2	169.4	125.0	124.3	131.2	140.4	226.2	158.3	212.6	104.9
Mar	155.7	152.1	151.6	151.7	170.1	125.2	124.6	134.8	141.2	226.6	158.4	213.0	106.1
Apr	156.3	152.7	152.3	151.8	170.1	125.4	124.8	134.9	143.1	227.0	158.6	213.3	110.0
May	156.6	152.5	152.0	152.0	170.1	126.7	124.4	133.7	144.4	227.4	158.8	214.1	112.9
June	156.7	153.1	152.6	152.7	170.7	128.4	124.5	130.8	144.0	227.8	159.0	214.0	113.1
July	157.0	153.6	153.2	153.6	171.9	129.0	124.7	128.3	143.5	228.7	159.0	214.6	112.5
Aug	157.3	154.2	153.7	154.0	172.3	129.4	124.8	128.1	142.8	229.2	159.2	216.3	111.6
Sept	157.8	155.0	154.6	153.9	172.0	129.8	125.1	131.5	143.2	229.4	159.8	218.3	111.7
Oct	158.3	155.8	155.4	154.0	172.5	128.7	125.0	133.4	143.9	230.1	160.1	218.8	110.5
Nov	158.6	156.2	155.9	153.9	172.4	128.4	124.8	133.4	144.8	230.5	160.7	219.2	111.1
Dec	158.6	156.6	156.3	154.0	172.3	129.4	125.0	130.3	145.2	230.6	160.8	218.7	112.2
1997: Jan	159.1	156.9	156.5	155.1	173.6	130.8	124.9	129.6	145.0	231.8	161.3	220.0	113.3
Feb	159.6	156.9	156.5	155.8	174.6	131.0	125.2	131.9	144.8	232.7	161.8	220.7	113.1
Mar	160.0	157.1	156.6	155.9	175.2	129.9	125.4	134.5	144.9	233.4	162.1	221.4	111.2
Apr	160.2	157.1	156.6	155.8	175.3	128.9	125.5	136.1	144.8	233.8	162.2	222.7	110.0
May	160.1	157.1	156.6	155.9	175.3	129.0	125.8	135.3	144.4	234.2	162.2	223.1	109.9
June	160.3	157.1	156.6	156.9	176.0	131.9	125.7	132.4	144.0	234.4	162.7	223.1	112.3
July	160.5	157.5	157.0	157.5	177.0	132.1	125.6	130.2	143.7	234.8	162.6	223.5	111.4
Aug	160.8	158.1	157.6	157.6	177.5	131.4	125.2	130.0	143.8	235.2	163.0	225.7	112.5
Sept	161.2	158.4	157.9	157.7	177.2	132.1	125.4	133.0	144.3	235.4	163.0	228.1	113.9
Oct	161.6	158.7	158.2	157.7	177.8	130.8	125.4	134.9	144.5	235.8	163.1	229.4	111.5
Nov	161.5	158.9	158.5	157.7	177.7	131.1	125.2	134.7	143.9	236.4	162.9	229.9	110.7
Dec	161.3	159.1	158.7	157.7	178.1	130.0	125.1	131.6	143.2	237.1	163.1	230.1	108.4

[1] Includes alcoholic beverages, not shown separately.
[2] Household fuels—gas (piped), electricity, fuel oil, etc.—and motor fuel. Motor oil, coolant, etc. also included through 1982.
Note.—Data beginning 1983 incorporate a rental equivalence measure for homeowners' costs.
Source: Department of Labor, Bureau of Labor Statistics.

TABLE B–61.—Consumer price indexes for selected expenditure classes, 1954–97

[For all urban consumers; 1982–84=100, except as noted]

Year or month	Food and beverages Total¹	Food Total	Food At home	Food Away from home	Shelter Total	Renters' costs Total²	Renters' costs Rent, residential	Homeowners' costs²	Maintenance and repairs	Fuel Total	Fuels Total	Fuel oil and other household fuel commodities	Gas (piped) and electricity (energy services)	Other utilities and public services
1954	....	28.2	30.1	21.9	22.5	....	35.1	....	20.9	22.6	....	12.6	20.2	....
1955	....	27.8	29.5	22.1	22.7	....	35.6	....	21.4	23.0	....	12.7	20.7	....
1956	....	28.0	29.6	22.6	23.1	....	36.3	....	22.3	23.6	....	13.3	20.9	....
1957	....	28.9	30.6	23.4	24.0	....	37.0	....	23.2	24.3	....	14.0	21.1	....
1958	....	30.2	32.0	24.1	24.5	....	37.6	....	23.6	24.8	....	13.7	21.9	....
1959	....	29.7	31.2	24.8	24.7	....	38.2	....	24.0	25.4	....	13.9	22.4	....
1960	....	30.0	31.5	25.4	25.2	....	38.7	....	24.4	26.0	....	13.8	23.3	....
1961	....	30.4	31.8	26.0	25.4	....	39.2	....	24.8	26.3	....	14.1	23.5	....
1962	....	30.6	32.0	26.7	25.8	....	39.7	....	25.0	26.3	....	14.2	23.5	....
1963	....	31.1	32.4	27.3	26.1	....	40.1	....	25.3	26.6	....	14.4	23.5	....
1964	....	31.5	32.7	27.8	26.5	....	40.5	....	25.8	26.6	....	14.4	23.5	....
1965	....	32.2	33.5	28.4	27.0	....	40.9	....	26.3	26.6	....	14.6	23.5	....
1966	....	33.8	35.2	29.7	27.8	....	41.5	....	27.5	26.7	....	15.0	23.6	....
1967	35.0	34.1	35.1	31.3	28.8	....	42.2	....	28.9	27.1	21.4	15.5	23.7	46.6
1968	36.2	35.3	36.3	32.9	30.1	....	43.3	....	30.6	27.4	21.7	16.0	23.9	47.1
1969	38.1	37.1	38.0	34.9	32.6	....	44.7	....	33.2	28.0	22.1	16.3	24.3	48.4
1970	40.1	39.2	39.9	37.5	35.5	....	46.5	....	35.8	29.1	23.1	17.0	25.4	50.0
1971	41.4	40.4	40.9	39.4	37.0	....	48.7	....	38.6	31.1	24.7	18.2	27.1	53.4
1972	43.1	42.1	42.7	41.0	38.7	....	50.4	....	40.6	32.5	25.7	18.3	28.5	56.2
1973	48.8	48.2	49.7	44.2	40.5	....	52.5	....	43.6	34.3	27.5	21.1	29.9	57.8
1974	55.5	55.1	57.1	49.8	44.4	....	55.2	....	49.5	40.7	34.4	33.2	34.5	60.7
1975	60.2	59.8	61.8	54.5	48.8	....	58.0	....	54.1	45.4	39.4	36.4	40.1	63.9
1976	62.1	61.6	63.1	58.2	51.5	....	61.1	....	57.6	49.4	43.3	38.8	44.7	67.7
1977	65.8	65.5	66.8	62.6	54.9	....	64.8	....	62.0	54.7	49.0	43.9	50.5	70.8
1978	72.2	72.0	73.8	68.3	60.5	....	69.3	....	67.2	58.5	53.0	46.2	55.0	73.7
1979	79.9	79.9	81.8	75.9	68.9	....	74.3	....	74.0	64.8	61.3	62.4	61.0	74.3
1980	86.7	86.8	88.4	83.4	81.0	....	80.9	....	82.4	75.4	74.8	86.1	71.4	77.0
1981	93.5	93.6	94.8	90.9	90.5	....	87.9	....	90.7	86.4	87.2	104.6	81.9	84.3
1982	97.3	97.4	98.1	95.8	96.9	....	94.6	....	96.4	94.9	95.6	103.4	93.2	93.3
1983	99.5	99.4	99.1	100.0	99.1	103.0	100.1	102.5	99.9	100.2	100.5	97.2	101.5	99.5
1984	103.2	103.2	102.8	104.2	104.0	108.6	105.3	107.3	103.7	104.8	104.0	99.4	105.4	107.2
1985	105.6	105.6	104.3	108.3	109.8	115.4	111.8	113.1	106.5	106.5	104.5	95.9	107.1	112.1
1986	109.1	109.0	107.3	112.5	115.8	121.9	118.3	119.4	107.9	104.1	99.2	77.6	105.7	117.9
1987	113.5	113.5	111.9	117.0	121.3	128.1	123.1	124.8	111.8	103.0	97.3	77.9	103.8	120.1
1988	118.2	118.2	116.6	121.8	127.1	133.6	127.8	131.1	114.7	104.4	98.0	78.1	104.6	122.9
1989	124.9	125.1	124.2	127.4	132.8	138.9	132.8	137.3	118.0	107.8	100.9	81.7	107.5	127.1
1990	132.1	132.4	132.3	133.4	140.0	146.7	138.4	144.6	122.2	111.6	104.5	99.3	109.3	131.7
1991	136.8	136.3	135.8	137.9	146.3	155.6	143.3	150.2	126.3	115.3	106.7	94.6	112.6	137.9
1992	138.7	137.9	136.8	140.7	151.2	160.9	146.9	155.3	128.6	117.8	108.1	90.7	114.8	142.5
1993	141.6	140.9	140.1	143.2	155.7	165.0	150.3	160.2	130.6	121.3	111.2	90.3	118.5	147.0
1994	144.9	144.3	144.1	145.7	160.5	169.4	154.0	165.5	130.8	122.8	111.7	88.8	119.2	150.2
1995	148.9	148.4	148.8	149.0	165.7	174.3	157.8	171.0	135.0	123.7	111.5	88.1	119.2	152.8
1996	153.7	153.3	154.3	152.7	171.0	180.2	162.0	176.5	139.0	127.5	115.2	99.2	122.1	157.2
1997	157.7	157.3	158.1	157.0	176.3	186.4	166.7	181.5	143.7	130.8	117.9	99.8	125.1	161.6
1996: Jan	151.4	151.0	151.9	150.6	168.6	176.6	160.0	174.3	136.3	124.7	112.2	97.6	118.7	154.4
Feb	151.3	150.8	151.4	150.9	169.4	178.8	160.4	174.6	137.0	125.0	112.5	97.7	119.1	154.9
Mar	152.1	151.6	152.5	151.2	170.1	180.4	160.6	175.0	137.5	125.2	111.9	99.3	118.2	156.4
Apr	152.7	152.3	153.3	151.6	170.1	179.7	160.9	175.3	138.0	125.4	112.9	102.1	118.9	155.4
May	152.5	152.0	152.6	152.0	170.1	178.9	161.2	175.6	138.8	126.7	114.0	99.6	120.6	156.9
June	153.1	152.6	153.4	152.3	170.7	180.0	161.7	176.0	138.8	128.4	116.5	94.6	124.1	157.6
July	153.6	153.2	154.1	152.8	171.9	183.0	162.2	176.6	139.4	129.0	117.4	92.3	125.6	157.5
Aug	154.2	153.7	154.8	153.1	172.3	183.4	162.5	177.0	139.7	129.4	117.9	92.2	126.1	158.0
Sept	155.0	154.6	155.9	153.5	172.0	180.9	162.9	177.5	139.9	129.8	118.4	95.6	126.2	158.3
Oct	155.8	155.4	156.8	154.2	172.5	181.3	163.3	178.1	140.2	128.7	116.2	102.9	122.7	158.6
Nov	156.2	155.9	157.2	154.7	172.4	179.9	163.7	178.6	141.1	128.4	115.7	105.9	121.7	158.9
Dec	156.6	156.3	157.7	155.0	172.3	179.1	164.0	178.8	141.5	129.4	117.1	110.3	122.8	159.1
1997: Jan	156.9	156.5	157.9	155.3	173.6	182.7	164.4	179.1	141.5	130.8	119.1	111.5	124.9	159.7
Feb	156.9	156.5	157.7	155.6	174.6	185.3	164.8	179.5	142.3	131.0	119.2	109.6	125.3	160.2
Mar	157.1	156.6	157.7	156.0	175.2	186.8	165.1	179.8	142.4	129.9	117.2	105.5	123.4	160.5
Apr	157.1	156.6	157.5	156.2	175.3	186.3	165.5	180.2	142.5	128.9	115.3	102.1	121.7	160.8
May	157.1	156.6	157.5	156.3	175.3	185.3	165.9	180.6	143.2	129.0	115.3	100.4	121.9	161.1
June	157.1	156.6	157.3	156.6	176.0	186.6	166.4	181.1	143.3	131.9	119.8	98.0	127.5	161.7
July	157.5	157.0	157.7	157.1	177.0	188.4	166.8	181.7	145.4	132.1	119.6	94.7	127.8	162.4
Aug	158.1	157.6	158.5	157.4	177.5	189.1	167.3	182.2	145.5	131.4	118.6	93.5	126.7	162.1
Sept	158.4	157.9	158.6	157.8	177.2	186.8	167.8	182.8	146.2	132.1	119.7	93.7	128.1	162.3
Oct	158.7	158.2	159.0	158.2	177.8	187.7	168.2	183.3	144.7	130.8	117.4	95.3	125.1	162.5
Nov	158.9	158.5	159.1	158.6	177.7	185.9	168.7	183.9	144.9	131.1	117.7	96.6	125.3	162.8
Dec	159.1	158.7	159.2	159.0	178.1	186.1	169.1	184.3	145.6	130.0	115.8	97.2	123.0	162.9

¹ Includes alcoholic beverages, not shown separately.
² December 1982=100.

See next page for continuation of table.

TABLE B–61.—*Consumer price indexes for selected expenditure classes, 1954–97*—Continued

[For all urban consumers; 1982–84=100, except as noted]

Year or month	Transportation Total	Private transportation						Public transportation	Medical care Total	Medical care commodities	Medical care services
		Total³	New cars	Used cars	Motor fuel⁴	Automobile maintenance and repair	Other				
1954	26.1	27.1	46.5	22.7	21.8	22.7		18.0	17.8	42.0	15.3
1955	25.8	26.7	44.8	21.5	22.1	23.2		18.5	18.2	42.5	15.7
1956	26.2	27.1	46.1	20.7	22.8	24.2		19.2	18.9	43.4	16.3
1957	27.7	28.6	48.5	23.2	23.8	25.0		19.9	19.7	44.6	17.0
1958	28.6	29.5	50.0	24.0	23.4	25.4		20.9	20.6	46.1	17.9
1959	29.8	30.8	52.2	26.8	23.7	26.0		21.5	21.5	46.8	18.7
1960	29.8	30.6	51.5	25.0	24.4	26.5		22.2	22.3	46.9	19.5
1961	30.1	30.8	51.5	26.0	24.1	27.1		23.2	22.9	46.3	20.2
1962	30.8	31.4	51.3	28.4	24.3	27.5		24.0	23.5	45.6	20.9
1963	30.9	31.6	51.0	28.7	24.2	27.8		24.3	24.1	45.2	21.5
1964	31.4	32.0	50.9	30.0	24.1	28.2		24.7	24.6	45.1	22.0
1965	31.9	32.5	49.7	29.8	25.1	28.7		25.2	25.2	45.0	22.7
1966	32.3	32.9	48.8	29.0	25.6	29.2		26.1	26.3	45.1	23.9
1967	33.3	33.8	49.3	29.9	26.4	30.4	37.9	27.4	28.2	44.9	26.0
1968	34.3	34.8	50.7		26.8	32.1	39.2	28.7	29.9	45.0	27.9
1969	35.7	36.0	51.5	30.9	27.6	34.1	41.6	30.9	31.9	45.4	30.2
1970	37.5	37.5	53.0	31.2	27.9	36.6	45.2	35.2	34.0	46.5	32.3
1971	39.5	39.4	55.2	33.0	28.1	39.3	48.6	37.8	36.1	47.3	34.7
1972	39.9	39.7	54.7	33.1	28.4	41.1	48.9	39.3	37.3	47.4	35.9
1973	41.2	41.0	54.8	35.2	31.2	43.2	48.4	39.7	38.8	47.5	37.5
1974	45.8	46.2	57.9	36.7	42.2	47.6	50.2	40.6	42.4	49.2	41.4
1975	50.1	50.6	62.9	43.8	45.1	53.7	53.5	43.5	47.5	53.3	46.6
1976	55.1	55.6	66.9	50.3	47.0	57.6	61.8	47.8	52.0	56.5	51.3
1977	59.0	59.7	70.4	54.7	49.7	61.9	67.2	50.0	57.0	60.2	56.4
1978	61.7	62.5	75.8	55.8	51.8	67.0	69.9	51.5	61.8	64.4	61.2
1979	70.5	71.7	81.8	60.2	70.1	73.7	75.2	54.9	67.5	69.0	67.2
1980	83.1	84.2	88.4	62.3	97.4	81.5	84.3	69.0	74.9	75.4	74.8
1981	93.2	93.8	93.7	76.9	108.5	89.2	91.4	85.6	82.9	83.7	82.8
1982	97.0	97.1	97.4	88.8	102.8	96.0	97.7	94.9	92.5	92.3	92.6
1983	99.3	99.3	99.9	98.7	99.4	100.3	99.8	99.5	100.6	100.2	100.7
1984	103.7	103.6	102.8	112.5	97.9	103.8	103.5	105.7	106.8	107.5	106.7
1985	106.4	106.2	106.1	113.7	98.7	106.8	109.0	110.5	113.5	115.2	113.2
1986	102.3	101.2	110.6	108.8	77.1	110.3	115.1	117.0	122.0	122.8	121.9
1987	105.4	104.2	114.6	113.1	80.2	114.8	120.8	121.1	130.1	131.0	130.0
1988	108.7	107.6	116.9	118.0	80.9	119.7	127.9	123.3	138.6	139.9	138.3
1989	114.1	112.9	119.2	120.4	88.5	124.9	135.8	129.5	149.3	150.8	148.9
1990	120.5	118.8	121.0	117.6	101.2	130.1	142.5	142.6	162.8	163.4	162.7
1991	123.8	121.9	125.3	118.1	99.4	136.0	149.1	148.9	177.0	176.8	177.1
1992	126.5	124.6	128.4	123.2	99.0	141.3	153.2	151.4	190.1	188.1	190.5
1993	130.4	127.5	131.5	133.9	98.0	145.9	156.8	167.0	201.4	195.0	202.9
1994	134.3	131.4	136.0	141.7	98.5	150.2	162.1	172.0	211.0	200.7	213.4
1995	139.1	136.3	139.0	156.5	100.0	154.0	170.6	175.9	220.5	204.5	224.2
1996	143.0	140.0	141.4	157.0	106.3	158.4	173.9	181.9	228.2	210.4	232.4
1997	144.3	141.0	141.7	151.1	106.2	162.7	177.5	186.7	234.6	215.3	239.1
1996: Jan	139.9	137.4	141.1	157.9	98.6	156.2	172.7	171.6	225.2	207.7	229.3
Feb	140.4	137.5	141.3	157.5	98.2	156.6	173.2	177.4	226.2	208.5	230.3
Mar	141.2	138.3	141.5	157.3	101.4	156.9	172.5	178.9	226.6	208.9	230.7
Apr	143.1	140.3	141.3	157.4	108.6	157.2	173.0	179.3	227.0	209.6	231.1
May	144.4	141.7	141.2	157.6	113.6	157.5	173.1	180.2	227.4	209.7	231.6
June	144.0	141.0	141.3	157.2	111.2	157.7	173.1	182.2	227.8	210.5	231.9
July	143.5	140.5	141.0	156.9	108.9	158.1	173.5	182.7	228.7	211.0	232.9
Aug	142.8	139.9	140.7	156.6	106.4	158.6	174.1	181.4	229.2	211.1	233.4
Sept	143.2	140.0	141.0	157.0	106.2	160.0	174.1	184.6	229.4	211.2	233.6
Oct	143.9	140.5	141.5	157.0	105.9	160.5	175.4	187.2	230.1	212.4	234.2
Nov	144.8	141.5	142.3	156.5	107.8	160.5	176.2	187.3	230.5	211.9	234.9
Dec	145.2	141.7	143.0	155.6	108.6	160.6	176.0	189.9	230.6	212.0	235.0
1997: Jan	145.0	141.8	143.0	154.7	108.6	161.1	176.2	185.8	231.8	212.8	236.3
Feb	144.8	141.9	142.9	154.4	108.1	161.2	177.1	182.4	232.7	213.9	237.1
Mar	144.9	141.5	142.9	154.4	106.4	161.5	177.4	188.1	233.4	214.7	237.7
Apr	144.8	141.3	142.6	154.3	106.0	161.9	177.3	189.8	233.8	215.2	238.1
May	144.4	141.0	142.1	153.9	105.7	162.2	177.0	188.1	234.2	215.6	238.5
June	144.0	140.7	141.7	151.8	105.9	162.6	176.7	186.6	234.4	216.0	238.7
July	143.7	140.1	141.1	149.9	103.9	162.9	177.5	189.4	234.8	216.0	239.2
Aug	143.8	140.8	140.4	148.5	107.6	163.3	177.4	183.4	235.2	215.5	239.8
Sept	144.3	141.0	140.0	148.2	109.3	163.5	176.9	186.0	235.4	215.3	240.0
Oct	144.5	140.9	140.6	147.9	106.7	163.9	178.4	190.9	235.8	215.6	240.5
Nov	143.9	140.6	141.3	147.6	104.6	164.0	179.0	185.9	236.4	215.8	241.2
Dec	143.2	140.0	141.5	147.9	101.9	164.7	178.9	184.3	237.1	216.8	241.8

³ Includes other new vehicles, not shown separately. Includes direct pricing of new trucks and motorcycles beginning 1982.
⁴ Includes direct pricing of diesel fuel and gasohol beginning 1981.

Note.—See Note, Table B–60.

Source: Department of Labor, Bureau of Labor Statistics.

TABLE B–62.—*Consumer price indexes for commodities, services, and special groups, 1954–97*

[For all urban consumers; 1982–84=100, except as noted]

Year or month	All items (CPI–U)	Commodities			Services			Special indexes				
		All commodities	Food	Commodities less food	All services	Medical care services	Services less medical care	All items less food	All items less energy	All items less food and energy	All items less medical care	CPI–U–X1 (all items) (Dec. 1982 =97.6)[1]
1954	26.9	31.6	28.2	33.8	20.0	15.3	....	26.6	....	....	....	29.2
1955	26.8	31.3	27.8	33.6	20.4	15.7	....	26.6	....	....	....	29.1
1956	27.2	31.6	28.0	33.9	20.9	16.3	....	27.1	....	....	....	29.6
1957	28.1	32.6	28.9	34.9	21.8	17.0	22.8	28.0	28.9	28.9	28.7	30.5
1958	28.9	33.3	30.2	35.3	22.6	17.9	23.6	28.6	29.7	29.6	29.5	31.4
1959	29.1	33.3	29.7	35.8	23.3	18.7	24.2	29.2	29.9	30.2	29.8	31.6
1960	29.6	33.6	30.0	36.0	24.1	19.5	25.0	29.7	30.4	30.6	30.2	32.2
1961	29.9	33.8	30.4	36.1	24.5	20.2	25.4	30.0	30.7	31.0	30.5	32.5
1962	30.2	34.1	30.6	36.3	25.0	20.9	25.9	30.3	31.1	31.4	30.8	32.8
1963	30.6	34.4	31.1	36.6	25.5	21.5	26.3	30.7	31.5	31.8	31.1	33.3
1964	31.0	34.8	31.5	36.9	26.0	22.0	26.8	31.1	32.0	32.3	31.5	33.7
1965	31.5	35.2	32.2	37.2	26.6	22.7	27.4	31.6	32.5	32.7	32.0	34.2
1966	32.4	36.1	33.8	37.7	27.6	23.9	28.3	32.3	33.5	33.5	33.0	35.2
1967	33.4	36.8	34.1	38.6	28.8	26.0	29.3	33.4	34.4	34.7	33.7	36.3
1968	34.8	38.1	35.3	40.0	30.3	27.9	30.8	34.9	35.9	36.3	35.1	37.7
1969	36.7	39.9	37.1	41.7	32.4	30.2	32.9	36.8	38.0	38.4	37.0	39.4
1970	38.8	41.7	39.2	43.4	35.0	32.3	35.6	39.0	40.3	40.8	39.2	41.3
1971	40.5	43.2	40.4	45.1	37.0	34.7	37.5	40.8	42.0	42.7	40.8	43.1
1972	41.8	44.5	42.1	46.1	38.4	35.9	38.9	42.0	43.4	44.0	42.1	44.4
1973	44.4	47.8	48.2	47.7	40.1	37.5	40.6	43.7	46.1	45.6	44.8	47.2
1974	49.3	53.5	55.1	52.8	43.8	41.4	44.3	48.0	50.6	49.4	49.8	51.9
1975	53.8	58.2	59.8	57.6	48.0	46.6	48.3	52.5	55.1	53.9	54.3	56.2
1976	56.9	60.7	61.6	60.5	52.0	51.3	52.2	56.0	58.2	57.4	57.2	59.4
1977	60.6	64.2	65.5	63.8	56.0	56.4	55.9	59.6	61.9	61.0	60.8	63.2
1978	65.2	68.8	72.0	67.5	60.8	61.2	60.7	63.9	66.7	65.5	65.4	67.5
1979	72.6	76.6	79.9	75.3	67.5	67.2	67.5	71.2	73.4	71.9	72.9	74.0
1980	82.4	86.0	86.8	85.7	77.9	74.8	78.2	81.5	81.9	80.8	82.8	82.3
1981	90.9	93.2	93.6	93.1	88.1	82.8	88.7	90.4	90.1	89.2	91.4	90.1
1982	96.5	97.0	97.4	96.9	96.0	92.6	96.4	96.3	96.1	95.8	96.8	95.6
1983	99.6	99.8	99.4	100.0	99.4	100.7	99.2	99.7	99.6	99.6	99.6	99.6
1984	103.9	103.2	103.2	103.1	104.6	106.7	104.4	104.0	104.3	104.6	103.7	103.9
1985	107.6	105.4	105.6	105.2	109.9	113.2	109.6	108.0	108.4	109.1	107.2	107.6
1986	109.6	104.4	109.0	101.7	115.4	121.9	114.6	109.8	112.6	113.5	108.8	109.6
1987	113.6	107.7	113.5	104.3	120.2	130.0	119.1	113.6	117.2	118.2	112.6	113.6
1988	118.3	111.5	118.2	107.7	125.7	138.3	124.3	118.3	122.3	123.4	117.0	118.3
1989	124.0	116.7	125.1	112.0	131.9	148.9	130.1	123.7	128.1	129.0	122.4	124.0
1990	130.7	122.8	132.4	117.4	139.2	162.7	136.8	130.3	134.7	135.5	128.8	130.7
1991	136.2	126.6	136.3	121.3	146.3	177.1	143.3	136.1	140.9	142.1	133.8	136.2
1992	140.3	129.1	137.9	124.2	152.0	190.5	148.4	140.8	145.4	147.3	137.5	140.3
1993	144.5	131.5	140.9	126.3	157.9	202.9	153.6	145.1	150.0	152.2	141.2	144.5
1994	148.2	133.8	144.3	127.9	163.1	213.4	158.4	149.0	154.1	156.5	144.7	148.2
1995	152.4	136.4	148.4	129.8	168.7	224.2	163.5	153.1	158.7	161.2	148.6	152.4
1996	156.9	139.9	153.3	132.6	174.1	232.4	168.7	157.5	163.1	165.6	152.8	156.9
1997	160.5	141.8	157.3	133.4	179.4	239.1	173.9	161.1	167.1	169.5	156.3	160.5
1996: Jan	154.4	137.8	151.0	130.6	171.3	229.3	165.9	155.0	161.0	163.4	150.4	154.4
Feb	154.9	138.0	150.8	131.0	172.2	230.3	166.8	155.7	161.6	164.2	150.9	154.9
Mar	155.7	139.2	151.6	132.4	172.6	230.7	167.2	156.5	162.3	164.9	151.7	155.7
Apr	156.3	140.2	152.3	133.5	172.7	231.1	167.3	157.0	162.5	165.0	152.3	156.3
May	156.6	140.4	152.0	134.0	173.1	231.6	167.7	157.4	162.5	165.1	152.6	156.6
June	156.7	139.9	152.6	133.0	173.9	231.9	168.5	157.5	162.7	165.2	152.7	156.7
July	157.0	139.5	153.2	132.0	174.8	232.9	169.4	157.7	163.1	165.5	153.0	157.0
Aug	157.3	139.5	153.7	131.7	175.3	233.4	169.9	157.9	163.4	165.8	153.2	157.3
Sept	157.8	140.3	154.6	132.5	175.6	233.6	170.2	158.4	164.0	166.4	153.8	157.8
Oct	158.3	141.0	155.4	133.2	175.8	234.2	170.4	158.8	164.7	167.0	154.2	158.3
Nov	158.6	141.5	155.9	133.7	175.9	234.9	170.4	159.0	164.9	167.2	154.5	158.6
Dec	158.6	141.4	156.3	133.3	176.1	235.0	170.6	159.0	164.8	167.0	154.5	158.6
1997: Jan	159.1	141.5	156.5	133.3	177.0	236.3	171.5	159.6	165.3	167.5	155.0	159.1
Feb	159.6	141.8	156.5	133.8	177.7	237.1	172.2	160.2	165.9	168.3	155.5	159.6
Mar	160.0	142.0	156.6	134.1	178.2	237.7	172.7	160.6	166.5	169.0	155.9	160.0
Apr	160.2	142.3	156.6	134.4	178.3	238.1	172.8	160.8	166.8	169.4	156.0	160.2
May	160.1	142.1	156.6	134.1	178.4	238.5	172.8	160.7	166.8	169.3	155.9	160.1
June	160.3	141.5	156.6	133.3	179.3	238.7	173.8	161.0	166.7	169.2	156.1	160.3
July	160.5	141.0	157.0	132.3	180.1	239.2	174.6	161.1	167.0	169.5	156.3	160.5
Aug	160.8	141.4	157.6	132.6	180.3	239.8	174.8	161.3	167.3	169.6	156.6	160.8
Sept	161.2	142.1	157.9	133.5	180.6	240.0	175.1	161.8	167.6	170.0	157.1	161.2
Oct	161.6	142.4	158.2	133.8	181.0	240.5	175.5	162.2	168.3	170.8	157.4	161.6
Nov	161.5	142.3	158.5	133.5	181.0	241.2	175.4	162.1	168.3	170.8	157.3	161.5
Dec	161.3	141.7	158.7	132.6	181.0	241.8	175.4	161.8	168.3	170.7	157.0	161.3

[1] CPI–U–X1 is a rental equivalence approach to homeowners' costs for the consumer price index for years prior to 1983, the first year for which the official index (CPI–U) incorporates such a measure. CPI–U–X1 is rebased to the December 1982 value of the CPI–U (1982–84=100); thus it is identical with CPI–U data for December 1982 and all subsequent periods. Data prior to 1967 estimated by moving the series at the same rate as the CPI–U for each year.

Note.—See Note, Table B–60.

Source: Department of Labor, Bureau of Labor Statistics.

TABLE B–63.—*Changes in special consumer price indexes, 1960–97*

[For all urban consumers; percent change]

Year or month	All items (CPI–U)		All items less food		All items less energy		All items less food and energy		All items less medical care	
	Dec. to Dec.[1]	Year to year	Dec. to Dec.[1]	Year to year	Dec. to Dec.[1]	Year to year	Dec. to Dec.[1]	Year to year	Dec. to Dec.[1]	Year to year
1960	1.4	1.7	1.0	1.7	1.3	1.7	1.0	1.3	1.3	1.3
1961	.7	1.0	1.3	1.0	.7	1.0	1.3	1.3	.3	1.0
1962	1.3	1.0	1.0	1.0	1.3	1.3	1.3	1.3	1.3	1.0
1963	1.6	1.3	1.6	1.3	1.9	1.3	1.6	1.3	1.6	1.0
1964	1.0	1.3	1.0	1.3	1.3	1.6	1.2	1.6	1.0	1.3
1965	1.9	1.6	1.6	1.6	1.9	1.6	1.5	1.2	1.9	1.6
1966	3.5	2.9	3.5	2.2	3.4	3.1	3.3	2.4	3.4	3.1
1967	3.0	3.1	3.3	3.4	3.2	2.7	3.8	3.6	2.7	2.1
1968	4.7	4.2	5.0	4.5	4.9	4.4	5.1	4.6	4.7	4.2
1969	6.2	5.5	5.6	5.4	6.5	5.8	6.2	5.8	6.1	5.4
1970	5.6	5.7	6.6	6.0	5.4	6.1	6.6	6.3	5.2	5.9
1971	3.3	4.4	3.0	4.6	3.4	4.2	3.1	4.7	3.2	4.1
1972	3.4	3.2	2.9	2.9	3.5	3.3	3.0	3.0	3.4	3.2
1973	8.7	6.2	5.6	4.0	8.2	6.2	4.7	3.6	9.1	6.4
1974	12.3	11.0	12.2	9.8	11.7	9.8	11.1	8.3	12.2	11.2
1975	6.9	9.1	7.3	9.4	6.6	8.9	6.7	9.1	6.7	9.0
1976	4.9	5.8	6.1	6.7	4.8	5.6	6.1	6.5	4.5	5.3
1977	6.7	6.5	6.4	6.4	6.7	6.4	6.5	6.3	6.7	6.3
1978	9.0	7.6	8.3	7.2	9.1	7.8	8.5	7.4	9.1	7.6
1979	13.3	11.3	14.0	11.4	11.1	10.0	11.3	9.8	13.4	11.5
1980	12.5	13.5	13.0	14.5	11.7	11.6	12.2	12.4	12.5	13.6
1981	8.9	10.3	9.8	10.9	8.5	10.0	9.5	10.4	8.8	10.4
1982	3.8	6.2	4.1	6.5	4.2	6.7	4.5	7.4	3.6	5.9
1983	3.8	3.2	4.1	3.5	4.5	3.6	4.8	4.0	3.6	2.9
1984	3.9	4.3	3.9	4.3	4.4	4.7	4.7	5.0	3.9	4.1
1985	3.8	3.6	4.1	3.8	4.0	3.9	4.3	4.3	3.5	3.4
1986	1.1	1.9	.5	1.7	3.8	3.9	3.8	4.0	.7	1.5
1987	4.4	3.6	4.6	3.5	4.1	4.1	4.2	4.1	4.3	3.5
1988	4.4	4.1	4.2	4.1	4.7	4.4	4.7	4.4	4.2	3.9
1989	4.6	4.8	4.5	4.6	4.6	4.7	4.4	4.5	4.5	4.6
1990	6.1	5.4	6.3	5.3	5.2	5.2	5.2	5.0	5.9	5.2
1991	3.1	4.2	3.3	4.5	3.9	4.6	4.4	4.9	2.7	3.9
1992	2.9	3.0	3.2	3.5	3.0	3.2	3.3	3.7	2.7	2.8
1993	2.7	3.0	2.7	3.1	3.1	3.2	3.2	3.3	2.6	2.7
1994	2.7	2.6	2.6	2.7	2.6	2.7	2.6	2.8	2.5	2.5
1995	2.5	2.8	2.7	2.8	2.9	3.0	3.0	3.0	2.5	2.7
1996	3.3	3.0	3.1	2.9	2.9	2.8	2.6	2.7	3.3	2.8
1997	1.7	2.3	1.8	2.3	2.1	2.5	2.2	2.4	1.6	2.3

	Percent change from preceding month									
	Unadjusted	Seasonally adjusted	Unadjusted	Seasonally adjusted	Unadjusted	Seasonally adjusted	Unadjusted	Seasonally adjusted	Unadjusted	Seasonally adjusted
1996: Jan	0.6	0.4	0.5	0.4	0.5	0.2	0.4	0.2	0.5	0.3
Feb	.3	.3	.5	.3	.4	.2	.5	.2	.3	.3
Mar	.5	.3	.5	.3	.4	.2	.4	.2	.5	.3
Apr	.4	.3	.3	.4	.1	.2	.1	.2	.4	.3
May	.2	.3	.3	.3	0	.2	.1	.2	.2	.3
June	.1	.1	.1	0	.1	.2	.1	.2	.1	.1
July	.2	.3	.1	.3	.2	.3	.2	.2	.2	.3
Aug	.2	.2	.1	.1	.2	.1	.1	.1	.1	.1
Sept	.3	.3	.3	.3	.4	.4	.4	.3	.4	.3
Oct	.3	.3	.3	.3	.4	.2	.4	.2	.3	.3
Nov	.2	.3	.1	.3	.1	.2	.1	.2	.2	.3
Dec	0	.3	0	.3	-.1	.1	-.1	.2	0	.3
1997: Jan	.3	.1	.4	.2	.3	.1	.3	.1	.3	.1
Feb	.3	.3	.4	.2	.4	.2	.5	.2	.3	.3
Mar	.3	.1	.2	.1	.4	.2	.4	.2	.3	0
Apr	.1	.1	.1	.2	.2	.2	.2	.3	.1	.1
May	-.1	.1	-.1	-.1	0	.2	-.1	.2	-.1	0
June	.1	.1	.2	.1	-.1	.1	-.1	.1	.1	.1
July	.1	.2	.1	.2	.2	.2	.2	.2	.1	.2
Aug	.2	.2	.1	.1	.2	.1	.1	.1	.2	.2
Sept	.2	.2	.3	.3	.2	.2	.2	.3	.3	.3
Oct	.2	.2	.2	.2	.4	.2	.5	.2	.2	.2
Nov	-.1	.1	-.1	.1	0	.1	0	.1	-.1	.1
Dec	-.1	.1	-.2	.1	0	.2	-.1	.2	-.2	.1

[1] Changes from December to December are based on unadjusted indexes.

Note.—See Note, Table B–60.

Source: Department of Labor, Bureau of Labor Statistics.

TABLE B–64.—*Changes in consumer price indexes for commodities and services, 1929–97*

[For all urban consumers; percent change]

Year	All items (CPI–U) Dec. to Dec.[1]	Year to year	Commodities Total Dec. to Dec.[1]	Year to year	Food Dec. to Dec.[1]	Year to year	Services Total Dec. to Dec.[1]	Year to year	Medical care Dec. to Dec.[1]	Year to year	Medical care[2] Dec. to Dec.[1]	Year to year	Energy[3] Dec. to Dec.[1]	Year to year
1929	0.6	0	.....	.....	2.5	1.2	.....	.....	.....	.....	.....	.....	.....	.....
1933	.8	−5.1	.....	.....	6.9	−2.8	.....	.....	.....	.....	.....	.....	.....	.....
1939	0	−1.4	−0.7	−2.0	−2.5	−2.5	0	0	1.2	1.2	1.0	0	.....	.....
1940	.7	.7	1.4	.7	2.5	1.7	.8	.8	0	0	0	1.0	.....	.....
1941	9.9	5.0	13.3	6.7	15.7	9.2	2.4	.8	1.2	0	1.0	0	.....	.....
1942	9.0	10.9	12.9	14.5	17.9	17.6	2.3	3.1	3.5	3.5	3.8	2.9	.....	.....
1943	3.0	6.1	4.2	9.3	3.0	11.0	2.3	2.3	5.6	4.5	4.6	4.7	.....	.....
1944	2.3	1.7	2.0	1.0	0	−1.2	2.2	2.2	3.2	4.3	2.6	3.6	.....	.....
1945	2.2	2.3	2.9	3.0	3.5	2.4	.7	1.5	3.1	3.1	2.6	2.6	.....	.....
1946	18.1	8.3	24.8	10.6	31.3	14.5	3.6	1.4	9.0	5.1	8.3	5.0	.....	.....
1947	8.8	14.4	10.3	20.5	11.3	21.7	5.6	4.3	6.4	8.7	6.9	8.0	.....	.....
1948	3.0	8.1	1.7	7.2	−.8	8.3	5.9	6.1	6.9	7.1	5.8	6.7	.....	.....
1949	−2.1	−1.2	−4.1	−2.7	−3.9	−4.2	3.7	5.1	1.6	3.3	1.4	2.8	.....	.....
1950	5.9	1.3	7.8	.7	9.8	1.6	3.6	3.0	4.0	2.4	3.4	2.0	.....	.....
1951	6.0	7.9	5.9	9.0	7.1	11.0	5.2	5.3	5.3	4.7	5.8	5.3	.....	.....
1952	.8	1.9	−.9	1.3	−1.0	1.8	4.4	4.5	5.8	6.7	4.3	5.0	.....	.....
1953	.7	.8	−.3	−.3	−1.1	−1.4	4.2	4.3	3.4	3.5	3.5	3.6	.....	.....
1954	−.7	.7	−1.6	−.9	−1.8	−.4	2.0	3.1	2.6	3.4	2.3	2.9	.....	.....
1955	.4	−.4	−.3	−.9	−.7	−1.4	2.0	2.0	3.2	2.6	3.3	2.2	.....	.....
1956	3.0	1.5	2.6	1.0	2.9	.7	3.4	2.5	3.8	3.8	3.2	3.8	.....	.....
1957	2.9	3.3	2.8	3.2	2.8	3.2	4.2	4.3	4.8	4.3	4.7	4.2	.....	.....
1958	1.8	2.8	1.2	2.1	2.4	4.5	2.7	3.7	4.6	5.3	4.5	4.6	−0.9	0
1959	1.7	.7	.6	0	−1.0	−1.7	3.9	3.1	4.9	4.5	3.8	4.4	4.7	1.9
1960	1.4	1.7	1.2	.9	3.1	1.0	2.5	3.4	3.7	4.3	3.2	3.7	1.3	2.3
1961	.7	1.0	0	.6	−.7	1.3	2.1	1.7	3.5	3.6	3.1	2.7	−1.3	.4
1962	1.3	1.0	.9	.9	1.3	.7	1.6	2.0	2.9	3.5	2.2	2.6	2.2	.4
1963	1.6	1.3	1.5	.9	2.0	1.6	2.4	2.0	2.8	2.9	2.5	2.6	−.9	0
1964	1.0	1.3	.9	1.2	1.3	1.3	1.6	2.0	2.3	2.3	2.1	2.1	0	−.4
1965	1.9	1.6	1.4	1.1	3.5	2.2	2.7	2.3	3.6	3.2	2.8	2.4	1.8	1.8
1966	3.5	2.9	2.5	2.6	4.0	5.0	4.8	3.8	8.3	5.3	6.7	4.4	1.7	1.7
1967	3.0	3.1	2.5	1.9	1.2	.9	4.3	4.3	8.0	8.8	6.3	7.2	1.7	2.1
1968	4.7	4.2	4.0	3.5	4.4	3.5	5.8	5.2	7.1	7.3	6.2	6.0	1.7	1.7
1969	6.2	5.5	5.4	4.7	7.0	5.1	7.7	6.9	7.3	8.2	6.2	6.7	2.9	2.5
1970	5.6	5.7	3.9	4.5	2.3	5.7	8.1	8.0	8.1	7.0	7.4	6.6	4.8	2.8
1971	3.3	4.4	2.8	3.6	4.3	3.1	4.1	5.7	5.4	7.4	4.6	6.2	3.1	3.9
1972	3.4	3.2	3.4	3.0	4.6	4.2	3.4	3.8	3.7	3.5	3.3	3.3	2.6	2.6
1973	8.7	6.2	10.4	7.4	20.3	14.5	6.2	4.4	6.0	4.5	5.3	4.0	17.0	8.1
1974	12.3	11.0	12.8	11.9	12.0	14.3	11.4	9.2	13.2	10.4	12.6	9.3	21.6	29.6
1975	6.9	9.1	6.2	8.8	6.6	8.5	8.2	9.6	10.3	12.6	9.8	12.0	11.4	10.5
1976	4.9	5.8	3.3	4.3	.5	3.0	7.2	8.3	10.8	10.1	10.0	9.5	7.1	7.1
1977	6.7	6.5	6.1	5.8	8.1	6.3	8.0	7.7	9.0	9.9	8.9	9.6	7.2	9.5
1978	9.0	7.6	8.8	7.2	11.8	9.9	9.3	8.6	9.3	8.5	8.8	8.4	7.9	6.3
1979	13.3	11.3	13.0	11.3	10.2	11.0	13.6	11.0	10.5	9.8	10.1	9.2	37.5	25.1
1980	12.5	13.5	11.0	12.3	10.2	8.6	14.2	15.4	10.1	11.3	9.9	11.0	18.0	30.9
1981	8.9	10.3	6.0	8.4	4.3	7.8	13.0	13.1	12.6	10.7	12.5	10.7	11.9	13.6
1982	3.8	6.2	3.6	4.1	3.1	4.1	4.3	9.0	11.2	11.8	11.0	11.6	1.3	1.5
1983	3.8	3.2	2.9	2.9	2.7	2.1	4.8	3.5	6.2	8.7	6.4	8.8	−.5	.7
1984	3.9	4.3	2.7	3.4	3.8	3.8	5.4	5.2	5.8	6.0	6.1	6.2	.2	1.0
1985	3.8	3.6	2.5	2.1	2.6	2.3	5.1	5.1	6.8	6.1	6.8	6.3	1.8	.7
1986	1.1	1.9	−2.0	−.9	3.8	3.2	4.5	5.0	7.9	7.7	7.7	7.5	−19.7	−13.2
1987	4.4	3.6	4.6	3.2	3.5	4.1	4.3	4.2	5.6	6.6	5.8	6.6	8.2	.5
1988	4.4	4.1	3.8	3.5	5.2	4.1	4.8	4.6	6.9	6.4	6.9	6.5	.5	.8
1989	4.6	4.8	4.1	4.7	5.6	5.8	5.1	4.9	8.6	7.7	8.5	7.7	5.1	5.6
1990	6.1	5.4	6.6	5.2	5.3	5.8	5.7	5.5	9.9	9.3	9.6	9.0	18.1	8.3
1991	3.1	4.2	1.2	3.1	1.9	2.9	4.6	5.1	8.0	8.9	7.9	8.7	−7.4	.4
1992	2.9	3.0	2.0	2.0	1.5	1.2	3.6	3.9	7.0	7.6	6.6	7.4	2.0	.5
1993	2.7	3.0	1.5	1.9	2.9	2.2	3.8	3.9	5.9	6.5	5.4	5.9	−1.4	1.2
1994	2.7	2.6	2.3	1.7	2.9	2.4	2.9	3.3	5.4	5.2	4.9	4.8	2.2	.4
1995	2.5	2.8	1.4	1.9	2.1	2.8	3.5	3.4	4.4	5.1	3.9	4.5	−1.3	.6
1996	3.3	3.0	3.2	2.6	4.3	3.3	3.3	3.2	3.2	3.7	3.0	3.5	8.6	4.7
1997	1.7	2.3	.2	1.4	1.5	2.6	2.8	3.0	2.9	2.9	2.8	2.8	−3.4	1.3

[1] Changes from December to December are based on unadjusted indexes.
[2] Commodities and services.
[3] Household fuels—gas (piped), electricity, fuel oil, etc.—and motor fuel. Motor oil, coolant, etc. also included through 1982.

Note.—See Note, Table B–60.

Source: Department of Labor, Bureau of Labor Statistics.

TABLE B-65.—*Producer price indexes by stage of processing, 1954–97*

[1982=100]

Year or month	Total finished goods	Consumer foods			Finished goods excluding consumer foods					Total finished consumer goods
		Total	Crude	Processed	Total	Consumer goods			Capital equipment	
						Total	Durable	Non-durable		
1954	30.4	34.2	37.5	34.0		31.1	39.8	26.7	26.7	31.7
1955	30.5	33.4	39.1	32.7		31.3	40.2	26.8	27.4	31.5
1956	31.3	33.3	39.1	32.7		32.1	41.6	27.3	29.5	32.0
1957	32.5	34.4	38.5	34.1		32.9	42.8	27.9	31.3	32.9
1958	33.2	36.5	41.0	36.1		32.9	43.4	27.8	32.1	33.6
1959	33.1	34.8	37.3	34.7		33.3	43.9	28.2	32.7	33.3
1960	33.4	35.5	39.8	35.2		33.5	43.8	28.4	32.8	33.6
1961	33.4	35.4	38.0	35.3		33.4	43.6	28.4	32.9	33.6
1962	33.5	35.7	38.4	35.6		33.4	43.4	28.4	33.0	33.7
1963	33.4	35.3	37.8	35.2		33.4	43.1	28.5	33.1	33.5
1964	33.5	35.4	38.9	35.2		33.3	43.3	28.4	33.4	33.6
1965	34.1	36.8	39.0	36.8		33.6	43.2	28.8	33.8	34.2
1966	35.2	39.2	41.5	39.2		34.1	43.4	29.3	34.6	35.4
1967	35.6	38.5	39.6	38.8	35.0	34.7	44.1	30.0	35.8	35.6
1968	36.6	40.0	42.5	40.0	35.9	35.5	45.1	30.6	37.0	36.5
1969	38.0	42.4	45.9	42.3	36.9	36.3	45.9	31.5	38.3	37.9
1970	39.3	43.8	46.0	43.9	38.2	37.4	47.2	32.5	40.1	39.1
1971	40.5	44.5	45.8	44.7	39.6	38.7	48.9	33.5	41.7	40.2
1972	41.8	46.9	48.0	47.2	40.4	39.4	50.0	34.1	42.8	41.5
1973	45.6	56.5	63.6	55.8	42.0	41.2	50.9	36.1	44.2	46.0
1974	52.6	64.4	71.6	63.9	48.8	48.2	55.5	44.0	50.5	53.1
1975	58.2	69.8	71.7	70.3	54.7	53.2	61.0	48.9	58.2	58.2
1976	60.8	69.6	76.7	69.0	58.1	56.5	63.7	52.4	62.1	60.4
1977	64.7	73.3	79.5	72.7	62.2	60.6	67.4	56.8	66.1	64.3
1978	69.8	79.9	85.8	79.4	66.7	64.9	73.6	60.0	71.3	69.4
1979	77.6	87.3	92.3	86.8	74.6	73.5	80.8	69.3	77.5	77.5
1980	88.0	92.4	93.9	92.3	86.7	87.1	91.0	85.1	85.8	88.6
1981	96.1	97.8	104.4	97.2	95.6	96.1	96.4	95.8	94.6	96.6
1982	100.0	100.0	100.0	100.0	100.0	100.0	100.0	100.0	100.0	100.0
1983	101.6	101.0	102.4	100.9	101.8	101.2	102.8	100.5	102.8	101.3
1984	103.7	105.4	111.4	104.9	103.2	102.2	104.5	101.1	105.2	103.3
1985	104.7	104.6	102.9	104.8	104.6	103.3	106.5	101.7	107.5	103.8
1986	103.2	107.3	105.6	107.4	101.9	98.5	108.9	93.3	109.7	101.4
1987	105.4	109.5	107.1	109.6	104.0	100.7	111.5	94.9	111.7	103.6
1988	108.0	112.6	109.8	112.7	106.5	103.1	113.8	97.3	114.3	106.2
1989	113.6	118.7	119.6	118.6	111.8	108.9	117.6	103.8	118.8	112.1
1990	119.2	124.4	123.0	124.4	117.4	115.3	120.4	111.5	122.9	118.2
1991	121.7	124.1	119.3	124.4	120.9	118.7	123.9	115.0	126.7	120.5
1992	123.2	123.3	107.6	124.4	123.1	120.8	125.7	117.3	129.1	121.7
1993	124.7	125.7	114.4	126.5	124.4	121.7	128.0	117.6	131.4	123.0
1994	125.5	126.8	111.3	127.9	125.1	121.6	130.9	116.2	134.1	123.3
1995	127.9	129.0	118.8	129.8	127.5	124.0	132.7	118.8	136.7	125.6
1996	131.3	133.6	129.2	133.8	130.5	127.6	134.2	123.3	138.3	129.5
1997	131.8	134.5	126.4	135.1	130.9	128.2	133.8	124.3	138.3	130.2
1996:Jan	129.4	130.7	125.0	131.1	129.0	125.4	134.2	120.1	138.3	127.1
Feb	129.4	130.7	121.9	131.3	128.9	125.3	134.3	119.9	138.4	127.0
Mar	130.1	132.0	145.3	131.0	129.5	126.1	134.3	121.2	138.3	128.0
Apr	130.6	131.2	131.7	131.1	130.4	127.4	134.0	123.1	138.3	128.7
May	131.1	131.5	117.3	132.5	130.9	128.2	134.2	124.1	138.2	129.3
June	131.7	133.6	128.8	133.9	131.0	128.3	134.4	124.2	138.2	130.0
July	131.5	133.9	123.7	134.6	130.8	128.0	133.8	124.0	138.1	129.9
Aug	131.9	135.3	121.5	136.3	130.9	128.1	133.7	124.2	138.2	130.4
Sept	131.8	135.6	128.2	136.2	130.5	128.0	132.4	124.6	137.3	130.4
Oct	132.7	136.6	136.3	136.6	131.5	128.8	135.2	124.5	138.9	131.2
Nov	132.6	136.1	136.2	136.1	131.5	128.8	135.2	124.5	138.7	131.1
Dec	132.7	135.5	134.8	135.5	131.7	129.2	135.0	125.2	138.7	131.2
1997:Jan	132.6	134.1	130.3	134.3	132.1	129.5	134.9	125.7	139.0	131.0
Feb	132.2	133.8	133.2	133.9	131.7	129.0	135.0	124.9	138.9	130.6
Mar	132.1	135.2	140.4	134.8	131.1	128.2	135.0	123.8	138.8	130.4
Apr	131.6	134.3	121.5	135.2	130.7	127.7	134.5	123.2	138.6	129.8
May	131.6	135.2	124.4	135.9	130.5	127.6	133.6	123.5	138.1	130.0
June	131.6	134.0	116.0	135.4	130.9	128.1	133.4	124.4	138.1	130.0
July	131.3	134.0	115.7	135.3	130.4	127.6	132.4	124.1	137.8	129.7
Aug [1]	131.7	134.9	117.3	136.1	130.7	128.1	132.3	124.8	137.7	130.3
Sept	131.8	134.8	122.8	135.6	130.8	128.5	131.5	125.7	137.1	130.5
Oct	132.4	135.0	132.3	135.2	131.5	128.8	134.9	124.7	138.7	130.8
Nov	131.8	134.5	129.4	134.9	130.9	128.1	134.4	123.8	138.4	130.1
Dec	131.1	134.2	133.0	134.2	130.2	127.2	133.9	122.8	138.0	129.4

[1] Data have been revised through August 1997 to reflect the availability of late reports and corrections by respondents. All data are subject to revision 4 months after original publication.

See next page for continuation of table.

TABLE B–65.—*Producer price indexes by stage of processing, 1954–97*—Continued

[1982=100]

Year or month	Intermediate materials, supplies, and components								Crude materials for further processing				
				Materials and components		Processed fuels and lubricants	Containers	Supplies			Other		
	Total	Foods and feeds²	Other	For manufacturing	For construction				Total	Foodstuffs and feedstuffs	Total	Fuel	Other
1954	27.9		27.2	29.8	29.1	15.8	28.5	31.7	31.6	42.3		8.9	26.1
1955	28.4		28.0	30.5	30.3	15.8	28.9	31.2	30.4	38.4		8.9	27.5
1956	29.6		29.3	32.0	31.8	16.3	31.0	32.0	30.6	37.6		9.5	28.6
1957	30.3		30.1	32.7	32.0	17.2	32.4	32.3	31.2	39.2		10.1	28.2
1958	30.4		30.1	32.8	32.0	16.2	33.2	33.1	31.9	41.6		10.2	27.1
1959	30.8		30.5	33.3	32.9	16.2	33.0	33.5	31.1	38.8		10.4	28.1
1960	30.8		30.7	33.3	32.7	16.6	33.4	33.3	30.4	38.4		10.5	26.9
1961	30.6		30.3	32.9	32.2	16.8	33.2	33.7	30.2	37.9		10.5	27.2
1962	30.6		30.2	32.7	32.1	16.7	33.6	34.5	30.5	38.6		10.4	27.1
1963	30.7		30.1	32.7	32.2	16.6	33.2	35.0	29.9	37.5		10.5	26.7
1964	30.8		30.3	33.1	32.5	16.2	32.9	34.7	29.6	36.6		10.5	27.2
1965	31.2		30.7	33.6	32.8	16.5	33.5	35.0	31.1	39.2		10.6	27.7
1966	32.0		31.3	34.3	33.6	16.8	34.5	36.5	33.1	42.7		10.9	28.3
1967	32.2	41.8	31.7	34.5	34.0	16.9	35.0	36.8	31.3	40.3	21.1	11.3	26.5
1968	33.0	41.5	32.5	35.3	35.7	16.5	35.9	37.1	31.8	40.9	21.6	11.5	27.1
1969	34.1	42.9	33.6	36.5	37.7	16.6	37.2	37.8	33.9	44.1	22.5	12.0	28.4
1970	35.4	45.6	34.8	38.0	38.3	17.7	39.0	39.7	35.2	45.2	23.8	13.8	29.1
1971	36.8	46.7	36.2	38.9	40.8	19.5	40.8	40.8	36.0	46.1	24.7	15.7	29.4
1972	38.2	49.5	37.7	40.4	43.0	20.1	42.7	42.5	39.9	51.5	27.0	16.8	32.3
1973	42.4	70.3	40.6	44.1	46.5	22.2	45.2	51.7	54.5	72.6	34.3	18.6	42.9
1974	52.5	83.6	50.5	56.0	55.0	33.6	53.3	56.8	61.4	76.4	44.1	24.8	54.5
1975	58.0	81.6	56.6	61.7	60.1	39.4	60.0	61.8	61.6	77.4	43.7	30.6	50.0
1976	60.9	77.4	60.0	64.0	64.1	42.3	63.1	65.8	63.4	76.8	48.2	34.5	54.9
1977	64.9	79.6	64.1	67.4	69.3	47.7	65.9	69.3	65.5	77.5	51.7	42.0	56.3
1978	69.5	84.8	68.6	72.0	76.5	49.9	71.0	72.9	73.4	87.3	57.5	48.2	61.9
1979	78.4	94.5	77.4	80.9	84.2	61.6	79.4	80.2	85.9	100.0	69.6	57.3	75.5
1980	90.3	105.5	89.4	91.7	91.3	85.0	89.1	89.9	95.3	104.6	84.6	69.4	91.8
1981	98.6	104.6	98.2	98.7	97.9	100.6	96.7	96.9	103.0	103.9	101.8	84.8	109.8
1982	100.0	100.0	100.0	100.0	100.0	100.0	100.0	100.0	100.0	100.0	100.0	100.0	100.0
1983	100.6	103.6	100.5	101.2	102.8	95.4	100.4	101.8	101.3	101.8	100.7	105.1	98.8
1984	103.1	105.7	103.0	104.1	105.6	95.7	105.9	104.1	103.5	104.7	102.2	105.1	101.0
1985	102.7	97.3	103.0	103.3	107.3	92.8	109.0	104.4	95.8	94.8	96.9	102.7	94.3
1986	99.1	96.2	99.3	102.2	108.1	72.7	110.3	105.6	87.7	93.2	81.6	92.2	76.0
1987	101.5	99.2	101.7	105.3	109.8	73.3	114.5	107.7	93.7	96.2	87.9	84.1	88.5
1988	107.1	109.5	106.9	113.2	116.1	71.2	120.1	113.7	96.0	106.1	85.5	82.1	85.9
1989	112.0	113.8	111.9	118.1	121.3	76.4	125.4	118.1	103.1	111.2	93.4	85.3	95.8
1990	114.5	113.3	114.5	118.7	122.9	85.9	127.7	119.4	108.9	113.1	101.5	84.8	107.3
1991	114.4	111.1	114.6	118.1	124.5	85.3	128.1	121.4	101.2	105.5	94.6	82.9	97.5
1992	114.7	110.7	114.9	117.9	126.5	84.5	127.7	122.7	100.4	105.1	93.5	84.0	94.2
1993	116.2	112.7	116.4	118.9	132.0	84.7	126.4	125.0	102.4	108.4	94.7	87.1	94.1
1994	118.5	114.8	118.7	122.1	136.6	83.1	129.7	127.0	101.8	106.5	94.8	82.4	97.0
1995	124.9	114.8	125.5	130.4	142.1	84.2	148.8	132.1	102.7	105.8	96.8	72.1	105.8
1996	125.7	128.1	125.6	128.6	143.6	90.0	141.1	135.9	113.8	121.5	104.5	92.6	105.7
1997	125.6	125.4	125.7	128.3	146.5	89.3	135.9	135.9	110.9	112.2	106.0	100.4	103.5
1996:Jan	125.2	123.0	125.4	129.5	141.9	85.2	148.2	135.3	108.8	114.7	100.8	86.1	103.9
Feb	124.7	123.0	124.8	129.0	142.0	84.0	146.1	135.3	111.1	115.0	104.4	97.1	102.8
Mar	124.9	123.4	125.0	128.6	142.2	85.8	144.6	135.4	110.0	116.2	102.0	88.2	104.4
Apr	125.4	125.3	125.4	128.3	142.5	89.3	143.0	135.7	114.4	119.6	106.7	93.9	108.3
May	126.2	130.3	126.0	128.8	143.5	91.4	141.6	136.2	115.9	127.7	103.8	90.1	106.1
June	126.2	131.2	125.9	128.8	144.0	91.3	140.1	136.1	113.3	129.0	98.7	82.3	102.9
July	125.9	131.9	125.6	128.3	143.7	91.1	139.6	136.4	115.6	130.9	101.2	89.2	102.6
Aug	126.1	132.7	125.7	128.3	144.1	91.9	138.4	136.4	116.0	129.5	102.8	90.2	104.6
Sept	126.7	133.5	126.3	128.6	144.8	93.6	138.5	136.8	112.9	124.9	100.8	80.5	107.1
Oct	126.0	130.7	125.8	128.3	144.3	92.3	137.9	135.9	111.3	119.6	101.8	79.1	109.5
Nov	125.7	126.2	125.7	128.0	144.9	91.3	137.5	135.4	114.8	117.7	108.7	100.4	107.6
Dec	126.0	125.6	126.1	128.2	144.7	92.7	137.9	135.5	121.6	113.6	122.5	134.1	109.0
1997:Jan	126.3	124.6	126.4	128.4	145.0	93.4	137.8	135.5	112.2		131.0	149.8	112.8
Feb	126.1	124.8	126.2	128.4	145.7	92.1	136.9	135.5	116.1	110.0	115.2	116.6	108.1
Mar	125.6	127.2	125.6	128.6	146.2	88.7	136.0	135.8	107.6	114.1	99.4	82.1	104.0
Apr	125.3	127.5	125.2	128.4	146.8	87.0	135.1	136.0	107.9	116.7	98.1	79.6	103.5
May	125.4	128.3	125.3	128.4	147.2	87.2	134.6	136.2	110.4	117.4	101.8	86.3	105.3
June	125.8	124.6	125.7	128.3	147.0	89.8	134.2	136.0	107.1	111.3	100.5	90.4	100.8
July	125.5	124.6	125.6	128.2	147.2	88.9	134.1	135.9	107.1	112.0	99.9	88.0	101.4
Aug¹	125.8	124.6	125.8	128.3	147.1	90.0	133.4	135.9	107.5	111.6	100.9	88.9	102.3
Sept	126.0	126.2	126.0	128.4	146.7	90.9	135.4	136.1	108.2	111.1	102.4	95.1	101.0
Oct	125.5	122.6	125.7	128.2	146.4	88.7	136.8	135.8	111.6	109.4	108.9	108.9	102.9
Nov	125.6	124.3	125.6	128.4	146.6	88.2	137.3	135.9	110.2	112.0	119.2	101.6	101.6
Dec	125.0	123.3	125.2	128.0	146.6	86.2	139.6	135.9	107.4	108.8	102.5	99.9	98.4

² Intermediate materials for food manufacturing and feeds.

Source: Department of Labor, Bureau of Labor Statistics.

TABLE B–66.—*Producer price indexes by stage of processing, special groups, 1974–97*

[1982=100]

Year or month	Finished goods						Intermediate materials, supplies, and components				Crude materials for further processing			
				Excluding foods and energy										
	Total	Foods	Energy	Total	Capital equipment	Consumer goods excluding foods and energy	Total	Foods and feeds[1]	Energy	Other	Total	Foodstuffs and feedstuffs	Energy	Other
1974	52.6	64.4	26.2	53.6	50.5	55.5	52.5	83.6	33.1	54.0	61.4	76.4	27.8	83.3
1975	58.2	69.8	30.7	59.7	58.2	60.6	58.0	81.6	38.7	60.2	61.6	77.4	33.3	69.3
1976	60.8	69.6	34.3	63.1	62.1	63.7	60.9	77.4	41.5	63.8	63.4	76.8	35.3	80.2
1977	64.7	73.3	39.7	66.9	66.1	67.3	64.9	79.6	46.8	67.6	65.5	77.5	40.4	79.8
1978	69.8	79.9	42.3	71.9	71.3	72.2	69.5	84.8	49.1	72.5	73.4	87.3	45.2	87.8
1979	77.6	87.3	57.1	78.3	77.5	78.8	78.4	94.5	61.1	80.7	85.9	100.0	54.9	106.2
1980	88.0	92.4	85.2	87.1	85.8	87.8	90.3	105.5	84.9	90.3	95.3	104.6	73.1	113.1
1981	96.1	97.8	101.5	94.6	94.6	94.6	98.6	104.6	100.5	97.7	103.0	103.9	97.7	111.7
1982	100.0	100.0	100.0	100.0	100.0	100.0	100.0	100.0	100.0	100.0	100.0	100.0	100.0	100.0
1983	101.6	101.0	95.2	103.0	102.8	103.1	100.6	103.6	95.3	101.6	101.3	101.8	98.7	105.3
1984	103.7	105.4	91.2	105.5	105.2	105.7	103.1	105.7	95.5	104.7	103.5	104.7	98.0	111.7
1985	104.7	104.6	87.6	108.1	107.5	108.4	102.7	97.3	92.6	105.2	95.8	94.8	93.3	104.9
1986	103.2	107.3	63.0	110.6	109.7	111.1	99.1	96.2	72.6	104.9	87.7	93.2	71.8	103.1
1987	105.4	109.5	61.8	113.3	111.7	114.2	101.5	99.2	73.0	107.8	93.7	96.2	75.0	115.7
1988	108.0	112.6	59.8	117.0	114.3	118.5	107.1	109.5	70.9	115.2	96.0	106.1	67.7	133.0
1989	113.6	118.7	65.7	122.1	118.8	124.0	112.0	113.8	76.1	120.2	103.1	111.2	75.9	137.9
1990	119.2	124.4	75.0	126.6	122.9	128.8	114.5	113.3	85.5	120.9	108.9	113.1	85.9	136.3
1991	121.7	124.1	78.1	131.1	126.7	133.7	114.4	111.1	85.1	121.4	101.2	105.5	80.4	128.2
1992	123.2	123.3	77.8	134.2	129.1	137.3	114.7	110.7	84.3	122.0	100.4	105.1	78.8	128.4
1993	124.7	125.7	78.0	135.8	131.4	138.5	116.2	112.7	84.6	123.8	102.4	108.4	76.7	140.2
1994	125.5	126.8	77.0	137.1	134.1	139.0	118.5	114.8	83.0	127.1	101.8	106.5	72.1	156.2
1995	127.9	129.0	78.1	140.0	136.7	141.9	124.9	114.8	84.1	135.2	102.7	105.8	69.4	173.6
1996	131.3	133.6	83.2	142.0	138.3	144.3	125.7	128.1	89.8	134.0	113.8	121.5	85.0	155.8
1997	131.8	134.5	83.4	142.5	138.3	145.1	125.6	125.4	89.0	134.2	110.9	112.2	86.8	156.5
1996: Jan	129.4	130.7	78.5	141.8	138.3	143.9	125.2	123.0	85.0	134.8	108.8	114.7	78.1	162.1
Feb	129.4	130.7	77.8	141.9	138.4	144.1	124.7	123.0	83.8	134.4	111.1	115.0	82.7	162.3
Mar	130.1	132.0	80.1	141.8	138.3	144.0	124.9	123.4	85.7	134.1	110.0	116.2	80.6	159.2
Apr	130.6	131.2	83.3	141.7	138.3	143.8	125.4	125.3	89.1	133.9	114.4	119.6	87.3	157.6
May	131.1	131.5	84.6	142.0	138.2	144.3	126.2	130.3	91.2	134.1	115.9	127.7	83.3	158.1
June	131.7	133.6	84.7	142.0	138.2	144.4	126.2	131.2	91.1	134.0	113.3	129.0	77.6	155.3
July	131.5	133.9	84.2	141.9	138.1	144.3	125.9	131.9	90.9	133.6	115.6	130.9	81.8	152.4
Aug	131.9	135.3	84.6	141.9	138.2	144.2	126.1	132.7	91.7	133.6	116.0	129.5	83.8	152.9
Sept	131.8	135.6	85.3	141.1	137.3	143.5	126.7	133.5	93.3	133.9	112.9	124.9	81.0	153.5
Oct	132.7	136.6	84.8	142.7	138.9	145.0	126.0	130.7	92.1	133.6	111.3	119.6	82.7	152.3
Nov	132.6	136.1	84.4	142.5	138.7	144.9	125.7	126.2	91.0	133.7	114.8	117.7	91.9	151.7
Dec	132.7	135.5	85.7	142.6	138.7	145.1	126.0	125.6	92.4	133.9	121.6	113.6	109.6	152.5
1997: Jan	132.6	134.1	86.5	142.8	139.0	145.1	126.3	124.6	93.2	134.1	126.3	112.2	119.4	156.6
Feb	132.2	133.8	85.2	142.7	138.9	145.1	126.1	124.8	91.8	134.2	116.1	111.0	98.0	158.9
Mar	132.1	135.2	83.0	142.8	138.8	145.3	125.6	127.2	88.5	134.2	107.6	114.1	77.1	159.6
Apr	131.6	134.3	81.8	142.7	138.6	145.2	125.3	127.5	86.7	134.2	107.9	116.7	76.4	156.4
May	131.6	135.2	82.2	142.3	138.1	144.9	125.4	128.3	87.0	134.2	107.4	117.4	80.8	157.8
June	131.6	134.0	83.6	142.2	138.1	144.8	125.8	126.4	89.5	134.2	107.1	111.3	79.2	157.4
July	131.3	134.0	83.1	141.9	137.8	144.4	125.5	124.6	88.6	134.2	107.1	112.0	79.1	155.6
Aug[2]	131.7	134.9	84.2	141.8	137.7	144.4	125.8	124.6	89.7	134.2	107.5	111.6	79.7	157.5
Sept	131.8	134.8	85.2	141.6	137.1	144.4	126.0	126.2	90.6	134.3	108.2	111.1	82.1	156.1
Oct	132.4	135.0	83.5	143.1	138.7	145.9	125.5	122.6	88.4	134.4	111.6	109.4	90.9	155.6
Nov	131.8	134.5	82.0	142.9	138.4	145.7	125.6	124.3	88.0	134.4	113.8	110.2	95.4	154.1
Dec	131.1	134.2	80.2	142.7	138.0	145.6	125.0	123.3	85.9	134.3	107.4	108.8	83.4	152.7

[1] Intermediate materials for food manufacturing and feeds.
[2] Data have been revised through August 1997 to reflect the availability of late reports and corrections by respondents. All data are subject to revision 4 months after original publication.

Source: Department of Labor, Bureau of Labor Statistics.

TABLE B–67.—*Producer price indexes for major commodity groups, 1954–97*

[1982=100]

Year or month	Farm products and processed foods and feeds			Industrial commodities				
	Total	Farm products	Processed foods and feeds	Total	Textile products and apparel	Hides, skins, leather, and related products	Fuels and related products and power [1]	Chemicals and allied products [1]
1954	38.5	43.2	35.4	27.2	48.2	29.5	13.2	33.8
1955	36.6	40.5	33.8	27.8	48.2	29.4	13.2	33.7
1956	36.4	40.0	33.8	29.1	48.2	31.2	13.6	33.9
1957	37.7	41.1	34.8	29.9	48.3	31.2	14.3	34.6
1958	39.4	42.9	36.5	30.0	47.4	31.6	13.7	34.9
1959	37.6	40.2	35.6	30.5	48.1	35.9	13.7	34.8
1960	37.7	40.1	35.6	30.5	48.6	34.6	13.9	34.8
1961	37.7	39.7	36.2	30.4	47.8	34.9	14.0	34.5
1962	38.1	40.4	36.5	30.4	48.2	35.3	14.0	33.9
1963	37.7	39.6	36.8	30.3	48.2	34.3	13.9	33.5
1964	37.5	39.0	36.7	30.5	48.5	34.4	13.5	33.6
1965	39.0	40.7	38.0	30.9	48.8	35.9	13.8	33.9
1966	41.6	43.7	40.2	31.5	48.9	39.4	14.1	34.0
1967	40.2	41.3	39.8	32.0	48.9	38.1	14.4	34.2
1968	41.1	42.3	40.6	32.8	50.7	39.3	14.3	34.1
1969	43.4	45.0	42.7	33.9	51.8	41.5	14.6	34.2
1970	44.9	45.8	44.6	35.2	52.4	42.0	15.3	35.0
1971	45.8	46.6	45.5	36.5	53.3	43.4	16.6	35.6
1972	49.2	51.6	48.0	37.8	55.5	50.0	17.1	35.6
1973	63.9	72.7	58.9	40.3	60.5	54.5	19.4	37.6
1974	71.3	77.4	68.0	49.2	68.0	55.2	30.1	50.2
1975	74.0	77.0	72.6	54.9	67.4	56.5	35.4	62.0
1976	73.6	78.8	70.8	58.4	72.4	63.9	38.3	64.0
1977	75.9	79.4	74.0	62.5	75.3	68.3	43.6	65.9
1978	83.0	87.7	80.6	67.0	78.1	76.1	46.5	68.0
1979	92.3	99.6	88.5	75.7	82.5	96.1	58.9	76.0
1980	98.3	102.9	95.9	88.0	89.7	94.7	82.8	89.0
1981	101.1	105.2	98.9	97.4	97.6	99.3	100.2	98.4
1982	100.0	100.0	100.0	100.0	100.0	100.0	100.0	100.0
1983	102.0	102.4	101.8	101.1	100.3	103.2	95.9	100.3
1984	105.5	105.5	105.4	103.3	102.7	109.0	94.8	102.9
1985	100.7	95.1	103.5	103.7	102.9	108.9	91.4	103.7
1986	101.2	92.9	105.4	100.0	103.2	113.0	69.8	102.6
1987	103.7	95.5	107.9	102.6	105.1	120.4	70.2	106.4
1988	110.0	104.9	112.7	106.3	109.2	131.4	66.7	116.3
1989	115.4	110.9	117.8	111.6	112.3	136.3	72.9	123.0
1990	118.6	112.2	121.9	115.8	115.0	141.7	82.3	123.6
1991	116.4	105.7	121.9	116.5	116.3	138.9	81.2	125.6
1992	115.9	103.6	122.1	117.4	117.8	140.4	80.4	125.9
1993	118.4	107.1	124.0	119.0	118.0	143.7	80.0	128.2
1994	119.1	106.3	125.5	120.7	118.3	148.5	77.8	132.1
1995	120.5	107.4	127.0	125.5	120.8	153.7	78.0	142.5
1996	129.7	122.4	133.3	127.3	122.4	150.5	85.8	142.1
1997	127.0	112.8	134.0	127.7	122.6	154.3	85.9	143.7
1996: Jan	125.5	116.4	130.0	126.4	121.8	149.0	80.6	140.8
Feb	125.8	116.6	130.3	126.3	121.9	149.3	80.9	140.9
Mar	126.7	119.5	130.3	126.4	122.0	149.7	82.0	141.1
Apr	127.9	121.7	130.9	127.3	122.0	148.4	86.2	141.4
May	131.2	128.1	132.7	127.5	122.3	149.2	86.6	142.2
June	132.5	129.6	134.0	127.1	122.3	149.2	85.2	142.2
July	133.2	129.9	134.8	127.0	122.6	149.4	85.9	142.0
Aug	133.6	128.6	136.1	127.3	122.5	150.3	86.8	142.5
Sept	132.4	125.1	136.0	127.4	123.0	150.2	87.1	143.3
Oct	130.8	120.2	136.0	127.5	122.9	153.1	86.8	143.0
Nov	129.1	117.9	134.7	128.0	122.7	153.6	88.5	142.8
Dec	127.8	114.8	134.2	129.3	122.7	154.4	93.3	143.2
1997: Jan	126.7	113.0	133.4	130.3	122.6	155.3	96.1	143.6
Feb	126.3	113.0	132.9	128.9	122.5	156.2	90.3	143.8
Mar	128.4	116.2	134.5	127.1	122.6	156.8	83.4	143.7
Apr	128.6	116.7	134.5	126.7	122.5	157.5	82.2	143.5
May	129.4	117.4	135.4	127.0	122.6	156.1	83.4	143.5
June	126.8	111.6	134.3	127.2	122.6	153.6	84.5	143.4
July	126.5	111.6	133.9	127.0	122.6	151.6	83.9	143.7
Aug [2]	126.7	111.4	134.3	127.3	122.6	152.2	84.9	143.7
Sept	126.7	111.5	134.2	127.6	122.6	152.1	86.2	143.7
Oct	125.8	110.4	133.5	128.1	122.5	152.5	86.7	144.0
Nov	126.1	110.6	133.7	128.2	122.5	154.3	87.0	143.9
Dec	125.3	110.1	132.9	126.9	122.5	153.5	82.8	143.5

[1] Prices for some items in this grouping are lagged and refer to 1 month earlier than the index month.
[2] Data have been revised through August 1997 to reflect the availability of late reports and corrections by respondents. All data are subject to revision 4 months after original publication.

See next page for continuation of table.

[1982=100]

Year or month	Rubber and plastic products	Lumber and wood products	Pulp, paper, and allied products	Metals and metal products	Machinery and equipment	Furniture and household durables	Non-metallic mineral products	Transportation equipment Total	Motor vehicles and equipment	Miscellaneous products
1954	37.5	32.5	29.6	25.5	26.3	44.9	26.6		33.4	31.3
1955	42.4	34.1	30.4	27.2	27.2	45.1	27.3		34.3	31.3
1956	43.0	34.6	32.4	29.6	29.3	46.3	28.5		36.3	31.7
1957	42.8	32.8	33.0	30.2	31.4	47.5	29.6		37.9	32.6
1958	42.8	32.5	33.4	30.0	32.1	47.9	29.9		39.0	33.3
1959	42.6	34.7	33.7	30.6	32.8	48.0	30.3		39.9	33.4
1960	42.7	33.5	34.0	30.6	33.0	47.8	30.4		39.3	33.6
1961	41.1	32.0	33.0	30.5	33.0	47.5	30.5		39.2	33.7
1962	39.9	32.2	33.4	30.2	33.0	47.2	30.5		39.2	33.9
1963	40.1	32.8	33.1	30.3	33.1	46.9	30.3		38.9	34.2
1964	39.6	33.5	33.0	31.1	33.3	47.1	30.4		39.1	34.4
1965	39.7	33.7	33.3	32.0	33.7	46.8	30.4		39.2	34.7
1966	40.5	35.2	34.2	32.8	34.7	47.4	30.7		39.2	35.3
1967	41.4	35.1	34.6	33.2	35.9	48.3	31.2		39.8	36.2
1968	42.8	39.8	35.0	34.0	37.0	49.7	32.4		40.9	37.0
1969	43.6	44.0	36.0	36.0	38.2	50.7	33.6	40.4	41.7	38.1
1970	44.9	39.9	37.5	38.7	40.0	51.9	35.3	41.9	43.3	39.8
1971	45.2	44.7	38.1	39.4	41.4	53.1	38.2	44.2	45.7	40.8
1972	45.3	50.7	39.3	40.9	42.3	53.8	39.4	45.5	47.0	41.5
1973	46.6	62.2	42.3	44.0	43.7	55.7	40.7	46.1	47.4	43.3
1974	56.4	64.5	52.5	57.0	50.0	61.8	47.8	50.3	51.4	48.1
1975	62.2	62.1	59.0	61.5	57.9	67.5	54.4	56.7	57.6	53.4
1976	66.0	72.2	62.1	65.0	61.3	70.3	58.2	60.5	61.2	55.6
1977	69.4	83.0	64.6	69.3	65.2	73.2	62.6	64.6	65.2	59.4
1978	72.4	96.9	67.7	75.3	70.3	77.5	69.6	69.5	70.0	66.7
1979	80.5	105.5	75.9	86.0	76.7	82.8	77.6	75.3	75.8	75.5
1980	90.1	101.5	86.3	95.0	86.0	90.7	88.4	82.9	83.1	93.6
1981	96.4	102.8	94.8	99.6	94.4	95.9	96.7	94.3	94.6	96.1
1982	100.0	100.0	100.0	100.0	100.0	100.0	100.0	100.0	100.0	100.0
1983	100.8	107.9	103.3	101.8	102.7	103.4	101.6	102.8	102.2	104.8
1984	102.3	108.0	110.3	104.8	105.1	105.7	105.4	105.2	104.1	107.0
1985	101.9	106.6	113.3	104.4	107.2	107.1	108.6	107.9	106.4	109.4
1986	101.9	107.2	116.1	103.2	108.8	108.2	110.0	110.5	109.1	111.6
1987	103.0	112.8	121.8	107.1	110.4	109.9	110.0	112.5	111.7	114.9
1988	109.3	118.9	130.4	118.7	113.2	113.1	111.2	114.3	113.1	120.2
1989	112.6	126.7	137.8	124.1	117.4	116.9	112.6	117.7	116.2	126.5
1990	113.6	129.7	141.2	122.9	120.7	119.2	114.7	121.5	118.2	134.2
1991	115.1	132.1	142.9	120.2	123.0	121.2	117.2	126.4	122.1	140.8
1992	115.1	146.6	145.2	119.2	123.4	122.2	117.3	130.4	124.9	145.3
1993	116.0	174.0	147.3	119.2	124.0	123.7	120.0	133.7	128.0	145.4
1994	117.6	180.0	152.5	124.8	125.1	126.1	124.2	137.2	131.4	141.9
1995	124.3	178.1	172.2	134.5	126.6	128.2	129.0	139.7	133.0	145.4
1996	123.8	176.1	168.7	131.0	126.5	130.4	131.0	141.7	134.1	147.7
1997	123.2	183.8	167.9	131.8	125.9	130.8	133.2	141.6	132.8	150.9
1996: Jan	123.9	172.9	174.1	132.8	127.3	129.6	130.0	141.7	134.5	147.7
Feb	123.7	173.0	173.2	131.8	127.3	129.9	130.2	141.7	134.5	146.6
Mar	123.6	172.8	171.1	131.8	127.0	129.9	130.2	141.8	134.5	146.4
Apr	123.4	171.9	169.2	132.0	126.6	130.0	130.5	141.6	134.1	146.4
May	123.7	175.8	168.0	132.4	126.4	130.3	130.8	141.6	134.1	147.8
June	123.8	176.8	167.5	131.9	126.2	130.2	130.9	141.7	134.2	147.8
July	123.9	175.0	167.0	130.4	126.3	130.6	131.2	141.3	133.5	148.3
Aug	124.2	177.0	166.6	130.0	126.4	130.5	131.2	141.4	133.3	148.1
Sept	124.1	180.2	166.9	130.0	126.3	130.6	131.6	140.0	131.0	147.9
Oct	123.7	177.8	166.9	129.4	126.2	130.9	131.7	142.9	135.2	148.3
Nov	123.7	180.2	166.9	129.4	126.2	130.9	132.0	142.7	134.9	148.4
Dec	123.7	179.7	167.2	129.9	126.2	130.9	131.9	142.6	134.8	148.5
1997: Jan	123.2	180.6	167.6	131.0	126.4	130.9	132.3	142.9	134.6	148.7
Feb	123.1	183.4	167.1	131.6	126.3	130.9	132.5	142.8	134.5	148.9
Mar	122.9	184.8	166.5	132.2	126.3	131.0	132.6	142.7	134.3	149.5
Apr	123.2	185.4	166.3	131.8	126.2	130.7	133.3	142.3	133.7	150.6
May	123.3	186.8	166.1	132.2	125.9	130.9	133.3	141.5	132.5	150.9
June	123.2	185.4	166.4	132.5	125.9	130.9	133.4	141.4	132.3	150.9
July	123.3	185.9	166.9	132.0	126.0	130.9	133.4	140.5	131.0	151.0
Aug [2]	123.4	185.0	167.8	132.2	125.7	130.7	133.5	140.5	131.0	151.0
Sept	123.3	183.7	168.7	132.0	125.6	130.9	133.3	139.3	129.3	152.4
Oct	123.2	180.8	169.5	131.9	125.6	130.9	133.6	142.5	134.3	152.3
Nov	123.2	181.9	170.4	131.3	125.6	130.6	133.7	142.0	133.5	152.3
Dec	123.1	181.9	171.2	130.6	125.4	130.7	133.7	141.5	132.6	152.7

Source: Department of Labor, Bureau of Labor Statistics.

[Percent change]

Year or month	Total finished goods		Finished consumer foods		Finished goods excluding consumer foods						Finished energy goods		Finished goods excluding foods and energy	
					Total		Consumer goods		Capital equipment					
	Dec. to Dec.[1]	Year to year	Dec. to Dec.[1]	Year to year	Dec. to Dec.[1]	Year to year	Dec. to Dec.[1]	Year to year	Dec. to Dec.[1]	Year to year	Dec. to Dec.[1]	Year to year	Dec. to Dec.[1]	Year to year
1960	1.8	0.9	5.3	2.0			0.3	0.6	0.3	0.3				
1961	-.6	0	-1.9	-.3			-.3	-.3	0	.3				
1962	.3	.3	.6	.8			0	0	.3	.3				
1963	-.3	-.3	-1.4	-1.1			0	0	.6	.3				
1964	.6	.3	.6	.3			.3	-.3	.9	.9				
1965	3.3	1.8	9.1	4.0			.9	.9	1.5	1.2				
1966	2.0	3.2	1.3	6.5			1.8	1.5	3.8	2.4				
1967	1.7	1.1	-.3	-1.8			2.0	1.8	3.1	3.5				
1968	3.1	2.8	4.6	3.9	2.5	2.6	2.0	2.3	3.0	3.4				
1969	4.9	3.8	8.1	6.0	3.3	2.8	2.8	2.3	4.8	3.5				
1970	2.1	3.4	-2.3	3.3	4.3	3.5	3.8	3.0	4.8	4.7				
1971	3.3	3.1	5.8	1.6	2.0	3.7	2.1	3.5	2.4	4.0				
1972	3.9	3.2	7.9	5.4	2.3	2.0	2.1	1.8	2.1	2.6				
1973	11.7	9.1	22.7	20.5	6.6	4.0	7.5	4.6	5.1	3.3				
1974	18.3	15.4	12.8	14.0	21.1	16.2	20.3	17.0	22.7	14.3			17.7	11.4
1975	6.6	10.6	5.6	8.4	7.2	12.1	6.8	10.4	8.1	15.2	16.3	17.2	6.0	11.4
1976	3.8	4.5	-2.5	-.3	6.2	6.2	6.0	6.2	6.5	6.7	11.6	11.7	5.7	5.7
1977	6.7	6.4	6.9	5.3	6.8	7.1	6.7	7.3	7.2	6.4	12.0	15.7	6.2	6.0
1978	9.3	7.9	11.7	9.0	8.3	7.2	8.5	7.1	8.0	7.9	8.5	6.5	8.4	7.5
1979	12.8	11.2	7.4	9.3	14.8	11.8	17.6	13.3	8.8	8.7	58.1	35.0	9.4	8.9
1980	11.8	13.4	7.5	5.8	13.4	16.2	14.1	18.5	11.4	10.7	27.9	49.2	10.8	11.2
1981	7.1	9.2	1.5	5.8	8.7	10.3	8.6	10.3	9.2	10.3	14.1	19.1	7.7	8.6
1982	3.6	4.1	2.0	2.2	4.2	4.6	4.2	4.1	3.9	5.7	-.1	-1.5	4.9	5.7
1983	.6	1.6	2.3	1.0	0	1.8	-.9	1.2	2.0	2.8	-9.2	-4.8	1.9	3.0
1984	1.7	2.1	3.5	4.4	1.1	1.4	.8	1.0	1.8	2.3	-4.2	-4.2	2.0	2.4
1985	1.8	1.0	.6	-.8	2.2	1.4	2.1	1.1	2.7	2.2	-.2	-3.9	2.7	2.5
1986	-2.3	-1.4	2.8	2.6	-4.0	-2.6	-6.6	-4.6	2.1	2.0	-38.1	-28.1	2.7	2.3
1987	2.2	2.1	-.2	2.1	3.2	2.1	4.1	2.2	1.3	1.8	11.2	-1.9	2.1	2.4
1988	4.0	2.5	5.7	2.8	3.2	2.4	3.1	2.4	3.6	2.3	-3.6	-3.2	4.3	3.3
1989	4.9	5.2	5.2	5.4	4.8	5.0	5.3	5.6	3.8	3.9	9.5	9.9	4.2	4.4
1990	5.7	4.9	2.6	4.8	6.9	5.0	8.7	5.9	3.4	3.5	30.7	14.2	3.5	3.7
1991	-.1	2.1	-1.5	-.2	.3	3.0	-.7	2.9	2.5	3.1	-9.6	4.1	3.1	3.6
1992	1.6	1.2	1.6	-.6	1.6	1.8	1.6	1.8	1.7	1.9	-.3	-.4	2.0	2.4
1993	.2	1.2	2.4	1.9	-.4	1.1	-1.4	.7	1.8	1.8	-4.1	.3	.4	1.2
1994	1.7	.6	1.1	.9	1.9	.6	2.0	-.1	2.0	2.1	3.5	-1.3	1.6	1.0
1995	2.3	1.9	1.9	1.7	2.3	1.9	2.3	2.0	2.2	1.9	1.1	1.4	2.6	2.1
1996	2.8	2.7	3.4	3.6	2.6	2.4	3.7	2.9	.4	1.2	11.7	6.5	.6	1.4
1997	-1.2	.4	-1.0	.7	-1.1	.3	-1.5	.5	-.5	0	-6.4	.2	.1	.4

	Percent change from preceding month													
	Unadjusted	Seasonally adjusted	Unadjusted	Seasonally adjusted	Unadjusted	Seasonally adjusted	Unadjusted	Seasonally adjusted	Unadjusted	Seasonally adjusted	Unadjusted	Seasonally adjusted	Unadjusted	Seasonally adjusted
1996:Jan	0.2	0.1	-0.2	-0.2	0.5	0.2	0.6	0.3	0.1	0	2.3	1.4	0.1	0
Feb	0	0	0	-.2	-.1	-.1	-.1	0	.1	0	-.9	-.6	.1	.1
Mar	.5	.5	1.0	.8	.5	.5	.6	.6	-.1	.1	3.0	2.5	-.1	0
Apr	.4	.2	-.6	-.3	.7	.4	1.0	.5	0	0	4.0	2.1	-.1	0
May	.4	.2	.2	.2	.4	.1	.6	.2	-.1	0	1.6	-.6	.2	.2
June	.5	.3	1.6	1.4	.1	-.1	.1	-.1	0	.1	.1	-.8	0	.1
July	-.2	0	.2	.1	-.2	.1	-.2	.1	-.1	0	-.6	.4	-.1	0
Aug	.3	.3	1.0	.7	.1	.2	.1	.2	.1	.1	.5	.6	0	.1
Sept	-.1	.3	.2	.4	-.3	.3	-.1	.3	-.7	.1	.8	.7	-.6	.1
Oct	.7	.4	.7	.8	.8	.2	.6	.4	1.2	-.1	-.6	1.7	1.1	.1
Nov	-.1	.2	-.4	0	0	.2	0	.3	-.1	0	.1	.9	-.1	0
Dec	.1	.5	-.4	-.2	.2	.8	.3	1.0	0	0	.9	3.3	.1	.1
1997:Jan	-.1	-.3	-1.0	-1.0	.3	-.1	.2	-.1	.2	.1	.9	-.2	.1	0
Feb	-.3	-.3	-.2	-.4	-.3	-.3	-.4	-.4	-.1	-.1	-1.5	-1.2	-.1	-.1
Mar	-.1	-.2	1.0	.8	-.5	-.5	-.6	-.7	-.1	0	-2.6	-3.1	.1	.1
Apr	-.4	-.5	-.7	-.4	-.3	-.6	-.4	-.9	-.1	-.1	-1.4	-3.2	-.1	-.1
May	0	-.2	.7	.4	-.2	-.5	-.1	-.5	-.4	-.2	.5	-1.3	-.3	-.2
June	0	-.2	-.9	-.9	.3	.2	.4	.2	0	.1	1.7	.5	.1	.1
July	-.2	-.1	0	-.2	-.4	-.2	-.4	-.2	-.2	-.1	-.6	.2	-.2	-.2
Aug[2]	.3	.3	.7	.2	.2	.4	.4	.6	-.1	0	1.3	1.5	-.1	.1
Sept	.1	.5	-.1	.1	.1	.6	.3	.7	-.4	.3	1.2	1.2	-.1	.4
Oct	.5	.1	.1	.4	.5	0	.2	.1	1.2	-.1	-2.0	.1	1.1	0
Nov	-.5	-.2	-.4	-.1	-.5	-.2	-.5	-.3	-.2	-.1	-1.8	-.8	-.1	-.1
Dec	-.5	-.2	-.2	-.1	-.5	-.2	-.7	-.1	-.3	.2	-2.2	-.2	-.1	-.1

[1] Changes from December to December are based on unadjusted indexes.
[2] Data have been revised through August 1997 to reflect the availability of late reports and corrections by respondents. All data are subject to revision 4 months after original publication.

Source: Department of Labor, Bureau of Labor Statistics.

MONEY STOCK, CREDIT, AND FINANCE

TABLE B–69.—*Money stock, liquid assets, and debt measures, 1959–97*

[Averages of daily figures, except debt; billions of dollars, seasonally adjusted]

Year and month	M1	M2	M3	L	Debt[1]	Percent change from year or 6 months earlier[2]			
	Sum of currency, demand deposits, travelers checks, and other checkable deposits (OCDs)	M1 plus retail MMMF balances, savings deposits (including MMDAs), and small time deposits	M2 plus large time deposits, RPs, Euro-dollars, and institution-only MMMF balances	M3 plus other liquid assets	Debt of domestic nonfinancial sectors (monthly average of adjacent month-end levels)	M1	M2	M3	Debt
December:									
1959	140.0	297.8	299.7	388.6	687.6	....	....	....	7.6
1960	140.7	312.4	315.2	403.5	723.0	0.5	4.9	5.2	5.1
1961	145.2	335.5	340.8	430.6	765.7	3.2	7.4	8.1	5.9
1962	147.8	362.7	371.3	465.9	818.4	1.8	8.1	8.9	6.9
1963	153.3	393.2	405.9	503.6	873.3	3.7	8.4	9.3	6.7
1964	160.3	424.7	442.4	540.3	936.8	4.6	8.0	9.0	7.3
1965	167.8	459.2	482.1	584.3	1,003.7	4.7	8.1	9.0	7.1
1966	172.0	480.2	505.4	615.1	1,070.9	2.5	4.6	4.8	6.7
1967	183.3	524.8	557.9	667.3	1,145.2	6.6	9.3	10.4	6.9
1968	197.4	566.8	607.2	729.9	1,236.8	7.7	8.0	8.8	8.0
1969	203.9	587.9	615.9	764.4	1,326.7	3.3	3.7	1.4	7.3
1970	214.4	626.5	677.1	814.8	1,416.1	5.1	6.6	9.9	6.7
1971	228.3	710.2	776.0	902.6	1,549.6	6.5	13.4	14.6	9.4
1972	249.2	802.3	886.0	1,022.8	1,705.7	9.2	13.0	14.2	10.1
1973	262.8	855.5	985.0	1,141.5	1,890.8	5.5	6.6	11.2	10.9
1974	274.2	902.4	1,070.0	1,248.5	2,063.5	4.3	5.5	8.6	9.1
1975	287.4	1,017.0	1,172.0	1,366.5	2,251.2	4.8	12.7	9.5	9.1
1976	306.3	1,152.7	1,312.0	1,516.6	2,495.5	6.6	13.3	11.9	10.9
1977	331.2	1,271.5	1,472.5	1,705.3	2,811.5	8.1	10.3	12.2	12.7
1978	358.4	1,368.0	1,646.8	1,911.3	3,201.2	8.2	7.6	11.8	13.9
1979	382.9	1,475.7	1,806.6	2,121.2	3,590.0	6.8	7.9	9.7	12.1
1980	408.9	1,601.1	1,992.2	2,330.0	3,932.0	6.8	8.5	10.3	9.5
1981	436.8	1,756.2	2,240.9	2,601.8	4,329.0	6.8	9.7	12.5	10.1
1982	474.6	1,910.8	2,442.3	2,845.9	4,758.0	8.7	8.8	9.0	9.9
1983	521.2	2,127.7	2,684.8	3,150.6	5,324.9	9.8	11.4	9.9	11.9
1984	552.2	2,312.2	2,979.8	3,518.6	6,106.8	5.9	8.7	11.0	14.7
1985	619.9	2,497.6	3,198.3	3,827.0	7,024.8	12.3	8.0	7.3	15.0
1986	724.4	2,733.9	3,486.4	4,122.3	7,905.0	16.9	9.5	9.0	12.5
1987	749.7	2,832.7	3,672.5	4,339.9	8,659.9	3.5	3.6	5.3	9.5
1988	787.0	2,996.3	3,912.9	4,663.5	9,429.2	5.0	5.8	6.5	8.9
1989	794.2	3,160.9	4,065.9	4,892.8	10,150.8	.9	5.5	3.9	7.7
1990	825.8	3,279.5	4,125.9	4,976.6	10,825.4	4.0	3.8	1.5	6.6
1991	897.3	3,379.6	4,180.4	5,006.2	11,301.9	8.7	3.1	1.3	4.4
1992	1,025.0	3,434.0	4,190.4	5,078.0	11,842.0	14.2	1.6	.2	4.8
1993	1,129.8	3,486.6	4,254.4	5,167.8	12,462.1	10.2	1.5	1.5	5.2
1994	1,150.7	3,502.1	4,327.3	5,308.4	13,078.0	1.8	.4	1.7	4.9
1995	1,129.0	3,655.0	4,592.5	5,697.6	13,773.3	-1.9	4.4	6.1	5.3
1996	1,081.1	3,821.8	4,920.5	6,071.7	14,496.6	-4.2	4.6	7.1	5.3
1997 *p*	1,068.7	4,019.3	5,333.0	....	....	-1.1	5.2	8.4	....
1996: Jan	1,122.2	3,669.9	4,620.1	5,720.8	13,822.8	-4.0	4.8	5.6	4.4
Feb	1,119.8	3,685.0	4,652.9	5,739.5	13,895.8	-4.2	4.5	5.6	4.9
Mar	1,126.2	3,714.0	4,689.4	5,789.7	13,972.0	-2.7	5.2	6.2	5.3
Apr	1,123.6	3,724.5	4,706.3	5,826.0	14,035.3	-2.1	5.2	6.2	5.3
May	1,117.1	3,725.4	4,728.9	5,846.5	14,088.1	-2.8	4.7	6.6	5.2
June	1,115.6	3,741.6	4,751.4	5,889.6	14,147.7	-2.4	4.7	6.9	5.4
July	1,108.9	3,749.1	4,769.4	5,914.2	14,219.7	-2.4	4.3	6.5	5.7
Aug	1,099.9	3,759.7	4,787.7	5,942.1	14,273.7	-3.6	4.1	5.8	5.4
Sept	1,093.3	3,769.7	4,816.5	5,981.5	14,322.1	-5.8	3.0	5.4	5.0
Oct	1,080.3	3,780.1	4,850.2	6,005.7	14,383.7	-7.7	3.0	6.1	5.0
Nov	1,080.1	3,799.8	4,877.6	6,040.0	14,446.6	-6.6	4.0	6.3	5.1
Dec	1,081.1	3,821.8	4,920.5	6,071.7	14,496.6	-6.2	4.3	7.1	4.9
1997: Jan	1,079.7	3,836.9	4,943.7	6,087.5	14,538.1	-5.3	4.7	7.3	4.5
Feb	1,080.7	3,852.3	4,984.3	6,138.7	14,595.8	-3.5	4.9	8.2	4.5
Mar	1,075.4	3,867.9	5,019.0	6,186.5	14,657.5	-3.3	5.2	8.4	4.7
Apr	1,065.3	3,885.7	5,058.4	6,243.7	14,728.7	-2.8	5.6	8.6	4.8
May	1,062.8	3,883.3	5,063.0	6,263.3	14,775.7	-3.2	4.4	7.6	4.6
June	1,063.1	3,896.8	5,080.9	6,287.5	14,805.5	-3.3	3.9	6.5	4.3
July	1,062.1	3,907.1	5,121.2	6,318.8	14,860.6	-3.3	3.7	7.2	4.4
Aug	1,069.6	3,941.3	5,168.2	6,380.1	14,917.8	-2.1	4.6	7.4	4.4
Sept	1,060.8	3,959.8	5,204.9	6,421.2	14,975.9	-2.7	4.8	7.4	4.3
Oct	1,057.4	3,974.9	5,237.1	6,444.7	15,042.5	-1.5	4.6	7.1	4.3
Nov	1,064.0	3,997.8	5,285.0	6,507.5	15,107.9	.2	5.9	8.8	4.5
Dec *p*	1,068.7	4,019.3	5,333.0	....	....	1.1	6.3	9.9	....

[1] Consists of outstanding credit market debt of the U.S. Government, State and local governments, and private nonfinancial sectors; data derived from flow of funds accounts.
[2] Annual changes are from December to December; monthly changes are from 6 months earlier at a simple annual rate.

Note.—See Table B–70 for components.

Source: Board of Governors of the Federal Reserve System.

TABLE B–70.—*Components of money stock measures and liquid assets, 1959–97*

[Averages of daily figures; billions of dollars, seasonally adjusted, except as noted]

Year and month	Currency	Travelers checks	Demand deposits	Other checkable deposits (OCDs)	Small denomination time deposits [1]	Savings deposits, including money market deposit accounts (MMDAs) [2]	Money market mutual fund (MMMF) balances Retail	Institution only
December:								
1959	28.8	0.3	110.8	0.0	11.4	146.5	0.0	0.0
1960	28.7	.3	111.6	.0	12.5	159.1	.0	.0
1961	29.3	.4	115.5	.0	14.8	175.5	.0	.0
1962	30.3	.4	117.1	.0	20.1	194.7	.0	.0
1963	32.2	.4	120.6	.1	25.6	214.4	.0	.0
1964	33.9	.5	125.8	.1	29.2	235.3	.0	.0
1965	36.0	.5	131.3	.1	34.5	256.9	.0	.0
1966	38.0	.6	133.4	.1	55.0	253.2	.0	.0
1967	40.0	.6	142.5	.1	77.8	263.7	.0	.0
1968	43.0	.7	153.6	.1	100.6	268.9	.0	.0
1969	45.7	.8	157.3	.2	120.4	263.6	.0	.0
1970	48.6	.9	164.7	.1	151.2	260.9	.0	.0
1971	52.0	1.0	175.1	.2	189.8	292.2	.0	.0
1972	56.2	1.2	191.6	.2	231.7	321.4	.0	.0
1973	60.8	1.4	200.3	.3	265.8	326.7	.1	.0
1974	67.0	1.7	205.0	.4	287.9	338.6	1.7	.2
1975	72.8	2.1	211.6	.9	337.8	388.8	2.8	.5
1976	79.5	2.6	221.6	2.7	390.7	453.2	2.5	.6
1977	87.4	2.9	236.7	4.2	445.5	492.2	2.6	1.0
1978	96.0	3.3	250.6	8.5	520.9	481.9	6.7	3.4
1979	104.8	3.5	257.7	16.8	634.2	423.8	34.8	10.2
1980	115.4	3.9	261.4	28.1	728.5	400.2	63.4	15.9
1981	122.6	4.1	231.4	78.7	823.1	343.9	152.4	38.6
1982	132.5	4.1	234.0	104.1	850.9	400.1	185.2	49.4
1983	146.1	4.7	238.3	132.1	784.0	684.9	137.5	41.4
1984	156.1	5.0	243.7	147.4	888.8	704.7	166.5	62.1
1985	167.9	5.6	266.6	179.8	885.7	815.2	176.8	64.5
1986	180.7	6.1	302.1	235.6	858.3	940.9	210.4	85.1
1987	196.8	6.6	286.8	259.5	921.0	937.4	224.6	92.0
1988	212.3	7.0	286.8	280.9	1,037.1	926.3	245.9	92.3
1989	222.7	6.9	279.3	285.3	1,151.4	893.7	321.7	110.3
1990	246.8	7.8	277.4	293.9	1,172.8	923.8	357.1	138.0
1991	267.3	7.8	289.6	332.5	1,065.4	1,045.0	371.9	185.5
1992	292.9	8.1	339.5	384.4	868.3	1,187.3	353.5	207.5
1993	322.2	7.9	385.2	414.5	782.6	1,219.2	354.9	209.5
1994	354.4	8.5	384.1	403.8	817.5	1,149.6	384.3	198.5
1995	372.6	8.9	391.1	356.5	933.7	1,137.1	455.2	246.9
1996	395.2	8.6	402.6	274.8	945.7	1,271.0	523.9	299.3
1997 p	426.0	8.2	391.7	242.8	963.7	1,395.4	591.5	359.5
1996: Jan	373.0	8.9	394.4	345.9	934.3	1,153.8	459.6	250.1
Feb	373.4	8.9	397.3	340.3	934.1	1,165.1	466.0	259.7
Mar	375.4	8.9	404.6	337.3	930.8	1,180.2	476.8	263.7
Apr	376.4	8.8	404.5	333.9	929.5	1,190.1	481.4	263.4
May	377.7	8.7	407.2	323.5	928.5	1,195.6	484.2	263.6
June	379.9	8.7	410.7	316.4	928.8	1,204.1	493.2	269.7
July	382.8	8.6	408.8	308.7	930.5	1,211.0	498.7	274.0
Aug	385.2	8.4	405.9	300.4	934.1	1,222.7	503.0	278.8
Sept	387.6	8.5	405.1	292.2	937.3	1,231.5	507.5	285.2
Oct	390.2	8.6	398.4	283.2	941.0	1,246.3	512.5	288.1
Nov	392.5	8.6	402.2	276.8	943.9	1,259.0	516.8	292.0
Dec	395.2	8.6	402.6	274.8	945.7	1,271.0	523.9	299.3
1997: Jan	397.0	8.6	401.6	272.5	946.8	1,282.5	527.9	296.3
Feb	400.5	8.6	404.3	267.3	948.2	1,290.5	532.9	305.4
Mar	402.4	8.5	403.1	261.5	947.4	1,304.3	540.8	311.8
Apr	403.7	8.3	395.6	257.7	948.9	1,321.1	550.5	311.6
May	406.1	8.2	395.7	252.8	953.3	1,320.9	546.4	311.6
June	407.7	8.0	397.2	250.1	957.9	1,325.4	550.5	318.9
July	410.2	8.2	396.4	247.2	960.2	1,329.9	554.9	324.1
Aug	412.1	8.3	402.0	247.2	960.8	1,341.4	569.4	329.2
Sept	415.4	8.1	390.6	246.7	961.6	1,356.7	580.8	338.9
Oct	418.0	8.1	386.4	244.8	963.2	1,370.2	584.2	345.3
Nov	421.9	8.2	391.0	243.0	963.2	1,380.2	590.4	346.4
Dec p	426.0	8.2	391.7	242.8	963.7	1,395.4	591.5	359.5

[1] Small denomination deposits are those issued in amounts of less than $100,000.
[2] Data prior to 1982 are savings deposits only; MMDA data begin December 1982.

See next page for continuation of table.

362

[Averages of daily figures; billions of dollars, seasonally adjusted, except as noted]

Year and month	Large denomination time deposits[3]	Overnight and term repurchase agreements (RPs) (net)	Overnight and term Eurodollars (net)	Savings bonds	Short-term Treasury securities	Bankers acceptances	Commercial paper
December:							
1959	1.2	0.0	0.7	46.1	38.6	0.6	3.6
1960	2.0	.0	.8	45.7	36.7	.9	5.1
1961	3.9	.0	1.5	46.5	37.0	1.1	5.2
1962	7.0	.0	1.6	46.9	39.8	1.1	6.8
1963	10.8	.0	1.9	48.1	40.7	1.2	7.7
1964	15.2	.0	2.4	49.0	38.5	1.3	9.1
1965	21.2	.0	1.8	49.6	40.7	1.6	10.2
1966	23.1	.0	2.2	50.2	43.2	1.8	14.4
1967	30.9	.0	2.2	51.2	38.7	1.8	17.8
1968	37.4	.0	2.9	51.8	46.1	2.3	22.5
1969	20.4	4.9	2.7	51.7	59.5	3.3	34.0
1970	45.1	3.0	2.4	52.0	49.0	3.5	33.2
1971	57.6	5.2	2.9	54.3	36.1	3.8	32.3
1972	73.3	6.6	3.9	57.6	40.8	3.5	35.1
1973	111.0	12.8	5.8	60.4	49.4	5.0	41.6
1974	144.7	14.2	8.5	63.3	52.8	12.6	49.7
1975	129.7	14.7	10.2	67.2	68.5	10.7	48.1
1976	118.1	25.1	15.4	71.8	69.9	10.8	52.2
1977	145.2	32.9	21.9	76.4	78.4	14.1	64.1
1978	195.6	44.6	35.1	80.3	81.4	22.0	80.9
1979	223.1	47.7	49.8	79.5	108.2	27.1	99.7
1980	260.2	57.4	57.7	72.3	133.9	32.0	99.5
1981	303.8	65.3	77.0	67.8	149.4	39.9	103.8
1982	324.8	67.4	89.8	68.0	182.9	44.5	108.3
1983	316.4	94.5	104.8	71.1	213.2	45.0	136.5
1984	403.2	105.4	96.9	74.2	261.9	45.4	157.3
1985	422.4	119.9	94.0	79.5	298.2	42.1	208.9
1986	420.2	143.3	103.9	91.8	275.8	37.1	231.2
1987	467.0	172.6	108.2	100.6	249.5	44.5	272.7
1988	518.3	189.0	117.0	109.4	266.8	40.2	334.3
1989	541.5	158.0	95.2	117.5	324.0	40.7	344.6
1990	480.9	138.8	88.7	126.0	334.1	36.1	354.4
1991	416.5	119.5	79.3	137.9	328.8	23.8	335.2
1992	353.4	128.6	67.0	156.6	344.7	20.8	365.5
1993	333.4	158.6	66.4	171.5	340.5	14.8	386.6
1994	363.1	182.9	80.8	180.2	383.0	14.0	403.9
1995	419.8	182.1	88.7	184.8	469.9	11.2	439.3
1996	491.4	194.1	113.9	187.0	456.5	12.2	495.5
1997[p]	579.2	235.9	139.1	....	....	....	....
1996: Jan	420.9	187.2	92.0	185.0	464.5	11.3	440.0
Feb	426.3	188.9	93.0	185.2	448.2	10.2	443.0
Mar	432.6	187.8	91.5	185.4	458.7	9.9	446.3
Apr	435.4	189.0	94.0	185.8	464.4	10.2	459.3
May	442.5	202.9	94.5	186.1	452.8	10.7	468.0
June	448.9	195.6	95.6	186.4	470.5	11.1	470.1
July	455.9	194.5	95.8	186.7	473.6	11.5	473.0
Aug	460.4	192.6	96.3	186.9	478.1	11.7	477.7
Sept	468.3	194.4	98.9	187.1	483.9	12.0	482.0
Oct	480.9	196.0	105.1	187.1	476.7	12.1	479.6
Nov	483.4	195.3	107.1	187.0	479.9	12.2	483.2
Dec	491.4	194.1	113.9	187.0	456.5	12.2	495.5
1997: Jan	494.8	198.3	117.5	186.8	436.1	11.9	509.1
Feb	504.7	202.1	119.7	186.4	437.7	12.7	517.5
Mar	517.0	200.6	121.7	186.3	441.7	13.5	525.9
Apr	530.4	204.1	126.6	186.2	448.5	12.8	537.8
May	530.0	204.5	133.5	186.2	457.1	13.1	543.9
June	537.7	198.7	128.8	186.3	451.7	12.6	555.9
July	552.4	207.1	130.5	186.4	431.5	12.9	566.8
Aug	553.9	208.6	135.3	186.5	448.1	13.3	563.9
Sept	563.1	205.7	137.4	186.5	453.3	13.0	563.5
Oct	565.3	217.6	133.8	186.5	439.0	13.2	568.9
Nov	573.4	233.5	133.9	186.5	445.8	12.7	577.4
Dec[p]	579.2	235.9	139.1	....	....	....	....

[3] Large denomination deposits are those issued in amounts of more than $100,000.

Note.—See also Table B–69.

Source: Board of Governors of the Federal Reserve System.

[Averages of daily figures [1]; millions of dollars; seasonally adjusted, except as noted]

| Year and month | Adjusted for changes in reserve requirements [2] | | | | | Borrowings of depository institutions from the Federal Reserve, NSA | | |
| | Reserves of depository institutions | | | | Monetary base | | | |
	Total	Nonborrowed	Nonborrowed plus extended credit	Required	Monetary base	Total	Seasonal	Extended credit
December:								
1959	11,109	10,168	10,168	10,603	40,880	941		
1960	11,247	11,172	11,172	10,503	40,977	74		
1961	11,499	11,366	11,366	10,915	41,853	133		
1962	11,604	11,344	11,344	11,033	42,957	260		
1963	11,730	11,397	11,397	11,239	45,003	332		
1964	12,011	11,747	11,747	11,605	47,161	264		
1965	12,316	11,872	11,872	11,892	49,620	444		
1966	12,223	11,690	11,690	11,884	51,565	532		
1967	13,180	12,952	12,952	12,805	54,579	228		
1968	13,767	13,021	13,021	13,341	58,357	746		
1969	14,168	13,049	13,049	13,882	61,569	1,119		
1970	14,558	14,225	14,225	14,309	65,013	332		
1971	15,230	15,104	15,104	15,049	69,108	126		
1972	16,645	15,595	15,595	16,361	75,167	1,050		
1973	17,021	15,723	15,723	16,717	81,073	1,298	41	
1974	17,550	16,823	16,970	17,292	87,535	727	32	147
1975	17,822	17,692	17,704	17,556	93,887	130	14	12
1976	18,388	18,335	18,335	18,115	101,515	53	13	
1977	18,990	18,420	18,420	18,800	110,324	569	55	
1978	19,753	18,885	18,885	19,521	120,445	868	135	
1979	20,720	19,248	19,248	20,279	131,143	1,473	82	
1980	22,015	20,325	20,328	21,501	142,004	1,690	116	3
1981	22,443	21,807	21,956	22,124	149,021	636	54	148
1982	23,600	22,966	23,152	23,100	160,127	634	33	186
1983	25,367	24,593	24,595	24,806	175,467	774	96	2
1984	26,854	23,668	26,272	26,000	187,333	3,186	113	2,604
1985	31,463	30,144	30,643	30,426	203,609	1,318	56	499
1986	38,972	38,146	38,449	37,603	223,651	827	38	303
1987	38,895	38,118	38,601	37,849	239,799	777	93	483
1988	40,428	38,712	39,957	39,381	256,905	1,716	130	1,244
1989	40,522	40,257	40,277	39,600	267,625	265	84	20
1990	41,797	41,471	41,494	40,132	293,190	326	76	23
1991	45,563	45,371	45,371	44,584	317,403	192	38	1
1992	54,383	54,260	54,260	53,228	351,347	124	18	1
1993	60,545	60,463	60,463	59,482	386,880	82	31	0
1994	59,404	59,195	59,195	58,236	418,484	209	100	0
1995	56,386	56,129	56,129	55,108	434,523	257	40	0
1996	50,063	49,908	49,908	48,639	452,669	155	68	0
1997	47,196	46,872	46,872	45,513	481,230	324	79	0
1996: Jan	55,691	55,653	55,653	54,206	434,518	38	7	0
Feb	54,810	54,775	54,775	53,959	433,584	35	8	0
Mar	55,613	55,592	55,592	54,476	436,733	21	10	0
Apr	55,155	55,064	55,064	54,035	437,075	91	34	0
May	54,168	54,040	54,040	53,308	437,881	127	105	0
June	54,038	53,652	53,652	52,888	439,686	386	192	0
July	53,221	52,854	52,854	52,156	442,262	368	284	0
Aug	52,181	51,847	51,847	51,221	443,999	334	309	0
Sept	51,280	50,912	50,912	50,242	445,812	368	306	0
Oct	50,076	49,789	49,789	48,905	447,077	287	212	0
Nov	49,811	49,597	49,597	48,776	449,365	214	109	0
Dec	50,063	49,908	49,908	48,639	452,669	155	68	0
1997: Jan	49,517	49,472	49,472	48,293	454,137	45	19	0
Feb	49,008	48,966	48,966	47,977	456,284	42	21	0
Mar	48,312	48,155	48,155	47,151	457,623	156	37	0
Apr	47,430	47,170	47,170	46,420	458,235	261	88	0
May	47,048	46,805	46,805	45,808	459,602	243	173	0
June	47,108	46,741	46,741	45,828	461,401	367	243	0
July	46,885	46,476	46,476	45,683	464,212	409	330	0
Aug	47,414	46,816	46,816	46,161	466,456	598	385	0
Sept	46,666	46,229	46,229	45,371	469,353	438	368	0
Oct	46,454	46,184	46,184	45,058	472,022	270	227	0
Nov	46,865	46,712	46,712	45,248	476,484	153	115	0
Dec	47,196	46,872	46,872	45,513	481,230	324	79	0

[1] Data are prorated averages of biweekly (maintenance period) averages of daily figures.
[2] Aggregate reserves incorporate adjustments for discontinuities associated with regulatory changes to reserve requirements. For details on aggregate reserves series see *Federal Reserve Bulletin*.

Note.—NSA indicates data are not seasonally adjusted.

Source: Board of Governors of the Federal Reserve System.

TABLE B–72.—*Bank credit at all commercial banks, 1972–97*

[Monthly average; billions of dollars, seasonally adjusted [1]]

Year and month	Total bank credit	Securities in bank credit			Loans and leases in bank credit							
		Total securities	U.S. Government securities	Other securities	Total loans and leases [2]	Commercial and industrial	Real estate			Consumer	Security	Other
							Total	Revolving home equity	Other			
December:												
1972	572.5	182.4	89.0	93.4	390.1	137.1	98.1	....	....	86.3	15.6	53.0
1973	647.8	187.6	88.2	99.4	460.2	165.0	117.3	....	....	98.6	12.9	66.4
1974	713.7	193.8	86.3	107.5	519.9	196.6	130.1	....	....	102.4	12.7	78.1
1975	745.1	227.9	116.7	111.2	517.2	189.3	134.4	....	....	104.9	13.5	75.1
1976	804.6	249.8	136.3	113.5	554.8	190.9	148.8	....	....	116.3	17.7	81.1
1977	891.5	259.3	136.6	122.7	632.3	211.0	175.2	....	....	138.3	21.0	86.8
1978	1,013.9	266.8	137.6	129.2	747.1	246.2	210.5	....	....	164.7	19.7	106.0
1979	1,135.6	286.2	144.3	141.9	849.4	291.4	241.9	....	....	184.5	18.7	112.9
1980	1,238.6	325.0	170.6	154.4	913.5	325.7	262.6	....	....	179.2	18.0	128.0
1981	1,307.0	339.8	179.3	160.5	967.3	355.4	284.1	....	....	182.5	21.4	123.9
1982	1,400.4	366.5	201.7	164.8	1,033.9	392.5	299.9	....	....	188.2	25.3	128.0
1983	1,552.2	428.3	259.2	169.1	1,123.9	414.2	331.0	....	....	212.9	28.0	137.8
1984	1,722.9	400.7	259.8	140.9	1,322.2	473.2	376.3	....	....	254.2	35.0	183.5
1985	1,910.4	449.8	270.8	179.0	1,460.6	500.2	425.9	....	....	295.0	43.3	196.2
1986	2,093.7	504.0	310.1	193.9	1,589.7	536.7	494.1	....	....	315.4	40.3	203.2
1987	2,241.2	531.6	335.8	195.8	1,709.6	566.4	587.2	....	....	328.2	34.5	193.3
New series												
1988	2,435.5	562.2	367.4	194.9	1,873.3	607.6	675.2	40.0	635.2	357.2	40.7	192.6
1989	2,609.2	585.1	401.0	184.2	2,024.1	638.8	770.3	50.2	720.1	377.7	41.5	195.7
1990	2,754.6	634.9	457.0	177.9	2,119.7	641.1	856.3	62.3	794.0	383.2	45.4	193.9
1991	2,858.9	745.7	566.0	179.7	2,113.2	619.6	880.6	69.6	811.0	366.4	55.4	191.3
1992	2,958.4	843.0	666.2	176.8	2,115.4	596.2	901.5	73.5	828.0	358.9	65.6	193.3
1993	3,118.3	917.6	732.7	184.9	2,200.7	586.6	941.5	73.0	868.4	391.2	90.3	191.3
1994	3,332.5	951.9	730.6	221.2	2,380.6	646.0	1,003.4	75.3	928.1	452.4	79.1	199.7
1995	3,616.2	996.0	707.9	288.1	2,620.2	718.2	1,079.9	79.1	1,000.8	496.5	86.6	239.0
1996	3,770.3	989.8	705.4	284.5	2,780.4	782.2	1,129.0	84.8	1,044.2	521.0	78.5	269.8
1997	4,110.4	1,101.6	751.5	350.1	3,008.8	857.0	1,225.9	98.3	1,127.6	509.7	97.1	319.2
1996: Jan	3,630.6	990.2	702.1	288.1	2,640.4	723.7	1,085.4	79.5	1,005.9	498.1	87.9	245.4
Feb	3,650.6	1,001.4	711.1	290.4	2,649.2	727.5	1,091.1	79.8	1,011.3	497.5	87.2	245.9
Mar	3,649.8	990.6	703.6	287.0	2,659.2	729.0	1,096.7	79.9	1,016.8	500.2	84.6	248.7
Apr	3,667.2	991.8	707.8	284.0	2,675.4	733.1	1,098.7	80.2	1,018.5	504.0	84.7	254.9
May	3,664.8	992.3	711.6	280.7	2,672.5	736.4	1,101.7	79.9	1,021.8	503.2	76.6	254.6
June	3,672.0	983.4	707.4	275.9	2,688.7	740.2	1,104.1	79.4	1,024.7	508.6	78.8	256.9
July	3,685.8	985.1	708.2	277.0	2,700.7	744.7	1,104.8	80.1	1,024.7	511.8	77.9	261.5
Aug	3,678.1	974.7	703.5	271.3	2,703.4	746.6	1,109.7	81.0	1,028.7	514.0	72.1	261.1
Sept	3,697.5	972.5	704.5	268.0	2,725.0	760.6	1,112.4	81.9	1,030.6	517.3	73.3	261.4
Oct	3,716.9	969.5	701.6	267.9	2,747.4	769.9	1,116.2	83.0	1,033.2	519.2	75.8	266.3
Nov	3,742.8	980.5	705.6	274.9	2,762.3	773.9	1,122.6	83.7	1,038.8	520.5	76.9	268.5
Dec	3,770.3	989.8	705.4	284.5	2,780.4	782.2	1,129.0	84.8	1,044.2	521.0	78.5	269.8
1997: Jan	3,803.6	1,005.2	706.3	298.8	2,798.4	784.5	1,135.6	85.2	1,050.5	521.8	81.3	275.2
Feb	3,839.5	1,020.7	703.5	317.2	2,818.8	793.2	1,141.1	85.9	1,055.2	520.5	82.8	281.2
Mar	3,858.6	1,014.3	707.7	306.6	2,844.3	797.7	1,154.6	87.3	1,067.3	517.9	87.3	286.6
Apr	3,897.7	1,033.1	722.3	310.8	2,864.6	803.5	1,168.1	89.2	1,078.9	515.1	89.4	288.5
May	3,902.2	1,014.0	721.9	292.1	2,888.1	808.4	1,179.1	90.4	1,088.6	516.5	88.3	295.9
June	3,922.3	1,010.2	724.9	285.3	2,912.1	813.8	1,189.4	91.9	1,097.5	517.7	92.6	298.6
July	3,957.6	1,031.6	726.7	305.0	2,926.0	817.0	1,198.2	93.2	1,105.1	517.6	93.5	299.7
Aug	3,971.2	1,025.4	715.5	309.9	2,945.7	825.6	1,205.5	94.3	1,111.2	518.8	93.3	302.6
Sept	3,996.0	1,032.1	724.4	307.6	2,963.9	837.6	1,214.0	95.5	1,118.5	515.2	94.5	302.6
Oct	4,030.2	1,046.1	731.9	314.2	2,984.1	844.3	1,219.3	96.4	1,122.9	509.2	104.4	306.9
Nov	4,075.4	1,081.1	745.3	335.8	2,994.2	847.2	1,225.8	97.4	1,128.4	509.7	97.6	314.0
Dec	4,110.4	1,101.6	751.5	350.1	3,008.8	857.0	1,225.9	98.3	1,127.6	509.7	97.1	319.2

[1] Data are Wednesday values or prorated averages of Wednesday values for domestically chartered commercial banks, branches and agencies of foreign banks, New York State investment companies (through September 1996), and Edge Act and agreement corporations. Beginning 1988, data are adjusted for breaks caused by reclassifications of assets.

[2] Excludes Federal funds sold to, reverse repurchase agreements (RPs) with, and loans to commercial banks in the United States.

Note.—Data are not strictly comparable because of breaks in the series.

Source: Board of Governors of the Federal Reserve System.

TABLE B-73.—*Bond yields and interest rates, 1929-97*

[Percent per annum]

Year and month	U.S. Treasury securities Bills (new issues)[1] 3-month	6-month	Constant maturities[2] 3-year	10-year	30-year	Corporate bonds (Moody's) Aaa	Baa	High-grade municipal bonds (Standard & Poor's)	New-home mortgage yields[3]	Commercial paper, 6 months[4]	Prime rate charged by banks[5]	Discount rate, Federal Reserve Bank of New York[5]	Federal funds rate[6]
1929						4.73	5.90	4.27		5.85	5.50–6.00	5.16	
1933	0.515					4.49	7.76	4.71		1.73	1.50–4.00	2.56	
1939	.023					3.01	4.96	2.76		.59	1.50	1.00	
1940	.014					2.84	4.75	2.50		.56	1.50	1.00	
1941	.103					2.77	4.33	2.10		.53	1.50	1.00	
1942	.326					2.83	4.28	2.36		.66	1.50	7 1.00	
1943	.373					2.73	3.91	2.06		.69	1.50	7 1.00	
1944	.375					2.72	3.61	1.86		.73	1.50	7 1.00	
1945	.375					2.62	3.29	1.67		.75	1.50	7 1.00	
1946	.375					2.53	3.05	1.64		.81	1.50	7 1.00	
1947	.594					2.61	3.24	2.01		1.03	1.50–1.75	1.00	
1948	1.040					2.82	3.47	2.40		1.44	1.75–2.00	1.34	
1949	1.102					2.66	3.42	2.21		1.49	2.00	1.50	
1950	1.218					2.62	3.24	1.98		1.45	2.07	1.59	
1951	1.552					2.86	3.41	2.00		2.16	2.56	1.75	
1952	1.766					2.96	3.52	2.19		2.33	3.00	1.75	
1953	1.931		2.47	2.85		3.20	3.74	2.72		2.52	3.17	1.99	
1954	.953		1.63	2.40		2.90	3.51	2.37		1.58	3.05	1.60	
1955	1.753		2.47	2.82		3.06	3.53	2.53		2.18	3.16	1.89	1.78
1956	2.658		3.19	3.18		3.36	3.88	2.93		3.31	3.77	2.77	2.73
1957	3.267		3.98	3.65		3.89	4.71	3.60		3.81	4.20	3.12	3.11
1958	1.839		2.84	3.32		3.79	4.73	3.56		2.46	3.83	2.15	1.57
1959	3.405	3.832	4.46	4.33		4.38	5.05	3.95		3.97	4.48	3.36	3.30
1960	2.928	3.247	3.98	4.12		4.41	5.19	3.73		3.85	4.82	3.53	3.22
1961	2.378	2.605	3.54	3.88		4.35	5.08	3.46		2.97	4.50	3.00	1.96
1962	2.778	2.908	3.47	3.95		4.33	5.02	3.18		3.26	4.50	3.00	2.68
1963	3.157	3.253	3.67	4.00		4.26	4.86	3.23	5.89	3.55	4.50	3.23	3.18
1964	3.549	3.686	4.03	4.19		4.40	4.83	3.22	5.83	3.97	4.50	3.55	3.50
1965	3.954	4.055	4.22	4.28		4.49	4.87	3.27	5.81	4.38	4.54	4.04	4.07
1966	4.881	5.082	5.23	4.92		5.13	5.67	3.82	6.25	5.55	5.63	4.50	5.11
1967	4.321	4.630	5.03	5.07		5.51	6.23	3.98	6.46	5.10	5.61	4.19	4.22
1968	5.339	5.470	5.68	5.65		6.18	6.94	4.51	6.97	5.90	6.30	5.16	5.66
1969	6.677	6.853	7.02	6.67		7.03	7.81	5.81	7.81	7.83	7.96	5.87	8.20
1970	6.458	6.562	7.29	7.35		8.04	9.11	6.51	8.45	7.71	7.91	5.95	7.18
1971	4.348	4.511	5.65	6.16		7.39	8.56	5.70	7.74	5.11	5.72	4.88	4.66
1972	4.071	4.466	5.72	6.21		7.21	8.16	5.27	7.60	4.73	5.25	4.50	4.43
1973	7.041	7.178	6.95	6.84		7.44	8.24	5.18	7.96	8.15	8.03	6.44	8.73
1974	7.886	7.926	7.82	7.56		8.57	9.50	6.09	8.92	9.84	10.81	7.83	10.50
1975	5.838	6.122	7.49	7.99		8.83	10.61	6.89	9.00	6.32	7.86	6.25	5.82
1976	4.989	5.266	6.77	7.61		8.43	9.75	6.49	9.00	5.34	6.84	5.50	5.04
1977	5.265	5.510	6.69	7.42	7.75	8.02	8.97	5.56	9.02	5.61	6.83	5.46	5.54
1978	7.221	7.572	8.29	8.41	8.49	8.73	9.49	5.90	9.56	7.99	9.06	7.46	7.93
1979	10.041	10.017	9.71	9.44	9.28	9.63	10.69	6.39	10.78	10.91	12.67	10.28	11.19
1980	11.506	11.374	11.55	11.46	11.27	11.94	13.67	8.51	12.66	12.29	15.27	11.77	13.36
1981	14.029	13.776	14.44	13.91	13.45	14.17	16.04	11.23	14.70	14.76	18.87	13.42	16.38
1982	10.686	11.084	12.92	13.00	12.76	13.79	16.11	11.57	15.14	11.89	14.86	11.02	12.26
1983	8.63	8.75	10.45	11.10	11.18	12.04	13.55	9.47	12.57	8.89	10.79	8.50	9.09
1984	9.58	9.80	11.89	12.44	12.41	12.71	14.19	10.15	12.38	10.16	12.04	8.80	10.23
1985	7.48	7.66	9.64	10.62	10.79	11.37	12.72	9.18	11.55	8.01	9.93	7.69	8.10
1986	5.98	6.03	7.06	7.68	7.78	9.02	10.39	7.38	10.17	6.39	8.33	6.33	6.81
1987	5.82	6.05	7.68	8.39	8.59	9.38	10.58	7.73	9.31	6.85	8.21	5.66	6.66
1988	6.69	6.92	8.26	8.85	8.96	9.71	10.83	7.76	9.19	7.68	9.32	6.20	7.57
1989	8.12	8.04	8.55	8.49	8.45	9.26	10.18	7.24	10.13	8.80	10.87	6.93	9.21
1990	7.51	7.47	8.26	8.55	8.61	9.32	10.36	7.25	10.05	7.95	10.01	6.98	8.10
1991	5.42	5.49	6.82	7.86	8.14	8.77	9.80	6.89	9.32	5.85	8.46	5.45	5.69
1992	3.45	3.57	5.30	7.01	7.67	8.14	8.98	6.41	8.24	3.80	6.25	3.25	3.52
1993	3.02	3.14	4.44	5.87	6.59	7.22	7.93	5.63	7.20	3.30	6.00	3.00	3.02
1994	4.29	4.66	6.27	7.09	7.37	7.96	8.62	6.19	7.49	4.93	7.15	3.60	4.21
1995	5.51	5.59	6.25	6.57	6.88	7.59	8.20	5.95	7.87	5.93	8.83	5.21	5.83
1996	5.02	5.09	5.99	6.44	6.71	7.37	8.05	5.75	7.80	5.42	8.27	5.02	5.30
1997	5.07	5.18	6.10	6.35	6.61	7.27	7.87	5.55	7.71		8.44	5.00	5.46

[1] Rate on new issues within period; bank-discount basis.

[2] Yields on the more actively traded issues adjusted to constant maturities by the Department of the Treasury.

[3] Effective rate (in the primary market) on conventional mortgages, reflecting fees and charges as well as contract rate and assuming, on the average, repayment at end of 10 years. Rates beginning January 1973 not strictly comparable with prior rates.

[4] Bank-discount basis; prior to November 1979, data are for 4–6 months paper. Series no longer published by Federal Reserve (FR). See FR release H.15 *Selected Interest Rates* dated May 12, 1997.

[5] For monthly data, high and low for the period. Prime rate for 1929–33 and 1947–48 are ranges of the rate in effect during the period.

[6] Since July 19, 1975, the daily effective rate is an average of the rates on a given day weighted by the volume of transactions at these rates. Prior to that date, the daily effective rate was the rate considered most representative of the day's transactions, usually the one at which most transactions occurred.

[7] From October 30, 1942, to April 24, 1946, a preferential rate of 0.50 percent was in effect for advances secured by Government securities maturing in 1 year or less.

See next page for continuation of table.

TABLE B–73.—*Bond yields and interest rates, 1929–97*—Continued

[Percent per annum]

Year and month	U.S. Treasury securities Bills (new issues)[1]		U.S. Treasury securities Constant maturities[2]			Corporate bonds (Moody's)		High-grade munici-pal bonds (Stand-ard & Poor's)	New-home mort-gage yields[3]	Com-mer-cial paper, 6 months[4]	Prime rate charged by banks[5]	Discount rate, Federal Reserve Bank of New York[5]	Federal funds rate[6]
	3-month	6-month	3-year	10-year	30-year	Aaa	Baa						
												High-low	High-low
1993:													
Jan	3.06	3.17	4.93	6.60	7.34	7.91	8.67	6.18	7.82	3.35	6.00–6.00	3.00–3.00	3.02
Feb	2.95	3.08	4.58	6.26	7.09	7.71	8.39	5.87	7.77	3.27	6.00–6.00	3.00–3.00	3.03
Mar	2.97	3.08	4.40	5.98	6.82	7.58	8.15	5.65	7.46	3.24	6.00–6.00	3.00–3.00	3.07
Apr	2.89	3.00	4.30	5.97	6.85	7.46	8.14	5.78	7.46	3.19	6.00–6.00	3.00–3.00	2.96
May	2.96	3.07	4.40	6.04	6.92	7.43	8.21	5.81	7.37	3.20	6.00–6.00	3.00–3.00	3.00
June	3.10	3.23	4.53	5.96	6.81	7.33	8.07	5.73	7.23	3.38	6.00–6.00	3.00–3.00	3.04
July	3.05	3.15	4.43	5.81	6.63	7.17	7.93	5.60	7.20	3.35	6.00–6.00	3.00–3.00	3.06
Aug	3.05	3.17	4.36	5.68	6.32	6.85	7.60	5.50	7.05	3.33	6.00–6.00	3.00–3.00	3.03
Sept	2.96	3.06	4.17	5.36	6.00	6.66	7.34	5.31	6.95	3.25	6.00–6.00	3.00–3.00	3.09
Oct	3.04	3.13	4.18	5.33	5.94	6.67	7.31	5.29	6.80	3.27	6.00–6.00	3.00–3.00	2.99
Nov	3.12	3.27	4.50	5.72	6.21	6.93	7.66	5.47	6.80	3.43	6.00–6.00	3.00–3.00	3.02
Dec	3.08	3.25	4.54	5.77	6.25	6.93	7.69	5.35	6.92	3.40	6.00–6.00	3.00–3.00	2.96
1994:													
Jan	3.02	3.19	4.48	5.75	6.29	6.92	7.65	5.30	6.95	3.30	6.00–6.00	3.00–3.00	3.05
Feb	3.21	3.38	4.83	5.97	6.49	7.08	7.76	5.44	6.85	3.62	6.00–6.00	3.00–3.00	3.25
Mar	3.52	3.79	5.40	6.48	6.91	7.48	8.13	5.93	6.99	4.08	6.25–6.00	3.00–3.00	3.34
Apr	3.74	4.13	5.99	6.97	7.27	7.88	8.52	6.28	7.31	4.40	6.75–6.25	3.00–3.00	3.56
May	4.19	4.64	6.34	7.18	7.41	7.99	8.62	6.26	7.43	4.92	7.25–6.75	3.50–3.00	4.01
June	4.18	4.58	6.27	7.10	7.40	7.97	8.65	6.14	7.62	4.86	7.25–7.25	3.50–3.50	4.25
July	4.39	4.81	6.48	7.30	7.58	8.11	8.80	6.19	7.71	5.13	7.25–7.25	3.50–3.50	4.26
Aug	4.50	4.91	6.50	7.24	7.49	8.07	8.74	6.19	7.67	5.19	7.75–7.25	4.00–3.50	4.47
Sept	4.64	5.02	6.69	7.46	7.71	8.34	8.98	6.33	7.70	5.32	7.75–7.75	4.00–4.00	4.73
Oct	4.96	5.39	7.04	7.74	7.94	8.57	9.20	6.50	7.76	5.70	7.75–7.75	4.00–4.00	4.76
Nov	5.25	5.69	7.44	7.96	8.08	8.68	9.32	6.96	7.81	6.01	8.50–7.75	4.75–4.00	5.29
Dec	5.64	6.21	7.71	7.81	7.87	8.46	9.10	6.76	7.83	6.62	8.50–8.50	4.75–4.75	5.45
1995:													
Jan	5.81	6.31	7.66	7.78	7.85	8.46	9.08	6.53	8.18	6.63	8.50–8.50	4.75–4.75	5.53
Feb	5.80	6.10	7.25	7.47	7.61	8.26	8.85	6.24	8.28	6.38	9.00–8.50	5.25–4.75	5.92
Mar	5.73	5.91	6.89	7.20	7.45	8.12	8.70	6.10	8.21	6.30	9.00–9.00	5.25–5.25	5.98
Apr	5.67	5.80	6.68	7.06	7.36	8.03	8.60	6.01	8.15	6.19	9.00–9.00	5.25–5.25	6.05
May	5.70	5.73	6.27	6.63	6.95	7.65	8.20	5.90	7.99	6.07	9.00–9.00	5.25–5.25	6.01
June	5.50	5.46	5.80	6.17	6.57	7.30	7.90	5.83	7.73	5.79	9.00–9.00	5.25–5.25	6.00
July	5.47	5.41	5.89	6.28	6.72	7.41	8.04	5.98	7.78	5.68	9.00–8.75	5.25–5.25	5.85
Aug	5.41	5.40	6.10	6.49	6.86	7.57	8.19	6.07	7.75	5.75	8.75–8.75	5.25–5.25	5.74
Sept	5.26	5.28	5.89	6.20	6.55	7.32	7.93	5.88	7.69	5.66	8.75–8.75	5.25–5.25	5.80
Oct	5.30	5.34	5.77	6.04	6.37	7.12	7.75	5.77	7.58	5.71	8.75–8.75	5.25–5.25	5.76
Nov	5.35	5.29	5.57	5.93	6.26	7.02	7.68	5.61	7.46	5.59	8.75–8.75	5.25–5.25	5.80
Dec	5.16	5.15	5.39	5.71	6.06	6.82	7.49	5.42	7.40	5.43	8.75–8.50	5.25–5.25	5.60
1996:													
Jan	5.02	4.97	5.20	5.65	6.05	6.81	7.47	5.42	7.32	5.23	8.50–8.50	5.25–5.00	5.56
Feb	4.87	4.79	5.14	5.81	6.24	6.99	7.63	5.45	7.20	4.99	8.50–8.25	5.00–5.00	5.22
Mar	4.96	4.96	5.79	6.27	6.60	7.35	8.03	5.82	7.49	5.26	8.25–8.25	5.00–5.00	5.31
Apr	4.99	5.08	6.11	6.51	6.79	7.50	8.19	5.93	7.76	5.38	8.25–8.25	5.00–5.00	5.22
May	5.02	5.12	6.27	6.74	6.93	7.62	8.30	5.98	7.80	5.42	8.25–8.25	5.00–5.00	5.24
June	5.11	5.26	6.49	6.91	7.06	7.71	8.40	6.03	8.05	5.57	8.25–8.25	5.00–5.00	5.27
July	5.17	5.32	6.45	6.87	7.03	7.65	8.35	5.91	8.01	5.67	8.25–8.25	5.00–5.00	5.40
Aug	5.09	5.17	6.21	6.64	6.84	7.46	8.18	5.72	8.08	5.51	8.25–8.25	5.00–5.00	5.22
Sept	5.15	5.29	6.41	6.83	7.03	7.66	8.35	5.86	7.98	5.66	8.25–8.25	5.00–5.00	5.30
Oct	5.01	5.12	6.08	6.53	6.81	7.39	8.07	5.71	7.95	5.45	8.25–8.25	5.00–5.00	5.24
Nov	5.03	5.07	5.82	6.20	6.48	7.10	7.79	5.59	7.80	5.40	8.25–8.25	5.00–5.00	5.31
Dec	4.87	5.02	5.91	6.30	6.55	7.20	7.89	5.62	7.79	5.44	8.25–8.25	5.00–5.00	5.29
1997:													
Jan	5.05	5.11	6.16	6.58	6.83	7.42	8.09	5.72	7.81	5.48	8.25–8.25	5.00–5.00	5.25
Feb	5.00	5.05	6.03	6.42	6.69	7.31	7.94	5.63	7.78	5.42	8.25–8.25	5.00–5.00	5.19
Mar	5.14	5.24	6.38	6.69	6.93	7.55	8.18	5.78	7.88	5.61	8.50–8.25	5.00–5.00	5.39
Apr	5.17	5.35	6.61	6.89	7.09	7.73	8.34	5.88	8.03	5.79	8.50–8.50	5.00–5.00	5.51
May	5.13	5.35	6.42	6.71	6.94	7.58	8.20	5.71	8.01	5.78	8.50–8.50	5.00–5.00	5.50
June	4.92	5.14	6.24	6.49	6.77	7.41	8.02	5.60	7.95	5.69	8.50–8.50	5.00–5.00	5.56
July	5.07	5.12	6.00	6.22	6.51	7.14	7.75	5.41	7.78	5.60	8.50–8.50	5.00–5.00	5.52
Aug	5.13	5.17	6.06	6.30	6.58	7.22	7.82	5.47	7.59	5.59	8.50–8.50	5.00–5.00	5.54
Sept	4.97	5.11	5.98	6.21	6.50	7.15	7.70	5.38	7.61		8.50–8.50	5.00–5.00	5.54
Oct	4.95	5.09	5.84	6.03	6.33	7.00	7.57	5.37	7.54		8.50–8.50	5.00–5.00	5.50
Nov	5.15	5.17	5.76	5.88	6.11	6.87	7.42	5.38	7.40		8.50–8.50	5.00–5.00	5.52
Dec	5.16	5.24	5.74	5.81	5.99	6.76	7.32	5.22	7.40		8.50–8.50	5.00–5.00	5.50

Sources: Department of the Treasury, Board of Governors of the Federal Reserve System, Federal Housing Finance Board, Moody's Investors Service, and Standard & Poor's Corporation.

TABLE B–74.—*Credit market borrowing, 1988–97*

[Billions of dollars; quarterly data at seasonally adjusted annual rates]

Item	1988	1989	1990	1991	1992	1993	1994	1995	1996
NONFINANCIAL SECTORS									
DOMESTIC	764.6	716.3	662.7	470.6	539.9	619.6	594.0	698.2	714.2
FEDERAL GOVERNMENT	155.1	146.4	246.9	278.2	304.0	256.1	155.9	144.4	145.0
Treasury securities	137.7	144.7	238.7	292.0	303.8	248.3	155.7	142.9	146.6
Budget agency securities and mortgages	17.4	1.6	8.2	–13.8	.2	7.8	.2	1.5	–1.6
NONFEDERAL, BY INSTRUMENT	609.4	569.9	415.8	192.4	235.9	363.4	438.1	553.7	569.2
Commercial paper	11.9	21.4	9.7	–18.4	8.6	10.0	21.4	18.1	–.9
Municipal securities and loans	59.3	52.9	49.3	87.8	30.5	74.8	–35.9	–48.2	1.3
Corporate bonds	103.1	73.8	47.1	78.8	67.6	75.2	23.3	73.3	72.5
Bank loans n.e.c.	40.3	28.2	4.3	–42.3	–12.0	6.4	75.2	102.0	66.8
Other loans and advances	52.6	55.7	61.8	–55.4	5.7	–18.9	37.3	46.5	21.5
Mortgages	298.8	293.7	231.8	152.5	131.5	155.3	191.9	223.1	319.2
Home	229.3	235.2	222.3	177.7	189.1	184.1	199.0	192.4	268.1
Multifamily residential	17.7	10.6	–1.4	–3.2	–10.7	–6.0	1.7	10.4	17.7
Commercial	56.5	50.3	12.4	–22.2	–47.4	–23.9	–11.0	18.8	30.9
Farm	–4.8	–2.5	–1.6	.3	.5	1.0	2.2	1.6	2.6
Consumer credit	43.4	44.2	11.9	–10.7	3.9	60.7	124.9	138.9	88.8
NONFEDERAL, BY SECTOR	609.4	569.9	415.8	192.4	235.9	363.4	438.1	553.7	569.2
Household sector	250.3	257.8	247.4	176.4	191.1	246.2	343.7	354.9	362.9
Nonfinancial business	304.6	261.0	119.9	–67.4	23.7	54.9	140.8	241.8	193.7
Corporate	230.9	191.1	118.4	–53.8	39.6	49.1	135.3	213.7	147.9
Nonfarm noncorporate	83.9	69.3	.5	–15.6	–16.4	3.2	2.2	26.6	43.4
Farm	–10.2	.6	1.0	2.0	.5	2.6	3.3	1.5	2.4
State and local governments	54.5	51.1	48.5	83.3	21.1	62.3	–46.4	–42.9	12.7
FOREIGN BORROWING IN THE UNITED STATES	7.4	10.2	23.9	15.1	24.1	69.8	–14.0	71.1	70.5
Commercial paper	8.7	13.1	12.3	6.8	5.6	–9.6	–26.1	13.5	11.3
Bonds	6.9	4.9	21.4	15.0	16.8	82.9	12.2	49.7	49.4
Bank loans n.e.c.	–1.8	–.1	–2.9	3.1	2.3	.7	1.4	8.5	9.1
Other loans and advances	–6.4	–7.6	–7.0	–9.8	–.6	–4.2	–1.5	–.5	.8
NONFINANCIAL DOMESTIC AND FOREIGN BORROWING	772.0	726.4	686.6	485.7	564.0	689.3	579.9	769.2	784.7
FINANCIAL SECTORS									
BY INSTRUMENT	249.2	225.0	211.3	156.8	240.2	293.6	464.3	448.4	536.3
Federal Government related	119.8	149.5	167.4	145.7	155.8	165.3	287.5	204.1	231.5
Government-sponsored enterprises securities	44.9	25.2	17.1	9.2	40.3	80.6	176.9	105.9	90.4
Mortgage pool securities	74.9	124.3	150.3	136.6	115.6	84.7	115.4	98.2	141.1
U.S. Government loans	.0	.0	–.1	–.0	–.0	.0	–4.8	.0	.0
Private financial sectors	129.5	75.5	44.0	11.1	84.4	128.3	176.8	244.3	304.9
Open market paper	54.8	31.3	8.6	–32.3	–1.1	–5.5	40.5	42.7	92.2
Corporate bonds	52.2	40.8	54.7	72.9	84.8	122.2	117.6	188.2	156.5
Bank loans n.e.c.	2.7	13.5	4.0	7.3	.7	–14.4	–13.7	4.2	16.8
Other loans and advances	19.4	–10.5	–23.9	–37.3	–.6	22.4	22.6	3.4	27.9
Mortgages	.3	.3	.6	.5	.6	3.6	9.8	5.9	11.4
BY SECTOR	249.2	225.0	211.3	156.8	240.2	293.6	464.3	448.4	536.3
Commercial banking	2.0	5.2	–26.8	–13.2	10.0	13.4	20.1	22.5	13.0
Savings institutions	21.6	–15.0	–30.9	–44.7	–7.0	11.3	12.8	2.6	25.5
Government-sponsored enterprises	44.9	25.2	17.0	9.1	40.2	80.6	172.1	105.9	90.4
Federally related mortgage pools	74.9	124.3	150.3	136.6	115.6	84.7	115.4	98.2	141.1
Asset-backed securities issuers	37.6	27.7	59.5	54.4	57.3	82.8	68.8	132.9	132.0
Finance companies	23.9	27.4	23.1	16.0	–3.1	–1.4	48.7	50.2	45.9
Funding corporations	38.0	12.5	16.8	–4.0	16.2	6.3	23.1	34.9	64.1
Other [1]	6.3	17.7	2.3	2.5	11.1	15.9	3.3	1.2	24.4
ALL SECTORS									
BY INSTRUMENT	1,021.2	951.5	898.0	642.5	804.2	982.9	1,044.3	1,217.7	1,321.0
Open market paper	75.4	65.9	30.7	–44.0	13.1	–5.1	35.7	74.3	102.6
U.S. Government securities	274.9	295.8	414.4	424.0	459.8	421.4	448.1	348.5	376.5
Municipal securities and loans	59.3	52.9	49.3	87.8	30.5	74.8	–35.9	–48.2	1.3
Corporate and foreign bonds	162.2	119.5	123.1	166.7	169.1	280.3	153.2	311.1	278.4
Bank loans n.e.c.	41.2	41.5	5.5	–31.8	–8.9	–7.2	62.9	114.7	92.6
Other loans and advances	65.7	37.7	30.8	–102.4	4.6	–.8	53.6	49.3	50.2
Mortgages	299.1	294.0	232.4	153.0	132.1	158.9	201.7	229.0	330.6
Consumer credit	43.4	44.2	11.9	–10.7	3.9	60.7	124.9	138.9	88.8

[1] Credit unions, life insurance companies, mortgage companies, real estate investment trusts, and brokers and dealers.

See next page for continuation of table.

368

Item	1996				1997		
	I	II	III	IV	I	II	III
NONFINANCIAL SECTORS							
DOMESTIC	857.1	695.7	677.6	626.3	691.7	562.8	646.6
FEDERAL GOVERNMENT	227.3	62.7	163.2	126.9	81.2	-97.1	40.9
Treasury securities	229.6	60.5	166.3	130.2	82.6	-97.3	41.9
Budget agency securities and mortgages	-2.3	2.2	-3.1	-3.3	-1.4	.2	-.9
NONFEDERAL, BY INSTRUMENT	629.9	633.0	514.4	499.4	610.5	659.9	605.6
Commercial paper	25.4	9.2	-14.2	-24.1	7.8	21.4	15.5
Municipal securities and loans	-4.1	30.2	-65.2	44.2	23.2	76.5	40.4
Corporate bonds	60.9	71.5	67.8	89.9	79.4	86.1	122.9
Bank loans n.e.c.	47.5	49.7	136.2	33.6	147.6	105.4	25.8
Other loans and advances	20.4	33.9	46.4	-14.5	15.5	4.0	51.0
Mortgages	359.9	323.7	261.6	331.6	267.5	308.7	307.4
Home	316.9	255.4	248.2	251.6	242.0	217.8	223.1
Multifamily residential	13.9	18.4	11.9	26.8	5.4	19.6	19.6
Commercial	27.5	45.1	-.6	51.5	18.1	67.2	60.4
Farm	1.6	4.9	2.2	1.6	2.1	4.1	4.3
Consumer credit	119.9	114.7	81.9	38.6	69.6	57.8	42.7
NONFEDERAL, BY SECTOR	629.9	633.0	514.4	499.4	610.5	659.9	605.6
Household sector	446.2	378.1	345.5	281.6	333.3	295.1	245.9
Nonfinancial business	176.0	216.9	219.7	162.0	242.3	280.6	308.4
Corporate	131.7	172.2	193.0	94.6	190.0	205.4	240.8
Nonfarm noncorporate	44.2	38.5	29.2	61.5	48.1	67.6	63.2
Farm	.1	6.2	-2.5	6.0	4.2	7.6	4.4
State and local governments	7.7	38.0	-50.8	55.8	35.0	84.2	51.3
FOREIGN BORROWING IN THE UNITED STATES	52.3	36.1	105.7	87.9	26.2	56.3	82.2
Commercial paper	-6.3	9.6	37.5	4.4	15.4	10.3	-11.6
Bonds	47.7	11.2	60.2	78.5	11.0	34.3	89.2
Bank loans n.e.c.	8.7	15.1	4.7	7.8	-.7	11.5	7.3
Other loans and advances	2.3	.1	3.4	-2.7	.5	.2	-2.7
NONFINANCIAL DOMESTIC AND FOREIGN BORROWING	909.5	731.9	783.3	714.2	718.0	619.1	728.7
FINANCIAL SECTORS							
BY INSTRUMENT	342.0	721.7	436.8	644.8	323.4	665.8	526.2
Federal Government related	148.8	301.4	222.9	252.8	105.7	286.2	161.0
Government-sponsored enterprises securities	31.4	126.9	80.0	123.3	-8.9	198.1	46.4
Mortgage pool securities	117.4	174.5	142.9	129.6	114.6	88.1	114.6
U.S. Government loans	.0	.0	.0	.0	.0	.0	.0
Private financial sectors	193.2	420.3	213.9	392.0	217.7	379.7	365.2
Open market paper	17.1	105.4	84.4	162.0	175.9	77.8	168.2
Corporate bonds	150.5	230.9	80.7	164.0	38.9	215.0	129.9
Bank loans n.e.c.	23.4	20.6	2.6	20.4	7.0	9.9	15.6
Other loans and advances	-5.5	52.7	33.3	31.2	-20.1	63.0	37.5
Mortgages	7.7	10.8	12.9	14.3	16.0	14.0	14.0
BY SECTOR	342.0	721.7	436.8	644.8	323.4	665.8	526.2
Commercial banking	-34.2	44.5	14.7	26.8	13.7	81.7	30.1
Savings institutions	11.0	42.1	25.8	23.0	-16.8	31.9	21.2
Government-sponsored enterprises	31.4	126.9	80.0	123.3	-8.9	198.1	46.4
Federally related mortgage pools	117.4	174.5	142.9	129.6	114.6	88.1	114.6
Asset-backed securities issuers	138.9	162.5	88.0	138.6	62.2	9.7	165.2
Finance companies	41.4	67.8	30.7	43.8	6.4	124.6	.1
Funding corporations	37.2	62.7	33.7	123.0	129.4	-16.1	129.3
Other [1]	-1.1	40.7	21.0	36.8	22.8	63.9	19.2
ALL SECTORS							
BY INSTRUMENT	1,251.5	1,453.5	1,220.1	1,359.0	1,041.4	1,284.9	1,255.0
Open market paper	36.2	124.2	107.7	142.3	199.2	109.5	172.0
U.S. Government securities	376.1	364.1	386.1	379.7	186.9	189.1	201.9
Municipal securities and loans	-4.1	30.2	-65.2	44.2	23.2	76.5	40.4
Corporate and foreign bonds	259.1	313.6	208.7	332.4	129.3	335.4	341.9
Bank loans n.e.c.	79.5	85.5	143.5	61.8	153.8	126.7	48.7
Other loans and advances	17.2	86.7	83.0	14.0	-4.1	67.2	85.9
Mortgages	367.6	334.5	274.5	345.9	283.5	322.7	321.4
Consumer credit	119.9	114.7	81.9	38.6	69.6	57.8	42.7

Source: Board of Governors of the Federal Reserve System.

TABLE B-75.—*Mortgage debt outstanding by type of property and of financing, 1945–97*

[Billions of dollars]

End of year or quarter	All proper-ties	Farm proper-ties	Nonfarm properties				Nonfarm properties by type of mortgage					
							Government underwritten				Conventional [2]	
			Total	1- to 4-family houses	Multi-family proper-ties	Com-mercial proper-ties	Total [1]	1- to 4-family houses			Total	1-to 4-family houses
								Total	FHA insured	VA guar-anteed		
1945	35.5	4.8	30.8	18.6	5.7	6.4	4.3	4.3	4.1	0.2	26.5	14.3
1946	41.8	4.9	36.9	23.0	6.1	7.7	6.3	6.1	3.7	2.4	30.6	16.9
1947	48.9	5.1	43.9	28.2	6.6	9.1	9.8	9.3	3.8	5.5	34.1	18.9
1948	56.2	5.3	50.9	33.3	7.5	10.2	13.6	12.5	5.3	7.2	37.3	20.8
1949	62.7	5.6	57.1	37.6	8.6	10.8	17.1	15.0	6.9	8.1	40.0	22.6
1950	72.8	6.1	66.7	45.2	10.1	11.5	22.1	18.8	8.5	10.3	44.7	26.3
1951	82.3	6.7	75.6	51.7	11.5	12.5	26.6	22.9	9.7	13.2	49.1	28.9
1952	91.4	7.2	84.2	58.5	12.3	13.4	29.3	25.4	10.8	14.6	54.9	33.2
1953	101.3	7.7	93.6	66.1	12.9	14.5	32.1	28.1	12.0	16.1	61.5	38.0
1954	113.7	8.2	105.4	75.7	13.5	16.3	36.2	32.1	12.8	19.3	69.3	43.6
1955	129.9	9.0	120.9	88.2	14.3	18.3	42.9	38.9	14.3	24.6	78.0	49.3
1956	144.5	9.8	134.6	99.0	14.9	20.7	47.8	43.9	15.5	28.4	86.8	55.1
1957	156.5	10.4	146.1	107.6	15.3	23.2	51.6	47.2	16.5	30.7	94.6	60.4
1958	171.8	11.1	160.7	117.7	16.8	26.1	55.2	50.1	19.7	30.4	105.5	67.6
1959	190.8	12.1	178.7	130.9	18.7	29.2	59.3	53.8	23.8	30.0	119.4	77.0
1960	207.5	12.8	194.7	141.9	20.3	32.4	62.3	56.4	26.7	29.7	132.3	85.5
1961	228.0	13.9	214.1	154.6	23.0	36.5	65.6	59.1	29.5	29.6	148.5	95.5
1962	251.4	15.2	236.2	169.3	25.8	41.1	69.4	62.2	32.3	29.9	166.9	107.1
1963	278.5	16.8	261.7	186.4	29.0	46.2	73.4	65.9	35.0	30.9	188.2	120.5
1964	305.9	18.9	287.0	203.4	33.6	50.0	77.2	69.2	38.3	30.9	209.8	134.1
1965	333.3	21.2	312.1	220.5	37.2	54.5	81.2	73.1	42.0	31.1	231.0	147.4
1966	356.5	23.1	333.4	232.9	40.3	60.1	84.1	76.1	44.8	31.3	249.3	156.9
1967	381.2	25.1	356.1	247.3	43.9	64.8	88.2	79.9	47.4	32.5	267.9	167.4
1968	411.1	27.5	383.5	264.8	47.3	71.4	93.4	84.4	50.6	33.8	290.1	180.4
1969	441.6	29.4	412.2	283.2	52.2	76.9	100.2	90.2	54.5	35.7	312.0	193.0
1970	473.7	30.5	443.2	297.4	60.1	85.6	109.2	97.3	59.9	37.3	333.9	200.2
1971	524.2	32.4	491.8	325.9	70.1	95.9	120.7	105.2	65.7	39.5	371.1	220.7
1972	597.4	35.4	562.0	366.5	82.8	112.7	131.1	113.0	68.2	44.7	430.9	253.5
1973	672.6	39.8	632.8	407.9	93.1	131.7	135.0	116.2	66.2	50.0	497.7	291.7
1974	732.5	44.9	687.5	440.7	100.0	146.9	140.2	121.3	65.1	56.2	547.3	319.4
1975	791.9	49.9	742.0	482.1	100.6	159.3	147.0	127.7	66.1	61.6	595.0	354.3
1976	878.6	55.4	823.2	546.3	105.7	171.2	154.1	133.5	66.5	67.0	669.0	412.8
1977	1,010.3	63.9	946.4	642.7	114.0	189.7	161.7	141.6	68.0	73.6	784.6	501.0
1978	1,163.0	72.8	1,090.2	753.5	124.9	211.8	176.4	153.4	71.4	82.0	913.9	600.2
1979	1,328.4	86.8	1,241.7	870.5	134.9	236.3	199.0	172.9	81.0	92.0	1,042.7	697.6
1980	1,463.0	97.5	1,365.5	969.0	141.0	255.5	225.1	195.2	93.6	101.6	1,140.4	773.9
1981	1,572.8	107.2	1,465.5	1,049.1	138.9	277.5	238.9	207.6	101.3	106.2	1,226.7	841.5
1982	1,650.7	111.3	1,539.3	1,096.4	140.8	302.2	248.9	217.9	108.0	109.9	1,290.5	878.5
1983	1,841.9	113.7	1,728.2	1,219.4	154.0	354.8	279.8	248.8	127.4	121.4	1,448.4	970.5
1984	2,071.1	112.4	1,958.7	1,360.4	177.0	421.4	294.8	265.9	136.7	129.1	1,663.9	1,094.5
1985	2,333.9	105.9	2,228.0	1,535.6	205.2	487.2	328.3	288.8	153.0	135.8	1,899.7	1,246.8
1986	2,634.8	95.2	2,539.5	1,741.6	238.4	559.6	370.5	328.6	185.5	143.1	2,169.1	1,413.0
1987	2,985.2	87.7	2,897.5	1,976.5	260.8	660.1	431.4	387.9	235.5	152.4	2,466.0	1,588.6
1988	3,280.3	83.0	3,197.4	2,217.4	277.5	702.4	459.7	414.2	258.8	155.4	2,737.7	1,803.3
1989	3,580.8	80.5	3,500.4	2,459.2	288.3	752.9	486.8	440.1	282.8	157.3	3,013.5	2,019.1
1990	3,803.1	78.9	3,724.2	2,672.2	286.9	765.1	517.9	470.9	310.9	160.0	3,206.3	2,201.3
1991	3,956.1	79.2	3,876.9	2,849.9	283.9	743.2	537.2	493.3	330.6	162.7	3,339.7	2,356.6
1992	4,088.2	79.7	4,008.4	3,038.9	273.4	696.2	533.3	489.8	326.0	163.8	3,475.1	2,549.2
1993	4,261.2	80.7	4,180.4	3,225.4	270.0	685.0	513.4	469.5	303.2	166.2	3,667.0	2,755.9
1994	4,462.8	83.0	4,379.9	3,424.4	274.9	680.5	559.3	514.2	336.8	177.3	3,820.5	2,910.2
1995	4,691.8	84.6	4,607.3	3,616.8	287.2	703.2	584.3	537.1	352.3	184.7	4,023.0	3,079.7
1996	5,022.5	87.1	4,935.3	3,851.2	312.4	771.7	623.2	574.1	379.2	194.9	4,312.1	3,277.1
1995: I	4,503.7	82.4	4,421.3	3,457.1	276.0	688.3	565.4	520.3	341.7	178.6	3,855.9	2,936.8
II	4,571.5	83.6	4,487.9	3,514.1	280.2	693.7	571.3	525.8	345.5	180.3	3,916.6	2,988.2
III	4,643.8	84.3	4,559.5	3,578.1	283.3	698.1	578.4	531.0	348.5	182.5	3,981.2	3,047.1
IV	4,691.8	84.6	4,607.3	3,616.8	287.2	703.2	584.3	537.1	352.3	184.7	4,023.0	3,079.7
1996: I	4,770.5	85.0	4,685.6	3,682.8	291.3	711.4	592.3	544.3	357.2	187.2	4,093.3	3,138.5
II	4,861.4	86.2	4,775.2	3,720.2	300.5	754.5	599.5	551.9	362.5	189.3	4,175.7	3,168.4
III	4,940.7	86.7	4,854.0	3,793.0	304.5	756.5	611.0	562.3	370.3	192.0	4,243.0	3,230.6
IV	5,022.5	87.1	4,935.3	3,851.2	312.4	771.7	623.2	574.1	379.2	194.9	4,312.1	3,277.1
1997: I	5,080.7	87.7	4,993.1	3,899.0	315.1	778.9	631.0	581.4	384.3	197.0	4,362.1	3,317.7
II	5,168.3	88.7	5,079.7	3,960.4	321.1	798.1	641.7	591.3	391.6	199.7	4,438.0	3,369.1
III p	5,259.9	89.8	5,170.1	4,027.4	327.2	815.5	647.1	596.6	395.6	201.0	4,523.0	3,430.8

[1] Includes FHA insured multifamily properties, not shown separately.
[2] Derived figures. Total includes commercial properties, and multifamily properties, not shown separately.

Source: Board of Governors of the Federal Reserve System, based on data from various Government and private organizations.

[Billions of dollars]

End of year or quarter	Total	Major financial institutions				Other holders	
		Total	Savings institutions [1]	Commercial banks [2]	Life insurance companies	Federal and related agencies [3]	Individuals and others [4]
1945	35.5	21.0	9.6	4.8	6.6	2.4	12.1
1946	41.8	26.0	11.5	7.2	7.2	2.0	13.8
1947	48.9	31.8	13.8	9.4	8.7	1.8	15.3
1948	56.2	37.8	16.1	10.9	10.8	1.8	16.6
1949	62.7	42.9	18.3	11.6	12.9	2.3	17.5
1950	72.8	51.7	21.9	13.7	16.1	2.8	18.4
1951	82.3	59.5	25.5	14.7	19.3	3.5	19.3
1952	91.4	66.9	29.8	15.9	21.3	4.1	20.4
1953	101.3	75.1	34.9	16.9	23.3	4.6	21.7
1954	113.7	85.7	41.1	18.6	26.0	4.8	23.2
1955	129.9	99.3	48.9	21.0	29.4	5.3	25.3
1956	144.5	111.2	55.5	22.7	33.0	6.2	27.1
1957	156.5	119.7	61.2	23.3	35.2	7.7	29.1
1958	171.8	131.5	68.9	25.5	37.1	8.0	32.3
1959	190.8	145.5	78.1	28.1	39.2	10.2	35.1
1960	207.5	157.6	87.0	28.8	41.8	11.5	38.4
1961	228.0	172.6	98.0	30.4	44.2	12.2	43.1
1962	251.4	192.5	111.1	34.5	46.9	12.6	46.3
1963	278.5	217.1	127.2	39.4	50.5	11.8	49.5
1964	305.9	241.0	141.9	44.0	55.2	12.2	52.7
1965	333.3	264.6	154.9	49.7	60.0	13.5	55.2
1966	356.5	280.8	161.8	54.4	64.6	17.5	58.2
1967	381.2	298.8	172.3	59.0	67.5	20.9	61.4
1968	411.1	319.9	184.3	65.7	70.0	25.1	66.1
1969	441.6	339.1	196.4	70.7	72.0	31.1	71.4
1970	473.7	355.9	208.3	73.3	74.4	38.3	79.4
1971	524.2	394.2	236.2	82.5	75.5	46.4	83.6
1972	597.4	450.0	273.7	99.3	76.9	54.6	92.8
1973	672.6	505.4	305.0	119.1	81.4	64.8	102.4
1974	732.5	542.6	324.2	132.1	86.2	82.2	107.7
1975	791.9	581.2	355.8	136.2	89.2	101.1	109.6
1976	878.6	647.5	404.6	151.3	91.6	116.7	114.4
1977	1,010.3	745.2	469.4	179.0	96.8	140.5	124.6
1978	1,163.0	848.2	528.0	214.0	106.2	170.6	144.3
1979	1,328.4	938.2	574.6	245.2	118.4	216.0	174.3
1980	1,463.0	996.8	603.1	262.7	131.1	256.8	209.4
1981	1,572.8	1,040.5	618.5	284.2	137.7	289.4	242.9
1982	1,650.7	1,021.3	578.1	301.3	142.0	355.4	273.9
1983	1,841.9	1,108.2	626.7	330.5	151.0	433.4	300.3
1984	2,071.1	1,245.9	709.7	379.5	156.7	490.6	334.6
1985	2,333.9	1,361.5	760.5	429.2	171.8	581.9	390.5
1986	2,634.8	1,474.3	778.0	502.5	193.8	733.7	426.7
1987	2,985.2	1,665.3	860.5	592.4	212.4	858.9	461.0
1988	3,280.3	1,831.5	924.6	674.0	232.9	937.8	511.1
1989	3,580.8	1,931.5	910.3	767.1	254.2	1,067.3	582.0
1990	3,803.1	1,914.3	801.6	844.8	267.9	1,258.9	629.9
1991	3,956.1	1,841.0	705.4	876.1	259.5	1,422.5	692.7
1992	4,088.2	1,764.5	628.0	894.5	242.0	1,558.1	765.5
1993	4,261.2	1,763.4	598.4	940.6	224.4	1,682.8	814.9
1994	4,462.8	1,811.0	596.2	1,003.9	210.9	1,787.7	864.1
1995	4,691.8	1,884.7	596.8	1,080.5	207.5	1,877.1	930.0
1996	5,022.5	1,968.9	628.3	1,135.1	205.4	2,012.3	1,041.3
1995: I	4,503.7	1,837.2	601.8	1,025.0	210.4	1,791.7	874.8
II	4,571.5	1,864.0	599.7	1,053.2	211.0	1,807.2	900.4
III	4,643.8	1,891.1	604.6	1,072.9	213.6	1,834.4	918.3
IV	4,691.8	1,884.7	596.8	1,080.5	207.5	1,877.1	930.0
1996: I	4,770.5	1,897.3	602.6	1,087.4	207.4	1,905.8	967.4
II	4,861.4	1,919.6	611.7	1,099.6	208.2	1,949.2	992.5
III	4,940.7	1,945.1	628.0	1,112.9	204.1	1,981.8	1,013.8
IV	5,022.5	1,968.9	628.3	1,135.1	205.4	2,012.3	1,041.3
1997: I	5,080.7	1,982.8	626.4	1,149.9	206.5	2,035.2	1,062.7
II	5,168.3	2,023.4	629.1	1,186.3	208.1	2,055.0	1,089.9
III *p*	5,259.9	2,055.8	629.8	1,216.6	209.4	2,081.5	1,122.6

[1] Includes savings banks and savings and loan associations. Data reported by Federal Savings and Loan Insurance Corporation-insured institutions include loans in process for 1987 and exclude loans in process beginning 1988.

[2] Includes loans held by nondeposit trust companies, but not by bank trust departments.

[3] Includes Government National Mortgage Association (GNMA), Federal Housing Administration, Veterans Administration, Farmers Home Administration (FmHA), Federal Deposit Insurance Corporation, Resolution Trust Corporation (through 1995), and in earlier years Reconstruction Finance Corporation, Homeowners Loan Corporation, Federal Farm Mortgage Corporation, and Public Housing Administration. Also includes U.S.-sponsored agencies such as Federal National Mortgage Association (FNMA), Federal Land Banks, Federal Home Loan Mortgage Corporation (FHLMC), and mortgage pass-through securities issued or guaranteed by GNMA, FHLMC, FNMA or FmHA. Other U.S. agencies (amounts small or current separate data not readily available) included with "individuals and others."

[4] Includes private mortgage pools.

Source: Board of Governors of the Federal Reserve System, based on data from various Government and private organizations.

TABLE B–77.—*Consumer credit outstanding, 1955–97*

[Amount outstanding (end of month); billions of dollars, seasonally adjusted]

Year and month	Total consumer credit [1]	Automobile	Revolving [2]	Other [3]
December:				
1955	41.9	13.5	....	28.4
1956	45.4	14.5	....	30.9
1957	48.1	15.5	....	32.6
1958	48.3	14.3	....	34.1
1959	55.9	16.6	....	39.3
1960	60.0	18.1	....	41.9
1961	62.2	17.7	....	44.5
1962	68.1	20.0	....	48.1
1963	76.6	22.9	....	53.7
1964	86.0	25.9	....	60.1
1965	96.0	29.4	....	66.6
1966	101.9	31.0	....	70.8
1967	106.9	31.1	....	75.7
1968	117.4	34.4	2.0	81.0
1969	127.1	36.9	3.6	86.6
1970	131.5	36.3	4.9	90.2
1971	146.9	40.5	8.3	98.1
1972	166.1	47.8	9.4	108.9
1973	190.0	53.7	11.3	124.9
1974	198.8	54.2	13.2	131.3
1975	203.6	56.8	14.5	132.3
1976	224.8	65.9	16.6	142.3
1977	257.5	79.0	36.7	141.8
1978	302.1	95.8	45.2	161.0
1979	343.5	108.7	53.4	181.5
1980	350.1	112.0	55.1	183.0
1981	367.6	119.8	61.1	186.7
1982	384.6	127.5	66.5	190.7
1983	433.7	146.2	79.1	208.4
1984	512.8	175.3	100.3	237.2
1985	592.7	210.8	124.7	257.1
1986	646.3	247.1	141.2	258.0
1987	676.3	266.1	160.9	249.4
1988 [4]	719.0	285.3	184.6	249.2
1989	779.0	290.8	211.2	277.0
1990	789.3	283.5	238.6	267.2
1991	777.2	263.4	263.7	250.1
1992	779.9	262.7	278.2	239.1
1993	838.6	288.0	309.9	240.7
1994	959.7	327.9	365.5	266.4
1995	1,094.2	364.2	443.0	287.0
1996	1,179.9	392.4	499.2	288.3
1996: Jan	1,102.3	367.0	447.3	288.1
Feb	1,113.3	370.5	454.0	288.8
Mar	1,123.2	373.7	460.2	289.4
Apr	1,133.0	376.8	466.3	289.8
May	1,141.4	380.0	471.1	290.2
June	1,151.0	383.8	474.8	292.4
July	1,161.5	388.1	479.5	293.9
Aug	1,169.9	388.8	483.3	297.8
Sept	1,170.7	389.9	485.3	295.6
Oct	1,177.3	391.4	490.6	295.4
Nov	1,179.5	390.4	495.0	294.1
Dec	1,179.9	392.4	499.2	288.3
1997: Jan	1,189.7	393.4	505.3	291.0
Feb	1,195.4	393.8	509.3	292.3
Mar	1,197.3	392.6	509.5	295.2
Apr	1,206.2	396.5	512.4	297.3
May	1,209.5	397.5	514.3	297.7
June	1,211.7	399.8	516.2	295.8
July	1,216.1	403.2	520.2	292.6
Aug	1,222.2	403.2	523.7	295.3
Sept	1,223.8	405.7	526.4	291.7
Oct	1,235.2	410.4	529.9	294.9
Nov [p]	1,231.0	409.1	528.1	293.8

[1] Covers most short- and intermediate-term credit extended to individuals through regular business channels, usually to finance the purchase of consumer goods and services or to refinance debts incurred for such purposes. Credit secured by real estate is excluded.

[2] Consists of credit cards at retailers, gasoline companies, and commercial banks, and check credit at commercial banks. Excludes 30-day charge credit held by travel and entertainment companies. Prior to 1968, included in "other." Beginning 1977, includes open-end credit at retailers, previously included in "other." Also beginning 1977, some retail credit was reclassified from commercial into consumer credit.

[3] Includes mobile home loans and all other loans not included in automobile or revolving credit, such as loans for education, boats, trailers, or vacations. These loans may be secured or unsecured.

[4] Data newly available in January 1989 result in breaks in many series between December 1988 and subsequent months.

Source: Board of Governors of the Federal Reserve System.

TABLE B–78.—*Federal receipts, outlays, surplus or deficit, and debt, selected fiscal years, 1929–99*

[Billions of dollars; fiscal years]

Fiscal year or period	Total			On-budget			Off-budget			Federal debt (end of period)		Addendum: Gross domestic product
	Receipts	Outlays	Surplus or deficit (–)	Receipts	Outlays	Surplus or deficit (–)	Receipts	Outlays	Surplus or deficit (–)	Gross Federal	Held by the public	
1929	3.9	3.1	0.7	3.9	3.1	0.7	....	....	....	¹16.9	....	....
1933	2.0	4.6	–2.6	2.0	4.6	–2.6	....	....	....	¹22.5	....	57.4
1939	6.3	9.1	–2.8	5.8	9.2	–3.4	0.5	–0.0	0.5	48.2	41.4	88.9
1940	6.5	9.5	–2.9	6.0	9.5	–3.5	.6	–.0	.6	50.7	42.8	96.5
1941	8.7	13.7	–4.9	8.0	13.6	–5.6	.7	.0	.7	57.5	48.2	113.9
1942	14.6	35.1	–20.5	13.7	35.1	–21.3	.9	.1	.8	79.2	67.8	144.2
1943	24.0	78.6	–54.6	22.9	78.5	–55.6	1.1	.1	1.0	142.6	127.8	180.0
1944	43.7	91.3	–47.6	42.5	91.2	–48.7	1.3	.1	1.2	204.1	184.8	209.0
1945	45.2	92.7	–47.6	43.8	92.6	–48.7	1.3	.1	1.2	260.1	235.2	221.4
1946	39.3	55.2	–15.9	38.1	55.0	–17.0	1.2	.2	1.0	271.0	241.9	222.9
1947	38.5	34.5	4.0	37.1	34.2	2.9	1.5	.3	1.2	257.1	224.3	234.9
1948	41.6	29.8	11.8	39.9	29.4	10.5	1.6	.4	1.2	252.0	216.3	256.6
1949	39.4	38.8	.6	37.7	38.4	–.7	1.7	.4	1.3	252.6	214.3	271.7
1950	39.4	42.6	–3.1	37.3	42.0	–4.7	2.1	.5	1.6	256.9	219.0	273.6
1951	51.6	45.5	6.1	48.5	44.2	4.3	3.1	1.3	1.8	255.3	214.3	321.3
1952	66.2	67.7	–1.5	62.6	66.0	–3.4	3.6	1.7	1.9	259.1	214.8	348.9
1953	69.6	76.1	–6.5	65.5	73.8	–8.3	4.1	2.3	1.8	266.0	218.4	373.1
1954	69.7	70.9	–1.2	65.1	67.9	–2.8	4.6	2.9	1.7	270.8	224.5	378.0
1955	65.5	68.4	–3.0	60.4	64.5	–4.1	5.1	4.0	1.1	274.4	226.6	395.3
1956	74.6	70.6	3.9	68.2	65.7	2.5	6.4	5.0	1.5	272.7	222.2	427.6
1957	80.0	76.6	3.4	73.2	70.6	2.6	6.8	6.0	.8	272.3	219.3	450.5
1958	79.6	82.4	–2.8	71.6	74.9	–3.3	8.0	7.5	.5	279.7	226.3	460.6
1959	79.2	92.1	–12.8	71.0	83.1	–12.1	8.3	9.0	–.7	287.5	234.7	491.8
1960	92.5	92.2	.3	81.9	81.3	.5	10.6	10.9	–.2	290.5	236.8	518.2
1961	94.4	97.7	–3.3	82.3	86.0	–3.8	12.1	11.7	.4	292.6	238.4	530.9
1962	99.7	106.8	–7.1	87.4	93.3	–5.9	12.3	13.5	–1.3	302.9	248.0	567.5
1963	106.6	111.3	–4.8	92.4	96.4	–4.0	14.2	15.0	–.8	310.3	254.0	598.3
1964	112.6	118.5	–5.9	96.2	102.8	–6.5	16.4	15.7	.6	316.1	256.8	640.0
1965	116.8	118.2	–1.4	100.1	101.7	–1.6	16.7	16.5	.2	322.3	260.8	686.7
1966	130.8	134.5	–3.7	111.7	114.8	–3.1	19.1	19.7	–.6	328.5	263.7	752.8
1967	148.8	157.5	–8.6	124.4	137.0	–12.6	24.4	20.4	4.0	340.4	266.6	811.9
1968	153.0	178.1	–25.2	128.1	155.8	–27.7	24.9	22.3	2.6	368.7	289.5	868.1
1969	186.9	183.6	3.2	157.9	158.4	–.5	29.0	25.2	3.7	365.8	278.1	947.9
1970	192.8	195.6	–2.8	159.3	168.0	–8.7	33.5	27.6	5.9	380.9	283.2	1,009.0
1971	187.1	210.2	–23.0	151.3	177.3	–26.1	35.8	32.8	3.0	408.2	303.0	1,077.7
1972	207.3	230.7	–23.4	167.4	193.8	–26.4	39.9	36.9	3.1	435.9	322.4	1,176.9
1973	230.8	245.7	–14.9	184.7	200.1	–15.4	46.1	45.6	.5	466.3	340.9	1,306.8
1974	263.2	269.4	–6.1	209.3	217.3	–8.0	53.9	52.1	1.8	483.9	343.7	1,438.1
1975	279.1	332.3	–53.2	216.6	271.9	–55.3	62.5	60.4	2.0	541.9	394.7	1,554.5
1976	298.1	371.8	–73.7	231.7	302.2	–70.5	66.4	69.6	–3.2	629.0	477.4	1,730.4
Transition quarter	81.2	96.0	–14.7	63.2	76.6	–13.3	18.0	19.4	–1.4	643.6	495.5	454.8
1977	355.6	409.2	–53.7	278.7	328.5	–49.8	76.8	80.7	–3.9	706.4	549.1	1,971.4
1978	399.6	458.7	–59.2	314.2	369.1	–54.9	85.4	89.7	–4.3	776.6	607.1	2,212.6
1979	463.3	504.0	–40.7	365.3	404.1	–38.7	98.0	100.0	–2.0	829.5	640.3	2,495.9
1980	517.1	590.9	–73.8	403.9	476.6	–72.7	113.2	114.3	–1.1	909.1	709.8	2,718.9
1981	599.3	678.2	–79.0	469.1	543.1	–74.0	130.2	135.2	–5.0	994.8	785.3	3,049.1
1982	617.8	745.8	–128.0	474.3	594.4	–120.1	143.5	151.4	–7.9	1,137.3	919.8	3,211.3
1983	600.6	808.4	–207.8	453.2	661.3	–208.0	147.3	147.1	.2	1,371.7	1,131.6	3,421.9
1984	666.5	851.9	–185.4	500.4	686.1	–185.7	166.1	165.8	.3	1,564.7	1,300.5	3,812.0
1985	734.1	946.4	–212.3	547.9	769.6	–221.7	186.2	176.8	9.4	1,817.5	1,499.9	4,102.1
1986	769.2	990.5	–221.2	569.0	807.0	–238.0	200.2	183.5	16.7	2,120.6	1,736.7	4,374.3
1987	854.4	1,004.1	–149.8	641.0	810.3	–169.3	213.4	193.8	19.6	2,346.1	1,888.7	4,605.1
1988	909.3	1,064.5	–155.2	667.8	861.8	–194.0	241.5	202.7	38.8	2,601.3	2,050.8	4,953.5
1989	991.2	1,143.7	–152.5	727.5	932.8	–205.2	263.7	210.9	52.8	2,868.0	2,189.9	5,351.8
1990	1,032.0	1,253.2	–221.2	750.3	1,028.1	–277.8	281.7	225.1	56.6	3,206.6	2,410.7	5,684.5
1991	1,055.0	1,324.4	–269.4	761.2	1,082.7	–321.6	293.9	241.7	52.2	3,598.5	2,688.1	5,858.8
1992	1,091.3	1,381.7	–290.4	788.9	1,129.3	–340.5	302.4	252.3	50.1	4,002.1	2,998.8	6,143.2
1993	1,154.4	1,409.4	–255.0	842.5	1,142.8	–300.4	311.9	266.6	45.3	4,351.4	3,247.5	6,475.1
1994	1,258.6	1,461.7	–203.1	923.6	1,182.4	–258.8	335.0	279.4	55.7	4,643.7	3,432.1	6,845.7
1995	1,351.8	1,515.7	–163.9	1,000.8	1,227.1	–226.3	351.1	288.7	62.4	4,921.0	3,603.4	7,194.8
1996	1,453.1	1,560.5	–107.5	1,085.6	1,259.6	–174.0	367.5	300.9	66.6	5,181.9	3,733.0	7,529.8
1997	1,579.3	1,601.2	–21.9	1,187.3	1,290.6	–103.3	392.0	310.6	81.4	5,369.7	3,771.1	7,972.4
1998²	1,657.9	1,667.8	–10.0	1,241.9	1,348.1	–106.3	416.0	319.7	96.3	5,543.6	3,796.8	8,348.0
1999²	1,742.7	1,733.2	9.5	1,308.6	1,404.4	–95.7	434.1	328.9	105.3	5,738.1	3,807.3	8,684.6

¹ Not strictly comparable with later data.
² Estimates.

Note.—Through fiscal year 1976, the fiscal year was on a July 1–June 30 basis; beginning October 1976 (fiscal year 1977), the fiscal year is on an October 1–September 30 basis. The 3-month period from July 1, 1976 through September 30, 1976 is a separate fiscal period known as the transition quarter.
Refunds of receipts are excluded from receipts and outlays.
See *Budget of the United States Government, Fiscal Year 1999*, February 1998, for additional information.

Sources: Department of Commerce (Bureau of Economic Analysis), Department of the Treasury, and Office of Management and Budget.

—*Federal budget receipts, outlays, surplus or deficit, and debt, as percent of gross domestic product, fiscal years 1934–99*

[Percent; fiscal years]

Fiscal year or period	Receipts	Outlays		Surplus or deficit (−)	Federal debt (end of period)	
		Total	National defense		Gross Federal	Held by public
1934	4.8	10.7		−5.9		
1935	5.2	9.2		−4.0		
1936	5.0	10.5		−5.5		
1937	6.1	8.6		−2.5		
1938	7.6	7.7		−.1		
1939	7.1	10.3		−3.2	54.2	46.6
1940	6.8	9.8	1.7	−3.0	52.5	44.3
1941	7.6	12.0	5.6	−4.3	50.5	42.3
1942	10.1	24.4	17.8	−14.2	54.9	47.0
1943	13.3	43.6	37.1	−30.3	79.2	71.0
1944	20.9	43.7	37.9	−22.8	97.6	88.4
1945	20.4	41.9	37.5	−21.5	117.5	106.2
1946	17.6	24.8	19.1	−7.1	121.6	108.5
1947	16.4	14.7	5.5	1.7	109.5	95.5
1948	1C.2	11.6	3.5	4.6	98.2	84.3
1949	14.5	14.3	4.8	.2	93.0	78.9
1950	14.4	15.6	5.0	−1.1	93.9	80.1
1951	16.1	14.2	7.3	1.9	79.5	66.7
1952	19.0	19.4	13.2	−.4	74.3	61.6
1953	18.7	20.4	14.2	−1.7	71.3	58.5
1954	18.4	18.7	13.0	−.3	71.6	59.4
1955	16.6	17.3	10.8	−.8	69.4	57.3
1956	17.4	16.5	9.9	.9	63.8	52.0
1957	17.8	17.0	10.1	.8	60.4	48.7
1958	17.3	17.9	10.2	−.6	60.7	49.1
1959	16.1	18.7	10.0	−2.6	58.5	47.7
1960	17.8	17.8	9.3	.1	56.1	45.7
1961	17.8	18.4	9.3	−.6	55.1	44.9
1962	17.6	18.8	9.2	−1.3	53.4	43.7
1963	17.8	18.6	8.9	−.8	51.9	42.5
1964	17.6	18.5	8.6	−.9	49.4	40.1
1965	17.0	17.2	7.4	−.2	46.9	38.0
1966	17.4	17.9	7.7	−.5	43.6	35.0
1967	18.3	19.4	8.8	−1.1	41.9	32.8
1968	17.6	20.5	9.4	−2.9	42.5	33.4
1969	19.7	19.4	8.7	.3	38.6	29.3
1970	19.1	19.4	8.1	−.3	37.8	28.1
1971	17.4	19.5	7.3	−2.1	37.9	28.1
1972	17.6	19.6	6.7	−2.0	37.0	27.4
1973	17.7	18.8	5.9	−1.1	35.7	26.1
1974	18.3	18.7	5.5	−.4	33.6	23.9
1975	18.0	21.4	5.6	−3.4	34.9	25.4
1976	17.2	21.5	5.2	−4.3	36.3	27.6
Transition quarter	17.9	21.1	4.9	−3.2	35.4	27.2
1977	18.0	20.8	4.9	−2.7	35.8	27.9
1978	18.1	20.7	4.7	−2.7	35.1	27.4
1979	18.6	20.2	4.7	−1.6	33.2	25.7
1980	19.0	21.7	4.9	−2.7	33.4	26.1
1981	19.7	22.2	5.2	−2.6	32.6	25.8
1982	19.2	23.2	5.8	−4.0	35.4	28.6
1983	17.6	23.6	6.1	−6.1	40.1	33.1
1984	17.5	22.3	6.0	−4.9	41.0	34.1
1985	17.9	23.1	6.2	−5.2	44.3	36.6
1986	17.6	22.6	6.2	−5.1	48.5	39.7
1987	18.6	21.8	6.1	−3.3	50.9	41.0
1988	18.4	21.5	5.9	−3.1	52.5	41.4
1989	18.5	21.4	5.7	−2.8	53.6	40.9
1990	18.2	22.0	5.3	−3.9	56.4	42.4
1991	18.0	22.6	4.7	−4.6	61.4	45.9
1992	17.8	22.5	4.9	−4.7	65.1	48.8
1993	17.8	21.8	4.5	−3.9	67.2	50.2
1994	18.4	21.4	4.1	−3.0	67.8	50.1
1995	18.8	21.1	3.8	−2.3	68.4	50.1
1996	19.3	20.7	3.5	−1.4	68.8	49.6
1997	19.8	20.1	3.4	−.3	67.4	47.3
1998[1]	19.9	20.0	3.2	−.1	66.4	45.5
1999[1]	20.1	20.0	3.1	.1	66.1	43.8

[1] Estimates.

Note.—See Note, Table B–78.

Sources: Department of the Treasury and Office of Management and Budget.

TABLE B–80.—*Federal receipts and outlays, by major category, and surplus or deficit, fiscal years 1940–99*

[Billions of dollars; fiscal years]

Fiscal year or period	Receipts (on-budget and off-budget)					Outlays (on-budget and off-budget)											Surplus or deficit (–) (on-budget and off-budget)
	Total	Individual income taxes	Corporation income taxes	Social insurance and retirement receipts	Other	Total	National defense		International affairs	Health	Medicare	Income security	Social security	Net interest	Other	
							Total	Department of Defense, military								
1940	6.5	0.9	1.2	1.8	2.7	9.5	1.7		0.1	0.1		1.5	0.0	0.9	5.3	-2.9
1941	8.7	1.3	2.1	1.9	3.3	13.7	6.4		.1	.1		1.9	.1	.9	4.1	-4.9
1942	14.6	3.3	4.7	2.5	4.2	35.1	25.7		1.0	.1		1.8	.1	1.1	5.4	-20.5
1943	24.0	6.5	9.6	3.0	4.9	78.6	66.7		1.3	.1		1.7	.2	1.5	7.0	-54.6
1944	43.7	19.7	14.8	3.5	5.7	91.3	79.1		1.4	.2		1.5	.2	2.2	6.6	-47.6
1945	45.2	18.4	16.0	3.5	7.3	92.7	83.0		1.9	.2		1.1	.3	3.1	3.1	-47.6
1946	39.3	16.1	11.9	3.1	8.2	55.2	42.7		1.9	.2		2.4	.4	4.1	3.6	-15.9
1947	38.5	17.9	8.6	3.4	8.5	34.5	12.8		5.8	.2		2.8	.5	4.2	8.2	4.0
1948	41.6	19.3	9.7	3.8	8.8	29.8	9.1		4.6	.2		2.5	.6	4.3	8.5	11.8
1949	39.4	15.6	11.2	3.8	8.9	38.8	13.2		6.1	.2		3.2	.7	4.5	11.1	.6
1950	39.4	15.8	10.4	4.3	8.9	42.6	13.7		4.7	.3		4.1	.8	4.8	14.2	-3.1
1951	51.6	21.6	14.1	5.7	10.2	45.5	23.6		3.6	.3		3.4	1.6	4.7	8.4	6.1
1952	66.2	27.9	21.2	6.4	10.6	67.7	46.1		2.7	.3		3.7	2.1	4.7	8.1	-1.5
1953	69.6	29.8	21.2	6.8	11.7	76.1	52.8		2.1	.3		3.8	2.7	5.2	9.1	-6.5
1954	69.7	29.5	21.1	7.2	11.9	70.9	49.3		1.6	.3		4.4	3.4	4.8	7.1	-1.2
1955	65.5	28.7	17.9	7.9	11.0	68.4	42.7		2.2	.3		5.1	4.4	4.9	8.9	-3.0
1956	74.6	32.2	20.9	9.3	12.2	70.6	42.5		2.4	.4		4.7	5.5	5.1	10.1	3.9
1957	80.0	35.6	21.2	10.0	13.2	76.6	45.4		3.1	.5		5.4	6.7	5.4	10.1	3.4
1958	79.6	34.7	20.1	11.2	13.6	82.4	46.8		3.4	.5		7.5	8.2	5.6	10.3	-2.8
1959	79.2	36.7	17.3	11.7	13.5	92.1	49.0		3.1	.7		8.2	9.7	5.8	15.5	-12.8
1960	92.5	40.7	21.5	14.7	15.6	92.2	48.1		3.0	.8		7.4	11.6	6.9	14.4	.3
1961	94.4	41.3	21.0	16.4	15.7	97.7	49.6		3.2	.9		9.7	12.5	6.7	15.2	-3.3
1962	99.7	45.6	20.5	17.0	16.5	106.8	52.3	50.1	5.6	1.2		9.2	14.4	6.9	17.2	-7.1
1963	106.6	47.6	21.6	19.8	17.6	111.3	53.4	51.1	5.3	1.5		9.3	15.8	7.7	18.3	-4.8
1964	112.6	48.7	23.5	22.0	18.5	118.5	54.8	52.6	4.9	1.8		9.7	16.6	8.2	22.6	-5.9
1965	116.8	48.8	25.5	22.2	20.3	118.2	50.6	48.8	5.3	1.8		9.5	17.5	8.6	25.0	-1.4
1966	130.8	55.4	30.1	25.5	19.8	134.5	58.1	56.6	5.6	2.5	0.1	9.7	20.7	9.4	28.5	-3.7
1967	148.8	61.5	34.0	32.6	20.7	157.5	71.4	70.1	5.6	3.4	2.7	10.3	21.7	10.3	32.1	-8.6
1968	153.0	68.7	28.7	33.9	21.7	178.1	81.9	80.4	5.3	4.4	4.6	11.8	23.9	11.1	35.1	-25.2
1969	186.9	87.2	36.7	39.0	23.9	183.6	82.5	80.8	4.6	5.2	5.7	13.1	27.3	12.7	32.6	3.2
1970	192.8	90.4	32.8	44.4	25.2	195.6	81.7	80.1	4.3	5.9	6.2	15.7	30.3	14.4	37.2	-2.8
1971	187.1	86.2	26.8	47.3	26.8	210.2	78.9	77.5	4.2	6.8	6.6	22.9	35.9	14.8	40.0	-23.0
1972	207.3	94.7	32.2	52.6	27.8	230.7	79.2	77.6	4.8	8.7	7.5	27.7	40.2	15.5	47.3	-23.4
1973	230.8	103.2	36.2	63.1	28.3	245.7	76.7	75.0	4.1	9.4	8.1	28.3	49.1	17.3	52.8	-14.9
1974	263.2	119.0	38.6	75.1	30.6	269.4	79.3	77.9	5.7	10.7	9.6	33.7	55.9	21.4	52.9	-6.1
1975	279.1	122.4	40.6	84.5	31.5	332.3	86.5	84.9	7.1	12.9	12.9	50.2	64.7	23.2	74.8	-53.2
1976	298.1	131.6	41.4	90.8	34.3	371.8	89.6	87.9	6.4	15.7	15.8	60.8	73.9	26.7	82.7	-73.7
Transition quarter	81.2	38.8	8.5	25.2	8.8	96.0	22.3	21.8	2.5	3.9	4.3	15.0	19.8	6.9	21.4	-14.7
1977	355.6	157.6	54.9	106.5	36.6	409.2	97.2	95.1	6.4	17.3	19.3	61.1	85.1	29.9	93.0	-53.7
1978	399.6	181.0	60.0	121.0	37.7	458.7	104.5	102.3	7.5	18.5	22.8	61.5	93.9	35.5	114.7	-59.2
1979	463.3	217.8	65.7	138.9	40.8	504.0	116.3	113.6	7.5	20.5	26.5	66.4	104.1	42.6	120.2	-40.7
1980	517.1	244.1	64.6	157.8	50.6	590.9	134.0	130.9	12.7	23.2	32.1	86.6	118.5	52.5	131.3	-73.8
1981	599.3	285.9	61.1	182.7	69.5	678.2	157.5	153.9	13.1	26.9	39.1	99.7	139.6	68.8	133.5	-79.0
1982	617.8	297.7	49.2	201.5	69.3	745.8	185.3	180.7	12.3	27.4	46.6	107.7	156.0	85.0	125.4	-128.0
1983	600.6	288.9	37.0	209.0	65.6	808.4	209.9	204.4	11.8	28.6	52.6	122.6	170.7	89.8	122.2	-207.8
1984	666.5	298.4	56.9	239.4	71.8	851.9	227.4	220.9	15.9	30.4	57.5	112.7	178.2	111.1	118.6	-185.4
1985	734.1	334.5	61.3	265.2	73.1	946.4	252.7	245.2	16.2	33.5	65.8	128.2	188.6	129.5	131.8	-212.3
1986	769.2	349.0	63.1	283.9	73.2	990.5	273.4	265.5	14.2	35.9	70.2	119.8	198.8	136.0	142.2	-221.2
1987	854.4	392.6	83.9	303.3	74.6	1,004.1	282.0	274.0	11.6	40.0	75.1	123.3	207.4	138.7	126.1	-149.8
1988	909.3	401.2	94.5	334.3	79.3	1,064.5	290.4	281.9	10.5	44.5	78.9	129.4	219.3	151.8	139.7	-155.2
1989	991.2	445.7	103.3	359.4	82.8	1,143.7	303.6	294.9	9.6	48.4	85.0	136.1	232.5	169.3	159.3	-152.5
1990	1,032.0	466.9	93.5	380.0	91.5	1,253.2	299.3	289.8	13.8	57.7	98.1	147.1	248.6	184.2	204.3	-221.2
1991	1,055.0	467.8	98.1	396.0	93.1	1,324.4	273.3	262.4	15.9	71.2	104.5	170.3	269.0	194.5	225.7	-269.4
1992	1,091.3	476.0	100.3	413.7	101.4	1,381.7	298.4	286.9	16.1	89.5	119.0	197.0	287.6	199.4	174.7	-290.4
1993	1,154.4	509.7	117.5	428.3	98.9	1,409.4	291.1	278.6	17.2	99.4	130.6	207.3	304.6	198.8	160.4	-255.0
1994	1,258.6	543.1	140.4	461.5	113.7	1,461.7	281.6	268.6	17.1	107.1	144.7	214.1	319.6	203.0	174.5	-203.1
1995	1,351.8	590.2	157.0	484.5	120.1	1,515.7	272.1	259.4	16.4	115.4	159.9	220.5	335.8	232.2	163.4	-163.9
1996	1,453.1	656.4	171.8	509.4	115.4	1,560.5	265.7	253.2	13.5	119.4	174.2	226.0	349.7	241.1	170.9	-107.5
1997	1,579.3	737.5	182.3	539.4	120.2	1,601.2	270.5	258.3	15.2	123.8	190.0	230.9	365.3	244.0	161.5	-21.9
1998 [1]	1,657.9	767.8	190.8	571.4	127.9	1,667.8	264.1	251.4	14.5	131.8	198.1	239.3	381.5	242.7	195.8	-10.0
1999 [1]	1,742.7	791.5	198.0	595.9	157.4	1,733.2	265.5	252.7	14.5	141.5	207.3	252.8	396.2	241.8	213.8	9.5

[1] Estimates.

Note.—See Note, Table B–78.

Sources: Department of the Treasury and Office of Management and Budget.

[Millions of dollars; fiscal years]

Description	Actual					Estimates	
	1993	1994	1995	1996	1997	1998	1999
RECEIPTS AND OUTLAYS:							
Total receipts	1,154,401	1,258,627	1,351,830	1,453,062	1,579,292	1,657,858	1,742,736
Total outlays	1,409,414	1,461,731	1,515,729	1,560,512	1,601,235	1,667,815	1,733,217
Total surplus or deficit (-)	-255,013	-203,104	-163,899	-107,450	-21,943	-9,957	9,519
On-budget receipts	842,467	923,601	1,000,751	1,085,570	1,187,302	1,241,867	1,308,608
On-budget outlays	1,142,827	1,182,359	1,227,065	1,259,608	1,290,609	1,348,140	1,404,355
On-budget surplus or deficit (-)	-300,360	-258,758	-226,314	-174,038	-103,307	-106,273	-95,747
Off-budget receipts	311,934	335,026	351,079	367,492	391,990	415,991	434,128
Off-budget outlays	266,587	279,372	288,664	300,904	310,626	319,675	328,862
Off-budget surplus or deficit (-)	45,347	55,654	62,415	66,588	81,364	96,316	105,266
OUTSTANDING DEBT, END OF PERIOD:							
Gross Federal debt	4,351,416	4,643,705	4,921,018	5,181,934	5,369,707	5,543,589	5,738,119
Held by Government accounts	1,103,945	1,211,588	1,317,645	1,448,967	1,598,559	1,746,773	1,930,829
Held by the public	3,247,471	3,432,117	3,603,373	3,732,968	3,771,148	3,796,816	3,807,290
Federal Reserve System	325,653	355,150	374,114	390,924	424,507		
Other	2,921,818	3,076,967	3,229,259	3,342,043	3,346,641		
RECEIPTS: ON-BUDGET AND OFF-BUDGET	1,154,401	1,258,627	1,351,830	1,453,062	1,579,292	1,657,858	1,742,736
Individual income taxes	509,680	543,055	590,244	656,417	737,466	767,768	791,454
Corporation income taxes	117,520	140,385	157,004	171,824	182,293	190,842	197,965
Social insurance and retirement receipts	428,300	461,475	484,473	509,414	539,371	571,374	595,886
On-budget	116,366	126,450	133,394	141,922	147,381	155,383	161,758
Off-budget	311,934	335,026	351,079	367,492	391,990	415,991	434,128
Excise taxes	48,057	55,225	57,484	54,014	56,924	55,540	72,009
Estate and gift taxes	12,577	15,225	14,763	17,189	19,845	20,436	20,541
Customs duties and fees	18,802	20,099	19,301	18,670	17,928	18,363	18,175
Miscellaneous receipts:							
Deposits of earnings by Federal Reserve System	14,908	18,023	23,378	20,477	19,636	24,991	24,642
All other [1]	4,557	5,141	5,183	5,057	5,829	8,544	22,064
OUTLAYS: ON-BUDGET AND OFF-BUDGET	1,409,414	1,461,731	1,515,729	1,560,512	1,601,235	1,667,815	1,733,217
National defense	291,086	281,642	272,066	265,748	270,473	264,112	265,489
International affairs	17,248	17,083	16,434	13,496	15,228	14,480	14,463
General science, space, and technology	17,030	16,227	16,724	16,709	17,174	17,093	17,616
Energy	4,319	5,219	4,936	2,844	1,483	403	-1,045
Natural resources and environment	20,239	21,064	22,078	21,614	21,369	23,822	23,237
Agriculture	20,363	15,046	9,778	9,159	9,032	10,580	11,017
Commerce and housing credit	-21,853	-4,228	-17,808	-10,472	-14,624	3,525	3,541
On-budget	-23,294	-5,331	-15,839	-10,292	-14,575	1,804	2,695
Off-budget	1,441	1,103	-1,969	-180	-49	1,721	846
Transportation	35,004	38,066	39,350	39,565	40,767	41,535	42,259
Community and regional development	9,052	10,454	10,641	10,685	11,005	11,802	10,918
Education, training, employment, and social services	50,012	46,307	54,263	52,001	53,008	55,114	59,488
Health	99,415	107,122	115,418	119,378	123,843	131,772	141,457
Medicare	130,552	144,747	159,855	174,225	190,016	198,135	207,271
Income security	207,299	214,089	220,493	225,989	230,886	239,349	252,808
Social security	304,585	319,565	335,846	349,676	365,257	381,499	396,217
On-budget	6,236	5,683	5,476	5,807	6,885	9,660	8,911
Off-budget	298,349	313,881	330,370	343,869	358,372	371,839	387,306
Veterans benefits and services	35,671	37,584	37,890	36,985	39,313	43,114	43,272
Administration of justice	14,955	15,256	16,216	17,548	20,197	22,274	25,524
General government	13,009	11,303	13,835	11,892	12,768	12,878	17,173
Net interest	198,811	202,957	232,169	241,090	244,013	242,694	241,754
On-budget	225,599	232,160	265,474	277,597	285,227	289,424	293,377
Off-budget	-26,788	-29,203	-33,305	-36,507	-41,214	-46,730	-51,623
Allowances							3,250
Undistributed offsetting receipts	-37,386	-37,772	-44,455	-37,620	-49,973	-46,366	-42,492
On-budget	-30,970	-31,362	-38,023	-31,342	-43,490	-39,211	-34,825
Off-budget	-6,416	-6,409	-6,432	-6,278	-6,483	-7,155	-7,667

[1] Beginning 1984, includes universal service fund receipts. Beginning 1999, includes receipts from tobacco legislation.

Note.—See Note, Table B-78.

Sources: Department of the Treasury and Office of Management and Budget.

TABLE B–82.—*Federal Government receipts and current expenditures, national income and product accounts (NIPA), 1978–97*

[Billions of dollars; quarterly data at seasonally adjusted annual rates]

Year or quarter	Receipts					Current expenditures								
							Consumption expenditures		Transfer payments		Grants-in-aid to State and local governments	Net interest paid	Subsidies less current surplus of government enterprises	Current surplus or deficit (−) (NIPA)
	Total	Personal tax and nontax receipts	Corporate profits tax accruals	Indirect business tax and nontax accruals	Contributions for social insurance	Total[1]	Total	National defense	To persons	To rest of the world (net)				
Fiscal:														
1978	429.2	185.5	67.4	27.9	148.4	467.5	165.5	116.2	179.3	3.5	74.7	33.1	11.6	−38.3
1979	497.0	221.6	75.3	29.9	170.2	514.8	181.2	126.9	198.5	4.0	79.1	40.2	11.7	−17.8
1980	546.7	249.1	70.4	36.2	190.9	597.0	207.5	145.3	235.4	4.3	86.7	50.1	13.0	−50.3
1981	633.5	287.9	69.3	54.3	222.0	690.1	239.0	168.6	274.6	5.2	90.1	66.1	15.2	−56.6
1982	653.7	308.4	51.6	51.5	242.2	758.5	263.7	192.2	305.6	6.3	83.4	81.8	17.7	−104.8
1983	658.1	291.0	56.4	51.6	259.1	836.2	291.4	211.6	339.9	7.0	86.2	89.9	21.4	−178.1
1984	723.7	300.7	75.1	57.4	290.5	878.7	298.8	224.1	342.4	9.0	91.6	107.2	29.9	−155.1
1985	798.7	337.8	75.0	58.9	326.9	957.2	333.5	250.1	360.7	12.3	98.6	125.4	26.6	−158.6
1986	836.4	353.6	80.5	53.7	348.7	1,017.9	359.1	271.3	380.6	13.3	108.2	129.9	26.7	−181.4
1987	922.5	398.3	99.3	56.4	368.5	1,051.1	373.4	283.0	399.4	10.7	103.3	134.2	30.2	−128.6
1988	981.5	407.9	107.7	60.4	405.6	1,106.4	385.4	296.3	420.5	11.1	108.4	146.5	34.4	−124.9
1989	1,069.9	458.3	119.1	61.7	430.8	1,173.4	401.4	301.8	449.7	11.7	115.8	161.9	32.9	−103.5
1990	1,112.5	477.3	116.5	63.6	455.1	1,261.9	419.9	308.8	490.7	14.9	128.4	178.5	29.5	−149.4
1991	1,141.5	477.4	111.5	75.8	476.7	1,319.9	444.4	326.0	535.7	−26.0	147.1	187.1	31.7	−178.4
1992	1,181.0	485.8	115.4	80.9	499.0	1,455.3	447.6	318.0	595.8	11.5	168.4	197.9	34.1	−274.3
1993	1,251.8	513.3	130.6	85.2	522.7	1,512.6	449.9	313.2	634.3	17.3	180.3	192.2	38.7	−260.8
1994	1,356.5	555.2	152.5	97.1	551.7	1,555.1	445.6	305.7	661.9	16.4	197.2	195.6	38.4	−198.6
1995	1,452.2	598.6	180.0	95.2	578.4	1,628.9	444.9	300.5	699.9	14.3	211.9	220.3	37.5	−176.7
1996	1,551.9	668.6	192.4	91.1	599.8	1,672.2	442.1	298.1	737.3	13.6	215.3	226.2	37.7	−120.2
1997	1,691.9	757.3	206.0	92.1	635.5	1,736.2	457.5	307.5	774.1	12.2	220.0	234.2	38.2	−44.3
Calendar:														
1978	446.5	193.8	71.4	28.9	152.4	478.1	168.8	118.4	182.4	3.8	77.3	34.6	11.4	−31.7
1979	511.1	229.7	74.4	30.1	176.8	529.5	185.9	130.7	205.7	4.1	80.5	42.1	11.3	−18.4
1980	561.5	256.2	70.3	39.7	195.3	622.5	215.2	150.9	247.0	5.0	88.7	52.7	13.9	−61.0
1981	649.3	297.2	65.7	57.3	229.1	707.1	246.0	174.3	282.1	5.0	87.9	71.7	14.4	−57.8
1982	646.4	302.9	49.0	49.7	244.8	781.0	270.0	197.6	316.4	7.0	83.9	84.4	19.4	−134.7
1983	671.9	293.0	61.3	53.3	264.2	846.3	293.0	214.9	340.0	7.8	87.0	92.8	25.4	−174.4
1984	746.9	308.3	75.2	57.9	305.3	902.9	314.1	236.3	344.6	9.7	94.4	113.3	27.1	−156.0
1985	811.3	343.7	76.3	58.2	333.1	974.2	342.5	257.6	366.9	12.2	100.3	126.9	25.2	−162.9
1986	850.1	358.3	83.8	53.2	354.7	1,027.6	362.3	272.7	386.2	12.9	107.6	130.5	28.0	−177.5
1987	937.4	402.4	103.2	57.8	374.1	1,066.3	378.2	287.6	401.8	11.2	102.9	137.8	34.4	−128.9
1988	997.2	414.4	111.0	60.9	410.9	1,118.5	387.8	297.9	425.8	11.4	111.2	148.4	33.8	−121.3
1989	1,079.3	463.4	117.1	61.7	437.1	1,192.7	405.2	303.3	460.3	11.4	118.2	166.7	30.8	−113.4
1990	1,129.8	485.7	118.0	65.1	461.1	1,284.5	426.6	312.7	500.0	13.3	132.4	179.9	32.4	−154.7
1991	1,149.0	476.9	109.8	79.7	482.6	1,345.0	445.9	325.4	550.1	−27.9	153.4	192.7	30.8	−196.0
1992	1,198.5	490.8	118.6	81.9	507.1	1,479.4	451.0	319.7	608.5	16.6	172.2	195.8	35.1	−280.9
1993	1,275.1	522.6	138.3	86.9	527.3	1,525.7	447.3	311.1	642.6	17.3	185.8	192.7	40.1	−250.7
1994	1,374.8	562.3	156.7	98.7	557.1	1,561.4	443.2	301.6	666.6	16.4	199.2	200.0	35.9	−186.7
1995	1,463.2	605.8	182.1	93.5	581.8	1,637.6	443.5	298.6	709.4	11.5	211.9	224.8	36.4	−174.4
1996	1,587.6	686.7	194.5	95.8	610.5	1,698.1	451.5	305.7	747.2	16.3	218.3	227.1	37.7	−110.5
1997 P	....	773.6	....	91.3	645.8	1,751.9	464.1	311.2	782.3	13.2	223.8	230.4	38.2	....
1992: I	1,183.4	481.0	119.6	80.8	502.0	1,450.7	445.8	317.2	598.7	12.4	165.4	196.8	31.8	−267.4
II	1,193.1	481.6	125.3	80.2	506.1	1,472.8	446.3	317.3	606.9	15.0	173.0	198.4	33.1	−279.6
III	1,187.0	490.7	106.0	80.2	510.1	1,484.5	454.4	323.5	611.3	12.9	174.2	196.4	35.3	−297.5
IV	1,230.5	510.0	123.7	86.5	510.3	1,509.5	457.7	320.7	617.2	26.1	176.3	191.8	40.3	−279.0
1993: I	1,227.1	500.8	125.2	82.6	518.5	1,505.3	447.1	312.4	634.5	12.6	177.2	192.2	41.7	−278.2
II	1,268.8	519.1	138.5	85.5	525.8	1,518.0	445.8	311.5	640.9	14.8	181.9	193.1	41.6	−249.2
III	1,277.2	527.1	135.0	85.9	529.3	1,527.8	447.0	310.6	645.8	15.5	187.3	192.9	39.2	−250.6
IV	1,327.2	543.4	154.5	93.8	535.5	1,551.9	449.2	309.8	649.3	26.2	196.9	192.5	37.8	−224.6
1994: I	1,324.5	542.0	136.9	98.2	547.4	1,533.5	442.4	299.8	659.5	11.2	194.5	189.9	36.0	−209.0
II	1,381.1	574.3	153.4	98.1	555.3	1,544.3	439.2	300.7	663.9	12.9	196.2	196.6	35.4	−163.2
III	1,383.8	561.6	163.4	99.3	559.5	1,571.4	450.5	308.7	668.1	15.7	199.6	202.8	34.8	−187.6
IV	1,409.5	571.1	173.2	99.0	566.2	1,596.4	440.8	297.3	674.9	25.8	206.6	210.8	37.5	−186.8
1995: I	1,429.0	581.4	179.0	94.3	574.3	1,620.6	444.8	299.9	697.5	12.0	212.2	218.8	35.3	−191.5
II	1,459.0	608.2	178.7	93.8	578.3	1,638.5	444.0	299.8	707.0	11.0	216.5	223.9	36.1	−179.5
III	1,472.8	607.5	186.9	93.7	584.7	1,649.3	449.0	303.2	713.8	11.3	210.6	227.5	37.0	−176.5
IV	1,491.9	626.0	183.8	92.2	589.9	1,642.0	436.3	291.6	719.4	11.8	208.5	229.0	37.2	−150.2
1996: I	1,526.3	644.9	192.1	91.7	597.6	1,679.9	444.6	298.2	738.4	19.2	213.7	226.6	37.4	−153.6
II	1,583.8	688.8	197.2	90.0	607.8	1,695.4	453.7	307.8	746.3	11.2	223.2	223.5	37.5	−111.6
III	1,598.6	695.7	196.7	91.5	614.8	1,698.2	454.0	309.3	749.7	11.9	218.7	226.6	37.4	−99.5
IV	1,641.6	717.5	192.0	110.2	622.0	1,718.8	453.6	307.6	754.4	22.9	217.5	231.8	38.5	−77.1
1997: I	1,675.3	746.9	204.9	88.2	635.3	1,730.8	458.0	306.4	775.5	10.5	219.6	228.9	38.4	−55.5
II	1,709.3	767.9	207.7	92.2	641.5	1,746.0	464.2	311.3	780.5	10.8	222.5	229.8	38.1	−36.8
III	1,741.8	781.9	219.3	92.4	648.2	1,752.6	464.7	311.6	784.5	10.0	224.2	231.2	37.9	−10.8
IV P	....	797.6	....	92.5	658.2	1,778.3	469.4	315.5	788.6	21.7	228.8	231.5	38.3	....

[1] Includes an item for the difference between wage accruals and disbursements, not shown separately.

Note.—See Note, Table B–78.

Source: Department of Commerce, Bureau of Economic Analysis.

TABLE B–83.—*Federal and State and local government receipts and current expenditures, national income and product accounts (NIPA), 1959–97*

[Billions of dollars; quarterly data at seasonally adjusted annual rates]

Year or quarter	Total government Receipts	Total government Current expenditures	Total government Current surplus or deficit (−) (NIPA)	Federal Government Receipts	Federal Government Current expenditures	Federal Government Current surplus or deficit (−) (NIPA)	State and local government Receipts	State and local government Current expenditures	State and local government Current surplus or deficit (−) (NIPA)	Addendum: Grants-in-aid to State and local governments
1959	128.8	116.6	12.2	90.6	88.0	2.6	45.0	35.4	9.6	6.8
1960	138.8	121.5	17.3	97.0	89.6	7.4	48.3	38.4	9.9	6.5
1961	144.1	130.8	13.3	99.0	96.1	2.9	52.4	42.0	10.4	7.2
1962	155.8	141.3	14.5	107.2	104.4	2.8	56.6	44.8	11.7	8.0
1963	167.5	149.1	18.4	115.5	110.2	5.4	61.1	48.1	13.0	9.1
1964	172.9	157.3	15.6	116.2	115.4	.9	67.1	52.4	14.7	10.4
1965	187.0	168.6	18.5	125.8	122.4	3.4	72.3	57.2	15.1	11.1
1966	210.7	190.8	19.9	143.5	140.9	2.6	81.5	64.3	17.3	14.4
1967	226.4	217.5	8.9	152.6	160.9	−8.3	89.8	72.5	17.3	15.9
1968	260.9	243.7	17.2	176.8	179.7	−2.8	102.7	82.6	20.0	18.6
1969	293.9	264.1	29.8	199.5	190.8	8.7	114.8	93.7	21.1	20.3
1970	299.6	292.9	6.7	195.1	209.1	−14.1	129.0	108.2	20.8	24.4
1971	319.6	323.2	−3.7	203.3	228.6	−25.3	145.3	123.7	21.7	29.0
1972	364.8	353.1	11.6	232.6	253.1	−20.5	169.7	137.5	32.2	37.5
1973	408.8	386.5	22.2	264.0	275.1	−11.1	185.3	152.0	33.4	40.6
1974	451.8	438.3	13.6	295.1	312.0	−16.9	200.6	170.2	30.5	43.9
1975	468.4	514.7	−46.3	297.4	371.3	−73.9	225.6	198.0	27.6	54.6
1976	535.9	557.1	−21.3	343.1	400.3	−57.2	253.9	217.9	35.9	61.1
1977	603.9	605.5	−1.5	389.6	435.9	−46.3	281.9	237.1	44.7	67.5
1978	678.5	657.5	20.9	446.5	478.1	−31.7	309.3	256.7	52.6	77.3
1979	761.1	727.3	33.8	511.1	529.5	−18.4	330.6	278.3	52.3	80.5
1980	834.2	840.8	−6.6	561.5	622.5	−61.0	361.4	307.0	54.4	88.7
1981	952.2	954.6	−2.4	649.3	707.1	−57.8	390.8	335.4	55.4	87.9
1982	971.5	1,054.9	−83.4	646.4	781.0	−134.7	409.0	357.7	51.3	83.9
1983	1,028.6	1,138.1	−109.5	671.9	846.3	−174.4	443.6	378.8	64.9	87.0
1984	1,144.5	1,213.7	−69.1	746.9	902.9	−156.0	492.0	405.1	86.9	94.4
1985	1,239.7	1,311.7	−71.9	811.3	974.2	−162.9	528.7	437.8	91.0	100.3
1986	1,313.1	1,395.7	−82.6	850.1	1,027.6	−177.5	570.6	475.7	94.9	107.6
1987	1,429.4	1,474.5	−45.1	937.4	1,066.3	−128.9	594.9	511.1	83.8	102.9
1988	1,517.3	1,552.7	−35.4	997.2	1,118.5	−121.3	631.4	545.5	85.9	111.2
1989	1,642.1	1,660.4	−18.3	1,079.3	1,192.7	−113.4	681.0	585.9	95.1	118.2
1990	1,726.4	1,800.9	−74.5	1,129.8	1,284.5	−154.7	728.9	648.8	80.1	132.4
1991	1,779.8	1,900.0	−120.2	1,149.0	1,345.0	−196.0	784.2	708.4	75.8	153.4
1992	1,870.6	2,065.2	−194.6	1,198.5	1,479.4	−280.9	844.3	758.0	86.3	172.2
1993	1,983.7	2,146.9	−163.2	1,275.1	1,525.7	−250.7	894.4	807.0	87.4	185.8
1994	2,124.7	2,214.5	−89.8	1,374.8	1,561.4	−186.7	949.2	852.3	96.8	199.2
1995	2,250.2	2,321.6	−71.4	1,463.2	1,637.6	−174.4	999.0	895.9	103.1	211.9
1996	2,412.7	2,417.8	−5.1	1,587.6	1,698.1	−110.5	1,043.4	938.0	105.3	218.3
1997 ᵖ	....	2,510.9	....	....	1,751.9	....	....	982.7	....	223.8
1992: I	1,841.4	2,024.0	−182.6	1,183.4	1,450.7	−267.4	823.4	738.6	84.8	165.4
II	1,858.9	2,051.9	−193.0	1,193.1	1,472.8	−279.6	838.8	752.2	86.6	173.0
III	1,860.1	2,075.7	−215.5	1,187.0	1,484.5	−297.5	847.3	765.4	82.0	174.2
IV	1,921.8	2,109.1	−187.3	1,230.5	1,509.5	−279.0	867.7	775.9	91.7	176.3
1993: I	1,917.5	2,118.0	−200.4	1,227.1	1,505.3	−278.2	867.6	789.8	77.8	177.2
II	1,970.8	2,138.7	−167.9	1,268.8	1,518.0	−249.2	883.9	802.6	81.3	181.9
III	1,989.8	2,153.4	−163.6	1,277.2	1,527.8	−250.6	899.9	812.9	86.9	187.3
IV	2,056.7	2,177.6	−120.9	1,327.2	1,551.9	−224.6	926.3	822.6	103.7	196.9
1994: I	2,051.9	2,176.2	−124.3	1,324.5	1,533.5	−209.0	922.0	837.2	84.7	194.5
II	2,125.9	2,194.3	−68.4	1,381.1	1,544.3	−163.2	941.0	846.2	94.8	196.2
III	2,141.1	2,230.3	−89.2	1,383.8	1,571.4	−187.6	956.9	858.4	98.4	199.6
IV	2,179.8	2,257.3	−77.5	1,409.5	1,596.4	−186.8	976.8	867.5	109.3	206.6
1995: I	2,205.2	2,289.0	−83.8	1,429.0	1,620.6	−191.5	988.4	880.6	107.7	212.2
II	2,240.3	2,314.1	−73.8	1,459.0	1,638.5	−179.5	997.7	892.1	105.6	216.5
III	2,264.2	2,339.5	−75.4	1,472.8	1,649.3	−176.5	1,002.0	900.9	101.1	210.6
IV	2,291.3	2,343.6	−52.4	1,491.9	1,642.0	−150.2	1,007.8	910.0	97.8	208.5
1996: I	2,337.5	2,387.0	−49.6	1,526.3	1,679.9	−153.6	1,024.9	920.8	104.1	213.7
II	2,407.6	2,404.8	2.8	1,583.8	1,695.4	−111.6	1,046.9	932.5	114.4	223.2
III	2,426.7	2,423.6	3.1	1,598.6	1,698.2	−99.5	1,046.7	944.2	102.6	218.7
IV	2,479.0	2,455.8	23.2	1,641.6	1,718.8	−77.1	1,054.9	954.5	100.4	217.5
1997: I	2,526.6	2,477.4	49.2	1,675.3	1,730.8	−55.5	1,070.9	966.1	104.7	219.6
II	2,566.8	2,498.7	68.1	1,709.3	1,746.0	−36.8	1,080.0	975.1	104.9	222.5
III	2,616.7	2,516.1	100.6	1,741.8	1,752.6	−10.8	1,099.1	987.7	111.4	224.2
IV ᵖ	....	2,551.5	....	....	1,778.3	....	....	1,001.9	....	228.8

Note.—Federal grants-in-aid to State and local governments are reflected in Federal current expenditures and State and local receipts. Total government receipts and current expenditures have been adjusted to eliminate this duplication.

Source: Department of Commerce, Bureau of Economic Analysis.

378

TABLE B–84.—*Federal and State and local government receipts and current expenditures, national income and product accounts (NIPA), by major type, 1959–97*

[Billions of dollars; quarterly data at seasonally adjusted annual rates]

Year or quarter	Receipts					Current expenditures									Addendum: Grants-in-aid to State and local governments
	Total	Personal tax and nontax receipts	Corporate profits tax accruals	Indirect business tax and nontax accruals	Contributions for social insurance	Total¹	Consumption expenditures	Transfer payments	Net interest paid		Less: Dividends received by government²	Less: Interest received by government²	Subsidies less current surplus of government enterprises	Current surplus or deficit (−) (NIPA)	
									Total	Interest paid					
1959	128.8	44.5	23.6	41.9	18.8	116.6	82.7	27.5	6.3	....	....	....	0.1	12.2	6.8
1960	138.8	48.7	22.7	45.5	21.9	121.5	85.0	29.3	6.9	10.1	3.3	....	.3	17.3	6.5
1961	144.1	50.3	22.8	48.1	22.9	130.8	89.6	33.6	6.4	9.9	3.5	....	1.3	13.3	7.2
1962	155.8	54.8	24.0	51.7	25.4	141.3	98.2	34.7	6.9	10.8	3.9	....	1.5	14.5	8.0
1963	167.5	58.0	26.2	54.7	28.5	149.1	104.2	36.6	7.4	11.6	4.2	....	.9	18.4	9.1
1964	172.9	56.0	28.0	58.8	30.1	157.3	109.9	38.1	7.9	12.5	4.6	....	1.4	15.6	10.4
1965	187.0	61.9	30.9	62.7	31.6	168.6	117.6	41.1	8.1	13.2	5.1	....	1.7	18.5	11.1
1966	210.7	71.0	33.7	65.4	40.6	190.8	133.5	45.8	8.5	14.5	6.0	....	3.0	19.9	14.4
1967	226.4	77.9	32.7	70.4	45.5	217.5	151.2	54.5	8.9	15.7	6.8	....	2.9	8.9	15.9
1968	260.9	92.1	39.4	79.0	50.4	243.7	167.8	62.6	10.3	18.1	7.7	0.1	3.1	17.2	18.6
1969	293.9	109.9	39.7	86.6	57.8	264.1	179.9	69.3	11.5	19.8	8.3	.2	3.6	29.8	20.3
1970	299.6	109.0	34.4	94.3	62.0	292.9	192.1	83.8	12.4	22.3	9.9	.2	4.9	6.7	24.4
1971	319.6	108.7	37.7	103.6	69.6	323.2	206.7	99.4	12.5	23.1	10.6	.3	5.1	−3.7	29.0
1972	364.8	132.0	41.9	111.4	79.5	353.1	223.6	110.9	12.9	24.8	11.9	.3	6.4	11.6	37.5
1973	408.8	140.6	49.3	121.0	97.9	386.5	239.4	126.6	15.2	29.6	14.4	.5	5.9	22.2	40.6
1974	451.8	159.1	51.8	129.3	111.7	438.3	267.2	150.5	16.3	33.6	17.3	.9	4.5	13.6	43.9
1975	468.4	156.4	50.9	140.0	121.1	514.7	299.9	189.2	18.5	37.7	19.2	.9	8.1	−46.3	54.6
1976	535.9	182.3	64.2	151.6	137.7	557.1	321.4	206.5	22.8	43.6	20.9	.9	7.4	−21.3	61.1
1977	603.9	210.0	73.0	165.5	155.4	605.5	351.5	220.9	24.4	47.9	23.5	1.3	10.1	−1.5	67.5
1978	678.5	240.1	83.5	177.8	177.0	657.5	383.3	238.6	26.5	56.8	30.3	1.7	11.1	20.9	77.3
1979	761.1	280.2	88.0	188.7	204.2	727.3	421.8	266.9	28.7	68.6	39.9	2.0	11.7	33.8	80.5
1980	834.2	312.4	84.8	212.0	225.0	840.8	476.4	317.6	33.4	83.9	50.5	1.9	15.2	−6.6	88.7
1981	952.2	360.2	81.1	249.3	261.6	954.6	531.3	360.7	48.1	110.2	62.1	2.3	16.9	−2.4	87.9
1982	971.5	371.4	63.1	256.4	280.6	1,054.9	577.9	403.3	55.5	130.6	75.0	2.9	21.1	−83.4	83.9
1983	1,028.6	369.3	77.2	280.1	301.9	1,138.1	619.2	434.4	61.8	146.7	84.9	3.4	25.6	−109.5	87.0
1984	1,144.5	395.5	94.0	309.5	345.5	1,213.7	664.9	448.2	79.1	174.7	95.6	3.9	25.5	−69.1	94.4
1985	1,239.7	437.7	96.5	329.6	375.9	1,311.7	725.1	480.9	88.0	195.9	107.9	4.5	21.9	−71.9	100.3
1986	1,313.1	459.9	106.5	344.7	402.0	1,395.7	775.0	510.9	89.8	208.0	118.2	5.1	25.1	−82.6	107.6
1987	1,429.4	514.2	127.1	364.8	423.3	1,474.5	819.3	533.7	96.3	216.0	119.7	5.9	31.0	−45.1	102.9
1988	1,517.3	532.0	137.0	385.5	462.8	1,552.7	859.1	568.3	103.7	229.7	125.9	6.9	28.5	−35.4	111.2
1989	1,642.1	594.9	141.3	414.7	491.2	1,660.4	912.4	616.3	115.5	251.0	135.5	8.1	24.2	−18.3	118.2
1990	1,726.4	624.8	140.5	442.6	518.5	1,800.9	976.7	679.8	128.2	268.6	140.4	9.0	25.3	−74.5	132.4
1991	1,779.8	624.8	133.4	478.1	543.5	1,900.0	1,025.4	721.1	139.4	282.8	143.5	9.5	23.6	−120.2	153.4
1992	1,870.6	650.5	143.0	505.6	571.4	2,065.2	1,054.7	852.3	141.2	282.7	141.5	10.1	27.1	−194.6	172.2
1993	1,983.7	690.0	165.2	532.5	596.0	2,146.9	1,078.9	907.1	140.3	279.0	138.7	10.5	31.1	−163.2	185.8
1994	2,124.7	739.1	186.6	568.5	630.5	2,214.5	1,107.0	947.3	144.9	286.4	141.5	11.4	26.6	−89.8	199.2
1995	2,250.2	795.1	213.2	582.8	659.1	2,321.6	1,142.1	1,001.5	165.2	314.1	148.9	12.5	25.2	−71.4	211.9
1996	2,412.7	886.9	229.0	604.8	692.0	2,417.8	1,182.4	1,058.3	165.4	317.7	152.3	13.6	25.4	−5.1	218.3
1997p	....	987.9	....	619.5	732.0	2,510.9	1,227.0	1,107.3	165.1	319.2	154.0	14.6	26.1	....	223.8
1992:I	1,841.4	636.7	143.9	495.7	565.1	2,024.0	1,038.4	828.8	142.0	283.2	141.2	9.8	24.6	−182.6	165.4
II	1,858.9	640.0	150.9	497.9	570.1	2,051.9	1,047.1	846.0	143.5	285.1	141.6	10.1	25.4	−193.0	170.0
III ...	1,860.1	650.6	127.6	507.1	574.8	2,075.7	1,061.8	855.4	141.7	282.9	141.3	10.1	26.9	−215.5	174.2
IV ...	1,921.8	674.8	149.7	521.7	575.7	2,109.1	1,071.3	879.1	137.6	279.4	141.9	10.3	31.5	−187.3	176.3
1993:I	1,917.5	662.5	149.2	520.6	585.3	2,118.0	1,068.6	887.5	139.1	278.4	139.3	10.2	33.0	−200.4	177.2
II	1,970.8	685.6	165.4	525.9	594.0	2,138.7	1,074.7	900.9	140.8	279.6	138.8	10.4	32.8	−167.9	181.9
III ...	1,989.8	695.5	161.2	534.4	598.7	2,153.4	1,082.0	910.8	141.0	279.6	138.6	10.5	30.2	−163.6	187.3
IV ...	2,056.7	716.4	184.9	549.4	606.1	2,177.6	1,090.4	929.3	140.2	278.4	138.2	10.8	28.5	−120.9	196.9
1994:I	2,051.9	712.9	163.0	556.9	619.2	2,176.2	1,094.0	928.5	136.7	275.5	138.8	11.1	28.1	−124.3	194.5
II	2,125.9	750.5	182.8	564.4	628.2	2,194.3	1,098.4	939.2	142.1	282.4	140.3	11.3	25.9	−68.4	196.2
III ...	2,141.1	739.9	194.6	573.2	633.4	2,230.3	1,119.0	950.5	147.2	289.1	142.0	11.4	25.1	−89.2	199.6
IV ...	2,179.8	753.0	206.2	579.4	641.2	2,257.3	1,116.8	971.2	153.6	298.6	145.0	11.7	27.4	−77.5	206.6
1995:I	2,205.2	766.5	209.6	578.9	650.1	2,289.0	1,131.7	984.4	160.2	307.4	147.3	12.1	24.8	−83.8	212.2
II	2,240.3	795.1	209.1	580.9	655.1	2,314.1	1,140.2	996.5	164.5	313.9	149.4	12.3	25.1	−73.8	216.5
III ...	2,264.2	798.9	218.8	584.0	662.4	2,339.5	1,151.4	1,007.7	167.5	316.6	149.1	12.6	25.7	−75.4	210.6
IV ...	2,291.3	820.0	215.3	587.3	668.6	2,343.6	1,145.1	1,017.4	168.6	318.5	149.9	12.9	25.5	−52.4	208.5
1996:I	2,337.5	840.0	226.2	594.0	677.3	2,387.0	1,162.2	1,046.7	166.0	317.4	151.4	13.3	25.3	−49.6	213.7
II	2,407.6	887.8	232.2	599.0	688.7	2,404.8	1,180.7	1,050.2	162.3	314.6	152.3	13.6	25.2	2.8	223.2
III ...	2,426.7	897.3	231.6	600.9	696.8	2,423.6	1,189.8	1,058.2	164.4	318.1	153.7	13.7	24.9	3.1	218.7
IV ...	2,479.0	922.6	226.0	625.3	705.1	2,455.8	1,197.0	1,078.0	168.8	320.7	152.0	14.0	26.0	23.2	217.5
1997:I	2,526.6	955.7	241.2	610.2	719.5	2,477.4	1,209.7	1,091.0	164.9	317.9	153.0	14.3	26.1	49.2	219.6
II	2,566.8	979.2	244.5	616.2	726.9	2,498.7	1,221.6	1,100.8	164.9	319.1	154.1	14.7	26.0	68.1	222.5
III ...	2,616.7	998.0	258.2	625.4	735.0	2,516.1	1,230.8	1,108.5	165.6	319.7	154.1	14.7	25.8	100.6	224.2
IVp ...	....	1,018.5	....	626.2	746.6	2,551.5	1,245.9	1,129.0	165.2	320.0	154.8	14.9	26.4	....	228.8

¹ Includes an item for the difference between wage accruals and disbursements, not shown separately.
² Prior to 1968, dividends received is included in interest received.

Source: Department of Commerce, Bureau of Economic Analysis.

TABLE B–85.—*State and local government receipts and current expenditures, national income and product accounts (NIPA), 1959–97*

[Billions of dollars; quarterly data at seasonally adjusted annual rates]

Year or quarter	Receipts						Current expenditures					Current surplus or deficit (−) (NIPA)
	Total	Personal tax and nontax receipts	Corporate profits tax accruals	Indirect business tax and nontax accruals	Contributions for social insurance	Federal grants-in-aid	Total[1]	Consumption expenditures	Transfer payments to persons	Net interest paid less dividends received	Subsidies less current surplus of government enterprises	
1959	45.0	4.6	1.2	29.3	3.1	6.8	35.4	30.9	5.6	0.1	−1.2	9.6
1960	48.3	5.2	1.2	32.0	3.4	6.5	38.4	33.7	5.9	.1	−1.3	9.9
1961	52.4	5.7	1.3	34.4	3.7	7.2	42.0	36.7	6.5	.1	−1.4	10.4
1962	56.6	6.3	1.5	37.0	3.9	8.0	44.8	39.1	7.0	.2	−1.4	11.7
1963	61.1	6.7	1.7	39.4	4.2	9.1	48.1	42.2	7.5	.1	−1.7	13.0
1964	67.1	7.5	1.8	42.6	4.7	10.4	52.4	46.0	8.2	−.1	−1.7	14.7
1965	72.3	8.1	2.0	46.1	5.0	11.1	57.2	50.5	8.8	−.3	−1.7	15.1
1966	81.5	9.5	2.2	49.7	5.7	14.4	64.3	56.5	10.1	−.6	−1.7	17.3
1967	89.8	10.6	2.6	53.9	6.7	15.9	72.5	62.9	12.1	−.9	−1.6	17.3
1968	102.7	12.7	3.3	60.8	7.2	18.6	82.6	70.8	14.5	−1.1	−1.6	20.0
1969	114.8	15.2	3.6	67.4	8.3	20.3	93.7	79.8	16.7	−1.4	−1.5	21.1
1970	129.0	16.7	3.7	74.8	9.2	24.4	108.2	91.6	20.1	−2.0	−1.6	20.8
1971	145.3	18.7	4.3	83.1	10.2	29.0	123.7	102.9	24.0	−1.7	−1.4	21.7
1972	169.7	24.2	5.3	91.2	11.5	37.5	137.5	113.4	27.5	−1.8	−1.6	32.2
1973	185.3	26.3	6.0	99.5	13.0	40.6	152.0	126.4	30.4	−3.4	−1.5	33.4
1974	200.6	28.2	6.7	107.2	14.6	43.9	170.2	144.0	32.3	−5.3	−.9	30.5
1975	225.6	31.0	7.3	115.8	16.8	54.6	198.0	164.9	38.9	−5.4	−.4	27.6
1976	253.9	35.8	9.6	127.8	19.5	61.1	217.9	179.7	43.6	−5.0	−.4	35.9
1977	281.9	41.0	11.4	139.9	22.1	67.5	237.1	196.1	47.4	−6.0	−.3	44.7
1978	309.3	46.3	12.1	148.9	24.7	77.3	256.7	214.5	52.4	−9.8	−.3	52.6
1979	330.6	50.5	13.6	158.6	27.4	80.5	278.3	235.9	57.2	−15.3	.4	52.3
1980	361.4	56.2	14.5	172.3	29.7	88.7	307.0	261.3	65.7	−21.2	1.2	54.4
1981	390.8	63.0	15.4	192.0	32.5	87.9	335.4	285.3	73.6	−25.9	2.4	55.4
1982	409.0	68.5	14.0	206.8	35.8	83.9	357.7	307.9	79.9	−31.8	1.7	51.3
1983	443.6	76.2	15.9	226.8	37.7	87.0	378.8	326.2	86.6	−34.4	.2	64.9
1984	492.0	87.1	18.8	251.5	40.2	94.4	405.1	350.8	93.9	−38.0	−1.6	86.9
1985	528.7	94.0	20.2	271.4	42.8	100.3	437.8	382.6	101.9	−43.4	−3.3	91.0
1986	570.6	101.6	22.7	291.5	47.3	107.6	475.7	412.7	111.8	−45.8	−3.0	94.9
1987	594.9	111.8	23.9	307.1	49.2	102.9	511.1	441.1	120.7	−47.4	−3.4	83.8
1988	631.4	117.6	26.0	324.6	51.9	111.2	545.5	471.3	131.0	−51.5	−5.3	85.9
1989	681.0	131.4	24.2	353.0	54.1	118.2	585.9	507.2	144.5	−59.3	−6.6	95.1
1990	728.9	139.1	22.5	377.6	57.4	132.4	648.8	550.1	166.5	−60.7	−7.1	80.1
1991	784.2	147.8	23.6	398.4	60.9	153.4	708.4	579.4	199.0	−62.8	−7.2	75.8
1992	844.3	159.7	24.4	423.7	64.3	172.2	758.0	603.6	227.2	−64.8	−8.0	86.3
1993	894.4	167.4	26.9	445.6	68.7	185.8	807.0	631.6	247.2	−62.9	−9.0	87.4
1994	949.2	176.8	29.9	469.8	73.4	199.2	852.3	663.8	264.3	−66.5	−9.3	96.8
1995	999.0	189.4	31.1	489.3	77.3	211.9	895.9	698.6	280.6	−72.1	−11.2	103.1
1996	1,043.4	200.2	34.5	508.9	81.4	218.3	938.0	730.9	294.8	−75.3	−12.3	105.3
1997ᵖ		214.3		528.2	86.2	223.8	982.7	762.9	311.8	−79.8	−12.1	
1992: I	823.4	155.7	24.3	414.9	63.1	165.4	738.6	592.6	217.7	−64.5	−7.2	84.8
II	838.8	158.4	25.7	417.7	64.0	173.0	752.2	600.8	224.1	−65.0	−7.7	86.6
III	847.3	159.9	21.6	427.0	64.7	174.2	765.4	607.4	231.2	−64.9	−8.3	82.0
IV	867.7	164.9	25.9	435.2	65.4	176.3	775.9	613.6	235.8	−64.5	−8.9	91.7
1993: I	867.6	161.6	24.1	438.0	66.8	177.2	789.8	621.4	240.4	−63.3	−8.7	77.8
II	883.9	166.5	26.9	440.4	68.2	181.9	802.6	628.9	245.2	−62.7	−8.8	81.3
III	899.9	168.4	26.3	448.5	69.4	187.3	812.9	635.0	249.5	−62.4	−9.1	86.9
IV	926.3	172.9	30.4	455.5	70.6	196.9	822.6	641.1	253.8	−63.1	−9.2	103.7
1994: I	922.0	170.8	26.1	458.7	71.8	194.5	837.2	651.6	257.9	−64.3	−7.9	84.7
II	941.0	176.1	29.4	466.3	72.9	196.2	846.2	659.2	262.3	−65.8	−9.5	94.8
III	956.9	178.3	31.3	473.8	73.9	199.6	858.4	668.6	266.6	−67.0	−9.7	98.4
IV	976.8	182.0	32.9	480.4	74.9	206.6	867.5	676.0	270.5	−68.9	−10.1	109.3
1995: I	988.4	185.1	30.6	484.6	75.8	212.2	880.6	686.9	274.9	−70.7	−10.6	107.7
II	997.7	187.0	30.4	487.1	76.8	216.5	892.1	696.2	278.6	−71.7	−11.0	105.6
III	1,002.0	191.3	32.0	490.4	77.7	210.6	900.9	702.4	282.6	−72.6	−11.4	101.1
IV	1,007.8	194.0	31.5	495.1	78.7	208.5	910.0	708.8	286.3	−73.4	−11.7	97.8
1996: I	1,024.9	195.0	34.1	502.3	79.7	213.7	920.8	717.6	289.1	−73.8	−12.1	104.1
II	1,046.9	198.9	35.0	508.9	80.9	223.2	932.5	727.0	292.7	−74.8	−12.3	114.4
III	1,046.7	201.7	34.9	509.4	82.0	218.7	944.2	735.9	296.6	−75.9	−12.4	102.6
IV	1,054.9	205.1	34.0	515.1	83.1	217.5	954.5	743.3	300.6	−77.0	−12.5	100.4
1997: I	1,070.9	208.7	36.4	522.0	84.2	219.6	966.1	751.7	305.1	−78.3	−12.3	104.7
II	1,080.0	211.3	36.8	524.0	85.4	222.5	975.1	757.4	309.5	−79.6	−12.2	104.9
III	1,099.1	216.1	38.9	533.0	86.8	224.2	987.7	766.1	314.0	−80.3	−12.1	111.4
IVᵖ		220.9		533.7	88.3	228.8	1,001.9	776.5	318.7	−81.3	−12.0	

[1] Includes an item for the difference between wage accruals and disbursements, not shown separately.

Source: Department of Commerce, Bureau of Economic Analysis.

TABLE B–86.—*State and local government revenues and expenditures, selected fiscal years, 1927–94*

[Millions of dollars]

Fiscal year [1]	General revenues by source [2]							General expenditures by function [2]				
	Total	Property taxes	Sales and gross receipts taxes	Individual income taxes	Corporation net income taxes	Revenue from Federal Government	All other [3]	Total	Education	Highways	Public welfare	All other [4]
1927	7,271	4,730	470	70	92	116	1,793	7,210	2,235	1,809	151	3,015
1932	7,267	4,487	752	74	79	232	1,643	7,765	2,311	1,741	444	3,269
1934	7,678	4,076	1,008	80	49	1,016	1,449	7,181	1,831	1,509	889	2,952
1936	8,395	4,093	1,484	153	113	948	1,604	7,644	2,177	1,425	827	3,215
1938	9,228	4,440	1,794	218	165	800	1,811	8,757	2,491	1,650	1,069	3,547
1940	9,609	4,430	1,982	224	156	945	1,872	9,229	2,638	1,573	1,156	3,862
1942	10,418	4,537	2,351	276	272	858	2,123	9,190	2,586	1,490	1,225	3,889
1944	10,908	4,604	2,289	342	451	954	2,269	8,863	2,793	1,200	1,133	3,737
1946	12,356	4,986	2,986	422	447	855	2,661	11,028	3,356	1,672	1,409	4,591
1948	17,250	6,126	4,442	543	592	1,861	3,685	17,684	5,379	3,036	2,099	7,170
1950	20,911	7,349	5,154	788	593	2,486	4,541	22,787	7,177	3,803	2,940	8,867
1952	25,181	8,652	6,357	998	846	2,566	5,763	26,098	8,318	4,650	2,788	10,342
1953	27,307	9,375	6,927	1,065	817	2,870	6,252	27,910	9,390	4,987	2,914	10,619
1954	29,012	9,967	7,276	1,127	778	2,966	6,897	30,701	10,557	5,527	3,060	11,557
1955	31,073	10,735	7,643	1,237	744	3,131	7,584	33,724	11,907	6,452	3,168	12,197
1956	34,667	11,749	8,691	1,538	890	3,335	8,465	36,711	13,220	6,953	3,139	13,399
1957	38,164	12,864	9,467	1,754	984	3,843	9,252	40,375	14,134	7,816	3,485	14,940
1958	41,219	14,047	9,829	1,759	1,018	4,865	9,699	44,851	15,919	8,567	3,818	16,547
1959	45,306	14,983	10,437	1,994	1,001	6,377	10,516	48,887	17,283	9,592	4,136	17,876
1960	50,505	16,405	11,849	2,463	1,180	6,974	11,634	51,876	18,719	9,428	4,404	19,325
1961	54,037	18,002	12,463	2,613	1,266	7,131	12,563	56,201	20,574	9,844	4,720	21,063
1962	58,252	19,054	13,494	3,037	1,308	7,871	13,489	60,206	22,216	10,357	5,084	22,549
1963	62,890	20,089	14,456	3,269	1,505	8,722	14,850	64,816	23,776	11,136	5,481	24,423
1962–63	62,269	19,833	14,446	3,267	1,505	8,663	14,556	63,977	23,729	11,150	5,420	23,678
1963–64	68,443	21,241	15,762	3,791	1,695	10,002	15,951	69,302	26,286	11,664	5,766	25,586
1964–65	74,000	22,583	17,118	4,090	1,929	11,029	17,250	74,678	28,563	12,221	6,315	27,579
1965–66	83,036	24,670	19,085	4,760	2,038	13,214	19,269	82,843	33,287	12,770	6,757	30,029
1966–67	91,197	26,047	20,530	5,825	2,227	15,370	21,197	93,350	37,919	13,932	8,218	33,281
1967–68	101,264	27,747	22,911	7,308	2,518	17,181	23,598	102,411	41,158	14,481	9,857	36,915
1968–69	114,550	30,673	26,519	8,908	3,180	19,153	26,118	116,728	47,238	15,417	12,110	41,963
1969–70	130,756	34,054	30,322	10,812	3,738	21,857	29,971	131,332	52,718	16,427	14,679	47,508
1970–71	144,927	37,852	33,233	11,900	3,424	26,146	32,374	150,674	59,413	18,095	18,226	54,940
1971–72	167,541	42,877	37,518	15,227	4,416	31,342	36,162	168,549	65,814	19,021	21,117	62,597
1972–73	190,222	45,283	42,047	17,994	5,425	39,264	40,210	181,357	69,714	18,615	23,582	69,446
1973–74	207,670	47,705	46,098	19,491	6,015	41,820	46,541	198,959	75,833	19,946	25,085	78,096
1974–75	228,171	51,491	49,815	21,454	6,642	47,034	51,735	230,722	87,858	22,528	28,156	92,180
1975–76	256,176	57,001	54,547	24,575	7,273	55,589	57,191	256,731	97,216	23,907	32,604	103,004
1976–77	285,157	62,527	60,641	29,246	9,174	62,444	61,124	274,215	102,780	23,058	35,906	112,472
1977–78	315,960	66,422	67,596	33,176	10,738	69,592	68,436	296,984	110,758	24,609	39,140	122,477
1978–79	343,236	64,944	74,247	36,932	12,128	75,164	79,821	327,517	119,448	28,440	41,898	137,731
1979–80	382,322	68,499	79,927	42,080	13,321	83,029	95,466	369,086	133,211	33,311	47,288	155,277
1980–81	423,404	74,969	85,971	46,426	14,143	90,294	111,599	407,449	145,784	34,603	54,105	172,957
1981–82	457,654	82,067	93,613	50,738	15,028	87,282	128,926	436,733	154,282	34,520	57,996	189,935
1982–83	486,753	89,105	100,247	55,129	14,258	90,007	138,008	466,516	163,876	36,655	60,906	205,079
1983–84	542,730	96,457	114,097	64,529	17,141	96,935	153,570	505,008	176,108	39,419	66,414	223,068
1984–85	598,121	103,757	126,376	70,361	19,152	106,158	172,317	553,899	192,686	44,989	71,479	244,745
1985–86	641,486	111,709	135,005	74,365	19,994	113,099	187,314	605,623	210,819	49,368	75,868	269,568
1986–87	686,860	121,203	144,091	83,935	22,425	114,857	200,350	657,134	226,619	52,355	82,650	295,510
1987–88	726,762	132,212	156,452	88,350	23,663	117,602	208,482	704,921	242,683	55,621	89,090	317,528
1988–89	786,129	142,400	166,336	97,806	25,926	125,824	227,838	762,360	263,898	58,105	97,879	342,479
1989–90	849,502	155,613	177,885	105,640	23,566	136,802	249,996	834,818	288,148	61,057	110,518	375,095
1990–91	902,207	167,999	185,570	109,341	22,242	154,099	262,955	908,108	309,302	64,937	130,402	403,467
1991–92	979,137	180,337	197,731	115,638	23,880	179,174	282,376	981,253	324,652	67,351	158,723	430,526
1992–93	1,041,567	189,793	209,649	123,235	26,417	198,591	293,932	1,033,167	342,287	68,370	170,705	451,805
1993–94	1,100,441	197,140	223,628	128,810	28,320	215,445	307,098	1,077,665	353,287	72,067	183,384	468,917

[1] Fiscal years not the same for all governments. See Note.
[2] Excludes revenues or expenditures of publicly owned utilities and liquor stores, and of insurance-trust activities. Intergovernmental receipts and payments between State and local governments are also excluded.
[3] Includes other taxes and charges and miscellaneous revenues.
[4] Includes expenditures for libraries, hospitals, health, employment security administration, veterans' services, air transportation, water transport and terminals, parking facilities, and transit subsidies, police protection, fire protection, correction, protective inspection and regulation, sewerage, natural resources, parks and recreation, housing and community development, solid waste management, financial administration, judicial and legal, general public buildings, other government administration, interest on general debt, and general expenditures, n.e.c.

Note.—Data for fiscal years listed from 1962–63 to 1993–94 are the aggregations of data for government fiscal years that ended in the 12-month period from July 1 to June 30 of those years. Data for 1963 and earlier years include data for government fiscal years ending during that particular calendar year.

Data are not available for intervening years.

Source: Department of Commerce, Bureau of the Census.

[Millions of dollars]

End of year or month	Total interest-bearing public debt securities	Marketable				Nonmarketable				
		Total [1]	Treasury bills	Treasury notes	Treasury bonds	Total	U.S. savings securities [2]	Foreign series [3]	Government account series	Other [4]
Fiscal year:										
1967	322,286	[5]210,672	58,535	49,108	97,418	111,614	51,213	1,514	56,155	2,732
1968	344,401	226,592	64,440	71,073	91,079	117,808	51,712	3,741	59,526	2,829
1969	351,729	226,107	68,356	78,946	78,805	125,623	51,711	4,070	66,790	3,052
1970	369,026	232,599	76,154	93,489	62,956	136,426	51,281	4,755	76,323	4,067
1971	396,289	245,473	86,677	104,807	53,989	150,816	53,003	9,270	82,784	5,759
1972	425,360	257,202	94,648	113,419	49,135	168,158	55,921	18,985	89,598	3,654
1973	456,353	262,971	100,061	117,840	45,071	193,382	59,418	28,524	101,738	3,702
1974	473,238	266,575	105,019	128,419	33,137	206,663	61,921	25,011	115,442	4,289
1975	532,122	315,606	128,569	150,257	36,779	216,516	65,482	23,216	124,173	3,645
1976	619,254	392,581	161,198	191,758	39,626	226,673	69,733	21,500	130,557	4,883
1977	697,629	443,508	156,091	241,692	45,724	254,121	75,411	21,799	140,113	16,798
1978	766,971	485,155	160,936	267,865	56,355	281,816	79,798	21,680	153,271	27,067
1979	819,007	506,693	161,378	274,242	71,073	312,314	80,440	28,115	176,360	27,399
1980	906,402	594,506	199,832	310,903	83,772	311,896	72,727	25,158	189,848	24,163
1981	996,495	683,209	223,388	363,643	96,178	313,286	68,017	20,499	201,052	23,718
1982	1,140,883	824,422	277,900	442,890	103,631	316,461	67,274	14,641	210,462	24,084
1983	1,375,751	1,024,000	340,733	557,525	125,742	351,751	70,024	11,450	234,684	35,593
1984	1,559,570	1,176,556	356,798	661,687	158,070	383,015	72,832	8,806	259,534	41,843
1985	1,821,010	1,360,179	384,220	776,449	199,510	460,831	77,011	6,638	313,928	63,254
1986	2,122,684	[1]1,564,329	410,730	896,884	241,716	558,355	85,551	4,128	365,872	102,804
1987	2,347,750	[1]1,675,980	378,263	1,005,127	277,590	671,769	97,004	4,350	440,658	129,757
1988	2,599,877	[1]1,802,905	398,451	1,089,578	299,875	796,972	106,176	6,320	536,455	148,021
1989	2,836,309	[1]1,892,763	406,597	1,133,193	337,974	943,546	114,025	6,818	663,677	159,026
1990	3,210,943	[1]2,092,759	482,454	1,218,081	377,224	1,118,184	122,152	36,041	779,412	180,579
1991	3,662,759	[1]2,390,660	564,589	1,387,717	423,354	1,272,099	133,512	41,639	908,406	188,542
1992	4,061,801	[1]2,677,476	634,287	1,566,349	461,840	1,384,325	148,266	37,039	1,011,020	188,000
1993	4,408,567	[1]2,904,910	658,381	1,734,161	497,367	1,503,657	167,024	42,459	1,114,289	179,885
1994	4,689,524	[1]3,091,602	697,295	1,867,507	511,800	1,597,922	176,413	41,996	1,211,689	167,824
1995	4,950,644	[1]3,260,447	742,462	1,980,343	522,643	1,690,197	181,181	40,950	1,324,270	143,796
1996	5,220,790	[1]3,418,371	761,232	2,098,670	543,469	1,802,419	184,147	37,488	1,454,690	126,094
1997	5,407,528	[1]3,439,616	701,909	2,122,172	576,151	1,967,912	182,665	34,909	1,608,478	141,860
1996: Jan	4,983,247	[1]3,331,836	756,723	2,038,955	521,158	1,651,411	182,238	39,678	1,299,967	129,528
Feb	5,012,872	[1]3,387,122	795,328	2,042,732	534,062	1,625,750	182,691	40,361	1,274,699	127,999
Mar	5,082,952	[1]3,375,055	811,919	2,014,074	534,062	1,707,897	182,992	40,361	1,357,647	126,897
Apr	5,097,989	[1]3,367,197	769,061	2,049,074	534,062	1,730,792	183,481	40,362	1,380,433	126,516
May	5,124,422	[1]3,387,187	782,756	2,055,370	534,061	1,737,235	183,594	38,004	1,387,235	128,402
June	5,126,748	[1]3,348,433	773,612	2,025,761	534,061	1,778,315	183,770	37,781	1,428,508	128,256
July	5,184,908	[1]3,411,190	789,809	2,072,321	534,060	1,773,718	183,949	37,615	1,427,185	124,969
Aug	5,173,734	[1]3,395,960	781,044	2,056,447	543,469	1,777,774	184,037	37,615	1,429,850	126,272
Sept	5,220,790	[1]3,418,371	761,232	2,098,670	543,469	1,802,419	184,147	37,488	1,454,690	126,094
Oct	5,243,339	[1]3,431,060	763,392	2,109,198	543,469	1,812,280	184,301	37,842	1,462,867	127,270
Nov	5,263,423	[1]3,444,643	802,272	2,072,410	554,962	1,818,780	184,379	37,635	1,466,961	129,805
Dec	5,317,188	[1]3,459,691	777,414	2,112,315	554,962	1,857,497	182,442	37,427	1,505,937	131,691
1997: Jan	5,308,048	[1]3,441,468	762,591	2,108,916	554,961	1,866,579	182,138	37,067	1,514,451	132,923
Feb	5,344,143	[1]3,477,535	762,198	2,127,559	565,417	1,866,608	182,644	36,767	1,514,154	133,043
Mar	5,375,139	[1]3,504,361	785,558	2,131,003	565,416	1,870,778	182,619	36,767	1,516,613	134,761
Apr	5,348,249	[1]3,464,512	741,401	2,126,823	565,416	1,883,737	182,625	35,559	1,529,858	135,695
May	5,308,468	[1]3,415,897	719,679	2,099,890	565,416	1,892,570	182,624	35,509	1,538,241	136,196
June	5,370,459	[1]3,433,058	704,135	2,132,574	565,416	1,937,401	182,664	35,359	1,581,467	137,911
July	5,367,593	[1]3,433,094	706,149	2,122,205	565,415	1,934,499	182,683	35,209	1,580,082	136,525
Aug	5,367,587	[1]3,430,768	722,074	2,093,189	576,151	1,936,819	182,641	35,059	1,580,074	139,045
Sept	5,407,528	[1]3,439,616	701,909	2,122,172	576,151	1,967,912	182,665	34,909	1,608,478	141,860
Oct	5,421,664	[1]3,438,686	703,011	2,111,648	576,151	1,982,978	182,853	34,609	1,616,693	148,823
Nov	5,426,155	[1]3,433,599	718,906	2,079,406	587,335	1,992,556	183,055	34,459	1,622,966	152,076
Dec	5,494,913	[1]3,456,817	715,394	2,106,049	587,335	2,038,096	181,209	36,159	1,666,650	154,078

[1] Includes Federal Financing Bank securities, not shown separately, in the amount of 15,000 million dollars. Beginning February 1997, also includes Treasury inflation-indexed notes, not shown separately, in amounts (millions of dollars): February—7,361; March—7,383; April—15,872; May—15,912; June—15,933; July—24,325; August—24,354; September—24,384; October—32,876; November—32,952; and December—33,039.

[2] Series previously shown as U.S. savings bonds. Beginning February 1997, includes U.S. retirement plan bonds, U.S. individual retirement bonds, and U.S. savings notes previously included in "other" nonmarketable interest-bearing public debt securities in this table. Data prior to February 1997 do not reflect this change.

[3] Nonmarketable certificates of indebtedness, notes, bonds, and bills in the Treasury foreign series of dollar-denominated and foreign-currency denominated issues.

[4] Includes depository bonds, retirement plan bonds, Rural Electrification Administration bonds, State and local bonds, and special issues held only by U.S. Government agencies and trust funds and the Federal home loan banks. See footnote 2.

[5] Includes $5,610 million in certificates not shown separately.

Note.—Through fiscal year 1976, the fiscal year was on a July 1–June 30 basis; beginning October 1976 (fiscal year 1977), the fiscal year is on an October 1–September 30 basis.

Source: Department of the Treasury.

TABLE B-88.—*Maturity distribution and average length of marketable interest-bearing public debt securities held by private investors, 1967–97*

End of year or month	Amount outstanding, privately held	Maturity class					Average length [1]	
		Within 1 year	1 to 5 years	5 to 10 years	10 to 20 years	20 years and over		
	Millions of dollars						Years	Months
Fiscal year:								
1967	150,321	56,561	53,584	21,057	6,153	12,968	5	1
1968	159,671	66,746	52,295	21,850	6,110	12,670	4	5
1969	156,008	69,311	50,182	18,078	6,097	12,337	4	2
1970	157,910	76,443	57,035	8,286	7,876	8,272	3	8
1971	161,863	74,803	58,557	14,503	6,357	7,645	3	6
1972	165,978	79,509	57,157	16,033	6,358	6,922	3	3
1973	167,869	84,041	54,139	16,385	8,741	4,564	3	1
1974	164,862	87,150	50,103	14,197	9,930	3,481	2	11
1975	210,382	115,677	65,852	15,385	8,857	4,611	2	8
1976	279,782	150,296	90,578	24,169	8,087	6,652	2	7
1977	326,674	161,329	113,319	33,067	8,428	10,531	2	11
1978	356,501	163,819	132,993	33,500	11,383	14,805	3	3
1979	380,530	181,883	127,574	32,279	18,489	20,304	3	7
1980	463,717	220,084	156,244	38,809	25,901	22,679	3	9
1981	549,863	256,187	182,237	48,743	32,569	30,127	4	0
1982	682,043	314,436	221,783	75,749	33,017	37,058	3	11
1983	862,631	379,579	294,955	99,174	40,826	48,097	4	1
1984	1,017,488	437,941	332,808	130,417	49,664	66,658	4	6
1985	1,185,675	472,661	402,766	159,383	62,853	88,012	4	11
1986	1,354,275	506,903	467,348	189,995	70,664	119,365	5	3
1987	1,445,366	483,582	526,746	209,160	72,862	153,016	5	9
1988	1,555,208	524,201	552,993	232,453	74,186	171,375	5	9
1989	1,654,660	546,751	578,333	247,428	80,616	201,532	6	0
1990	1,841,903	626,297	630,144	267,573	82,713	235,176	6	1
1991	2,113,799	713,778	761,243	280,574	84,900	273,304	6	0
1992	2,363,802	808,705	866,329	295,921	84,706	308,141	5	11
1993	2,562,336	858,135	978,714	306,663	94,345	324,479	5	10
1994	2,719,861	877,932	1,128,322	289,998	88,208	335,401	5	8
1995	2,870,781	1,002,875	1,157,492	290,111	87,297	333,006	5	4
1996	3,011,185	1,058,558	1,212,258	306,643	111,360	322,366	5	3
1997	2,998,846	1,017,913	1,206,993	321,622	154,205	298,113	5	4
1996: Jan	2,937,115	1,050,406	1,174,222	292,525	93,339	326,622	5	2
Feb	2,994,090	1,078,387	1,189,173	299,298	95,090	332,141	5	3
Mar	2,980,688	1,097,120	1,158,416	298,496	94,990	331,666	5	2
Apr	2,968,878	1,055,822	1,188,828	297,917	94,820	331,491	5	3
May	2,983,624	1,061,225	1,199,184	298,842	111,981	312,391	5	3
June	2,943,097	1,052,190	1,168,683	299,042	111,395	311,787	5	3
July	2,996,840	1,067,689	1,196,678	309,371	110,820	312,282	5	2
Aug	2,989,680	1,074,540	1,176,091	305,079	112,150	321,820	5	3
Sept	3,011,185	1,058,558	1,212,258	306,643	111,360	322,366	5	3
Oct	3,021,881	1,062,308	1,207,999	317,522	111,893	322,160	5	3
Nov	3,028,647	1,084,720	1,198,931	302,951	128,832	313,214	5	3
Dec	3,032,551	1,061,459	1,231,746	301,103	128,054	310,188	5	3
1997: Jan	3,025,762	1,049,217	1,230,524	302,878	128,679	314,464	5	3
Feb	3,052,688	1,062,767	1,225,904	315,125	126,023	322,870	5	4
Mar	3,082,541	1,087,199	1,224,620	323,173	125,228	322,322	5	3
Apr	2,997,163	1,035,135	1,199,000	327,320	119,853	315,855	5	3
May	2,988,194	1,024,615	1,182,510	331,276	143,676	306,117	5	5
June	2,989,260	1,007,563	1,206,304	330,005	141,299	304,090	5	4
July	3,002,678	1,016,588	1,208,014	331,086	142,476	304,514	5	4
Aug	2,995,863	1,033,763	1,184,038	321,471	155,967	300,624	5	5
Sept	2,998,846	1,017,913	1,206,993	321,622	154,205	298,113	5	4
Oct	2,998,652	1,020,602	1,200,942	320,882	154,778	301,488	5	4
Nov	2,988,004	1,039,059	1,155,293	330,129	153,997	309,526	5	5
Dec	2,988,654	1,027,280	1,170,833	328,855	153,224	308,462	5	5

[1] Treasury inflation-indexed notes, first offered in 1997, are excluded from the average length calculation.

Note.—All issues classified to final maturity.

Through fiscal year 1976, the fiscal year was on a July 1–June 30 basis; beginning October 1976 (fiscal year 1977), the fiscal year is on an October 1–September 30 basis.

Source: Department of the Treasury.

TABLE B–89.—*Estimated ownership of public debt securities by private investors, 1976–97*

[Par values;[1] billions of dollars]

End of month	Total	Commercial banks[2]	Held by private investors — Nonbank investors — Total	Individuals[3] Total	Individuals[3] Savings bonds[4]	Individuals[3] Other securities	Insurance companies	Money market funds	Corporations[5]	State and local governments[6]	Foreign and international[7]	Other investors[8]
1976: June	376.4	92.5	283.9	96.1	69.6	26.5	10.7	0.8	23.3	36.7	69.8	46.5
Dec	409.5	103.8	305.7	101.6	72.0	29.6	12.7	1.1	23.5	44.3	78.1	44.4
1977: June	421.0	102.9	318.1	104.9	74.4	30.5	13.0	.8	22.1	56.7	87.9	32.7
Dec	461.3	102.0	359.3	107.8	76.7	31.1	15.1	.9	18.2	68.1	109.6	39.6
1978: June	477.8	99.6	378.2	109.0	79.1	29.9	14.2	1.3	17.3	82.6	119.5	34.3
Dec	508.6	95.3	413.3	114.0	80.7	33.3	15.3	1.5	17.3	93.1	133.1	39.0
1979: June	516.6	94.6	422.0	115.5	80.6	34.9	16.0	3.8	18.6	102.7	114.9	50.5
Dec	540.5	95.6	444.9	118.0	79.9	38.1	15.6	5.6	17.0	100.2	119.0	69.5
1980: June	558.2	98.5	459.7	116.5	73.4	43.1	15.3	5.3	14.0	100.1	118.2	90.3
Dec	616.4	111.5	504.9	117.1	72.5	44.6	18.1	3.5	19.3	114.2	129.7	103.0
1981: June	651.2	115.0	536.2	107.4	69.2	38.2	19.9	9.0	19.9	128.1	136.6	115.3
Dec	694.5	113.8	580.7	110.8	68.1	42.7	21.6	21.5	17.9	135.9	136.6	136.4
1982: June	740.9	114.7	626.2	114.1	67.4	46.7	24.4	22.4	17.6	157.9	137.2	152.6
Dec	848.4	134.0	714.4	116.5	68.3	48.2	30.6	42.6	24.5	163.2	149.5	187.5
1983: June	948.6	167.4	781.2	121.3	69.7	51.6	37.8	28.3	32.8	184.3	160.1	216.6
Dec	1,022.6	179.5	843.1	133.4	71.5	61.9	46.0	22.8	39.7	199.1	166.3	235.8
1984: June	1,102.2	180.6	921.6	142.2	72.9	69.3	51.2	14.9	45.3	218.7	171.6	277.7
Dec	1,212.5	181.5	1,031.0	143.8	74.5	69.3	64.5	25.9	50.1	233.9	205.9	306.9
1985: June	1,292.0	195.6	1,096.4	148.7	76.7	72.0	69.1	24.8	54.9	267.7	213.8	317.4
Dec	1,417.2	189.4	1,227.8	154.8	79.8	75.0	80.5	25.1	59.0	341.5	224.8	342.1
1986: June	1,502.7	194.4	1,308.3	159.5	83.8	75.7	87.9	22.8	61.2	381.2	250.9	344.8
Dec	1,602.0	197.7	1,404.3	162.7	92.3	70.4	101.6	28.6	68.8	418.5	263.4	360.7
1987: June	1,658.1	192.5	1,465.6	165.6	96.8	68.8	104.7	20.6	79.7	464.3	281.1	349.6
Dec	1,731.4	194.4	1,537.0	172.4	101.1	71.3	108.1	14.6	84.6	478.3	299.7	379.3
1988: June	1,786.7	190.8	1,595.9	182.0	106.2	75.8	113.5	13.4	87.6	482.7	345.4	371.3
Dec	1,858.5	185.3	1,673.2	190.4	109.6	80.8	118.6	11.8	86.0	488.1	362.2	416.1
1989: June	1,909.1	178.4	1,730.7	211.7	114.0	97.7	120.6	11.3	91.0	482.6	369.1	444.4
Dec	2,015.8	165.3	1,850.5	216.4	117.7	98.7	123.9	14.9	93.4	493.9	429.6	478.4
1990: June	2,141.8	177.3	1,964.5	229.6	121.9	107.7	133.7	28.0	96.9	545.2	427.3	503.8
Dec	2,288.3	172.1	2,116.2	233.8	126.2	107.6	138.2	45.5	108.9	550.3	458.4	581.1
1991: June	2,397.9	196.2	2,201.7	243.5	133.2	110.3	156.8	55.2	130.8	565.9	473.6	575.8
Dec	2,563.2	232.5	2,330.7	263.9	138.1	125.8	181.8	80.0	150.8	583.0	491.7	579.5
1992: June	2,712.4	267.0	2,445.4	275.1	145.4	129.7	192.8	79.4	175.0	576.8	529.6	616.7
Dec	2,839.9	294.4	2,545.5	289.2	157.3	131.9	197.5	79.7	192.5	562.7	549.7	674.2
1993: Mar	2,895.0	310.2	2,584.8	297.7	163.6	134.1	208.0	77.9	199.3	582.5	564.2	655.2
June	2,936.3	307.2	2,629.1	303.0	166.5	136.4	217.8	76.2	206.1	596.1	567.7	662.1
Sept	2,983.0	313.9	2,669.1	305.8	169.1	136.7	229.4	74.8	215.6	596.8	591.3	655.3
Dec	3,047.4	322.2	2,725.2	309.9	171.9	137.9	234.5	80.8	213.0	609.2	622.9	655.0
1994: Mar	3,094.6	344.4	2,750.2	315.1	175.0	140.1	233.4	69.3	216.3	614.4	633.3	668.3
June	3,088.2	330.1	2,758.1	321.1	177.1	144.0	238.0	59.9	226.3	595.9	633.2	683.7
Sept	3,127.8	313.2	2,814.6	327.2	178.6	148.6	243.7	59.9	229.3	569.1	655.8	729.6
Dec	3,168.0	290.4	2,877.6	331.2	180.5	150.7	240.1	67.6	224.5	540.2	688.6	785.5
1995: Mar	3,239.2	308.1	2,931.1	342.8	181.4	161.4	244.2	67.7	230.3	525.3	729.2	791.6
June	3,245.0	298.4	2,946.6	344.2	182.6	161.6	245.0	58.7	227.7	485.5	784.2	801.2
Sept	3,279.5	289.4	2,990.1	345.9	183.5	162.4	245.2	64.2	224.1	454.2	848.4	808.1
Dec	3,294.9	278.7	3,016.2	347.7	185.0	162.7	241.5	71.5	228.8	421.5	862.2	843.0
1996: Mar	3,382.8	284.0	3,098.8	347.2	185.8	161.4	239.4	85.7	229.0	423.4	931.5	842.6
June	3,347.3	280.2	3,067.1	347.6	186.5	161.1	229.5	82.1	230.9	403.1	959.8	814.1
Sept	3,386.2	274.8	3,111.4	353.8	186.8	167.0	226.8	85.2	249.1	326.4	1,030.9	839.2
Dec	3,411.2	261.7	3,149.5	356.6	187.0	169.6	214.1	91.6	258.5	363.7	1,131.8	733.2
1997: Mar	3,451.7	282.3	3,169.4	355.4	186.5	168.9	214.3	84.0	262.5	348.0	1,215.4	689.8
June	3,361.7	265.7	3,096.0	355.4	186.3	169.1	203.4	77.4	261.0	337.4	1,246.9	614.5
Sept	3,388.9	260.0	3,128.9	354.8	186.2	168.6	192.0	76.4	266.5	333.5	1,292.4	613.3

[1] U.S. savings bonds, series A–F and J, are included at current redemption value.
[2] Includes domestically chartered banks, U.S. branches and agencies of foreign banks, New York investment companies majority owned by foreign banks, and Edge Act corporations owned by domestically chartered banks, foreign banks, and banks in U.S. affiliated territories.
[3] Exclusive of banks and personal trust accounts.
[4] Includes U.S. savings notes. Sales began May 1, 1967, and were discontinued June 30, 1970.
[5] Exclusive of banks and insurance companies.
[6] State and local government holdings (beginning 1979) include their fully defeased debt that is backed by U.S. Treasury securities. Includes State and local pension funds.
[7] Consists of the investments of foreign and international accounts (both official and private) in U.S. public debt issues. Reflects 1978 benchmark through December 1984; December 1984 benchmark through 1989; and December 1989 benchmark thereafter.
[8] Includes savings and loan associations, credit unions, nonprofit institutions, mutual savings banks, corporate pension trust funds, dealers and brokers, certain Government deposit accounts, and Government-sponsored enterprises.

Source: Department of the Treasury.

TABLE B–90.—*Corporate profits with inventory valuation and capital consumption adjustments,*
1959–97

[Billions of dollars; quarterly data at seasonally adjusted annual rates]

Year or quarter	Corporate profits with inventory valuation and capital consumption adjustments	Corporate profits tax liability	Corporate profits after tax with inventory valuation and capital consumption adjustments		Undistributed profits with inventory valuation and capital consumption adjustments
			Total	Dividends	
1959	52.9	23.6	29.2	12.7	16.5
1960	51.4	22.7	28.7	13.4	15.3
1961	52.5	22.8	29.7	14.0	15.7
1962	60.5	24.0	36.5	15.0	21.5
1963	66.3	26.2	40.1	16.1	24.0
1964	73.3	28.0	45.3	18.0	27.3
1965	84.1	30.9	53.3	20.2	33.1
1966	89.8	33.7	56.2	20.9	35.2
1967	87.4	32.7	54.7	22.1	32.7
1968	94.2	39.4	54.9	24.6	30.2
1969	90.9	39.7	51.3	25.2	26.0
1970	78.7	34.4	44.4	23.7	20.7
1971	92.0	37.7	54.3	23.7	30.5
1972	106.7	41.9	64.8	25.8	39.0
1973	120.1	49.3	70.8	28.1	42.7
1974	109.2	51.8	57.4	30.4	27.0
1975	128.2	50.9	77.3	30.1	47.2
1976	154.9	64.2	90.7	35.9	54.8
1977	184.3	73.0	111.3	40.8	70.5
1978	209.0	83.5	125.5	46.0	79.5
1979	213.1	88.0	125.1	52.5	72.6
1980	188.3	84.8	103.5	59.3	44.1
1981	207.0	81.1	125.9	69.5	56.4
1982	182.3	63.1	119.2	69.8	49.4
1983	235.2	77.2	157.9	80.8	77.2
1984	290.1	94.0	196.1	83.2	112.8
1985	304.0	96.5	207.5	92.8	114.7
1986	293.8	106.5	187.3	110.2	77.1
1987	333.2	127.1	206.1	107.0	99.1
1988	382.1	137.0	245.1	116.8	128.3
1989	380.0	141.3	238.7	138.9	99.7
1990	397.1	140.5	256.6	151.9	104.7
1991	411.3	133.4	277.9	163.1	114.8
1992	428.0	143.0	285.0	169.5	115.5
1993	492.8	165.2	327.6	195.8	131.9
1994	570.5	186.6	383.8	216.2	167.6
1995	650.0	213.2	436.7	264.4	172.4
1996	735.9	229.0	506.9	304.8	202.1
1992: I	444.2	143.9	300.3	162.1	138.2
II	437.2	150.9	286.3	164.6	121.7
III	376.1	127.6	248.5	170.9	77.6
IV	454.6	149.7	304.9	180.4	124.5
1993: I	459.2	149.2	309.9	188.0	121.9
II	478.2	165.4	312.8	192.5	120.3
III	492.8	161.2	331.5	198.3	133.2
IV	541.2	184.9	356.3	204.2	152.1
1994: I	512.0	163.0	348.9	203.2	145.8
II	562.0	182.8	379.3	211.6	167.7
III	590.1	194.6	395.5	220.0	175.5
IV	617.7	206.2	411.5	230.2	181.3
1995: I	613.2	209.6	403.6	255.5	148.1
II	628.0	209.1	418.9	260.8	158.1
III	672.8	218.8	454.0	266.8	187.2
IV	685.7	215.3	470.4	274.4	196.0
1996: I	717.7	226.2	491.5	300.7	190.8
II	738.5	232.2	506.3	303.7	202.6
III	739.6	231.6	508.0	305.7	202.3
IV	747.8	226.0	521.8	309.1	212.6
1997: I	779.6	241.2	538.4	326.8	211.5
II	795.1	244.5	550.6	333.0	217.6
III	827.3	258.2	569.1	339.1	230.0

Source: Department of Commerce, Bureau of Economic Analysis.

TABLE B–91.—*Corporate profits by industry, 1959–97*

[Billions of dollars; quarterly data at seasonally adjusted annual rates]

		Corporate profits with inventory valuation adjustment and without capital consumption adjustment										
		Domestic industries										
			Financial[1]			Nonfinancial						
Year or quarter	Total	Total	Total	Federal Reserve banks	Other	Total	Manu-facturing[2]	Trans-portation and public utilities	Whole-sale trade	Retail trade	Other	Rest of the world
1959	53.1	50.4	7.0	0.7	6.3	43.4	26.5	7.1	2.8	3.3	3.6	2.7
1960	51.0	47.8	7.7	.9	6.7	40.2	23.8	7.5	2.5	2.8	3.6	3.1
1961	51.3	48.0	7.5	.8	6.8	40.4	23.4	7.9	2.5	3.0	3.6	3.3
1962	56.4	52.6	7.6	.9	6.8	45.0	26.3	8.5	2.8	3.4	3.9	3.8
1963	61.2	57.1	7.3	1.0	6.4	49.8	29.6	9.5	2.8	3.6	4.4	4.1
1964	67.5	63.0	7.5	1.1	6.4	55.5	32.4	10.2	3.4	4.5	5.1	4.5
1965	77.6	72.9	7.9	1.3	6.5	65.0	39.7	11.0	3.8	4.9	5.6	4.7
1966	83.0	78.5	9.2	1.7	7.5	69.3	42.4	11.9	3.9	4.8	6.2	4.5
1967	80.3	75.5	9.5	2.0	7.6	66.0	39.0	10.9	4.0	5.6	6.4	4.8
1968	86.9	81.3	10.9	2.5	8.4	70.4	41.7	11.0	4.5	6.4	6.8	5.6
1969	83.2	76.6	11.6	3.1	8.5	65.0	37.0	10.6	4.8	6.4	6.2	6.6
1970	71.8	64.7	13.1	3.5	9.6	51.6	27.1	8.2	4.3	6.0	5.9	7.1
1971	85.5	77.7	15.2	3.3	11.9	62.5	34.8	8.9	5.1	7.2	6.6	7.9
1972	97.9	88.4	16.4	3.3	13.1	72.0	41.4	9.4	6.8	7.4	7.1	9.5
1973	110.9	96.0	17.5	4.5	13.0	78.5	46.7	9.0	8.0	6.6	8.2	14.9
1974	103.4	85.9	16.2	5.7	10.5	69.7	40.7	7.6	11.3	2.3	7.7	17.5
1975	129.4	114.8	15.9	5.6	10.3	98.9	54.5	10.9	13.6	8.2	11.6	14.6
1976	158.9	142.3	19.9	5.9	14.0	122.4	70.7	15.3	12.7	10.5	13.3	16.5
1977	186.8	167.7	25.7	6.1	19.6	142.0	78.5	18.5	15.4	12.4	17.1	19.1
1978	213.1	190.2	31.8	7.6	24.1	158.4	89.6	21.7	15.4	12.3	19.4	22.9
1979	220.2	185.6	31.6	9.4	22.2	153.9	88.3	16.9	18.5	9.8	20.5	34.6
1980	198.3	162.9	24.3	11.8	12.6	138.5	75.8	18.3	16.7	6.1	21.6	35.5
1981	204.1	174.4	18.7	14.4	4.3	155.7	87.5	20.1	21.9	9.8	16.3	29.7
1982	166.8	139.4	15.6	15.2	.4	123.8	63.4	20.9	19.0	13.1	7.4	27.4
1983	203.7	173.1	24.8	14.6	10.2	148.3	72.8	29.7	18.7	18.7	8.4	30.6
1984	238.5	205.8	20.5	16.4	4.1	185.3	86.6	39.7	27.8	21.5	9.8	32.7
1985	230.5	197.1	29.0	16.3	12.6	168.1	81.6	34.3	20.6	22.5	9.1	33.4
1986	234.0	199.3	36.4	15.5	20.9	162.9	60.2	38.1	22.9	23.7	18.0	34.6
1987	272.9	231.3	37.1	15.7	21.4	194.2	85.0	41.7	16.7	23.9	26.9	41.6
1988	325.0	274.3	43.0	17.6	25.4	231.2	115.1	48.7	19.3	19.6	28.5	50.7
1989	330.6	272.6	53.1	20.2	32.9	219.6	109.3	42.6	20.4	20.7	26.6	58.0
1990	358.2	292.5	68.6	21.4	47.2	223.8	112.3	43.2	17.2	20.6	30.6	65.7
1991	378.2	309.5	87.4	20.3	67.1	222.1	92.7	53.9	20.6	26.1	28.9	68.7
1992	398.9	334.0	83.7	17.8	65.9	250.3	96.3	57.8	23.0	32.2	41.0	64.9
1993	456.9	383.0	82.9	16.1	66.8	300.1	116.7	69.4	24.3	38.9	50.9	73.9
1994	519.1	445.7	69.4	17.8	51.7	376.3	151.6	83.1	29.4	46.0	66.2	73.4
1995	598.4	511.7	97.6	22.2	75.4	414.1	181.3	86.4	26.9	41.9	77.6	86.7
1996	674.1	578.2	103.5	22.0	81.5	474.7	205.5	91.7	38.3	48.9	90.3	95.9
1992:I	411.4	341.7	105.1	18.8	86.3	236.6	92.0	61.2	14.6	32.0	36.8	69.7
II	404.3	337.6	96.9	18.4	78.5	240.7	89.6	57.4	21.8	34.3	37.5	66.7
III	359.4	295.6	49.7	17.3	32.4	245.9	98.4	54.3	27.4	25.2	40.6	63.9
IV	420.5	361.2	83.1	16.7	66.4	278.1	105.1	58.3	28.3	37.3	49.3	59.3
1993:I	419.2	339.7	76.6	16.4	60.2	263.1	95.8	65.5	20.5	34.7	46.5	79.5
II	444.4	374.5	84.7	16.0	68.6	289.8	115.1	68.2	26.3	36.6	43.6	69.9
III	459.8	382.7	79.4	16.0	63.4	303.3	113.8	70.0	24.8	41.4	53.3	77.1
IV	504.1	435.2	91.0	15.9	75.0	344.2	142.2	73.8	25.4	42.7	60.2	68.9
1994:I	470.8	398.9	44.1	16.1	28.1	354.7	149.7	74.0	28.1	41.6	61.3	71.9
II	510.2	437.9	72.3	16.8	55.5	365.6	138.8	82.3	33.8	47.4	63.2	72.3
III	535.0	460.7	81.3	18.2	63.1	379.5	151.6	85.1	27.3	47.2	68.3	74.2
IV	560.3	485.2	80.0	20.0	60.0	405.3	166.2	90.8	28.6	47.8	71.8	75.0
1995:I	560.4	476.9	89.5	21.6	67.9	387.3	161.9	85.5	25.5	41.0	73.5	83.5
II	577.2	486.8	96.3	22.5	73.8	390.4	170.3	85.2	20.3	42.3	72.3	90.4
III	621.4	540.9	107.1	22.4	84.7	433.8	194.5	88.8	28.5	42.2	79.7	80.4
IV	634.5	542.1	97.4	22.1	75.2	444.7	198.4	86.0	33.2	42.1	85.0	92.4
1996:I	659.8	568.7	110.4	21.8	88.6	458.3	197.1	88.9	37.2	46.0	89.1	91.1
II	676.8	583.5	111.5	21.9	89.6	472.0	204.8	96.0	30.8	50.6	89.7	93.3
III	676.4	584.6	104.0	22.0	82.0	480.7	210.5	91.2	37.7	50.6	90.6	91.8
IV	683.4	575.8	88.1	22.3	65.8	487.8	209.7	90.5	47.4	48.3	91.9	107.5
1997:I	711.9	614.5	116.5	22.8	93.7	498.0	208.2	91.5	49.0	55.1	94.2	97.4
II	725.7	624.9	117.5	23.2	94.3	507.4	221.0	89.6	49.5	54.9	92.4	100.8
III	757.1	657.2	119.4	23.7	95.7	537.8	240.4	90.0	54.1	57.9	95.3	99.9

[1] Consists of the following industries: Depository institutions; nondepository credit institutions; security and commodity brokers; insurance carriers; regulated investment companies; small business investment companies; and real estate investment trusts.

[2] See Table B–92 for industry detail.

Note.—The industry classification is on a company basis and is based on the 1987 Standard Industrial Classification (SIC) beginning 1987, and on the 1972 SIC for earlier years shown.

Source: Department of Commerce, Bureau of Economic Analysis.

TABLE B–92.—*Corporate profits of manufacturing industries, 1959–97*

[Billions of dollars; quarterly data at seasonally adjusted annual rates]

| | | Corporate profits with inventory valuation adjustment and without capital consumption adjustment | | | | | | | | | | | |
| | | Durable goods | | | | | | | Nondurable goods | | | | |
Year or quarter	Total manufac- turing	Total	Pri- mary metal indus- tries	Fabri- cated metal prod- ucts	Indus- trial machin- ery and equip- ment	Elec- tronic and other electric equip- ment	Motor vehicles and equip- ment	Other	Total	Food and kindred prod- ucts	Chem- icals and allied prod- ucts	Petro- leum and coal prod- ucts	Other
1959	26.5	13.7	2.3	1.1	2.2	1.7	3.0	3.5	12.8	2.5	3.5	2.6	4.3
1960	23.8	11.7	2.0	.8	1.8	1.3	3.0	2.8	12.1	2.2	3.1	2.6	4.2
1961	23.4	11.4	1.6	1.0	1.9	1.3	2.5	3.1	12.0	2.4	3.3	2.2	4.2
1962	26.3	14.1	1.6	1.2	2.4	1.5	4.0	3.5	12.2	2.4	3.2	2.2	4.4
1963	29.6	16.4	2.0	1.3	2.5	1.6	4.9	4.0	13.2	2.7	3.7	2.2	4.7
1964	32.4	18.0	2.5	1.4	3.3	1.7	4.6	4.5	14.4	2.7	4.1	2.3	5.3
1965	39.7	23.2	3.1	2.1	4.0	2.7	6.2	5.2	16.4	2.8	4.6	2.9	6.1
1966	42.4	23.9	3.6	2.4	4.5	3.0	5.1	5.3	18.4	3.3	4.9	3.4	6.8
1967	39.0	21.2	2.7	2.5	4.1	3.0	4.0	5.0	17.8	3.2	4.3	3.9	6.4
1968	41.7	22.4	1.9	2.3	4.1	2.9	5.5	5.7	19.2	3.2	5.2	3.7	7.0
1969	37.0	19.0	1.4	2.0	3.7	2.3	4.8	4.9	18.0	3.0	4.6	3.3	7.0
1970	27.1	10.4	.8	1.1	3.0	1.3	1.3	3.0	16.8	3.2	3.9	3.6	6.1
1971	34.8	16.6	.8	1.5	3.0	1.9	5.1	4.2	18.2	3.5	4.5	3.7	6.5
1972	41.4	22.6	1.6	2.2	4.3	2.8	5.9	5.7	18.8	2.9	5.2	3.2	7.5
1973	46.7	25.0	2.3	2.6	4.7	3.2	5.9	6.3	21.7	2.5	6.1	5.2	7.9
1974	40.7	15.1	5.0	1.8	3.1	.5	.7	4.1	25.7	2.6	5.2	10.7	7.2
1975	54.5	20.3	2.7	3.2	4.8	2.6	2.2	4.8	34.1	8.6	6.3	9.8	9.4
1976	70.7	31.2	2.1	3.9	6.7	3.8	7.4	7.4	39.5	7.1	8.2	13.3	11.0
1977	78.5	37.6	1.0	4.5	8.3	5.8	9.3	8.6	41.0	6.8	7.7	12.9	13.6
1978	89.6	45.0	3.6	5.0	10.4	6.6	8.9	10.5	44.6	6.1	8.2	15.5	14.8
1979	88.3	36.5	3.5	5.2	9.1	5.4	4.6	8.6	51.8	5.8	7.1	24.5	14.6
1980	75.8	17.9	2.6	4.3	7.5	5.0	–4.3	2.8	57.8	6.0	5.5	33.6	12.9
1981	87.5	18.1	3.0	4.4	8.2	4.9	.2	–2.7	69.4	9.0	7.6	38.6	14.2
1982	63.4	4.9	–4.7	2.6	3.4	1.3	–.3	2.7	58.5	7.3	4.7	31.6	14.9
1983	72.8	18.6	–5.0	3.0	3.7	3.4	5.2	8.3	54.2	6.1	6.9	22.5	18.6
1984	86.6	36.7	–.5	4.6	5.5	5.1	8.9	13.0	49.9	6.5	7.7	16.1	19.6
1985	81.6	30.1	–.8	4.7	5.5	2.5	7.3	10.8	51.6	8.6	6.1	17.3	19.6
1986	60.2	28.6	.9	5.2	2.7	2.7	4.4	12.7	31.7	7.3	8.0	–5.8	22.1
1987	85.0	40.1	2.7	5.4	4.7	6.5	3.8	17.0	45.0	11.3	15.1	–3.8	22.4
1988	115.1	49.2	5.9	6.3	9.4	5.7	5.7	16.2	65.9	11.9	19.3	10.4	24.3
1989	109.3	49.3	6.0	6.5	11.1	9.5	2.2	13.9	60.0	11.0	19.0	5.0	25.0
1990	112.3	40.9	3.3	6.2	10.2	8.4	–2.2	15.0	71.4	14.5	17.0	17.0	22.9
1991	92.7	30.5	1.3	5.4	4.3	8.9	–5.4	16.0	62.1	18.2	15.7	5.9	22.3
1992	96.3	37.1	–.1	6.5	5.6	10.0	–1.1	16.2	59.1	18.3	16.5	–1.6	26.0
1993	116.7	54.5	.3	7.4	7.5	15.3	5.5	18.6	62.2	16.5	17.4	2.3	26.0
1994	151.6	76.7	2.2	11.0	12.7	22.5	7.5	20.9	74.8	20.0	24.5	.1	30.2
1995	181.3	85.2	6.5	12.4	22.0	19.2	–.2	25.3	96.0	27.1	30.3	6.0	32.6
1996	205.5	99.0	5.6	17.1	25.8	23.9	–3.2	29.8	106.5	28.5	31.2	10.0	36.8
1992: I	92.0	33.4	.5	6.2	4.7	9.8	–2.0	14.2	58.6	15.9	17.1	1.8	23.8
II	89.6	35.3	.3	6.4	5.4	8.5	–.2	14.8	54.3	20.2	15.2	–6.9	25.8
III	98.4	37.2	–.5	7.2	6.0	9.7	–2.8	17.6	61.2	20.0	16.2	–1.8	26.8
IV	105.1	42.6	–.8	6.4	6.4	11.8	.4	18.4	62.4	17.2	17.3	.4	27.6
1993: I	95.8	39.1	–1.9	5.4	4.2	13.8	–.3	18.0	56.7	18.1	18.3	–6.1	26.4
II	115.1	52.9	1.2	7.3	8.1	12.4	4.7	19.2	62.2	15.9	15.2	2.7	28.3
III	113.8	55.9	–.3	7.6	9.3	16.8	4.7	17.8	57.9	16.4	15.2	3.8	22.5
IV	142.2	70.3	2.1	9.1	8.4	18.3	12.9	19.4	71.9	15.6	20.9	8.8	26.6
1994: I	149.7	77.0	2.2	10.6	9.8	20.1	14.1	20.1	72.7	19.3	22.6	.0	30.8
II	138.8	73.7	1.7	10.0	12.5	20.8	8.8	20.0	65.1	18.5	23.7	–9.2	32.1
III	151.6	73.3	2.3	10.8	12.2	23.6	3.7	20.7	78.3	19.7	24.0	4.7	29.9
IV	166.2	83.0	2.6	12.7	16.3	25.5	3.3	22.7	83.2	22.5	27.8	5.0	27.9
1995: I	161.9	81.1	4.5	11.2	19.7	20.1	2.5	23.1	80.8	25.4	25.7	–.9	30.6
II	170.3	78.6	7.6	12.6	19.8	16.9	–1.9	23.7	91.7	27.4	30.0	5.2	29.1
III	194.5	88.3	6.6	12.4	23.0	19.8	.1	26.4	106.2	27.5	33.2	12.7	32.8
IV	198.4	93.0	7.4	13.4	25.5	20.0	–1.4	28.2	105.4	28.2	32.1	7.1	37.9
1996: I	197.1	94.5	5.9	16.2	27.0	19.0	–2.7	29.2	102.7	27.3	31.8	5.2	38.3
II	204.8	98.9	4.4	16.2	25.9	21.7	–.1	30.8	105.8	23.8	32.4	12.8	36.9
III	210.5	102.9	7.0	18.0	25.6	25.2	–1.5	28.6	107.7	28.8	31.5	10.0	37.3
IV	209.7	99.7	5.1	18.1	24.6	29.6	–8.3	30.6	109.9	34.2	28.9	11.9	34.9
1997: I	208.2	101.3	3.9	17.4	24.0	31.4	–1.3	25.9	106.9	28.0	28.8	12.4	37.7
II	221.0	111.8	5.6	18.4	27.8	33.3	–3.5	30.2	109.2	28.2	29.9	10.3	40.8
III	240.4	128.1	7.6	20.8	32.5	36.7	.4	30.0	112.3	29.1	30.0	12.4	40.9

Note.—The industry classification is on a company basis and is based on the 1987 Standard Industrial Classification (SIC) beginning 1987 and on the 1972 SIC for earlier years shown. In the 1972 SIC, the categories shown here as "industrial machinery and equipment" and "electronic and other electric equipment" were identified as "machinery, except electrical" and "electric and electronic equipment," respectively.

Source: Department of Commerce, Bureau of Economic Analysis.

TABLE B–93.—*Sales, profits, and stockholders' equity, all manufacturing corporations, 1952–97*

[Billions of dollars]

Year or quarter	All manufacturing corporations				Durable goods industries				Nondurable goods industries			
	Sales (net)	Profits		Stock-holders' equity[2]	Sales (net)	Profits		Stock-holders' equity[2]	Sales (net)	Profits		Stock-holders' equity[2]
		Before income taxes[1]	After income taxes			Before income taxes[1]	After income taxes			Before income taxes[1]	After income taxes	
1952	250.2	22.9	10.7	103.7	122.0	12.9	5.5	49.8	128.0	10.0	5.2	53.9
1953	265.9	24.4	11.3	108.2	137.9	14.0	5.8	52.4	128.0	10.4	5.5	55.7
1954	248.5	20.9	11.2	113.1	122.8	11.4	5.6	54.9	125.7	9.6	5.6	58.2
1955	278.4	28.6	15.1	120.1	142.1	16.5	8.1	58.8	136.3	12.1	7.0	61.3
1956	307.3	29.8	16.2	131.6	159.5	16.5	8.3	65.2	147.8	13.2	7.8	66.4
1957	320.0	28.2	15.4	141.1	166.0	15.8	7.9	70.5	154.1	12.4	7.5	70.6
1958	305.3	22.7	12.7	147.4	148.6	11.4	5.8	72.8	156.7	11.3	6.9	74.6
1959	338.0	29.7	16.3	157.1	169.4	15.8	8.1	77.9	168.5	13.9	8.3	79.2
1960	345.7	27.5	15.2	165.4	173.9	14.0	7.0	82.3	171.8	13.5	8.2	83.1
1961	356.4	27.5	15.3	172.6	175.2	13.6	6.9	84.9	181.2	13.9	8.5	87.7
1962	389.4	31.9	17.7	181.4	195.3	16.8	8.6	89.1	194.1	15.1	9.2	92.3
1963	412.7	34.9	19.5	189.7	209.0	18.5	9.5	93.3	203.6	16.4	10.0	96.3
1964	443.1	39.6	23.2	199.8	226.3	21.2	11.6	98.5	216.8	18.3	11.6	101.3
1965	492.2	46.5	27.5	211.7	257.0	26.2	14.5	105.4	235.2	20.3	13.0	106.3
1966	554.2	51.8	30.9	230.3	291.7	29.2	16.4	115.2	262.4	22.6	14.6	115.1
1967	575.4	47.8	29.0	247.6	300.6	25.7	14.6	125.0	274.8	22.0	14.4	122.6
1968	631.9	55.4	32.1	265.9	335.5	30.6	16.5	135.6	296.4	24.8	15.5	130.3
1969	694.6	58.1	33.2	289.9	366.5	31.5	16.9	147.6	328.1	26.6	16.4	142.3
1970	708.8	48.1	28.6	306.8	363.1	23.0	12.9	155.1	345.7	25.2	15.7	151.7
1971	751.1	52.9	31.0	320.8	381.8	26.5	14.5	160.4	369.3	26.5	16.5	160.5
1972	849.5	63.2	36.5	343.4	435.8	33.6	18.4	171.4	413.7	29.6	18.0	172.0
1973	1,017.2	81.4	48.1	374.1	527.3	43.6	24.8	188.7	489.9	37.8	23.3	185.4
1973: IV	275.1	21.4	13.0	386.4	140.1	10.8	6.3	194.7	135.0	10.6	6.7	191.7
New series:												
1973: IV	236.6	20.6	13.2	368.0	122.7	10.1	6.2	185.8	113.9	10.5	7.0	182.1
1974	1,060.6	92.1	58.7	395.0	529.0	41.1	24.7	196.0	531.6	51.0	34.1	199.0
1975	1,065.2	79.9	49.1	423.4	521.1	35.3	21.4	208.1	544.1	44.6	27.7	215.3
1976	1,203.2	104.9	64.5	462.7	589.6	50.7	30.8	224.3	613.7	54.3	33.7	238.4
1977	1,328.1	115.1	70.4	496.7	657.3	57.9	34.8	239.9	670.8	57.2	35.5	256.8
1978	1,496.4	132.5	81.1	540.5	760.7	69.6	41.8	262.6	735.7	62.9	39.3	277.9
1979	1,741.8	154.2	98.7	600.5	865.7	72.4	45.2	292.5	876.1	81.8	53.5	308.0
1980	1,912.8	145.8	92.6	668.1	889.1	57.4	35.6	317.7	1,023.7	88.4	56.9	350.4
1981	2,144.7	158.6	101.3	743.4	979.5	67.2	41.6	350.4	1,165.2	91.3	59.6	393.0
1982	2,039.4	108.2	70.9	770.2	913.1	34.7	21.7	355.5	1,126.4	73.6	49.3	414.7
1983	2,114.3	133.1	85.8	812.8	973.5	48.7	30.0	372.4	1,140.8	84.4	55.8	440.4
1984	2,335.0	165.6	107.6	864.2	1,107.6	75.5	48.9	395.6	1,227.5	90.0	58.8	468.5
1985	2,331.4	137.0	87.6	866.2	1,142.6	61.5	38.6	420.9	1,188.8	75.6	49.1	445.3
1986	2,220.9	129.3	83.1	874.7	1,125.5	52.1	32.6	436.3	1,095.4	77.2	50.5	438.4
1987	2,378.2	173.0	115.6	900.9	1,178.0	78.0	53.0	444.3	1,200.3	95.1	62.6	456.6
1988	2,596.2	216.1	154.6	957.6	1,284.7	91.7	67.1	468.7	1,311.5	124.4	87.5	488.9
1989	2,745.1	188.8	136.3	999.0	1,356.6	75.2	55.7	501.3	1,388.5	113.5	80.6	497.7
1990	2,810.7	159.6	111.6	1,043.8	1,357.2	57.6	40.9	515.0	1,453.5	102.0	70.6	528.9
1991	2,761.1	99.8	67.5	1,064.1	1,304.0	14.1	7.4	506.8	1,457.1	85.7	60.1	557.4
1992[3]	2,890.2	32.5	23.2	1,034.7	1,389.8	−33.5	−23.7	473.9	1,500.4	66.0	47.0	560.8
1993	3,015.1	118.6	83.9	1,039.7	1,490.2	39.0	27.6	482.7	1,524.9	79.6	56.4	557.1
1994	3,255.8	245.3	176.6	1,110.1	1,657.6	121.6	87.6	533.3	1,598.2	123.7	89.1	576.8
1995	3,528.3	276.5	200.2	1,240.6	1,807.1	131.2	94.8	613.7	1,720.6	145.3	105.4	627.0
1996	3,757.2	308.7	227.0	1,347.6	1,940.7	147.1	106.6	673.7	1,816.5	161.6	120.4	674.0
1995: I	843.0	73.4	52.5	1,194.6	431.6	36.3	26.1	588.8	411.5	37.1	26.4	605.8
II	889.0	79.5	57.6	1,234.8	457.6	39.5	29.2	616.4	431.4	40.0	28.4	618.4
III	881.2	70.8	50.7	1,254.7	445.9	29.2	20.8	619.0	435.3	41.5	29.9	635.8
IV	915.1	52.8	39.4	1,278.4	472.7	26.1	18.7	630.5	442.4	26.7	20.7	647.9
1996: I	884.8	70.4	51.4	1,299.4	457.5	31.8	22.7	644.2	427.3	38.7	28.7	655.2
II	948.4	82.7	59.4	1,328.1	492.5	42.9	31.1	665.0	455.9	39.8	28.3	663.1
III	946.6	84.7	62.6	1,358.6	484.0	38.2	27.8	680.5	462.6	46.5	34.8	678.0
IV	977.3	70.9	53.6	1,404.4	506.7	34.2	25.1	704.9	470.6	36.6	28.5	699.5
1997: I	934.0	82.9	61.1	1,427.9	486.8	38.7	26.9	718.6	447.2	44.3	34.2	709.3
II	987.6	92.2	66.8	1,452.8	527.6	49.2	36.1	731.6	460.0	43.0	30.7	721.2
III	987.0	87.0	62.7	1,478.2	519.2	41.6	29.2	754.3	467.8	45.4	33.5	723.9

[1] In the old series, "income taxes" refers to Federal income taxes only, as State and local income taxes had already been deducted. In the new series, no income taxes have been deducted.
[2] Annual data are average equity for the year (using four end-of-quarter figures).
[3] Data for 1992 (most significantly 1992:I) reflect the early adoption of Financial Accounting Standards Board Statement 106 (Employer's Accounting for Post-Retirement Benefits Other Than Pensions) by a large number of companies during the fourth quarter of 1992. Data for 1993:I also reflect adoption of Statement 106. Corporations must show the cumulative effect of a change in accounting principle in the first quarter of the year in which the change is adopted.

Note.—Data are not necessarily comparable from one period to another due to changes in accounting principles, industry classifications, sampling procedures, etc. For explanatory notes concerning compilation of the series, see "Quarterly Financial Report for Manufacturing, Mining, and Trade Corporations," Department of Commerce, Bureau of the Census.

Source: Department of Commerce, Bureau of the Census.

TABLE B–94.—*Relation of profits after taxes to stockholders' equity and to sales, all manufacturing corporations, 1947–97*

Year or quarter	Ratio of profits after income taxes (annual rate) to stockholders' equity—percent [1]			Profits after income taxes per dollar of sales—cents		
	All manufacturing corporations	Durable goods industries	Nondurable goods industries	All manufacturing corporations	Durable goods industries	Nondurable goods industries
1947	15.6	14.4	16.6	6.7	6.7	6.7
1948	16.0	15.7	16.2	7.0	7.1	6.8
1949	11.6	12.1	11.2	5.8	6.4	5.4
1950	15.4	16.9	14.1	7.1	7.7	6.5
1951	12.1	13.0	11.2	4.9	5.3	4.5
1952	10.3	11.1	9.7	4.3	4.5	4.1
1953	10.5	11.1	9.9	4.3	4.2	4.3
1954	9.9	10.3	9.6	4.5	4.6	4.4
1955	12.6	13.8	11.4	5.4	5.7	5.1
1956	12.3	12.8	11.8	5.3	5.2	5.3
1957	10.9	11.3	10.6	4.8	4.8	4.9
1958	8.6	8.0	9.2	4.2	3.9	4.4
1959	10.4	10.4	10.4	4.8	4.8	4.9
1960	9.2	8.5	9.8	4.4	4.0	4.8
1961	8.9	8.1	9.6	4.3	3.9	4.7
1962	9.8	9.6	9.9	4.5	4.4	4.7
1963	10.3	10.1	10.4	4.7	4.5	4.9
1964	11.6	11.7	11.5	5.2	5.1	5.4
1965	13.0	13.8	12.2	5.6	5.7	5.5
1966	13.4	14.2	12.7	5.6	5.6	5.6
1967	11.7	11.7	11.8	5.0	4.8	5.3
1968	12.1	12.2	11.9	5.1	4.9	5.2
1969	11.5	11.4	11.5	4.8	4.6	5.0
1970	9.3	8.3	10.3	4.0	3.5	4.5
1971	9.7	9.0	10.3	4.1	3.8	4.5
1972	10.6	10.8	10.5	4.3	4.2	4.4
1973	12.8	13.1	12.6	4.7	4.7	4.8
1973: IV	13.4	12.9	14.0	4.7	4.5	5.0
New series:						
1973: IV	14.3	13.3	15.3	5.6	5.0	6.1
1974	14.9	12.6	17.1	5.5	4.7	6.4
1975	11.6	10.3	12.9	4.6	4.1	5.1
1976	13.9	13.7	14.2	5.4	5.2	5.5
1977	14.2	14.5	13.8	5.3	5.3	5.3
1978	15.0	16.0	14.2	5.4	5.5	5.3
1979	16.4	15.4	17.4	5.7	5.2	6.1
1980	13.9	11.2	16.3	4.8	4.0	5.6
1981	13.6	11.9	15.2	4.7	4.2	5.1
1982	9.2	6.1	11.9	3.5	2.4	4.4
1983	10.6	8.1	12.7	4.1	3.1	4.9
1984	12.5	12.4	12.5	4.6	4.4	4.8
1985	10.1	9.2	11.0	3.8	3.4	4.1
1986	9.5	7.5	11.5	3.7	2.9	4.6
1987	12.8	11.9	13.7	4.9	4.5	5.2
1988	16.1	14.3	17.9	6.0	5.2	6.7
1989	13.6	11.1	16.2	5.0	4.1	5.8
1990	10.7	8.0	13.4	4.0	3.0	4.9
1991	6.3	1.5	10.8	2.4	.6	4.1
1992 [2]	2.2	-5.0	8.4	.8	-1.7	3.1
1993	8.1	5.7	10.1	2.8	1.9	3.7
1994	15.9	16.4	15.4	5.4	5.3	5.6
1995	16.1	15.5	16.8	5.7	5.2	6.1
1996	16.8	15.8	17.9	6.0	5.5	6.6
1995: I	17.6	17.7	17.4	6.2	6.1	6.4
II	18.6	18.9	18.4	6.5	6.4	6.6
III	16.2	13.5	18.8	5.8	4.7	6.9
IV	12.3	11.8	12.8	4.3	3.9	4.7
1996: I	15.8	14.1	17.5	5.8	5.0	6.7
II	17.9	18.7	17.1	6.3	6.3	6.2
III	18.4	16.3	20.5	6.6	5.7	7.5
IV	15.3	14.2	16.3	5.5	5.0	6.1
1997: I	17.1	15.0	19.3	6.5	5.5	7.6
II	18.4	19.8	17.0	6.8	6.8	6.7
III	17.0	15.5	18.5	6.3	5.6	7.2

[1] Annual ratios based on average equity for the year (using four end-of-quarter figures). Quarterly ratios based on equity at end of quarter only.
[2] See footnote 3, Table B–93.
Note.—Based on data in millions of dollars.
See Note, Table B–93.
Source: Department of Commerce, Bureau of the Census.

| Year or month | Common stock prices [1] | | | | | | Common stock yields (S&P)(percent) [4] | |
| | New York Stock Exchange indexes (Dec. 31, 1965=50) [2] | | | | | Dow Jones industrial average [2] | Standard & Poor's composite index (1941–43=10) [2] | Dividend-price ratio [5] | Earnings-price ratio [6] |
	Composite	Industrial	Transpor-tation	Utility [3]	Finance				
1955	21.54	....	....	....	....	442.72	40.49	4.08	7.95
1956	24.40	....	....	....	....	493.01	46.62	4.09	7.55
1957	23.67	....	....	....	....	475.71	44.38	4.35	7.89
1958	24.56	....	....	....	....	491.66	46.24	3.97	6.23
1959	30.73	....	....	....	....	632.12	57.38	3.23	5.78
1960	30.01	....	....	....	....	618.04	55.85	3.47	5.90
1961	35.37	....	....	....	....	691.55	66.27	2.98	4.62
1962	33.49	....	....	....	....	639.76	62.38	3.37	5.82
1963	37.51	....	....	....	....	714.81	69.87	3.17	5.50
1964	43.76	....	....	....	....	834.05	81.37	3.01	5.32
1965	47.39	....	....	....	....	910.88	88.17	3.00	5.59
1966	46.15	46.18	50.26	90.81	44.45	873.60	85.26	3.40	6.63
1967	50.77	51.97	53.51	90.86	49.82	879.12	91.93	3.20	5.73
1968	55.37	58.00	50.58	88.38	65.85	906.00	98.70	3.07	5.67
1969	54.67	57.44	46.96	85.60	70.49	876.72	97.84	3.24	6.08
1970	45.72	48.03	32.14	74.47	60.00	753.19	83.22	3.83	6.45
1971	54.22	57.92	44.35	79.05	70.38	884.76	98.29	3.14	5.41
1972	60.29	65.73	50.17	76.95	78.35	950.71	109.20	2.84	5.50
1973	57.42	63.08	37.74	75.38	70.12	923.88	107.43	3.06	7.12
1974	43.84	48.08	31.89	59.58	49.67	759.37	82.85	4.47	11.59
1975	45.73	50.52	31.10	63.00	47.14	802.49	86.16	4.31	9.15
1976	54.46	60.44	39.57	73.94	52.94	974.92	102.01	3.77	8.90
1977	53.69	57.86	41.09	81.84	55.25	894.63	98.20	4.62	10.79
1978	53.70	58.23	43.50	78.44	56.65	820.23	96.02	5.28	12.03
1979	58.32	64.76	47.34	76.41	61.42	844.40	103.01	5.47	13.46
1980	68.10	78.70	60.61	74.69	64.25	891.41	118.78	5.26	12.66
1981	74.02	85.44	72.61	77.81	73.52	932.92	128.05	5.20	11.96
1982	68.93	78.18	60.41	79.49	71.99	884.36	119.71	5.81	11.60
1983	92.63	107.45	89.36	93.99	95.34	1,190.34	160.41	4.40	8.03
1984	92.46	108.01	85.63	92.89	89.28	1,178.48	160.46	4.64	10.02
1985	108.09	123.79	104.11	113.49	114.21	1,328.23	186.84	4.25	8.12
1986	136.00	155.85	119.87	142.72	147.20	1,792.76	236.34	3.49	6.09
1987	161.70	195.31	140.39	148.59	146.48	2,275.99	286.83	3.08	5.48
1988	149.91	180.95	134.12	143.53	127.26	2,060.82	265.79	3.64	8.01
1989	180.02	216.23	175.28	174.87	151.88	2,508.91	322.84	3.45	7.42
1990	183.46	225.78	158.62	181.20	133.26	2,678.94	334.59	3.61	6.47
1991	206.33	258.14	173.99	185.32	150.82	2,929.33	376.18	3.24	4.79
1992	229.01	284.62	201.09	198.91	179.26	3,284.29	415.74	2.99	4.22
1993	249.58	299.99	242.49	228.90	216.42	3,522.06	451.41	2.78	4.46
1994	254.12	315.25	247.29	209.06	209.73	3,793.77	460.33	2.82	5.83
1995	291.15	367.34	269.41	220.30	238.45	4,493.76	541.64	2.56	6.09
1996	358.17	453.98	327.33	249.77	303.89	5,742.89	670.83	2.19	5.24
1997	456.54	574.52	414.60	283.82	424.48	7,441.15	872.72	1.77	....
1996: Jan	329.22	412.71	300.30	254.07	273.73	5,179.37	614.42	2.31	
Feb	346.46	435.92	315.29	257.80	290.97	5,518.73	649.54	2.22	
Mar	346.73	439.56	324.76	245.77	290.45	5,612.24	647.07	2.22	5.27
Apr	347.50	441.99	326.42	244.87	287.92	5,579.86	647.17	2.24	
May	354.84	452.63	334.66	249.73	290.43	5,616.71	661.23	2.21	
June	358.32	458.30	331.57	247.20	294.42	5,671.51	668.50	2.21	5.21
July	345.52	438.58	316.60	245.31	287.89	5,496.26	644.07	2.28	
Aug	354.59	449.41	321.61	244.74	302.95	5,685.50	662.68	2.22	
Sept	360.96	459.69	323.12	242.25	308.16	5,804.01	674.88	2.20	5.24
Oct	373.54	473.98	332.93	249.61	324.42	5,996.21	701.46	2.11	
Nov	388.75	490.60	348.32	258.85	345.30	6,318.36	735.67	2.01	
Dec	391.61	494.38	352.28	257.09	350.01	6,435.87	743.25	2.01	5.23
1997: Jan	403.58	509.64	359.40	263.91	361.45	6,707.03	766.22	1.95	
Feb	418.57	524.30	364.15	271.36	388.75	6,917.48	798.39	1.89	
Mar	416.72	523.08	372.87	264.78	387.21	6,901.12	792.16	1.91	5.31
Apr	401.00	506.69	366.67	253.18	364.25	6,657.50	763.93	1.98	
May	433.36	549.65	395.50	268.18	392.32	7,242.36	833.09	1.85	
June	457.07	578.57	410.94	280.48	419.12	7,599.60	876.29	1.77	4.58
July	480.94	610.42	433.75	288.51	441.59	7,990.65	925.29	1.66	
Aug	481.53	609.54	439.71	287.63	446.93	7,948.43	927.74	1.65	
Sept	489.74	617.94	451.63	291.87	459.86	7,866.59	937.02	1.65	4.29
Oct	499.25	625.22	466.04	302.83	476.70	7,875.82	951.16	1.61	
Nov	492.08	615.57	453.49	307.52	465.29	7,677.36	938.92	1.65	
Dec	504.66	623.57	461.04	325.60	490.30	7,909.82	962.37	1.62	....

[1] Averages of daily closing prices, except NYSE data through May 1964 are averages of weekly closing prices.
[2] Includes stocks as follows: for NYSE, all stocks listed (more than 3,000); for Dow-Jones industrial average, 30 stocks; and for S&P composite index, 500 stocks.
[3] Effective April 1993, the NYSE doubled the value of the utility index to facilitate trading of options and futures on the index. Annual indexes prior to 1993 reflect the doubling.
[4] Based on 500 stocks in the S&P composite index.
[5] Aggregate cash dividends (based on latest known annual rate) divided by aggregate market value based on Wednesday closing prices. Monthly data are averages of weekly figures; annual data are averages of monthly figures.
[6] Quarterly data are ratio of earnings (after taxes) for 4 quarters ending with particular quarter to price index for last day of that quarter. Annual data are averages of quarterly ratios.

Note.—All data relate to stocks listed on the New York Stock Exchange.

Sources: New York Stock Exchange (NYSE), Dow Jones & Co., Inc., and Standard & Poor's Corporation (S&P).

TABLE B–96.—Business formation and business failures, 1955–97

Year or month	Index of net business formation (1967= 100)	New business incorporations (number)	Business failure rate [2]	Business failures [1]					
				Number of failures			Amount of current liabilities (millions of dollars)		
				Total	Liability size class		Total	Liability size class	
					Under $100,000	$100,000 and over		Under $100,000	$100,000 and over
1955	96.6	139,915	41.6	10,969	10,113	856	449.4	206.4	243.0
1956	94.6	141,163	48.0	12,686	11,615	1,071	562.7	239.8	322.9
1957	90.3	137,112	51.7	13,739	12,547	1,192	615.3	267.1	348.2
1958	90.2	150,781	55.9	14,964	13,499	1,465	728.3	297.6	430.7
1959	97.9	193,067	51.8	14,053	12,707	1,346	692.8	278.9	413.9
1960	94.5	182,713	57.0	15,445	13,650	1,795	938.6	327.2	611.4
1961	90.8	181,535	64.4	17,075	15,006	2,069	1,090.1	370.1	720.0
1962	92.6	182,057	60.8	15,782	13,772	2,010	1,213.6	346.5	867.1
1963	94.4	186,404	56.3	14,374	12,192	2,182	1,352.6	321.0	1,031.6
1964	98.2	197,724	53.2	13,501	11,346	2,155	1,329.2	313.6	1,015.6
1965	99.8	203,897	53.3	13,514	11,340	2,174	1,321.7	321.7	1,000.0
1966	99.3	200,010	51.6	13,061	10,833	2,228	1,385.7	321.5	1,064.1
1967	100.0	206,569	49.0	12,364	10,144	2,220	1,265.2	297.9	967.3
1968	108.3	233,635	38.6	9,636	7,829	1,807	941.0	241.1	699.9
1969	115.8	274,267	37.3	9,154	7,192	1,962	1,142.1	231.3	910.8
1970	108.8	264,209	43.8	10,748	8,019	2,729	1,887.8	269.3	1,618.4
1971	111.1	287,577	41.7	10,326	7,611	2,715	1,916.9	271.3	1,645.6
1972	119.3	316,601	38.3	9,566	7,040	2,526	2,000.2	258.8	1,741.5
1973	119.1	329,358	36.4	9,345	6,627	2,718	2,298.6	235.6	2,063.0
1974	113.2	319,149	38.4	9,915	6,733	3,182	3,053.1	256.9	2,796.3
1975	109.9	326,345	42.6	11,432	7,504	3,928	4,380.2	298.6	4,081.6
1976	120.4	375,766	34.8	9,628	6,176	3,452	3,011.3	257.8	2,753.4
1977	130.8	436,170	28.4	7,919	4,861	3,058	3,095.3	208.3	2,887.0
1978	138.1	478,019	23.9	6,619	3,712	2,907	2,656.0	164.7	2,491.3
1979	138.3	524,565	27.8	7,564	3,930	3,634	2,667.4	179.9	2,487.5
1980	129.9	533,520	42.1	11,742	5,682	6,060	4,635.1	272.5	4,362.6
1981	124.8	581,242	61.3	16,794	8,233	8,561	6,955.2	405.8	6,549.3
1982	116.4	566,942	88.4	24,908	11,509	13,399	15,610.8	541.7	15,069.1
1983	117.5	600,420	109.7	31,334	15,572	15,762	16,072.9	635.1	15,437.8
1984	121.3	634,991	107.0	52,078	33,527	18,551	29,268.6	409.8	28,858.8
1985	120.9	664,235	115.0	57,253	36,551	20,702	36,937.4	423.9	36,513.5
1986	120.4	702,738	120.0	61,616	38,908	22,708	44,724.0	838.3	43,885.7
1987	121.2	685,572	102.0	61,111	38,949	22,162	34,723.8	746.0	33,977.8
1988	124.1	685,095	98.0	57,097	38,300	18,797	39,573.0	686.9	38,886.1
1989	124.8	676,565	65.0	50,361	33,312	17,049	42,328.8	670.5	41,658.2
1990	120.7	647,366	74.0	60,747	40,833	19,914	56,130.1	735.6	55,394.5
1991	115.2	628,604	107.0	88,140	60,617	27,523	96,825.3	1,044.9	95,780.4
1992	116.3	666,800	110.0	97,069	68,264	28,805	94,317.5	1,096.7	93,220.8
1993	121.1	706,537	109.0	86,133	61,188	24,945	47,755.5	947.6	46,807.9
1994	125.5	741,778	86.0	71,558	50,814	20,744	28,977.9	845.0	28,132.9
1995	(3)	766,988	82.0	71,128	49,495	21,633	37,283.6	866.1	36,417.4
1996	(3)	790,332	80.0	71,811	49,547	22,264	34,021.1	913.1	33,108.0
Seasonally adjusted									
1996: Jan	(3)	69,345	....	6,038	4,217	1,821	4,310.3	66.9	4,243.4
Feb	(3)	69,617	....	5,547	3,888	1,659	1,905.8	65.2	1,840.7
Mar	(3)	60,449	....	6,637	4,561	2,076	1,656.6	81.4	1,575.2
Apr	(3)	67,180	....	6,720	4,634	2,086	3,000.3	90.4	2,909.9
May	(3)	68,186	....	7,233	4,954	2,279	2,427.0	89.0	2,338.0
June	(3)	61,513	....	6,272	4,326	1,946	1,537.2	80.3	1,456.8
July	(3)	73,060	....	4,530	3,171	1,359	4,281.0	48.4	4,232.5
Aug	(3)	62,164	....	4,977	3,340	1,637	1,518.4	73.9	1,444.4
Sept	(3)	62,515	....	4,760	3,374	1,386	2,892.1	49.1	2,843.0
Oct	(3)	69,898	....	6,541	4,483	2,058	2,166.5	92.6	2,073.9
Nov	(3)	60,665	....	6,258	4,304	1,954	1,401.5	88.1	1,313.4
Dec	(3)	66,542	....	6,393	4,377	2,016	6,142.0	83.3	6,058.7
1997: Jan	(3)	74,963	....	7,383	4,948	2,435	11,286.0	91.4	11,194.6
Feb	(3)	70,808	....	6,782	4,518	2,264	1,213.5	88.5	1,125.0
Mar	(3)	65,405	....	7,438	4,933	2,505	1,530.7	99.6	1,431.1
Apr	(3)	67,556	....	7,654	5,083	2,571	4,049.8	108.0	3,941.8
May	(3)	67,530	....	7,211	4,827	2,384	2,084.9	97.3	1,987.6
June	(3)	65,063	....	6,917	4,700	2,217	1,565.6	94.3	1,471.3
July	(3)	....	....	7,292	4,852	2,440	10,464.1	98.8	10,365.3
Aug	(3)	....	....	6,811	4,679	2,132	1,920.1	86.0	1,834.1
Sept	(3)	....	....	7,155	4,775	2,380	3,446.8	93.3	3,353.5
Oct	(3)	....	....	7,420	5,053	2,367	1,318.8	99.4	1,219.4
Nov	(3)	....	....	6,022	4,021	2,001	1,715.5	80.3	1,635.2

[1] Commercial and industrial failures only through 1983, excluding failures of banks, railroads, real estate, insurance, holding, and financial companies, steamship lines, travel agencies, etc.
Data beginning 1984 are based on expanded coverage and new methodology and are therefore not generally comparable with earlier data.
Data for 1996 and 1997 are preliminary and subject to revision.
[2] Failure rate per 10,000 listed enterprises.
[3] Series discontinued in 1995.

Sources: Department of Commerce (Bureau of Economic Analysis) and The Dun & Bradstreet Corporation.

TABLE B–97.—*Farm income, 1945–97*

[Billions of dollars; quarterly data at seasonally adjusted annual rates]

Year or quarter	Income of farm operators from farming						Net farm income
	Gross farm income					Produc-tion expenses	
	Total[1]	Cash marketing receipts			Value of inventory changes[2]		
		Total	Livestock and products	Crops			
1945	25.4	21.7	12.0	9.7	-0.4	13.1	12.3
1946	29.6	24.8	13.8	11.0	.0	14.5	15.1
1947	32.4	29.6	16.5	13.1	-1.8	17.0	15.4
1948	36.5	30.2	17.1	13.1	1.7	18.8	17.7
1949	30.8	27.8	15.4	12.4	-.9	18.0	12.8
1950	33.1	28.5	16.1	12.4	.8	19.5	13.6
1951	38.3	32.9	19.6	13.2	1.2	22.3	15.9
1952	37.8	32.5	18.2	14.3	.9	22.8	15.0
1953	34.4	31.0	16.9	14.1	-.6	21.5	13.0
1954	34.2	29.8	16.3	13.6	.5	21.8	12.4
1955	33.5	29.5	16.0	13.5	.2	22.2	11.3
1956	34.0	30.4	16.4	14.0	-.5	22.7	11.3
1957	34.8	29.7	17.4	12.3	.6	23.7	11.1
1958	39.0	33.5	19.2	14.2	.8	25.8	13.2
1959	37.9	33.6	18.9	14.7	.0	27.2	10.7
1960	38.6	34.0	19.0	15.0	.4	27.4	11.2
1961	40.5	35.2	19.5	15.7	.3	28.6	12.0
1962	42.3	36.5	20.2	16.3	.6	30.3	12.1
1963	43.4	37.5	20.0	17.4	.6	31.6	11.8
1964	42.3	37.3	19.9	17.4	-.8	31.8	10.5
1965	46.5	39.4	21.9	17.5	1.0	33.6	12.9
1966	50.5	43.4	25.0	18.4	-.1	36.5	14.0
1967	50.5	42.8	24.4	18.4	.7	38.2	12.3
1968	51.8	44.2	25.5	18.7	.1	39.5	12.3
1969	56.4	48.2	28.6	19.6	.1	42.1	14.3
1970	58.8	50.5	29.5	21.0	.0	44.5	14.4
1971	62.1	52.7	30.5	22.3	1.4	47.1	15.0
1972	71.1	61.1	35.6	25.5	.9	51.7	19.5
1973	98.9	86.9	45.8	41.1	3.4	64.6	34.4
1974	98.2	92.4	41.3	51.1	-1.6	71.0	27.3
1975	100.6	88.9	43.1	45.8	3.4	75.0	25.5
1976	102.9	95.4	46.3	49.0	-1.5	82.7	20.2
1977	108.8	96.2	47.6	48.6	1.1	88.9	19.9
1978	128.4	112.4	59.2	53.2	1.9	103.2	25.2
1979	150.7	131.5	69.2	62.3	5.0	123.3	27.4
1980	149.3	139.7	68.0	71.7	-6.3	133.1	16.1
1981	166.3	141.6	69.2	72.5	6.5	139.4	26.9
1982	164.1	142.6	70.3	72.3	-1.4	140.3	23.8
1983	153.9	136.8	69.6	67.2	-10.9	139.6	14.2
1984	168.0	142.8	72.9	69.9	6.0	142.0	26.0
1985	161.2	144.1	69.8	74.3	-2.3	132.6	28.6
1986	156.1	135.4	71.6	63.8	-2.2	125.2	30.9
1987	168.4	141.8	76.0	65.8	-2.3	131.0	37.4
1988	177.9	151.2	79.6	71.6	-4.1	139.9	38.0
1989	191.9	160.8	83.9	76.9	3.8	146.7	45.3
1990	198.1	169.5	89.2	80.3	3.3	153.3	44.8
1991	191.9	167.9	85.8	82.1	-.2	153.3	38.6
1992	200.5	171.4	85.6	85.7	4.2	152.9	47.5
1993	203.6	177.7	90.2	87.5	-4.5	160.5	43.1
1994	215.7	181.2	88.2	93.1	8.2	167.5	48.3
1995	210.9	187.7	87.0	100.7	-3.9	174.2	36.7
1996	233.5	202.3	92.9	109.4	2.7	181.3	52.2
1995: I	208.7	182.5	83.4	99.2	-4.8	171.0	37.7
II	206.8	183.0	81.8	101.2	-4.5	174.0	32.8
III	219.2	201.9	96.3	105.6	-3.5	176.1	43.1
IV	209.0	183.4	86.6	96.8	-2.8	175.6	33.4
1996: I	239.4	203.7	90.1	113.6	3.3	177.6	61.9
II	238.8	206.0	90.6	115.4	3.1	182.1	56.6
III	230.8	206.3	96.7	109.6	2.5	182.4	48.4
IV	225.0	193.3	94.2	99.1	2.0	183.1	41.9
1997: I[p]	240.4	204.1	91.9	112.2	1.6	182.3	58.1
II[p]	245.2	212.1	95.2	116.9	1.6	185.1	60.1

[1] Cash marketing receipts and inventory changes plus Government payments, other farm cash income, and nonmoney income furnished by farms.

[2] Physical changes in end-of-period inventory of crop and livestock commodities valued at average prices during the period.

Note.—Data include net Commodity Credit Corporation loans and operator households.

Source: Department of Agriculture, Economic Research Service.

[Billions of dollars]

End of year	Total assets	Physical assets					Financial assets		Claims			
			Nonreal estate									
		Real estate	Livestock and poultry [1]	Machinery and motor vehicles	Crops [2]	Purchased inputs [3]	Investments in cooperatives	Other [4]	Total claims	Real estate debt [5]	Nonreal estate debt [6]	Proprietors' equity
1950	121.6	75.4	17.1	12.3	7.1		2.7	7.0	121.6	5.2	5.7	110.7
1951	136.1	83.8	19.5	14.3	8.2		2.9	7.3	136.1	5.7	6.9	123.7
1952	133.0	85.1	14.8	15.0	7.9		3.2	7.1	133.0	6.2	7.1	119.7
1953	128.7	84.3	11.7	15.6	6.8		3.3	7.0	128.7	6.6	6.3	115.7
1954	132.6	87.8	11.2	15.7	7.5		3.5	6.9	132.6	7.1	6.7	118.7
1955	137.0	93.0	10.6	16.3	6.5		3.7	6.9	137.0	7.8	7.3	121.9
1956	145.7	100.3	11.0	16.9	6.8		4.0	6.7	145.7	8.5	7.4	129.8
1957	154.5	106.4	13.9	17.0	6.4		4.2	6.6	154.5	9.0	8.2	137.3
1958	168.7	114.6	17.7	18.1	6.9		4.5	6.9	168.7	9.7	9.4	149.7
1959	173.0	121.2	15.2	19.3	6.2		4.8	6.2	173.0	10.6	10.7	151.7
1960	174.3	123.3	15.6	19.1	6.4		4.2	5.8	174.3	11.3	11.1	151.9
1961	181.6	129.1	16.4	19.3	6.5		4.5	5.9	181.6	12.3	11.8	157.5
1962	188.9	134.6	17.3	19.9	6.5		4.6	5.9	188.9	13.5	13.2	162.2
1963	196.7	142.4	15.9	20.4	7.4		5.0	5.7	196.7	15.0	14.6	167.1
1964	204.2	150.5	14.5	21.2	7.0		5.2	5.8	204.2	16.9	15.3	172.1
1965	220.8	161.5	17.6	22.4	7.9		5.4	6.0	220.8	18.9	16.9	185.0
1966	234.0	171.2	19.0	24.1	8.1		5.7	6.0	234.0	20.7	18.5	194.8
1967	246.0	180.9	18.8	26.3	7.9		5.8	6.1	246.0	22.6	19.6	203.7
1968	257.2	189.4	20.2	27.7	7.4		6.1	6.3	257.2	24.7	19.2	213.2
1969	267.8	195.3	22.8	28.6	8.3		6.4	6.4	267.8	26.4	20.0	221.4
1970	278.9	202.4	23.7	30.4	8.7		7.2	6.5	278.9	27.5	21.2	230.1
1971	301.7	217.6	27.3	32.4	9.9		7.9	6.7	301.7	29.3	24.0	248.5
1972	339.9	243.0	33.7	34.6	12.9		8.7	6.9	339.9	32.0	26.7	281.2
1973	418.5	298.3	42.4	39.7	21.3		9.7	7.1	418.5	36.1	31.6	350.8
1974 [7]	449.1	335.6	24.6	48.5	22.5		11.2	6.9	449.1	40.8	35.1	373.3
1975	510.7	383.6	29.4	57.4	20.5		13.0	6.9	510.7	45.3	39.7	425.7
1976	590.7	456.5	29.0	63.3	20.6		14.3	6.9	590.7	50.5	45.6	494.6
1977	651.5	509.3	31.9	69.3	20.4		13.5	7.0	651.5	58.4	52.4	540.6
1978	767.3	601.8	50.1	68.5	23.8		16.1	7.1	767.3	66.7	60.7	639.9
1979	898.1	706.1	61.4	75.4	29.9		18.1	7.3	898.1	79.7	71.8	746.6
1980	983.2	782.8	60.6	80.3	32.7		19.3	7.4	983.2	89.7	77.1	816.4
1981	982.3	785.6	53.5	85.5	29.5		20.6	7.6	982.3	98.8	83.6	799.9
1982	944.5	750.0	53.0	86.0	25.8		21.9	7.8	944.5	101.8	87.0	755.7
1983	943.3	753.4	49.5	85.8	23.6		22.8	8.1	943.3	103.2	87.9	752.2
1984	857.0	661.8	49.5	85.0	26.1	2.0	24.3	8.3	857.0	106.7	87.1	663.3
1985	772.7	586.2	46.3	82.9	22.9	1.2	24.3	9.0	772.7	100.1	77.5	595.1
1986	724.8	542.3	47.8	81.9	16.3	2.1	24.4	10.0	724.8	90.4	66.6	567.8
1987	756.1	563.5	58.0	78.7	17.7	3.2	25.3	9.9	756.1	82.4	62.0	611.7
1988	792.5	586.8	62.2	81.0	23.6	3.5	25.1	10.4	792.5	78.1	61.7	652.6
1989	817.7	604.3	66.2	84.1	23.7	2.6	26.3	10.5	817.7	76.2	61.9	679.6
1990	844.6	623.3	70.9	86.3	23.0	2.8	27.5	10.9	844.6	74.9	63.2	706.4
1991	848.3	628.9	68.1	85.9	22.2	2.6	28.7	11.8	848.3	75.1	64.3	708.8
1992	873.8	646.3	71.0	85.3	24.2	3.9	29.4	13.6	873.8	75.6	63.6	734.5
1993	910.7	678.3	72.8	85.9	23.3	3.8	31.3	15.3	910.7	76.3	65.9	768.5
1994	943.0	712.4	67.9	86.7	23.1	5.0	32.4	15.5	943.0	78.0	69.1	795.9
1995	985.4	761.3	57.8	86.7	27.2	3.4	34.1	14.9	985.4	79.6	71.5	834.3
1996	1,034.9	805.4	60.1	85.5	30.6	4.4	34.9	14.0	1,034.9	81.9	74.2	878.7

[1] Excludes commercial broilers; excludes horses and mules beginning 1959; excludes turkeys beginning 1986.
[2] Non-Commodity Credit Corporation (CCC) crops held on farms plus value above loan rate for crops held under CCC.
[3] Includes fertilizer, chemicals, fuels, parts, feed, seed, and other supplies.
[4] Currency and demand deposits.
[5] Includes CCC storage and drying facilities loans.
[6] Does not include CCC crop loans.
[7] Beginning 1974, data are for farms included in the new farm definition, that is, places with sales of $1,000 or more annually.

Note.—Data exclude operator households.
Beginning 1959, data include Alaska and Hawaii.

Source: Department of Agriculture, Economic Research Service.

TABLE B–99.—*Farm output and productivity indexes, 1948–94*

[1992=100]

Year	Farm output					Productivity indicators[3]	
	Total[1]	Livestock and products	Crops			Farm output per unit of total factor input	Farm output per unit of farm labor
			Total[2]	Feed crops	Food grains	Oil crops		
1948	44	49	42	47	47	17	43	13
1949	44	52	40	43	41	15	40	14
1950	44	54	38	44	38	18	40	14
1951	46	57	40	42	37	16	41	15
1952	47	58	41	44	48	16	43	16
1953	48	59	42	43	44	16	44	17
1954	48	61	41	45	39	18	45	18
1955	50	62	42	47	37	20	44	18
1956	50	63	42	46	38	23	45	19
1957	50	63	42	51	36	23	45	20
1958	52	64	46	54	53	29	47	23
1959	54	66	46	54	43	25	47	23
1960	55	66	48	57	51	27	48	24
1961	56	69	48	53	47	32	50	26
1962	56	69	49	54	43	32	51	26
1963	58	71	51	56	45	33	52	28
1964	58	73	49	52	50	33	53	29
1965	59	71	52	59	52	40	54	30
1966	59	72	51	58	52	43	54	33
1967	61	74	54	64	59	45	57	36
1968	62	75	55	62	62	51	58	38
1969	63	75	57	64	57	52	59	39
1970	63	78	55	59	54	53	58	39
1971	67	79	61	72	63	59	63	43
1972	68	80	61	70	60	59	63	43
1973	70	80	65	73	66	71	64	45
1974	66	79	59	61	71	57	60	46
1975	71	75	68	72	84	71	65	49
1976	72	79	67	73	83	60	64	50
1977	76	80	73	78	78	82	69	55
1978	77	80	76	84	73	87	67	58
1979	82	82	83	89	85	105	69	64
1980	79	85	75	76	94	81	66	64
1981	86	87	87	91	111	92	74	69
1982	87	86	87	93	108	101	76	72
1983	76	88	68	61	92	76	69	64
1984	86	87	85	90	101	87	78	74
1985	89	89	89	100	95	96	84	82
1986	87	90	84	95	83	89	84	84
1987	88	91	85	84	84	88	87	87
1988	82	94	75	62	76	72	82	76
1989	89	94	86	85	83	88	90	87
1990	94	95	92	88	107	87	93	91
1991	94	98	91	86	82	94	93	89
1992	100	100	100	100	100	100	100	100
1993	94	101	89	76	96	85	94	99
1994	105	105	106	102	96	115	104	110

[1] Gross production.
[2] Includes items not included in groups shown.
[3] See Table B–100 for farm inputs.

Source: Department of Agriculture, Economic Research Service.

TABLE B-100.—Farm input use, selected inputs, 1948-97

Year	Farm population, April [1] Number (thousands)	As percent of total population [2]	Farm employment (thousands) [3] Total	Self-employed and unpaid workers [4]	Hired workers	Crops harvested (millions of acres) [5]	Selected indexes of input use (1992=100) Total	Farm labor	Farm real estate	Durable equipment	Energy	Agricultural chemicals [6]	Feed, seed, and purchased livestock [7]	Other purchased inputs
1948	24,383	16.6	10,363	8,026	2,337	356	104	336	102	62	70	33	58	42
1949	24,194	16.2	9,964	7,712	2,252	360	110	329	103	74	78	35	60	72
1950	23,048	15.2	9,926	7,597	2,329	345	110	316	105	85	80	42	60	72
1951	21,890	14.2	9,546	7,310	2,236	344	112	303	107	95	83	41	62	77
1952	21,748	13.9	9,149	7,005	2,144	349	111	294	108	103	86	42	62	79
1953	19,874	12.5	8,864	6,775	2,089	348	110	278	109	107	89	41	63	75
1954	19,019	11.7	8,651	6,570	2,081	346	106	271	110	112	88	42	58	72
1955	19,078	11.5	8,381	6,345	2,036	340	112	274	111	114	91	44	65	75
1956	18,712	11.1	7,852	5,900	1,952	324	112	260	111	115	91	49	68	74
1957	17,656	10.3	7,600	5,660	1,940	324	111	243	111	113	89	47	71	77
1958	17,128	9.8	7,503	5,521	1,982	324	111	231	111	111	87	48	75	80
1959	16,592	9.3	7,342	5,390	1,952	324	114	231	111	111	88	55	76	92
1960	15,635	8.7	7,057	5,172	1,885	324	113	225	111	112	89	56	75	91
1961	14,803	8.1	6,919	5,029	1,890	302	111	219	108	110	91	59	72	89
1962	14,313	7.7	6,700	4,873	1,827	295	111	216	107	109	93	54	75	91
1963	13,367	7.1	6,518	4,738	1,780	298	111	211	108	109	94	60	77	90
1964	12,954	6.7	6,110	4,506	1,604	298	109	199	107	110	96	65	75	90
1965	12,363	6.4	5,610	4,128	1,482	298	108	193	107	112	97	69	74	90
1966	11,595	5.9	5,214	3,854	1,360	294	110	180	106	115	99	79	80	91
1967	10,875	5.5	4,903	3,650	1,253	306	109	171	108	119	98	76	80	93
1968	10,454	5.2	4,749	3,535	1,213	300	107	165	107	125	98	65	81	91
1969	10,307	5.1	4,596	3,419	1,176	290	108	163	105	127	100	70	86	89
1970	9,712	4.7	4,523	3,348	1,175	293	108	161	105	128	100	73	88	86
1971	9,425	4.5	4,436	3,275	1,161	305	107	158	107	129	98	77	86	84
1972	9,610	4.6	4,373	3,228	1,146	294	108	156	105	129	97	82	88	84
1973	9,472	4.5	4,337	3,169	1,168	321	110	156	109	132	99	91	88	91
1974	9,264	4.3	4,389	3,075	1,314	328	110	145	111	139	94	96	88	96
1975	8,864	4.1	4,331	3,021	1,310	336	108	145	110	144	110	88	83	94
1976	8,253	3.8	4,363	2,992	1,371	337	111	143	110	148	124	97	88	97
1977	[8]6,194	[8]2.8	4,143	2,852	1,291	345	110	138	110	152	130	95	83	98
1978	[8]6,501	[8]2.9	3,937	2,680	1,256	338	116	132	109	156	136	105	96	117
1979	[8]6,241	[8]2.8	3,765	2,495	1,270	348	118	128	110	161	124	115	103	125
1980	[8]6,051	[8]2.7	3,699	2,401	1,298	352	120	124	112	166	121	127	109	114
1981	[8]5,850	[8]2.5	[9]3,582	[9]2,324	[9]1,258	366	117	126	112	166	116	127	103	107
1982	[8]5,628	[8]2.4	[9]3,466	[9]2,248	[9]1,218	362	114	120	110	163	109	96	106	102
1983	[8]5,787	[8]2.5	[9]3,349	[9]2,171	[9]1,178	306	110	118	102	155	106	89	108	105
1984	5,754	2.4	[9]3,233	[9]2,095	[9]1,138	348	110	116	108	147	110	101	97	105
1985	5,355	2.2	3,116	2,018	1,098	342	106	109	107	139	98	96	99	97
1986	5,226	2.2	2,912	1,873	1,039	325	103	102	104	130	91	106	99	86
1987	4,986	2.1	2,897	1,846	1,051	302	101	102	100	120	102	96	97	93
1988	4,951	2.1	2,954	1,967	1,037	297	100	109	100	113	102	89	96	96
1989	4,801	2.0	2,863	1,935	928	318	99	103	102	108	101	92	91	99
1990	4,591	1.9	2,891	2,000	892	322	100	103	101	105	100	95	99	101
1991	4,632	1.9	2,877	1,968	910	318	102	105	100	103	101	99	99	102
1992	....	....	2,810	1,944	866	319	100	100	100	100	100	100	100	100
1993	....	....	2,800	1,942	857	308	100	95	98	97	100	105	101	108
1994	....	....	2,767	1,925	842	321	101	96	99	94	103	106	102	113
1995	....	....	2,836	1,967	869	314	......	......	......	......	......	......	......	......
1996	....	....	2,842	2,010	832	326	......	......	......	......	......	......	......	......
1997 P	....	....	2,870	1,991	879	333	......	......	......	......	......	......	......	......

[1] Farm population as defined by Department of Agriculture and Department of Commerce, i.e., civilian population living on farms in rural areas, regardless of occupation. See also footnote 8. Series discontinued in 1992.

[2] Total population of United States including Armed Forces overseas, as of July 1.

[3] Includes persons doing farmwork on all farms. These data, published by the Department of Agriculture, differ from those on agricultural employment by the Department of Labor (see Table B-35) because of differences in the method of approach, in concepts of employment, and in time of month for which the data are collected.

[4] Prior to 1982 this category was termed "family workers" and did not include nonfamily unpaid workers.

[5] Acreage harvested plus acreages in fruits, tree nuts, and farm gardens.

[6] Fertilizer, lime, and pesticides.

[7] Includes purchases of broiler- and egg-type chicks and turkey poults and livestock imports for purposes other than immediate slaughter.

[8] Based on new definition of a farm. Under old definition of a farm, farm population (in thousands and as percent of total population) for 1977, 1978, 1979, 1980, 1981, 1982, and 1983 is 7,806 and 3.6; 8,005 and 3.6; 7,553 and 3.4; 7,241 and 3.2; 7,014 and 3.1; 6,880 and 3.0; 7,029 and 3.0, respectively.

[9] Basis for farm employment series was discontinued for 1981 through 1984. Employment is estimated for these years.

Note.—Population includes Alaska and Hawaii beginning 1960.

Sources: Department of Agriculture (Economic Research Service) and Department of Commerce (Bureau of the Census).

TABLE B–101.—*Indexes of prices received and prices paid by farmers, 1975–97*

[1990–92=100, except as noted]

Year or month	Prices received by farmers			Prices paid by farmers											Ad;dendum: Average farm real estate value per acre (dollars)[3]
	All farm products	Crops	Livestock and products	All commodities, services, interest, taxes, and wage rates[1]	Production items									Wage rates	
					Total[2]	Feed	Livestock and poultry	Fertilizer	Agricultural chemicals	Fuels	Farm machinery	Farm services	Rent		
1975	73	88	62	47	55	83	39	87	72	40	38	48		44	340
1976	75	87	64	50	59	83	47	74	78	43	43	52		48	397
1977	73	83	64	53	61	82	48	72	71	46	47	57		51	474
1978	83	89	78	58	67	80	65	72	66	48	51	60		55	531
1979	94	98	90	66	76	89	88	77	67	61	56	66		60	628
1980	98	107	89	75	85	98	85	96	71	86	63	81		65	737
1981	100	111	89	82	92	110	80	104	77	98	70	89		70	819
1982	94	98	90	86	94	99	78	105	83	97	76	96		74	823
1983	98	108	88	86	92	107	76	100	87	94	81	82		76	788
1984	101	111	91	89	94	112	73	103	90	93	85	86		77	801
1985	91	98	86	86	91	95	74	98	90	93	85	85		78	713
1986	87	87	88	85	86	88	73	90	89	76	83	83		81	640
1987	89	86	91	87	87	83	85	86	87	76	85	84		85	599
1988	99	104	93	91	90	104	91	94	89	77	89	85		87	632
1989	104	109	100	96	95	110	93	99	93	83	94	91		95	668
1990	104	103	105	99	99	103	102	97	95	100	96	96	96	96	683
1991	100	101	99	99	100	100	98	102	103	101	104	100	99	100	703
1992	98	101	97	101	101	99	96	100	103	96	104	103	104	105	713
1993	101	102	100	104	103	101	104	96	109	93	107	109	100	108	736
1994	100	105	95	106	106	105	94	105	112	95	113	112	108	110	782
1995	102	112	92	110	109	104	82	120	115	94	120	118	116	114	832
1996	112	126	99	115	115	130	75	124	119	105	125	118	119	117	890
1997	107	115	99	116	116	122	93	121	121	103	128	118	119	123	942
1996: Jan	108	121	94	113	112	124	74	125	118	100	123	118	119	119	890
Feb	106	123	93	113	113	125	73	127	118	98	123	117	119	119	....
Mar	109	129	94	114	114	128	72	128	119	104	124	117	119	119	....
Apr	108	129	93	114	114	130	69	128	119	105	124	117	119	117	....
May	112	131	97	115	115	138	70	126	118	106	124	117	119	117	....
June	118	140	100	115	115	137	73	124	118	97	125	118	119	117	....
July	119	136	102	115	116	139	75	121	118	98	125	119	119	113	....
Aug	117	133	104	115	116	139	78	119	119	99	126	119	119	113	....
Sept	116	126	105	116	116	135	80	120	121	107	126	119	119	113	....
Oct	112	119	103	115	115	124	79	122	121	114	127	118	119	120	....
Nov	110	116	102	115	114	120	82	123	121	114	128	117	119	120	....
Dec	109	113	103	115	115	121	82	124	121	116	126	117	119	120	....
1997: Jan	108	116	98	116	115	121	85	124	121	115	126	117	119	124	942
Feb	105	113	98	116	115	122	89	124	118	113	127	117	119	124	....
Mar	108	118	99	117	116	127	89	124	119	104	127	117	119	124	....
Apr	107	116	100	117	117	128	93	124	119	105	127	117	119	123	....
May	108	117	100	117	117	129	95	124	121	101	127	117	119	123	....
June	108	119	98	117	117	124	95	122	121	98	127	118	119	123	....
July	107	114	100	116	116	119	100	121	120	95	127	118	119	119	....
Aug	108	116	99	116	116	118	97	119	121	100	127	118	119	119	....
Sept	107	114	99	116	116	121	96	119	121	101	127	119	119	119	....
Oct	107	114	97	116	115	116	94	119	122	102	129	118	119	126	....
Nov	107	115	98	116	115	116	93	117	123	102	129	118	119	126	....
Dec	105	111	97	116	115	116	94	115	123	94	129	117	119	126	....

[1] Includes items used for family living, not shown separately.
[2] Includes other production items not shown separately.
[3] Average for 48 States. Annual data are: March 1 for 1975, February 1 for 1976–81, April 1 for 1982–85, February 1 for 1986–89, and January 1 for 1990–97.

Note—Data on a 1990–92 base prior to 1975 have not been calculated by Department of Agriculture.

Source: Department of Agriculture (National Agricultural Statistics Service and Economic Research Service).

TABLE B–102.—U.S. exports and imports of agricultural commodities, 1940–97

[Billions of dollars]

Year	Exports							Imports					Agricultural trade balance
	Total[1]	Feed grains	Food grains[2]	Oilseeds and products	Cotton	Tobacco	Animals and products	Total[1]	Crops, fruits, and vegetables[3]	Animals and products	Coffee	Cocoa beans and products	
1940	0.5	(4)	(4)	(4)	0.2	(4)	0.1	1.3	(4)	0.2	0.1	(4)	-0.8
1941	.7	(4)	0.1	(4)	.1	0.1	.3	1.7	0.1	.3	.2	(4)	-1.0
1942	1.2	(4)	(4)	(4)	.1	.1	.8	1.3	(4)	.5	.2	(4)	-.1
1943	2.1	(4)	.1	0.1	.2	.2	1.2	1.5	.1	.4	.3	(4)	.6
1944	2.1	(4)	.1	.1	.1	.1	1.3	1.8	.1	.3	.3	(4)	.3
1945	2.3	(4)	.4	(4)	.3	.2	.9	1.7	.1	.4	.3	(4)	.5
1946	3.1	0.1	.7	(4)	.5	.4	.9	2.3	.2	.4	.5	0.1	.8
1947	4.0	.4	1.4	.1	.4	.3	.7	2.8	.1	.4	.6	.2	1.2
1948	3.5	.1	1.5	.2	.5	.2	.5	3.1	.2	.6	.7	.2	.3
1949	3.6	.3	1.1	.3	.9	.3	.4	2.9	.2	.4	.8	.1	.7
1950	2.9	.2	.6	.2	1.0	.3	.3	4.0	.2	.7	1.1	.2	-1.1
1951	4.0	.3	1.1	.3	1.1	.3	.5	5.2	.2	1.1	1.4	.2	-1.1
1952	3.4	.3	1.1	.2	.9	.2	.3	4.5	.2	.7	1.4	.2	-1.1
1953	2.8	.3	.7	.2	.5	.3	.4	4.2	.2	.6	1.5	.2	-1.3
1954	3.1	.2	.5	.3	.8	.3	.5	4.0	.2	.5	1.5	.3	-.9
1955	3.2	.3	.6	.4	.5	.4	.6	4.0	.2	.5	1.4	.2	-.8
1956	4.2	.4	1.0	.5	.7	.3	.7	4.0	.2	.4	1.4	.2	.2
1957	4.5	.3	1.0	.5	1.0	.4	.7	4.0	.2	.5	1.4	.2	.6
1958	3.9	.5	.8	.4	.7	.4	.5	3.9	.2	.7	1.2	.2	(4)
1959	4.0	.6	.9	.6	.4	.3	.6	4.1	.2	.8	1.1	.2	-.1
1960	4.8	.5	1.2	.6	1.0	.4	.6	3.8	.2	.6	1.0	.2	1.0
1961	5.0	.5	1.4	.6	.9	.4	.6	3.7	.2	.7	1.0	.2	1.3
1962	5.0	.8	1.3	.7	.5	.4	.6	3.9	.2	.9	1.0	.2	1.2
1963	5.6	.8	1.5	.8	.6	.4	.7	4.0	.3	.9	1.0	.2	1.6
1964	6.3	.9	1.7	1.0	.7	.4	.8	4.1	.3	.8	1.2	.2	2.3
1965	6.2	1.1	1.4	1.2	.5	.4	.8	4.1	.3	.9	1.1	.1	2.1
1966	6.9	1.3	1.8	1.2	.4	.5	.7	4.5	.4	1.2	1.1	.1	2.4
1967	6.4	1.1	1.5	1.3	.5	.5	.7	4.5	.4	1.1	1.0	.2	1.9
1968	6.3	.9	1.4	1.3	.5	.5	.7	5.0	.5	1.3	1.2	.2	1.3
1969	6.0	.9	1.2	1.3	.3	.6	.8	5.0	.5	1.4	.9	.2	1.1
1970	7.3	1.1	1.4	1.9	.4	.5	.9	5.8	.5	1.6	1.2	.3	1.5
1971	7.7	1.0	1.3	2.2	.6	.5	1.0	5.8	.6	1.5	1.2	.2	1.9
1972	9.4	1.5	1.8	2.4	.5	.7	1.1	6.5	.7	1.8	1.3	.2	2.9
1973	17.7	3.5	4.7	4.3	.9	.7	1.6	8.4	.8	2.6	1.7	.3	9.3
1974	21.9	4.6	5.4	5.7	1.3	.8	1.8	10.2	.8	2.2	1.6	.5	11.7
1975	21.9	5.2	6.2	4.5	1.0	.9	1.7	9.3	.8	1.8	1.7	.5	12.6
1976	23.0	6.0	4.7	5.1	1.0	.9	2.4	11.0	.9	2.3	2.9	.6	12.0
1977	23.6	4.9	3.6	6.6	1.5	1.1	2.7	13.4	1.2	2.3	4.2	1.0	10.2
1978	29.4	5.9	5.5	8.2	1.7	1.4	3.0	14.8	1.5	3.1	4.0	1.4	14.6
1979	34.7	7.7	6.3	8.9	2.2	1.2	3.8	16.7	1.7	3.9	4.2	1.2	18.0
1980	41.2	9.8	7.9	9.4	2.9	1.3	3.8	17.4	1.7	3.8	4.2	.9	23.8
1981	43.3	9.4	9.6	9.6	2.3	1.5	4.2	16.9	2.0	3.5	2.9	.9	26.4
1982	36.6	6.4	7.9	9.1	2.0	1.5	3.9	15.3	2.3	3.7	2.9	.7	21.3
1983	36.1	7.3	7.4	8.7	1.8	1.5	3.8	16.5	2.3	3.8	2.8	.8	19.6
1984	37.8	8.1	7.5	8.4	2.4	1.5	4.2	19.3	3.1	4.1	3.3	1.1	18.5
1985	29.0	6.0	4.5	5.8	1.6	1.5	4.1	20.0	3.5	4.2	3.3	1.4	9.1
1986	26.2	3.1	3.8	6.5	.8	1.2	4.5	21.5	3.6	4.5	4.6	1.1	4.7
1987	28.7	3.8	3.8	6.4	1.6	1.1	5.2	20.4	3.6	4.9	2.9	1.2	8.3
1988	37.1	5.9	5.9	7.7	2.0	1.3	6.4	21.0	3.8	5.2	2.5	1.0	16.1
1989	40.1	7.7	7.1	6.3	2.2	1.3	6.4	21.9	4.2	5.0	2.4	1.0	18.2
1990	39.5	7.0	4.8	5.7	2.8	1.4	6.7	22.9	4.9	5.6	1.9	1.1	16.6
1991	39.4	5.7	4.2	6.4	2.5	1.4	7.1	22.9	4.8	5.5	1.9	1.1	16.5
1992	43.1	5.7	5.4	7.2	2.0	1.7	8.0	24.8	4.9	5.7	1.7	1.1	18.3
1993	42.9	5.0	5.6	7.3	1.5	1.3	8.1	25.2	5.0	5.9	1.5	1.0	17.7
1994	46.2	4.7	5.3	7.2	2.7	1.3	9.3	27.1	5.4	5.8	2.5	1.0	19.1
1995	56.3	8.2	6.7	8.9	3.7	1.4	11.0	30.3	5.9	6.0	3.3	1.1	26.0
1996	60.4	9.4	7.4	10.8	2.7	1.4	11.3	33.6	6.9	6.1	2.8	1.4	26.8
Jan–Nov:													
1996	55.2	8.6	7.1	9.5	2.4	1.3	10.4	30.7	8.1	5.6	2.5	1.3	24.5
1997[5]	52.0	5.5	4.7	10.6	2.4	1.4	10.5	33.0	8.3	5.9	3.5	1.3	19.0

[1] Total includes items not shown separately.
[2] Rice, wheat, and wheat flour.
[3] Includes nuts, fruits, and vegetable preparations.
[4] Less than $50 million.
[5] For 1997, totals include transshipments through Canada that are not reflected in commodity groupings. Prior data reflect the transshipments.

Note.—Data derived from official estimates released by the Bureau of the Census, Department of Commerce. Agricultural commodities are defined as (1) nonmarine food products and (2) other products of agriculture which have not passed through complex processes of manufacture. Export value, at U.S. port of exportation, is based on the selling price and includes inland freight, insurance, and other charges to the port. Import value, defined generally as the market value in the foreign country, excludes import duties, ocean freight, and marine insurance.

Source: Department of Agriculture, Economic Research Service.

TABLE B–103.—*U.S. international transactions, 1946–97*

[Millions of dollars; quarterly data seasonally adjusted, except as noted. Credits (+), debits (−)]

Year or quarter	Goods[1]			Services					Investment income			Unilateral transfers, net[3]	Balance on current account
	Exports	Imports	Net	Net military transactions[2][3]	Net travel and transportation receipts	Other services, net	Balance on goods and services	Receipts on U.S. assets abroad	Payments on foreign assets in U.S.	Net			
1946	11,764	−5,067	6,697	−424	733	310	7,316	772	−212	560	−2,991	4,885
1947	16,097	−5,973	10,124	−358	946	145	10,857	1,102	−245	857	−2,722	8,992
1948	13,265	−7,557	5,708	−351	374	175	5,906	1,921	−437	1,484	−4,973	2,417
1949	12,213	−6,874	5,339	−410	230	208	5,367	1,831	−476	1,355	−5,849	873
1950	10,203	−9,081	1,122	−56	−120	242	1,188	2,068	−559	1,509	−4,537	−1,840
1951	14,243	−11,176	3,067	169	298	254	3,788	2,633	−583	2,050	−4,954	884
1952	13,449	−10,838	2,611	528	83	309	3,531	2,751	−555	2,196	−5,113	614
1953	12,412	−10,975	1,437	1,753	−238	307	3,259	2,736	−624	2,112	−6,657	−1,286
1954	12,929	−10,353	2,576	902	−269	305	3,514	2,929	−582	2,347	−5,642	219
1955	14,424	−11,527	2,897	−113	−297	299	2,786	3,406	−676	2,730	−5,086	430
1956	17,556	−12,803	4,753	−221	−361	447	4,618	3,837	−735	3,102	−4,990	2,730
1957	19,562	−13,291	6,271	−423	−189	482	6,141	4,180	−796	3,384	−4,763	4,762
1958	16,414	−12,952	3,462	−849	−633	486	2,466	3,790	−825	2,965	−4,647	784
1959	16,458	−15,310	1,148	−831	−821	573	69	4,132	−1,061	3,071	−4,422	−1,282
1960	19,650	−14,758	4,892	−1,057	−964	639	3,508	4,616	−1,238	3,379	−4,062	2,824
1961	20,108	−14,537	5,571	−1,131	−978	732	4,195	4,999	−1,245	3,755	−4,127	3,822
1962	20,781	−16,260	4,521	−912	−1,152	912	3,370	5,618	−1,324	4,294	−4,277	3,387
1963	22,272	−17,048	5,224	−742	−1,309	1,036	4,210	6,157	−1,560	4,596	−4,392	4,414
1964	25,501	−18,700	6,801	−794	−1,146	1,161	6,022	6,824	−1,783	5,041	−4,240	6,823
1965	26,461	−21,510	4,951	−487	−1,280	1,480	4,664	7,437	−2,088	5,350	−4,583	5,431
1966	29,310	−25,493	3,817	−1,043	−1,331	1,497	2,940	7,528	−2,481	5,047	−4,955	3,031
1967	30,666	−26,866	3,800	−1,187	−1,750	1,742	2,604	8,021	−2,747	5,274	−5,294	2,583
1968	33,626	−32,991	635	−596	−1,548	1,759	250	9,367	−3,378	5,990	−5,629	611
1969	36,414	−35,807	607	−718	−1,763	1,964	91	10,913	−4,869	6,044	−5,735	399
1970	42,469	−39,866	2,603	−641	−2,038	2,330	2,254	11,748	−5,515	6,233	−6,156	2,331
1971	43,319	−45,579	−2,260	653	−2,345	2,649	−1,303	12,707	−5,435	7,272	−7,402	−1,433
1972	49,381	−55,797	−6,416	1,072	−3,063	2,965	−5,443	14,765	−6,572	8,192	−8,544	−5,795
1973	71,410	−70,499	911	740	−3,158	3,406	1,900	21,808	−9,655	12,153	−6,913	7,140
1974	98,306	−103,811	−5,505	165	−3,184	4,231	−4,292	27,587	−12,084	15,503	−9,249	1,962
1975	107,088	−98,185	8,903	1,461	−2,812	4,854	12,404	25,351	−12,564	12,787	−7,075	18,116
1976	114,745	−124,228	−9,483	931	−2,558	5,027	−6,082	29,375	−13,311	16,063	−5,686	4,295
1977	120,816	−151,907	−31,091	1,731	−3,565	5,680	−27,246	32,354	−14,217	18,137	−5,226	−14,335
1978	142,075	−176,002	−33,927	857	−3,573	6,879	−29,763	42,088	−21,680	20,408	−5,788	−15,143
1979	184,439	−212,007	−27,568	−1,313	−2,935	7,251	−24,565	63,834	−32,961	30,873	−6,593	−285
1980	224,250	−249,750	−25,500	−1,822	−997	8,912	−19,407	72,606	−42,532	30,073	−8,349	2,317
1981	237,044	−265,067	−28,023	−844	144	12,552	−16,172	86,529	−53,626	32,903	−11,702	5,030
1982	211,157	−247,642	−36,485	112	−992	13,209	−24,156	86,200	−56,412	29,788	−17,075	−11,443
1983	201,799	−268,901	−67,102	−563	−4,227	14,124	−57,767	85,200	−53,700	31,500	−17,718	−43,985
1984	219,926	−332,418	−112,492	−2,547	−8,438	14,404	−109,073	104,756	−74,036	30,720	−20,598	−98,951
1985	215,915	−338,088	−122,173	−4,390	−9,798	14,483	−121,880	93,679	−73,087	20,592	−22,700	−123,987
1986	223,344	−368,425	−145,081	−5,181	−8,484	18,139	−140,605	91,186	−79,095	12,091	−24,679	−153,193
1987	250,208	−409,765	−159,557	−3,844	−7,613	17,661	−153,353	100,511	−91,302	9,209	−23,909	−168,053
1988	320,230	−447,189	−126,959	−6,320	−2,591	19,969	−115,900	129,366	−115,722	13,644	−25,988	−128,245
1989	362,120	−477,365	−115,245	−6,749	4,043	25,662	−92,288	153,659	−138,639	15,020	−26,963	−104,231
1990	389,307	−498,337	−109,030	−7,599	8,002	27,401	−81,225	163,324	−139,402	23,921	−34,588	−91,892
1991	416,913	−490,981	−74,068	−5,274	17,032	31,284	−31,027	141,408	−121,159	20,249	5,122	−5,657
1992	440,352	−536,458	−96,106	−1,448	19,974	38,373	−39,207	125,852	−107,836	18,016	−35,192	−56,383
1993	456,832	−589,441	−132,609	1,269	19,764	39,274	−72,301	129,844	−110,176	19,668	−38,137	−90,771
1994	502,398	−668,590	−166,192	1,874	16,519	43,383	−104,416	154,510	−144,787	9,723	−38,845	−133,538
1995	575,871	−749,431	−173,560	3,866	21,197	46,640	−101,857	196,880	−190,072	6,808	−34,046	−129,095
1996	612,069	−803,239	−191,170	3,786	24,713	51,631	−111,040	206,400	−203,577	2,824	−39,968	−148,184
1995:												
I	138,389	−182,790	−44,401	722	4,312	11,062	−28,305	47,218	−45,171	2,047	−8,451	−34,709
II	143,181	−190,739	−47,558	984	4,333	11,442	−30,799	50,303	−47,080	3,223	−8,128	−35,704
III	145,360	−188,180	−42,820	1,289	5,755	11,892	−23,884	49,130	−49,531	−401	−8,847	−33,132
IV	148,941	−187,722	−38,781	871	6,796	12,240	−18,874	50,230	−48,290	1,940	−8,620	−25,554
1996:												
I	150,048	−192,973	−42,925	485	5,194	12,707	−24,539	49,277	−47,216	2,061	−10,406	−32,884
II	153,411	−200,973	−47,562	1,214	5,818	12,751	−27,779	50,188	−49,305	883	−8,689	−35,585
III	150,764	−203,257	−52,493	792	6,559	12,626	−32,516	51,893	−53,263	−1,370	−8,947	−42,833
IV	157,846	−206,036	−48,190	1,295	7,147	13,550	−26,198	55,043	−53,793	1,250	−11,926	−36,874
1997:												
I	162,527	−212,314	−49,787	437	6,195	13,855	−29,300	55,269	−57,259	−1,990	−8,682	−39,972
II	171,411	−218,545	−47,134	1,048	6,413	14,028	−25,645	59,129	−62,376	−3,247	−8,960	−37,852
III p	170,579	−222,128	−51,549	1,040	6,788	14,090	−29,631	60,608	−63,929	−3,321	−9,204	−42,156

[1] Adjusted from Census data for differences in valuation, coverage, and timing; excludes military.
[2] Quarterly data are not seasonally adjusted.
[3] Includes transfers of goods and services under U.S. military grant programs.

See next page for continuation of table.

TABLE B–103.—*U.S. international transactions, 1946–97*—Continued

[Millions of dollars; quarterly data seasonally adjusted, except as noted]

Year or quarter	U.S. assets abroad, net [increase/capital outflow (−)]				Foreign assets in the U.S., net [increase/capital inflow (+)]			Allocations of special drawing rights (SDRs)	Statistical discrepancy	
	Total	U.S. official reserve assets [2][5]	Other U.S. Government assets [2]	U.S. private assets	Total	Foreign official assets [2]	Other foreign assets		Total (sum of the items with sign reversed)	Of which: Seasonal adjustment discrepancy
1946		−623								
1947		−3,315								
1948		−1,736								
1949		−266								
1950		1,758								
1951		−33								
1952		−415								
1953		1,256								
1954		480								
1955		182								
1956		−869								
1957		−1,165								
1958		2,292								
1959		1,035								
1960	−4,099	2,145	−1,100	−5,144	2,294	1,473	821		−1,019	
1961	−5,538	607	−910	−5,235	2,705	765	1,939		−989	
1962	−4,174	1,535	−1,085	−4,623	1,911	1,270	641		−1,124	
1963	−7,270	378	−1,662	−5,986	3,217	1,986	1,231		−360	
1964	−9,560	171	−1,680	−8,050	3,643	1,660	1,983		−907	
1965	−5,716	1,225	−1,605	−5,336	742	134	607		−457	
1966	−7,321	570	−1,543	−6,347	3,661	−672	4,333		629	
1967	−9,757	53	−2,423	−7,386	7,379	3,451	3,928		−205	
1968	−10,977	−870	−2,274	−7,833	9,928	−774	10,703		438	
1969	−11,585	−1,179	−2,200	−8,206	12,702	−1,301	14,002		−1,516	
1970	−9,337	2,481	−1,589	−10,229	6,359	6,908	−550	867	−219	
1971	−12,475	2,349	−1,884	−12,940	22,970	26,879	−3,909	717	−9,779	
1972	−14,497	−4	−1,568	−12,925	21,461	10,475	10,986	710	−1,879	
1973	−22,874	158	−2,644	−20,388	18,388	6,026	12,362		−2,654	
1974	−34,745	−1,467	[4] 366	−33,643	35,341	10,546	24,796		−2,558	
1975	−39,703	−849	−3,474	−35,380	17,170	7,027	10,143		4,417	
1976	−51,269	−2,558	−4,214	−44,498	38,018	17,693	20,326		8,955	
1977	−34,785	−375	−3,693	−30,717	53,219	36,816	16,403		−4,099	
1978	−61,130	732	−4,660	−57,202	67,036	33,678	33,358		9,236	
1979	−66,054	−1,133	−3,746	−61,176	40,852	−13,665	54,516	1,139	24,349	
1980	−86,967	−8,155	−5,162	−73,651	62,612	15,497	47,115	1,152	20,886	
1981	−114,147	−5,175	−5,097	−103,875	86,232	4,960	81,272	1,093	21,792	
1982	−122,335	−4,965	−6,131	−111,239	96,418	3,593	92,826		37,359	
1983	−61,573	−1,196	−5,006	−55,372	88,780	5,845	82,934		16,779	
1984	−36,313	−3,131	−5,489	−27,694	118,032	3,140	114,892		17,231	
1985	−39,889	−3,858	−2,821	−33,211	146,383	−1,119	147,501		17,494	
1986	−106,753	312	−2,022	−105,044	230,211	35,648	194,563		29,735	
1987	−72,617	9,149	1,006	−82,771	248,383	45,387	202,996		−7,713	
1988	−100,221	−3,912	2,967	−99,275	246,065	39,758	206,307		−17,600	
1989	−168,744	−25,293	1,259	−144,710	224,390	8,503	215,887		48,585	
1990	−74,011	−2,158	2,307	−74,160	140,992	33,910	107,082		24,911	
1991	−57,881	5,763	2,911	−66,555	109,641	17,389	92,253		−46,103	
1992	−68,774	3,901	−1,657	−71,018	168,776	40,477	128,299		−43,619	
1993	−194,537	−1,379	−342	−192,817	279,671	71,753	207,918		5,637	
1994	−160,516	5,346	−352	−165,510	297,337	40,385	256,952		−3,283	
1995	−307,207	−9,742	−549	−296,916	451,234	110,729	340,505		−14,931	
1996	−352,444	6,668	−690	−358,422	547,555	122,354	425,201		−46,927	
1995:										
I	−59,625	−5,318	−158	−54,149	97,652	22,098	75,554		−3,318	5,658
II	−110,548	−2,722	−184	−107,642	122,714	37,138	85,576		23,538	−775
III	−40,679	−1,893	266	−39,052	125,839	39,585	86,254		−52,028	−6,985
IV	−96,356	191	−473	−96,074	105,029	11,908	93,121		16,881	2,106
1996:										
I	−70,768	17	−210	−70,575	88,233	52,014	36,219		15,419	6,228
II	−49,698	−523	−358	−48,817	106,114	13,154	92,960		−20,831	−1,076
III	−77,542	7,489	162	−85,193	158,629	24,089	134,540		−38,254	−7,830
IV	−154,436	−315	−284	−153,837	194,579	33,097	161,482		−3,269	2,669
1997:										
I	−127,969	4,480	−21	−132,428	182,238	28,891	153,347		−14,297	7,059
II	−90,935	−236	−268	−90,431	143,015	−5,374	148,389		−14,228	−1,713
III *p*	−101,564	−730	482	−101,316	169,540	22,498	147,042		−25,820	−8,560

[4] Includes extraordinary U.S. Government transactions with India.
[5] Consists of gold, special drawing rights, foreign currencies, and the U.S. reserve position in the International Monetary Fund (IMF).
Source: Department of Commerce, Bureau of Economic Analysis.

[Billions of dollars; quarterly data seasonally adjusted]

Year or quarter	Exports							Imports						
			Nonagricultural products							Nonpetroleum products				
	Total	Agricultural products	Total	Industrial supplies and materials	Capital goods except automotive	Automotive	Other	Total	Petroleum and products	Total	Industrial supplies and materials	Capital goods except automotive	Automotive	Other
1965	26.5	6.3	20.2	7.6	8.1	1.9	2.6	21.5	2.0	19.5	9.1	1.5	0.9	8.0
1966	29.3	6.9	22.4	8.2	8.9	2.4	2.9	25.5	2.1	23.4	10.2	2.2	1.8	9.2
1967	30.7	6.5	24.2	8.5	9.9	2.8	3.0	26.9	2.1	24.8	10.0	2.5	2.4	9.9
1968	33.6	6.3	27.3	9.6	11.1	3.5	3.2	33.0	2.4	30.6	12.0	2.8	4.0	11.8
1969	36.4	6.1	30.3	10.3	12.4	3.9	3.7	35.8	2.6	33.2	11.8	3.4	4.9	13.0
1970	42.5	7.4	35.1	12.3	14.7	3.9	4.3	39.9	2.9	36.9	12.4	4.0	5.5	15.0
1971	43.3	7.8	35.5	10.9	15.4	4.7	4.5	45.6	3.7	41.9	13.8	4.3	7.4	16.4
1972	49.4	9.5	39.9	11.9	16.9	5.5	5.6	55.8	4.7	51.1	16.3	5.9	8.7	20.2
1973	71.4	18.0	53.4	17.0	22.0	6.9	7.6	70.5	8.4	62.1	19.6	8.3	10.3	23.9
1974	98.3	22.4	75.9	26.3	30.9	8.6	10.0	103.8	26.6	77.2	27.8	9.8	12.0	27.5
1975	107.1	22.2	84.8	26.8	36.6	10.6	10.8	98.2	27.0	71.2	24.0	10.2	11.7	25.3
1976	114.7	23.4	91.4	28.4	39.1	12.1	11.7	124.2	34.6	89.7	29.8	12.3	16.2	31.4
1977	120.8	24.3	96.5	29.8	39.8	13.4	13.5	151.9	45.0	106.9	35.7	14.0	18.6	38.6
1978 [1]	142.1	29.9	112.2	34.2	47.5	15.2	15.3	176.0	42.6	133.4	40.7	19.3	25.0	48.4
1979	184.4	35.5	149.0	52.2	60.2	17.9	18.7	212.0	60.4	151.6	47.5	24.6	26.6	52.8
1980	224.3	42.0	182.2	65.1	76.3	17.4	23.4	249.8	79.5	170.2	53.0	31.6	28.3	57.4
1981	237.0	44.1	193.0	63.6	84.2	19.7	25.5	265.1	78.4	186.7	56.1	37.1	31.0	62.4
1982	211.2	37.3	173.9	57.7	76.5	17.2	22.4	247.6	62.0	185.7	48.6	38.4	34.3	64.3
1983	201.8	37.1	164.7	52.7	71.7	18.5	21.8	268.9	55.1	213.8	53.7	43.7	43.0	73.3
1984	219.9	38.4	181.5	56.8	77.0	22.4	25.3	332.4	58.1	274.4	66.1	60.4	56.5	91.4
1985	215.9	29.6	186.3	54.8	79.3	24.9	27.2	338.1	51.4	286.7	62.6	61.3	64.9	97.9
1986	223.3	27.2	196.2	59.4	82.8	25.1	28.9	368.4	34.3	334.1	69.9	72.0	78.1	114.2
1987	250.2	29.8	220.4	63.7	92.7	27.6	36.4	409.8	42.9	366.8	70.8	85.1	85.2	125.7
1988	320.2	38.8	281.4	82.6	119.1	33.4	46.3	447.2	39.6	407.6	83.1	102.2	87.9	134.4
1989	362.1	42.2	319.9	91.8	138.9	34.9	54.3	477.4	50.9	426.5	84.5	112.2	87.4	142.5
1990	389.3	40.2	349.1	96.9	152.5	36.5	63.2	498.3	62.3	436.1	82.9	116.1	88.5	148.6
1991	416.9	40.1	376.8	101.7	166.5	40.0	68.6	491.0	51.7	439.2	81.2	120.8	85.7	151.5
1992	440.4	44.0	396.3	101.7	176.1	47.0	71.5	536.5	51.6	484.9	89.0	134.3	91.8	169.8
1993	456.8	43.7	413.1	105.0	182.1	52.5	73.5	589.4	51.5	538.0	101.0	152.3	102.4	182.3
1994	502.4	47.1	455.3	112.6	205.2	57.8	79.8	668.6	51.3	617.3	113.7	184.4	118.3	201.0
1995	575.9	57.2	518.6	135.5	233.8	61.8	87.6	749.4	56.2	693.3	128.8	221.4	123.8	219.2
1996	612.1	61.5	550.6	137.9	253.1	65.0	94.5	803.2	72.7	730.5	136.8	229.0	128.9	235.8
1995: I	138.4	13.8	124.6	32.8	54.4	15.9	21.4	182.8	13.2	169.6	31.6	51.3	32.3	54.3
II	143.2	13.5	129.7	34.9	58.1	15.1	21.7	190.7	14.9	175.8	34.4	54.8	31.5	55.1
III	145.4	14.8	130.5	34.2	59.3	15.2	21.7	188.2	14.4	173.8	31.4	57.0	30.2	55.3
IV	148.9	15.1	133.8	33.6	61.9	15.6	22.7	187.7	13.7	174.0	31.4	58.3	29.7	54.5
1996: I	150.0	15.9	134.2	33.8	62.0	15.7	22.7	193.0	14.6	178.4	32.9	57.8	31.0	56.7
II	153.4	15.1	138.3	35.4	63.2	16.0	23.7	201.0	18.5	182.5	35.4	56.6	32.3	58.2
III	150.8	15.1	135.7	33.9	61.7	16.6	23.5	203.3	19.1	184.2	34.3	56.8	33.4	59.6
IV	157.8	15.5	142.4	34.8	66.3	16.8	24.5	206.0	20.6	185.5	34.1	57.9	32.2	61.3
1997: I	162.5	14.3	148.2	36.0	69.0	17.7	25.5	212.3	19.2	193.1	35.8	59.3	35.6	62.5
II	171.4	14.1	157.3	37.9	74.2	18.4	26.9	218.5	17.7	200.8	37.3	62.9	34.6	66.0
III ᴾ	170.6	14.5	156.0	36.8	74.6	18.3	26.3	222.1	17.5	204.6	36.0	65.5	35.9	67.1

[1] End-use categories beginning 1978 are not strictly comparable with data for earlier periods. See *Survey of Current Business*, June 1988.

Note.—Data are on an international transactions basis and exclude military.

In June 1990, end-use categories for goods exports were redefined to include reexports; beginning with data for 1978, reexports (exports of foreign goods) are assigned to detailed end-use categories in the same manner as exports of domestic goods.

Source: Department of Commerce, Bureau of Economic Analysis.

[Billions of dollars]

Item	1988	1989	1990	1991	1992	1993	1994	1995	1996	1997 first 3 quarters at annual rate[1]
EXPORTS	320.2	362.1	389.3	416.9	440.4	456.8	502.4	575.9	612.1	672.7
Industrial countries	207.3	234.2	253.8	261.3	265.1	270.6	295.2	338.1	354.3	386.3
Canada	74.3	81.1	83.5	85.9	91.4	101.2	114.8	127.6	134.6	151.2
Japan	37.2	43.9	47.8	47.2	46.9	46.7	51.8	63.1	66.0	65.5
Western Europe[2]	86.4	98.4	111.4	116.8	114.5	111.3	115.3	132.4	137.2	152.6
Australia, New Zealand, and South Africa	9.4	10.9	11.2	11.4	12.4	11.5	13.2	15.0	16.5	17.0
Australia	6.8	8.1	8.3	8.3	8.7	8.1	9.6	10.5	11.7	12.1
Other countries, except Eastern Europe	109.1	122.2	130.6	150.4	169.5	179.8	201.7	232.1	250.4	278.8
OPEC[3]	13.8	12.7	12.7	18.4	19.7	18.7	17.1	18.4	20.3	22.7
Other[4]	95.3	109.5	117.9	132.0	149.8	161.1	184.6	213.7	230.1	256.1
Eastern Europe[2]	3.8	5.5	4.3	4.8	5.6	6.2	5.3	5.7	7.4	7.6
International organizations and unallocated	.1	.2	.6	.4	.1	.2	.1			
IMPORTS	447.2	477.4	498.3	491.0	536.5	589.4	668.6	749.4	803.2	870.6
Industrial countries	283.2	292.5	299.9	294.3	316.3	347.8	389.8	425.3	443.1	474.5
Canada	84.6	89.9	93.1	93.0	100.9	113.3	131.1	147.1	158.6	170.6
Japan	89.8	93.5	90.4	92.3	97.4	107.2	119.1	123.5	115.2	121.5
Western Europe[2]	102.6	102.4	109.2	102.0	111.4	120.9	132.9	147.7	161.6	173.5
Australia, New Zealand, and South Africa	6.2	6.6	7.3	7.0	6.6	6.4	6.7	7.1	7.7	9.0
Australia	3.5	3.9	4.4	4.1	3.7	3.3	3.2	3.4	3.9	4.9
Other countries, except Eastern Europe	161.8	182.8	196.1	194.9	218.2	238.1	272.9	317.1	353.1	387.8
OPEC[3]	23.0	29.2	37.0	33.4	32.4	32.6	31.7	35.6	44.4	46.3
Other[4]	138.8	153.6	159.1	161.5	185.8	205.4	241.3	281.5	308.8	341.5
Eastern Europe[2]	2.2	2.1	2.3	1.8	2.0	3.5	5.8	7.0	7.0	8.3
International organizations and unallocated										
BALANCE (excess of exports +)	−127.0	−115.2	−109.0	−74.1	−96.1	−132.6	−166.2	−173.6	−191.2	−198.0
Industrial countries	−75.9	−58.2	−46.1	−33.0	−51.2	−77.2	−94.6	−87.2	−88.8	−88.2
Canada	−10.3	−8.8	−9.6	−7.1	−9.5	−12.2	−16.3	−19.5	−24.0	−19.4
Japan	−52.6	−49.7	−42.6	−45.0	−50.5	−60.5	−67.3	−60.3	−49.2	−56.0
Western Europe[2]	−16.2	−4.0	2.2	14.8	3.1	−9.7	−17.6	−15.2	−24.4	−20.8
Australia, New Zealand, and South Africa	3.2	4.2	3.9	4.4	5.8	5.2	6.6	7.9	8.9	8.0
Australia	3.3	4.2	3.9	4.2	5.0	4.8	6.4	7.1	7.8	7.2
Other countries, except Eastern Europe	−52.7	−60.6	−65.5	−44.5	−48.7	−58.3	−71.2	−85.1	−102.7	−109.0
OPEC[3]	−9.2	−16.6	−24.3	−15.0	−12.7	−14.0	−14.6	−17.2	−24.1	−23.5
Other[4]	−43.5	−44.1	−41.2	−29.5	−36.0	−44.3	−56.6	−67.8	−78.7	−85.5
Eastern Europe[2]	1.6	3.5	2.1	3.0	3.7	2.7	−.5	−1.3	.4	−.7
International organizations and unallocated	.1	.2	.6	.4	.1	.2	.1			

[1] Preliminary; seasonally adjusted.
[2] The former German Democratic Republic (East Germany) included in Western Europe beginning fourth quarter 1990 and in Eastern Europe prior to that time.
[3] Organization of Petroleum Exporting Countries, consisting of Algeria, Ecuador (through 1992), Gabon, Indonesia, Iran, Iraq, Kuwait, Libya, Nigeria, Qatar, Saudi Arabia, United Arab Emirates, and Venezuela.
[4] Latin America, other Western Hemisphere, and other countries in Asia and Africa, less members of OPEC.

Note.—Data are on an international transactions basis and exclude military.

Source: Department of Commerce, Bureau of Economic Analysis.

Table B–106.—U.S. international trade in goods on balance of payments (BOP) and Census basis, and trade in services on BOP basis, 1974–97

[Billions of dollars; monthly data seasonally adjusted]

Year or month	Goods: Exports (f.a.s. value) [1][2]							Goods: Imports (customs value, except as noted) [5]							Services (BOP basis)	
	Total, BOP basis [3]	Census basis (by end-use category)						Total, BOP basis	Census basis (by end-use category)						Exports	Imports
		Total, Census basis [3][4]	Foods, feeds, and beverages	Industrial supplies and materials	Capital goods except automotive	Automotive vehicles, parts, and engines	Consumer goods (nonfood) except automotive		Total, Census basis [4]	Foods, feeds, and beverages	Industrial supplies and materials	Capital goods except automotive	Automotive vehicles, parts, and engines	Consumer goods (nonfood) except automotive		
		F.a.s. value [2]							F.a.s. value [2]							
1974	98.3	99.4						103.8	103.3						22.6	21.4
1975	107.1	108.9						98.2	99.3						25.5	22.0
1976	114.7	116.8						124.2	124.6						28.0	24.6
1977	120.8	123.2						151.9	151.5						31.5	27.6
1978	142.1	145.8						176.0	176.1						36.4	32.2
1979	184.4	186.4						212.0	210.3						39.7	36.7
1980	224.3	225.6						249.8	245.3						47.6	41.5
									Customs value						
1981	237.0	238.7						265.1	261.0						57.4	45.5
1982	211.2	216.4	31.3	61.7	72.7	15.7	14.3	247.6	244.0	17.1	112.0	35.4	33.3	39.7	64.1	51.7
1983	201.8	205.6	30.9	56.7	67.2	16.8	13.4	268.9	258.0	18.2	107.0	40.9	40.8	44.9	64.3	55.0
1984	219.9	224.0	31.5	61.7	72.0	20.6	13.3	332.4	[6]330.7	21.0	123.7	59.8	53.5	60.0	71.2	67.7
1985	215.9	[7]218.8	24.0	58.5	73.9	22.9	12.6	338.1	[6]336.5	21.9	113.9	65.1	66.8	68.3	73.2	72.9
1986	223.3	[7]227.2	22.3	57.3	75.8	21.7	14.2	368.4	365.4	24.4	101.3	71.8	78.2	79.4	86.3	81.8
1987	250.2	254.1	24.3	66.7	86.2	24.6	17.7	409.8	406.2	24.8	111.0	84.5	85.2	88.7	98.6	92.3
1988	320.2	322.4	32.3	85.1	109.2	29.3	23.1	447.2	441.0	24.8	118.3	101.4	87.7	95.9	111.0	100.0
1989	362.1	363.8	37.2	99.3	138.8	34.8	36.4	477.4	473.2	25.1	132.3	113.3	86.1	102.9	127.1	104.2
1990	389.3	393.6	35.1	104.4	152.7	37.4	43.3	498.3	495.3	26.6	143.2	116.4	87.3	105.7	147.8	120.0
1991	416.9	421.7	35.7	109.7	166.7	40.0	45.9	491.0	488.5	26.5	131.6	120.7	85.7	108.0	164.2	121.2
1992	440.4	448.2	40.3	109.1	175.9	47.0	51.4	536.5	532.7	27.6	138.6	134.3	91.8	122.7	177.2	120.3
1993	456.8	465.1	40.6	111.8	181.7	52.4	54.7	589.4	580.7	27.9	145.6	152.4	102.4	134.0	186.7	126.4
1994	502.4	512.6	42.0	121.4	205.0	57.8	60.0	668.6	663.3	31.0	162.1	184.4	118.3	146.3	197.2	135.5
1995	575.9	584.7	50.5	146.2	233.0	61.8	64.4	749.4	743.5	33.2	181.8	221.4	123.8	159.9	218.7	147.0
1996	612.1	625.1	55.5	147.7	252.9	65.0	70.1	803.2	795.3	35.7	204.5	229.1	128.9	171.0	236.8	156.6
1996: Jan	48.9	49.6	4.7	11.9	20.0	5.3	5.6	64.4	64.1	2.8	15.9	19.3	10.4	13.6	18.7	12.7
Feb	50.4	51.2	4.5	12.1	21.1	5.3	5.8	63.5	63.1	2.8	15.0	19.0	10.5	13.8	18.4	13.0
Mar	50.7	51.6	4.9	12.6	20.8	5.1	5.7	65.1	63.8	3.0	15.6	19.5	10.1	13.6	19.9	13.0
Apr	50.8	51.6	4.6	12.7	21.1	5.1	5.7	66.7	65.1	3.1	16.9	18.7	10.5	13.7	19.2	13.0
May	51.3	52.4	4.7	12.5	21.1	5.4	5.9	68.1	66.9	3.0	17.4	19.0	11.0	14.3	20.0	13.1
June	51.3	52.2	4.5	12.3	20.9	5.6	5.9	66.2	65.3	2.9	16.7	18.8	10.8	13.9	19.6	12.8
July	49.1	50.5	4.7	11.6	20.1	5.3	5.6	66.8	66.4	2.9	17.3	18.7	11.0	14.1	19.4	13.3
Aug	51.3	52.6	4.7	12.3	21.2	5.5	5.9	68.0	67.2	3.0	17.4	19.0	11.2	14.4	19.9	13.1
Sept	50.4	51.7	4.4	12.2	20.4	5.7	5.9	68.4	68.1	3.0	17.8	19.1	11.2	14.8	20.0	12.9
Oct	52.5	53.6	4.5	12.7	22.0	5.4	6.1	67.8	67.5	3.0	18.3	18.9	10.2	15.0	20.6	13.2
Nov	53.2	54.5	5.0	12.3	22.2	5.9	6.1	68.4	68.1	3.0	17.6	19.3	11.2	14.7	20.8	13.2
Dec	52.1	53.4	4.4	12.5	22.1	5.5	6.0	69.8	69.6	3.2	18.7	19.6	10.8	15.1	20.3	13.2
1997: Jan	51.7	52.2	4.3	12.1	21.6	5.6	6.1	69.8	69.6	3.1	17.9	19.5	11.8	15.1	20.2	13.6
Feb	53.7	54.4	4.3	12.7	22.7	5.9	6.3	70.4	70.0	3.1	17.6	19.4	12.1	15.3	20.6	13.7
Mar	57.2	58.1	4.2	13.7	24.7	6.2	6.5	72.0	70.6	3.3	18.0	20.4	11.7	14.9	21.0	13.9
Apr	57.2	57.9	4.2	13.5	25.0	6.2	6.3	72.7	71.7	3.4	17.6	20.7	11.4	16.2	21.2	13.8
May	56.9	57.9	4.1	13.4	24.8	5.9	6.7	73.2	72.3	3.4	17.9	21.0	11.6	16.1	21.1	13.9
June	57.4	58.2	3.9	13.9	24.5	6.3	6.7	72.6	71.7	3.3	17.6	21.3	11.6	15.7	21.0	14.1
July	56.7	57.8	3.8	13.2	24.9	6.3	6.4	73.6	73.4	3.4	17.5	21.6	12.3	16.1	21.1	14.0
Aug	57.3	58.4	4.2	13.4	24.9	6.2	6.4	73.9	73.6	3.3	17.9	22.1	11.8	16.0	21.6	14.1
Sept	56.4	57.5	4.3	13.1	24.8	5.8	6.4	74.9	74.6	3.4	18.3	22.0	11.8	16.7	21.7	14.4
Oct	58.5	59.5	4.7	13.2	25.4	6.5	6.8	74.9	74.7	3.3	18.4	22.4	11.3	16.6	21.8	14.4
Nov [P]	57.8	58.4	4.6	13.1	24.6	6.9	6.6	72.9	72.6	3.2	17.1	21.4	11.8	16.8	21.4	14.4

[1] Department of Defense shipments of grant-aid military supplies and equipment under the Military Assistance Program are excluded from total exports through 1985 and included beginning 1986.
[2] F.a.s. (free alongside ship) value basis at U.S. port of exportation for exports and at foreign port of exportation for imports.
[3] Includes undocumented exports to Canada through 1988. Beginning 1989, undocumented exports to Canada are included in the appropriate end-use category.
[4] Total includes "other" exports or imports, not shown separately.
[5] Total arrivals of imported goods other than intransit shipments.
[6] Total includes revisions not reflected in detail.
[7] Total exports are on a revised statistical month basis; end-use categories are on a statistical month basis.

Note.—Goods on a Census basis are adjusted to a BOP basis by the Bureau of Economic Analysis, in line with concepts and definitions used to prepare international and national accounts. The adjustments are necessary to supplement coverage of Census data, to eliminate duplication of transactions recorded elsewhere in international accounts, and to value transactions according to a standard definition. Data include trade of the U.S. Virgin Islands.

Source: Department of Commerce (Bureau of the Census and Bureau of Economic Analysis).

[Billions of dollars]

Type of investment	1988	1989	1990	1991	1992	1993	1994	1995	1996
NET INTERNATIONAL INVESTMENT POSITION OF THE UNITED STATES:									
With direct investment at current cost	−161.8	−243.8	−246.4	−326.0	−473.0	−370.1	−411.7	−687.7	−870.5
With direct investment at market value	−12.6	−70.5	−207.0	−319.9	−529.5	−274.9	−321.5	−637.5	−831.3
U.S. ASSETS ABROAD:									
With direct investment at current cost	1,841.0	2,076.0	2,180.0	2,285.1	2,325.0	2,742.5	2,899.0	3,272.7	3,720.7
With direct investment at market value	2,006.6	2,348.1	2,291.7	2,468.4	2,464.2	3,055.3	3,178.0	3,700.4	4,284.5
U.S. official reserve assets	144.2	168.7	174.7	159.2	147.4	164.9	163.4	176.1	160.7
Gold [1]	107.4	105.2	102.4	92.6	87.2	102.6	100.1	101.3	96.7
Special drawing rights	9.6	10.0	11.0	11.2	8.5	9.0	10.0	11.0	10.3
Reserve position in the International Monetary Fund	9.7	9.0	9.1	9.5	11.8	11.8	12.0	14.6	15.4
Foreign currencies	17.4	44.6	52.2	45.9	40.0	41.5	41.2	49.1	38.3
U.S. Government assets other than official reserves	86.1	84.5	82.0	79.1	80.7	81.0	81.4	81.9	82.6
U.S. credits and other long-term assets	85.4	83.9	81.4	77.5	79.1	79.1	79.3	80.0	80.8
Repayable in dollars	83.9	82.4	80.0	76.3	78.0	78.1	78.4	79.2	80.0
Other	1.5	1.5	1.3	1.2	1.1	1.0	.9	.8	.7
U.S. foreign currency holdings and U.S. short-term assets	.7	.6	.6	1.6	1.6	1.9	2.1	1.9	1.8
U.S. private assets:									
With direct investment at current cost	1,610.7	1,822.8	1,923.3	2,046.8	2,096.8	2,496.6	2,654.3	3,014.8	3,477.4
With direct investment at market value	1,776.3	2,094.9	2,035.1	2,230.0	2,236.0	2,809.3	2,933.3	3,442.5	4,041.2
Direct investment abroad:									
At current cost	526.8	560.4	620.0	643.3	659.4	714.8	797.8	884.3	970.8
At market value	692.5	832.5	731.8	827.5	798.6	1,027.5	1,076.8	1,312.0	1,534.6
Foreign securities	232.8	314.3	342.3	455.8	515.1	853.5	889.7	1,054.4	1,273.4
Bonds	104.2	116.9	144.7	176.8	200.8	309.7	303.1	355.3	398.0
Corporate stocks	128.7	197.3	197.6	279.0	314.3	543.9	586.6	699.1	875.5
U.S. claims on unaffiliated foreigners reported by U.S. nonbanking concerns	197.8	234.3	265.3	256.3	254.3	242.0	273.7	308.0	369.1
U.S. claims reported by U.S. banks, not included elsewhere	653.2	713.8	695.7	690.4	668.0	686.2	693.1	768.1	864.1
FOREIGN ASSETS IN THE UNITED STATES:									
With direct investment at current cost	2,002.8	2,319.8	2,426.4	2,611.1	2,798.0	3,112.6	3,310.7	3,960.4	4,591.3
With direct investment at market value	2,019.2	2,418.6	2,498.7	2,788.3	2,993.7	3,330.2	3,499.5	4,337.9	5,115.8
Foreign official assets in the United States	322.0	341.9	375.3	401.7	442.8	516.2	545.7	678.5	805.1
U.S. Government securities	260.9	263.7	295.0	315.9	335.7	388.3	415.0	498.9	610.2
U.S. Treasury securities	253.0	257.3	287.9	307.1	323.0	371.2	393.4	471.5	579.0
Other	8.0	6.4	7.1	8.8	12.7	17.1	21.6	27.4	31.2
Other U.S. Government liabilities	15.2	15.4	17.2	18.6	20.8	22.1	24.5	25.2	25.9
U.S. liabilities reported by U.S. banks, not included elsewhere	31.5	36.5	39.9	38.4	55.0	69.7	73.4	107.4	112.1
Other foreign official assets	14.4	26.3	23.2	28.7	31.3	36.1	32.9	46.9	56.9
Other foreign assets in the United States:									
With direct investment at current cost	1,680.8	1,977.9	2,051.1	2,209.4	2,355.3	2,596.4	2,765.0	3,282.0	3,786.1
With direct investment at market value	1,697.1	2,076.7	2,123.3	2,386.6	2,550.9	2,814.0	2,953.7	3,659.5	4,310.7
Direct investment in the United States:									
At current cost	375.2	435.9	467.3	491.9	500.5	550.9	585.0	654.5	729.1
At market value	391.5	534.7	539.6	669.1	696.2	768.4	773.7	1,032.0	1,253.6
U.S. Treasury securities	100.9	166.5	162.4	189.5	225.1	253.9	266.7	389.4	530.6
U.S. currency	84.2	90.1	108.9	124.3	137.7	156.6	180.0	192.3	209.6
U.S. securities other than U.S. Treasury securities	392.3	482.9	467.4	559.2	620.2	730.6	752.8	999.5	1,225.5
Corporate and other bonds	191.3	231.7	245.7	287.3	319.8	389.9	413.9	534.1	654.1
Corporate stocks	201.0	251.2	221.7	271.9	300.4	340.6	338.9	465.4	571.3
U.S. liabilities to unaffiliated foreigners reported by U.S. nonbanking concerns	144.5	167.1	213.4	208.9	220.7	229.0	197.3	232.9	271.5
U.S. liabilities reported by U.S. banks, not included elsewhere	583.7	635.5	631.6	635.6	651.0	675.5	783.3	813.4	819.9

[1] Valued at market price.

Note.—For details regarding these data, see *Survey of Current Business,* July 1997.

Source: Department of Commerce, Bureau of Economic Analysis.

Year or quarter	United States	Canada	Japan	European Union[1]	France	Germany[2]	Italy	United Kingdom
	Industrial production (Index, 1992=100)[3]							
1972	65.3	68.9	51.9	72.0	74	69.2	67.3	76.7
1973	70.6	77.0	59.6	77.2	79	73.6	73.9	83.6
1974	69.6	78.5	57.3	77.8	82	73.4	76.8	81.9
1975	63.4	72.8	51.2	72.6	96	68.8	70.0	77.4
1976	69.3	77.6	56.9	78.0	82	75.1	78.5	80.0
1977	74.9	80.3	59.3	79.9	84	76.5	78.0	84.1
1978	79.3	83.0	63.0	82.1	86	78.6	79.7	86.5
1979	82.0	87.1	67.5	85.9	93.0	82.4	85.0	89.9
1980	79.7	84.1	70.6	85.6	93.0	82.6	89.4	84.0
1981	81.0	85.8	71.4	84.0	92.3	81.0	87.4	81.3
1982	76.7	77.4	71.7	82.9	91.4	78.5	84.7	82.9
1983	79.5	82.4	73.9	83.8	90.7	79.0	82.7	85.9
1984	86.6	92.4	80.7	85.6	91.2	81.2	85.4	86.0
1985	88.0	97.6	83.6	88.4	91.3	84.9	86.6	90.7
1986	89.0	96.8	83.5	90.4	91.9	86.6	90.2	92.9
1987	93.2	101.6	86.4	92.3	93.0	86.9	92.6	96.6
1988	97.4	106.9	95.3	96.1	97.3	90.3	99.1	101.2
1989	99.1	106.8	99.9	99.8	100.9	94.6	103.0	103.4
1990	98.9	103.2	104.2	101.8	102.4	99.5	102.2	103.1
1991	97.0	98.9	106.1	101.1	101.2	102.4	101.3	99.6
1992	100.0	100.0	100.0	100.0	100.0	100.0	100.0	100.0
1993	103.6	105.1	95.8	96.9	96.2	92.7	97.9	102.2
1994	109.2	111.4	97.0	101.8	100.0	96.2	104.0	107.6
1995	114.5	116.0	100.2	105.9	102.0	98.1	110.3	110.0
1996	118.5	117.7	102.9	106.0	102.3	98.6	107.2	111.2
1997 ᴾ	124.5	....	....	....	....	....	....	....
1996: I	116.1	115.8	101.7	105.3	102.0	97.5	108.0	110.5
II	118.2	116.6	101.3	105.2	102.1	98.6	107.5	110.8
III	119.3	118.8	103.2	106.1	102.7	99.9	107.1	111.5
IV	120.4	119.7	105.5	106.9	102.6	99.6	106.0	112.0
1997: I	121.9	121.0	108.0	107.8	103.2	101.0	107.5	112.1
II	123.3	123.0	107.9	109.5	105.5	102.0	109.9	112.9
III	125.1	125.2	107.5	....	107.1	104.1	110.3	114.2
IV ᴾ	127.4	....	....	....	....	....	....	....
	Consumer prices (Index, 1982–84=100)							
1972	41.8	37.9	42.9	30.8	32.2	58.7	19.0	25.5
1973	44.4	40.8	47.9	33.5	34.5	62.8	20.9	27.9
1974	49.3	45.2	59.0	38.0	39.3	67.1	25.0	32.3
1975	53.8	50.1	65.9	43.4	43.9	71.1	29.3	40.2
1976	56.9	53.8	72.2	48.6	48.2	74.2	34.1	46.8
1977	60.6	58.1	78.1	54.5	52.7	76.9	40.3	54.2
1978	65.2	63.3	81.4	59.4	57.5	79.0	45.3	58.7
1979	72.6	69.1	84.4	65.6	63.7	82.2	52.4	66.6
1980	82.4	76.1	90.9	74.3	72.3	86.7	63.5	78.5
1981	90.9	85.6	95.3	83.5	82.0	92.2	75.3	87.9
1982	96.5	94.9	98.1	92.3	91.6	97.1	87.7	95.4
1983	99.6	100.4	99.8	100.2	100.5	100.3	100.8	99.8
1984	103.9	104.8	102.1	107.4	107.9	102.7	111.5	104.8
1985	107.6	108.9	104.1	114.0	114.2	104.8	121.1	111.1
1986	109.6	113.4	104.8	118.2	117.2	104.7	128.5	114.9
1987	113.6	118.4	104.8	122.0	120.9	104.9	134.4	119.7
1988	118.3	123.2	105.6	126.5	124.2	106.3	141.1	125.6
1989	124.0	129.3	108.1	133.2	128.6	109.2	150.4	135.4
1990	130.7	135.5	111.4	140.8	133.0	112.2	159.5	148.2
1991	136.2	143.1	115.0	148.1	137.2	116.3	169.8	156.9
1992	140.3	145.2	116.9	154.7	140.6	122.1	178.8	162.7
1993	144.5	147.9	118.4	160.2	143.5	127.6	186.3	165.3
1994	148.2	148.2	119.3	165.2	145.9	131.1	193.6	169.3
1995	152.4	151.4	119.1	170.2	148.4	133.5	204.0	175.2
1996	156.9	153.7	119.3	174.5	151.5	135.5	212.0	179.4
1997 ᴾ	160.5	156.2	121.3	....	153.2	137.8	215.7	185.1
1996: I	155.0	152.5	118.7	173.0	150.5	134.8	209.6	177.3
II	156.5	153.7	119.5	174.6	151.7	135.4	212.1	179.6
III	157.4	153.9	119.3	174.9	151.4	135.9	212.6	179.9
IV	158.5	154.9	119.7	175.6	152.0	135.8	213.7	181.0
1997: I	159.6	155.7	119.4	176.6	152.7	137.0	214.7	182.0
II	160.2	156.2	121.9	177.5	153.1	137.5	215.5	184.3
III	160.8	156.6	121.9	178.4	153.3	138.5	215.9	186.2
IV ᴾ	161.5	156.5	122.2	....	153.8	138.3	217.1	187.6

[1] Consists of Austria, Belgium, Denmark, Finland, France, Germany, Greece, Ireland, Italy, Luxembourg, Netherlands, Portugal, Spain, Sweden, and United Kingdom.
[2] Prior to 1991 data are for West Germany only.
[3] All data exclude construction. Quarterly data are seasonally adjusted.

Sources: National sources as reported by Department of Commerce (International Trade Administration, Office of Trade and Economic Analysis), Department of Labor (Bureau of Labor Statistics), and Board of Governors of the Federal Reserve System.

TABLE B-109.—*Civilian unemployment rate, and hourly compensation, major industrial countries, 1972–97*

[Quarterly data seasonally adjusted]

Year or quarter	United States	Canada	Japan	France	Germany[1]	Italy	United Kingdom
Civilian unemployment rate (Percent)[2]							
1972	5.6	6.2	1.4	2.9	0.7	3.8	4.2
1973	4.9	5.5	1.3	2.8	.7	3.7	3.2
1974	5.6	5.3	1.4	2.9	1.6	3.1	3.1
1975	8.5	6.9	1.9	4.2	3.4	3.4	4.6
1976	7.7	7.2	2.0	4.6	3.4	3.9	5.9
1977	7.1	8.1	2.0	5.2	3.4	4.1	6.4
1978	6.1	8.4	2.3	5.4	3.3	4.1	6.3
1979	5.8	7.5	2.1	6.1	2.9	4.4	5.4
1980	7.1	7.5	2.0	6.5	2.8	4.4	7.0
1981	7.6	7.6	2.2	7.6	4.0	4.9	10.5
1982	9.7	11.0	2.4	8.3	5.6	5.4	11.3
1983	9.6	11.9	2.7	8.6	[3] 6.9	5.9	11.8
1984	7.5	11.3	2.8	10.0	7.1	5.9	11.7
1985	7.2	10.5	2.6	10.5	7.2	6.0	11.2
1986	7.0	9.6	2.8	10.6	6.6	[3] 7.5	11.2
1987	6.2	8.9	2.9	10.8	6.3	7.9	10.3
1988	5.5	7.8	2.5	10.3	6.3	7.9	8.6
1989	5.3	7.5	2.3	9.6	5.7	7.8	7.2
1990	[3] 5.6	8.1	2.1	9.1	5.0	7.0	6.9
1991	6.8	10.4	2.1	9.6	p 4.3	[3] 6.9	8.8
1992	7.5	11.3	2.2	[3] 10.4	p 4.6	p 7.3	10.1
1993	6.9	11.2	2.5	11.8	p 5.7	[3] p 10.2	10.5
1994	[3] 6.1	10.4	2.9	12.3	p 6.5	p 11.3	9.7
1995	5.6	9.5	3.2	11.8	p 6.5	p 12.0	8.7
1996	5.4	9.7	3.4	12.6	p 7.2	p 12.1	p 8.2
1997	4.9	9.2	....	....	....	p 12.3	....
1996:I	5.6	9.5	3.3	12.3	6.9	12.0	8.3
II	5.4	9.6	3.5	12.5	7.1	12.5	8.3
III	5.3	9.8	3.4	12.7	7.2	11.9	8.2
IV	5.3	9.9	3.3	12.7	7.5	12.0	7.9
1997:I	5.3	9.6	3.3	12.6	7.7	12.3	7.5
II	4.9	9.4	3.5	12.7	7.7	12.7	7.3
III	4.9	9.0	3.4	12.7	7.8	11.9	6.9
IV	4.7	8.9	....	....	....	12.2	....
Manufacturing hourly compensation in U.S. dollars (Index, 1992=100)[4]							
1972	26.6	25.8	9.2	13.6	12.6	12.6	12.0
1973	28.6	27.7	12.5	17.7	17.2	14.9	13.4
1974	31.8	32.6	15.3	19.4	20.0	17.4	15.4
1975	35.6	35.8	17.5	26.6	23.2	21.9	19.5
1976	38.6	42.3	18.8	27.4	24.4	21.4	18.3
1977	42.0	43.5	23.0	30.2	28.9	23.8	20.0
1978	45.4	43.6	31.5	37.2	36.0	28.5	25.7
1979	49.8	46.8	32.0	44.6	42.3	35.3	33.8
1980	55.8	51.8	32.9	51.8	46.3	40.3	44.6
1981	61.3	58.2	36.1	46.6	39.7	36.6	45.1
1982	67.2	62.5	33.5	45.7	38.9	36.2	42.9
1983	69.0	66.4	36.1	43.6	38.7	37.8	39.9
1984	71.4	66.1	37.2	41.3	36.4	37.5	38.0
1985	75.3	66.0	38.5	43.5	37.2	38.8	40.4
1986	78.6	67.4	57.3	58.7	52.6	51.7	49.6
1987	80.8	72.7	68.3	70.2	66.5	62.8	61.5
1988	84.0	81.8	78.4	73.5	70.7	65.0	71.2
1989	86.8	88.2	77.3	72.3	69.2	67.8	69.7
1990	91.0	94.5	79.3	89.2	86.4	86.3	84.3
1991	95.7	102.4	90.3	90.3	89.4	92.5	93.2
1992	100.0	100.0	100.0	100.0	100.0	100.0	100.0
1993	102.9	93.7	119.3	96.8	100.1	83.9	90.7
1994	105.6	90.3	132.4	101.4	108.0	81.5	95.3
1995	108.7	91.5	148.4	114.3	128.2	82.6	99.0
1996	112.2	96.1	130.1	113.8	128.1	93.5	101.6

[1] Data are for West Germany only.

[2] Civilian unemployment rates, approximating U.S. concepts. Quarterly data for France and Germany should be viewed as less precise indicators of unemployment under U.S. concepts than the annual data.

[3] There are breaks in the series for Germany (1983), France (1992), Italy (1986, 1991, and 1993), and United States (1990 and 1994). Based on the prior series, the rate for Germany was 7.2 percent in 1983, the rate for France was 10.5 in 1992, 11.9 in 1993, 12.7 in 1994 and 12.3 in 1995, and the rate for Italy was 6.3 percent in 1986 and 6.6 in 1991. The break in 1993 raised Italy's rate by approximately 1 percentage point. For details on break in series in 1990 and 1994 for United States, see footnote 5, Table B–35.

[4] Hourly compensation in manufacturing, U.S. dollar basis. Data relate to all employed persons (wage and salary earners and the self-employed) in the United States, Canada, Japan, France, and Germany, and to all employees (wage and salary earners) in the other countries. For France and United Kingdom, compensation adjusted to include changes in employment taxes that are not compensation to employees, but are labor costs to employers.

Source: Department of Labor, Bureau of Labor Statistics.

TABLE B–110.—*Foreign exchange rates, 1972–97*

[Currency units per U.S. dollar, except as noted]

Period	Belgium (franc)	Canada (dollar)	France (franc)	Germany (mark)	Italy (lira)	Japan (yen)
March 1973	39.408	0.9967	4.5156	2.8132	568.17	261.90
1972	44.020	0.9907	5.0444	3.1886	583.70	303.13
1973	38.955	1.0002	4.4535	2.6715	582.41	271.31
1974	38.959	.9780	4.8107	2.5868	650.81	291.84
1975	36.800	1.0175	4.2877	2.4614	653.10	296.78
1976	38.609	.9863	4.7825	2.5185	833.58	296.45
1977	35.849	1.0633	4.9161	2.3236	882.78	268.62
1978	31.495	1.1405	4.5091	2.0097	849.13	210.39
1979	29.342	1.1713	4.2567	1.8343	831.11	219.02
1980	29.238	1.1693	4.2251	1.8175	856.21	226.63
1981	37.195	1.1990	5.4397	2.2632	1138.58	220.63
1982	45.781	1.2344	6.5794	2.4281	1354.00	249.06
1983	51.123	1.2325	7.6204	2.5539	1519.32	237.55
1984	57.752	1.2952	8.7356	2.8455	1756.11	237.46
1985	59.337	1.3659	8.9800	2.9420	1908.88	238.47
1986	44.664	1.3896	6.9257	2.1705	1491.16	168.35
1987	37.358	1.3259	6.0122	1.7981	1297.03	144.60
1988	36.785	1.2306	5.9595	1.7570	1302.39	128.17
1989	39.409	1.1842	6.3802	1.8808	1372.28	138.07
1990	33.424	1.1668	5.4467	1.6166	1198.27	145.00
1991	34.195	1.1460	5.6468	1.6610	1241.28	134.59
1992	32.148	1.2085	5.2935	1.5618	1232.17	126.78
1993	34.581	1.2902	5.6669	1.6545	1573.41	111.08
1994	33.426	1.3664	5.5459	1.6216	1611.49	102.18
1995	29.472	1.3725	4.9864	1.4321	1629.45	93.96
1996	30.970	1.3638	5.1158	1.5049	1542.76	108.78
1997	35.807	1.3849	5.8393	1.7348	1703.81	121.06
1996: I	30.206	1.3691	5.0379	1.4694	1572.47	105.83
II	31.274	1.3647	5.1557	1.5215	1555.26	107.46
III	30.846	1.3705	5.0930	1.4973	1521.33	108.97
IV	31.550	1.3508	5.1763	1.5312	1522.27	112.91
1997: I	34.190	1.3593	5.5926	1.6575	1637.48	121.16
II	35.388	1.3864	5.7813	1.7148	1691.18	119.80
III	37.305	1.3850	6.0845	1.8065	1761.83	118.02
IV	36.283	1.4087	5.8886	1.7577	1722.20	125.39

Period	Netherlands (guilder)	Sweden (krona)	Switzerland (franc)	United Kingdom (pound) [1]	Multilateral trade-weighted value of the U.S. dollar (March 1973=100)	
					Nominal	Real [2]
March 1973	2.8714	4.4294	3.2171	2.4724	100.0	100.0
1972	3.2098	4.7571	3.8186	2.5034	109.1	
1973	2.7946	4.3619	3.1688	2.4525	99.1	98.9
1974	2.6879	4.4387	2.9805	2.3403	101.4	99.4
1975	2.5293	4.1531	2.5839	2.2217	98.5	94.0
1976	2.6449	4.3580	2.5002	1.8048	105.7	97.6
1977	2.4548	4.4802	2.4065	1.7449	103.4	93.3
1978	2.1643	4.5207	1.7907	1.9184	92.4	84.4
1979	2.0073	4.2893	1.6644	2.1224	88.1	83.2
1980	1.9875	4.2310	1.6772	2.3246	87.4	84.9
1981	2.4999	5.0660	1.9675	2.0243	103.4	101.0
1982	2.6719	6.2839	2.0327	1.7480	116.6	111.8
1983	2.8544	7.6718	2.1007	1.5159	125.3	117.4
1984	3.2085	8.2708	2.3500	1.3368	138.2	128.9
1985	3.3185	8.6032	2.4552	1.2974	143.0	132.4
1986	2.4485	7.1273	1.7979	1.4677	112.2	103.7
1987	2.0264	6.3469	1.4918	1.6398	96.9	90.9
1988	1.9778	6.1370	1.4643	1.7813	92.7	88.2
1989	2.1219	6.4559	1.6369	1.6382	98.6	94.4
1990	1.8215	5.9231	1.3901	1.7841	89.1	86.0
1991	1.8720	6.0521	1.4356	1.7674	89.8	86.4
1992	1.7587	5.8258	1.4064	1.7663	86.6	83.2
1993	1.8585	7.7956	1.4781	1.5016	93.2	89.6
1994	1.8190	7.7161	1.3667	1.5319	91.3	88.3
1995	1.6044	7.1406	1.1812	1.5785	84.2	82.1
1996	1.6863	6.7082	1.2361	1.5607	87.3	86.1
1997	1.9525	7.6446	1.4514	1.6376	96.4	95.6
1996: I	1.6451	6.7817	1.1914	1.5305	86.4	84.7
II	1.7022	6.7327	1.2428	1.5237	88.0	86.5
III	1.6797	6.6341	1.2227	1.5539	87.1	86.0
IV	1.7179	6.6858	1.2875	1.6359	87.9	87.1
1997: I	1.8630	7.3744	1.4357	1.6314	93.7	93.1
II	1.9289	7.7099	1.4460	1.6354	95.7	94.8
III	2.0340	7.8318	1.4883	1.6254	98.6	97.6
IV	1.9809	7.6499	1.4343	1.6587	97.5	96.6

[1] Value is U.S. dollars per pound.
[2] Adjusted by changes in consumer prices.

Note.—Certified noon buying rates in New York.

Source: Board of Governors of the Federal Reserve System.

[Millions of SDRs; end of period]

Area and country	1952	1962	1972	1982	1992	1995	1996	1997 Oct	1997 Nov
All countries	49,388	62,851	146,658	361,239	726,149	981,688	1,122,994	1,233,522	....
Industrial countries [1]	39,280	53,502	113,362	214,025	424,229	514,117	575,014	605,986	....
United States	24,714	17,220	12,112	29,918	52,995	59,467	53,694	50,346	50,327
Canada	1,944	2,561	5,572	3,439	8,662	10,243	14,310	15,877	13,783
Australia	920	1,168	5,656	6,053	8,429	8,279	10,384	12,129	12,217
Japan	1,101	2,021	16,916	22,001	52,937	124,125	151,511	164,893	167,691
New Zealand	183	251	767	577	2,239	2,967	4,140	3,137	....
Austria	116	1,081	2,505	5,544	9,703	13,020	16,277	15,024	14,912
Belgium	1,133	1,753	3,564	4,757	10,914	11,601	12,326	12,838	12,762
Denmark	150	256	787	2,111	8,090	7,468	9,892	15,101	14,290
Finland	132	237	664	1,420	3,862	6,809	4,866	8,174	....
France	686	4,049	9,224	17,850	22,522	20,930	21,500	24,348	25,045
Germany	960	6,958	21,908	43,909	69,489	60,517	61,176	59,341	59,977
Greece	94	287	950	916	3,606	10,064	12,292	8,029	9,148
Iceland	8	32	78	133	364	209	317	....	....
Ireland	318	359	1,038	2,390	2,514	5,818	5,719	5,435	5,523
Italy	722	4,068	5,605	15,108	22,438	25,815	34,287	41,669	42,194
Netherlands	953	1,943	4,407	10,723	17,492	23,897	19,832	20,144	19,997
Norway	164	304	1,220	6,273	8,725	15,190	18,482	22,566	23,048
Portugal	603	680	2,129	1,179	14,474	11,225	11,632	11,458	....
Spain	134	1,045	4,618	7,450	33,640	23,746	40,831	49,976	50,986
Sweden	504	802	1,453	3,397	16,667	16,344	13,452	10,685	....
Switzerland	1,667	2,919	6,961	16,930	27,100	27,411	29,642	28,259	28,767
United Kingdom	1,956	3,308	5,201	11,904	27,300	28,910	28,390	....	....
Developing countries: Total [2]	9,648	9,349	33,295	147,213	301,920	467,571	547,980	627,537	....
By area:									
Africa	1,786	2,110	3,962	7,737	12,868	17,461	21,107	30,282	....
Asia [2]	3,793	2,772	8,130	44,490	164,775	254,340	299,955	331,728	....
Europe	269	381	2,680	5,359	15,354	57,380	61,907	75,369	....
Middle East	1,183	1,805	9,436	64,039	44,149	50,768	56,152	67,727	....
Western Hemisphere	2,616	2,282	9,089	25,563	64,774	87,623	108,859	122,430	....
Memo:									
Oil-exporting countries	1,699	2,030	9,956	67,108	46,144	44,707	55,981	65,432	....
Non-oil developing countries [2]	7,949	7,319	23,339	80,105	255,776	422,865	491,999	562,105	....

[1] Includes data for Luxembourg.
[2] Includes data for Taiwan Province of China.

Note.—International reserves is comprised of monetary authorities' holdings of gold (at SDR 35 per ounce), special drawing rights (SDRs), reserve positions in the International Monetary Fund, and foreign exchange.
U.S. dollars per SDR (end of period) are: 1952 and 1962—1.00000; 1972—1.08571; 1982—1.10311; 1992—1.37500; 1995—1.48649; 1996—1.43796; October 1997—1.38362; and November 1997—1.36184.

Source: International Monetary Fund, *International Financial Statistics.*

TABLE B–112.—*Growth rates in real gross domestic product, 1979–97*

[Percent change at annual rate]

Area and country	1979–88	1989	1990	1991	1992	1993	1994	1995	1996	1997[1]
World	3.4	3.8	2.7	1.8	2.8	2.8	4.1	3.7	4.1	4.2
Advanced economies	2.9	3.7	2.7	1.2	1.9	1.2	3.2	2.5	2.7	3.0
Major industrial countries	2.8	3.5	2.4	.8	1.8	1.0	2.8	2.0	2.4	2.8
United States	2.7	3.4	1.2	−.9	2.7	2.3	3.5	2.0	2.8	3.7
Japan	3.8	4.8	5.1	3.8	1.0	.3	.6	1.4	3.5	1.1
Germany[2]	1.8	3.6	5.7	5.0	2.2	−1.1	2.9	1.9	1.4	2.3
France	2.2	4.3	2.5	.8	1.2	−1.3	2.8	2.1	1.5	2.2
Italy	2.7	2.9	2.2	1.1	.6	−1.2	2.2	2.9	.7	1.2
United Kingdom[3]	2.5	2.2	.4	−2.0	−.5	2.1	4.3	2.7	2.3	3.3
Canada	3.2	2.4	−.2	−1.8	.8	2.2	4.1	2.3	1.5	3.7
Other advanced economies	3.6	4.5	3.9	2.9	2.4	2.0	4.5	4.2	3.7	3.9
Developing countries	4.3	4.2	4.1	4.9	6.6	6.6	6.8	6.0	6.5	6.2
Africa	2.3	3.5	2.2	1.7	.8	1.0	2.9	2.8	5.2	3.7
Asia	6.8	6.1	5.6	6.6	9.5	9.4	9.6	8.9	8.2	7.6
Middle East and Europe	2.3	2.8	5.6	3.4	6.2	4.6	.4	3.5	4.8	4.6
Western Hemisphere	2.7	1.8	1.1	3.6	3.1	3.7	5.0	1.3	3.4	4.1
Countries in transition	2.9	2.1	−3.6	−7.7	−10.9	−6.2	−6.5	−.8	.1	1.8
Central and eastern Europe	....	....	....	−10.4	−7.9	−3.9	−1.8	1.6	1.5	2.1
Russia, Transcaucasus, and central Asia	....	....	....	−5.2	−13.9	−8.7	−12.3	−3.9	−1.9	1.5

[1] All figures are forecasts as published by the International Monetary Fund. For United States, preliminary estimates by the Department of Commerce show that real GDP grew 3.8 percent in 1997.
[2] Through 1991 data are for West Germany only.
[3] Average of expenditure, income, and output estimates of GDP at market prices.

Sources: Department of Commerce (Bureau of Economic Analysis) and International Monetary Fund.

○

ISBN 0-16-049419-2

90000

9 780160 494192